THE AMERICAN NEGRO

HIS HISTORY AND LITERATURE

TWENTIETH CENTURY NEGRO LITERATURE

Edited by D. W. Culp

ARNO PRESS and THE NEW YORK TIMES

NEW YORK 1969

General Editor
WILLIAM LOREN KATZ

"TWENTIETH CENTURY NEGRO LITERATURE," subtitled "A CYCLOPEDIA OF THOUGHT ON THE VITAL TOPICS RELATING TO THE AMERICAN NEGRO BY ONE HUNDRED OF AMERICA'S GREATEST NEGROES," is a large, 472-page encyclopedia of a book published at the turn of the century that tried to summarize and point up the strivings and achievements of the American Negro (despite great obstacles) during the nineteenth century and to show what the Negro should do to make greater progress in the upcoming twentieth century.

The plan of the book was to select thirty or forty topics or subjects and get three, four, or five different outstanding Negroes or scholars to write pieces on each subject, thus creating a symposium on each topic. There are also a short biography and a good photograph of each contributor to the book. The symposium approach makes for much repetition, but much variety and different viewpoints are also thus achieved. Some of the essays are short and slight, but many others are much longer, quite authoritative, and written by scholars in the various fields.

All of the important subjects of the turn-of-the-century period are here: Negro history and achievements, education, voting, civil rights and politics, southern and nothern race relations, Negro crime and the treatment of Negroes in the courts; Negro women, business, the professions, morality, mortality and health, youth, intelligence, the Negro churches and their ministers, Negro laborers and farmers, teachers, writers, inventors, Negro newspapers, Negro self-help, opportunities in Africa, and possibilities for the future in America.

The great names, as well as the near great, are here in profusion as contributors: George Washington Carver, W. H. Crogman, T. Thomas Fortune, Francis J. Grimké, Bishop J. W. Hood, J. W. E. Bowen, Kelly Miller, Henry A. Rucker, W. S. Scarborough, Mary Church Terrell, Charles Henry Turner, Bishop H. M. Turner, Bishop L. H. Holsey, Booker T. Washington, Congressman George H. White, Henry E. Baker, J. W. Cromwell, Mrs. Paul Laurence Dunbar, and many others. There are twelve women and eighty-eight men essayists.

Culp's book, published in 1902, was the second large Negro reference book or encyclopedia. It followed William J. Simmons' mammoth 1,100-page *Men of Mark: Eminent, Progressive and Rising*, published in 1887. Coming just after the Paris Exposition of 1900, the piece by Henry E. Baker on "The Negro as an Inventor" in Culp's book devotes about eight and a half pages to the eleven-page list of colored inventors in the United States that was included in the Exposition. Daniel Murray's eight-page *Preliminary List of Books and Pamphlets by Negro Authors*, also in the 1900 Paris Exposition, is not included in this book.

A monument to Negro striving and struggle in the nineteenth century against very great odds, *Twentieth Century Negro Literature* was a vitally necessary and fine contribution for its time.

Ernest Kaiser
THE SCHOMBURG COLLECTION

TWENTIETH CENTURY
NEGRO LITERATURE

Dr. D. W. Culp

TWENTIETH CENTURY
NEGRO LITERATURE

OR

A CYCLOPEDIA OF THOVGHT

ON THE

VITAL TOPICS RELATING
TO THE AMERICAN NEGRO

BY

ONE HUNDRED OF AMERICA'S
GREATEST NEGROES

EDITED AND ARRANGED

BY

D. W. CULP, A. M., M. D.

AN AUTHOR AND LECTURER, ETC.

COPIOVSLY ILLVSTRATED

WITH

One Hundred Fine Photo Engravings

PUBLISHED BY

J. L. NICHOLS & CO.

MANUFACTURING PUBLISHERS
ON THE EXCLUSIVE TERRITORY PLAN

TORONTO, CAN.   NAPERVILLE, ILL   ATLANTA, GA.

❦❦❦

Dedication.

———

To all persons of whatever race and of whatever section of our country,
who in any way contributed, in the Nineteenth Century,
to the financial, intellectual, moral and spiritual elevation of the Negro,
the editor dedicates this book with the ardent hope,
that before this century shall have ended,
the Negro,
through his own manly efforts,
aided by his friends,
shall reach that point in the American civilization,
where he will be recognized and treated as any other American citizen.

❦❦❦

PREFACE

The idea of putting this book on the market originated in the following considerations:

First. There is considerable ignorance, on the part of the white people of this country, of the intellectual ability of the Negro, and, as a consequence, the educated Negro does not receive, at the hands of the whites, that respectful consideration to which his education entitles him.

Second. At this time, when the attainments made in the nineteenth century by the other races and nationalities are being paraded, the friends of the Negro are particularly interested to know something of the attainments made by him in that century.

Third. There is a strong desire, on the part of those white people who are deeply interested in the American race problem, to know what the educated Negroes are thinking on the topics touching this problem, since it is believed that, if this problem is to be correctly solved, it will be solved by the combined efforts of the intelligent elements of both races.

Fourth. A book, in which the aspiring Negro youth of the land can study the character sketches and the literary productions of the scholarly men of their own race, along with their study of the character sketches and the choice literary productions of the scholarly white men of the country, is a desideratum.

Fifth. The majority of the Negroes need to be enlightened on those vital topics relating to themselves, and on those questions touching their development in civilization.

The object of this book is, therefore: (1) To enlighten the uninformed white people on the intellectual ability of the Negro. (2) To give to those, who are interested in the Negro race, a better idea of the extent to which he contributed to the promotion of America's civilization, and of the intellectual attainments made by him in the nineteenth century. (3) To reflect the views of the most scholarly and prominent Negroes of America on those topics, touching the Negro, that are now engaging the attention of the civilized world. (4) To point out, to the aspiring Negro youth, those men and women of their own race who, by their scholarship, by their integrity of character, and by their earnest efforts in the work of uplifting their own race, have made themselves illustrious; also, to enlighten such youth on those ethical, political, and sociological questions, touching the Negro that will sooner or later engage their attention. (5) To enlighten the Negroes on that perplexing problem, commonly called the "Race Problem," that has necessarily grown out of their contact with their ex-masters and their descendants; and also to stimulate them to make greater efforts to ascend to that plane of civilization occupied by the other enlightened peoples of the world.

Now, among all the books on the Negro, there is none whose object is so worthy, comprehensive, and specific as that above set forth. In this the superiority of this book to all others, on the Negro, may be seen. And the superior value of this book is also apparent from the following considerations: (1) This is the only book in which there is such a magnificent array of Negro talent. Other Negro books of a biographical character are objected to, by the intelligent people who have read them, on the ground that they contain too few sketches of scholarly Negroes, and too many of Negroes of ordinary ability. But such a criticism cannot be made on this book since, as a matter of fact, all of the one hundred men and women, appearing in it, are among the best educated Negroes in the world. (2) This is the only book from which one can get anything like a definite and correct idea of the progress made by the Negro since his Emancipation along all lines. (3) There is no book but this one in which there can be found expressed the thoughts of any considerable number of educated Negroes on so many political, religious, civil, moral and sociological problems touching the Negro, which are interesting alike to the politician, the moralist and the sociologist.

But it is not to be understood that the one hundred men and women mentioned in this book are the only Negro scholars in this country. So far from this, there are hundreds of other Negroes who are as scholarly, as prominent and as active in the work of uplifting their race as the one hundred herein given. These one hundred appear here, rather than others, for no other reason than that they are better known to the editor. Now, in sending forth this book, the editor ardently hopes that it will not only accomplish the objects herein set forth, but that it will also do much towards bringing about a better understanding between the two races in the South.

D. W. CULP, Palatka, Fla.

W. H. Crogman, A. M.

PROF. W. H. CROGMAN, A. M.

Prof. W. H. Crogman, A. M., who occupies the chair of Greek and Latin in Clark University, Atlanta, in Christian character, scholarship in his department, literary ability, general culture and distinguished services stands, it is safe to say, among the first four, if not at the head of the Negro race. In all the particulars mentioned, he would honor a professorship in any college in the land.

Prof. Crogman was born on the island of St. Martin, May 5, 1841. In 1855, Mr. B. L. Boomer, chief mate of the vessel, visiting the island, became interested in the boy, then an orphan, and induced him to come to the United States. Mr. Boomer took him to his home in Middleboro, Mass., sent him to district school in the winter, and always took great interest in him. Mr. Boomer's brothers were all seafaring men, captains or officers of vessels. With one of these the boy, Willie, began to follow the sea. This beginning afterward led to a life of eleven years on the ocean. He visited many lands, and observant and thoughtful, obtained a wide knowledge of various nationalities and parts of the world. His visits included especially England, various points on the Continent of Europe, Calcutta and Bombay in Asia, various places in South America and Australia.

In 1866, at the suggestion of Mr. Boomer, that an academic education would make him useful, Prof. Crogman, then at the age of twenty-five, began to earn means to attend an academy. He worked and laid by money till two years later in 1868, he entered Pierce Academy, in Middleboro, Mass. He remained there two years, taking an English course with French and bookkeeping.

After completing his academic course, in the Fall of 1870, Prof. Crogman started for the South to give his life to the Christian education and elevation of his race. He was recommended by the Boston Preachers' Meeting to the work in South Carolina, and was employed by Rev. T. W. Lewis as instructor in English branches, at Claflin University, Orangeburg, S. C. Here he remained three years. In this work he became impressed with the need of a knowledge of Greek and Latin and began the study of Latin by himself. To gain a knowledge of these branches he went to Atlanta University in the Fall of 1873. This resulted in his completing there the full classical course in 1876. Prof. Francis, of Atlanta University, who was one of his teachers there, was present at the reception and in a most happy speech paid a high tribute to Prof. Crogman's manhood, industry, thorough scholarship and rapid advancement during his college life, completing as he did the four years' course in three years. He spoke also of Prof. Crogman's carrying off as his bride one of their noblest and most gifted and cultured young ladies, Miss Lavinia C. Mott, of Charlotte, N. C. Immediately on his graduating from Atlanta University, Prof. Crogman was called to a position on the faculty of Clark University, where he has been ever since, having occupied his present chair since 1880. Letters expressive of their highest appreciation of him and his work were read from several of his students, who now themselves occupy prominent positions.

Prof. Crogman is author of "Talks for the Times," a book in which almost every phase of the Race Problem is discussed in a very practical and fascinating style. Speaking of this book, the "Independent" says:

"We notice this collection of 'Talks for the Times' with unusual pleasure. They are worthy of the strong and cultivated gentleman who is their author. They deal largely with Negro education, educational institutions and educators, but occasionally deal with general topics, such as 'Life's Deeper Meanings.' The author speaks of his race and speaks in strong, polished English, full of nerve and rich in the music of good English prose."

The "California Christian Advocate" says:

"We are minded to say, 'here is a volume that must be intensely interesting to all who are interested in the culture and continued advancement of the Negro.' But why should we thus write? It would be nearer our deliberate estimate to say, 'Here is a book made up of manly and vigorous addresses by a vigorous, scholarly and independent thinker.' Whoever values the result of scholarly investigation will be interested in this volume. We do not hesitate to say that but for the noble identification of the author with his own people in such addresses as 'The Negro's Need,' 'The Negro's Claims,' and 'The Negro Problem,' no one who reads this book would guess that Professor Crogman was other than a vigorous minded Anglo-Saxon. And yet to our thinking, it is much to say that 'Talks for the Times' is the production of a ripe scholar who is of almost pure African blood—a man who almost entirely by his own exertion has climbed steadily up the ladder of scholarship until he is no mean exponent of the culture of our day."

INTRODUCTION.

BY PROF. W. H. CROGMAN.

I am requested to write an introduction to this volume of essays, written by representative men and women of the Negro race and touching almost every phase of the Negro question. Certainly it is a hopeful sign that the Negro is beginning, with some degree of seriousness, to turn his eyes inward, to study himself, and try to discover what are his possibilities, and what the obstructions that lie in the way to his larger development. Undoubtedly this is a rational method of procedure, and the one most likely to reward his effort; for it is only in proportion as we become interested in ourselves that we enlist the interest of others, and only in proportion as we respect ourselves that we command the respect of others. The story is told of a Negro who, at some time during the War of the Rebellion, being asked why he did not enlist in the army, replied: "De Norf and de Souf am two dogs fightin' over a bone. De nigger am de bone and takes no part in de conflict." That this is not the language of an intelligent Negro is quite evident, if, indeed, it be the language of a Negro at all. So common has it been in this country to caricature the black man, to represent him as a driveler in speech and a buffoon in action, that I am always loath to accept as his those many would-be-witty sayings which, too often, originating with others, have been attributed to him. But be the author of that remark whosoever he may, one thing now is perfectly apparent—the Negro has reached beyond the "bone" stage. He is no longer content with being a passive observer, a quiet looker-on, while his character and interests are under discussion. He is now disposed to speak for himself, to "take part in the conflict." Any one desiring evidence of this will find it in the following pages of "Twentieth Century Negro Literature."

This book will do good. It will enlighten many of both races on topics respecting which they seem to be profoundly ignorant. Not very long ago a Negro delivered an address in one of the largest churches in Atlanta. It was an occasion in which a goodly number of white people was present. They expressed themselves as being delighted. One man said to a colored bishop that he didn't know there was a Negro in the state that could have delivered such an address. The fact is, both the good bishop and the writer of these lines might have found him twenty who could, at least, deliver an address as good, and ten, probably, who could deliver a better. Well, we don't know each other—we white and black folk. We are neighbors, yet strangers. Our thoughts, our motives, our desires are unknown to each other. Between the best white and black people, in whom alone vests the possibility of a rational and peaceful solution of the race question, there is absolutely no communication, no opportunity for exchange of views. Herein lies the danger; for both people, as a consequence, are suspicious, the one of the other. Not infrequently, with much uncharitableness, we attribute wrong motives to those who are truly our friends. Were we acquainted with one another, as we ought to be, we would doubtless be surprised to discover how little we differ in our thinking with reference to many of the vexed questions confronting us. Indeed, it has always been the belief of the writer, frequently expressed, that neither of the races is as bad as it appears to the other. May we not hope, then, that "Twentieth Century Negro Literature" may have the good fortune of falling into the hands of many white friends.

On the other hand, the book must be stimulating to the Negro people, especially to those of the younger generation, now blessed with large educational privilege. It must awaken in them self-respect, self-reliance, and the ambition to be and to do. By the perusal of its pages they will be led to see more clearly the path of duty, and to feel more sensibly the weight of responsibility resting upon them. The first generation of Negroes after emancipation exhibited to a painful degree the spirit of dependence, an inclination to lean on something and on somebody—now on the politician, now on the philanthropist. The reason for this, of course, is not far to fetch. The spirit of dependence is invariably a characteristic of weakness. It was not to be expected that the first generation emerging from slavery would possess all the heroic qualities. Gradually, however, the Negro is realizing the importance of self-help. Good books, among other agencies, will deepen this impression, and ultimately lead him to imbibe in all its fulness the sentiment of the poet,

"Destiny is not about thee, but within;
Thyself must make thyself."

The contributors to this volume are worthy of notice. They are among the best we have. Some of them are personally known to the writer. They are men of experience, scholarly men, shunning rather than courting notoriety—just the class of men to guide a people, alas, too easily led astray by pretentious ignorance. From a number so large and so meritorious it would seem invidious to select any for special mention. It may not be out of place, however, to say a few words with reference to the editor and compiler, Dr. D. W. Culp. Born a slave in Union County, South Carolina, like many a black boy, he has had to forge his way to the front. In 1876 we find him graduating in a class of one from Biddle University—the first college graduate from that school. In the fall of the same year he entered Princeton Theological Seminary, and at the same time pursued studies in philosophy, history, and psychology in the university under the eminent Doctor McCosh. His first appearance in the university was the signal for a display of race prejudice. To the Southern students especially his presence was very obnoxious. Several of them immediately left the college and went home. To the credit of their parents, it should be said, they were led to return. Before the expiration of three years Mr. Culp, by exemplary conduct and good scholarship, won the respect and friendship of the students in both university and seminary, the Southerners included. He was graduated from the seminary in 1879, and immediately found work as pastor under the Freedmen's Board of the Northern Presbyterian Church. He served in the pastorate several years in different states, was for a time principal of a school in Jacksonville, Florida, the largest school in the state. Becoming, however, more and more interested in the physical salvation of his race, he entered upon the study of medicine in the University of Michigan; but was finally graduated with honor from the Ohio Medical University, in 1891, since which time he has followed the practice of medicine. For a passionate love of knowledge, and for persistent effort in trying to secure it, Dr. Culp is a noble and inspiring example to the young and aspiring Negro.

Clark University, South Atlanta, Georgia,
    December 16, 1901.

ALPHABETICAL LIST OF WRITERS AND ILLUSTRATIONS.

The writers of this book are one hundred (one for each year in the century) of the most scholarly and prominent Negroes of America.

12   *LIST OF WRITERS.*

CONTENTS.

THE FOLLOWING TOPICS ARE DISCUSSED IN THIS BOOK BY ONE HUNDRED WRITERS:

CONTENTS.

THE EDITOR'S BIOGRAPHY, BY WALTER I. LEWIS.

Daniel Wallace Culp, compiler and editor of this book, was born about forty-seven years ago, of slave parents, four miles from Union Court House in South Carolina. His mother, Marilla by name, was an excellent type of the devout Christian woman of her day; she believed firmly in that God, whose inscrutable wisdom directed the ways of her race through paths that were truly hard. She hesitated not to teach her son Daniel to love, fear and obey the God in whom she trusted, using whatever light she had.

Christopher Brandon, to whom Daniel and his mother belonged, was one of those slave-holders in South Carolina who did not believe in the institution of slavery, but being uncertain as to whether his slaves would be better off if he freed them, he held them, establishing a sort of patrimony in which his slaves were allowed such superior opportunities and advantages that the less favored neighbors styled them "Brandon's free Negroes." This distinction carried with it its disadvantages as well, for on account of the ease and comfort allowed them, they were despised alike by the hard-hearted slave-owners and the less fortunate slaves. Brandon was kind to his slaves, who were made to work enough to keep a plenty at home to live upon. He also protected them against whatever ill treatment begrudging neighbors might be prompted to offer.

Brandon was a bachelor. He made a favorite and close companion of Daniel to the extent of having him occupy the same bed with him. This affection of the bachelor master lasted until his death, which occurred several years after the emancipation.

It is said that in his expiring moments this good man, Brandon, called for young Daniel, who was then too far away to be on hand in time to hear what was to have been said before death ensued. Thus died a man who was brave enough, in the midst of environments that were exacting to the extent of active ostracism for his assertion of his belief that the Negro is a real human being, possessed of a mind, soul and rights to happiness, and should share in the community of responsibilities.

At an early age Daniel became anxious to know what is in books. This ambition was fed by his former master, who became his first teacher. This make-shift tutelage continued until 1869, when this rapid little learner caught a sight of better intellectual food. Accordingly he left his rural home, his soul charged with greater things, and entered Biddle Memorial Institute, now Biddle University, at Charlotte, N. C.

As a student Daniel did not attract any special attention until he had passed the preparatory and entered the regular classical course of that institution. It was here that he won great distinction in his faculty for acquiring a ready knowledge of the languages and the higher mathematics. So rapidly did he advance in these studies that it was found necessary to place him in a class alone, none of his mates being able to keep up with him. This separation was from a class of about twenty young men from the Carolinas, Virginia, Georgia and Tennessee. For five years he studied, making an advancement that was frequently a marvel to the teachers, some of whom were at times puzzled to sustain their place of superiority over him.

In 1876 Daniel Wallace Culp graduated from Biddle University, being the first graduate from the classical department of that institution, with the degree of Bachelor of Arts.

Having decided to study theology, he, in the fall of the same year in which he graduated from Biddle, entered Princeton Theological Seminary. At the same time he entered Princeton College to study the History of Philosophy and Psychology under the great Dr. McCosh.

The presence of a colored student in the classes at Princeton College (which has no connection with the Theological Seminary) was particularly obnoxious to the young men of the South, of whom there were several then in attendance. This brought on a crisis. The young white men of the South packed their trunks and left for their homes, declaring with much emphasis that they would not sit in the lecture room with a "nigger." But, strange to relate, their parents showed better sense by requiring them to promptly return. In the meanwhile efforts were made to have Dr. Culp discontinue his attendance at these lectures, all of which he positively refused to do. The young men from the South finally became friendly, and things moved on smoothly, Dr. Culp winning the respect of all the students by his gentlemanly conduct and scholarship.

In the Theological Seminary he was regarded as one of the brightest students in his class, excelling in the study of the Hebrew language and theology. He graduated from this seminary in the spring of 1879.

Now came the most trying time in the life of the young man who had been sated with frequent conquests while in the pursuit of knowledge. Dr. Culp was assigned to an humble Presbyterian Church at Laurens, S. C., under the auspices of the Freedman's

Board of the Northern Presbyterian Church. His work was to preach and teach at that place. He remained at Laurens one year, when he was called to the pastorate of Laura Street Presbyterian Church in Jacksonville, Fla.

In the fall of 1881 he was appointed principal of Stanton Institute, the largest colored college in the state of Florida. For a while he filled both the pastorate of the church and the principalship of Stanton, but finding it impracticable to hold both he finally resigned the pastorate, after having served the church for five years. He was principal of Stanton four years. Rev. F. J. Grimke, D. D., succeeded Dr. Culp as pastor of Laura Street Presbyterian Church.

Desiring to help his people in what is known as the "black belt" of Florida, he severed his connection with the Stanton Institute and went to Lake City and established the Florida Normal and Industrial Institute. There he prepared many young men and women to teach in the district schools. This school was operated under the General Congregational Association of Florida, of which Dr. Culp is a member.

In 1886 he accepted an appointment from the American Missionary Association to take charge of the church and school at Florence, Ala. He did not remain there long before the same board appointed him to the pastorate of the First Congregational Church in Nashville, Tenn. It was here that Dr. Culp became deeply concerned about the physical salvation of his race. To fit himself to do actual work along this line, he resigned his pastorate over the strongest protests of his members, and entered the Medical School of the University of Michigan, at Ann Arbor. After remaining in this college for some time, studying with the avidity and success of former years, he left and entered the Ohio Medical College, where he could enjoy the advantages of the study of the superior hospital facilities. Here he graduated with honors in 1891, and again came South, locating in Augusta, Ga.

Shortly after his arrival in Augusta, Dr. Culp having demonstrated his high capabilities and fitness, was elected by the City Council to be superintendent and resident physician of the Freedmen's Hospital in that city. This position was coveted by several white physicians, hence the election of Dr. Culp created no small stir. The excitement was great for some time. Finally it became apparent that to continue to hold this position would be hazardous in a number of ways, and upon the advice of his wife and friends Dr. Culp resigned, after serving one year.

Afterwards he built up an excellent practice of medicine in the city of Augusta, but owing to the fast failing health of his family he moved to Palatka, Fla., and after two years of successful practice he moved to Jacksonville to give his children, a promising girl and boy, the advantages of the schools.

After remaining in Jacksonville for about seven years, Dr. Culp yielded to the entreaties of the people of Palatka and returned to that city, where he now is, having won the fullest confidence of the people as a successful physician.

Dr. Culp married Mrs. Mary Emily Jefferson, of Jacksonville, in 1884. She was at that time a prominent teacher in the public schools of that city. His union has been blessed with two children, a girl, Charlotte Marilla, fourteen years old, and Julian McKenzie, twelve years old.

Dr. and Mrs. Culp are both profoundly interested in the education of these children, hoping to fit them to be useful to their race.

Dr. Culp is classed as a thorough race man. Freed from the monstrous visions which many delight to parade as arguments, he abides by a strong faith in the destiny of the valuable elements of his race. That his people are destined to reach a high point in civilization has been his private conviction for years, not being very free, however, to say that this will be attained in America.

Dr. Culp also seriously believes that if the race problem is ever solved in this country, it will be done by the combined efforts of the intelligent elements of both races. His great interest in the physical salvation of his race has moved him to both lecture extensively and write books and pamphlets on health topics during the past seven years. Notable among these are his books on smallpox and vaccination, consumption, etc., all of which have done good among the people whose means of information on the proper care of health are the poorest.

Dr. Culp has good standing with the editors of the leading magazines. By these he has been invited repeatedly to write articles on the Race Problem. This invitation he has accepted more than once, and when he writes, he displays a degree of literary ability that is striking. His purpose in compiling and editing this book is but one of the several great plans he has in reserve to publicly demonstrate what he regards as actual service for the inspiration of his day and generation.

Mrs. Mary B. Talbert.

MRS. MARY B. TALBERT.

Mary Burnett Talbert was born at Oberlin, Ohio, in 1866, her father's family having gone there from Chapel Hill, N. C. She is descended on her maternal side from Richard Nichols, who compelled Peter Stuyvesant to surrender New Amsterdam and who for a short while was Governor of the State of New York.

She graduated at the early age of sixteen from the Oberlin High School, and through the generosity of Ex-President James H. Fairchild was enabled to attend Oberlin College.

When applying for admission to the class in trigonometry, the instructor doubtfully admitted her, as so many of the High School pupils had found the subject very hard and preferred a review of other mathematics. She entered the class, however, on trial, and made a term's record of 5 per cent, with an examination of 5.5 per cent, 6 per cent being the highest mark for lessons in college.

During the next term she entered the class of mechanics, and made a perfect record for term's work and examination.

While attending school she was well liked by her classmates, being made Treasurer of Aeolian, one of the two college societies for young women, and was also one of six representatives chosen for Class Day Exercises. She was given the place of honor upon the programme, and recited an original poem, "The Lament of the Old College Bell, Once First, Now Second."

Mrs. Talbert graduated from Oberlin at the early age of nineteen, being the only colored member of her class after the withdrawal of the late Lieutenant John Alexander.

She started out in life equipped not only with a great love of learning but with all the encouragement which made it possible for her to follow the inclinations of her mind.

In 1886 she accepted a position in Bethel University, Little Rock, Ark.

Some women make themselves teachers, but Mrs. Talbert was a born teacher. The late Professor John M. Ellis, in writing of her, said: "She is a lady of Christian character and pleasing address. As a student she has an excellent record and standing in her class, showing good abilities and industry and fidelity in her work. She has the qualities natural and acquired to make a superior teacher."

In January, 1887, she was elected Assistant Principal of the Little Rock High School, the highest position held by any woman in the State of Arkansas, and the only colored woman who has ever held the position. Mrs. Talbert resigned her place after her marriage to Mr. William H. Talbert, one of Buffalo's leading colored young men, and was urged after marriage to reconsider her resignation and take up her work again.

Leading educators and literary men, such as Charles Dudley Warner, Samuel A. Greene of Boston, L. S. Holden of St. Louis, and others who visited her classes, and, having seen them at work, registered their names with written comments.

Professor Albert A. Wright of Oberlin writes as follows: "Mary Burnett received her education in the public schools and college of this place, where her parents have resided for many years. She has won the respect and approval of her teachers by her successful accomplishments of the tasks set before her." Mrs. Talbert received the degree granted to students of the Literary Course in 1894, and is a member of the Association of Collegiate Alumnae, being the only colored woman in the city of Buffalo eligible.

TWENTIETH CENTURY NEGRO LITERATURE.

TOPIC I.

DID THE AMERICAN NEGRO MAKE, IN THE NINETEENTH CENTURY, ACHIEVEMENTS ALONG THE LINES OF WEALTH, MORALITY, EDUCATION, ETC., COMMENSURATE WITH HIS OPPORTUNITIES? IF SO, WHAT ACHIEVEMENTS DID HE MAKE?

BY MARY B. TALBERT.

As the hand upon the dial of the nineteenth century clock pointed to its last figure, it showed that the American Negro had ceased to be a thing, a commodity that could be bought and sold, a mere animal; but was indeed a human being possessing all the qualities of mind and heart that belong to the rest of mankind, capable of receiving education and imparting it to his fellow man, able to think, act, feel, and develop those intellectual and moral qualities, such as characterize mankind generally.

Let us glance at the intellectual Negro and see if he has made any progress commensurate with his opportunities during the nineteenth century.

Intuitively we turn to that great historian of our race—who for seven years worked with such care and zeal to write a thoroughly trustworthy history of the American Negro, and to-day stands as our first and greatest historian—George W. Williams. In prefacing his second volume, he says: "I have tracked my bleeding countrymen through widely scattered documents of American history; I have listened to their groans, their clanking chains, and melting prayers, until the woes of a race and the agonies of centuries seem to crowd upon my soul as a bitter reality. Many pages of this history have been blistered with my tears; and although having lived but a little more than a generation my mind feels as if it were cycles old.

"A short time ago the schools of the entire North were shut in his

17

face; and the few separate schools accorded him were given grudgingly. They were usually held in the lecture room of some colored church or thrust off to one side in a portion of the city or town toward which aristocratic ambition would never turn. These schools were generally poorly equipped; and the teachers were either colored persons whose opportunities of securing an education had been poor, or white persons whose mental qualifications would not encourage them to make an honest living among their own race."

It will not be necessary to enumerate the various insults and discouragements which faced the noble pioneers of our race who, seeing their fellow men denied the opportunities and privileges of securing an education, scorned by the press and pulpit, in public and private gatherings for their ignorance, set about to lift the Negro from his low social and mental condition.

The Negro turned his attention to the education of himself and his children; schools were commenced, churches organized, and a new era of self-culture and general improvement began.

In Boston we see Thomas Paul, Leonard A. Grimes, John T. Raymond, Robert Morris and John V. DeGrasse.

In 1854 John V. DeGrasse was admitted to the Massachusetts Medical Society, being the first instance of such an honor being conferred upon a colored man in this country.

In New York we find Rev. Henry Highland Garnet, Dr. Charles B. Ray, Charles L. Reason and Jacob Day doing what they could to elevate the Negro and place him on a higher intellectual plane.

Philadelphia also added her quota to the list of noble men who were striving to show to the world that the American Negro, although enslaved, was a human being. We find such men as Robert Purvis, William Still and Stephen Smith.

In Western Pennsylvania and New York were John Peck, John B. Vashon and Peyton Harris and all through the North, each state held colored men who were anxious to do what they could to elevate the race, and it seems as if God gave each one a special duty to perform, which combined, made one mighty stimulus to the young colored youth to do what he could to build up the Negro race.

Do you ask if the Negro has advanced intellectually, I need only to refer you to the showing made by the men and women of our race to-day. The works of Frederick Douglass, John M. Langston, Blanche K. Bruce,

J. C. Price, are living testimonials of what the Negro accomplished a generation ago.

When we consider the fact that the Negro was of such import that laws were made making it a misdemeanor to educate the Negro, both before and after the Civil War; when we consider the Greek text books of Professor Scarborough of Wilberforce used by one of the oldest Colleges in America; when we consider the Presidents and Principals of various Negro schools in our country, such as Livingston, N. C.; Spellman Seminary, Atlanta, Ga.; Wilberforce, Ohio; Virginia Normal and Collegiate; Shaw University; when we consider the place that our honored clergy occupy among the intellectual men of the world; when we consider the work of Booker T. Washington, we must admit that the love of knowledge seems to be intuitive. No people ever learned more in so short a time.

Every year since the Civil War the American Negro has been taking on better and purer traits of character.

The Negro of to-day is materially different from the Negro of yesterday. He delights in the education of his children, and from every section of our Southland come letters asking for competent colored teachers and educated ministers. The young man and woman who educate themselves in our Northern colleges and normal schools do not always have to turn their attention to the far South to seek fields of labor, but in an honest competition, gain places of honor and trust in the North.

Think of the scores of young colored women all over our Northern states teaching the "young idea how to shoot," and not a black face in the class. We find colored women with large classes of white pupils in St. Paul, Minn.; Chicago, Ill.; Detroit, Mich.; Cleveland, Ohio; Buffalo, N. Y.; and other Northern cities. "From the state of semi-civilization," says Williams, "in which he cared only for the comforts of the present, his desires and wants have swept outward and upward into the years to come and toward the Mysterious Future."

Several hundred weekly newspapers, a dozen monthly magazines, conducted by Negroes, are feeding the mind of the race, binding communities together by the cords of common interest and racial sympathy. The conditions around which the Negro was surrounded years ago have disappeared and the Negro is as proud of his own society as the whites are of theirs. Sociological study and laws have given to our present generation the will power and tenacity to establish and maintain a social standing equal with any of the races of the world. Without a question of doubt he has shown moral qualities far in advance of those which dominated in slave history and under which he was constantly subjected.

Has the Negro made any achievements along the lines of wealth? needs only a review of statistics to answer the above question, for where once was the rude cabin, and one-room hut, we now see the beautiful homes with well kept stock and farm, hygienic stables as well as artistic lawns. The first experiment the general masses of negroes had in the saving of money was under that institution known as "The Freedman's Saving and Trust Company." The institution started out under the most favorable auspices. The depositors numbered among its rank and file, day laborers, farmers, mechanics, house-servants, barbers and washerwomen; thus showing to the entire country that the emancipated Negro was not only working but by industry and economy was saving his earnings. We know too well of the misplaced confidence in that bank and how after a short time the bank failed and thousands of colored men and women lost their earnings. During the brief period of its existence $57,000,000 were deposited. Although the Freedman's Bank caused many a colored person to shrink from any banking institution, yet some were hopeful and again began to save money. Throughout the entire South we find scores of colored men who have excellent farms, elegant homes and small fortunes.

"In Baltimore a company of colored men own a ship-dock and transact a large business. Some of the largest orange plantations in Florida are owned by colored men. On most of the plantations, and in many of the large towns and cities colored mechanics are quite numerous."

The total amount of property owned by the colored people in all the states is rated at over $400,000,000.

In the North, East and West we see many colored men with handsome estates run high into the hundred thousands. Almost every large city and town will show among her population a Negro here and there whose wealth is rated between five and ten thousand dollars or more.

Rev. A. G. Davis of Raleigh, N. C., in an address at the North Carolina Agricultural Fair, said, "Scan, if you will, the long line of eight million Negroes as they march slowly but surely up the road of progress, and you will find in her ranks such men as Granville T. Woods, of Ohio, the electrician, mechanical engineer, manufacturer of telephones, telegraph and electrical instruments; William Still, of Philadelphia, the

Mrs. Josephine Silone Yates

MRS. JOSEPHINE SILONE YATES.

Mrs. Josephine Yates, youngest daughter of Alexander and Parthenia Reeve-Silone, was born in Mattiluck, Suffolk County, N. Y., where her parents, grandparents and great-grandparents were long and favorably known as individuals of sterling worth, morally, intellectually and physically speaking. On the maternal side Mrs. Yates is a niece of the Rev. J. B. Reeve, D. D., of Phildelphia.

Mrs. Silone, a woman of education and great refinement of character, began the work of educating this daughter in her quiet, Christian home, and both parents hoping that she might develop into a useful woman spared no pains in endeavoring to secure for her the education the child very early showed a desire to obtain; and with this end in view she was sent to Newport, R. I., in her fourteenth year, having already spent one year at the Institute for Colored Youth in Philadelphia, and Mrs. Coppin, then Miss Fannie Jackson, with her vigorous intellect, aided the inspiration the mother had begun. In 1877 Miss Silone graduated as valedictorian of a large class from Rogers High School of Newport; and although the only Colored member of her class, and the first graduate of color, invariably she was treated with the utmost courtesy by teachers, scholars and such members of the School Board as Thomas Wentworth Higginson, T. Coggeshall, and others.

Two years later she graduated from the Rhode Island State Normal School in Providence, and soon began her life work as a teacher. During the eight years spent in Lincoln Institute, Jefferson City, Mo., she had charge of the Department of Natural Science, and was the first woman to be elected to a professorship in that institution.

In 1889 Miss Silone was married to Prof. W. W. Yates, principal of Phillips School, Kansas City, Mo., and removed to that city, where since she has been engaged in either public or private school work.

From the age of nine years she has been writing for the press, and her articles have appeared in many leading periodicals—for a long time under the signature "R. K. Potter." Mrs. Yates has long been a zealous club worker and is well known as a lecturer East and West. She was one of the organizers and the first President of the Kansas City Woman's League; and in the summer of 1901 was elected President of the National Association of Colored Women, which organization she had already served as Treasurer for a period of four years.

Mrs. Yates is the mother of two children, whose education she carefully superintends, and is ever ready to comfort the sick or to stop her round of duties to give counsel or render help along any line possible to the many young people and others who seek her door.

coal dealer; Henry Tanner, the artist; John W. Terry, foreman of the iron and fitting department of the Chicago West Division Street Car Company; J. D. Baltimore, engineer, machinist, and inventor, of Washington, D. C.; Wiley Jones, of Pine Bluff, Arkansas, the owner of a street car railroad, race track and park; Richard Hancock, foreman of the pattern shops of the Eagle Works and Manufacturing Company, and draughtsman; John Beack, the inventor, whose inventions are worth tens of thousands of dollars; W. C. Atwood, the lumber merchant and capitalist."

And now in review let me add that the social conditions of the American Negro are such that he has shown to the world his aptitude for study and general improvement.

Before character, education and wealth, all barriers will melt, and these are necessary to develop the growth of the race.

From abject serfdom and pauperism he has risen to a plane far above the masses of any race of people.

By his industry and frugality he has made himself master of any situation into which he has been placed, and none will deny that his achievements along all lines have been commensurate with his opportunities.

SECOND PAPER.

DID THE AMERICAN NEGRO MAKE, IN THE NINETEENTH CENTURY, ACHIEVEMENTS ALONG THE LINES OF WEALTH, MORALITY, EDUCATION, ETC., COMMENSURATE WITH HIS OPPORTUNITIES? IF SO, WHAT ACHIEVEMENTS DID HE MAKE?

BY JOSEPHINE SILONE YATES.

The measure of the success of a race is the depths from which it has come, and the condition under which it has developed. To know what the Negro actually accomplished in the nineteenth century, one must know something of his life and habitat previous to the year 1619, when against his will or wish, he was brought to the Virginian coast; must also know his life as a slave, and his opportunities since emancipation.

History shows that the Negroes brought from Africa to this country to be sold into slavery were at the time in a more or less primitive stage of uncivilized life; while the methods used to capture and transport them to this "land of the free and home of the brave," recently revived through the vivid pen pictures and other illustrations running in serial form in Scribner's, Pearson's and other reliable periodicals (accounts which bear the impress of truth, and are hardly liable to the charge of having been written within too close range of time and space, or vice versa, to be strictly truthful), indicate the demoralizing and debasing effects of the "system" from its initial period, this followed up by the blighting influences of slave life, even under the most favorable conditions, for nearly two hundred and fifty years, left upon Negro life and character just the traits it would have left upon any other people subjected to similar conditions for the same length of time.

It may be said, and with truth, that slavery gave to the Negro some of the arts of civilized life; but it must be added, that, denying him the inalienable rights of manhood, denying him the right to the product of his labor, it left him no noble incentive to labor at these arts, and thus tended to render him improvident, careless, shiftless, in short, to demoralize his entire nature.

It is further stated that the system gave him Christianity. Did it give him piety? Could it give him morality in the highest sense of these terms?

Constantine could march the refractory Saxons to the banks of a stream and give them their option between Christianity and the sword, but the haughty monarch soon found that a religion forced in this peremptory and wholesale fashion did not change the moral nature of the soldier; and we submit that Christianity, language, and the arts of civilized life, absorbed amidst the debasing influences of a cruel and infamous bondage could not be productive of a harmonious development of body, mind and soul; of strong moral and intellectual fiber; or of ideas of the dignity of labor; of habits of thrift, economy, the careful expenditure of time and money; or knowledge of the intimate relationship of these two great factors in the process of civilization. These are results attained only where the rights of manhood and womanhood are acknowledged and respected. The lack of these results or basic impulses to advancement represent defects in the Negro character, preventing a more rapid development in the nineteenth century and directly traceable to his enslaved state; and the origin or cause, the growth and subsequent development of these, and other defects, must be taken into consideration before the Negro is stamped as the greatest criminal on earth, wholly irredeemable; before he is condemned in wholesale manner for not having made more rapid strides toward advanced civilization in little more than one generation of freedom. Indeed, it speaks well for the intrinsic merit of the race, that although public opinion freely admits that the natural outcome of bondage is a cowardly, thieving, brutal, or abject specimen of humanity, even in the darkest hours of slavery, there were many, many, high-born souls who, if necessary, at the price of life itself, maintained their integrity, rose superior to their surroundings, taught these same lofty sentiments to others.

Emancipation and certain constitutional amendments brought freedom to the material body of the erstwhile slave, but the soul, the higher self, could not be so easily freed from the evils that slavery had fastened upon it through centuries of debasement; and because of this soul degradation the Negro, no less than the South, needed to be physically, mentally and morally reconstructed.

Reconstruction, the eradication of former characteristics, the growth and development of new and more favorable ones, is with any race the work of time. Generations must pass, and still it need not be expected that the process will be full and complete; meanwhile, what measure of success is the Negro achieving? Were his achievements in the nineteenth century, educationally, morally, financially and otherwise at all commensurate with his opportunities?

The year 1863 saw four million Negroes come forth from a state of cruel bondage with little of this world's goods that constitute capital; with few of those incentives to labor that universally are requisites to the full and free development of labor and capital. The knowledge the Negro had of agriculture, of domestic life, and in some cases, his high-grade mechanical skill, gave him something of a vantage ground, but for nearly two hundred and fifty years he had been so "worked" that it would be expecting too much to demand that he at once comprehend the true dignity of labor. Nor was it to be expected that to his untutored mind freedom and work were terms to be intimately associated. Then there was a certain amount of constitutional inertia to be overcome, a natural heritage of the native of a tropical or semi-tropical climate, but quite incompatible with the fierce competition of American civilization, or with the material conditions of a people who owned in the entire country forty years ago, only a few thousand dollars; and among whom education was limited to the favored few whose previous estate either of freedom, or by other propitious circumstance, had rendered its acquisition possible. Organizations for business enterprise or any purpose of reform and advancement, outside of the Northern cities, was practically unknown.

Evidently one of the first things to be done by which the Negro could be reconstructed and become an intelligent member of society was to educate him; teach him to provide for himself; making him more provident and painstaking; teaching him self-reliance and self-control; teaching him the value of time, of money, and the intimate relationship of the two. Certainly not a light task. These lessons could only be learned in the practical school of experience, then, not in a day. And what has been accomplished? Forty years ago there was not in the entire Southland a single Negro school; before the close of the nineteenth century there were twenty thousand Negro school houses, thirty thousand Negro teachers, and three million Negro school children happily wending their way to the "Pierian Spring."

Under the "system," generally speaking, it had been considered a crime to teach the Negro to read or write; and the census of 1870 shows that only two-tenths of all the Negroes of the United States, over ten years of age, could write. Ten years later, the proportion had increased to three-tenths of the whole number; while in 1890 only a generation after emancipation, forty-three per cent of those ten years and over were able to read and write; this proportion before the close of the century reached forty-five per cent.

To wipe out forty-five per cent of illiteracy in less than forty years; to find millions of children in the common schools; to find twenty thousand Negroes learning trades under the soul inspiring banner of free labor; to find other thousands successfully operating many commercial enterprises; among these, several banks, one cotton mill, and one silk mill; to find Negroes performing four-fifths of the free labor of the South, thus becoming a strong industrial factor of the section is to furnish proof of achievements in the nineteenth century of which we need not be ashamed; and considering the restrictions of labor unions, the fields or classes of labor from which the Negro is practically barred regardless of section, quite commensurate with the opportunities afforded him during the period in question.

Within forty years the system of instruction in the American schools has undergone some radical changes for the better; and if the system in vogue at the beginning of this period, with the study of the classics as the pivotal point, did not fit the practical needs of the average Anglo-Saxon youth, with his heritage of centuries of culture, it is not strange if some blunders were made in attempting to shape this same classical education into a working basis for a people emerging from a state of bondage in which to impart even the elements of education, was considered a crime, generally speaking.

Industrial, manual, or technical training had not, forty years ago, taken firm hold upon the educational system, and school courses for Negroes were planned after classical models, perhaps better suited in many instances for students of a more advanced mentality and civilization; for humanity at large can scarcely hope to escape the slow and inevitable stages and processes of evolution. Individual genius, however, bound by no law, may leap and bound from stage to stage; and we point with pride to Negroes whose classic education in the early decades of freedom served not only to prove their own individual ability, but the capacity of the race for, and susceptibility to, a high degree of culture at a time when such demonstration was a prime necessity.

We do not consider that any mistake was made in at once providing for the classical or higher education of those who were mentally able to receive it, and as brilliant achievements of the nineteenth century from an educational standpoint, we refer with a keen sense of gratification to the two thousand five hundred and twenty-five or more college graduates who are helping to raise the standard of the race from all points of view; to the real genius of the race that has given us Douglass, Langston, Bruce, Washington, Tanner, Scarborough, Page, Grisham, Miller, Dubois, Wright, Bowen, Crogman, Johnson, Dunbar, Chestnutt and others too numerous to mention, whose names should be enshrined in the hearts of present and future generations; to the forty thousand Negro students pursuing courses in higher institutions of learning; to the twelve thousand pursuing classical courses; to the one hundred and twenty thousand taking scientific courses; to the one hundred and fifty-six institutions for the higher education of Negroes; to the two thousand practicing physicians; to the three hundred newspapers and the five hundred books written and published by Negroes; to a gradually increasing discrimination in all those matters of taste and form which mark the social status of a people, and give to the individual, or the mass, the, perhaps, indefinable, but at the same time, distinctive, stamp of culture.

These achievements, alone, within less than forty years of freedom, serve to demonstrate our fitness for civilization, and also, that as the years pass there is a still greater necessity for Negroes who possess a broad, a liberal, a well balanced education; and at the same time a similar need for Negroes possessing shrewd, business ability; a high degree of mechanical skill; extensive knowledge of industrial arts and sciences, and of profitably invested capital.

From the early years of freedom a few leaders, as at Hampton, realized, that the great mass of Negroes needed first of all experimental knowledge of the dignity of labor such as could never result from labor performed under the conditions of slavery; that they needed to know more of skilled labor in order to be able to meet and enter the fierce competition of American industrial life, or even to live upon the plane of American civilization; and in spite of adverse criticism, these leaders proceeded to establish industrial and manual training schools for the Negro, with such elementary training as from their point of view seemed most beneficial. That the methods chosen have been rich in results, it is only necessary to know something of the deep and extensive influence of Hampton, Tuskegee, Normal, and other industrial schools, in directly, or indirectly, improving the environment and daily life of the masses.

The insidious and ultimate effect of slavery upon the normal and spiritual nature of the enslaved is to blunt, to entirely efface the finer instincts and sensibilities, to take away those germs of manhood and womanhood that distinguish the lowest savage from the beasts of the field. Continue this soul-debasement for centuries, deny the slave the right to home, the right to family—ties which universally prove the greatest stimulus to courage, patriotism, morality, civilization—then declare the emancipated slave a brute, for whom education does nothing, because in little more than a generation he has not wiped out all of the degradation that the conditions of generations instilled and intensified!

Criminologists, discussing the apparent increase of crime in this country, assert that this apparent increase is largely due to the more complete records kept of criminals within the last forty years than formerly, and the better facilities for ferreting out crime and for subjecting offenders to the penalty of the law; and it may be added, in the Negro's case, as recently stated by a Kansas City judge, a native of Georgia, noted for his unprejudiced views and fair dealing, "It takes less evidence to convict a Negro than it does a white man; and a longer term in the peni-

.tentiary will be given a Negro for the same offense than will be given a white offender. That is why I have been so frequently compelled to cut down the sentence of Negroes." The entire history of the chain-gang system corroborates these statements—a system that helps to increase the reported number of criminals; and although race riots, lynchings and massacres may seem to indicate the opposite to the uninitiated, the Negro is not a lawless element of society. In the United States a natural restlessness has possessed him since emancipation, and it requires time to work out and adjust conditions under which he can develop normally from the standpoint of morality as well as from other points of view. Meanwhile, the prime necessity to raise the moral status is the development and upbuilding of that which in its highest embodiment, was denied him in the days of bondage—the home. We need homes, homes, homes, where intelligence and morality rule. And what was accomplished in this line in the nineteenth century? From owning comparatively few homes forty years ago, the Negro advanced before the close of the century to the position of occupying one million five hundred thousand farms and homes; and of owning two hundred and seventy-five thousand of these; many of them, as shown by views, forming a part of the exhibit at the Paris Exposition and elsewhere, compare favorably with the homes of any people.

As to the intelligence and morality that constitute the environment of the great mass of these homes owned by Negroes, the statistics of education and of crime show that Negro criminals do not, as a rule, come from the refined and educated classes, but from the most illiterate, the stupid, and the besotted element; from the class that has not been reached by the moral side of education, if at all. Says the compiler of the eleventh census: "Of juvenile criminals the smallest ratio is found among Negroes." This speaks well for the general atmosphere of the home life of our youth; while the bravery displayed by the colored man in every war of American independence has demonstrated his ability to risk life fearlessly "in defense of a country in which too many states permit his exclusion from the rights of citizenship." Such sacrifice presupposes a moral ideal of the highest type.

The position of the women of the race, always an index to the real progress of a people, in spite of slanderous attacks from unscrupulous members of her own and other races, is gradually improving, and was materially aided and abetted by the liberal ideas that especially obtained in the latter half of the century with reference to the development of women—irrespective of race or color—along the line of education, the professions, the industrial arts, etc.

As to the advancement of the Negro from a financial standpoint, it is possible that his achievements during the period in question might have been greater; yet both from within and without there have been many hindrances to overcome in the matter of accumulating wealth.

One of the greatest crimes of the slave system was that in practically denying to the slave the right to the product of his labor or any part thereof; it, to all intents and purposes destroyed his acquisitive faculty; thus he had small incentive to labor when free; and as the years went by, accumulated little in the shape of capital; showed little interest in profitable investment of his savings, if he were so fortunate as to have any. The great number of secret orders, and other schemes for the unwary, the main object of which apparently was to "bury the people" with great pomp and show, drained his pockets of most of the surplus change.

The Freedmen's Bureau sought to establish Negroes as peasant proprietors of the soil on the farms and plantations of the stricken South, and dreams of "forty acres and a mule" for a long time possessed the more ambitious only, in many instances, to meet a rude awakening; but notwithstanding the fact that the system of renting land, combined with the credit system of obtaining the necessities of life while waiting for the production and sale of the crop, is not conducive to the ownership of land on the part of the tenant; notwithstanding the very natural tendency on the part of the Negro to disassociate ideas of freedom and of tilling the soil, added to a desire to segregate in large cities in place of branching out to the sparsely settled districts of the great West and Northwest, there to take up rich farming lands and by a pioneer life to mend his fortunes in company with the peasants of other nations who are thus acquiring a firm foothold and a competence for their descendants; we repeat—in spite of the facts mentioned—before the close of the century the Negro had accumulated farms and homes valued in the neighborhood of seven hundred and fifty million dollars; personal property valued at one hundred and seventy millions; and had raised eleven millions for educational purposes. From these, and such other statistics as are available, relative to the achievements of the Negro in the United States during the nineteenth century, bearing in mind our first propo-

J. W. E. Bowen, D. D.

J. W. E. BOWEN, A. M., PH. D., D. D.

Dr. John Wesley Edward Bowen was born in New Orleans. His father, Edward Bowen, went to New Orleans from Washington, D. C. He was a free man, a boss carpenter and builder by trade, and able to read, write and cipher. He was highly esteemed, was prosperous in business, accumulated some money and lived in comfort. Dr. Bowen's mother, Rose Bowen, he says, was the grand-daughter of an African Princess of the Jolloffer tribe, on the west coast of Africa. When he was three years old his father bought him and his mother out of slavery. When he was thirteen he went to the preparatory school of New Orleans University for colored people, established after the war by the Methodist Episcopal church. When he was seventeen he entered the University proper, and five years later he was graduated with the degree of A. B. At the age of seventeen he was converted in a Methodist revival meeting, and nine months later was licensed as a local preacher, and has been preaching ever since.

Soon after his graduation Dr. Bowen became Professor of Latin and Greek in the Central Tennessee College, at Nashville, in which position he remained for four years. In 1882 he resigned his professorship and entered Boston University, where he studied four years, taking the degree of B. D. in 1885; and the degree of Ph. D. in 1887 from the school of all sciences of Boston University. He also did special advanced work in Greek, Latin, Hebrew, Chaldee, Arabic and German, and in Metaphysics and Psychology.

He was the first colored man in the Methodist church to take the degree of Ph. D. and the second colored man to take the degree in any university in this country.

Soon after leaving the university, Dr. Bowen joined the New England Methodist Conference, and was appointed pastor of the Revere Street Church. While in New England he also preached acceptably in many white churches—serving one for a month, and was asked to become their pastor after this period. After serving St. John's colored church in Newark three years, he became pastor of the Centennial Methodist Episcopal church in Baltimore, and at the same time professor of church history in the Morgan college for colored people in that city. During this pastorate he conducted a phenomenal revival in which there were 735 conversions.

Dr. Bowen next was the pastor of Asbury Methodist Episcopal church in Washington for three years, and at the same time Professor of Hebrew in Howard University for colored people in that city. He here acquired a national fame as a scholar, orator and thinker. During this pastorate he pursued the study of the Semitic languages in the school of correspondence of Dr. W. R. Harper, then at Yale University. When he resigned his positions at Washington, he became for one year a Field Secretary of the Missionary Society of the Methodist Episcopal church, retaining his Washington residence.

Dr. Bowen was next elected Professor of Historical Theology in Gammon Theological Seminary for colored people at Atlanta, Ga., which position he still holds. In consequence of the resignation of the president, the Rev. Dr. Thierkield, he has been for several months the chairman of the faculty, and the executive officer of the institution. He is also the Secretary of the Stewart Foundation for Africa, a member of the American Negro Academy, and a member of the American Historical Association, which last society numbers among its members some of the most learned men in this and other countries. Dr. Bowen received the degree of A. M. from the University of New Orleans in 1886, and that of D. D. from Gammon Theological Seminary in 1892.

Amid all these engrossing occupations, Dr. Bowen has been a voluminous writer and an indefatigable lecturer. His publications include a volume of sermons and addresses, "Plain Talks to the Colored People of America," "Appeal to the King," "The Comparative Status of the Negro at the Close of the War and To-day," "The Struggle for Supremacy Between Church and State in the Middle Ages," and "The American and the African Negro." He has now ready for the press a volume of "University Addresses" and a volume of "Discussions in Philosophy and Theory;" also "The History of the Education of the Negro Race."

Dr. Bowen was voted for at the last General Conference for Bishop. He stood second on first ballot. His friends predict that he will be elected at the forthcoming General Conference.

sition—the measure of the success of a people is the depths from which it has come—we conclude that educationally, morally, financially, the Negro has accomplished by means of the opportunities at his command about all that could be expected of him or any other race under similar conditions.

That the Negro has made mistakes goes without saying. All races as well as all individuals have made them, but—"Let the dead past bury its dead."

The great problem confronting this and future generations is and will be, how to surpass or even equal our ancestors in bringing about results that make for the upbuilding of sterling character; how with our superior advantages to make the second forty years of freedom and the entire future life proportionally worthy of honorable mention.

> "Build to-day, then strong and sure,
>   With a firm and ample base,
> And ascending and secure
>   Shall to-morrow find its place.
> Thus alone can we attain
>   To those turrets, where the eye
> Sees the world as one vast plain,
>   And one boundless reach of sky."

THIRD PAPER.

DID THE AMERICAN NEGRO MAKE, IN THE NINETEENTH CENTURY, ACHIEVEMENTS ALONG THE LINES OF WEALTH, MORALITY, EDUCATION, ETC., COMMENSURATE WITH HIS OPPORTUNITIES? IF SO, WHAT ACHIEVEMENTS DID HE MAKE?

BY REV. J. W. E. BOWEN, D. D.

Inference and conjecture are the stock methods of argument of the unintelligent or the superficially informed. Such indisposition or incapacity leads to erroneous conclusions. Nothing but an appeal to facts involving careful and painstaking labor and a wise sifting of facts, that myth and legend be eliminated, should claim the attention of thinking men. It must be confessed, however, that in any discussion that relates to the comparative status of the Negro over against his standing in slavery full and accurate data are lacking. The statistical science of to-day was unknown then, and it is next to the impossible to affirm positively the relative superiority or inferiority of present day growth over those of that day. This statement is not made to deny the truth of the immense stride of the latter times, but it is made as a reasonable off-set to those prejudicial and dogmatic declarations of the superior conditions of slavery over those of freedom. Dogmatism is the argument of the bigot. It is not wide of the truth, to say that the claims of certain writers that the Negro has retrograded physically, morally and socially, lacks the confirmation of veritable data. It is admitted that the modern diseases of civilized life have made inroads into his hardy nature, but the universal declaration of inferiority is not proved. It is also true that in isolated cases physicians of that day noted the comparative freedom of the blacks from the maladies of ennui and bacchanalian feastings, but no half-kept record of that day is before us to justify the statement that the Negro of to-day is superior to his mighty sire of ante-bellum fame that stood between the plow handles all day and danced or shouted all night. The increase of zymotic diseases is admitted, but there has been a corresponding increase of power in many lines that will more than counteract this baleful growth.

Again, over against this admission may be placed another statement of fact, not to minify the truth already alluded to, but to illustrate the futility of basing an entire argument upon one arm of a syllogism, viz.: the Negro's numerical growth since freedom sung in his ears, is a clear evidence of physical vitality. This growth has kept pace with the glowing prophecies of statisticians.

Let us subdivide the subject, that the facts may be grouped in a logical order. Let us study the growth of the race under three heads: Numerical growth, material growth, moral and social growth.

Growth in numbers is growth in power of resistance, and this is basal in the life of any people. If there be not found in a people a power to resist the forces of death and to reproduce itself by the natural laws of race increase, then such a people should not be counted in the struggle of races. In other words, race fecundity contains the germs of intellectual and national existence.

At the distance of forty years from slavery, the declarations of the early extinction of the Negro, under the conditions of freedom, are comical and absurd. It was affirmed with all the authority of divine prophecy that the Negro race could not exist under any other condition than slavery, and this concern became a basis for contending for his continued enslavement.

The unvarnished facts brought to light by cold mathematicians are now before us, and a few interesting and startling discoveries are placed before us. In the next place growth in material productions and the possession of the fruits of civilized life deserve attention.

The story of the burdens and disadvantages of the Negro at the beginning of his days of freedom has not yet been committed to paper. It will require a black writer to perform this deed. But it is within the limits of truth to affirm that history can furnish no burdens upon a race's shoulders parallel to those upon the shoulders of the untutored black man when he was shot out of the mouth of the cannon into freedom's arena. A Hindoo poet, of English blood, has written a beautiful poem upon the "White Man's Burden," but it is poetry. "The Black Man's Burden" is a burden that rests upon his heart, and, like the deepest feelings of the human heart, it cannot be reduced to cold type. Thomas Nelson Page describes the untoward beginnings of the race:

"No other people ever had more disadvantages to contend with on their issue into freedom. They were seduced, deceived, misled. Their habits of industry were destroyed, and they were fooled into believing that they could be legislated into immediate equality with a race that, without mentioning superiority of ability and education, had a thousand years' start of them. They were made to believe that their only salvation lay in aligning themselves against the other race, and following blindly the adventurers who came to lead them to a new promised land. It is no wonder that they committed great blunders and great excesses. For nearly a generation they have been pushed along the wrong road. But now, in place of political leaders, who were simply firebrands, is arising a new class of leaders, which, with a wider horizon, a deeper sagacity and a truer patriotism, are endeavoring to establish a foundation of morality, industry and knowledge, and to build upon them a race that shall be capable of availing itself of every opportunity that the future may present, and worthy of whatever fortune it may bring."

Slavery did not teach him economy; on the contrary, it taught him profligacy, and, where he learned to economize, it was in spite of the system. His wastefulness is not yet a thing of the past, but he has made commendable advance in learning how to save. What are the facts? In the state of Georgia alone, the Negro has dug out of the hills more than

$30,000,000 of taxable property. This amount represents more than five times the entire wealth of all the Negroes of the United States, North and South, bond and free, taxable and personal, at the birth of freedom. But when we collect together the wealth of the entire race, the figures read like romance.

Some facts for reflection:

Four millions of slaves were valued at $3,500,000,000. Negroes own 87 per cent of their homes in fee simple; 89 per cent of their farms are unencumbered.

They own, Banks	3
Magazines	5
Newspapers	400

Value of Libraries	$ 500,000
Drug stores	500,000
School property	20,000,000
Church property	42,000,000
160,000 farms	400,000,000
150,000 homes	350,000,000
Personal property	200,000,000

With these facts undisputed, the question, Has the Negro kept pace with his opportunities? contains its own affirmative answer. It is an incomparable achievement that the Negro should have accumulated and saved this vast amount of wealth within the short space of forty years.

In the social and intellectual life the Negro has surpassed all hopes. There can be furnished by the race a thoroughly equipped man for any chair of learning for a university. He began with the blue-back spelling book and has steadily grown in learning and power until he now occupies a respectable position in the literary world.

But the pivotal point that is determinative in this discussion, and that which is considered the conclusion of the whole matter, is the moral and social question, as well as the domestic virtues of which woman is the queen. The accumulation of property, and the achievements in the world of letters, admirable as they are in themselves, and for purposes of civilization, are secondary and valueless in the final analysis, if there is no corresponding moral development and social power. The evolution of the family, based upon monogamy, is one of the chief glories of Christianity over against the libertinism and polygamous practices of paganism.

Speaking of the women of our race, we cannot but speak the things which we have seen and heard. With Dr. Crummell, "In her girlhood all the delicate tenderness of her sex has been rudely outraged. In the field, in the rude cabin, in the press-room and in the factory, she was thrown into the companionship of coarse and ignorant men. No chance was given her for delicate reserve or tender modesty. From her girlhood she was the doomed victim of the grossest passions. All the virtues of her sex were utterly ignored. If the instinct of chastity asserted itself, then she had to fight like a tigress for the ownership and possession of her own person, and oftentimes had to suffer pains and lacerations for her virtuous self assertion. When she reached maturity all the tender instincts of her womanhood were ruthlessly violated. At the age of marriage, always prematurely anticipated under slavery, she was mated as the stock of the plantation were mated, not to be the companion of a loved and chosen husband, but to be the breeder of human cattle for the field or auction block."

Has this condition of affairs changed? I answer unequivocally, yea, a thousand times, yea. A negative answer would be the quintessence of ignorance. From a recent careful survey of every Southern state through nearly one hundred trusty observers, I have the testimony that the young women are pure in large numbers, and are rapidly increasing in an intense desire and determination to preserve themselves chaste and pure from the lustful approaches of the sinner, and that the number of legally and lovingly married families, purely preserved in the domestic and social virtues among husbands and wives, sons and daughters, is so far beyond the days of slavery that a comparison would minify the difference.

The marvel is, that the Negro has sufficient moral vitality left to cut his way through the whirlpool of licentiousness to the solid rock of Christian character. From the harem life of promiscuous and unnameable sins of slavery, some of which were the natural and fatal growth of pagan vices, others the fruit of prostitution, to the making of one clean, beautiful, noble and divine family and home, covers a period of intense, moral, spiritual and intellectual development, more significant than the geologic transformation of ages. Be it known that this one family can be duplicated by a hundred thousand and more.

The moral and social darkness has not been increased either in quality or intensity. The splendid results of philanthropic effort have served only as a small tallow candle which has been brought into the darkness of this Egyptian night, and the darkness has thickened relatively only because the light has been brought in. That faint and flickering light reveals how great the darkness has been, and is. Some think that the shadows are lengthening into eternal night for the Negro, but that flickering light within has upon it the breath of God which will some day fan it into the white and penetrating blazes of the electro-carbon searchlight, that shall chase away the curse of slavery. Thus, from every point of view, the growth of the Negro has more than kept pace with his opportunities.

FOURTH PAPER.

DID THE AMERICAN NEGRO MAKE, IN THE NINETEENTH CENTURY, ACHIEVEMENTS ALONG THE LINES OF WEALTH, MORALITY, EDUCATION, ETC., COMMENSURATE WITH HIS OPPORTUNITIES? IF SO, WHAT ACHIEVEMENTS DID HE MAKE?

BY REV. M. C. B. MASON.

The progress made by the Negro since emancipation has challenged the admiration and wonder of the world. In all the annals of the world's history, there is no parallel to it, and this progress, remarkable as it is, has been in all lines, and in all departments of his life and activity. Indeed, it would be quite a problem to be able to declare in what particular line he has made the most progress. To secure some adequate conception of what he is to-day, we must compare him with what he was yesterday. In no other way can we come to any comprehensive idea of the progress which he has made and the work which he has accomplished.

A generation ago, he had practically nothing. He started out with scarcely a name—poor, ignorant, degraded, demoralized, as slavery left him. Without a home, without a foot of land, without the true sense of real manhood, ragged, destitute, so freedom found him. He stood at one end of the cotton row with his master at the other and as he stepped out into the new and inexperienced life before him his master still claimed him and the very clothes upon his back. Under these peculiar circumstances and amid these peculiar difficulties he began life for himself. He had, however, learned how to work; so much he brought out of slavery with him; and right royal service it has rendered him. What

Rev. M. C. B. Mason, Ph. D.

REV. M. C. B. MASON, PH. D.

Rev. Dr. M. C. B. Mason, senior corresponding secretary of the Freedmen's Aid and Southern Education Society of the Methodist Episcopal Church, was born of slave parents near Houma, La., March 27, 1859. In 1857, two years before young Mason was born, his father purchased his own freedom, paying $1,350. The papers were never legally made out and his father had to wait with other members of the family for the Emancipation Proclamation to secure their freedom.

Young Mason was twelve years of age before he had ever seen a school-house, having entered school in July, 1871, and mastered the alphabet the first day. Subsequently he attended a school of higher grade and in 1888 graduated from the New Orleans University from the regular classical course. Two years afterward he entered the Gammon Theological Seminary at Atlanta, Ga., graduating therefrom in 1891. Immediately after his graduation he matriculated in the Syracuse University, at Syracuse, N. Y., taking the "non-resident course" leading to the degree of Doctor of Philosophy.

In July of the same year he was elected Field Agent of the Freedmen's Aid Society of the Methodist Episcopal Church, being the first colored man ever called to such a position. So successfully did he prosecute his work that at the General Committee meeting, which met in New York in 1893, he was elected Assistant Corresponding Secretary, and in May, 1896, at the General Conference in Cleveland, composed of 537 representatives, only 69 of whom were colored, he was elected Corresponding Secretary, with a majority of 104 votes against 11 competitors, all of whom were white. Four years later at the General Conference which assembled in Chicago, Dr. Mason was re-elected and made Senior Corresponding Secretary, receiving the largest vote ever given to any General Conference Secretary in the history of the Methodist Episcopal Church. This is all the more remarkable when it is remembered that there were 14 candidates in a body composed of 701 representatives, of whom only 73 were colored. It will be remembered also that the salary paid a General Conference Officer of the Methodist Episcopal Church is the same as that paid to the Bishops, and Dr. Mason is no exception to the rule.

The Doctor is quite a success as a money raiser and has secured hundreds of thousands of dollars during the ten years he has been connected with this great educational institution of the Methodist Episcopal Church. The Freedmen's Aid and Southern Educational Society has educated hundreds and thousands of men and women of our race, and has an average attendance of over seven thousand young men and women of color in its schools every year. Dr. Mason is thus brought in contact with more young men and women of the race than any other Negro in America. And the whole race is very largely indebted to him for the work which, through this institution, he is accomplishing.

As an orator the Doctor has no superiors, and few equals. He is in great demand all over the country, especially in the North. We are told that he has been offered $6,000 per year with a guarantee for ten years, if he would resign his present position and take the lecture platform. This offer he has constantly refused preferring to remain in the work where he can be more useful to his own people.

During a recent trip to Europe he was in constant demand for lectures in London, Glasgow, Belfast and among the English colony in France.

is he to-day? From this humble beginning of a generation ago when he had absolutely nothing he has begun to acquire something of this world's goods. He has been getting for himself a home, some land, some money in bank, and some interest in stocks and bonds. His industry, thrift and economy are everywhere in evidence and he is bravely and consciously struggling toward the plane where his vindication as a man and a citizen is what he is and what he has acquired. In Louisiana he pays taxes on twelve millions, in Georgia on fourteen millions and in South Carolina on thirteen millions. A recent statistician, writing for the New York Sun, estimates his wealth North and South at four hundred millions. During the last few years much of this accumulation of property is in farm land which everywhere is rapidly increasing in value. In this matter of securing a home and some land, the Negro's achievements are certainly commensurate with his opportunities.

In education his progress is even more clearly manifest. There are to-day 2,912,912 Negro children of school age in the United States. Of these 1,511,618 are enrolled in the public schools and the average attendance is sixty-seven per cent of the enrollment. In addition to the 1,511,618 who are enrolled in the public schools 50,000 more are attending schools under the care and maintenance of the church. In this work all the leading denominations of the country are represented. The Freedmen's Aid and Southern Educational Society of the Methodist Episcopal Church among the first, if not the very first to engage in this work, has under its care forty-seven institutions of Christian learning, twenty of which are mainly for the education of the colored people. These institutions are scattered all over the sixteen former slave states and have possibly sent out more graduates as teachers, preachers, physicians, dentists, pharmacists and industrial workers than any other institution or set of institutions doing work in the South. In addition to the work of the Freedmen's Aid and Southern Educational Society there are the American Missionary Association, under Congregational auspices, the Baptist Home Missionary Society, the Presbyterian Home Missionary Society, the Lutheran Evangelical Society—all of which support institutions for Christian learning for the education of the colored people throughout the South. These schools are mainly for the higher and secondary education of the Negro and have accomplished untold good. There are to-day nearly 30,000 Negro teachers in the United States and a careful estimate will show that these church schools have sent out over 20,000 of them. And these teachers, prepared by these church schools, commonly so called, were the first to take their places in the public schools as rapidly as they were opened and these, in the very nature of the case, represent a very large per cent of the teaching force even at the present time.

Again distinctively Negro bodies of churchmen, especially Baptists and Methodists, are also carrying forward a commendable work of Christian education among their own people. Some schools of excellent standing in the African Methodist Episcopal, the African Methodist Episcopal Zion and the Colored Methodist Episcopal Churches are doing most effective work and the results are being felt in all directions.

The work of industrial education is steadily growing in all sections of the South, and is destined more and more to occupy a prominent place in the education of our people. The emphasis placed upon this line of education at Hampton Institute, Hampton, Va., Claflin University at Orangeburg, S. C., and Tuskegee Institute at Tuskegee, Ala., is having its effect in many other places. New Orleans, Louisiana, Wilmington, Delaware, Nashville, Tennessee, and several other cities have adopted some lines of industrial education in their public schools, and in some places it is compulsory. Consequently, industrial education, which, a few years ago, was mainly confined to a few institutions, has been, in some form or other, adopted in a large number of cities both in the North and in the South. The results of this line of work are already seen. Hundreds of industrial artisans and trained mechanics are scattered here and there all over the South, and are practically and effectively solving the problem.

In addition to the work of general education, Negroes have entered all the learned professions, and are succeeding beyond the most sanguine expectations of their friends. This is especially true in medicine, pharmacy and dentistry. The Negro lawyer has done well. He has had a difficult field, and the fact that some have acquired sufficient ability and influence to practice before the Supreme Court of the United States, speaks well for the race in this difficult field. But, the success of the Negro physician is perhaps the most remarkable in any line of professional work to which he has aspired. From the results of careful study made by an eminent statistician, it was found that the average salary of white physicians in the United States is about $700, and the average salary of Negro physicians is $1,444 per annum. The encouraging feature about this whole matter is that as physicians among us increase, the greater is the increase in the average salary. While dentists and pharmacists have not succeeded quite so well, yet the success of the physician has directly opened an avenue for the pharmacists, and has indirectly helped the dentist. Consequently, in nearly every town of any considerable size in the South to-day, there are four or five prosperous Negro physicians, with two or three drug stores, where Negro pharmacists carefully compound their prescriptions, and have the confidence and respect of the entire community.

The Negro is progressing morally. From whatever standpoint you view him he is getting away from the past and wiping the reproach of Egypt from him. Any careful observer will see at once that in the field of ethics and morals a veritable revolution has taken place among the Negroes during the present generation. There is still, however, much room for improvement, and to this perhaps, more than to any one thing, the race must now turn its attention. Some questions regarding his inability to learn have all been settled by the remarkable achievements which he has made in all lines of intellectual endeavor, but it must still be confessed that in the field of morals and manners, the charge is still made, and that not without some semblance of truth, that evidences of the essential qualities of sturdy and manly character are not as clearly manifest among us as they should be.

Here the problem comes home and the Negro, as ever, is the most important factor. The pertinent question is not what shall be done with the Negro, but rather what will the Negro do with himself. This is the question, and the answer he gives to it will largely depend, in no small degree, whether he shall continue to be an insignificant element in this Nation or become more a living factor in its growth and development. Here I repeat it, is the question and this is the problem. Intellectual ability is good, but individual purity is better. Rights and privileges are in themselves good, but to make ourselves worthy of them is infinitely better. It is encouraging and gratifying to know that so many are getting a correct interpretation of life's deeper meanings and are daily coming into possession of higher and purer ideals. Who can say that the Negro has not made progress commensurate with his opportunities?

FIFTH PAPER.

DID THE AMERICAN NEGRO MAKE, IN THE NINETEENTH CENTURY, ACHIEVEMENTS ALONG THE LINES OF WEALTH, MORALITY, EDUCATION, ETC., COMMENSURATE WITH HIS OPPORTUNITIES? IF SO, WHAT ACHIEVEMENTS DID HE MAKE?

BY REV. D. WEBSTER DAVIS.

To the superficial observer, it would sometimes appear that the American Negro did not make achievements commensurate with his opportunities, during the nineteenth century. Yet, on taking a more comprehensive view, the student of history and sociology must decide in the affirmative.

In deciding upon the comparative progress of a race, along the lines of a higher civilization, care must be taken as to the standard by which he is to be measured, and what has been his real opportunities. Civilization is a plant of slow growth, as evidenced by the history of all Nations that have accomplished great things in the past. There is a difference, as wide as the heavens, between the refined and cultured Englishman of to-day, and the rough, uncouth Norseman of the ninth century; but more than a thousand years were required to bring about that transformation. A difference, as wide as the poles, exists between the ancient Gauls, who were conquered by the Franks in the tenth century, and the Chesterfieldian Frenchman of to-day; yet the same time elapsed between these two periods. There is just as marked a difference, in many respects, between those twenty uncouth savages, brought to the shores of Virginia in 1620, and the best specimens of the American Negro of to-day, and yet only 287 years lie between the former and the latter.

The next question that naturally rises is, "What have been the real opportunities of the American Negro?" Brought here a savage from his native wilds, and thrown into abject, and, in many cases, cruel slavery, he yet received from this iniquitous institution something of God. As Dr. Booker T. Washington so well says: "He went into slavery, practically, without a language, and came out speaking the beautiful English, the finest language to convey thought, ever devised by the mind of man. He went in without a God, and came out with the Christian religion." These are powerful agencies for civilization, and yet, the debasing influence of slavery has done much to hinder, while it has done something to help him. Only a comparatively few Negroes came into direct contact

Rev. D. Webster Davis

REV. DANIEL WEBSTER DAVIS.

Randall and Charlotte Davis, who were valued servants on a Caroline County farm, found themselves, March 25, 1862, the parents of a little black boy, who brought gladness and sorrow to their hearts. Gladness, because the Lord had sent them a boy, and he was their boy, bone of their bone, flesh of their flesh, blood of their blood. Sorrow, because, while he was their child, he was *"Marster's"* child too; he belonged to *"Marster"* more than he did to them.

War was raging. The Negro cabins knew little else but muffled prayers, stifled songs, unuttered sermons—all for deliverance. From the cabin to the broad fields of tobacco these emotions and utterances were carried daily. Father preached, mother prayed. Singing was but the opening of the oppressed heart. Those were troublous years, heart-aching years. Years of consecration, fixed and unceasing, to the God of Freedom. In such an atmosphere the boy was nurtured and reared.

The war was over. The boy over whom mother and father had prayed had changed from a chattel, a thing of barter, to a free child, belonging only to mother and father. What a change!

Entering the public schools of Richmond, step by step, grade by grade was passed with honor and public commendation, until June, 1878, when D. Webster Davis graduated from the Richmond High and Normal School, receiving at the same time the Essayist Medal.

In 1880 the subject of our sketch commenced to teach in the public schools of Richmond and has taught therein continuously ever since, and is to-day rated as one of the best and most progressive in the system.

September 8, 1893, Mr. Davis married Miss Lizzie Smith, a teacher in the Richmond public schools. From this happy union three children have been born.

In October, 1895, feeling that the time had come for him to be about his Father's business he was ordained to the ministry.

From a child he babbled in verse, and the poetic muse brought in 1896, "Idle Moments," and in 1898, "Weh Down Souf." These two books established the name of Rev. Mr. Davis as a poet and have given him front rank with his contemporaries in verse-making.

Guadaloupe College, Seguin, Texas, recognizing the meritorious work of Rev. Davis bestowed upon him the degree of A. M. in 1898.

Rev. Mr. Davis is at present pastor of the Second Baptist Church of Manchester, where he has an ideal growing church of young folks, which work he began in 1895.

In the winter of 1900, the Central Lyceum Bureau of Rochester, N. Y., engaged the services of Rev. Davis for a four-weeks' reading tour, reading selections from his own works. The whole tour was an ovation, showing that texture of hair and color of skin cannot destroy that aristocracy of intellect, that charmed inner circle wherein "a man is a man for a' that."

The Lord has been good to Rev. Daniel Webster Davis, blessing him with intellectual force, blessing him with poetic utterance, blessing him with oratorical ability, blessing him in domestic felicity. Not yet in his prime, yet so richly endowed in the gifts which make men strong and powerful, it is hoped that he may be spared many years to work in the Master's vineyard, and many years to labor for the uplift of his race, oppressed and downtrodden.

May he expand and grow greater, remembering that he is God's servant, endowed for the benefit of his race, blessed, so that he may bless his people made strong, so that he may reach down and lift his people up, growing brighter and better unto the present day.

with the best side of American civilization, during slavery. The house-maids, coachmen, body-servants and, in many cases, the cooks came in direct contact with the civilization of the "Great House," and their superiority, and, in many cases, that of their ancestry, is still apparent. The "corn field Negro" (and they outnumbered the others 200 to 1) received none of the influences of this civilization, and none of the opportunities accorded the more favored servants around the "Great House."

When we take into consideration all of these circumstances, coupled with the fact that when "cut loose" from slavery in 1865, it was a matter of "root hog or die" with him for many years; and that only thirty-six years have passed away since this happy event, his achievements have been marvelous.

Optimist, as I try to be, I am not one of those who believe that the Negro has reached the delectable mountain, and that he is as good as anybody else. He is far from perfection, far from comparison with the more favored Anglo-Saxon, in wealth and culture, yet he has made progress commensurate with his opportunities.

It is a well-known philosophical axiom, that "action is equal to reaction, and in a contrary direction." The American Negro is now meeting the reaction consequent upon his violent action in the direction of civilization and culture; but, this reaction is only temporary, and, even the realization of his condition by the leading thinkers of his race, is a sign of hope, and an evidence of substantial progress that must tell for good.

Now, what achievements did he make? First, as to wealth: According to the census of 1900 he has forty million dollars in church property, and twelve millions in school property. He has 140,000 farms, worth $750,000,000, and 170 million dollars in personal property. This is the result of thirty-six years of freedom. One noticeable feature is that the great bulk of his wealth has been accumulated in the South, where the large majority of the American Negroes live. No one fact is more startling in history, than that a people, once held as slaves, have been able to live and thrive among the very people by whom they were held. This accentuates the fact that, after all, nowhere has the Negro better friends than can be found among the white people of the Southland. His property aggregates $75 per capita for every man, woman and child in this country, which is certainly no mean showing for thirty-six years of freedom.

As to education, he has reduced his illiteracy forty-five per cent, he has written more than 500 books, publishes 300 newspapers, three of them dailies; he has produced 2,000 lawyers, a still larger number of doctors and 32,000 teachers. He supports several colleges, seventeen academies, fifty high schools, five law schools, five medical schools and twenty-five theological seminaries. It is true that all of the education he is obtaining is not practical; and also true that many so-called educated ones are shiftless and trifling; but this is no more than was to be expected under the circumstances.

He has built 29,000 churches, and this must mean something. It is true that in the past, his ministers have in many cases appealed to the passions, rather than to the intellect; and yet, under these old preachers, many of them honest, earnest and Godly men, the Negro has made gigantic strides in morality. He is yet far, very far below what we would like to see him, but he is coming. The new gospel of work is striking a responsive chord in the American Negro's heart, and he is beginning to see that he must be able to *do* something if he would *be* something.

Happily for him he learned to work, during the dark days of the past, it only remained for him to learn to put brains in his work. This he is fast learning under the apostles of industrial training. Since the fiat went forth, amid the groves of Eden, when man lost his first estate, "by the sweat of thy brow shalt thou eat bread," God has never reversed his edict. Work must be his salvation, as it has been the salvation of all other races. To put into poetry the words of an old friend:

> I ain't got no edikashun,
>   But dis, kno', is true:
> Dat raisin' gals too good to wuch
>   Ain't nebber gwine to do;
> Dese boys, dat look good nuf to eat,
>   But too good to saw de logs,
> Am cay'in us, ez fas' ez smok'
>   To lan' us at de dogs.

These great achievements have not been accomplished alone. The great American Home Mission Society, the American Missionary Association, the Freedmen's Bureau, and the various churches and societies of the North and South have contributed liberally of their time and means to aid us in an upward struggle. The South itself has contributed its millions to the aid of their former slaves; they have given for his schools, they have aided him in building his churches, and there is scarcely a single home among us, humble or palatial, that has not been erected largely by the aid of Southern capital. But for the friendly aid of these people among whom the great bulk of the American Negroes live, we could never have climbed as far as we have on the ladder of progress. The Negro is fast learning that, if he would be free he, himself, must strike the blow, and he is teaching his children the gospel of self-help.

The heights are still beyond, but he is slowly rising, and day by day hope grows brighter. May God continue this progress until he shall stand shoulder to shoulder with the highest civilization and culture of the world.

TOPIC II.

WILL IT BE POSSIBLE FOR THE NEGRO TO ATTAIN, IN THIS COUNTRY, UNTO THE AMERICAN TYPE OF CIVILIZATION?

BY BISHOP H. M. TURNER, D. D., LL.D., D. C. L.

This interrogatory appears to presuppose that the seventeen or more millions of colored people in North and South America are not a part of the American population, and do not constitute a part of its civilization. But the term "this country" evidently refers to the United States of America, for this being the largest and the most powerful government on the American continent, not unfrequently, is made to represent the entire continent. So the Negro is regarded as a foreign and segregated race. The American people, therefore, who grade the type of American civilization are made up of white people, for the Indian, Chinamen, and the few Mexicans are not taken in account any more than the Negro is, by reason of their diminutive numbers, and not because they are regarded wanting in intellectual capacity, as the Negro is.

The above is an interrogatory that can be easily answered if the term "American" is to include the United States and the powers that enact its laws and proclaim its judicial decisions, as we have no civilization in the aggregate. Civilization contemplates that fraternity, civil and political equality between man and man, that makes his rights, privileges and immunities inviolable and sacred in the eyes and hearts of his fellows, whatever may be his nationality, language, color, hair texture, or anything else that may make an external variation.

Civility comprehends harmony, system, method, complacency, urbanity, refinement, politeness, courtesy, justice, culture, general enlightenment and protection of life and person to any man, regardless of his color or nationality. It is enough for a civilized community to know that you are a human being, to pledge surety of physical and political safety to you, and this has been the sequence in all ages among civilized people. But such is not the condition of things as they apply to this country, I mean the United States. True, we have a National Congress, State Legislature, Subordinate and Supreme Courts, and almost every form of government, necessary to regulate the affairs of a civilized coun-

42

Bishop H. M. Turner.

BISHOP H. M. TURNER, D. D., LL. D.

Bishop H. M. Turner, D. D., LL. D., D. C. L., was born near Newbury Court House, South Carolina, February 1, 1833 or 1834. His mother's maiden name was Sarah Greer, the youngest daughter of David Greer, who was brought to this country when a boy and sold in Charleston, S. C. Greer was the son of an African king. His father, the African king, sent seven African slaves for the return of his son, but the captain of the slave ship dying before he returned, the son received his freedom when South Carolina was still under British rule, upon the ground that Royal blood could not be enslaved. Henry McNeal Turner was the oldest son of Hardy Turner and Sarah Greer Turner. Henry grew up on the cotton fields of South Carolina, and when eight or nine years old he dreamed he was on a high mountain and millions of people were looking up at him for instruction, white and colored. He then procured a spelling book and commenced to learn to read and write, to prepare to give that vast multitude instruction. He got a white boy to teach him his alphabet and how to spell to three syllables. By this time he was large enough to wait in a law office at Abbeville Court House, S. C. The young lawyers took great pleasure in giving him instruction in their leisure moments for pastime. He gained a respectable knowledge of history, arithmetic, geography, astronomy and some other branches, but would not study grammar, as he thought he could talk well enough without a knowledge of grammar.

He made such remarkably rapid progress that by the time he was fifteen years old he had read the Bible through five times, and by the aid of Walker's Pronouncing Dictionary and the young white lawyers he became a good reader, and read Watson's Apology for the Bible, Buck's Theological Dictionary and very largely in Dr. Adam Clark's Commentary and other books. He became acquainted with the African M. E. Church, joined the same, leaving the M. E. Church South, met the Conference in St. Louis, Mo., and was admitted after an examination. Bishop D. A. Payne, D. D., LL. D., appointed him to a mission in Baltimore city. While he served his appointment he studied English Grammar, Latin, Greek, German and the Hebrew languages, and became what was regarded as an excellent scholar. He studied the rules of elocution under Dr. Cummings of the Protestant Episcopal Church, and was regarded as quite an orator. He was appointed in charge of Israel Church, Washington, D. C., and his fame became so notable that President Lincoln appointed him Chaplain, the first colored man that was ever made a commissioned officer in the United States Army. He served his regiment so faithfully and gained such a reputation that President Johnson commissioned him a Chaplain in the regular service of the United States Army. He resigned in a short time and commenced the organization of the A. M. E. Church in Georgia, and was so abundantly successful that the General Conference elected him manager of the Publication Department in 1876. He served there four years with headquarters in Philadelphia, and in 1880 the General Conference sitting in St. Louis, Mo., elected him Bishop, and on the 20th of May he was consecrated to that holy office. Bishop Turner has worked up territory enough as an organizer of the A. M. E. Church to demand five conferences. He has organized four conferences in Africa, making eleven conferences that he is the founder of.

Dr. Turner was for many years superintendent in the church for the whole State of Georgia and was the first Bishop of Africa, which position he held for eight years, while having his regular conferences in the United States. He says he has received over forty-three thousand on probation in the African M. E. Church. He has been a member of the Georgia Legislature twice, a member of the Constitutional Convention, Postmaster, Inspector of Customs and held other minor positions, and was at one time regarded one of the greatest orators of his race in the United States.

try. But above these, and above law and order, which these legislative and judicial bodies have been organized to observe, and execute justice in the land, we are often confronted through the public press with reports of the most barbarous and cruel outrages, that can be perpetrated upon human beings, known in the history of the world. No savage nation can exceed the atrocities which are often heralded through the country and accepted by many as an incidental consequence. Men are hung, shot and burnt by bands of murderers who are almost invariably represented as the most influential and respectable citizens in the community, while the evidences of guilt of what is charged against the victims, who are so inhumanly outraged, are never established by proof in any court, and all we can learn about the guilt and horrible deeds charged upon the murdered victims comes from the mouth of the bloody handed wretches who perpetrate the murders, yet they are not known according to published accounts. But enough is known to get from their mouths same horrible statements as to why this and that brutal murder was done, and invariably, it is told with such oily tongues, and the whole narrative is polished over and glossed with such skillfully constructed lies, that the ruling millions lift up their hands in holy horror and exclaim "they done him right."

Why, the very judges surrounded with court officers are powerless before these bloody mobs. Prisoners are cruelly, fiendishly and inhumanly dragged from their very custody. Sheriffs are as helpless as newborn babes. I do not pretend to say that in no instance have the victims been guilty as a whole or in part of some blood-curdling crime, for men perpetrate lawless acts, revolting deeds, disgraceful and brutal crimes, regardless of nationality, language or color, at times. But civilization presurmises legal adjudication and the intervention of that judicial authority which civilized legislation produces. And when properly administered the accused is innocent till he gets a fair trial; no verdict of guilt from a drunken lawless mob should be accepted by a civilized country; and when they do accept it they become a barbarous people. And a barbarous people make a barbarous nation. Civilization knows no marauders, mobs or lynchers and any one adjudged guilty by a drunken band of freebooters is not guilty in the eyes of a civilized people. For the ruthless and violent perpetrators of lawless deeds, especially when they are incarnate, are murderers to all intents and purposes, and popular approval does not diminish the magnitude of the crime. Millions may say, "Well done," but God, reason and civilization stamp them as culprits.

I confess that the United States has the highest form of civilized institutions that any nation has had. Let us take a cursory glance at the institutions in this country. It has common schools by the tens of thousands; colleges and universities of every grade by the hundred; millions of daily newspapers are flying from the press, and weekly papers and monthly magazines on all imaginary subjects; it has a Congress and President, Governors and State Legislatures without end, judges, various courts and law officers in countless numbers. Hundreds of thousands of school teachers, professors, and college presidents, and Doctors of Divinity, thousands of lecturers and public declaimers on all subjects, railroads, telegraphs and telephones in such vast numbers as stagger imagination itself, churches and pulpits that are filled by at least a hundred and twenty-five thousand ministers of the gospel, and Bibles enough to build a pyramid that would almost reach to heaven; a land of books upon every subject scattered among the people by the billions, and in short, we have all the forms and paraphernalia of civilization. But no one can say, who has any respect for truth, that the United States is a civilized nation, especially if we will take the daily papers and inspect them for a few moments, and see the deeds of horror that the ruling powers of the nation say "well done" to.

I know that thousands, yea millions and tens of millions would not plead guilty of having a part in the violent and gory outrages which are often perpetrated in this country upon human beings, chiefly because they are of African descent, and are not numerically strong enough to contend with the powers in governmental control. But that is no virtue that calls for admiration. As long as they keep silent and fail to lift up their voices in protestation and declaim against it, their very silence is a world-wide acquiescence. It is practically saying, well done. There are millions of people in the country who could not stand to kill a brute, such is their nervous sensitiveness, and I have heard of persons who would not kill a snake or a bug. But they are guilty of everything the drunken mobs do, as long as they hold their silence. Men may be ever so free from the perpetration of bloody deeds, personally, but their **failure** to object to any outrageous crime makes them particeps crimines.

I forgot to say in cataloguing the crimes committed in the United States that persons for the simple color of their skin are thrust into what are called Jim Crow cars on the public highways and charged as much as those who are riding in rolling palaces with every comfort that it is possible for man to enjoy. This is simple robbery on the public highways and the nine United States judges have approved of this robbery and said, "well done," by their verdict.

Such being the barbarous condition of the United States, and the low order of civilization which controls its institutions where right and justice should sit enthroned, I see nothing for the Negro to attain unto in this country. I have already admitted that this country has books and schools, and the younger members of the Negro race, like the younger members of the white race, should attend them and profit by them. But for the Negro as a whole, I see nothing here for him to aspire after. He can return to Africa, especially to Liberia where a Negro government is already in existence, and learn the elements of civilization in fact; for human life is there sacred, and no man is deprived of it or any other thing that involves his manhood, without due process of law. So my decision is that there is nothing in the United States for the Negro to learn or try to attain to.

SECOND PAPER.

WILL IT BE POSSIBLE FOR THE NEGRO TO ATTAIN, IN THIS COUNTRY, UNTO THE AMERICAN TYPE OF CIVILIZATION?

BY BISHOP L. H. HOLSEY.

This question is one of pre-eminent importance and interesting alike to both races. Civilization means culture and refinement. The American type of civilization is somewhat different from the European and Asiatic: but, in the main features or characteristics, the world's great civilizations have always been the same in tone and design. Patriotism, religion, and a thirst for power are the most prominent features of all civilizations. All civilizations have their imperfections. One of the strong features of the American type of civilization is the widespread and terrible social prejudice, which seems to be greatly increasing.

In this country the negro is despised and rejected, simply because he has a black skin, and social traits that distinguish him from other races. We cannot see, neither do we believe, that it is possible for the Negro to attain unto the American type of civilization, while he lives in the same territory and in immediate contact with the white people. This, however, applies especially to the former slave states. Eight-tenths of the Negroes are at present in the old slave states, and if they remain there, which is very questionable, they will never be brought into the political, religious and social fabrics. They can never become full-fledged and free citizens like the white people. As a race, the Negro cannot enjoy in this country, like the Anglo-Saxon, the immunities and privileges guaranteed to him by the Constitution. The civil rights, the ample protection and the broad and liberal sentiment that protect and inspire the white people, are nowhere in America accorded to the black man. He is everywhere proscribed, because he is a Negro. No matter how much culture and refinement he may possess, he does not receive at the hands of the prejudiced whites that respectful consideration to which his culture entitles him. If we enter the field of legislative enactments by the Southern people, we find the prejudice still more pronounced.

Every enactment that has found its way to the statutory documents of the Southern States, where the rights and privileges of the two races are involved, shows race prejudice; then this thing is getting no better, but worse. As the Negro rises from the darkness of the past and

Bishop L. H. Holsey

BISHOP L. H. HOLSEY.

Bishop Holsey was born a slave near Columbus, Ga., July 3, 1842. In 1862 he was married to Miss Harriet Turner, a young girl who belonged to Bishop Geo. F. Pierce, of the M. E. Church South, who performed the marriage ceremony in his own house. His early life was spent in Sparta, La. He was licensed to preach in 1868 in the M. E. Church South, and served the Hancock circuit for nearly two years. In 1870 he pastored the church in Savannah, Ga. Early in 1869 he became a member of the colored conference which belonged to the M. E. Church South. This conference was composed entirely of colored ministers. At this conference Bishop Holsey was ordained deacon by Bishop Pierce and a year later he was ordained elder. In the fall of 1870 his conference elected him a delegate to the first General Conference of the Colored Methodist Episcopal Church, held in America. This conference was held in Jackson, Tenn., where the first C. M. E. Church in America was organized. In 1871 he was sent to Augusta, Ga., as pastor of Trinity Church and served there until in 1873 he was elected Bishop of the C. M. E. Church. In 1881 he was sent to London, England, to represent the C. M. E. Church in the first ecumenical council. In that council Bishop Holsey represented his church well. He was also sent as delegate to the same council, which met in Washington, D. C., in 1897. He is the founder of Paine College in Augusta, Ga., which is now in a flourishing condition. Bishop Holsey has always taken an active part in all that concerns the C. M. E. Church. He has written all the messages but one to the General Conferences and has suggested its entire legislation up-to-date. He also wrote the Manual of Discipline, and composed the hymnal of the church, and he is the author of a book of Drawings and Lectures, containing an autobiography. He has written much for his church and done many other good things, too numerous to mention here.

approximates the American standard of civilization, the feeling against him becomes more intense, bitter and decisive, which does not speak well for the American civilization.

No Negro, however highly accomplished, can be brought into the social fabric. The lowest Greek, the dirtiest Jew, the vilest Russian, and the most treacherous Spaniard can be absorbed and assimilated into the social compact, but the Negro, because he is black, cannot enter into this compact.

Unless the Negro can enter the political and social compacts in some part of this country, there is no way for him to attain unto the American type of civilization. Can this be done? We think not, because as the Negro migrates to the North or to the Northwest, the process by which he enters the arena of full citizenship annuls and destroys his social characteristics in a greater or less degree.

There is, at present, among the majority of Negroes in the South, an unrest. Millions of them are waiting and wishing for somebody to lead them from the land of oppression and proscription to some more congenial clime, outside of the land of their nativity, but they do not want to depart, unless they can be assured that by so doing, they can better their condition. As it is, many are going to the North, East and West, and the time is fast approaching when the Black Belts of the South will be things of the past, unless the white people change their way of treating a Negro. The cotton fields and sugar farms now maintained by the Negroes will eventually be deserted by them, if the whites continue to oppress them. This, perhaps, would be beneficial to the South, as it would relieve them of the perplexing Race Problem. Now, if the Negroes were as free and as safe in their homes; if they had the same feeling of security of life and property; if they had the same treatment before the courts and had all the rights and privileges of a full citizen, as the white man, he would not be long in attaining to the American type of civilization. All Southern people, and many Northern people, for that matter, do not believe that the Negro is capable of as high a degree of civilization as the Anglo-Saxon. They believe him to be by nature inferior to the white man. But I contend that the Negro is not by nature inferior to the white man, but that he is as capable of reaching the American type of civilization as the white man. This is obvious from the phenomenal strides made by him within the past thirty-six years along material, moral and educational lines.

No one seems to take on and absorb the American civilization more readily than the American Negro, and if he has the same advantages and was allowed to enjoy the same full and free citizenship along with his white neighbor, his advancement in civilization would be as rapid as that of the white man.

There are to be found now not a few Negro men and women whose culture and refinement would not suffer by comparison with that of the best white people of this country. It is not native incapacity and the want of vital manhood that limit the Negro's progress in civilization, but it is the fight made against him on the ground of his previous condition. Remove this and give the Negro the white man's chance and he will keep pace with the white man in his march toward civilization.

THIRD PAPER.

WILL IT BE POSSIBLE FOR THE NEGRO TO ATTAIN, IN THIS COUNTRY, UNTO THE AMERICAN TYPE OF CIVILIZATION?

BY R. S. LOVINGGOOD, A. M.

I presume it is not necessary to show in detail what the American type of civilization is, or will be. Whatever that type is, or may be; will the Negro attain unto it in this country? Of the American type of civilization this much may be said, that this is a "government of the people, for the people and by the people; that all men are created with certain inalienable rights; that among these are life, liberty and the pursuit of happiness;" that governments derive "their just power from the consent of the governed;" that in such governments each individual is entitled to all the rights vouchsafed to any other individual in that government; that every one is entitled to stand on his merits as a citizen of the government.

Taking this view of the American type of civilization, will it be possible for the Negro to attain unto it? Will the time ever come when the Negro will stand on his merits in our government? Will it ever be that the Negro will stand the same chance to be Mayor, Congressman, Senator, Governor, President? That he will be tried for crimes as other men are tried? No one who believes in the innate capacity of the Negro to achieve as high a type of civilization as any other race, will question

R. S. Lovinggood, A. M.

PROF. R. S. LOVINGGOOD, A. M.

Prof. R. S. Lovinggood was born in Walhalla, S. C., in 1864. He came to Clark University, Atlanta, Ga., in 1881, and remained in school nine years, completing the college course and taking a course in carpentry. Immediately after graduating, he began to publish the "Atlanta Times," a weekly paper, which he continued for two years. He sold out his interest in the paper, and was elected principal of a city school in Birmingham, Ala., where he taught with great success for three years. Here he was married to Miss Lillie G. England, in 1894. In the fall of 1895, he was elected to the chair of Greek and Latin at Wiley University, Marshall, Texas, and entered upon his work with enthusiasm. His wife died in January, 1896, leaving him a boy only ten days old. He continued his work at Wiley University for five consecutive years. His success was notable in this position. He wrote a work which has received favorable mention in several papers of high grade. The title of the work is "Why Hic, Halc, Hoc for the Negro?"

He was married a second time on April 25, 1900, to Miss Mattie A. Townsend of Birmingham, Ala. In the fall of 1900, he was elected to the presidency of Samuel Houston College, Austin, Texas. His success here has been notable. Though this is a new school, he enrolled 205 the first year. This is its second year, and the enrollment will doubtless reach 300.

Prof. Lovinggood is a good scholar, a fluent speaker, and an earnest Christian. He was a delegate to the General Conference of the Methodist Episcopal Church in Chicago in 1900. He is quite popular with the preachers and the people wherever he goes. A bright future is before him and the young school of which he is president.

that it will be possible for him to achieve the American type of civilization along the lines of invention, commerce, philanthropy, scholarship, etc. The Negro *can be* industrious, patriotic, courageous. He can be useful in the community in which he lives. He can be as good as anybody else. No one doubts that he can be as meritorious as any other. Geographical lines cannot prevent the Negro from being meritorious. Now, if he is meritorious, will he be treated according to his merits in both church and state? Is it possible in this country that he will be treated according to his deserts? I take this to be the gist of the question, and it is a hard one to answer. The prejudice against the Negro is more severe than that against any other people, and the prejudice grows stronger. Even the Christian churches are yielding to it. I remember that the Plebeians in the Roman Empire, though of the same blood as the Patricians, were excluded from the Comitia, the Senate and all civil and priestly offices of the state for several hundred years. Though of the same color, the statute of Kilkenny prohibited the Irish and English from intermarrying in the fourteenth century. Prejudice ran high, and has not ended yet. The wail of sorrowful Ireland continues to go up before England for justice. I remember the sad story of Kosciusko and the Poles. The Poles were white.

Here we are of a different color, ex-slaves, poor, beaten back by prejudice. Who can tell our future? We can only hope and give the reason for the hope that is in us.

I believe it is *possible* for us to succeed in America. I should despair if I did not believe this. Why do I believe it? Here is my ground for hope: First, the Negro is the only race that has ever looked into the face of the blue-eyed Anglo-Saxon without being swept from the face of the earth. There is that docility, that perseverance, that endurance, long-suffering patience and that kindness in the Negro which rob the pangs of the hatred of the white man of much of their deadly poison. The Negro thrives on persecution. He never loses faith. Individuals may lose hope, but the race will never. The Negro does not run against the buzz-saw of destruction, and this fact should be put down to his credit. The saw will not whirl forever.

Second: The success of the last thirty-seven years gives hope of ultimate triumph. The Negro has increased in intelligence, in wealth, in moral worth, in population, etc. It is useless to give figures. All right-thinking men admit this.

I take no part in that view of a few pessimists, that the Negro race grows worse; that the "old time Negro" is better than the young "new Negro." The old Negro was submissive because he was not allowed to be otherwise. There is no character in slavish goodness. Character must be developed in freedom of action. Under freedom, a few young Negroes have gone to excess, but, thank God, under freedom, hundreds of thousands of young Negroes, in schools and out of schools, are struggling up the hill of virtue, of industry, of learning, not goaded on by the lash of the master, but impelled by a holy ambition that does not halt at temporary defeats.

Third: So I believe the Negro will be as good as any. He will produce his poets, historians, philosophers, inventors, his men of commerce, his humanitarians. His present disfranchisement will keep him along these lines. The best people in America are helping him. Besides the Negro's own efforts in such organizations as the A. M. E. Church, the American Missionary Association of the Congregational Church, the Freedmen's Aid and Southern Educational Society of the Methodist Episcopal Church, the Home Mission Society of the Baptist Church, and many other organizations are behind him with millions of dollars, with prayers and with the souls and the flesh and blood of the best men and women of the world. There are good men North and South—white men— who desire the Negro's success. Their number will grow. With these helps the Negro can become noble in character. He can merit the best at the hands of the American people. If he is as good and useful as any other class of people, will he be treated as any other class?

Fourth: Now, I will go a little further and say I know it is "possible" for the Negro to attain unto the American type of civilization; but, is it "probable"? I even believe it is probable.

The Negro is included in the "all men are created with certain inalienable rights." He is included in the "Our Father." He is included in the "Whatsoever ye would that men should do unto you, do you even so unto them." Now, if the nation adopts some separate and unjust manner of treatment of the Negro, it must repudiate the Declaration of Independence. It must repudiate the Lord's Prayer. It must repudiate the Golden Rule. Can it do that and survive? Can it practice injustice upon the Negro and survive? Sin recoils upon the sinner. Injustice to the Negro will destroy the Nation. For that reason good white men and women are striving to bring the Nation up to that high plane of righteousness where justice is meted out to all alike. These good white men and women ought to conquer. I believe they will. Not to-day, but to-morrow. Thus the Negro, striving to be the best in the community, the white men, striving to reduce to practice the Golden Rule, may it not come to pass that "They shall beat their swords into plowshares, and their spears into pruning hooks," and that the country of Lincoln shall thus become the "land of the free and the home of the brave," where all men of all races shall be treated in all departments of life according to their worth?

FOURTH PAPER.

WILL IT BE POSSIBLE FOR THE NEGRO TO ATTAIN, IN THIS COUNTRY, UNTO THE AMERICAN TYPE OF CIVILIZATION?

BY BISHOP J. W. HOOD, D. D., LL.D.

The subject of this article is one upon which much thought has been spent, and yet, excepting the color of the skin and the texture of the hair, the Negro has more the appearance of the white American than any other race. A cultured colored woman, with gloves on her hands and a veil on her face, is hard to distinguish from a cultured white woman a little way off.

And the same is true of men when the complexion is not seen. We shall take the position that the inherent possibility of the Negro is equal to that of any race. Notwithstanding his environments are against him, yet he has the inherent power to break through them, and will break through them and reach the highest plane of Christian civilization.

This is indicated by the progress he has made in the few years in which he has had any chance for development as an American citizen. Almost everything has been against him. Every possible effort has been employed by his enemies to keep him down; but in spite of all he rises. Like Israel of old, the more he is oppressed the more he prospers.

His possibility is indicated by the stock from which he comes.

It is the impression of many that the Negro has no history to which he can point. There could be no greater mistake than this. If it had been in the power of modern historians of the Caucasian race to rob him of his history it would have been done. But the Holy Bible has stood as an everlasting rock in the black man's defense. God himself has determined that the black man shall not be robbed of his record which he has made during the ages past.

The first and most illustrious of earth's historians has left on record statements which set forth the fact beyond reasonable doubt that an ancestor of the Negro race was the first of the earth's great monarchs; and that that race ruled the world for a long period; and the statements of Moses are confirmed by the testimonies of the earliest secular historians, whose writings have come down to our time. Ethiopia and Egypt were first among the early monarchies, and these countries were peopled by the descendants of Ham, through Cush and Mizraim.

Palestine was peopled by Canaan, the younger son of Ham, upon whom the curse was pronounced; and, notwithstanding the curse, his posterity ruled that land for hundreds of years. They were in it when the promise of it was made to Abraham; and four hundred years later, when Israel came out of Egypt, they were still in full possession of it. And, although the land was promised to Israel, yet two tribes, the Jebusites and Sidonians, resisted the attacks of Israel for more than four hundred years after they entered upon their promised possessions. Neither Joshua, nor the Judges of Israel, could drive them out. Not until David became King were the Jebusites driven out from the stronghold of Zion. (Even David failed to drive out the Sidonians.) It was from the ancient seat of the Jebusites, Jerusalem, also called Salem, the seat of royalty and power, that Melchizedek, the most illustrious king, priest and prophet of that race, came forth to bless Abraham, as seen in Gen. XIV., 18:19. There have been many wild notions respecting this personage, for which there is no good reason. Dr. Barnes, a standard author, whose commentaries have been adopted by the Presbyterian Board, takes the position that there can be no question but that Melchizedek was a Canaanite.

That the Phoenicians, who were the founders of Carthage in connection with the original Africans, were the descendants of Canaan there ought to be no question; but, since everything honorable to the Negro race is questioned, we will simply give the testimony of Rollin. He says: "The Canaanites are certainly the same people who are called almost always Phoenicians by the Greeks, for which name no reason can be given, any more than the oblivion of the true one." Thus it is seen, that up to Rollin's time there was no question as to the fact that the Phoenicians were Canaanites. Rollin did not know why this, instead of the true name, was given; neither do we know; but we may easily conjecture

Bishop J. W. Hood, D.D.

BISHOP J. W. HOOD, D. D., LL. D.

The subject of this sketch was born in Kennett Township, Chester County, Pa., May 30, 1831. His father's house being near the line between freedom and slavery was a station of the Underground Railroad. Hence, the boy was very early impressed with the evils of slavery and imbibed an intense hatred toward that institution, and an intense love for his afflicted race. This sentiment has been a great factor in shaping his conduct through life. His moral and religious convictions were fixed in early life. He was sensible of a call to the ministry, but hesitated a long time because he felt a lack of necessary qualification. He was licensed to preach in 1856; ordained a deacon in 1860; elder in 1862, and bishop in 1872. He entered upon a course of studies soon after he was licensed, and has been a hard student ever since.

His first appointment was to a mission in Nova Scotia. In December, 1861, he was appointed to missionary work in the South. Following the army, he reached New Berne, N. C., January 20, 1864. As a traveling minister he always had encouraging success, especially in North Carolina, in which State his denomination has a larger following than in any other. Two of its most important institutions are located there, namely, the Publication House at Charlotte and Livingstone College at Salisbury. Bishop Hood is one of the founders of the college, and has been President of the Board of Trustees during its entire history.

He has been married three times, and has six living children, all of whom have been mainly educated at this institution. The Bishop is an untiring worker, and has traveled as much as 20,000 miles a year. He once preached forty-five sermons in thirty-one days, driving from five to twenty-five miles a day. He is a natural presiding officer and governs his conferences with an ease and quietness' that is astonishing.

He is an author. His first work was a book of twenty-five sermons. The second a pamphlet, "Know, Do, and Be Happy." The third, a history of the A. M. E. Zion Church (625 pages).

The fourth a pamphlet, "The True Church, the Real Sacrifice, the Genuine Membership." His fifth, and most important, is, "The Plan of the Apocalypse." He has in manuscript, a work on the Millennium; also the material for a second book of sermons, and is now writing an Autobiography.

Bishop Haygood of the M. E. Church South, who wrote the introduction to the Book of Sermons, says: "Bishop Hood has traveled the continent to and fro. His ability, his eloquence, his zeal and usefulness, have commanded the respect and confidence of the best people of both races.

As one of the members of the Ecumenical Conference that met in London in 1881, Bishop Hood made a lasting impression.

These sermons speak for themselves. Their naturalness, their clearness, their force and their general soundness of doctrine, and wholesomeness of sentiment, commend them to sensible and pious people. I have found them as useful as interesting.

Those who still question whether the Negro in this country is capable of education and "uplifting," will modify their opinions when they read these sermons, or else will conclude that their author is a very striking exception to what they assume to be a general rule.

that, since it was the Greeks that gave this name instead of the true one, it may have been their purpose to hide the fact that the people to whom they were so greatly indebted were the descendants of the accursed son of Ham. This would be in perfect accord with the conduct of Caucasian authors now. We have also the testimony of Dr. Barnes that the Phoenicians were descended from the Canaanites. In his notes on Matt. XV., 22, of the woman of Canaan who met Jesus on the coasts of Tyre and Sidon, he says: "This woman is also called a Greek, a Syro-Phoenician by birth" (Mark VII., 26).

Anciently the whole land, including Tyre and Sidon, was in the possession of the Canaanites, and called Canaan. The Phoenicians were descended from the Canaanites. The country, including Tyre and Sidon, was called Phoenicia or Syro-Phoenicia. That country was taken by the Greeks under Alexander the Great, and these cities, in the time of Christ, were Greek cities. This woman was therefore a Gentile, living under the Greek government, and probably speaking that language. She was by birth a Syro-Phoenician, born in that country, and descended therefore from the ancient Canaanites." On the same text Dr. Abbott says: "The term Canaan was the older title of the country and the inhabitants were successively termed Canaanites and Phoenicians; as the inhabitants of England were successively called Britons or Englishmen."

Of Carthage we may remark that through all the hundreds of years of its existence as an independent government, it remained a republic. Rollin, speaking of the government, says: "The government of Carthage was founded upon principles of most consummate wisdom; and it is with reason that Aristotle ranks this republic in the number of those that were held in the greatest esteem by the ancients, and which were fit to serve as a model for others. He grounds his opinion on a reflection which does great honor to Carthage, by remarking that from the foundation to his time (that is, upward of five hundred years) no considerable sedition had disturbed the peace, nor any tyrant oppressed the liberty of the state. Indeed, mixed governments such as that of Carthage, where the power was divided betwixt the nobles and the people, are subject to the inconveniences either of degenerating into an abuse of liberty by the seditions of the populace, as frequently happened in Athens, and in all the Grecian republics, or in the oppression of the public liberty by the tyranny of the nobles; as in Athens, Syracuse, Corinth, Thebes, and Rome itself, under Sylla and Caesar. It is, therefore, giving Carthage the highest praise to observe that it had found out the art by the wisdom of its laws, and the harmony of the different parts of its government, to shun during so long a series of years, two rocks that are so dangerous, and on which others so often split. It were to be wished that some ancient author had left us an accurate and regular description of the customs and laws of the famous republic."

While we agree with Rollin in his lament of the want of a more complete history of that ancient Negro republic, yet, if those Caucasians who are wont to arrogate to themselves all the excellencies of the world, and deny that the Negro ever has been great, or ever can be, would take time to read what has been written with sufficient care to understand it, they would lose some of their self-conceit and add much to their store of knowledge.

That the ancient Egyptians were black, both the Holy Scriptures and the discoveries of science, as also the most ancient histories, most fully attest. But as some profess to have doubts on this point, we shall take some testimony, which, we think, no fair-minded man will attempt to dispute.

The Psalmist calls to memory the wonders which God wrought for his people, and celebrates in song his dealings with Israel in Egypt, and frequently calls Egypt the land of Ham. How can this be accounted for if Egypt was not peopled by the posterity of Ham? But he goes further than this; he calls their dwellings the tabernacles of Ham. "He smote the firstborn in Egypt; the chief of their strength in the tabernacles of Ham." Psalm lxxvii, 51: "Israel also came into Egypt; and Jacob sojourned in the land of Ham." Psalm cv, 23: "He sent Moses, his servant and Aaron whom he had chosen. They set among them his signs and wonders in the land of Ham." Psalm cv, 26:27: "They forget their God their Savior which had done great things in Egypt; wondrous things in the land of Ham." (Psalm xvi, 21:22.)

The man who, after reading these passages, can doubt that the Egyptians to whom Israel was in bondage were the descendants of Ham, is beyond the reach of reason. The repetition seems designed to settle this fact beyond question. We might add, if it were necessary, that the Book of Canticles is an allegory, based upon Solomon's affection for his beautiful black wife, the daughter of Pharaoh, King of Egypt.

In the sixty-eighth Psalm we have a prophecy which connects Egypt with Ethiopia, as follows: "Princes shall come out of Egypt. Ethiopia shall soon stretch forth her hands unto God."

Rollin, in speaking of the fact, that all callings in Egypt were honorable, gives this as a probable reason: "That as they all descended from Ham, their common father, the memory of their still recent origin, occurring to the minds of all in those first ages, established among them a kind of equality, and stamped in their opinion a nobility on every person descended from the common stock.

Again, treating of the history of the Kings of Egypt, Rollin says: "The ancient history of Egypt comprises two thousand one hundred and fifty-eight years; and is naturally divided into three periods. The first begins with the establishment of the Egyptian monarchy by Menes or Mizraim the son of Ham, in the year of the world 1816." On the next page he says of Ham: "He had four children, Cush, Mizraim, Phut and Canaan." After speaking of the settlements of the other sons he returns to Mizraim and says: "He is allowed to be the same as Menes, whom all historians declare to be the first king of Egypt."

In speaking of the sons of Ham, Rollin says: "Cush settled in Ethiopia, Mizraim in Egypt, which generally is called in Scripture after his name, and by that of Cham (Ham) his father."

That ancient Egypt was the seat of the arts and sciences, there can be no doubt; the evidences of this still remain. The cities built by the early kings of Egypt have been the wonder of all succeeding ages.

Sesostris stands at the head of the list of the great Egyptian warriors. Rollin says: "His father, whether by inspiration, caprice, or, as the Egyptians say, by the authority of an oracle, formed the design of making his son a conqueror. * * * " (See Rollin, Vol. I, p. 161.)

The record given by Rollin indicates that Sesostris was among the wisest, as well as among the most powerful monarchs of the earth. Napoleon was a great warrior, but he died in exile, a prisoner of war. Alexander was a great general, but he made a foolish march across a desert country almost to the destruction of his army, for the foolish purpose of worshipping at the shrine, and being called the son of Jupiter Ammon. This so discouraged his forces that he never accomplished the object of his ambition.

Sesostris made no such blunders in his campaigns. He went forth conquering until he met a providential interposition; his climax of wisdom was displayed in his turning back when he discovered that not merely mortal beings, but the Great Immortal, opposed his further conquest.

He returned to his own country to enjoy in peace and prosperity the fruits of his unparalleled victories. His conduct toward those cities which resisted in attacks most stubbornly was in striking contrast to that of Alexander. As Alexander advanced to invade Egypt, he found at Gaza a garrison so strong that he was obliged to besiege it. It held out a long time, during which he received two wounds; this provoked him to such a degree that when he had captured the place he treated the soldiers and inhabitants most cruelly.

Sesostris, on the other hand, was pleased with those who defended their possessions most bravely; the degree of resistance which he had to overcome was denoted by him in hieroglyphical figures on monuments. The more stubborn the resistance, the greater the achievement; and the more worthy the people to become his subjects.

If the descendants of the accursed son of Ham could establish and maintain for five hundred years a republic which was never disturbed by sedition nor tyranny, and enjoyed a civilization in some respects better than the boasted American civilization, there is no reason why any other branch of Ham's family may not attain to the highest and best civilization.

Our opinion is, that within two hundred and fifty years the American Negro will reach that Christian civilization taught by the Son of God to a degree equal to any race on the face of the globe. He has in him the elements for such a civilization to a degree not possessed by some other races.

But the limit allowed this article has been reached.

Hon. H. P. Cheatham

HENRY PLUMMER CHEATHAM.

Men who attain to real leadership and those who lift as they climb; broad in mental resource, generous, and strong in manly impulse, they forget self and become the embodiment of principles that make genuine progress and win the hearts of their comrades by the compelling force of character and personal magnetism. Promoting the well-being of a race, multiplying the happiness of the individual, these captains of moral thought practically accept the duty marked out by the Great Teacher and "cause two blades of grass to grow where but one grew before."

Such a man as pictured above is Henry Plummer Cheatham, one of the most successful forces in the public life of the twentieth century Negro. His career has been visited by success because he has richly deserved it. Mr. Cheatham was born in Henderson, N. C., some forty-odd years ago. He was educated in the public schools of his county and at Shaw University, of his native state. He was a promising lad, and with prophetic spirit laid deep the foundation upon which a brilliant character was to be built. His first public office was that of registrar of deeds in his native county. So conspicuous was his work and so worthily did he impress himself upon the judgment of the people, Mr. Cheatham was nominated and elected to the Fifty-first Congress, and was again chosen to sit in the Fifty-second Congress. When President McKinley reached the White House, one of his earliest appointments was that of Mr. Cheatham to be Recorder of Deeds for the District of Columbia, a post which has come to be regarded as carrying the insignia of leadership in the political councils of the race. That he has performed his duties capably and zealously, goes without saying. He is an ardent adherent of the merit system, and in both appointments and promotions the merit system has been his invariable guide, declining to be influenced by considerations of person, politics, religion or color. He has been instrumental in enrollng more Afro-Americans upon the governmental roster than any other Negro living.

Mr. Cheatham is a positive race man and is a foremost champion of the idea that the Negro's best development must come along natural lines, and that material progress is as much the result of sensible and persistent individual effort as of legislation and adventitious aid. He believes in practical education for the masses, technical education for the captains of professional thought and industrial leadership. He is unusually effective upon the "stump," and has been heard with pleasure and profit in many states during national campaigns.

TOPIC III.

HOW CAN THE FRIENDLY RELATIONS NOW EXISTING BETWEEN THE TWO RACES IN THE SOUTH BE STRENGTHENED AND MAINTAINED?

BY HON. H. P. CHEATHAM.

Prosperity to a nation is most secure when all elements and classes of that nation are at peace, one with the other. Christianity reaches the height of its sacred mission when the spirit of co-operation and brotherly love is most conspicuously in evidence. National prestige and the influence of a people in the councils of the world are invincible when the contributing forces of the land are happy and united. The problems of civilization are solved when wars are silenced and "rumors of wars" are heard no more.

America, as we have come to call the land of our birth, has not grown to her present proud proportions upon "flowery beds of ease." Her strong place among the powers of the earth has not been gained without resort to martial strife. But, it is a gratifying fact, that up to this hour every struggle against outside foes has made American people stronger from within, and every victory, in our long, unbroken line of successful campaigns, has bred a warmer spirit of homogeneity and knit us together in closer bonds as a national unit. Foreign foes offer our country no danger to-day. Our army and navy are without peers upon the globe, and, despite our marvelous sketch of coast line, we have nothing to fear from foreign invasion.

The disease that threatens us *most* is from within. If salvation be needed, we must pray to be "saved from ourselves." To "make clean our hearts"—to face in proper spirit the duty that lies before us—should be the earnest supplication of every true American citizen. A spirit of unity is our urgent need at the opening of the 20th century.

Thanks to the wise economic policies of those intrusted with the reins of legislation and government, our country is enjoying a period of unexampled commercial prosperity. Business is booming, money is easy, crops are abundant and labor is receiving a fair return for energy expended. But, in our mad rush for the material things of life are we not forgetting the spiritual wants of the citizen, are we not neglecting the

57

moral qualities that make nations enduring and the principles that must live when cities decay and dynasties cease to be? In fine are we not veering too far from the altruism of our fathers, in the apparent subordination of human rights to the acquisition of power and of wealth? This dangerous ambition breeds in our midst socialism and industrial unrest, exemplified in strikes and lockouts. It fosters anarchy—a spirit of lawlessness, from which but a few weeks ago the nation suffered the loss of a beloved chief magistrate. It stirs up racial antagonisms, and defies the ameliorating influences of Christian brotherhood. All difficulties surrounding our labor problems, however, are easy of solution, for while capital and mechanical industry may be frequently at war for one reason or another, the outbreaks are merely sporadic and short lived. They are invariably adjusted, from time to time, either through arbitration or equitable concessions. Capital and industry are of one color, and the complications are purely superficial. The one contention that "passeth all understanding" and which defies the skill of the ethnologist, the psychologist, and all who deal with the ancestral or philosophical aspects of mankind, is the "race problem."

I say "race problem" advisedly, because sociologists, in analyzing the issues growing out of the relations between the white American and the colored American, have eliminated from the discussion all difficulties surrounding their settlement—save the impossible effacement of race or color. All have admitted that the bronzed American may have character, intellect, capacity, wealth, industry and comeliness—yet he is a social "Pariah" because of his social identification. A problem that otherwise would be simple is thus converted into a perpetual issue by reason of race, and hence we have a "race problem." The race issue is particularly acute at the South—not because the Southern Negro differs materially from his Northern brother in character or attainments—but because in the Southern states the Negro abounds in the greatest numbers, and because upon her fertile soil he was once held in bondage. As a slave, the Negro came to be regarded as one whose inferiority must continue from generation to generation. The Civil War brought freedom in its wake, and one of its results was to clothe the emancipated servitor with the full vestments of citizenship. By proclamation and legislation, the ex-slave was made the political equal of his white master, and if numbers are to be counted the slave class became the superior force in the reconstructed Southland. That the new Negro citizen was honest and well meaning, no one doubts. It must be confessed, however, that the masses were ignorant of the high responsibilities charged to them, and it is but natural that many mistakes were unwittingly made. Indeed, the wonder is not that many errors could be laid at the door of the amateur "statesman," lawmakers and suffragists, but that more grievous blunders were not made. The result, all things considered, is highly creditable to the heads and hearts of the leaders of that trying epoch. The masters did not take kindly to the seeming domination of their former bondmen. The anomalous situation was made infinitely worse by the gross frauds and mal-administration of Northern white carpet-baggers, who misled the trusting Negro into false channels and bred in the minds of the landowners and former slave-magnates a bitter hatred for all that savored of the Negro and the party that they held responsible for their humiliation. Readers of history are familiar with the stirring scenes that went abreast with the efforts of the whites to free themselves from the consequences of the war. With the accession of President Hayes came the restoration of the democracy to local control in the Southern states. All are acquainted with the "reign of terror" and the depredations of red-shirted adventurers and night-riders. The instinct of white supremacy solidified that section, and later came the era of lynchings. General disorder prevailed wherever the racial problem was brought actively to the fore.

Of late we have heard much of "constitutional conventions," and the press has been filled with arguments pro and con as to the necessity for eliminating the Negro from politics or abridging his right to vote. There has been going on for years a seething cauldron, with the Negro as the burning impulse; but evidence is gradually accumulating to warrant the belief that a healthier atmosphere is coming out of the storm. Passions cool after full vent is given, and the sober second thought of races and nations invariably makes for peace, for law and for justice. Upon this established principle of metaphysics the Negro must base his hope for happier results in the near future. The South has awakened to its vast opportunities, and there seems to be a well-defined and determined effort on the part of the intelligence, the culture, and the wealth of that section to make the most of its bountiful resources. The commercial era opening in the South, gradually bringing into control the conservers of Christianity, of peace and of civil equity, will develop better conditions for the Negro; for among the aristocracy—among the landowners and mon-eyed classes—the black man has always found his best friends and most ardent sympathizers. They understand the Negro more thoroughly than many Negroes understand themselves, and the facts will bear me out in saying that when our people have needed advice, or have appealed for aid for churches, schools and for industrial opportunities, the high-grade white classes of the South have never turned a deaf ear. They have never been wanting in their approval of the self-respecting, thrifty and law-abiding Negro, and have always been ready to encourage him in the acquirement of a home, a farm or other real property—frequently lending the money for the first large payment. Many times they have exerted their influence to guarantee fair play for such Negroes in the courts—even when their causes were laid against a white man, or where white men had accused them of crime. It cannot be denied that injustice has been practiced against us in all sections of the South, and it is also true that the Negro's ignorance and credulity have made him an easy prey to the unscrupulous; but ignorant whites have suffered likewise, for he that knoweth little, no matter what his race, is the natural victim of the sharper. With the keenest of sleuths in our detective departments of the North, and with courts and juries of unimpeachable integrity, crime stalks boldly in its greatest cities, and arrogant corruption goes unwhipt of justice. So, in the Southland, there are crimes and criminals and the law will be powerless to bring them to book until a nobler sentiment is created by the supremacy of the better classes, and the relegation of the riotous element, through the vigorous and constant efforts of the rightful rulers of the South—the educated and peace-loving citizenry. In no case has any outrage against Negroes been given the approval of any responsible officer of the law. Violations of the letter and spirit of the statutes are committed over the protest of the authorities, and those who desire the aggressive execution of all the laws in the future must exercise more care in the selection of men intrusted with the power of administration. More attention must be paid to the character and personal fitness of candidates standing for office. The Negro can and will help to do this. The regeneration of existing conditions among the whites must come from an enlightened public spirit and a broader culture, such as are being bred through the public schools and through the introduction of improved methods in business and social life. First-class white men must take hold of the reins of government throughout the Southland. The Negro is an imitative creature, and he takes on the color of his environment. If it be charged that he is frequently immoral, dishonest

W. D. Chappelle, D. D.

WILLIAM D. CHAPPELLE.

Rev. William D. Chappelle was born in Fairfield County, South Carolina, November 16, 1857. At twelve years of age, he was sent to the common schools of Winnsboro, S. C., to Northern teachers. So eager was he to learn that he cut light wood up at night and carried it to town on his head, using the money thus obtained to buy his first book. After finishing the common schools, he entered Fairfield Normal Institute, and there prepared himself for a teacher, which vocation he pursued for several years. After his conversion he felt called to the ministry. Accordingly, he joined the Columbia Annual Conference in 1881, and feeling his inability to effectually preach the Gospel of Christ, he entered Allen University, there taking a collegiate course, at the same time serving missions near Columbia.

With a wife and one child, he found that the mission work was inadequate for his support, having very often to cease his studies in school and go out and teach for two or three months to relieve the wants of his family. This was very discouraging to him, but he courageously worked on until Bishop Dickerson relieved him of some of his responsibilities by giving him a room in his back yard. This he gladly accepted that he might earn some money with which to buy books and thus sustain himself in his struggle for an education.

I know of my own personal knowledge that he had very often to walk sixteen miles on Sundays and preach twice, getting back home at 11 or 12 o'clock at night to be enabled to make recitations on Monday. Nevertheless, he struggled on and graduated at the head of his class in 1887.

He was ordained deacon in Bethel A. M. E. Church, Columbia, S. C., March, 1883, by Bishop Dickerson, and ordained elder by Bishop James A. Shorter at Greenville, S. C., in 1885. He graduated from Allen University in 1887, in a class with six other young men—four preachers and two lawyers. In 1887 he was elected a delegate to the General Conference which met in Indianapolis, Ind., and he has been elected to each successive General Conference ever since. He served eight years as a pastor, holding three appointments, and ten years as a presiding elder. He was appointed to the Manning District in 1889, and after serving there four years he was appointed, by Bishop Salter, to the Orangeburg District, the largest district in the State, and served there five years. Bishop A. Grant appointed him to the Sumter District in 1898, which district he served until the General Conference met in Columbus, Ohio, 1900, where he was elected Corresponding Secretary and Editor of the Sunday School periodicals of the A. M. E. Church.

Dr. Chappelle also served two years as President of Allen University, his alma mater, being elected just ten years after his graduation from that institution.

He has had a successful career as teacher, as preacher and, now, as business manager and editor. He ranks, also, as one of the leaders of his race, as a scholar and writer of no mean ability. He is an able debater, having few superiors as an extemporaneous speaker. Acute in thought and incisive in speech, he is a fluent talker.

Unlike most men of a literary turn of mind, he combines fine business acumen with his intellectual ability, and has accumulated property, real and personal, to the amount of ten thousand dollars, situated in Columbia, S. C., and Nashville, Tenn.

and shiftless, the dissolute whites with whom he has been closely identified have furnished a model that he has copied only too faithfully. Let the Christian element become a more prominent factor in state affairs, and the Negro will at once grow in character and address by virtue of the inspiring example thus set for him.

This phase of the "Negro problem" carried to its logical conclusion becomes the "white man's problem." Will the Southern American rise in his majesty, dismiss his prejudice and prove equal to the lofty duty allotted to him? Will he give the Negro a man's chance in the battle of life, and depend upon his own natural gifts of mind and heart for his supremacy?

The political phase of the race problem I shall touch but briefly. There is no call for the Negro "to get *out of politics;*" as the term is popularly used. The fact is the Negro should begin "to *get into politics,*" in the truest sense of the word—that is, to begin at the a b c of political power and come up by the usual processes of individual development. The suffrage is a privilege conferred by the state. States make certain restrictions for their own protection as sovereign commonwealths. Although it is unfortunately a fact that the restrictions are enforced more rigidly against black illiterates and black non-property-holders than against the whites, of similar deficiencies, the conditions are there and can only be fought down by intelligently meeting the requirements, whatever they may be. No educated Negro is refused the right of suffrage by any constitutional enactment. No property-owner is made to feel himself outlawed by virtue of suffrage restrictions.

The moral is plain. Get education. Be thrifty and economical. Get lands and money. Get character and personal culture. These qualities, united, pass as good coin in any state North or South. They go far to minimize the disadvantages of color everywhere. Without them no race is strong anywhere. They are potent in allaying the race feeling aggravated by too many of us, through voting under the leadership of scheming politicians who are opposed to the best interests of the masters of the Southern soil, and who have no use for black men except on election day. In the matter of suffrage, I would suggest that the black voter place himself in touch with his white neighbors. The interests of each are identical. It is of far greater importance to the Negro to have the friendship, respect and confidence of his next-door neighbor than who shall be President of the United States. It is of more moment to him who shall be sheriff or member of the state legislature and city council than who shall go to Congress. This suggests that the Negro use clear judgment in casting his ballot, and that he use that instrument to identify himself with the law-abiding and progressive forces about him. The Negro's natural home will ever be in the South. The careful exercise of suffrage in promoting the interests of that section, eliminating partisan bitterness and vengeful spirit, will be one of the most powerful agencies in maintaining and strengthening friendly relations between the races there.

Further, let the Negro make for himself a place in the business world. Let him develop hotels, groceries, stores and shops of all kinds, thus affording employment to our competent young men and women. Let him perfect himself in the useful arts; till the soil, and become an indispensable factor in the uplift of the community which he calls home. The farmer, the artisan, and industrious wage-earner form the backbone of racial progress, for they support the church, are patrons of the schools, and are steady conservers of public morals. From this firm center, a lever is furnished which holds up the house of the minister, the editor, the teacher, physician, the artist, the lawyer, and all of the so-called "polite" professions. Let the Negro build up his own social circle, and strive to perfect it through an exemplary home life. While a part of the general social system the Negro people can be to the whites, as Booker T. Washington so well puts it, "separate as the fingers" in social contact, but "one as the hand" in all that tends to sustain and improve the State and Nation.

In short, let the white man be just, if he cannot be generous. Let him give the Negro what is due him. Weigh him honestly as to character and manly worth. Let the Negro be patient, persevering, philosophical, thrifty, self-respecting and far-seeing. Brains and energy will eventually win their legitimate place in the equation of civic virtue, and the forces of right will gravitate, the one towards the other, just as the flowering plant turns to the sunlight. In peaceful conditions, nurtured by mutual sympathy, mutual suffering and mutual triumphs, will be forged a bond that shall in due season draw the best in each of the great races of the South in closer and more friendly communion. Our beloved America shall throw off the shameful shackles of racial prejudice. Progress towards a sweeter civilization will be the watchword for all. Then, there shall be, indeed and in truth, for every class, color, condition and section in this land, "One God, one country, and one flag." There is hope ahead.

SECOND PAPER.

HOW CAN THE FRIENDLY RELATIONS NOW EXISTING BETWEEN THE TWO RACES IN THE SOUTH BE STRENGTHENED AND MAINTAINED?

BY REV. W. D. CHAPPELLE, D. D.

The subject above assigned me is a momentous one and involves an issue which is not settled, nor will it be settled until the relation which now exists between the two races is based upon that moral "ought" growing out of the ethical rule given by God for the government of man. For it must be conceded that all friendly relations are based upon ethical treatment. A relation upon any other basis is forced, and, therefore, not genuine. The so-called Negro problem which is being agitated by the public press is forced upon us by fictitious sentiment, conceived in prejudice, and watered by opportunity, and a disregard for law, and truthfulness of statements made concerning the Negro as a citizen.

When a relation is fixed by such undue advantages, that relation IS NOT, for it is ex-parte, and the party having the public ear creates the sentiment, and thus forces the party which is *not* heard to terms, whether those terms be satisfactory or not. Then, it can be plainly seen that such relations are not real, for they are not based upon that law under which all men are created and governed.

Now, I lay down the following as a general proposition which I think will stand the test of critics, whether they be of the North or South. It is the rule of international law to have a friendly relation between nations, states and individuals, and that relation is made by representatives of all the parties concerned. The agreement must be mutual and that mutuality must be based upon righteousness—that righteousness which makes sacred the rights of all the contending parties.

If the friendly relationship existing between the two races in the South is mutual, then the development of the Negro will fasten and rivet such a relation. But if it is not mutual, and undue advantages have been taken of him, his development will make it impossible for such relations to be strengthened and maintained.

To perpetuate a relationship, it must first be based upon the principles of right, guaranteed by the force of all competent power, that power being common to all parties concerned. This is the sum maximum of all ethical science and is complete. To add to it, or take from it, would change the rule. Then, the solution to all ills must be measured by that sense of conscience unimpaired, emanating from that innate rule of human duty based upon moral obligation.

Now, there must be a standard of righteousness, not fixed by man, but by a superior power; for it is not man's will which he must obey, but the will of his Maker. This will can be shown in two ways only. First, by revelation, and, second, by example, both of which have been verified and demonstrated in the sacrifice made by Christ for the world of mankind. This relationship can and will be sustained, because Christ sought to know the nature and power of the second party. He enters into a covenant fixing that relationship forever, between the two. Now, if the so-called superior race, with the boasted power of all the heavy centuries of the past, has given to the inferior race in its undeveloped condition, that consideration which is necessary to sustain and maintain the relationship which now exists, then, the relationship is real and the education and development of the Negro along economic and commercial lines will but make this relationship stronger. And the future of the two races in the South, under such conditions, must be bright and glorious.

But, I fear we have been hasty in our conclusions when we measure the relationship which now exists in the South, by constitutional rights and enactments. The Constitution of these United States makes the people a compact, and therefore equals in immunities, privileges and rights, with a common flag as the symbol of our common protection. Every citizen, then, of these United States—let him be of any race variety—owes to that flag its protection, and, in return, that flag is to protect him. So that the relationship of all the citizens of the United States to the flag is the same; being the same to the flag, they are the same to each other from a civic point of view.

I agree that there is such a thing as "State rights," but such rights must be local and subsidiary and must in no case conflict with, or counteract, the rights of a citizen growing out of a common Constitution whose jurisdiction holds the sisterhood of states together. To sustain and maintain such a sisterhood the compilers of the Constitution gave the general government the right to summons such states to protect her in the discharge of her duty. So that it is seen that the government is exercising a power that was given it by the sovereign people, acknowledging equal rights to all and special privileges to none. Among these are life, liberty and the peaceful pursuit of happiness. These are the rights which are guaranteed by the Constitution.

Now, an agreement entered into by the people of any part of these United States which does not conform to the stipulated rights mentioned above, is not a contract and can not be considered binding under the law. Therefore, a relationship based upon privileges of one and the denied rights of the other, cannot be friendly and must, sooner or later, be dissolved. I, for one, cannot concede that the relationship between the races in the South is friendly. It is, for the most part, peaceful, but that peace grows out of a fear of the law in the hands of an unfriendly and prejudiced people who feel that the Negro race has no rights which they are bound to respect. Accepting this position, the Negro quietly moves on, trying to make for himself and family a living, but he feels keenly the class legislation which proscribes him to the "Jim Crow" cars, to the rear seats in street cars, behind the doors in public restaurants, and a hundred other indignities heaped upon him. He is also denied the right to vote, which is the greatest evil done him and the only protection that the Constitution gives him.

Now, I ask, "Can there be friendly relations with such environments, and, if they are friendly, can they be sustained and maintained?" I assert that the infringement of any right is an unfriendly act, whether the one whose rights are infringed upon is conscious of the unfriendly act or not. If he is unconscious of it, it is all the more unfriendly. I assert further, that whenever existing conditions make it necessary for one race to suppress another, the suppression affects both races alike. The stronger race ceases to develop that strength which is necessary for the growth of a nation, and to prepare it to meet the great problems which are indispensable in the fostering of a government such as ours. And the weaker race is deprived of the opportunities which are necessary to cultivate those innate powers which are intended by God to be developed in the rounding out of good citizenship. In fact, the denial of freedom to any race, along any of the walks of life, has a tendency to teach that race irresponsibility; for responsibility must rest with the volition of the human family.

"The Nashville American," in a recent issue, admits that the Southern white people have made no progress in the great world of thought, because they had everything their way. The solid South practically destroyed its opportunities to develop thinkers in the political world, and the prejudice they entertain and foster by mere sentiment was not conducive to the production of strong men, or the development of great thinkers or leaders of distinguished constructive ability. In some sense the South has for some time lived in an eddy. There has not been that broad sweep of the current of thought which once made it strong and powerful. And the reason for this is assigned in their surroundings, their highest ambition being to suppress the Negro in the civil walks of life.

Now, we are confronted with a condition—call it a relation, if you please—in which the interest of the entire Southland is involved, and we, as the Negro race, are called upon to express ourselves as to the basis of this relationship and the perpetuity of the same. The facts above stated make it extremely difficult for one to conscientiously concede, first, that the relations are friendly; and, second, that they can be sustained and maintained. As a matter of fact, the subject assigned me can be easily answered by saying that the friendly relations which now exist can be sustained and maintained by destroying the system of public instruction; by making no protest against the encroachments upon our liberty; by destroying the medium of the Christian religion, pulling down our altars, demolishing our churches and hanging crape on the doorknobs of all places of public instruction. This we are unwilling to do, and, as God gives us strength and light to see our plain duty, we shall work, watch and wait for that surrounding which shall be congenial to a healthful development of a Christian manhood, when the sphinx of this age shall have passed into the oblivious past; and mankind, transformed from brutish prejudice to that lordly prince, divested of all racial prejudice, shall stand upon that plain of reason where all are equals. We must see that our rights under the Constitution are one thing and the enjoyment of those rights quite another thing.

Now, then, shall we, because these rights are denied us, fail to teach our children that these rights are ours? And can it not be seen that for us to concede that the relationship, now existing between the two races in the South, is friendly, is an admission of the righteousness upon which such relation is based? And even this very book will be brought in evidence against us.

A friendly relation grows out of real friendship, so that it is necessary here to explain friendship. Mr. Webster gives the meaning of friendship as a state of being friends; a friendly relation or attachment, to a person, or between persons; affection arising from mutual esteem and good will; friendliness; amity; good will.

"There is little friendship in the world," says Bacon. There can be no friendship without confidence, and no confidence without integrity.

Dryden says, "Aptness to unite; conformity; affinity; harmony, and correspondence are the signs of friendship." These grow out of that soil and are the forerunners of that friendship out of which a relation must be had to be called friendly.

Now let us analyze this term "friendship." "Amity"—from the Latin, amare to love, or friendship in a general way between individuals, societies or nations. "Goodwill"—I wish you well, peace and prosperity. "Integrity"—moral soundness; completeness; honesty; rectitude.

We have given some of the terms which Mr. Webster used in the explanation of the word friendship. Our purpose for so doing is to see if it is possible to base the relationship which now exists between the two races in the South, upon all the synonyms or any one of them. I confess with candor that I cannot see (nor can any lover of liberty who holds sacred the rights of the human family, regardless of race, color or previous condition of servitude) even a semblance of amity in the treatment which the Negro gets at the hands of the dominant race, in fact, it is just the opposite, the relationship is forced and also one sided.

The seemingly friendly relation is forced from the Negro; that is, he must show up friendly or be lynched by the first angry mob who becomes thirsty for Negro blood.

If we sustain a friendly relation based upon the integrity of the Southern whites, there could be no lynching; the friendship of the white man would cause it to cease at once.

Would to God that they would interpret our actions in the light in which they are rendered and not make us suffer for what somebody else has done, simply because we are weak and unable to protect ourselves against the insanity of the prejudice.

The Southern white people, in their haste, are making an unenviable history at which they will blush in the years to come.

Three innocent people in the State of Mississippi have just been taken from the officers and lynched, two of whom were women. Can a race of people said to be friendly towards another race reach such hasty conclusions? Would not friendship suggest an investigation in order that the facts in the case may be had? But we are living in the midst of a people whose civilization is christianized, thus having in it that friendship which characterized Christ in taking the sins of mankind upon himself. "Ye are my friends, if ye do whatsoever I command you" (Bible). This text makes friendship conditional and reciprocal; that is, there can be no friendship without mutuality; so that the relation which now exists is not based upon friendship, for the relation which is made to exist is not in accordance with that moral rule given for the government of man, therefore things are not what they seem to be in the Southland.

I tell you that the Negro is not satisfied with his condition and the more he learns of the common rights of the human family, the more he sees the great wrongs "perpetrated" upon him and the reasons for the same. You cannot educate a people and crush them, history does not narrate an instance.

THIRD PAPER.

HOW CAN THE FRIENDLY RELATIONS NOW EXISTING BETWEEN THE TWO RACES IN THE SOUTH BE STRENGTHENED AND MAINTAINED?

BY REV. S. N. BROWN.

Any superficial or narrow view of the present conditions existing between the Blacks and Whites of this country will surely be discouraging. It is a time for an unbiased, comprehensive, and discriminate study of the situation. This, I think, will point to a basis of a coming final adjustment.

No people have ever achieved lasting distinction or greatness without hardships. God's way of development seems to be through trial. The Negro has not been, and will not be, excepted in this regard. The tests of life have been well borne by him and he has clearly demonstrated certain essential elementary characteristics. From slavery is learned his amiability, vitality and patient endurance, and from freedom, the spirit of hope, forgiveness, and his ability for the highest improvement.

At this time, when the race problem is demanding renewed consideration, we note with interest the extreme as well as conservative views. The unfriendly discuss the Negro in the light of his savagery, his bondage and his mistakes. They read history "with their prejudices and not with their eyes."

Just as white men candidly and otherwise hold their individual view-

Rev. Sterling N. Brown

REV. STERLING N. BROWN, A. M., B. D.

Rev. Sterling N. Brown was born in Roane County, East Tennessee, November 21, 1857. He attended the first free school ever taught in his county. He entered Fisk University (Nashville, Tenn.) in 1875, and for some years, during his terms of vacation, taught school to provide the means with which to pursue his studies. He was converted when quite a boy and has been able since, almost continuously, to lead men to Christ. He began to preach early after his conversion, and many revivals have followed his ministry. The first great awakening where, under God, he was the instrument, was at Kingston, Tenn., where every child in school, of over one hundred in number, became Christians, and when the whole town was stirred as never before. Many hardened sinners were brought to Christ in the meeting. Several of the converts are now actively engaged in the ministry. Mr. Brown's acceptance as a preacher made it possible for him to spend the entire vacations of his last years at college in supplying the pulpits of his denomination in different parts of the South.

He graduated from the college course of Fisk University in 1885, and took the degree of A. M. in 1891. He is also a graduate from the Oberlin Theological Seminary with the degree of B. D. He was called, June 1, 1885, to the Mount Zion Congregational Church, Cleveland, Ohio, and was by that Church ordained to the gospel ministry. This church was composed of a few faithful but discouraged members. They worshipped in a small frame chapel without either attraction or convenience.

Soon the membership was increased, the church took new courage and a great ingathering came, the old building was torn away and in its place a beautiful and convenient house of worship was erected. Mr. Brown served Mt. Zion for nearly four years when he accepted a call from the Plymouth Congregational Church, Washington, D. C., April 1, 1889. This church, under his pastorate for eight years, had a steady and most healthful growth. In January, 1897, he gathered about him a few leading men and women of the race and organized a church in Northwest Washington, in the midst of a large unchurched population. Park Temple, the name of the new church, at once took an important place in the community and its influence for good was felt far and near. For five years the work grew and throbbed with life. Its lines of work, so practical and successful, awakened such interest in an older sister church nearby that overtures were made for a union, and so, October 1, 1901, the Lincoln Church and Park Temple were merged into a new organization to be known as Lincoln Temple, with the Rev. Mr. Brown as pastor. The new Institutional Church with a large main building and a branch work gives promise of an unusual church movement. The pastor of this church is one of the hardest worked men in the city. He was for three years a most active and influential member of the Washington Board of Education, and has been for seven years and is yet Professor in the Theological Department of Howard University. He is an able minister, a good pastor, and a practical man of affairs. His long public life in the city has added to his influence and in every best sense, he is still a growing man. He is full of sympathy and helpfulness, and so is continually drawn upon by all classes and conditions of people. He is regarded highly by public men of both races for his conservative views, good judgment and genuine public spirit.

Mr. Brown is a tireless worker, and one who looks always upon the bright side of things. He has an ear to hear man, but keeps also an ear attentive to the voice from the clouds. When he has settled upon a plan no discouragement can change him. Once convinced of the righteousness of his course he pushes ahead with no wavering. Many a time in his works he seemed headed for a stone wall, insurmountable and impassable, but he went up to the wall with as much courage and faith, as if there lay before him a beautiful green sward, inviting to his sandal. Thus through the years of school life and the years of his active ministry he has gone forward.

point of the subject, so do colored men differ as to their opinions. We, too, have extremists and conservatives among ourselves and friends. This is what ought to be expected. Why should an intelligent colored man be different in his thoughts and conclusions from his white brother of equal intelligence? What the American school and spirit do for the one may be expected for the other. There are certainly strong grounds for extreme views and for even more extreme measures. But who can rationally deny the wisdom of moderation and sensible counsel? Personally I cannot bring myself to accord with either one of these views. The extremist spits fire, swears vengeance and talks loudly. He might offer his life as a sacrifice, and yet he reckons without his host. The conservative builds without hope, is easily cast down, and thoroughly pessimistic. There is a middle ground that can and must be taken.

Were it not that we have unshaken faith in the great heart of our American government, we might, like the captive Jews, hang our harps upon the willows, and, as if in a strange land, find no song to sing.

The fact that the very warp and woof of American institutions are the eternal principles of right and justice encourages the hope that the incident of color, race or previous condition can not always be a bar to preferment. An equal chance and fair play to all the citizens are absolute essentials to the continued life of a republic such as ours is to be. It is in this self-evident truth that is found a sure ground of confidence. Upon this bed-rock of America's boasted pride for interest in her humblest citizen may be built the superstructure of the future of the race.

I do not share in any disparaging view of the ultimate outcome of conditions. The white man's attitude North and South towards the Negro is now well defined. There is to be no more special legislation in his direct interest; he will be expected more than ever "to weed his own row," and by self-endeavor continue to prove his right to be.

It would be amusing, if it were not so serious, to find the varied, strange theories for the black man's future well-being. Deportation, colonization, and a voluntary political self-effacement have all been advocated.

There is much said and written that would imply the need of some special kind of training suited alone for the Negro. If he has any special need whatsoever above his brother in white it is due to mistreatment and not to natural conditions. His phenomenal development along all lines indicates what is in him and what may be possible for him.

The race numbers from eight to ten millions, pays taxes upon property to the amount of nearly $300,000,000. They have graduated from universities, colleges, high, normal and professional schools about forty thousand. There are in all grades from the common school up about one and a half million pupils.

Men of the race own and control about three hundred newspapers, journals and periodicals. This is substantial progress for only thirty-six years, and yet this is no day for boasting or fine-spun flattery. As long as the great bulk of the race are in abject poverty and ignorance, and while more than a million of colored children of school age are not attending school for want of accommodation, and the number increasing more rapidly than facilities for education, and so long as the unsettled race question seriously agitates the American mind we do well to be deeply concerned. But it is unreasonable and not helpful to be over alarmed. It is time for the race to be sober and thoughtful, and if present conditions bring this about a sure blessing will result.

Among the mistakes of our years of freedom have been the surface view of life, and an ever present dependence upon politics and by-gone friends. The present shock from eliminating certain manhood rights in the Southland necessarily creates a sensation, but is also sure to quicken for us new life, purpose and hope.

The Negro question is only one aspect of America's larger problem. Can it be truthfully said that every worthy citizen shall have an equally fair opportunity in the race of life? It seems to me clear that racial adjustment at the South may be reasonably hoped for when the parties most interested unite upon the spirit of the golden rule. This and this alone will insure friendly relationship. The white man must make up in his mind to be fair, and just, and to recognize the fact that the Negro deserves a chance for the highest, broadest and best possible life. Will the Southern white man ever willingly accord this common right? Yes, I think so. But the alienation is not all on one side. For thirty-six years the fact has been specially emphasized that the Southern white man is the black man's enemy. The result is a natural one. Antagonism and race friction have enlarged rather than lessened. The time has fully come when the colored pulpit, press and leadership throughout the country and specially in the South should seek to make friends of these people with whom the blacks must necessarily live. We can not over-estimate the value of education and the getting hold of homesteads in the progress of the race, but these alone are not sufficient.

Our churches must mean more for right living. The sacredness of the home, of the married life, of honesty, of integrity, of uprightness and of right character must more than ever be impressed. The churches must be more practical and less sentimental. Instead of encouraging late hours—thus opening the evil way to our young—and spending long seasons in mere shouts and gesticulations, let there be training classes, mothers' and children's meetings, and those within reasonable hours. Let our pulpits and press rebuke crime among us as well as away from us. Let us organize and encourage good citizenship committees in all our churches and in every community. Let us draw the line between the idle and industrious among us. Let us urge vagrant laws upon that set of men who will not work but form the criminal class in all our cities. Let us more than ever show ourselves ready to help rid the community of objectionable persons and places. Let us not say less—if well said—for right public sentiment must be made, but let us do more. There must be a studied use of "Yankee" common sense. It is not to be expected that the Southern man's training, relative to the Negro, can be readily displayed. But having been born and reared under Southern skies and for parts of ten successive years taught there is one country, and having former slave-holders among some of my warmest friends, I am prepared to believe that there is no innate hindrance to a life of peace between the races.

I can not think that the best people of the South will long endure the savage methods of avenging their madness. They must have a better second thought and will ultimately welcome the spirit of maintaining law and order.

With all, there is but one way to settle the race question. It must be squarely and justly met upon the uncompromising basis of right. The Negro is a human being with clearly demonstrated capabilities, and it can not be that the world's foremost nation will need to further climb the ladder of fame by keeping the foot of the strong upon the neck of the weak.

When men are possessed and led by the Gospel of Jesus Christ then will there be peace and harmony and good will among all the people. "They shall" then "neither hurt nor destroy in all" His "holy mountain;" "for the earth shall be full of the knowledge of the Lord, as the waters cover the sea." God hasten that better day! Amen.

TOPIC IV.

SHOULD THE NEGRO BE GIVEN AN EDUCATION DIFFERENT FROM THAT GIVEN TO THE WHITES?

BY JAMES W. JOHNSON.

In answering the question involved in the above subject it becomes necessary to define the word "education"; for the term, "education given to the whites," is too loose and broad to be easily or logically handled. If the word is used in its ordinary sense, then it embraces every known form of education, from instruction in the elementary English branches on up through to instruction in the most abstruse sciences; and I can see no reason why the blacks should not receive the same instruction as the corresponding class among the whites. Mark you, I say, as the corresponding class among the whites.

If by the term, "education given to the whites," is meant higher education as opposed to industrial training, the question can not be answered in the form in which it is stated; for there is no "the Negroes" in the unit sense. Since its freedom the colored race has classified itself into almost as many grades, as regards ability and capacity, as there are to be found among the whites; it is, therefore, no longer possible to speak of "the Negroes," meaning that they are all upon the same mental and moral plain. It is as absurd to say that every Negro should be made to receive an industrial training as it is to say that every Negro should be given a college education.

The question of higher education or industrial training is one that depends entirely upon the individual; and there should be no limit placed upon the individual's right of development. I think it a great folly to educate a colored man beyond his capacity; I think it an equally great folly to so educate a white man.

It is needless, and not within the limits of the subject, for me to make any defense of higher education for Negroes; but, I do say that every man, be he black or white, should be allowed to make the most of all of his powers, his possibilities, and his opportunities. I recognize the fact that the great majority of Negroes must, and, I hope, will be engaged in agriculture and the trades; that is true of every race; but there is, and ought

72

Prof. J. W. Johnson

J. W. JOHNSON, A. B.

J. W. Johnson was born in Jacksonville, Fla., and after finishing the public schools of his native city he went to Atlanta University, from which institution he graduated with the degree of A. B. in 1894. The same year he was appointed principal of the Central Colored Grammar School, which position he now holds. In 1895 he edited and published the "Daily American," an afternoon paper. The publishing of this paper was one of the greatest and most creditable efforts in journalism ever made by any member of the race. In 1898 he was admitted to the bar, and in 1899 to the Supreme Court of Florida. In 1901 he was elected President of the Florida State Teachers' Association.

Mr. Johnson is a man of varied talents. He has a reputation as a pleasing speaker and fluent writer. He has devoted much of his time to literature, and is a contributor to the leading magazines. Mr. Johnson is a poet of more than ordinary talent and ability, and is widely known as the writer of the words of "Lift Every Voice and Sing," a national hymn for the Colored people of America. He is also the author of many songs and ballads, and also of the lyrics of two comic operas.

to be, no power to say that this or that individual in any grade of society shall not break through his environments, and rise above his conditions. And I think it safe to say that the proportion of colored men and women who have been given an education beyond their capacity for receiving and using, is very little larger than the same among the whites; and, in the years to come, as the race shall more and more fit itself to the grinding process which it takes to turn out a people, that proportion will become less and less, and each individual will settle to his level, or rise triumphant over obstacles and circumstances to the place for which his ability and aspirations fit him.

But let us consider our subject in a deeper sense; if by education is meant that training, those influences by which the habits, the character, the thoughts, and the ideals of a people are formed and developed, then, the answer hinges upon the answer to another question: Is the Negro to remain in this country a separate and distinct race, or is he to become one of the elements in the future composite American?

If, as some claim, the Negro is to remain in this country a separate and distinct race, then, in this deeper sense of the word, he should receive an education different from that given to the whites.

Because the Negro and the white race, although they have the same inherent powers, possess widely different characteristics. There are some things which the white race can do better than the Negro, and there are some things which the Negro can do better than the white race. This is no disparagement to either. It is no fault of the Negro that he has not that daring and restless spirit, that desire for founding new empires, that craving for power over weaker races, which makes the white race a pioneer; neither is it the fault of the white race that it has not that buoyancy of spirit, that cheerful patience, that music in the soul, that faith in a Higher Power, which supports the Negro under hardships that would crush or make pessimists of almost any other race on earth.

There have been given to each race certain talents, and for them each will be held accountable, and rewarded accordingly as they shall use them. Two boys in the same family may be gifted differently, one with an artistic, the other with a scientific, turn of mind; both cannot become artists, nor both scientists, yet they may each become equally great in their respective spheres. It is for the Negro to find out his own best and strongest powers, and make the most of them. He cannot by merely imitating the white man arrive at his fullest and truest racial development. He cannot and will not, as an absolutely distinct race, evolve, along the same lines, the *identical* civilization of the white race, but who shall say that along his own lines he may not evolve one equally as glorious and grand?

It is true, situated as he is among the most advanced people of the world in the very height of their power, with almost all of the ideals before him belonging to that people, the American Negro is greatly handicapped in distinct racial development; but the task is, perhaps, not an impossible one. Some of the most accessible means have not yet been fully employed; for instance, the race has never been made entirely familiar with the deeds and thoughts of the few men of mark it has already produced. In this deeper sense of education the knowing of one Crispus Attucks is worth more to the race than the knowing of one George Washington; and the knowing of one Dunbar is worth more than the knowing of all the Longfellows that America will ever produc

If the Negro is to remain in this country a separate and distinct race, and is, as such, to reach the highest development of his powers, he ought to be given an education different from that given to the whites; in that, in addition to whatever other instruction he may receive, those virtuous traits and characteristics which are peculiarly his should be developed to the highest degree possible.

If, on the other hand, he is to become, in time, one of the elements in the future American race—and this seems the more plausible answer to the question—his education ought to be purely American and not in any special way Negro.

History affords no precedent of two races, distinct yet equally powerful, living together in harmony; one has always reduced to a secondary position or destroyed the other, or the two have united. So it will be a question, if the Negro succeeds in making himself the equal of the white man in intellectual attainment, wealth, and power, whether or not what is now antipathy between the two races will develop into outright antagonism; and if we are to judge from human experience through all the past we must say that it will. If the Negro shall succeed in making a new record in history so well and so good; but if he is to follow the precedents of the past, it will be a far nobler destiny for him to become an integral part of the future American type than to drop into an acknowledged and permanent secondary position.

And may it not be in the great plan of Providence that the Negro shall

Prof. James Storum

PROF. JAMES STORUM.

Prof. James Storum was born in the city of Buffalo, New York, March 31, 1847. His mother, Mary Cannady, was a native of Sussex County, Virginia, where she lived for twelve years, when her father sold his farm and moved to Ohio and located with his wife and eight children near Urbana. His mother was a woman of strong character, deep religious convictions, and piety, and full of energy and enterprise, a counterpart of which is seen in her worthy son.

His grandfather, Charles Storum, of Duchess County, New York, was a soldier in the Revolutionary War, and did valiant service for the independence of this Republic. He died in 1843 at the age of one hundred years. Prof. Storum began his school life in the public schools of his native city. He was admired by his associates for his manly qualities and good fellowship, and was held in high esteem by his teachers for his studious habits and exemplary deportment. At the age of thirteen he embraced religion and united with the Michigan Street Baptist Church, where both his parents were useful and active members.

He frequently heard his parents express their purpose to send him to college, and as he grew older and better able to appreciate the value of education, the desire grew very strong within him to fit himself for a larger field of usefulness. In due time he entered Oberlin College, and after spending eighteen months in the preparatory department he entered the college proper, and graduated with the class of 1870.

Immediately after his graduation, Prof. Storum came to the city of Washington to teach in Wayland Seminary, one of the schools fostered by the Baptist Home Mission Society. He taught at Wayland thirteen years. Here, as in every walk in life, he exerted a most wholesome influence over the young men and women attending the seminary, whose graduates are found in all parts of this country. They delight to speak of the inspiration and high incentive they received from Prof. Storum while under his instruction.

After leaving Wayland, Prof. Storum taught in the public schools of Washington one year, whence he was called to the city of Petersburg, Virginia, to organize the Virginia Normal and Collegiate Institute, provided for by the Legislature of the "Old Dominion." He remained here three years and endeared himself to the pupils of the new school and to the citizens of Petersburg, irrespective of race, political bias or denominational creeds. He then returned to Washington and from that time until the present he has been teaching in the public high school.

Prof. Storum has ever been interested in and connected with the various enterprises whose aim has been the improvement and elevation of the Colored people. For five years he was secretary of the Capital Savings Bank of Washington and a member of the Board of Directors of the Industrial Building and Savings Company. For three consecutive years Prof. Storum was president of the Bethel Literary and Historical Society, the most prominent association of its kind in the country. Through his influence and by his energy the library and reading room were established and are now the most interesting and prominent features of the society.

In addition to his many and exacting duties, Prof. Storum has written and lectured on a great variety of subjects, religious, political, educational and financial.

He was happily married in 1872 to Mrs. Carrie Garrett Browne, a teacher in the public schools of Washington. There are three surviving children. Their domestic life has had its sunshine and its shadow. The darkest cloud that has overhung their household was the death of their oldest son, who died eight years ago at the age of eighteen, and who had given promise of being an unusually brilliant and useful man.

supply in the future American race the very elements that it shall lack and require to make it the most perfect race the world shall have seen?

If the Negro is to become an inseparable part of the great American nation his education should be in every way the same as that of other American citizens.

SECOND PAPER.

SHOULD THE NEGRO BE GIVEN AN EDUCATION DIFFERENT FROM THAT GIVEN TO THE WHITES?

BY PROF. JAMES STORUM, OF WASHINGTON, D. C.

The excuse for presenting this article is the oft repeated declaration that there should be one kind of education for the more favored class and another kind of education for the less favored class of our citizens. This declaration was never mooted until these latter years. The following incident will serve to illustrate the position taken by the advocates of this subject: A young man of more than ordinary ability, having a fine mind, and exceedingly apt and ambitious to learn, came to one of the schools in the South supported by Northern friends. He had had some advantages and had proved his capabilities to learn. He was giving great satisfaction to his teachers. He was prepared to take up one of the advanced studies, and did so and wrote to his friend telling him of the studies he was pursuing and the progress he was making. His friend, a would-be philanthropist, replied that he would not assist him if he pursued such studies. "You only need to learn to read, write, and cipher a little to teach your people." Yet this same man thought it necessary to take the common school course, a college course, and a professional course to teach his people. What class of people will have confidence in or give their support to a teacher, preacher, lawyer, or physician who knows only the A, B, C's of his profession? It is an historical as well as a scientific fact that no people have ever risen to influence and power without a strong intellectual and moral class permeating and leavening the entire mass. From the very beginning of our educational system the idea that the system and method of education should be different for the different classes of our people never entered the mind or thoughts of our educators nor any part of the body politic.

In the Southern part of our land the ruling class denied educational facilities to the colored people, and quite generally throughout the South it was made a penal offence to teach a colored man, woman, or child to read. The reason for this was well understood. Education produces intelligence and unfolds to one his powers and capabilities, and an intelligent people cannot be enslaved.

After the close of the war of the rebellion, schools were opened for the colored people. The newly-emancipated were not entirely oblivious to some of the advantages and benefits that follow from education, for they were constantly in touch with the master-class, so that when the opportunity was offered the colored people flocked to the schools in numbers far beyond the accommodations given. The colored people showed such avidity for learning and made such surprising progress that it seemed almost miraculous. Dr. Mayo says: "No people in human history have made such progress as the colored people of the United States." I can see no reason why the colored people should be differently educated from mankind generally; nor can I understand why persons should urge a different education unless they are hostile to and bitterly opposed to the progress of the colored people.

The aim or purpose of education is, always has been, and will ever be, preparation for complete living, that is, to be useful in one's day and generation and to live happily. "To secure this requires the acquisition of knowledge found in two fields of human endeavor. First, man and his experience and achievements and external nature; second, training to intelligent and productive activity in the use of this knowledge and the proper enjoyment of it."

What the education of the youth of a nation shall be depends upon the aim, purpose, and character of the government.

The history of the education of a people is the history of its civilization. Its civilization is not to be found in its material success, nor in its achievements in arms; but its civilization is manifest in its intellectual, moral, and esthetic development. It follows, then, that the education of a nation is to be found in the characteristics of its civilization; this includes religion, politics, justice, art, and mode of thought. The history of education fully attests this fact.

The government of Egypt was monarchical in form. The ruling classes were educated; the lower classes were not; yet while they were the beasts of burden and forced to toil under the most exacting task-masters they were of a mild and kind disposition, the result of their religious training.

The government of the Jews was Theocratic; their civilization was distinctively religious; their education was along religious lines. Their poets sing of the love, the power, the majesty, and the everlasting dominion of "I AM THAT I AM." Through the Jews indeed are all the nations of the earth blessed, in that they have preserved and transmitted through the ages the religion of their King and His Anointed.

Greece had two distinct ideas of government. The Dorian, as exemplified by the laws of Sparta, whose fundamental principle was that the individual existed for the state and must obey the behests of the state. The Ionian, as we find it in the constitution of Athens, whose basic principle was that the state existed for the individual and the individual was a freeman. The educational system of Sparta was entirely military, in keeping with the aim and purpose of the state. The boys at the tender age of seven years were taken from their homes and placed in state schools to be taught the art of war, and how to endure all of its hardships and privations. The educational system at Athens reflected the aim and purpose of the Athenian State; it was humanistic. The intellectual, ethical, and physical powers of the child were developed. In that little peninsula of Southern Europe there were two distinct civilizations having very little in common and always antagonistic. Sparta developed human machines, men of great physical force, but contributed nothing to the civilization of the world, nothing for the betterment of mankind. Liberty, patriotism, love of home and kindred, are the characteristics of the Athenian civilization. The contributions of Athens for the civilization of the world and the elevation of mankind are beyond human conception. The mind of man cannot conceive of the innumerable blessings that have flowed from Athenian civilization, the great reservoir of thought and perfected art. The profoundest thoughts of philosophy, the most electrifying words of statesmen and orators; the grand, sublime and patriotic strains of the muses, the illimitable beauty and symmetry of her art have been bequeathed to the world by Athens, "THE EYE OF GREECE." But above and beyond these is the principle of personal liberty and popular government that has come down to us from the Athenian Commonwealth. The aim and purpose of the Athenian Republic in its educational system was to train the children to become useful citizens, capable of aiding in the management of the state. Aristotle says: "Education should be regulated by the state for the ends of the state; * * * as the end purposed to the State, as the whole, is one, it is clear that the education of all the citizens must be one and the same and the super-intendence of it a public affair rather than in private hands."

The aim and purpose of the Roman government was to bequeath to humanity moral energy and jurisprudence, the latter of which is the basis of all modern law. A strong and an abiding faith subsisted between the Roman State and each of her citizens. "I am a Roman citizen," was the proudest allusion a man could make to himself, for he knew that the great Roman power was behind him to protect him in his rights. The children of the Romans were educated to be of use to the state. Cicero says: "The fatherland has produced us and brought us up that we may devote to its use the finest capabilities of our minds, talents, and understanding. Therefore, we must learn those arts whereby we may be of greatest service to the state, for that I hold to be the highest wisdom and virtue."

The aim and purpose of our government is to maintain and perpetuate the idea of constitutional liberty and to develop a popular government in which each inhabitant shall feel a personal interest in all that pertains to the government, and the government in turn shall feel itself obligated to protect and defend the interests of the humblest citizen within its dominion. Our government is "of the people, for the people, and by the people."

In this country there must be but one system of education welding all the people in one aim and purpose. Unity of thought, unity of action, and sympathy, unity in American life and duty, is and must ever be maintained in the stratification of American society. The government must be unique and homogeneous in its aim, purpose, and sympathy. The entire question of American citizenship is especially important in harmonizing the elements. Herbert Spencer says: "The education of the child must accord, both in mode and arrangement, with the education of mankind as considered historically; or, in other words, the genesis of knowledge in the individual must follow the same course as the genesis of knowledge in the race. * * * It follows that if there be an order in which the human race has mastered its various kinds of knowledge, there will arise in every child an aptitude to acquire these kinds of knowledge by the same order. As the mind of humanity placed in the midst of phenomena and striving to comprehend them, has, after endless comparisons, speculations, experiments and theories reached its present knowledge by a specific route, it may rationally be inferred that the relationship between mind and phenomena is such as to prevent this knowledge from being reached by any other route; and that as each child's mind stands in this same relationship to phenomena they can be accessible to it only through the same route."

Man is a trinity in his nature, consisting of mind, soul and body; these must be developed and the same means must be employed to bring it about. Intellectual, moral and physical training must characterize our system of education. The intellectual and the physical is being emphasized and the moral training must be made more prominent than it has been in the past. The aim and purpose of the founders of this Republic was to preserve in the substrata of the government those noble and lofty principles of the Christian religion for the maintenance of which they left their native land that they might plant these principles in the virgin soil of America.

Manual training is now being made an attractive feature in our schools, though by no means a new feature. Manual training must be made to strengthen the intellectual and moral training or it will fail in its purpose and end as an educational value. Trade schools are one thing, manual training schools another thing. It is not the purpose nor the end of manual training schools, as a branch of our school system, to teach trades *per se,* but rather to aid the pupils to find out their natural bent and to strengthen the trend of their ambition along chosen lines; or, in other words, to help the pupil to discover his powers, capabilities and capacity, to reveal the pupil to himself. Dr. Mayo says: "The higher education according to the last American interpretation is just this: The art of placing an educated mind, a consecrated heart, and a trained will, the whole of a refined manhood and womanhood, right at the ends of the ten fingers of both hands, so that whether you eat or drink or whatsoever you do you may do all to the glory of God."

There were two distinct civilizations attempted in this country; one was planted at Jamestown, Virginia, the other at Plymouth, Massachusetts. They were antagonistic in thought, aim and purpose. The civilization at Plymouth was an example of the "survival of the fittest," the errors of the one must be engulfed in the ever abiding principles of the other. The educational feature of the one must yield to the educational feature of the other. There must be but one system of education for all the people, great and small, black and white. This is essential for the peace, comfort, and prosperity of the nation.

This is an Anglo-Saxon country. The thought of this country is Anglo-Saxon. The progress of this country is Anglo-Saxon. The colored people of this country, like all others born and reared on our shores, are Anglo-Saxon in thought, in religion, in education, in training, and hence it is unsafe and dangerous, not to say impracticable, to educate them or any other class of our citizens along different lines. The people of this nation must be one in purpose, one in aim; there must be a common bond uniting them in a common sympathy and fraternity. To secure this end all the people must be trained to the highest wisdom. "The fear of God is the beginning of wisdom." Hence, says Milton: "To govern well is to train up a nation in true wisdom and virtue and that which springs from thence, magnanimity and likeness to God, which is called godliness. Other things follow as the shadow does the substance.

THIRD PAPER.

SHOULD THE NEGRO BE GIVEN AN EDUCATION DIFFERENT FROM THAT GIVEN TO THE WHITES?

BY REV. S. G. ATKINS.

"The education of a Negro is the education of a human being. In its essential characteristics the human mind is the same in every race and in every age. When a Negro child is taught that two and two are four he learns just what the white child learns when he is taught the same proposition. The teacher uses the same faculties of mind in imparting the truth as to the sum of two and two. The two children use the same faculties in learning the truth; it means the same thing to them both. In further teaching and training the methods may vary, but variations will depend less on differences of race than on peculiarities of the individual."—Bishop Haygood.

The above quotation from Bishop Haygood indicates my answer to the question. This question is simply a revival of the old superstition concerning the Negro that manifested itself in the inquiry as to whether the Negro had a soul. Civilization and fraternity have so far developed that it would be hard in these days to find a person whose skepticism concerning the Negro would find a doubtful expression as to the Negro's humanity. The light has become too strong for the existence of that kind

Rev. S. G. Atkins

PROF. S. G. ATKINS, A.M.

Prof. S. G. Atkins, President and Founder of The Slater Industrial and State Normal School, Winston-Salem, N. C., was born of a humble, yet high, because Christian, parentage, in Chatham County, North Carolina, June 11, 1863. Through this humble slave, yet Christian, parentage, there came to this youth principles of industry, morality and Christianity which formed the broad, deep, and solid foundation on which has rested his eventful and useful life. In early life he learned that "the fear of the Lord is the beginning of wisdom." In the days of youth he remembered his Creator.

Like many of the world's noblest and best characters, Prof. Atkins started life's journey at the plow handles; clearing the ground of roots and stumps, splitting rails, opening the furrow, planting and harvesting the crops, constituted the duty and pleasures of his early life.

Early evincing an insatiable thirst for knowledge, all the advantages of the village school were given him. His progress here was phenomenal. His eagerness to know truth; his power of mind to perceive, comprehend and analyze; his retentive memory, soon gave him first place among his fellows in the school in the village. A few years passed; he in the meantime having prepared himself, the master-mantle of the village school falls upon him. His work here caused a widening of his intellectual horizon. In the year 1880, therefore, he entered the Academic Department of St. Augustine Normal and Collegiate Institute, Raleigh, N. C., and graduated with distinction in 1884.

Immediately after leaving college, President J. C. Price, the famous colored orator, invited him to join the faculty at Livingstone College, Salisbury, N. C. At this post he proved himself one of the most useful men in the faculty. At times he filled various positions in the college. The Grammar School Department, under his management, was a model department, and was the pride of the college. He taught here, serving well and at a great sacrifice, six years. Prof. Atkins retired from the Livingstone College to enter the public school work in which he had long taken a deep interest. This interest had been manifested chiefly in connection with his devotion to the work of building up the North Carolina Teachers' Association, which body he helped to organize and of which he was President for three successive years. His first extended work in this field was as Principal of the Colored Graded School, of Winston, N. C. This position of responsibility he held, with increasing success, for five years, when he gave it up, against the protest of the Board of School Commissioners of Winston, to become President of The Slater Industrial and State Normal School. This Institution had already been projected by him to meet a want among the colored people in the community which he soon saw that the public school could not meet, viz.: a deeper ethical culture and the training of the youth of the community, not only in books, but also in some useful handicraft which would the sooner furnish the basis for strong personal character and sound home-life. His first step in this direction had been the founding of the settlement known as "Columbian Heights," to serve as a background for the Institution, which would do this. The settlement was founded in 1891, and the Institution projected in 1892. Prof. Atkins, as the first settler on Columbian Heights, and as the organizer and both Secretary and agent of the Board of Trustees, pushed the work of The Slater Industrial School, encouraged and supported by the industrious efforts of the members of the Board, until in 1895 he was called to the Presidency of the Institution. From that date to the present his labors have been an inseparable part of the history of the school.

Hon. C. H. Mebane, Superintendent of Public Instruction for North Carolina, says of him: "If I had fifty such men as Prof. Atkins in North Carolina, I could make a complete revolution in educational work in a short while, a complete revolution as to moral uplift and general good of the negro race."

In addition to his work as an educator, Prof. Atkins has taken much interest in the work of the American Academy of Social and Political Science, of which he is a member. He is also a member of the American Statistical Association, and has been twice elected Secretary of Education of the A. M. E. Zion Church.

The esteem in which he is held by leading men of the nation wherever he is known is fairly indicated in the following statement of Hon. J. L. M. Curry, LL. D., ex-minister to Spain and agent of the great Peabody and Slater Trusts for educational purposes. Dr. Curry says: "I regard President Atkins, of The Slater Industrial and State Normal School at Winston, N. C., as one of the most worthy and capable men connected with the education of the Negroes in the South. His intelligence, courtesy, good deportment, high character and efficiency as the head of a school have won the confidence and good-will of the people among whom he lives, and of all who best know his work and worth."

of mist; hence the unsympathetic critic has been forced to find a new way of putting his wish begotten thought.

There is still a higher authority for a negative answer to the question, "Should the Negroes be given an education different from that given to the whites?" in the following language: "God had made of one blood all nations of men for to dwell on the face of all the earth."

This declaration of St. Paul goes to the core of the matter, unless it is proposed to revive the old superstition that the Negro is not included as a part of the "nations of men." It is a strange fact that nobody ever proposes a modified or peculiar form of education for any other nationality.

It is the glory of the backward peoples of the earth that they are adopting the forms and methods of education which have made Western civilization the touch-stone of the world's progress.

But the implied contention that the Negro should be given an education of a different kind is not absolute. Most disputants on this subject —so far as published statements go—allow that after a long period of adaptation and modified training the American Negro may reach a stage in his mental evolution that he may assimilate the same kind of mental food that is admittedly suited to the Caucasian, Mongolian and others. This view of the matter leaves out of the count another great fact, viz., that the American Negro is more American than anything else, that he is not an alien either by birth or blood. Whatever exceptions might be alleged against Africa can no longer be made a bar to him.

But let us recur again to the evolution theory, and I will not undertake to consider this theory as Darwinian.

It is not generally advanced as a presumption that the Negro is not yet a thoroughbred, but it is presented in certain catchy and specious phrases such as suggest the necessity of beginning at the bottom rather than at the top, the necessity of giving to the colored American a kind of colored education, the necessity of making his civilization earthbound and breadwinning rather than heavenbound and soul-satisfying—the necessity of keeping him close to mother earth—as he "is of the earth earthy."

In those assumptions it is forgotten that education is not a question of mechanics; it is rather a question of ethics and immortality. Education is primarily an effort to realize in man his possibilities as a thinking and feeling being.

Man's inheritance is first from heaven, from above. That is the respect in which education differs from all merely constructive processes. The stimulating and quickening power is from above. Historically this is eminently true.

Education has been a process from above. It is not my intention to enter upon the discussion of the merits of any particular kind of education. My contention is that because the Negro is a part of humanity, because he is an American with an American consciousness and with a demonstrated capacity to take on training after the manner of an ordinary man he should not be treated as a monstrosity. Bishop Haygood sets forth the only proper line of distinction in education in the following sentence: "In further teaching and learning the methods may vary, but variations will depend less on differences of race than on peculiarities of the individual." The "peculiarities" here indicated unquestionably exist. They may be noted even in the same family, but these peculiarities are found in differences which lie deeper than the skin. There is no philosopher, unless he "is joined to idols," so bold as to base his presumption of difference in human beings upon the skin, for then his judgment might have to depend on whether the skin is dark, copper-colored, brown, white, yellow, freckled, red, etc. Human differences, all will admit, are essentially differences of *individual souls,* and this does not preclude the importance of environment and other incidental influences.

The great fact is that mind is mind—of like origin and like substance —and that it has been found to yield to like treatment among all nations and in all ages. There is no system of pedagogy that would hold together for a moment if the idea of the unity of the human race and the similarity of mind were invalidated. Philosophy itself would be threatened and all science would be in jeopardy. Investigation and practice never fail to support this theory of the solidarity of the human race. In the schools where it has been tried it has been found not to be a matter of color, nor even of blood—and certainly the differences have not depended on race affiliation. It has been a question of the individual and of local environment.

But so positive and indivisible is the human identity that even the influence of individualism and environments is overcome by the great universal processes of education, the great processes of mind quickening and mind development. In many of our best institutions there sit side by side the representatives of many nationalities and races, and it has never been found in the work of these institutions—as far as I have been

Prof. J. H. Jones, D.D.

REV. JOSHUA H. JONES.

The Rev. Joshua H. Jones was born at Pine Plains, South Carolina, June 15, 1856. He professed religion at ten years of age and joined the Shady Grove A. M. E. Church of the Bull Swamp Circuit, South Carolina. At the age of fourteen he was made Sunday School teacher, and at the age of sixteen Sunday School superintendent. By the time he was eighteen he had served in all the local spiritual offices of the church, and was then licensed as a local preacher by the quarterly conference of said circuit. The pastors soon discovered his usefulness and aid to them. He was a diligent student and an ardent churchman, and acquired education rapidly. At the age of twenty-one years he entered the Normal Department of Claflin University, Orangeburg, South Carolina, and in 1880 finished the Normal and College Preparatory Courses. He then taught and preached one year, after which he returned to Claflin University, and in 1885 graduated with the degree of A. B. Not daunted nor yet satisfied with his attainments he came north, studied awhile at Howard University, Washington, D. C., thence to Wilberforce University, were in 1887 he graduated from the Theological Course with the degree of B. D. In 1893 Wilberforce University conferred upon him the degree of D. D. in recognition of his superior worth and ability. In June, 1900, he was elected President of Wilberforce University, and a year later Claflin University conferred upon him the degree of M. A.

As a minister of the Gospel he has been pastor in charge of Williams Chapel, Orangeburg, South Carolina; Branchville Circuit, South Carolina; Fort Motte Circuit, South Carolina; Wheeling, West Virginia; The Holy Trinity Church, Wilberforce, Ohio; Lynn, Massachusetts; Providence, Rhode Island; Columbus, Ohio; and Presiding Elder of the Columbus District, Ohio Conference; Pastor at Zanesville, Ohio. In all an unbroken period of thirty-six years of church work and twenty-eight years in the ministry he has never known a failure. His labors have been indefatigable and his ministrations clean and inspiring.

In his public services he has been an inspiration to the race. For fourteen years he has been a Trustee of Wilberforce University, five years Trustee and Secretary of the Normal and Industrial Department at Wilberforce, and a constant and ardent helper in the establishment and development of the same. For six consecutive years he was elected and served as member of the Columbus Board of Education, and through his efforts six colored teachers were put into the mixed schools of Columbus, Ohio, as teachers.

In private affairs he has been industrious, frugal, economical and administrative. He has accumulated a comfortable estate and stands well with the banking and business circles of Columbus, Ohio, and pays taxes on a tax valuation of $10,000.

He has always been an ardent lover of his race, of his church, of his country and his God, and has always been a striking figure in the circles of men wherever his lot has fallen. Fifteen years ago he was elected Dean of Allen University, Columbia, South Carolina; eight years ago Professor of Theology in Payne Theological Seminary, neither of which he was able to accept because of heavy demands upon his energy elsewhere. In 1890 he was elected delegate to the Methodist Ecumenical Conference and has been several times delegate to the General Conference of the A. M. E. Church, and in 1900 was a strong candidate for the Bishopric, receiving fifty or more votes on the first ballot. In his present position he bids fair to give the church good service.

able to discover—that any one color or race could monopolize the benefits, but, on the contrary, it has been found that the benefits were realized according to individual temperament and power.

My position is not one in reference to non-essentials but essentials; it is not a contention based even so much on degree, but rather on quality and capability. I would not contend that environment would not make a whole group of children more or less backward, and I do not dispute the fact that because of better environments the whites represent as a whole a higher state of civilization. But I hold that this is true not because of race identity but rather because of individual embarrassment. Give a white child and a colored child the same environment and their progress or backwardness, I hold, would be essentially the same under the same stimulants and encouragements. Wherever colored and white children have been put to comparative tests too little attention has been paid to difference of environment, and too often there has been a dormant presumption that the same environment would not have produced the same results upon white children. Wherever these tests have been made it has been too often overlooked that the facilities for their education were not equal; they may have been nominally equal but the fact remains that they were not really equal.

Considering the inequalities of environment and educational facilities the results of most of the comparative tests are complimentary to the colored child and demonstrate the similarity of his mental susceptibilities—demonstrate that he is but a normal constituent part of the great human race with substantially the same limitations and capabilities as other members of the great human family.

FOURTH PAPER.

SHOULD THE NEGRO BE GIVEN AN EDUCATION DIFFERENT FROM THAT GIVEN TO THE WHITES?

BY PROF. J. H. JONES.

If this question is to be answered affirmatively or negatively, I emphatically say *no*. If the question be asked inquiringly, carrying with it the thought of race experience, race opportunity, race status and the variations growing out of these, then I would give the dubious answer, *yes and no.* In the first place, all things are educative and all forms of education have a definite relation to all other forms of education, and all educational processes have definite relations to all other educational processes, so all of these factors make for unity in education, and the completest education is that which embraces the greatest number of educational factors. It is perfectly true that educational processes may be varied so as to suit varying ideals or they may be varied so as to accomplish certain ends, for unvarying sequences follow definite antecedents; even so educational systems may be framed for the accomplishment of varying results or definite results as the framers of such systems may determine to suit the conditions of mankind as conceived at any given time. The end in view in an educational system is everything. What the chosen end of any system of education may be ought to depend upon the institution of the country in which a people lives and every educational system should be framed so as to utilize all of the agencies and involve all of the processes that make most rapidly for the achievement of the end in view.

If the end in view is serfdom for the Negro, then a vast amount of industrial training by rote, minus the natural sciences and mechanic arts for the generation of capacity, plus such rudiments in arithmetic, reading and writing as will enable him to be an efficient workman under the directions of others is the requisite. If it is the desire to make the Negro a useful agent in the production of wealth through the operation of the basal industries, in the largest quantity or the highest quality for the smallest amount of outlay, then a still higher class of training would be necessary, whether this production of wealth be for the good of self or for the common good of society. But if the end in view is to prepare him for the higher responsibilities of American citizenship, involving as that citizenship does the relationships, obligations and duties which devolve upon freemen and equally binding upon him as upon the whites in a democratic society or in a country of the people, for the people and by the people, it is evident that such a system must have structural affinity with such a system of education carried on by the whites and for the whites. In other words, such must be his education that his whole being is developed and in him there is the largest generation of capacity, insight, foresight, the power to think with proportions so as to give him that mastery over his environments and over the questions of common good which will enable him at all times to do the right things, the wisest things, the best things under any given circumstances in the midst of which he may be thrown. Any educational system that has an aim short of this as its end will certainly fail to prepare the Negro for the high duties which belong to a free individual in a democratic society.

Why should the Negro be given an education different from that given to the whites? Is he not a man? Is he not a free man? Is he not a citizen? Is he not held responsible by society for the performance of duties enjoined upon him by law? Is he not a subject of government? As a subject of government, ought he not participate in the affairs of the government? I think it will be admitted by all fair-minded men that all governments are for the welfare of the governed. Now, since the Negro is more interested in his own welfare than anybody else is and since to have a thing well done you had better do it yourself, since also his welfare is shaped by any government under which he lives, it must necessarily follow that his best good requires that he participate in the affairs of that government if he is to continue to be a free man. It is argued—and that not without some degree of reason—by part of the more favored people in this country, that the gift of the high privileges of citizenship carries with it the demand that the recipients of these gifts possess the capacity to exercise them for the common good of all who belong to the body politic. They also argue that human conditions for government are grounded in intelligence, virtue and property. So good, so well. But how is the Negro to acquire intelligence, virtue and property according to the American standard if his education is to be according to an un-American system? There are four fundamental American doctrines that both experience and philosophy attest as being right: (I) The right of education is a human right. (II) That the schools furnished by the state should be open to all of the children of the state. (III) The safety of the state depends upon the intelligence of our citizens of that state. (IV) As a matter of self-defense the state should compel all of its citizens to become intelligent. These doctrines have their root in the great truth that every individual is a member of society and that therefore society has an interest in him, in his capacity, in his intelligence, in his worth, and in turn is injured by his incapacity, his lack of worth, his ignorance. The great war-cry of American leadership is "Educate, educate, educate;" yea, more, "Educate your masters." No man lives unto himself. God has made every man dependent, associative and co-operative, and hence the good of every individual is found in the common good of society and the common good of society is found in the good of the individual. Every man who is not at his best or not doing his best is to that extent a failure and a hurt to the common good.

To me it is perfectly clear that if the Negro is to be in this country and not of it then his education should be different from that given to the whites. But if he is to be in the country and of the country it follows without argument that he must be educated in common with all of the people of the country so that the nation may have a common ideal and a common consciousness so that our whole society may have or feel a common interest in our common country. To be more explicit, whether or not the Negro should be given the same kind of education the whites are given depends upon whether or not the whites have the proper kind of education. I should rather contend that if the whites have the proper kind of education for mankind, then that given to the Negro should be exactly like it. If the whites have not the proper kind of education for mankind, then it follows that the Negro should be given a different kind, for whether or not one man should have the same thing as another depends upon whether or not that thing is fit for mankind in general. This would naturally force upon us the inquiry as to what kind of education the whites receive. If upon proper inquiry we find that theirs is the proper kind for man, in this same finding we should discover that this is the proper kind for the Negro.

Here differentiation begins, even in the field of education itself. A careful study of the constitution of man, involving the fundamentalities that grow out of his intellectual, moral, industrial, social and political nature will lead us, I think, to see that much of the white man's education is to be regretted and repudiated; much of it is to be approved and appropriated. All training given in avarice, hatred, prejudice, passion, sensuality, sin and wickedness, growing out of self-conceit and vanity, must assuredly be repudiated. But all things embraced in their education that make for the good, the true, the beautiful, the just and the elevation of mankind should be embraced, seized upon, masticated, digested and assimilated—transmuted into the elements of Negro character, forming a part of the very sub-consciousness of his being. In short, whatever education the whites have had or do get which makes for human enlargement, for righteousness, and brings man into closer relationship with God and gives him a fuller conception of the laws of God made manifest by the operation of His laws throughout the cosmos enabling him to discover the relationships which he sustains to God, to his fellow-men, to the lower creatures which inhabit this earthly sphere in which man lives and the laws that govern the universe, expressing modes of existence and orders of sequence, together with the principles of industry, frugality and economy, which determine the material accumulations necessary for the maintenance of life, these the Negro should know as largely as possible, for certainly they have been fields of educational processes found necessary for the white man through many generations. It is to be noticed that for centuries the white man has studied in order to get a thorough grasp, first of all, upon the intellectual tools—so to speak; in other words, to know how to read, write and cipher in terms of his own language, and at the same time to lay a foundation broad enough to pursue useful knowledge in all other directions possible. For instance, having mastered his own language to a reasonable degree, he takes the Latin and the Greek that he might acquaint himself with the development of the institutions out of which his own was evolved as well as to make double his hold upon his own; he studies Hebrew and the cognate languages to get mastery of the great truths, philosophy and institutions of a great people, adding to his own thereby; he studies the modern languages, German, French, Spanish and Italian, that he may gather the best fruits of the achievements of these nations and add them to his own store; yea, he covers the whole field of philology that he may add to his own store the best that has been garnered by all of the nations of the earth; he studies the literature, science and philosophy of all living races of his day and time with the same end in view and when he has swept the field of historic times he delves into the mysteries of geology and archæology and follows the mute footsteps of man through Neolithic and Paleolithic times to the very zero of human beginnings and comes back laden with truths to enrich the thought of his day.

He studies natural science as God manifested in nature, by observation and experiment; he commences with God through the discovery of the reign of law, classifying and systematizing the same and thus broadening his own vision and adding to the store of knowledge in our day and generation. As a preparation for this scientific research, he studies mathematics from the elementary principles through the largest elaborations of Euclid, Keppler, Newton and Copernicus, and their illustrious successors; he studies sociology, biology and mechanics; he studies civil and sociological laws and principles to the end that the intricacies of democratic business intercourse might be the more fully and clearly understood, mastered and applied in civilized processes. No form of industry has escaped him, no law of frugality has eluded him; whatever has in it an element of truth or virtue, he has pursued with a relentlessness that knows no failure. As a student, he has gone the rounds of the world in search of truth and has come back rich in the knowledge of the things that God would have us know.

How the Negro can live in the midst of a civilization created by such a people, drawing upon such vast resources as we have but faintly indicated and be given an education different from that of this people—and yet live among them with any degree of security—for the life of me, I cannot see. If, to keep up with the requirements of such a civilization as America furnishes to-day, a white child—notwithstanding his inheritance—has to go to school from his earliest days away into the years of his majority and be systematically trained in all of the subjects as taught in the kindergarten, the public schools, the secondary schools, the academies, the universities, and the professional schools, how much more imperatively necessary must it be that the Negro should have like training. It seems to me that he should not only have the same training but that he should have more of it than the white man has. His education should be physical, moral, intellectual, social, industrial and political, and his educational processes should have the highest structural affinity with the educational processes of the whites so that he may be brought into national and political assimilation with the white man's institutional life.

Hon. John P. Green

HON. JOHN P. GREEN.

Hon. John P. Green was born in 1845 at New Berne, N. C., of free parents. As a boy twelve years of age, he went with his widowed mother to Cleveland, Ohio. He was educated in the Cleveland public schools, graduating from the Central High School in 1869.

He was admitted to the bar of South Carolina in 1870. Returning to Cleveland, he for nine years served as justice of the peace. In 1881 he was elected member of the Ohio Legislature, serving three terms. In 1897 he was appointed to a position in the postoffice department by President McKinley.

He was also delegate to the National Republican Convention in 1872, in 1884 and 1896.

TOPIC V.

SHOULD THE IGNORANT AND NON-PROPERTY-HOLDING NEGRO BE ALLOWED TO VOTE?

BY JOHN P. GREEN.

All citizens who are industrious, honest, brave and patriotic should vote, without regard to their color; for, a man may possess all these characteristics and yet be "ignorant." Ignorance is only relative anyway.

(a) The Negro is a citizen. See XIV Amendment to Constitution, etc.

(b) He is industrious, and by his industry has not only helped to develop the resources of the United States but he has produced much of the property which is unjustly held by many white voters, and withheld from him; especially in the South.

The property of the South is due not more to the capital invested in the agricultural and manufacturing enterprises of that section than to the labor of the Negro, who furnishes the foundation of all wealth—labor—there.

(c) The untutored Negro has shown himself to be honest; he has never betrayed a trust imposed in him. During the great Civil War he was true to the trust imposed in him by his master at the front, who confided to his care the sustenance and even life of his wife and little ones. This was the supremest test of his honesty, which he sacredly discharged. Since the war, he has faithfully adhered to and followed the fortunes of the Republican party, by the mandate of which he was emancipated; even though in doing so he has suffered all the evils which a hostile opponent can invent to plague and swerve him from what he considers the path of gratitude and honor.

(d) He is brave; as the records of our wars will prove. His blood has stained many battlefields where, under "Old Glory," he fought for the Union and Liberty; not only on American soil, but also in foreign lands. The Negro, in contending in war, for the life and liberties of this Republic, has literally covered himself with glory.

(1) That he is patriotic goes without saying, in the light of what has

89

been written in the foregoing paragraph. With all his coarse and homely ignorance, the heart of the American Negro, when yet a slave, throbbed with patriotic love and loyalty; and this, too, at a time when his college-bred and intelligent (?) master was doing his uttermost to destroy this glorious fabric of Union.

It is only reasonable to assume that a man whose ignorance does not blind him from shooting right, can, and will, under proper instruction, which is given in prints and on the stump to all other voters, vote rightly.

(2) The first and most potent step in the direction of humiliating the Negro and relegating him to a condition of mental serfdom, is to deprive him of the ballot. It is the only token of real power which he possesses, aside from his brawn, which the white American really covets; and once shorn of that, he would, like Samson, be passive, in the hands of the Philistines.

(3) Another suggestion which may be urged in behalf of the suffrage rights of the "ignorant and non-property-holding Negro" is, that he is a hopeless minority; nor could he, by any means, control the destinies of this country, if the intelligent voters of the land would but be vigilant and prompt in the exercise of the franchise, imposed in them. It is a sad reflection that the alleged fraud and corruption which existed under "carpet-bag rule" in the South during the reconstruction period could never have existed had the white voters of the South, who were yet clothed with the elective franchise, given their countenance and affiliation to the Negro voters, instead of standing aloof from them and leaving them to be swayed by a set of *educated men,* many of whom were neither "to the manor born," nor particularly interested in the welfare of the several communities in which they operated.

(4) We must never lose sight of the fact that the welfare of the Republic is not resident altogether in the *brains* of the voters. The *heart* plays a very conspicuous part in the casting of a pure and salutary ballot. As between a voter possessing a pure, kind and patriotic heart but an uncultivated mind, and another endowed with all the learning of the universities, but swayed by ulterior and unpatriotic designs, one would experience little or no difficulty in making choice of the former, even though clad in a black skin.

(5) The fact that a Negro is a "non-property-holding Negro" should not militate against his right to exercise his rights of citizenship; for, many of the most useful and valuable of our voters, of both races, are

non-property-holding" voters. The fact of holding property is frequently predicated on conditions altogether fortuitous—a reverse of the wheel of fortune, a large or expensive family—a drought or flood, as well as many other contingencies all play conspicuous parts in preventing good and true citizens from accumulating property, even to the extent of an humble homestead; while fire, cyclone and flood often reduce a man of great possessions in a day to the conditions of a "non-property-holding" citizen; and did his right to vote depend on his property holding, he would be utterly bereft of it. On the contrary, it is no extraordinary thing to see a man of less than average intelligence endowed with "worldly goods" through a turn of the wheel of fortune or the expansion or contraction of a "margin," where men win or lose all on the casting of a die.

It does not seem to have occurred to many of those who are exceedingly anxious to deprive "ignorant and non-property-holding Negroes" of the ballot, that ignorance in a white man is just as vicious as ignorance in any other class of citizens; yet they go on eliminating, by laws of questionable validity, the hard working, wealth producing Negro of the South, while in most instances the ignorant, dilettante and faneant, with a white skin, is not only permitted to vote, but even protected in the exercise of the function.

Upon the whole, after mature reflection, an affirmative answer would seem to be the proper one to the foregoing proposition. Under our present Constitution, yes; the "ignorant and non-property-holding Negro" ought to vote.

TOPIC VI.

IS THE CRIMINAL NEGRO JUSTLY DEALT WITH IN THE COURTS OF THE SOUTH?

BY ATTORNEY R. S. SMITH.

At first glance the above question would seem to be fully answered with one word comprising but two letters, namely, N-o. And yet, upon second thought, it will be seen that that answer would not apply, for the reason that the alleged criminal Negro seldom reaches a court-house in the South before alleged summary justice is visited upon him by an unreasoning Judge Lynch.

The fact that the question is asked whether the criminal Negro is justly dealt with in the courts of the South, would imply that there is at least a doubt as to the genuineness of the justice meted out to him there. In legal phraseology, a criminal is one who has been duly convicted of crime. This being so, it would seem that my first inquiry should be, whether the Negro who has been legally ascertained to be a criminal is justly dealt with in the South, in the matter of his punishment therefor? This line of inquiry leads me into the investigation of the convict lease system which obtains in certain Southern states, and other unlawful abuses of colored criminals there.

It is not my purpose in the limited space allotted to consider this phase of the subject at great length, but rather to briefly point out its manifest injustice.

One of the greatest wrongs of the South is its convict lease system; and its lynch law, and its disfranchising statutes are like unto it. Although the emancipation proclamation, written and promulgated by the immortal Lincoln, has been operative for more than thirty-six years, yet a species of slavery still exists there, fostered and nurtured by the statutes authorizing the convict lease system. So vile became this evil in Anderson county, South Carolina, that the leading officials there denounced it as brutal and barbarous, a crime against nature and nature's God—a crime against civilization and humanity.

Some of the specific charges against the system were that these unfortunate beings, without regard to sex, were huddled together in

Atty. R. S. Smith

ATTORNEY REUBEN S. SMITH.

Reuben S. Smith, attorney-at-law, No. 420 Fifth Street, N. W., Washington, D. C., was born in Jackson County, Florida, April 1, 1854. He received his early education in the common schools of Marianna, in that county, and at Howard University, Washington, D. C. Before coming to Washington he taught school for a time and in 1876 served as an alternate delegate-at-large from Florida to the National Republican Convention, held at Cincinnati, Ohio. As a resident of the national capital he served as a clerk in the United States Treasury Department, in the office of the sixth auditor and in that of the second auditor. He was also Washington correspondent of several newspapers, but after graduating from the law department of the Howard University, in 1883, was admitted to the bar of the Supreme Court of the District of Columbia, and has since been successfully employed in the practice of his profession. He has not only established a lucrative private business, but has acted as attorney for a life insurance company and other corporations. In November, 1899, he was unanimously elected moderator of the conference of the Congregational churches of Virginia, Maryland, West Virginia and the District of Columbia, and is Superintendent of the Lincoln Memorial Congregational Church Sunday School.

Mr. Smith was a delegate to the National Republican Convention held at Chicago in 1880, and a special agent of the eleventh census of the United States (1890), assigned to the work of collecting the statistics of the recorded indebtedness of the State of Florida. It is therefore evident that he is a man of versatility as well as ability.— *Biographical Encyclopedia of the United States.*

The subject of this sketch also served as assistant sergeant-at-arms of the Philadelphia National Republican Convention of 1900. He has been attorney in several important cases in the Supreme Court of the District of Columbia, involving damage suits against large corporations, and has been generally successful. He has also been retained in many equity, real estate and contested will cases, wherein he has been equally successful. He has been almost exclusively engaged in civil practice during his experience of fourteen years as a practitioner before the Supreme Court of the District.

Mr. and Mrs. Smith are domiciled at No. 715 Second Street, Northwest, where they have resided for the past twenty years. Two children survive to them: Master Jerome Bonaparte, a student at Howard University and Miss Rosa Virginia, a pupil in the Washington High School.

prison quarters like so many cattle. It has been a foul blot upon the
escutcheon of the South, second only to the murderous stains made thereon by the lynchers. It is a disgrace even to the civilization of medieval
times. For cruelty and outrage it is unparalleled in the annals of civilized society. Siberia itself is preferable to the convict camp. Given
the worst form of human slavery plus the barbarities of prison life; add
to this the horrors of a Spanish prison, and you have somewhat of an idea
of the iniquitous institution of the barbarous convict lease system.

But as if compounding crime, it is asserted with many of the appearances of truth, that Negro boys and girls, upon trivial charges, are convicted and sent to the convict camp for the express purpose of securing
to the lessees of convicts the benefit of their unrequited toil until they
reach their majority. Thus confined among confirmed criminals they
naturally partake of the character of their environments, and conceive
and multiply vice and criminology. This system punishes the real criminal unjustly. The ill-gotten gain it offers furnishes the incentive to
thrust the innocent into prison pens.

Then, too, it is claimed with the appearance of truth that unscrupulous white men in certain Southern localities actually trump up charges
against Negro men and procure their convictions and sentence to the
convict camp for the double purpose of affording the lessees the comparatively free labor of the alleged criminals and to deprive them of the
right to vote. While heartily approving of such reasonable punishment
as shall deter crime, I can command no language strong and severe
enough to condemn in fitting terms the cruelties and deviltries heaped
upon the Negro in certain sections of the South in the name and for the
sake of those who profit by the convict lease system.

It is undisputed that some of those sent to the convict camp have
been properly found guilty; some have been illegally convicted; some
deserve proper punishment, while some, by reason of their tender years,
should have been put into reformatories, where they might have been
rescued from a life of crime and brought up as law-abiding citizens.
Such institutions may have been intended to protect society from the
dishonest and vicious and to repress crime, but they are really made
hotbeds of vice; and where sufficient vitality remains in the unfortu-
nates, they actually propagate and multiply criminals.

But if the question should become so varied as to inquire whether
the Negro in the South charged with crime is justly dealt with in the

courts thereof; in other words, is he afforded a fair trial there?—it could not be fully answered without taking into consideration the heinous crime with which the Negro is generally charged. There is nothing more revolting than rape, unless it be mob-rule. There is no true man, white or black, who would not rejoice to see condign punishment visited upon the brute legally proven guilty of this most diabolical crime.

The South justifies lynching on the ground that it shields the victim of the crime from the publicity to which a trial of the perpetrator would expose her. That is to say, the lynchers prefer to violate the organic law, which provides that no one shall be deprived of life, liberty, or property, without due process of law. They put the mob above the judicial system of the country, and arrogate to it greater power to protect the honor of the outraged female and uphold the majesty of the law than a court of justice. It is a sad reflection upon the administration of justice even to intimate that the mob which ruthlessly defies the law is better qualified to administer justice than the court established by law to try and determine the guilt or innocence of persons charged with the commission of crime.

In the dark ages of English history, it frequently happened that the person charged with the commission of crime was first executed and afterward his trial was had, and if a verdict of not guilty was found, his bones were disinterred and given a state funeral. But the Negro charged with the commission of crime in the South is frequently not granted a trial before or after execution; so that the Negro is not justly dealt with in the courts of the South, even after he has been hung, drawn and quartered, or burned.

In some instances where the Negro is fortunate enough to confront his accusers in a court in the South, the caste prejudice against him too often reduces his trial to a mere mockery of justice.

The cornerstone of the Republic is justice, to establish which, under liberty, its founders set foot upon these hostile shores in the early part of the seventeenth century. From that time to the present the slogan of every campaign, the rallying cry of every battle, has been justice in some form or other. And yet, in the alleged interest of innocence, justice, in certain localities, is often outraged, law dethroned, and mob rule exalted.

Whether or not the Negro charged with crime is justly dealt with in the courts of the South can only be answered relatively, for in some localities fair trials are granted even to Negroes charged with the commission of crime. But for the most part, it must be admitted that

Negroes brought into the courts of the South accused of crime against white people are not accorded a fair trial.

The reason of this unjust dealing with the Negro in the courts of the South is not far to seek; he is looked upon as an alien; then, too, the doctrine that he has no rights which a white man is bound to respect is exploded in certain localities only in theory, for in practice it is still unmistakably prevalent.

The crying need of the times is a wholesome respect for law and order, and a righteous condemnation of mob rule everywhere. Every pulpit North and South should speak out against mob rule and lynch law. The eloquent divine in Greenville, Miss., who recently denounced with righteous indignation the damnable outrages of mob violence in that state, was as a voice crying in the wilderness. For some reason his brethren of the cloth have not seen fit to join him in a crusade against this abominable sin. If the Southern clergy could only be induced to preach against this evil occasionally, there would soon be created throughout the sin-ridden districts such a healthy public sentiment and respect for law and order that these crimes against the state would soon become things of the past; nor could there be found throughout our broad land a miscreant, who, under the influence of the spirit of lawlessness, would take the life of our Chief Magistrate; nor would there be anywhere such an illiberal public sentiment as would openly criticise our Chief Executive for dining a representative member of the race whose feasts even Jupiter did not disdain to grace.

But let us consider the alleged crime for which lynching is attempted to be justified. L. H. Perkins, Esq., of the Kansas Bar Association, in an address to its annual meeting, in July, 1901, said:

"Lord Coke observes: 'There are crimes that are not so much as to be named among Christians.' It is difficult for us in Kansas to believe that certain crimes exist; crimes against nature, practiced by force upon defenseless childhood, disclosed in criminal records of great cities; but there is one crime in Kansas that we have learned to know. It ought not to be named, much less permitted in a Christian land. The crime and its fit punishment, can scarcely be discussed; but how else can it be expunged? Shall it be by fire? Must he who writes the story of this new-born age still further shock the world and foul the fair name of America by pictures of a howling mob, profaning every law of God and man; with every bulwark of our rights thrown down, the gates of hell unchained, and passion, loose, unbridled as hurricane, roaring above the prostrate guardians of the peace, annihilating in an hour the civilization of six thousand years?

"Death in flames! Savage, bloodthirsty vengeance! Three things this savory orgy lacks: salt and sweet herbs and a good appetite.

"There is a law that in the last extremity, in the presence of impending death, all barriers are removed, all ranks are leveled, all rights are equalized. Supreme necessity is supreme law. Can it be possible that some such overmastering impulse at times dethrones the public mind, and, while the fit is on, the latent cannibal runs riot in the land? It seems it must be so; and, if it be, 'twill be until we rise to the necessity.

"We may excoriate the cannibal, but which of us will now affirm the provocation is not great? Poor, helpless woman! Why don't she learn to shoot? This monstrous crime pursues her like a nightmare. It is an ever present peril to every woman in the land. Must she shun every alley and fly from every bush lest lascivious eyes be on her and unbridled, brutal passion block her way? Of all the hobgoblins abroad in the night, in fact or fancy or in song or story, there is none so hideous as the stealthy form of the lecherous brute that leaps forth out of darkness and drags defenseless woman to her ruin.

"And can it be that we who make the laws; we who have wives and daughters and sisters and mothers who are dearer than life itself; we who honor woman, not for her strength but for the very attributes that render her the prey of force; can it be that we can make no laws that will protect her, or satisfy the public that justice will be done?

"Concede that in the sight of God the crime of rape is worse than murder, yet is it plain that the punishment should be death? In the interest of woman herself were it not better that the brutal ravisher have somewhat more to bear if he do also murder? Else would not the motive to silence forever the most dangerous witness be complete?

"I offer the suggestion of three degrees for rape—the first to cover only ravishment by brutal violence and force; the second all the intermediate grades save statutory rape, which alone shall constitute the third degree. I am no firm believer in the justice of our age of consent, and would leave corporal punishment for statutory rape to the discretion of the trial court. The terms of imprisonment as now prescribed are doubtless long enough, but let us add to them the sting and shame of the ancient whipping post. For the third degree, in the court's discretion, not more than seven lashes. For the second degree two floggings of twenty lashes each, soundly administered within twelve months. And for the first degree, three several floggings of forty lashes each within twelve months, and then castration. There is much reason in this ancient penalty, and the time has come when it should be revived. If, as some say, this morbid and unbridled passion is disease, then treat it like appendicitis—remove the cause."

Mr. Perkins is on the right track. I am glad that he neither endorses lynching nor takes stock in the absurd report from certain sections of the South that all Negroes are ravishers of white women. I think his suggested remedy against rape a good one for white and black.

But to return to the consideration of the other phase of the question, I desire to say that Mrs. Helen Douglass, the widow of the lamented Frederick Douglass, is accepted authority on the convict lease system, and consequently I am indebted to her for most of the data used in this article touching that subject. In a well prepared lecture on convict leases, Mrs. Douglass introduces her theme as follows:

"We know what happens when manufactories are shut down and a vast amount of accumulated material is suddenly thrown upon the market. For 250 years the South had been manufacturing a peculiar article; had been literally stamping this article with its own lineaments and putting it upon a market created especially for it. The war came! The manufactories were closed; the material was on hand; what should be done with it? Never in the world, perhaps, has there been a clearer demonstration of the irrevocable nature of law, as affecting society, and the awful power of habit as the sum of reiterated choice."

At the Prison Reform Convention, held in Atlanta in 1888, Dr. P. D. Sims of Chattanooga, Tenn., said that, the impoverished condition of the South succeeding the War of the Rebellion, caused it to drift into the convict lease system, for which there were many excuses, but no justification. The lessee buys from the State the discipline of prisoners solely for gain; that neither the State nor the lessee had regard to the element of reform or consideration of a philanthropic character; that although many good men were engaged in it, the system was wrong. He presented the statistics of thirty-nine State prisons, showing that in the non-leasing prisons, the annual mortality was fifteen per thousand, while in the leasing, it was sixty-four per thousand, and that in the former, escapes were but five per thousand, and in the latter, they were fifty-one per thousand. He appealed to the South to change the system.

The lease system was adopted in Georgia in 1869, both Democrats and Republicans favoring it. The first year there were 350 convicts to be hired, and the second year the number doubled. An investigation showed that one company paid nothing to the State for the labor of its convicts, and that although the law provided for a chaplain, the State had none; that convicts were worked on Sundays contrary to law, and in some instances whipped to death. The evils of the system became so flagrant that a Senator on the floor of the Senate Chamber declared that the rich and powerful were allowed to go free, while the poor white person and the ignorant Negro were shown no mercy. It was proved that even a governor of the State was himself a lessee, working State convicts for private gain, under a $37,000 bond in force until 1899, although he was the convict's only protection against the wrongs of the lessee.

The ease and facility with which colored persons were sent to the penitentiary kept a goodly supply of prisoners on hand. While it was burdensome to taxpayers to keep them within walls, it was unjust to mechanics to allow them to learn trades; ergo, they were leased out to grade streets, to work on railroads, in mines and the like, where their physical powers might be availed of, but where they could learn nothing, save yes and no, axe and hoe.

By an act passed in 1876, by the legislature, the Marietta and North Georgia Railroad Company was leased 250 convicts for three years, to grade its road where the people were too poor to pay for it. The rest of the convicts the governor was authorized to lease to three penitentiary companies for twenty years for $500,000, to be paid in annual installments of $25,000. In a test case by two of these companies, in the Supreme Court of Georgia it was decided that the lessees acquired a vested right of property in the labor of these convicts, which the legislature could not disregard unless their labor was required by the State, in which case the lessee demanded compensation. The Supreme Court consequently granted an injunction restraining the keeper from delivering said convicts to said railroad company, thereby securing to the lessees a legal right of property in the labor of the convicts till the contract is legally terminated.

In an investigation of 1896, presided over by Governor Atkinson, Capt. Lowe, a lessee, testified:

"We do not think ourselves liable for the conduct of whipping bosses. They are given their commissions by the State, and we insist that they are answerable to the State alone. We cannot direct the whipping of convicts; it must be done by the bosses. If all the convicts were disabled by whipping, we think the State would be liable to us for loss of time, because the whipping bosses are the agents of the State."

Lessee Lowe admitted he was a close corporation, being president, secretary, treasurer, boss and everything else of the company, which held no meetings, had no stock, and declared no dividends.

Attorney-General Terrell held that the convicts were under the care of the lessees, whose duty it was to see that they were treated humanely, citing the order of 1887 by Governor Gordon, to prove that while the whipping bosses were appointed by the governor, they were under the control of the lessees. Governor Atkinson said that he did not dream for a moment that the lessees did not consider it their duty to see that the convicts were properly treated.

Mr. Huff, addressing the legislature, said, that "any attempt at reformation of the present system is an absurdity, a swindle and a fraud. It is a damnable outrage. The lessee contract would not stand fifteen minutes before a petit jury. I could hang any of the lessees before a petit jury in two and a half hours," said he.

One convict testified that in his case the skin came off with every blow inflicted by a soaked strap drawn through sand; that twenty bastard children were in one camp. A female convict testified that during her prison life of fourteen years she had borne seven children. A lessee testified that such irregularities as bastard children would occasionally occur as long as women were guarded by men.

Dr. Felton, addressing the Georgia Legislature, said:

"I stated ten years ago that the State was acting as a procuress for convict camps; the legislature is keeping up the supply in accordance with the demand. I repeat the accusation here and now."

In 1895 a number of convicts had their feet so frozen that the flesh and toes rotted off. Governor Atkinson enlightened the legislature of the deplorable condition existing in the convicts' camps through the report thereon by Hon. R. F. Wright, showing nearly fifty misdemeanor camps. In the chain-gangs were twenty-seven white and 768 colored convicts; generally both races and sexes being together day and night. Among these were eleven children under fourteen years of age. Some slept in rude floorless houses; some in tents on the bare ground, and a few in bunks. The bedding was scant and filthy, and full of vermin. The camps were poorly ventilated, the sleeping quarters being generally sweat-boxes, constructed to prevent escapes. There were no hospitals and no preparations for comfort or medical treatment. Female prisoners dressed in male attire, worked side by side with men.

A member of the legislature declared:

"Most lessees would rather see the devil in their camps than a Methodist or Baptist preacher. I do not urge the bill for the Negro, but for the safety of homes and property. Crime has increased in the United States more than in any other country on the globe. I plead for the orphan boys and girls of the State. Better send them to a bottomless hell than to James' camp."

Said the lamented Colonel Alston:

"The public knows how hard it is to get testimony in a case like the lease question. If a guard kills a man, he is not going to tell of it. If a lessee chooses to whip one to death, who is to know it? If he starves them, who is the wiser? I never expect to give up the agitation of this question till I can point to my native State redeemed, regenerated, and disenthralled from this great sin, and the finger of shame shall no longer be lifted at her, as a State that is banking on the crimes and misfortunes of her defenseless and ignorant population."

Three months after this Colonel Alston was shot dead in the State Capitol of Georgia, by a sub-lessee during a controversy arising from the leasing of some convicts; whereupon Governor Atkinson declared that, under heaven and by God's help, he meant to lift up the administration of the laws of the State to that high plane that will put an end to these things.

Mr. Byrd of Rome, Ga., by authority of Governor Atkinson, inspected the misdemeanor camps in 1897, and reported that private chain-gangs were being operated against law, and in spite of the decisions of the Supreme Court of Georgia, and that the average penal camp of the State penitentiary is a heaven, compared to the agony and torture endured by the misdemeanor convicts in many of these joints. He said that Mr. Wright did valiant service for humanity by showing that a bondage worse than slavery was being inflicted upon the convicts, who were confined in these "hells upon earth."

In one camp, he said, an ante-bellum residence had been converted into a prison by removing every window, and closing up every aperture, leaving not even an auger hole for light or air. In the center of a room only 18 feet by 20, was an open can, the reeking cesspool of this dungeon in which sat a sick Negro convict confined in this dark sweat-box, perishing.

In another camp, after the visit of Mr. Wright, the guards took turns at beating a convict to death and buried him in his shackles. A respectable citizen asserted that they caught the convict by the shackles and ran through the woods dragging him feet foremost, and that when these facts were sworn to before the Grand Jury of Pulaski County, it was thought best to hush them up and keep the matter out of the newspapers, and out of court, as the superintendent of the prison camp had friends on the jury.

Another case sworn to before the coroner's jury was that of a guard who had whipped nearly all the life out of an old Negro, who said: "Boss, is ye gwine to kill me?" The guard replied with an oath in the affirmative, whereupon the convict begged to be shot and thus freed from his sufferings. He was chained up to a tree where he died in thirty minutes.

In another camp a white convict was being boarded at a hotel ten miles away, and doing a prosperous business at painting, while another white convict who had been made night guard and given a gun and the keys to the camp, had it so free and easy that he threw up his job and decamped.

Mr. Boies of Pennsylvania, in his instructive work, discusses the convict lease system, and shows that the sentences of Negroes in the South are double those of white men for the same offenses; that for petty larceny a Negro may be condemned to the criminal class for life, albeit he had to steal or starve. He shows that the criminal machinery of the South is frequently used to nullify the Negro's right of suffrage; that no hand is extended to lift him up when he falls, and no effort is put forth for his reformation, and for this reason the South turns out one-third of the criminals of the whole country; that Massachusetts expends $20 per capita upon the children of her public schools, while Mississippi with a heavier tax, expends but $2 per capita.

In the Evening Star of Washington, D. C., of November 16, 1901, an exhaustive article on the prison camps of Florida appeared. Although guardedly, it favored the effort to make the criminal self-supporting, arguing that as he lives on the public when at large, he should not be permitted to continue to live on the public when in confinement. But it admits that the convict lease system is faulty. It says:

"At present, offenders of all grades and ages are thrown together, and the younger ones learn more evil than they knew at the time of their arrest, growing daily more depraved and vicious so long as they remain in bad company. It may be possible, however, to employ most of the convicts at tasks which will not require their close association, either at work or in quarters, and if that desideratum can be reached, the last argument against the leasing of prisoners will be met, and the system will be continued indefinitely, such minor matters as the corruption of inspectors, of which Alabama has complained, being capable of rebuke through legislation.

"There are now thirteen camps in Florida, each one of which is technically a State prison, and they are under the watch of a supervisor, who must visit them at least once in sixty days, examine the buildings, food, clothes, and bedding, question keepers and convicts as to work, punishment and health, enforce compliance with the laws and report to the governor every month. All leases are for four years, and the only cost of its criminals to the State are the salaries of supervisors and a sum of $300 a year for chaplain service.

"The country expends at least $200,000,000 per annum in maintaining its convicts. In the city of New York alone, the annual assessment for that purpose is $6 per citizen.

"Where the labor unions have not prevented it, society has made the criminal pay his own bills. In the South where the people are beginning to show a keenness for money that is not surpassed in the North, but where, as yet, capital is not gathered into such immense and usable sums as in the central and eastern States, a new policy has been adopted with regard to the offender. He is generally a Negro, hence he is sent back to slavery. He is sold to a farmer, a distiller, a phosphate miner, or a manufacturer, for a term of years, and his employer pays considerably less to the State than he would otherwise lay out in wages.

"In Alabama if a State prisoner or long-termer escapes from his employer, he must pay into the public treasury $200, and $100 if a county prisoner or short-termer escapes.

"When an inspector is present at a whipping, the turbulent convict may be given twenty-one lashes on his bare back; in the absence of the inspector, the whipping boss is limited to fifteen lashes.

"The guards are of the poor white class, dull and illiterate, and receive from $20 to $30 per month and their 'keep.'

"In Florida shackling is seldom practiced except as a punishment for running away, as it interferes with the work of the convict. Guns and bloodhounds are much in evidence in the convict camps. Nothing is done for the betterment of the convicts intellectually or otherwise. Missionaries are graciously permitted to distribute tracts among them.

"White convicts are generally assigned to offices and cook shops, or become gang foremen. For the white prisoner, whatever his offense, there is always a hope of pardon, but the Negro prisoner, unless he be a crap-shooter or chicken thief, congratulates himself on being consigned to open air work in the convict's camps, for he remembers how dreadfully easy in Florida it is for a Negro to be lynched."

Judge M. W. Gibbs of Arkansas said he had known white employers in the South to be in collusion with magistrates to have colored men committed on the flimsiest pretext, simply that they might obtain more free labor on their plantations by means of the convict lease system.

The eleventh census shows that in the United States there were 2,468 county jails and only 44 reformatories. There were no reformatories in Alabama, Arkansas, Florida, Georgia, Mississippi, North Carolina, South Carolina, Tennessee and Texas.

Great Britain supports over 400 reformatories and inebriate schools, and they have closed 56 out of 113 prisons and jails in ten years, and thereby reduced to that extent the amount of material for the manufacture of criminals.

Said Judge Calhoun, of a recorder's court in Georgia:

"I tremble when I contemplate the future of little boys who come before me for the first time, and are sentenced to the chain-gang. Some of them are bright-faced and intelligent; some are orphans; many thoroughly penitent; and, I believe, nearly all could be reclaimed, could they be sent to a reform school and surrounded with an atmosphere that would benefit instead of contaminate."

Mrs. Helen Cook, wife of Hon. John F. Cook, of Washington, D. C., has established an organization in the District of Columbia, known as "The Woman's League," which is doing a wonderful work in reducing the number of those who are brought into the courts to be justly or unjustly dealt with. Let the good women of the race throughout the country follow her example and do something to rescue the perishing.

In conclusion, let us hope and believe with the widow of the Sage of Anacostia, that "Meanwhile Hampton and Wilberforce, Howard and Shaw and Fiske and Atlanta and Tuskegee and other like institutions are silently setting the seal of manhood and womanhood upon a race whose face, with ours, is set toward a higher and better civilization."

SECOND PAPER.

IS THE CRIMINAL NEGRO JUSTLY DEALT WITH IN THE COURTS OF THE SOUTH?

BY ATTORNEY I. L. PURCELL.

First: What constitutes a court? In the South as in the North and other parts of the country, to constitute a court, there must be a judge, whose duty it is to preside over the court, a sheriff and deputies, and a State's solicitor, who looks after the interests of the State, and last, but by no means least, comes the jury, whose duty it is to discharge or pass on the innocence or guilt of the prisoner according to the law and evidence as offered; it requires all these to constitute an organized court of law.

First: The judge should be a man selected on account of his nobility of character, of heart, of soul and of mind; a man of experience and training, a man of affairs, learned in the affairs appertaining strictly to his branch, as also in literature and science; a man merciful, kind and generous, of a sterling character, temperate, though positive and un-biased by private opinion, in a word, he should be a man, the representative of justice, though not usurping that power as abiding in himself, but as the instrument of that power; whose moral character ought to be without blemish, a man whose habit, integrity, shrewd judgment and wise counsel place him above the average man, making him of the people and for the people.

Sheriffs and deputies ought to be honest and fearless, having the highest regard for the life and liberties of the people; they should be kind and generous, yet positive and fearless, ever ready to defend the life and liberties of the people, using their office only in consonance with the prescribed law in aiding the conviction of crime, but not as a means of revenging personal wrongs or injuries of the people whose color is their only sin.

J. L. Purcell

ISAAC LAWRENCE PURCELL.

Isaac Lawrence Purcell, the subject of this sketch, was born July 17, 1857, in Winnsboro, S. C. His father, John W. Purcell, by occupation a carpenter, was born in 1832 in Charleston, S. C., being one of the old free families.

Isaac Lawrence first attended a school provided by the Episcopal Church for Colored youths. He afterwards attended the public schools of his city and, in 1871, entered Brainard Institute, Chester, S. C., where he remained one term. In 1872 he entered Biddle University at Charlotte, N. C., where he remained until in the Fall of 1873, when the color line was removed at the South Carolina University. He entered the competitive examination for the scholarship in the South Carolina University from his county, being the only Colored applicant. In the Fall of 1873 he entered the South Carolina University, where he remained until the Spring of 1877, when the act of the Legislature of the State went into effect again drawing the color line, so he with the other Colored boys had to leave.

Mr. Purcell returned home, and under his father's instructions learned the carpenter's trade. He went to Palatka, Fla., in 1885, where he studied law, and was admitted to practice law in the Circuit and inferior courts October 8, 1889, and at once commenced the active work of his chosen profession at Palatka, Fla.

At the first term of the Circuit Court after his admittance he represented plaintiffs in several large damage suits, two against the city of Palatka; in both he got verdict for his clients; one was appealed to the Supreme Court. He was admitted to the State Supreme Court January 19, 1891, where he has successfully represented many cases. January 19, 1897, he was admitted to the United States Circuit and District Courts, and November 8, 1901, was duly admitted to the Supreme Court of the United States. He has represented some of the most important cases coming before the courts of his State. He came to Pensacola, his present home, in February, 1899, and has by his energy and ability built up a fine and growing business.

In politics he is a Republican, and has attended as a delegate every State, congressional and county convention since coming to the State, several times presided over State and congressional conventions, was for twelve years chairman of the Republican Executive Committee of his county, Putnam. For many years an alderman of the city of Palatka, Fla. In 1895 he was elected as a delegate to the Republican National Convention which convened in St. Louis, 1896. He has never held any office of profit, always honest and fearless in his opinions and his advocacy of right.

His private life has always been consistent; while not a member of any religious denomination, always attends the services of the Episcopal Church; is a temperate man; is generous and kind in disposition; was married October 24, 1895, to Miss E. L. Andrews, of Orangeburg, S. C.

THE JURY: The jury ought to be composed, if possible, of men of learning, whose moral character, love of truth, unbiased by racial prejudice or private opinions, being only representatives of the people, who in the name of the people adjudge, condemn or acquit according to the evidence, not from any private opinion, but governed by such law as is made in the statement of the judge bearing upon the case given previously to their retiring; if these men of learning can not be found, as in most cases, let others who, for the above qualifications minus learning, be substituted in their stead. In the selection of the jury in the most cases they come as the most refined element of the scum and refuse of the party class, whose labor in the election of some democratic officer, can only be rewarded under these terms; being unqualified to fill even the most inferior office of their party, in a majority of cases, not even one of these is acquainted with even the lowest element of learning, and if, perchance, one can be found, he is made foreman. The Negro is never thought of, but if, perchance, one should be selected, and in such a manner is he prominent, even his color makes him conspicuous, he also is on a par with his companions; men of influence are never selected. Before I conclude with the jury may I say a word of those who select them? In most States they are selected by the county commissioners, in some by a jury commissioner. These commissioners, in most cases, are none other than tools, instruments, who have no minds of their own, but like a reed before a gust of the mighty wind that blows nobody good, as serfs and pampered menials bend irrespective of that higher principle, that innate quality of man that places him above the brute creation, serving in abject slavery for the carrying out of party crime and cunning as well as subtle devices.

A court constituted of such elements as described, is an "Ideal One." One to be desired, and the only one at whose hands justice, and only that as gold refined, shall be tried, counterpoised and mete out to every man justice, in the name of Heaven and at the hands of man.

But may I ask how are our courts of the South constituted? are any two of the above qualities to be found in the most prominent of our Southern courts of criminal jurisdiction? If Diogenes of old would seek in our Southern courts for such a man, hereto,--as in Greece, such an one could not be found, for truth is no longer enthroned on its sacred altar.

Having defined the true elements of which the courts of our Southland are constituted, I shall pass to consider, THE MANNER IN WHICH THE

Negro is dealt with in these courts. Is the criminal Negro justly dealt with in the courts of the South? is a question that I think is more frequently asked than words can answer, language describe, or man's wisdom unravel. Our woes have gone out to the ends of the earth and, the stagnant waters can no longer contain its contaminating germs, and now, even on the other side of the globe, we hear the re-echo of our cries from this damnable cruelty wafted back to us by the zephyrs that sustain expectations impregnated with hope telling of some bright future.

What of the Negro in the sunny South? what of his rights as a citizen? what of his treatment at the bar of justice? are questions also propounded on the other side and since the trial cause of the alleged rape has been made clear, we expect and are looking forth to the dawn of a brighter future.

In our civil courts, in other words, our courts where property rights are tried, I must say, that where tenement rights are concerned, justice is meted out to the Negro even against the white man when elevated to our higher courts, this is the only sphere in which a lenient form of justice is prescribed and given the Negro. The same cannot be alleged of him when his life, his liberty, or reputation or citizenship is at stake.

Against a fellow Negro, he is in some instances protected, as against a white man, seldom, if ever. In this latter it is not justice that is the object of our courts, but the impeachment and condemnation of a fellow man, giving vent to a vindictive racial prejudice. Be the crime of the Negro ever so trivial, when against the white man, the sheriff, having to carry out the oath; the jury, their party plans; the judge, his selfish means; and, therefore, no evidence, however palpable, however substantial and convincing can shield the Negro under such instances. The skin of a white man being held sacred, cannot be violated or polluted by the touch of the Negro's hands, be it in self-defense, or in defense of his manhood, or in the defense of wife, daughter or some other female relative. On the other hand, seldom, if ever, can a white man be convicted when charged with striking a Negro, or for any insult he may offer to his wife, sister, daughter or mother; the juries being all white, they consider this no crime for a white man.

May we notice the following facts of the records of our courts; may I here testify and, without a fear of successful contradiction, that by these, as matter for the criminal statistics of the race serves no purpose.

First: Because our best citizens, the better class of our thinking men and the most virtuous of our people are not tried at the hands of an impartial jury, and innocence made to bear the stamp of guilt, can in no way be accounted justice; for instance, in a case of assault and battery, although the party charged is able and does prove, by legal evidence, that his actions were prompted only by resistance in self-defense, however convincing, if a white man can be found, if even he does not know anything, but can allege a negative, this unjust evidence counterpoises the balance of justice and the Negro is found guilty. If, on the other hand, larceny be charged, it is almost an impossibility even to attempt to defend, if there be a white witness against you, it being taken for granted that every Negro is a thief. Now in courts of justice according to my judgment, and according to the law, every man is presumed to be innocent until his guilt is proven beyond a reasonable doubt, by legal evidence, and such evidence must be furnished or obtained by the prosecution. But men are daily convicted in our courts, simply because they are Negroes.

In concluding, let me say, that a majority of my people labor under appalling disadvantages, but I hope that the time is not far distant when our courts will be constituted as the "Altars of Justice," the judges and their associates, as its priests, and the American citizen, be his color what it may, can come and there receive at the hands of unblemished and unspotted servants redresses for wrongs, compensation for impeached innocence and justice for his wrongs.

The time is coming when all racial prejudice shall have passed away, and when color will no longer impede our obtaining what is due us, and when the Negro will receive a fair and impartial trial before a jury of his peers; then will justice and equity rule sublime, and the Negro being protected in all his rights; his liberty, life and reputation will be held sacred, and virtue and worth will be considered; and man, the prince of God's creation will be crowned for doing justice unto man.

THIRD PAPER.

IS THE CRIMINAL NEGRO JUSTLY DEALT WITH IN THE COURTS OF THE SOUTH?

BY GEORGE T. ROBINSON, A. M., LL. B.

I answer this question in the negative.

There are some exceptions, but proof is too abundant to gainsay the assertion.

In the first place, all of the machinery of the law is in the hands of the white man. He is judge, jury, sheriff, constable, and policeman.

Race prejudice and antipathy so over-ride reason, that the average dispenser of justice is blinded to a sense of right, especially when a white man appears against an accused Negro. What is sop for the white man, is not always sop for the black man. As a matter of fact, the black man is discriminated against in everything in the South, and it would be unreasonable to expect the courts would do otherwise.

The presumption of law is that the accused is innocent, and that presumption stands as a witness in his favor until overcome by credible proof. But in the average court of the South, this applies to white men only. The Negro is presumed to be guilty, and the burden of proof is placed upon him to establish his innocence.

Cases have come under my observation where the accused Negro was not only tried without being represented by counsel, but on ex parte evidence, the black defendant not being permitted to testify in his own behalf or to introduce proof. These cases were not in courts of record.

The organic law of the land guarantees not only trial by jury on an indictment or presentment, but entitles the accused to be heard by himself and counsel and to introduce witnesses. In some instances, the accused is not even in court. The matter is prearranged and the imprisoned wretch is informed afterward and forced into agreeing to the "sentence," as the easiest way out of trouble. It is a rare thing now to see a Negro on a jury in the South.

Even the Federal courts are ignoring him. A white man does not consider a Negro his peer. Then from a white man's standpoint, a colored man tried by a white jury is not tried by his peers.

The Constitution is violated in letter and spirit, in order that the criminal Negro may not be justly dealt with. The greater the demand

Capt. Geo. J. Robinson

CAPTAIN GEORGE T. ROBINSON, A. M., LL. B.

George Thomas Robinson was born in Macon, Miss., January 12, 1854, of slave parents. An orphan, in 1865, he set out to fight life's battles with no one to guide and protect him. He has risen to a place of distinction—a journalist of note, a lawyer of high standing, a learned professor of law, an orator of repute, a molder of thought, and a reformer. He received his first inspiration from a remark which he heard Hon. C. S. Smith, now a bishop in the A. M. E. Church, make to a public school of which he was a pupil. It was: "A boy can make of himself whatever he has a mind to." George said to himself, "I will make speeches, too." Since that time Captain Robinson and Bishop Smith have delivered many addresses together. They spoke at the Emancipation Celebration in Nashville, 1st of January, 1892, which took place in the Representative Hall of the capitol. They were the principal speakers.

An afternoon paper on the 2nd said: "The ablest address of the occasion was delivered by Capt. George T. Robinson on Abraham Lincoln. The speaker electrified the audience."

"Cap." Robinson graduated from Fisk University in 1885 and from law in Central Tennessee College, now Walden University, both of Nashville, Tenn. He is a professor of law in the university.

In 1875 he refused a seat in the Legislature of Mississippi, in order to complete his education. In 1886 he delivered the commencement address at Lane College, Jackson, Tenn.; the same year he began the publication of the "Tennessee Star" in Nashville. In 1887 he was made a Captain in the Tennessee National Guard by Governor R. L. Taylor. In 1888 he was on the invitation committee to invite President Cleveland to Nashville and served on Gen. W. H. Jackson's staff as commander of a division in the parade. In 1893 he was a nominee on the Citizens' ticket for the city council. In 1896 he was appointed a member of the executive committee of the Negro department of the Tennessee Centennial and was chairman of the Military Committee. But the entire committee resigned before the exposition opened.

Settling in Nashville in 1886, he soon forged his way to the front and became a champion of Negro rights. Hon. George N. Tillman says of him: "He is one of the best and ablest men of his race in the State." Bishop Evans Tyree says: "Professor Robinson is a giant physically and mentally." Mr. Robinson's fame rests on his journalistic career.

The "Star" was regarded as one of the ablest edited Negro journals ever published. After several years of successful work for God and humanity, it consolidated with the "Indianapolis Freeman."

The "Star" made its advent in the midst of a big social scandal with a pastor of the most prominent Baptist Church in the city, the central figure. With the large following the divine had, it was not only unpopular, but dangerous to fight him, especially since he had been acquitted by the courts; and a large majority of his congregation endorsed the verdicts. The editor routed the opposition. He told the preacher that he had to quit that pulpit and leave the city.

This was the beginning of a reformation in colored society in the city which was far reaching, and brought editor Robinson into prominence. "He woke up one morning and found himself famous." His article, "A Pure Ministry," caused the reformer to be welcomed to Nashville as a Moses.

to keep the convict ranks filled up, the more unjustly is the black criminal dealt with in the severity of the sentence.

The very fact that Negroes are not permitted to serve on juries, even when all the parties are black, proves that it is for the purpose of preventing justice being done the accused Negro.

One of the most popular courts in the South is the Court of Judge Lynch. This "court" comes pretty nearly voicing the sentiment of the section where it thrives and does a large business. Members of this court are summoned as jurors to try Negroes, in legal courts, and thus the mob spirit is carried into the very temple of justice and is meted out to the black criminal in the name of the law. In such cases, who could expect a just verdict? Again, the professional juror, believing his job depends on the number and severity of the convictions of Negroes, is always ready to strain a point in order to convict.

Instead of giving the accused the benefit of the doubt, he seeks to ease his guilty conscience by rapping criminal laws.

The Negro who outrages the person of a female, is worthy of death— a legal death. His crime is no less heinous because his victim is colored —the crime in either case is blacker than the hinges of midnight.

A mob composed of white men takes the ravisher of a white female and burns him at the stake or hangs him and riddles his body with bullets or dismembers his body.

In such a case the criminal is not only unjustly dealt with, for both the moral and civil laws are violated, but a great sin is committed against society, the moral sensibilities are blunted and the crime intended to be suppressed is given new impetus.

Mob violence is the violation of every penal law. The victim has no show whatever.

A mob is not composed of men who have it in their hearts to respect the rights of the victim of their fury.

This is the cause of so many innocent, inoffensive Negro men, women and children perishing at the hands of mobs. Mob violence leads to the utter disregard for law and order, and increases crime, making criminals of "some of the best citizens."

There can be no such thing as dealing justly with the criminal Negro, as long as the rule is to deal unjustly with all Negroes.

For instance, take the black laws, notably the Jim Crow car laws and the infamous election laws, the most outrageous ever inflicted upon a free people. The Negro has been legislated out of the legislative halls, leaving the white man clear sailing in enacting unjust laws which discriminate against all Negroes alike, regardless of condition, culture, refinement, wealth, position or station.

The law places the mark of Cain upon him. His aspirations and ambitions must be curbed in spite of his fitness by character and training. The worthlessness of the Negro does not cause the opposition that the prosperity of the best of the race does. The legislator and constitution maker aims his darts at the latter class.

This state of affairs obtains in every Southern State; and the fact that the ballot, our only safeguard, has been taken from us, shows that the criminal Negro need not expect to be dealt with justly.

The nearest approach to fair play is to be had in the larger towns and cities of the South, and even here the chances are against the Negro. But it will not always be thus. A change will come sooner or later. Let us be courageous, do our best and trust in God.

FOURTH PAPER.

IS THE CRIMINAL NEGRO JUSTLY DEALT WITH IN THE COURTS OF THE SOUTH?

BY ATTORNEY J. THOMAS HEWIN.

For a man of color to approach a subject of this kind, first of all, he must crucify "self." He must not imagine that he is writing to suit the whims, fancies and caprices of a single individual, but must confine himself to the pure and unadulterated truth. To discuss this question from a lawyer's point of view, that is to say, by detailed cases, would be unintelligible to an ordinary layman's mind.

Therefore, we must confine ourselves to the subject from a layman's way of understanding legal matters. The Negro occupies to-day a peculiar position in the body politic. He is not wanted in politics, because his presence in official positions renders him obnoxious to his former masters and their descendants. He is not wanted in the industrial world as a trained handicraftsman, because he would be brought into competition with his white brother. He is not wanted in city positions, because positions of that kind are always saved for the white wardheeling poli-

J. Thomas Hewin.

J. THOMAS HEWIN.

J. Thomas Hewin was born in Dinwiddie County, Va., December 24, 1871. His parents were slaves. He was left an orphan at the age of thirteen, with no knowledge even of the alphabet. At the age of seventeen he was seized with a desire for an education. Finding no opportunity for mental improvement, he went to Richmond, Va., in 1889, where he found employment in a stone quarry. He took his books with him and studied at meal-time. In the fall he became janitor of a business college. Finding that he could do his janitor work mornings and evenings, he entered the public school of Richmond and afterward graduated from the Richmond Normal School as valedictorian of his class.

So thrifty was Mr. Hewin, that when he graduated from school, he had a bank account of $1,375 to his credit.

He also graduated from the Boston University Law School, and after returning to his native state was admitted to the bar. He was especially helpful to the unfortunate of his race.

He organized in Richmond the Anti-Deadly Weapon League among the young colored men of the place, for which he received the commendation of the press and people. He is a member of the Baptist Church, an ardent worker among his people, a power as an organizer and an orator of the Frederick Douglass type.

ticians. He is not wanted in State and Federal offices, because there is an unwritten law that a Negro shall not hold an office. He is not wanted on the Bench as a judge, because he would have to pass upon the white man's case also. Nor is he wanted on public conveyances, because here his presence is obnoxious to white people.

But let us not lose sight of our subject which is: Is the criminal Negro justly dealt with in the courts of the South? Permit the author of this article to say that there is no section in this country where there is not some prejudice against the Negro.

Whether the Negro be tried for a crime he commits in the North or South, he will get as fair a verdict upon the law and evidence as presented in a Southern court as in the courts of any State in this Union. When we see such awful examples of brutality and inhumanity as occur in some sections of our common country against the Negro, we do not wonder that people who live in distant lands say that there can be no justice for a Negro in the Southern States. This assertion has been repeated so often, that now it is a common thing for men to say that a Negro can get no justice in the South. Yet it is important for us to note that not one of these miscarriages of justice is traceable to the partiality of the courts. They are the result of men's prejudices, who are not willing for the Negro's case to be tested upon its merits, because they know that in nine cases in ten he would be acquitted in a court of justice; and for this reason they take the law into their own hands, rather than submit it to an intelligent, cool and unprejudiced judicial body as every court is. Is there a man under heaven who would charge this state of affairs up against the courts of the South? Certainly, no one can be found who would do it. It has been my experience in my State in the trial of criminal cases that in nine cases out of ten, the white juries are in sympathy with the poor, ignorant Negro. I think the same rule will hold good in other Southern States. When we approach the subject of criminal law, we must constantly bear in mind that the object of every criminal prosecution is twofold: (1) to reform the criminal; (2) to make an example of him, so that the public will be deterred from the commission of the same offense. It is not the severity of a criminal prosecution that deters crime, but it is the certainty of punishment, when crime is committed. While it is true that the courts of the South as constituted, at present, give the Negro equal justice upon the law and facts of his case, yet we must bear in mind that a criminal prosecution is not ended with judgment in the courts. There are other humane principles to be put into operation, in order that the criminal may receive the benefits of his punishment. The relation of the Southern courts towards the Negro in this respect is particularly weak. Splendid examples of this may be seen in the "Convict Lease System," prevailing in the States of South Carolina, Arkansas and other Southern States. Under this system a Negro may be convicted of a felony calling for a minimum term of imprisonment, and yet serve out a life-time in prison. It is a system which, instead of reforming the Negro, gradually re-enslaves him. It has become such an outrage upon justice and common decency that the eyes of the civilized world are upon the United States to see how long a democratic government will tolerate such an outrage upon common justice and a defenseless people. Yet, when we, at home, begin to trace the causes of this evil, we invariably ascribe them to the courts of the South. Wrong! Wrong! The courts of the South are not legislative bodies, but judicial bodies whose function it is to interpret the laws made, and not to make laws. That right in a republic, like ours, belongs exclusively to the legislative department, and not to the judiciary. The failure on the part of the public to distinguish between the legislative and judicial branches of the government accounts in a large measure for the criticism that has been made upon the courts of the South in their dealings with the criminal Negro. It is well for us to bear in mind that a court cannot make a law, but can only confine its opinion to the law as it is. It is a well-known fact that the United States and the several States composing the same are governed by written constitutions; also, that in a constitutional government all laws must be uniform in their operation. Hence, no law can be made that will operate more harshly upon a Negro than upon a white man who is guilty of the same offense. The criminal Negro naturally thinks that he is dealt with unjustly in the court. I have never seen in my practice a Negro who did not think that a white judge and a white jury were not his enemies, and that they were looking for false evidence upon which to convict him, and were not desirous of passing upon his case on the law and evidence as presented. This, in a large measure, accounts for the enormous fees paid by Negroes to white attorneys for the simplest trouble they may get into. They believe that a white man has more influence in a court than a Negro lawyer, as though the laws were based upon favors to individuals rather than upon fixed rules of judicial construction. As for the judiciary of other States, I cannot speak, but for Virginia, I can and will say, that for the integrity of her judiciary—a fairer and more impartial set of men cannot be found in this country. Never, in my life, has anyone of them treated me amiss in their courts, nor can I point to a single case where snap judgment was meted out to a man of color, for the simple reason that he was colored. The experience of my brother members of the Bar in other States seems to tally with mine in this respect. Though I did once read of a Missis-sippi judge who told some colored men who had assembled in his court to listen to the trial of one of their race that this was a white man's country, and that Negroes had no business in a court room, unless there on business. Lest we forget it, we will say it now that the greatest of all virtues is charity. The numerous complaints we hear about the mal-treatment of the Negro, do not come from within, but from without. They come from people who know nothing of the position we occupy in the South. They tell us that the Southern people are our enemies, that they are doing us all the harm that can be done to any people. Worst of all, our people in many instances, are silly enough to believe them—ignorant of the fact that their success depends upon making their next door neigh-bors their friends. The same people take this charge and lay it to the courts of justice. Shame that in a democratic government like ours a free people should be slaves to such tricksters whose only object is to create discord among a poor and defenseless people! When we hear people charging the Southern courts with treating the Negro unjustly, it reminds us of an old colored lady who was once warning a young colored man about dying in his sins. The young man wanted to know if the fire in hell was hot. The old lady said, "Hunney de olde sinners fetch their fire wid dem." If the Negro gets a harsh verdict at the Bar in a Southern court, it is because he brings his fire with him. Just why it is that the Negro cannot see things in the same light, I do not know. It is a rule of physics that action is equal to reaction and in the contrary direction. By the side of that we can put this statement, that a man is worked upon by that which he works. The Negro, as a rule, labors under the belief that he is an object of persecution and proscription, and in turn that insane belief so works upon him that it is useless for anybody to endeavor to make him believe otherwise. There is one thing I must say before I close and that is this, that if the Negro wants to break down the great undercurrent against him in the courts of the South, he must do all in his power to establish among his own people the element of caste—a line between the good and bad. He must frown upon those who do wrong, and uphold those who do right. He must lay aside the old adage that you must never do anything against your own color. If a man is my color, and he is wrong, I am against him. If a man is my color and he is right, I am for him. Let the Negro adopt this as a maxim, and justice in the courts of the South is his, now and forever.

Bishop Geo. W. Clinton.

BISHOP GEORGE WYLIE CLINTON, A. M., D. D.

The career of Bishop George Wylie Clinton, A. M., D. D., furnishes indisputable evidence that merit wins success, and that industry, joined with native and acquired ability, cannot be denied pre-eminence. His is a story of a man, who, starting life with a definite goal in view, has allowed neither the blandishments of flattery nor the frosts of discouragement to hinder his progress; but, impressing his great personality upon all with whom he came in contact, he moved steadily forward, and is now one of the best examples of erudition, eloquence and practicability in the Negro pulpit.

This remarkable man was born March 28, 1859, in Lancaster County, South Carolina. As a child he was religiously inclined and thoughtful beyond his years, and none who knew him was surprised, when at the age of ten years, he became a member of the A. M. E. Zion Church. When quite young he was sent to the public school, and afterwards to a private school where he remained until 1874, when he entered the South Carolina University. In 1876 when the Democrats succeeded in electing Wade Hampton governor, all the colored students were forced to withdraw from said university and thus, after finishing the Junior Classical year he went to Brainard Institute, Chester, S. C., from which he graduated with very high honors.

Young Clinton finished his education by taking Theology, Greek and Hebrew at Livingstone College. Realizing that the urgent need of his people was education, he became a successful and conspicuous educator. For ten years, with all his energy, he was engaged in the public education of his people, being at one time Principal of Lancaster (S. C.) High School and Industrial Institute; and he held a similar position in the Howard Graded School of Union, S. C. Both of the above schools made marvelous advancement while under his management. He founded a private school at Rock Hill, S. C., out of which has come the widely known Clinton Institute. As a writer, Bishop Clinton is easily among the best which the race has produced. In his style there is wonderful richness, energy and variety. His chaste, pleasing and conservative writings made the leading papers of his State seek his contributions.

He founded the A. M. E. Zion Quarterly Review, which he issued for two years with increasing success; and in 1892 he transferred it, free of debt, to the General Conference. His eminence as an editor was so pronounced that said General Conference elected him editor of the Star of Zion. During his incumbency in this office he added to his fame as a thoughtful, versatile writer, and inaugurated the plan by which the A. M. E. Zion publication was established.

Naturally, his greatest fame was made in the pulpit, for he is a most eloquent man, and possesses much magnetism. Added to a most pre-possessing personality, and a sonorous but well modulated voice, the Bishop has all the graces of a finished orator, and all the charms of a deep, earnest scholar. Like Martin Luther, he intended to study law; but the Bible overshadowed Blackstone. He began to preach at twenty years of age and in 1896 was elected Bishop in the A. M. E. Zion Church.

In spite of a multiplicity of duties, the Bishop finds time to serve as President of Atkinson College; and so well has he supervised and managed its affairs, that it is enjoying great popularity and is maintaining a high intellectual standing.

He was married, February 6, 1901, to Miss Marie Louise Clay of Huntsville, Ala. His wife is a highly accomplished lady, and a soloist of national repute. He has one son, George William, being the issue of his former marriage to the late Mrs. Annie K. Clinton. The Bishop lives in becoming style at Charlotte, N. C., where he owns some valuable and well-located property. His mother, for whom he has always manifested the deepest affection, makes her home with her distinguished son. Bishop Clinton is yet young; and the church and the race have every reason to hope for many more years of the distinguished services of this brilliant leader.

TOPIC VII.

TO WHAT EXTENT IS THE NEGRO PULPIT UPLIFTING THE RACE?

BY BISHOP GEORGE WYLIE CLINTON, M. A., D. D.

From the establishment of the gospel system the pulpit has occupied an important, unique and potential position in all things pertaining to man's well being along moral, social and spiritual lines.

It has not failed to concern itself about other affairs that tended to man's betterment. It may be stated in brief that at one time or another the pulpit has taken a deep interest and exerted a helpful, as well as a healthy influence in whatever has tended to man's highest and best welfare. Speaking of the Christian ministry, Daniel Webster on one occasion said: "The ministers of Christianity, departing from Asia-Minor, traversing Asia, Africa and Europe, to Iceland, Greenland and the poles of the earth, suffering all things, enduring all things, raising men everywhere from ignorance of idol worship to the knowledge of the true God, and everywhere bringing life and immortality to light, have only been acting in obedience to the divine instruction; and they still go forth. They have sought, and they still seek, to be able to preach the gospel to every creature under the whole heaven. And where was Christianity ever received, where were the truths ever poured into human hearts, where did its waters, springing up into everlasting life, ever burst forth, except in the track of a Christian ministry?

"Did we ever hear of an instance; does history record an instance, of any part of the globe Christianized by lay preachers or lay teachers? And descending from kingdoms and empires to cities, countries, to parishes and villages, do we not all know, that, wherever Christianity has been carried, and wherever it has been taught by human agency, that agency was the agency of the ministers of the gospel."

In the above high tribute from one of the greatest American statesmen since the Republic began its existence, we have set forth the peculiar work as well as the grand achievements of the pulpit. But as has been stated in the previous paragraph the pulpit has ever sought to uplift man on every line where his uplifting meant his highest good.

The Negro pulpit has not been an exception in the great work of uplifting mankind, especially that part of mankind with which it is ostensibly identified. No other pulpit ever had a more difficult task or labored under greater disadvantages than the Negro pulpit. In the very beginning the Negro pulpit had the leadership and the enlightenment of the race in spiritual and intellectual knowledge thrust upon it, when it was neither qualified nor regularly organized. Despite the disability within and the disadvantages without the Negro pulpit became the pioneer in the first movements to better the condition of the race by lifting it from the degradation and disorganized state in which it was left by slavery.

In almost every effort and successful plan which have been inaugurated since the race began its life of freedom the Negro pulpit has been the prime promoter and the advance guard. When other leaders have faltered, failed or retreated, the Negro pulpit has remained steadfast and redoubled its efforts.

As is indicated in the quotation from America's greatest orator, Daniel Webster, the chief and first work of the pulpit is spiritual instruction.

As an evidence of the success of the Negro pulpit along this line the race may point to a larger percentage of Negro Christians according to population than is true of any other people in this Christian land. While it is true the Negro brought the Christian religion over from slavery as the best heritage which that cruel system bequeathed to him, it remained for the Negro pulpit to give shape, tone and organic significance to Negro Christianity.

In organizing the Negro into separate and distinctly racial societies for the conduct of religious worship and church government the Negro pulpit did a work which has given the race greater prestige and more clearly demonstrated its capabilities and possibilities than any other work which has been done by or for the race toward uplifting it. When the Negro proved his ability to organize and conduct successfully a religious denomination of great size and strength, it proved its capacity to develop and govern itself along any other line. Surely the words of the prophet in which he speaks of a people "scattered and peeled," "a nation meted out and trodden down," seem fittingly applicable to the condition of the Negro just emerged from slavery.

It was this people, thus situated, that the Negro pulpit took hold of and formed into church societies and religious denominations, which now have followings which number up into the hundred thousands and possess property valued at millions of dollars deeded to, and held by and for the race.

Quickly seconding the work of organization followed the work of education. Before the free school began the Negro preacher became a teacher of his people to the full extent of his ability. Those who were sufficiently qualified found employment as public school teachers, while the more progressive and better qualified began to plan for institutions of higher grade to better qualify themselves and prepare teachers and leaders for the future weal of the race.

Whether we point to Wilberforce at Xenia, Ohio, secured to the A. M. E. Church through the late lamented Bishop D. A. Payne, D. D.; Livingstone College, over which that prince of American orators and foremost of Negro educators, Dr. Joseph Chas. Price, presided, from its permanent organization to his universally mourned death; the State University; the Chief Negro Baptist School located at Louisville, Kentucky, or the scores of other schools of high grade, it is a fact beyond dispute that the Negro pulpit began the initiative and has exerted the most helpful and controlling influence since they were founded.

A majority of the college, seminary and high school presidents and principals, as well as some of the strongest members of the several faculties, are men from the pulpit or men who do double duty by serving as best they can the pulpit and schoolroom.

In politics as well as in other spheres some of the most effective work which has been done for the uplifting of the race has been done by the Negro pulpit.

To the writer's personal knowledge some of the ablest, most faithful and useful men found in the constitutional conventions, legislatures and county offices during the reconstruction period were men from the Negro pulpit.

The Rev. James Walker Hood (A. M. E. Zion), now Bishop J. W. Hood, D. D., LL. D., in the Constitutional Convention of North Carolina, in the Legislature, and as Assistant Superintendent of Education for the State, did a work which contributed not only to the uplift of the race but to the best interest of all the people of the State.

Rev. Henry McNeal Turner, D. D., LL. D. (A. M. E. Church), as legislator in Georgia, exerted an influence which is still felt in that State.

Bishop B. W. Arnett, D. D. (A. M. E.), whose efforts in the Ohio

Legislature secured the repeal of the "Black Laws"; Rev. D. I. Walker (A. M. E. Zion), as school commissioner and State Senator from Chester County, South Carolina; Rev. J. E. Wilson (M. E.), as school commissioner and postmaster at Florence, South Carolina; Rev. Wm. Thomas (A. M. E.), and R. H. Cain (A. M. E.), Legislator, Congressman and later Bishop; Rev. H. R. Revels (M. E.), United States Senator, whose deportment in the United States Senate and in other walks of life called forth the highest encomiums from the Southern press; Rev. Henry Highland Garnett (Presbyterian), and Rev. M. G. Hopkins (Presbyterian), and Owen L. W. Smith (A. M. E. Zion), United States Minister to the Republic of Liberia, each and all have contributed much to the uplifting of the race in the political sphere. But the Negro pulpit has not confined its efforts along the line of race organization to the religious sphere. Knowing, as every thoughtful leader and man of the race must know, that material possessions, financial standing and social combination for material well being are indispensable, the Negro pulpit has not failed to project, foster and encourage organizations of a character to benefit the race along the above lines. In Masonry the Negro pulpit has ever held a commanding influence and served a most useful purpose. The same is to some extent true in Odd Fellowship and other societies which have been helpful to the race. But the most substantial organization now operated by and for the Negro race in this country are the True Reformers, Galilean Fishermen and Birmingham, Alabama, Penny Savings Bank.

The well-known and much lamented Rev. Wm. W. Brown (M. E.), C. C. Steward (A. M. E. Zion), W. R. Pettiford (Baptist), were the chief factors in founding and firmly establishing these healthy and helpful race institutions, which are still doing a thriving and widening business which is not only uplifting the race but benefitting the community at large. The Hale Infirmary, established by the widow of the late Elder Hale (A. M. E. Zion), of Montgomery, Alabama, in compliance with the expressed wish of her husband while living; the Orphanages of Charleston and Columbia, South Carolina, established and now being managed by Revs. Jenkins and E. A. Carroll (Baptist), in the above cities; also the Orphanage at Oxford, North Carolina, established by ministers of the Baptist Church, according to information obtained by the writer; the Episcopal Industrial School of Charlotte, North Carolina, founded by Rev. P. P. Alston (Episcopal), are but a few of the many ways in which the Negro pulpit is uplifting the race. In the literary sphere the Negro pulpit has made numerous and valuable contributions which stand to the credit of the race and add to American literary productions.

Bishops Payne, whose "History of the A. M. E. Church" and "Domestic Education;" B. T. Tanner's several works; Levi J. Coppin's "Key to the Bible," and "Baptized Children;" W. J. Gaines' "Negro and the White Man;" Dr. H. T. Johnson's "Logos;" Rev. Whitman's works; Rev. T. G. Steward's works; Bishop J. W. Hood's (A. M. E. Zion) "Negro in Christian Pulpit," "History of the A. M. E. Zion Church" and "Apocalypse Revealed;" Bishop J. B. Small's "Pulpiteer," "Human Heart" and "Predestination;" Dr. W. J. Simmon's (Baptist) "Men of Mark;" Bishop Holsey's (C. M. E.) sermons and addresses; Dr. C. H. Phillip's (C. M. E.) "C. M. E. Church History;" Dr. G. L. Blackwell's (A. M. E. Zion) "Model Home;" Rev. Geo. C. Lowe's (Congregational) poems; Rev. J. D. Corrother's (A. M. E. Zion) poems; Rev. W. H. Nelson's (M. E.) "A Walk With Jesus;" Dr. Alexander Crummell's (Episcopal) sermons and addresses and papers, with scores of books I can not mention for lack of space, besides others I have not seen or heard about, are contributions which cannot help but inspire and uplift the race. The greatest and most widely known race organization that is endeavoring to uplift the Negro along social lines and combat the prejudices, caste regulations and other efforts to crush out race-manhood and turn back the hand in the dial plate of the Negro's progress, is the Afro-American Council, headed by that born leader of men, the eminently pious and ever aggressive race leader, Bishop Alexander Walters, D. D. (A. M. E. Zion), and his most substantial following is made up of representatives of all the Negro pulpits in America.

In the Negro Press Association the Negro pulpit is largely and ably represented and the preacher editors are doing their work well. The above brief and partial (but partial only for lack of broader information and of more space) is but a feeble testimony to what the Negro pulpit is doing toward uplifting the race.

In the religious sphere the Negro pulpit stands out in bold prominence as the chief agency in the work of uplifting the race. In organizing and perpetuating existing organizations the Negro pulpit now, as before, leads all other agencies.

In the work of education the progressive pulpit is always a patron and supporter, as well as a workman which needeth not to be ashamed.

In the endeavor to constrain the people to a settled condition, instill the principles of Christianity in all the affairs of life, and promote peace and harmony between man and man, regardless of race, the Negro pulpit is doing a work which is ever adding new stones to the grand building of race progress and influence. I know no single agency which is accomplishing so much in the task of uplifting the race as the Negro pulpit. What the great Negro religious and social organizations are doing, especially in such establishments as the A. M. E. Zion, A. M. E. and Baptist Publication establishments at Charlotte, North Carolina; Philadelphia, Pennsylvania; Nashville, Tennessee, and Jackson, Tennessee, is due largely to the management and business skill of the Negro pulpit. Now as in the past the Negro pulpit constitutes the true leadership of the race.

Having been the pioneer in almost every race uplifting enterprise it will ever heartily co-operate with those who have come along in the paths blazed out by the Negro pulpit until the race shall take its place among the foremost peoples of the earth in every good work for the advancement of man and for the glory of God.

SECOND PAPER.

TO WHAT EXTENT IS THE NEGRO PULPIT UPLIFTING THE RACE?

BY REV. J. B. L. WILLIAMS, D. D.

The Christian pulpit has ever been acknowledged to be a great power for good among all people. Coming as it does divinely commissioned and bearing to man a divine massage, it has a claim upon the attention and the acceptation of mankind. Its claim to be heard is founded on the fact that it has something to say—some truth to communicate about God, His character, His purpose concerning man, His unbounded goodness and infinite love—about man, his duty and his destiny, and the great salvation offered to him. The Christian pulpit is peculiarly and inseparably interwoven in the social life, moral deportment and religious growth of the people. In its character it is to be the representation of the highest standard of ethical deportment and the best example of religious life. From it the people are to receive their inspiration for that which is pure, exalted and ennobling. To the Christian pulpit the people look for the

J. B. L. Williams, D. D.

REV. JOHN B. L. WILLIAMS, D. D.

Rev. John B. L. Williams, D. D., was born in Baltimore, Md., November 22, 1853. His parents, John W. Williams and Elizabeth Williams, were examples of piety, and were of prominent family connections in Baltimore. At an early age he was placed in a Roman Catholic School. Later in life he attended the city public schools and Douglass Institute. At 17 he was converted and joined the Methodist Episcopal church. At 18 he was divinely impressed with a call to the ministry. At 19 he became an apprentice at cabinet work and undertaking and completing his apprenticeship engaged in business for three years in Baltimore. In his 22d year he was licensed to preach by the Quarterly conference of John Wesley M. E. Church in Baltimore.

In March, 1876, he abandoned his business and left Baltimore to accept an appointment at Oak Hill, Ga. The same year he joined the Savannah Conference in its organization by Bishop Levi Scott, and he has rendered efficient service in the leading charges of the Conference: Newnan, three years; Loyd Street, Atlanta, one year; Presiding Elder Atlanta District, four years; M. E. Church at LaGrange, five years. He was honored by his brethren to the election of secretary of the Conference fifteen successive years. While pastor at Newnan he was principal of the city public school. At LaGrange he served two years as a member of the faculty of LaGrange Seminary and one year its principal. In 1882 he entered Clark University, taking studies in the college preparatory course. The same year he entered Gammon Theological Seminary and graduated in 1885 with honor. In 1891 he was transferred by Bishop H. W. Warren to the Florida Conference to take charge of Ebenezer M. E. Church in Jacksonville. He served Ebenezer Church five years, during which time its membership was doubled the last year, being marked by a great revival which lasted two weeks and resulted in the conversion of 130 persons. His next charge was Trinity Church, St. Augustine, where he served five years with success. He is now pastor of Trinity M. E. Church, Fernandina. As a preacher he is deliberate, convincing, persuasive and instructive. His sermons are well constructed, choicely worded, rhetorically polished, full of thought and eloquently delivered. He was honored with the degree of Doctor of Divinity by Wiley University of the Methodist Episcopal Church, Marshall, Texas, May 20, 1895.

loftiest ideals of life. In this respect the Negro more than any other people has been largely dependent upon the pulpit. Emerging as he did more than a quarter of a century ago from a thraldom which fettered his body and imprisoned his intellect and buried him in ignorance, it was the Christian pulpit represented at that time by the good old fathers of those dark and trying days—to whom the good and lamented Bishop Haygood paid high compliment in one of his addresses—they it was who saved their people from conditions which would have been vastly more deplorable but for such moral and religious instruction as they were able to impart. As a race we have moved an amazing distance from that ·period. Schools, seminaries and universities have sprung up as 'if by magic. Educated young men and young women have gone forth from these institutions determined to do their best for God and humanity. The Negro press has also arisen and swayed a mighty influence for moral and religious good, but neither the school nor the press has been recognized as an efficient substitute for the pulpit. What was true as regards the place and power of the pulpit to uplift the people in the dark days of the past is equally true now in these days of light and knowledge. The educated and Christian pulpit is an indispensable factor in the elevation of the race to-day.

The extent to which the Negro pulpit is uplifting the race is to be seen in the gradual but certain and permanent reformation taking place in the social and moral life of the race. Social distinction, based exclusively upon moral character, is being clearly defined and rigidly observed. The moral standard has been elevated and the conceptions of the race in relation to ethical life has been greatly improved and beautifully exemplified in the lives of thousands. The home life of the race is purer and the sacredness of the marriage vow is gaining pre-eminence over the divorce system. The home life of the masses is gradually being touched and improved by the far-reaching influence of the Negro Christian pulpit, and there are signs and indications of better things and happier conditions. From these pulpits the Gospel goes forth with simplicity and power. Its truth and teaching is made to touch, shape and direct the practical side of Christian life. The evils which exist and which are a menace to the best and purest modes of life are strongly denounced and openly rebuked by the Negro Christian pulpit, and the race is being led to understand that sound moral character is the foundation upon which to build a strong, symmetrical, well-rounded manhood.

The religious life of the race is being uplifted by the Negro Christian pulpit. Sound is being displaced by sense in the pulpit. Senseless emotion by thoughtful and reverential worship in the pew, and a clear conception and deep knowledge of divine truth is being gained by the people. The individual of pessimistic temperament may say that the masses are not being influenced and lifted up by the Negro pulpit, but this would be a mere statement and not an actual fact. The pessimist lives in an unwholesome atmosphere, he will not see the sunshine because he prefers to stay down in the valley beneath the cloud of doubt and surmounted with the fog of hopelessness. The educated Negro pulpit is mainly optimistic and sees beyond its immediate surroundings. It sees to it that the leaven of sound doctrine and moral ethics are being put into the meal, and from personal developments believes that in process of time the whole lump will be leavened. The Negro pulpit is awake to the gravity of its responsibility and it is putting forth its best efforts and mightiest endeavors to uplift the race socially, morally and religiously. Evidences of this aim and purpose are not difficult to be seen in all communities.

THIRD PAPER.

TO WHAT EXTENT IS THE NEGRO PULPIT UPLIFTING THE RACE?

BY REV. R. P. WYCHE, D. D.

The question has been raised as to the part taken by the pulpit in the uplift of the race. The most casual observer must conclude that there are influences at work which are elevating the Negro race, and it is interesting and instructive to trace out the work which is done by each individual agency.

The pulpit has long been recognized as a potent factor in the formation of character, and the Negro pulpit is not an exception to the general rule. Its influence may be elevating or degrading. The character and the ability of the man in the pulpit will determine its nature and extent.

The office itself implies an active interest in the elevation of man from the lower to the highest stage of life. But the uneducated ministry proved itself unequal to the task of teaching and leading the people along the difficult path to true excellence.

Some of the most stubborn opposition to the progress of the race was found in that class who had good reasons to fear the loss of power as the

Rev. R. P. Wyche.

REV. R. P. WYCHE, D. D.

Robert P. Wyche was born near Oxford, the county seat of Granville County, N. C. His father was a carpenter by trade and early taught his son the use of tools. In his humble home he was taught the dignity of labor, fidelity to duty, obedience to God and faith in prayer. These simple lessons shaped the course of his life probably more than any other influence. For a while he attended night school, as he worked in the day in order to earn the means to buy his books and to pay other necessary expenses. Robert was ambitious to excel. From the night school he went to a private school at Henderson, N. C. This school was conducted by the Rev. J. H. Crawford, a Presbyterian minister. Here Robert prosecuted his studies with eagerness, fitting himself to enter the preparatory department of Biddle University. The President of the university, the Rev. S. Mattoon, D. D., became interested in Robert, whom he esteemed as a promising student, and assured him that no worthy student should leave school for the want of means.

After graduating in 1877 his first thought was to enter the medical profession, but afterward he abandoned this idea and began seriously to consider the call to the ministry. After teaching school for a short period he returned to the seminary and took the full course in theology. He was licensed and ordained by the Presbytery of Catawba and was called to the pastorate of Seventh Street Presbyterian Church, at Charlotte, N. C. The degree of A. M. and the honorary degree of D. D. were conferred upon Rev. R. P. Wyche by Biddle University. He is at this time Moderator of the Synod of Catawba.

He married Miss Belle Butler, a popular educator, who unites with her husband in every measure for the true elevation of the Negro.

race advanced in intelligence. All of the higher interests of the people suffered at the hands of this class of leaders.

But let us now turn to another and better class of leaders. There are ministers who have enjoyed the benefits of a Christian education. This class of men form a strong factor in the elevation of the Negro. The present attainments of the pulpit are far-reaching in their beneficent influence upon the race.

The Negro pulpit is absolutely necessary to the higher moral development of the Negro. This development should lie at the foundation of all of his attainments, for men cannot reasonably hope to rise permanently along other lines while they neglect moral culture. The moral influence of the pulpit is now creating correct views of life in the Negro and leading him to good citizenship. The practical pulpit teaching along this line is having its effect in the moral uplift of the Negro. In this way the pulpit is serving as an uplifting force. Moral stability is the only solid foundation of an enduring elevation.

Considered from an intellectual point of view, the pulpit is of great value to the Negro race. The example set by the Negro pulpit in acquiring its intellectual status is worthy of imitation, and the youth of the rising generation will profit by it. The positive instruction and counsel coming from safe and trusted leaders will certainly yield its fruit. We cannot estimate the worth of the pulpit as the moulder of the thought, the character and the destiny of the race.

The financial status of the pulpit, under existing conditions, may be considered comparatively good. It has been made what it now is by industry, economy and self-denial, and stands as an object lesson for the benefit of those wishing to better their condition. The salaries paid Negro preachers are usually small, even less than the wages of mechanics. But these small earnings are carefully saved and wisely invested. As a result many of the Negro preachers have comfortable homes, while others of them have small bank accounts. The Negro minister has learned the dignity of labor and does not hesitate to labor with head and hands in order to attain to the position of usefulness and influence in the world. The people are taught in this practical manner the lessons of industry and economy more forcibly than in any other way, and they are thus led to secure homes, to enter into business and to educate their children.

Our elegant church edifices are largely due to the taste, tact and business qualities of the pulpit. These beautiful edifices exert a refining and uplifting influence upon the lives of men.

The spiritual power of the pulpit—this is the chief power that it is expected to wield in the world, for its mission is spiritual, and this great fact should ever be remembered. Our deepest needs are of a spiritual nature, and the pulpit offers to supply these deep-seated needs and to assist us to rise to the rank of "the sons of God."

The Gospel is the divinely appointed means to elevate men in Christian character. The promulgation of the Gospel and the exhibition of practical Christianity are the essential elements to an onward and upward progress.

_____

FOURTH PAPER.

TO WHAT EXTENT IS THE NEGRO PULPIT UPLIFTING THE RACE?

BY REV. I. D. DAVIS, D. D.

The influence of the Negro pulpit on the race is immeasurable. It is to the race what the lighthouse is to the ship laden with human souls upon the tempestuous sea. At the close of the war when the Negroes were in darkness, the Negro preachers were the first to come forward to lead them to the light, and whatever may be said to the contrary, the Negro preachers have done more for the Negro's uplift since his emancipation than any other class of persons. We delight to boast that the Negroes pay taxes on $400,000,000.00 worth of property, that they have thousands of well educated men and women, that their illiteracy has been reduced forty-five per cent, that they have hundreds of newspapers, that they have four hundred or more skilled physicians who are making good money, that they have hundreds of men who are engaged in business enterprises, that they have thousands of honest, sober, upright Christian men and women.

Now, to whom are we more indebted for all this than to the Negro preachers, who have faithfully taught their people to save their money and buy homes and lands, who have constantly advised them to send their sons and daughters to the schools, who have urged their people to patronize Negro business enterprises and Negro physicians and lawyers, who have shown their people the importance of taking Negro papers, who have enjoined them to be honest, sober, industrious citizens?

Rev. I. D. Davis, D. D.

REV. I. D. DAVIS, D. D.

The subject of this sketch was born at Laurens, S. C., in 1858. His parents were Nelson and Sarah Davis. In 1870 Rev. Charles Thompson (a Presbyterian Missionary from the North) came to Laurens and began services in a part of the town known as "Tin Pot Ally." The first to be enrolled in his Sunday School was the subject of our sketch.

After Rev. Thompson left Laurens our little hero went to school to another veteran, Mr. Wright, who soon learned to regard him highly. The late Rev. D. Gibbs now took charge of the church, and our subject was the first to enter his Sunday School. While the Rev. Gibbs was boarding at his father's home, the seed of the Presbyterian ministry was planted.

He now entered school under Rev. and Mrs. McDowell, and began the study of the Shorter Catechism. A polyglot Bible was offered for the most perfect recitation of the Catechism, and he won the first prize. In 1874 he took the examination and won the county scholarship for the State Normal at Columbia. From this examination he was given a teachers' certificate and taught his first school in the country; at the close of this school he accompanied Rev. and Mrs. McDowell to Statesville, N. C., and in November Rev. McDowell had arranged for him to go to Biddle University, Charlotte, N. C.

He returned home every summer and taught. So acceptable were his services that scholars were offered to him and held until his return from school. In 1877 on account of failing health he remained out of school, and was chosen as the principal of the city school at his native home. He was always known as the "Mocking Bird" of Laurens. He was the chorister in Sunday School and church. Returning to Biddle University in the fall of 1878, was taken under the care of Catawba Presbytery as a candidate for the ministry, and graduated with the degree of A. B. in 1881. In October, 1881, he entered the seminary of Biddle University, was licensed to preach the gospel in 1883, and was placed in charge of the Pleasant View Church, Greenville County, South Carolina, where he served so acceptably that he was desired as a settled pastor. In 1884 he graduated from the seminary, and was ordained to the full work of the gospel ministry the next day after graduating.

He took charge of the work at Lincolnton, N. C., where he served six years and six months, conducting both church and school, and was then re-elected principal of the city school.

The new church at McClintock was built under his administration. He was chosen moderator of the Presbytery of Catawba at Monroe, N. C., and in 1887 was sent as a commissioner from Catawba Presbytery to the General Assembly of the Presbyterian Church in the United States, which met at Omaha, Neb. In 1888 the degree of A. M. was conferred by Biddle University. In 1890 he accepted the call to Winnsboro, S. C., continuing in the church and school work here for four years very acceptably. In 1892 was sent as commissioner to the General Assembly at Saratoga, N. Y. In 1894 he accepted the work at Goodwill, Sumter Co., S. C., where he now serves the largest Colored Presbyterian Church in the United States. He administered communion to 2,000 communicants.

In connection with the church he has charge of the Goodwill Academy, with an enrollment of about 400 students. In 1895 he was chosen stated clerk of Fairfield Presbytery, which position he fills with accuracy and ability until to-day. In 1900 the degree of D. D. was conferred upon him by Biddle University.

He has been Moderator of Fairfield Presbytery and Atlantic Synod.

He is the secretary of the Sunday School Convention, chairman of the Committee on Vacancies and Supplies of the Fairfield Presbytery, and chairman of the Committee on Foreign Mission, Atlantic Synod.

NATHAN B. YOUNG.

Nathan B. Young was born in Newbern, Ala., September 18th, 1862. He was educated in the private schools at Tuscaloosa, Ala., at Talladega College, and at Oberlin College. He has taught school in Mississippi, Georgia, Florida, and Alabama. He is now President of the Florida State Normal and Industrial College, Tallahassee.

Prof. Nathan B. Young

TOPIC VIII.

IS IT TIME FOR THE NEGRO COLLEGES IN THE SOUTH TO BE PUT INTO THE HANDS OF NEGRO TEACHERS?

BY PROF. N. B. YOUNG.

The answer to this question depends upon what is meant by placing these schools in the hands of Negro teachers. If it means that they are to be manned and managed by them I answer, no. If, on the other hand, it means that they should have some hand in managing these schools, I answer, yes.

For two reasons I claim that the time has not arrived for the passing of these institutions into his sole control: the first is a *financial* reason, the second is an *intellectual* or *cultural* reason.

At present the majority of the Negro colleges and institutions of higher and professional learning are supported by white people, either directly or indirectly, and the withdrawal of white faculties and boards of trustees will mean a withdrawal of white supporters. Whether this withdrawal will be logical or ethical, it will nevertheless be a fact. Those whose duty it is to collect funds for these schools can testify to the certainty of such a result if the experiment should be made.

The white man is a very careful giver to charitable institutions of any kind, and he takes every precaution to see that his donations are wisely expended, and that, too, according to his standards. Hence, when he makes a charitable contribution he feels safer when one of his own race is a trustee, or dispenser of the contribution. This explains the fact that in cases where Negro schools under Negro management make an appeal for large endowment funds they find it necessary to appoint a white endowment committee to manage the fund.

The Negro has no standing in the financial world, because he has made no financial record. This is not so much his fault as it is his misfortune. He is without the financial experience that he would need in order to manage successfully large sums of money such as he would be called upon to collect and to manage in colleges. Without aid from the white donors these colleges would be unable to do the work of a college—in other words, with possibly one notable exception, it takes

125

a white man to get a white man's money, and since it is necessary to get a white man's money to support these institutions, it is also necessary to put their management into his hands. This condition will gradually change as the Negro race accumulates wealth within itself. This will naturally bring with it that experience which will eventually enable him to be a successful manager of these institutions.

It is generally known among those who are familiar with college management that the financial feature is the most difficult feature in this work. It requires a rare combination of qualities in a man to carry on successfully this phase of college work. The managing boards of white colleges find it exceedingly difficult to find white men fully equal to the task. If this takes place in the green tree, what may we expect in a dry?

At present the Negro race, to say the least, is too poor to take on itself the complete control of its colleges. Such a transfer would be a calamity, indeed, for under the white management these institutions are leading only a tolerable existence, are progressing but slowly and some of them not at all. To take these feeble institutions, then, and to connect them with a poorer source of supply would be practically to destroy them—certainly seriously to handicap them.

Besides, even if their financial support were guaranteed, at present a more serious obstacle would present itself. It would be impossible from the present supply of educated Negro men and women to get faculties for them. I mean, to get faculties every whit prepared for their progressive management. An up-to-date college must have not only strong financial backing but it must also have strong intellectual and moral backing. Each teacher should be so trained, intellectually and morally as to have a very keen appreciation of the deep significance of the work in which he is engaged. This means that he must in addition to a careful formal training, have a sort of intellectual and culture background to cause him to stand out in clear relief before his students as an embodiment of what he would have them become. He should, in very truth, be "a scholar and a gentleman."

The fact that a man or a woman is a graduate from some of these misnamed Southern *"universities"* or *"brevet"* colleges does not argue that he has a liberal education. The fact is that there are no Negro universities in this country and less than half a dozen *"bona fide"* colleges. These reputed "universities" and colleges are but indifferent high-schools for the most part, and their graduates without additional study, are not prepared to take a place on a college faculty. Strange to say, very few of these graduates feel the necessity of doing additional study before becoming anxious candidates for presidents of colleges or for professorships.

I stand by the statement that there are not enough really educated men fully equipped to manage the colleges such as we have, not to say anything of those that we ought to have. The race is not yet far enough removed from slavery to have that intellectual and moral background necessary to the bringing out of college professors and college presidents. It has taken the white race many generations to develop an Eliot, a Dwight, a Hadley, and an Angell, not to say anything about the Butlers, the Harrises, and the Wheelers. These men are developments—the very cream of the intellectual history of the Anglo-Saxon race in America. As I have indicated elsewhere, the trustees find it hard to fill their places when vacant.

The incipient Negro teacher and educator might as well admit the fact of their incompetency and with the admission bend themselves with renewed energy to hard study, laying aside all bogus degrees and meaningless titles, and acknowledge the fact that they are yet intellectual pigmies. If they will do this, perchance they themselves may not only add to their own statures but but they may also become the ancestors of intellectual giants, fully competent to occupy the positions which they fain would hold in the educational world.

Although the time has not yet come, as I believe, for the entire management of Negro colleges by Negroes, yet the time has come when he should have some hand in managing both as teacher and as trustee. It would be a sad commentary upon the Negro race and upon its white teachers to have these schools remain permanently under white tutelage and management. It would also be a sad commentary upon the Negro to have an alien race to continue giving its money to educate his children. He must be brought gradually to see the necessity of his supporting and managing his own institutions of learning. The only way to do this is to gradually place the managing of them upon his shoulders. Every Negro college ought to have one or more Negro trustees on the board, as well as one or more Negro teachers on the faculty. The only way to learn how to swim is to go into the water—

the only way for the Negro to learn how to manage his institutions is for him to have a hand in managing them.

Of the large number of Negro youth that are graduated every year from our colleges, there are not a few among them who have in them the making of fine professors if they were stimulated by the sure hope of securing a place on the faculty of their "alma mater." It is the imperative duty of the faculties of these schools to inspire these men to their best efforts and when they have done so it is the duty of the trustees to give them a place on the faculty.

I would not, however, make vacancies for them by moving efficient white teachers, but, when these white teachers fall out because of age or other reasons, I would appoint in their places competent Negro men. This policy would at once keep the support of the white donors and also the support of the Negro patrons. The Negro must have a larger hand in managing his institutions of learning even from the lowest to the highest.

I answer, then, that the time has not yet come for the complete transfer of Negro colleges to Negro management because the Negro is not yet able to assume the financial control of these institutions, nor the intellectual control; but he is able to have a larger hand in controlling them as donor, as trustee, and as teacher. This policy is being pursued by some of the educational agencies now at work in the South.

The efforts of the Negro churches, especially of the A. M. E. Zion church, the A. M. E. church, of the C. M. E. church, and a *wing* of the Baptist church, are to be commended in so far as they do not assume a hostile attitude toward other agencies which pursue a slightly different policy. There cannot be too much educational activity among Negroes for Negroes, and there certainly should be no antagonism among these agencies growing out of differences of opinion as to policies and methods of work. They should all make "a long pull, a strong pull, and a pull all together" for the educational, moral, and spiritual uplift of the masses of the Negro people.

D. J. Jordan, LL. B.

PROF. D. J. JORDAN, M. S., LL. B.

Nature has not been extravagant in her gift of geniuses. What has come to most of our leading men has come by hard work.

Although Prof. D. J. Jordan possesses talents about the average, he owes his success largely to persistent work. He was born near Cuthbert, Ga., October 18, 1866. His father was Rev. Giles D. Jordan who was for twenty-five years a highly respected minister in the A. M. E. Church in Georgia. He inherits many of his excellent traits of character from his mother, Julia Jordan.

In his early life he was unable to attend school more than three months of the year, but by close application while in school and faithful study during vacations, he was always able to make the next higher class at the beginning of the following school term.

After finishing the English branches he attended Payne High School at Cuthbert. In 1892 he graduated at Allen University, Columbia, S. C., with the degrees of B. S. and LL. B.

His record at this institution was in many respects remarkable. He was successful in passing the written examination given by the Supreme Court of South Carolina, and was admitted to practice in all the courts of that state, May, 1892.

After his graduation, he returned to his native city, taught a term and made preparations to enter upon the practice of the legal profession, but he was prevailed upon to accept a position on the faculty of Morris Brown College, in 1893.

He served here as Professor of Science and Dean of Law until November, 1895, when he resigned to accept the Presidency of Edward Waters College at Jacksonville, Fla.

He was married December 31, 1895, by Bishop A. Grant, to Miss Carrie J. Thomas, principal of one of the public schools of Atlanta. Four children have been born to them.

He was elected as a lay delegate to the General Conference of the A. M. E. Church which was held at Wilmington, N. C., in 1896.

In the spring of '96 he accepted the position of Professor of Literature at Morris Brown College, which position he held until September, 1898, when he was appointed Professor of Mathematics and Vice-President of the same institution. The degree of M. S. was conferred upon him by Allen University in 1900. In the Summer school, held at Clark University in 1901, Professor Jordan was instructor in mathematics. He has developed with the institution with which he has been connected, fitting himself for every promotion which has come to him.

Professor Jordan has an experience of eighteen years in the class room and is an excellent disciplinarian. The fact that he has filled four different chairs with credit is sufficient argument that he is an able "all-round scholar." His greatest strength, however, lies in his knowledge of English. His language is chaste; his diction, pure.

As one of the best writers and speakers of the race, he has contributed articles to our leading periodicals, including the "Atlanta Constitution," "Atlanta Journal," "A. M. E. Review" and "Indianapolis Freeman," and has delivered several commencement addresses.

SECOND PAPER.

IS IT TIME FOR THE NEGRO COLLEGES IN THE SOUTH TO BE PUT INTO THE HANDS OF NEGRO TEACHERS?

BY PROF. D. J. JORDAN, M. S., LL. B.

I am asked to say whether or not it is time for the Negro colleges in the South to be put into the hands of Negro teachers? The education of a people is the greatest question that can possibly concern them. It touches every phase of human interest and holds the key to the solution of every rational problem arising out of man's duty and destiny. The foundations of every helpful institution known to our social system rest upon such conceptions of right and wrong as the people's intelligence has called into being: for true teaching is not only the application of methods for the development of one's powers, but is also a directing or turning of those powers into proper channels. With any people it will not matter ultimately who now writes the laws, issues decrees, or enforces judgments if their youth are kept under wise, efficient instructors. How necessary, then, must it be to a race so conditioned as is the Negro in America that their schools should be conducted by only those who are most capable and worthy!

However, before we attempt to answer the question propounded, it is important that we fully comprehend its meaning. As I understand it, the matter might be stated in other words thus: Should Negroes exclusively be placed now on the faculties of the several missionary colleges which Northern philanthropy has established in the South since the close of the Civil War? There were then not only no schools for us, but there were no teachers and no money with which to employ teachers. No night in Egypt in the time of Israel was darker than those years immediately following the Negro's emancipation. And what must have been our condition to-day had not those pillars of light been placed in our starless sky? But what is more, for thirty years the same spirit and the same people who first made these colleges possible among us, have continued their aid, and still make them possible to-day.

And now let us see what advantages could be reasonably expected from such a change in management as the subject suggests. So far as I know, they who advocate the change establish themselves upon this proposition, namely, *"Negro teachers are best for Negro schools."*

And this is true, say they, (1) because being of the same race, there must of necessity exist such a spirit of sympathy and helpfulness between teacher and student as we could not reasonably expect were the teacher and the taught of different races; (2) because placing before students competent men and women of their own race as teachers sets before them an example and an object lesson of what the students themselves may become and do, that cannot fail to be inspiring; (3) because the employing of Negro teachers in Negro schools furnishes an honorable vocation to a large number of our own people who otherwise would possibly be unemployed; (5) because Negro teachers in Negro colleges, by their presence and work, increase the race pride among ourselves and win for us greater confidence and respect from others.

These are weighty considerations, and, *per se,* have my most hearty approval. But however complete may be our endorsement, we must not forget that unqualifiedly acting upon them in the matter under discussion would not be without its losses. Let us now consider what these might be, and then we shall be prepared to decide whether we would not—

> "* * * rather bear those ills we have
> Than fly to others we know not of."

In the first place, if the people who own and sustain these schools could be induced to sever their connection with them and turn them fully into the hands of Negroes, although the colleges are already built, equipped and advertised, yet, chiefly on account of our poverty, we should have to close the majority of them at once. This would be a most serious loss. The amount of ignorance and the lack of trained leaders among us, together with the small pittance done for us in the direction of even high-school education by the states and cities in which we live certainly do not suggest the advisability of ridding ourselves of even one agency for enlightenment. Far better would it be for us and for the country if they were increased tenfold.

This view takes into consideration the fact that the great majority of people who give of their means to support the schools do so because they have confidence in the ability, integrity and experience of those who control them. And if any one is so credulous as to believe that the schools under the management of Negroes could command the amount of interest and support as they now receive, I would ask him, why *have* Negroes, from Mr. Booker T. Washington down, who are trying to gain public confidence and assistance for their work, *find* it necessary to invite white men to accept membership on their boards of trustees? One need not go far to find the correct answer. In this connection, it will be in order to inquire also if there are, under the control of Negroes, any, colleges that receive anything like the amount of money for their support that is received by similar institutions under the management of white men?.

Furthermore, the placing of the colleges referred to wholly into the hands of Negroes would be an unnecessary drawing of the race line, and would very effectually close our mouths against making protest or complaint on account of our being .discriminated against for similar reasons.

Again, at this time, when there seems to be, on the part of certain persons of influence, a foul conspiracy against the Negro, it is of great importance that we have among us persons whose knowledge of the facts, and whose intellectual and social standing with those whose good opinion we value enable and impel them to speak out in our behalf. I recall with much gratification several instances where white persons connected with Negro schools have used the superior opportunities afforded them by the accident of race to say good things of us at a time when a spokesman who had the ear of the king was sorely needed. If, under present conditions, this class of people be sent from among us, I fear it might in a measure be with us as it was with a certain people in ancient times when "a new king arose who knew not Joseph."

And finally, would it not be highly presumptive and insolent on our part to demand of others that they deliver into our keeping, without price, property which they have purchased with their own money, and of which we have had the use and benefit for a third of a century? Until we shall be able to buy these colleges and properly support them, even the serious discussion of the question, it seems to me, is inappropriate and puerile. When, therefore, you ask me, if in my opinion the time has come when the Negro colleges in the South should be put into the hands of Negro teachers, I must answer you frankly, *no.*

I would not be understood, however, as placing my approval upon everything pertaining to the management of the schools under consideration. I do not deny that in some cases teachers are employed who are not possessed of the proper spirit for doing the best work among us. They are sometimes haughty, unsocial, and unsympathetic, and find themselves among us because there is offered better pay for less work than was found in their own neighborhoods. But these do not vitiate the schools; they are exceptions. I think, too, that the faculties of the several schools, together with the boards of trustees, should be as largely composed of competent, worthy Negroes as the interests of the institutions will allow. I am sure that such a policy would both encourage our people and train them in the management of such interests, and would be fully in harmony with the spirit and purpose of the institutions' founders. But we cannot state this as a demand based on what is justly ours; let it stand rather on its soundness as to what is best as a policy designed to accomplish the highest results. Before we find too many faults, though, with these missionary colleges, we ought to show by our full, loyal support of the few colleges we do control, that we are both able and willing to do the proper thing when the time shall come, if ever, for placing the Negro colleges in the South into the hands of Negro teachers.

THIRD PAPER.

IS IT TIME FOR THE NEGRO COLLEGES IN THE SOUTH TO BE PUT INTO THE HANDS OF NEGRO TEACHERS?

BY PROF. GEORGE A. GOODWIN.

In attempting to answer this question, I do so fully cognizant of the widely differing opinions which are superinduced by the present restive state of society. It is a delicate task. In this brief article it is not possible to be very extensive. Condensation is a necessity. Taking observations from ancient and modern civilizations as external evidence, and corroborating the experiences of the present age as internal evidence, my conclusion is reached. If my judgment is faulty, let us remember that trite aphorism: "To err is human, to forgive, divine."

If this be the question of the fawning element among us, then let us beware of the leaven of the separatists. If the liberal philanthropist makes the inquiry, let us demonstrate the wisdom of his investment by our exhibitions of gratitude and common sense. It cannot be a serious question with the learned sociologist, for he is too conversant with the philosophy of history and the laws of psychology. Of the popular idea of the over-ardent lovers of the race, it may be more comforting to an

Prof. G. A. Goodwin

REV. GEORGE A. GOODWIN.

George Augustus Goodwin was born at Augusta, Ga., February 20, 1861, being the eldest son of Mr. George and Mrs. Catherine Goodwin. His parents taught him until he was old enough to enter the public schools taught by "Yankee teachers." Having lost his father at an early age, he subsequently experienced some difficulty in remaining in school. However, his now sainted mother, by the assistance of his uncle, Mr. Charles Goodwin, kept him in school. For two consecutive years it was necessary for him to walk twelve miles daily in order to secure proper school advantages. While yet a lad he attracted the attention of both races and was several times offered good positions as a public school teacher. He, however, taught a private school four miles from the city and was thereby able to attend the Augusta Institute, now the Atlanta Baptist College. In the spring of 1879 he united with the historic Springfield Baptist Church, Augusta, Ga., where, for three generations, his parents and paternal grandparents had worshiped. May 29, 1884, he graduated from the Atlanta Baptist College as salutatorian.

On leaving school he took up teaching as a profession, in which he has been eminently successful in developing hundreds of young people. He has filled with credit and satisfaction the principalship of Eddy High School at Milledgeville, Ga., Union Academy, Gainesville, Fla., Preparatory Department, Livingstone College, Salisbury, N. C.; also Atlanta Baptist College and Waller Baptist Institute, Augusta, Ga. He was the prime factor in the movement which resulted in the organization of the present Georgia State Teachers' Association, of which he was secretary for a number of years. In the organization of the Florida Teachers' Association he was one of the original members. As an institute lecturer he is helpful in many ways.

Having received a call to the pastorate of the Second Baptist Church at Gainesville, Fla., his church at Augusta, Ga., ordained him to the ministry, January 6, 1889. He was very successful in this work in connection with his school duties. In July, 1895, he was happily married to the talented Miss Anna Laura Gardner of Augusta, Ga.

oppressed people; but truth is better than fiction—facts than theories. Therefore, with a conscience void of offence to all, and with the sincere hope that right will ultimately triumph before all is lost in the mad rush of the enthusiasts, I venture to express some of my convictions regarding this question. The proposition categorically stated would be: it is time for the Negro colleges in the South to be put in the hands of Negro teachers. Such an affirmation would imply, at least, that these colleges are elsewhere than in the South; that the colleges in the South are not wholly nor partially taught by Negro teachers; that those who teach in them for some cause, real or imaginary, are not equal to the demands of the times; that the Negro, exclusively, is superior for educating the Negro in the South; that a crisis is upon us making it imperative to man Negro colleges with Negro teachers. These inferences might be indefinitely multiplied; but they are harsh and fallacious—implications unworthy of the best thought interested in an issue involving the destiny of a race and this great republic. The facts in the case are so potent that I shall not attempt a critical refutation of the inferences deduced, but will consider the subject more freely on another line, in this way avoiding what might be a fearful indictment of those least prepared for it. Critically considering every contingency I see no valid reason for such a course as the question suggests. In answer thereto wisdom replies, *"It is NOT time for the Negro colleges in the South to be put in the hands of Negro teachers."*

This is an intensely practical age; in many respects, it is utilitarian. "The survival of the fittest," is the almost universal creed of the age. The American civilization is distinctly Anglo-Saxon. Whatever does not attain to that standard is out of harmony with real conditions. The Negro is here to stay. Two radically different civilizations cannot thrive in one country at the same time. One advances, the other retrogrades. Every chapter in history verifies the assertion. It is providential that the American Negro is brought into close touch with the highest ideals of American life through his most enlightened Anglo-Saxon brother. Only in this way can the Negro meet the rigid requirements of the ever-advancing standard of the proud, progressive Anglo-Saxon. The dominant race is naturally the criterion. Any other alternative would be abnormal and destructive in its far-reaching results. The ruling people in this country have the prestige of centuries of culture. Had the Negro's days of enslavement been years of culture

and refinement equal to that of the best people about him, present conditions would be greatly changed.   However desirable it may be to
elevate the Negro to places of dignity, it should be borne in mind that
his color is not a qualification.   These institutions will, in time, be more
generally under the management of Negro teachers, if the future proves
the work of the present *regime* non-productive of the highest results.
Such a change will greatly depend upon the ability of the Negro to appreciate his real condition and to utilize, to the best advantage, the
means and opportunities now afforded him.   Error now will prove
abortive and, perhaps, postpone indefinitely what might otherwise
sooner come in the natural course of events.   Such a transition must
not be revolutionary, but evolutionary if come it must, and come it will.
It were better to hope that all schools in the South were as they are in
the North for the most part.   That the Negro himself should so soon
contemplate this as practical is an anomaly.   That some evils exist I
do not deny.   But would separation and exclusion be a remedy?   No.
It is praiseworthy in the Negro that he, in a measure, has kept abreast
with the march of this civilization.   He has been responsive to the
magic touch and the benign influences of those who came to rescue him
from intellectual and moral darkness.   The Northern teachers and a
few Southern heroes began the work of educating the Negro, at a time,
when teaching the Negro was an extremely delicate innovation—nay,
dangerous experiment.   Through what perils, privations, ridicule, and
ostracism they passed, only such pioneers as Drs. H. M. Tupper, D. W.
Phillips, C. H. Corey, J. T. Robert, E. A. Ware, E. M. Cravath, Gen.
Armstrong, Miss S. B. Packard, and others of the immortal galaxy, are
permitted to speak from their high citadel of triumph.   Shall these of
blessed memory, together with their associates and workers of less prominence, be forgotten?   Shall they be revered, or shall they be calumniated?
Dumb be the lip, and palsied the hand that would, in any wise, dishonor
them and their efforts to uplift humanity!   It will not be remiss on my
part to ask for their successors in spirit and labor, and for their constituency that consideration which a superior statesmanship and a practical Christianity dictate.

These institutions, under their present management, have met the
exigencies of the times.   Granting that no human effort is perfect, the
fact remains that these institutions have lived up to the high purpose
for which they were founded, and are still being liberally supported and

endowed. What more could be required by rational beings? This couplet may be suggestive:

"He who does as best his circumstances will allow,
Does well, acts nobly, angels can do no more."

That others could have done better or equally as well remains to be seen. The history of the country from 1619-20 to 1865 is valid testimony. It was the influence of the Northern teachers, for the most part, that the best educated men among us were matriculated at the great Northern universities. It was by them that Negro schools were first operated in the South. The needs and magnitude of Negro education in the South have greatly intensified the philanthropic spirit of the Northern missionary societies and workers, each year resulting in a vast expenditure of money and energy. Shall those who believe "culture is colorless" be affronted; and shall their representatives be exiled by the beneficiaries? Is the wounded, dying traveler under the healing ministrations of the good Samaritan competent to protest against the merciful steward? Is such the subsequent of all human action? Let justice and reason answer! Formerly for the Negro literary culture was a sort of forbidden fruit in the Edenic South. For more than two centuries the cherubim of social pollution and moral degradation stood at the school-house gate with sword-like lash in hand, under governmental authority, to defy the return of the Negro to his pristine eminence in literary culture and moral probity held many years prior to the rise and supremacy of his now dominant kinsman. It was the northern missionaries, for such they are, who threw open the wicket-gate of opportunity unto the despairing Negro causing him to reach forth his hand unto the tree of life manifesting itself in the development of the higher faculties of a being with God's image. The Negro colleges in the South, with scarcely an exception, were built up by Northern philanthropy. They are the best institutions available to a great majority of those seeking the fullest possible development of their intellectual powers. As a rule, they are superior in equipment, in both standards of scholarship and discipline at least. This is true by virtue of the power vouchsafed to their management and teaching force through superior years of splendid environment. Under such circumstances the Northern missionary teachers are in their normal condition in prosecuting the work of Negro education. They are usually dispensers of exact scholarship, consecrated service, and broad culture. It is scarcely possible that the Negro, in less than forty years, a creature of misfortune many years prior to his enslavement, should now be the equal of his more favored brother in the acquisition of knowledge or his over-match in teaching ability. Physiologists are quite unanimous in making the Negro a member of the human race. He, therefore, has the same faculties and susceptibilities as other members of the human family. He is governed by the same laws of thought. In what then is the Negro constitutionally a better educator of the Negro? There is absolutely nothing in his skin nor sympathies that makes him a superior teacher of the Negro. Other things being equal preparation is the only synonym for superiority in teaching. If now the race has idiosyncrasies entirely different from the rest of the human family, as some wiseacres would imply by their persistency in making this demand for a change in the colleges, then maybe it were better to gratify their wish.

These colleges are more than so much material and apparatus. Through them the white brother is best prepared to represent the Negro to those who are to help in his uplift. The peculiar customs in the South weaken the authority of the Negro teacher in comparison with the *fiat* of the Anglo-Saxon teacher. The Negro teacher in the public schools, and in the schools distinctly his own, is not more successful, to be charitable, than the Northern teacher in securing and holding pupils. Nor has it been shown that the Negro teacher develops the powers of the child any faster, or in better ways of thinking and acting than does the Northern teacher. Coming to us as they do, their ability is rarely questioned. They are never anxious to advertise their fitness for the place by resorting to that unique process in promotions which seems so often the *naivete* of many another in similar spheres without hereditary influences as his legacy. At some time, in some way, I have been closely connected with schools of all grades in the South for the Negro—schools owned by the Negro, taught by the Negro exclusively, schools taught by the Negro and the Anglo-Saxon. I have been the pupil of Northern and Southern white teachers; for a brief while a pupil of the Negro teacher; and at one time janitor of a leading white academy in which help was mutually given by the janitor-tutor. I confess that I have yet to see the slightest difference in the general character of receiving and imparting knowledge, or in developing character on the principle of color *versus* culture. To accept any such doctrine would be pernicious.

These colleges are too important to be used as experimental stations even to gratify the caprice of the most cautious. Such a change in the work of these colleges, as the question suggests, should be looked upon with some degree of suspicion and as inimical to the best interests of the Negro. Without undervaluing the great importance of the public schools, it were better to try the experiment with them and the few secondary schools for Negro education connected with the several Southern States and managed by white trustees exclusively. What has been the history of the local academies and schools transferred to the Negro trustees and teachers not many years after the Civil War? What of those operated in later years as a monument to the creative genius of the Negro? For the most part, they remind us that they have seen better days. They speak a mighty truth which should be borne in mind by every class of inquirers on this subject. Self-help and worthy ambitions are commendable, but should be rational. The Negro needs the help of the Anglo-Saxon without regard to sections of country. He can advance more safely and rapidly as he walks arm in arm with his brother North and South. Far be it from me that I should, in any way, underestimate the heroic efforts of institutions wholly run by the Negro! Many of them are striking illustrations of what united effort can do; they serve a purpose which cannot be overlooked. Only in proportion as he is more a producer than a consumer, and as wealth and intelligence become common factors in his social life, will the Negro be able to assume entire control of these great institutions founded for him by the Northern societies. As to the ability of some members of the race to adorn any position in the gift of these colleges no one denies. There are men of superior scholarship, broad culture, sound character, tact, and executive ability even to grace similar places in white institutions. They are exceptions; and yet I do not hesitate to say that were their services in demand they could do so with comparatively more ease and satisfaction than if at the head of a strictly Negro institution. The reason is apparent to those experienced in such matters. Ability and adaptability are not the only requisites for this work.

If the Negro has not been able to acquire similar institutions by his own efforts aided by friends North and South, is there any guarantee that he would properly appreciate them if thus thrust upon him? To ask such a concession would be an admission of the point at issue. The South, commercially, believes in free trade; assuming it is right, it then would not be right to close the intellectual ports of the Negro against the cultured wares of his time honored benefactors in literary commerce. The Negro least of all should not ask it.

In Southern courts, where life and great interests are involved, the most intelligent Negro finds it to his advantage to employ legal talent of the opposite race because he is conditioned by the peculiar circumstances of a white judge and jury who, in most cases, seem to interpret law and weigh evidence in accordance with the prevailing opinions of the dominant class. In the work of Negro education vital interests are involved. The Anglo-Saxon teachers have the culture and the means at their command. They are actual competitors with the Negro and every other people in this particular missionary endeavor. They have given the world its highest civilization. Through them, as instrumentalities, the torch-light of civilization progresses; Christianity brightens every prospect in every land. Why should they be discriminated against in educating the Negro in the South? Should this service and philanthropy be directed to founding and supporting similar institutions for the more unfortunate class of the stronger race, there would be no question about the color of teachers though they be Indian or Japanese. The means used in maintaining these institutions is not obtained from the Negro nor by his influence. Would a change in the policy of the teaching force help or hinder in securing this aid? This change would establish more rigidly the color line so objectionable to the Negro himself. It would be a backward movement. In all probability the color of the darker races is due more largely to some sort of skin disease, than to other causes, transmitted through the ages since the flood. That is a very charitable Negro who wishes isolation to prevent inoculating the Anglo-Saxon if permitted to teach the Negro. The Negro has ample opportunity for his individuality in his societies and churches. He has gained absolutely nothing by completely divorcing himself from the fostering care of the Anglo-Saxon. Observe the contrast between those Negro churches wholly separated from the Anglo-Saxon and those partially controlled by the dominant race. Those who have been somewhat under the guardianship of the stronger race are usually the highest types of intelligent Christianity.

Mrs. Paul L. Dunbar

MRS. PAUL LAURENCE DUNBAR.

Mrs. Paul Laurence Dunbar (Alice Ruth Moore) was born in New Orleans, La., July 19, 1875. Attended public schools there and Straight University, and was graduated from the latter institution in 1892. Taught in the public schools of New Orleans until 1896, when she went to Boston and New York for study, taking a course in Manual Training at the Teachers' College. Was appointed a teacher in the public schools of Brooklyn, N. Y., in 1897, and taught there until her marriage to Mr. Paul Laurence Dunbar, in March, 1898.

In 1895, Mrs. Dunbar's first book, "Violets and Other Tales," was published by the Monthly Review Publishing Company, Boston. The next book, "The Goodness of St. Rocque," published by Dodd, Mead & Co., New York, in 1899, was favorably received by some of the best critics. Mrs. Dunbar has written a number of short stories for some of the leading magazines and newspapers in the country, among them McClures, the Smart Set, Ladies' Home Journal, the Southern Workman, Leslie's Weekly, the New York Sun, Boston Transcript, and for over a year did regular work on the Chicago News.

While teaching in Brooklyn, Mrs. Dunbar was actively interested in mission work on the East Side of New York, conducting classes in manual training and kindergarten after the regular hours of public school work was over. Since her marriage, Mrs. Dunbar has resided in Washington, and has done some of her best work in short story writing, as well as acting as secretary and general helpmeet for her husband.

Both races have suffered by the separation; but it is needless to say how much greater the Negro has suffered. The Negro has more to gain by co-operation with his Anglo-Saxon neighbors. Intelligence must be handed down from generation to generation, from race to race by contact, from individual to individual. In the schools of the American Baptist Home Mission Society, for the year 1898-1899, the annual report shows that out of 321 teachers employed, 124 were Negroes. It will be borne out by the report of each succeeding year. In a large measure, the other missionary societies North and South are about as liberal in recognizing the Negro teacher. Therefore to mix the faculties and boards of trustees of all these schools would be ideal in most respects. This would be a happy golden mean. Let us be patient, considerate, and faithful.

FOURTH PAPER.

IS IT TIME FOR THE NEGRO COLLEGES IN THE SOUTH TO BE PUT INTO THE HANDS OF NEGRO TEACHERS?

BY MRS. PAUL L. DUNBAR.

It seems a rather incongruous fact that so many of our Negro colleges in the South, whose purpose is avowedly the insistence of higher education of Negro youth, should deny that youth not only the privilege of teaching in the very institutions which have taught him, but also deny him the privilege of looking up to and reverencing his own people. For so long have the whites been held up to the young people as the only ones whom it is worth while taking as models; for so long have the ignorant of the race been taught that their best efforts after all, are hardly worth while, that wherever possible, it behooves us to place over the masses those of their own race who have themselves attained to that dignity to which the education of the schools tend.

It has been my good or ill fortune to number among my acquaintances a number of young boys and girls who could rattle off with fluency the names of Greek philosophers of ancient days; who could at a moment's notice tell you the leading writers of the Elizabethan period, or the minor Italian poets of the fifteenth century, but who were hopelessly ignorant of what members of their own race had done. They had, perhaps, a vague idea of an occasional name here and there, but what the owner of that name had done was a mystery. Happily these instances are decreasing in proportion as our schools are filled with teachers of our own race who can teach a proper appreciation of, and pride in the deeds of that race.

It is unreasonable to suppose that any teacher of another race, no matter how conscientious and scrupulous, is going to take the same interest in putting before his pupils the achievements of that people in contradistinction to the accepted course of study as laid down by the text books. How many young students of history in the white-taught schools remember being drilled to revere the glorious memory of Lincoln, and Sumner and Garrison and Wendell Phillips, and how few remember being drilled to remember Crispus Attucks and the fifty-fourth and fifty-fifth Massachusetts? How many students of literature are taught of the first woman writer in America to earn distinction, Margaret Hutchinson, but how few are reminded of her contemporary, Phyllis Wheatley? How many students remember the lachrymose career of Byron and how few know of his contemporary, Poushkin? The student of natural science is taught about Franklin, but not of Benjamin Banneker; the elocution classes remember Booth and Macready, and even how excellent an actor was Shakespeare, but they seldom hear of Ira Aldridge. How many of the mathematical students remember that Euclid was a black man? And the elementary classes in art, how glibly they can discuss Turner and Ruskin and the pre-Raphaelites and the style of Gibson, but they are likely not to know the name of the picture that the Paris Salon hung for Henry Tanner.

It is unreasonable, of course, to expect any Caucasian to remember these things, or if remembering them, to be able to point them out with the same amount of pride and persistence that a Negro in the same position would. And therein lies the secret of the foundation of a family, a government, a nation—pride. Pride in what has been done, in what may be done, in the ability to reach the very highest point that may be reached. With that quality instilled in the young from the very first, the foundation for individual achievement is firmly laid; and what more can we ask of any education?

It has been said that Negro boys and girls hearing of the deeds of some great man or woman have exclaimed, "Oh, well, no colored person could do that!" Fortunately, there are few of these now, but how much it is to be regretted that such an expression could ever have been made— at least within the last thirty years?

By all means let us have Negro teachers in our Negro schools and colleges. Let the boy who wants to be a farmer carry with him the memory of successful Negro farmers and of a Negro who knew enough about scientific agriculture to teach him to compete with the best white farmers in the country. It will be easier for him to reach his goal, and he will have more respect for his own ability and less cringing, servile admiration for his Caucasian rivals. Let the boy or girl whose inclinations tend to a profession get their instruction from some one whose complexion is akin to their own. It is a spur to ambition, a goal to be reached. The "what man has done, man may do" is so much easier from a successful brother than from a successful, though supercilious, neighbor.

Of course, the good effect of Negro teachers upon the youthful minds is the only point thus far touched upon. The other side of the question is obvious. What is the use of training teachers, of spending time and money acquiring college training if there is no place to use such training? There is room, and plenty of it, for the college bred man and woman, and for every place filled by our own teachers there is so much more money saved to our own race.

The closer the corporation, the wealthier it is. The tighter the lines drawn about distributing money outside our own great family the more affluent our family becomes. Every cent is an important item. More money for ourselves, a better opinion of our own achievements and ability to do more, higher regard for the raising of Negro ideals, and a deeper sense of the responsibility imposed on each individual to do his part towards leavening the lump; these things are dependent upon our teachers in our own schools.

By all means let us have Negro teachers in Negro colleges.

TOPIC IX.

WILL THE EDUCATION OF THE NEGRO SOLVE THE RACE PROBLEM?

BY BOOKER T. WASHINGTON.

"Will Education Solve the Race Problem?" is the title of an interesting article in the June number of The North American Review, by Professor John Roach Straton, of Macon, Georgia. My own belief is that education will finally solve the race problem. In giving some reasons for this faith, I wish to express my appreciation of the sincere and kindly spirit in which Professor Straton's article is written. I grant that much that he emphasizes as to present conditions is true. When we recall the past, these conditions could not be expected to be otherwise; but I see no reason for discouragement or loss of faith. When I speak of education as a solution for the race problem, I do not mean education in the narrow sense, but education which begins in the home and includes training in industry and in habits of thrift, as well as mental, moral and religious discipline, and the broader education which comes from contact with the public sentiment of the community in which one lives. Nor do I confine myself to the education of the Negro. Many persons in discussing the effect that education will have in working out the Negro question, overlook the helpful influence that will ultimately come through the broader and more generous education of all the race elements of the South. As all classes of whites in the South become more generally educated in the broader sense, race prejudice will be tempered and they will assist in lifting up the black man.

In our desire to see a better condition of affairs, we are too often inclined to grow impatient because a whole race is not elevated in a short time, very much as a house is built. In all the history of mankind there have been few such radical, social and economic changes in the policy of a nation as have been effected within thirty-five years in this country, with respect to the change of four million and a half of slaves into four million and a half of freemen (now nearly ten million). When all the conditions of the past are considered, and compared with the present, I think the White South, the North and the Negro are

Booker T. Washington.

PROF. BOOKER T. WASHINGTON, A. M.

Prof. B. T. Washington, the founder and principal of the Tuskegee, Alabama, Normal Industrial Institute, was born at Hale's Ford Postoffice, Franklin County, Virginia, about 1856 or 1857. At the age of nine he went with his mother and the rest of the family to Malden, Kanawha County, West Virginia. Here he attended the common schools until 1872. In the Fall of that year he left Malden and proceeded to Hampton Institute, at Hampton, Virginia. His means were scanty, but he thought he had money enough to reach that place. Upon his arrival at Richmond, he found himself minus enough to pay for a night's lodging. He took the next best, shelter under a sidewalk. Next morning he got employment in helping to unload a vessel, thus earning a sufficient sum with which to continue his journey to Hampton. At this institution the first year he paid his expenses by working, with a brother helping him some. The two remaining years he worked out his entire expenses as janitor. Graduating in 1875, he taught school several years at Malden, the place of his birth. In 1878 he entered Wayland Seminary and took a course of studies there. After leaving there he was given a position in Hampton Institute, which position he held two years, the last year having charge of the Indian boys. Meanwhile the Legislature of Alabama passed an act establishing a Normal School at Tuskegee, Alabama. The State Commissioners applied to Gen. S. C. Armstrong, principal of Hampton Institute, to recommend some one for principal. He recommended Mr. Washington, who went at once to Alabama, and organized the school July 4th, 1881. The buildings then occupied were a church and a small dwelling house, with thirty pupils and one teacher. Since that time it has made such wonderful progress that, to-day, the site of the institution is a city within itself. Mr. Carnegie recently donated to the institution $20,000, with which to build and equip a library. It is aided by friends both North and South. Mr. Washington is a splendid example of "grit and determination," and the history of his life is worthy the study of every colored youth in our land.

Professor Washington, in speaking of his experiences at Hampton, says: "While at Hampton, I resolved, if God permitted me to finish the course of study, I would enter the far South, the black belt of the Gulf States, and give my life in providing as best I could the same kind of chance for self-help for the youth of my race that I found ready for me when I went to Hampton, and so, in 1881, I left Hampton and went to Tuskegee and started the Normal and Industrial Institute."

Professor Washington is in great demand as a speaker in all educational gatherings. For several consecutive years he has addressed the National Educational Association, where from ten to fifteen thousand of the cream of the educational workers of the nation listen to his addresses with rapt attention. Without question he is the great leader of his race, and one of the great men of this age.

to be congratulated on the fact that conditions are no worse, but are as encouraging as they are. The sudden change from slavery to freedom, from restraint to liberty, was a tremendous one; and the wonder is, not that the Negro has not done better, but that he has done as well as he has. Every thoughtful student of the subject expected that the first two or three generations of freedom would lead to excesses and mistakes on the part of the Negro, which would in many cases cause moral and physical degeneration, such as would seem to the superficial observer to indicate conditions that could not be overcome. It was to be anticipated that, in the first generation at least, the tendency would be, among a large number, to seek the shadow instead of the substance; to grasp after the mere signs of the highest civilization instead of the reality; to be led into the temptation of believing that they could secure, in a few years, that which it has taken other races thousands of years to obtain. Any one who has the daily opportunity of studying the Negro at first hand cannot but gain the impression that there are indisputable evidences that the Negro throughout the country is settling down to a hard, common sense view of life; that he is fast learning that a race, like an individual, must pay for everything it gets— the price of beginning at the bottom of the social scale and gradually working up by natural processes to the highest civilization. The exaggerated impressions that the first years of freedom naturally brought are giving way to an earnest, practical view of life and its responsibilities.

Let us take a broad, generous survey of the Negro race as it came into the country, represented by twenty savages, in 1619, and trace its progress through slavery, through the Civil War period, and through freedom to the present moment. Who will be brave enough to say that the colored race, as a whole, has not increased in numbers and grown stronger mentally, morally, religiously, industrially, and in the accumulation of property? In a word, has not the Negro, at every stage, shown a tendency to grow into harmony with the best type of American civilization?

Professor Straton lays special stress upon the moral weakness of the race. Perhaps the worst feature of slavery was that it prevented the development of a family life, with all of its far-reaching significance. Except in rare cases the uncertainties of domicile made family life, during two hundred and fifty years of slavery, an impossibility. There is no institution so conducive to right and high habits of physical and moral life as the home. No race starting in absolute poverty could be expected, in the brief period of thirty-five years, to purchase homes and build up a family life and influence that would have a very marked impression upon the life of the masses. The Negro has not had time enough to collect the broken and scattered members of his family. For the sake of illustration, and to employ a personal reference, I do not know who my own father was; I have no idea who my grandmother was; I have or had uncles, aunts and cousins, but I have no knowledge as to where most of them now are. My case will illustrate that of hundreds of thousands of black people in every part of our country. Perhaps those who direct attention to the Negro's moral weakness, and compare his moral progress with that of the whites, do not consider the influence of the memories which cling about the old family homestead upon the character and aspirations of individuals. The very fact that the white boy is conscious that, if he fails in life, he will disgrace the whole family record, extending back through many generations, is of tremendous value in helping him to resist temptations. On the other hand, the fact that the individual has behind him and surrounding him proud family history and connections serves as a stimulus to make him overcome obstacles, when striving for success. All this should be taken into consideration, to say nothing of the physical, mental and moral training which individuals of the white race receive in their homes. We must not pass judgment on the Negro too soon. It requires centuries for the influence of home, school, church and public contact to permeate the mass of millions of people, so that the upward tendency may be apparent to the casual observer. It is too soon to decide what effect general education will have upon the rank and file of the Negro race, because the masses have not been educated.

Throughout the South, especially in the Gulf states, the great bulk of the black population lives in the country districts. In these districts the schools are rarely in session more than three months of the year. When this is considered, in connection with poor teachers, poor schoolhouses, and an almost entire lack of apparatus, it is obvious that we must wait longer before we can judge, even approximately, of the effect that general education will have upon the whole population. Most writers and speakers upon the subject of the Negro's non-progressiveness base their arguments upon alleged facts and statistics of the life of Negroes in the large cities. This is hardly fair. Before the Civil

War the Negro was not, to any considerable extent, a denizen of the large cities. Most of them lived on the plantations. The Negro living in the cities has undergone two marked changes: (1) the change from slavery to freedom; (2) the change from country life to city life. At first the tendency of both these changes was, naturally, to unsettle, to intoxicate and to lead the Negro to wrong ideas of life. The change from country life to city life, in the case of the white man, is about as marked as in the case of the Negro. The average Negro in the city, with all of its excitements and temptations, has not lived there more than half a generation. It is, therefore, too soon to reach a definite conclusion as to what the permanent effect of this life upon him will be. This, I think, explains the difference between the moral condition of the Negro, to which Professor Straton refers, in the states where there has been little change in the old plantation life, as compared with that in the more northern of the Atlantic states, where the change from country to city life is more marked.

Judging from close observation, my belief is that, after the Negro has overcome the false idea which city life emphasizes, two or three generations will bring about an earnestness and steadiness of purpose which do not now generally obtain. As the Negro secures a home in the city, learns the lessons of industry and thrift and becomes a tax-payer, his moral life improves. The influence of home surroundings, of the school, the church and public sentiment will be more marked and have a more potent effect in causing him to withstand temptations. But, notwithstanding the shortness of the time which the Negro has had in which to get schooled to his new life, any one who has visited the large cities of Europe will readily testify that the visible signs of immorality in those cities are far greater than among the colored people of America. Prostitution for gain is far more prevalent in the cities of Europe than among the colored people of our cities.

Professor Straton says that the Negro has degenerated in morals since he became free; in other words, that his condition in this respect is not as hopeful as it was during the early period of slavery. I do not think it wise to place too much reliance upon such a view of the matter, because there are too few facts upon which to base a comparison. The bald statement that the Negro was not given to crime during slavery proves little. Slavery represented an unnatural condition of life, in which certain physical checks were kept constantly upon the individual. To say that the Negro was at his best, morally, during the period of slavery is about the same as to say that the two thousand prisoners in the State prison and the city penal institutions in the city of Boston are the most righteous two thousand people in Boston. I question whether one can find two thousand persons in Boston who will equal these two thousand imprisoned criminals in the mere negative virtues. During the days of slavery the Negro was rarely brought into the court to be tried for crime; hence, there was almost no public record of crimes committed by him. Each master, in most cases, punished his slave as he thought best, and as little as possible was said about it outside of his little plantation world. The improper relations between the sexes, with which the black race is now frequently charged in most sections of the South, were encouraged or winked at, under the slavery system, because of the financial value of the slaves. A custom that was fostered for three centuries cannot be blotted out in one generation.

In estimating the progress of a race, we should not consider alone the degree of success which has been actually attained, but also the obstacles which have been overcome in reaching that success. Judged by the obstacles overcome, few races, if any, in history have made progress commensurate with that of the colored people of the United States, in the same length of time. It may be conceded that the present generation of colored people does not compare favorably with the present generation of the white race, because of the reasons I have already given, and the further reason that on account of the black man's poverty of means to employ lawyers to have his case properly appealed to the higher courts, and his inability to furnish bonds, his criminal record is much worse than that of the white race, both in the Northern and Southern states. The Southern states, as a whole, have not yet reached a point where they are able to provide reformatories for juvenile offenders, and consequently most of these are sent to the state prison, where the records show that the same individuals are often committed over and over again, because in the first instance, the child prisoner, instead of being reformed, becomes simply hardened to prison life. In the North, it is true, the Negro has the benefit of the reformatories; but the unreasonable prejudice which prevents him from securing employment in the shops and the factories more than offsets this advantage. Hundreds of Negroes in the North become criminals who would become strong and useful men if they were not discriminated against as bread winners.

In the matter of assault upon white women, the Negro is placed in a peculiar attitude. While this vile crime is always to be condemned in the strongest language, and it should be followed by the severest legal punishment, yet the custom of lynching a Negro when he is accused of committing such a crime calls the attention of the whole country to it, in such a way as is not always true in the case of a white man, North or South. Any one who reads the daily papers carefully knows that such assaults are constantly charged against white men in the North and in the South; but, because the white man, in most cases, is punished by the regular machinery of the courts, attention is seldom attracted to his crime outside of the immediate neighborhood where the offense is committed. This, to say nothing of the cases where the victim of lynch law could prove his innocence, if he were given a hearing before a cool, level-headed set of jurors in open court, makes the apparent contrast unfavorable to the black man. It is hardly proper, in summing up the value of any race, to dwell almost continually upon its weaker element. As other men are judged, so should the Negro be judged, by the best that the race can produce, rather than by the worst. Keep the searchlight constantly focused upon the criminal and worthless element of any people, and few among all the races and nations of the world can be accounted successful. More attention should be directed to individuals who have succeeded, and less to those who have failed. And Negroes who have succeeded grandly can be found in every corner of the South.

I doubt that much reliance can safely be placed upon mere ability to read and write a little as a means of saving any race. Education should go further. One of the weaknesses in the Negro's present condition grows out of failure, in the early years of his freedom, to teach him, in connection with thorough academic and religious branches, the dignity and beauty of labor, and to give him a working knowledge of the industries by which he must earn a subsistence. But the main question is: What is the present tendency of the race, where it has been given a fair opportunity, and where there has been thorough education of hand, head and heart? This question I answer from my own experience of nineteen years in the heart of the South, and from my daily contact with whites and blacks. In the first place, the social barrier prevents most white people from coming into real contact with the higher and better side of the Negro's social life. The Negro loafer, drunkard and gambler can be seen without social contact. The higher life cannot be seen without social contact. As I write these lines I am in the home of a Negro friend, where in the matter of cleanliness, sweetness, attractiveness, modern conveniences and other evidences of intelligence, morality and culture, the home would compare favorably with that of any white family in the neighborhood; and yet this Negro home is unknown outside of the little town where it exists. To really know the life of this family, one would have to become a part of it for days, as I have been. One of the most encouraging changes that have taken place in the life of the Negro race in the past thirty years is the creation of a growing public sentiment which draws a line between the good and bad, the clean and unclean. This change is fast taking place in every part of the country. It is one that cannot be accurately measured by any table of statistics. To be able to appreciate it fully, one must himself be a part of the social life of the race.

As to the effect of industrial education in the solution of the race problem, we should not expect too much from it in a short time. To the late General S. C. Armstrong, of Hampton Institute, in Virginia, should be given the credit, mainly, for inaugurating this system of education. When the Hampton Institute began the systematic, industrial training of the Negro, such training was unpopular among a large class of colored people. Later, when the same system was started by me at the Tuskegee Normal and Industrial Institute, in Alabama, it was still unpopular, especially in that part of the South. But the feeling against it has now almost disappeared in all parts of the country, so much so that I do not consider the opposition of a few people here and there as of material consequence. Where there is one who opposes it there are thousands who indorse it. So far as the colored people are concerned, I consider that the battle for this principle has been fought and the victory won. What the colored people are anxious about is that, with industrial education, they shall have thorough mental and religious training, and in this they are right. For bringing about this change in the attitude of the colored people, much credit should be given to the John F. Slater Fund, under the wise guidance of such men as Mr. Morris K. Jesup and Dr. J. L. M. Curry, as well as to Dr. H. B. Frissell, of the Hampton Institute. That such institutions for industrial training as the Hampton Institute and the Tuskegee Institute are always crowded with the best class of Negro students from nearly every state in the Union, and that every year they are compelled to refuse admission to hundreds of others, for lack of room and means, are sufficient evidence that the black race has come to appreciate the value of industrial education. The almost pathetic demand of the colored people for industrial education in every corner of the South is added evidence of the growing intelligence of the race. In saying what I do in regard to industrial education, I do not wish to be understood as meaning that the education of the Negro should be confined to that kind alone, because we need men and women well educated in other directions; but for the masses industrial education is the supreme need. I repeat that we must not expect too much from this training, in the redemption of a race, in the space of a few years.

There are few institutions in the South where industrial training is given upon a large and systematic scale, and the graduates from these institutions have not had time to make themselves felt to any very large extent upon the life of the rank and file of the people. But what are the indications? As I write, I have before me a record of graduates, which is carefully compiled each year. Of the hundreds who have been trained at the Tuskegee Institute, less than five per cent have failed because of any moral weakness. These graduates, as well as hundreds of other students who could not remain to finish the course, are now at work in the schoolroom, in the field, in the shop, in the home, or as teachers of industry, or in some way they are making their education felt in the lifting up of the colored people. Wherever these graduates go, they not only help their own race, but, in nearly every case, they win the respect and confidence of the white people.

Not long ago I sent a number of letters to white men, in all the Southern states, asking, among others, this question: "Judged by actual observation in your community, what is the effect of education upon the Negro?" In asking this question, I was careful to explain that by education I did not mean a mere smattering, but a thorough education of the head, heart and hand. I received about three hundred replies, and there was only one who said that education did not help the Negro. Most of the others were emphatic in stating that education made the Negro a better citizen. In all the record of crime in the South, there are very few instances where a black man, who has been thoroughly educated in the respects I have mentioned, has been ever charged with the crime of assaulting a woman. In fact, I do not know of a single instance of this kind, whether the man was educated in an industrial school or in a college.

The following extracts from a letter written by a Southern white man to the Daily Advertiser, of Montgomery, Alabama, contain most valuable testimony. The letter refers to convicts in Alabama, most of whom are colored:

"I was conversing not long ago with the warden of one of our mining prisons, containing about 500 convicts. The warden is a practical man, who has been in charge of prisoners for more than fifteen years, and has no theories of any kind to support. I remarked to him that I wanted some information as to the effect of manual training in preventing criminality, and asked him to state what per cent of the prisoners under his charge had received any manual training, besides the acquaintance with the crudest agricultural labor. He replied: 'Perhaps about one per cent.' He added: 'No; much less than that. We have here at present only one mechanic; that is, there is one man who claims to be a house painter.'

" 'Have you any shoemakers?'

" 'Never have had a shoemaker.'

" 'Have you any tailors?'

" 'Never have had a tailor.'

" 'Any printers?'

" 'Never have had a printer.'

" 'Any carpenters?'

" 'Never have had a carpenter. There is not a man in this prison that could saw to a straight line.' "

Now, these facts seem to show that manual training is almost as good a preventive for criminality as vaccination is for smallpox.

We can best judge further of the value of industrial and academic education by using a few statistics bearing upon the state of Virginia, where graduates from the Hampton Institute and other schools have gone in large numbers and have had an opportunity, in point of time, to make their influence apparent upon the Negro population. These statistics, based on census reports, were compiled mainly by persons connected with the Hampton Negro Conference:

"Taking taxation as a basis, the colored people of the State of Virginia contributed, in 1898, directly to the expenses of the State government, the sum of $9,576.76, and for schools $3,239.41 from their personal property, a total of $12,816.17; while, from their real estate, for the purpose of the commonwealth there was paid by them $34,303.53, and for schools $11,457.22, or a total of $45,760.75—a grand total of $58,576.92.

"The report for the same year shows them to own 987,118 acres of land, valued at $3,800,459, improved by buildings valued at $2,056,490, a total of $5,856,949. In the towns and cities, they own lots assessed at $2,154,331, improved by buildings valued at $3,400,636, a total of $5,554,976 for town property, and a grand total of $11,411,916 of their property of all kinds in the commonwealth. A comparative statement of different years would doubtless show a general upward tendency.

"The counties of Accomac, Essex, King and Queen, Middlesex, Mathews, Northampton, Northumberland, Richmond, Westmoreland, Gloucester, Princess Anne and Lancaster, all agricultural, show an aggregate of 114,197 acres held by Negroes in 1897, the last year accounted for in official reports, against 108,824 held the previous year, an increase of 5,379, or nearly five per cent. The total valuation of land owned by Negroes in the same counties for 1897, is $547,800, against $496,385 for the year next preceding, a gain of $51,150, or more than ten per cent. Their present property, as assessed in 1897, was $517,560, in 1896, $527,688, a loss of $10,128. Combining the real and personal property for 1897, we have $1,409,059, against $1,320,504 for 1896, a net gain of $88,555, an increase of six and one-half per cent.

"The records of Gloucester, Lancaster, Middlesex, Princess Anne, Northumberland, Northampton, King and Queen, Essex, and Westmoreland, where the colored population exceeds the white, show that the criminal expense for 1896 was $14,313.29, but for 1897 it was only $8,538.12, a saving of $5,774.17 to the State, or a falling off of forty per cent. This does not tell the whole story. In the first named year twenty-six persons were convicted of felonies, with sentences in the penitentiary, while in the year succeeding only nine, or one-third as many, were convicted of the graver offences of the law."

According to these returns, in 1892, when the colored people formed 41 per cent of the population, they owned 2.75 per cent of the total number of acres assessed for taxation, and 3.40 per cent of the buildings; in 1898, although not constituting more than 37 per cent of the population (by reason of white immigration), they owned 3.23 per cent of the acreage assessed, and 4.64 per cent of the buildings—a gain of nearly one-third in six years.

According to statistics gathered by a graduate of the Hampton Institute, in twelve counties in Virginia, there has been in the part of the state covered by the investigation an increase of 5,379 acres in the holdings of colored people, and an increase of $51,150 in the value of their land. In nine counties there has been a decrease in the number of persons charged with felonies and sent to the penitentiary from twenty-six in 1896 to nine in 1897.

I do not believe that the Negro will grow weaker in morals and less strong in numbers because of his immediate contact with the white race. The first class life insurance companies are considered excellent authorities as to the longevity of individuals and races; and the fact that most of them now seek to insure the educated class of blacks, is a good test of what these companies think of the effect of education upon the mortality of the race.

The case of Jamaica, in the West Indies, presents a good example by which to judge the future of the Negro of the United States, so far as mortality is concerned. The argument drawn from Jamaica is valuable, chiefly because the race there has been free for sixty-two years, instead of thirty-five, as in our own country. During the years of freedom, the blacks of Jamaica have been in constant contact with the white man. Slavery was abolished in Jamaica in 1838. The census of 1844 showed that there were 364,000 Negroes on the island. In 1871 there were 493,000, and in 1891 there were 610,597. In a history of Jamaica written by Mr. W. P. Livingston, who spent ten years studying the conditions of the island, we find that, immediately after emancipation on the island, there was something of the reaction that has taken place in some parts of our country; but that recently there has been a settling down to real, earnest life on the part of a large proportion of the race. After calling attention to certain weak and unsatisfactory phases in the life of the Jamaica Negro, Mr. Livingston says:

"This, then, is the race as it exists to-day, a product of sixty years of freedom; on the whole, a plain, honest, Anglicized people, with no peculiarity except a harmless ignorance and superstition. Looking at it in contrast with what it was at the beginning of the period, one cannot but be impressed with the wonderful progress it has made; and

Prof. John R. Hawkins.

JOHN RUSSELL HAWKINS.

John Russell Hawkins, the oldest son of Ossian and Christiana Hawkins, was born in the town of Warrenton, Warren County, North Carolina, on May 31, 1862. At the age of six years, he began attending the public school of his native town and made rapid progress in his studies.

When old enough to help his father work, he had to stop attending school regularly and apply himself to work on his father's farm. In the mean time, he kept up studies by attending night school and employing private tutors. At the age of fifteen, he went with four members of the highest class in the regular graded school to take the public examination for school teacher. Of the five examined, he made the highest grades and received an appointment as assistant teacher in the same school where he had received his first training.

In 1881, he left home and went to Hampton Institute, Hampton, Va., where he spent one year in special study preparatory for business.

In 1882, he left Hampton and accepted a position in the Government service, as railway postal clerk, on the line between Raleigh, N. C., and Norfolk, Va. Here he soon made a record that classed him among the best clerks in the service. In 1885, Mr. Hawkins returned to his native town and was elected as principal of the graded school. Here he spent two years teaching and reading law under private tutors.

In 1887, he was asked to go to Kittrell, N. C., to fill the position as business manager and treasurer of Kittrell College, then known as Kittrell Normal and Industrial Institute. So acceptably did Mr. Hawkins fill this position that in 1890 he was elected to the Presidency of Kittrell College which position he has filled with credit.

During the first eight years of his work at Kittrell, he developed that work so rapidly that the trustees deemed it wise to accept his recommendations and broaden the work so as to cover a regular college course. Mr. Hawkins has always been an ardent advocate of higher education for the Negro and worked hard to fit himself for giving such advantages to his students. For five years he spent his summers in the North, where he could get the best school advantages and keep himself in touch with best school methods.

Mr. Hawkins has been one of the most successful educators of the South and has raised large sums of money by public canvass among the philanthropists of the country. In his native State, North Carolina, he is a recognized leader among his people, and by his ability and standing has won the confidence and respect of all classes. A ripe scholar, a deep thinker, a ready writer and a polished orator, his services are almost constantly in demand. Indeed, it has been said of him that he is one of the finest public speakers on the stage. He speaks with such power of conviction as to touch the heart of his audiences and at once lead them into the subject under consideration with interest and profit.

In 1896 he was elected by the General Conference of the African Methodist Episcopal Church as Commissioner of Education and filled that office so acceptably that at the end of his first term in 1900, he was re-elected by acclamation. He is regarded as among the strongest laymen in his church and one of the best financiers of the race.

One of the finest qualities of Mr. Hawkins is his devotion to his family and his high ideals in home life.

In 1892 he married Miss Lillian M. Kennedy, of Sioux Falls, South Dakota, whose companionship and devotion has been a most important factor in contributing to her husband's success. They are the happy parents of two children, a girl and a boy, and are pleasantly located at Kittrell, N. C., in a very beautiful home.

where there has been steady progress in the past, there is infinite hope for the future. * * * The impact of Roman power and culture on the northern barbarians of the United Kingdom did not make itself felt for three hundred years. * * * Instead of dying off before civilization, he (the Negro) grows stronger as he comes within its best influences."

In comparing the black race of Jamaica with that of the United States, it should be borne in mind that the Negro in America enjoys advantages and encouragements which the race in Jamaica does not possess.

What I have said, I repeat, is based largely upon my own experience and observation, rather than upon statistics. I do not wish to convey the impression that the problem before our country is not a large and serious one; but I do believe that in a judicious system of industrial, mental and religious training we have found the method of solving it. What we most need is the money necessary to make the system effective. The indications are hopeful, not discouraging; and not the least encouraging is the fact that, in addition to the munificence of Northern philanthropists and the appropriations of the Southern state governments from common taxation, with the efforts of the Negro himself, we have now reached a point at which the solution of this problem is drawing to its aid some of the most thoughtful and cultured white men and women of the South, as is indicated by the article to which I have already referred, from the pen of Professor John Roach Straton.

SECOND PAPER.

WILL THE EDUCATION OF THE NEGRO SOLVE THE RACE PROBLEM?

BY PROF. J. R. HAWKINS.

Every nation of recognized merit and ability, chronicled in the world's history, is proud to revert to some special feature of its life, and point with pride to some one thing that has given character to its institutions and added to its national glory. As far back as history runs, we find nations, classes and races, pointing out different things as the stronghold, the ground work, the pillars on which their fame rests.

The thing to which the Negro can point with most pride, is the activity and progress made in the development of an ideal home life and the providing of a liberal education for his people. Indeed, it is worthy of note, that in both church and state, there is a growing interest in behalf of extending to all classes the privileges and benefits of at least a limited education. Nations that once thought of nothing but war and conquest are throwing their influence in the scale of popular education.

Countries that have long wielded the scepter of power, and held thousands subject to the will and opinion of one man or set of men, are being aroused to the importance of individual thought and individual responsibility. Churches and organizations that necessarily began their work with one or two as leaders, who had to do the thinking for hundreds of others, are now turning their attention to the work of training and developing the faculties and character of each one so as to enable him to think and act intelligently for himself; this is the spirit of the present age. In this lies the hope and destiny of all classes and all races.

Hence, if there be any particular problem as connected with the Negro race, in my opinion the solution of that problem will come only by following the rule of action applied to the uplifting and development of others.

The Negro is no new specie of nature; he is no new issue in the category of life; no new element in the citizenship of this country, and needs no special prescription to suit his needs. His case is one common to a people whose surroundings and environments have placed, or caused them to be placed, in a dependent attitude, and his only hope for rising above the common level of a menial slave is to so husband his resources as to change these environments and become the master of, rather than the helpless creature, of circumstances. The faithful pioneers who carried the torch of knowledge into darkened regions and cheered the lives of thousands with rays of hope and promise, opened the way for the liberation of great forces that had long lain dormant and smothered. Knowledge has been the torch in the civilizer's hand, and carrying this still we can find treasures still unearthed and truths still unlearned.

The glories already achieved in the field of science, art and literature have but aroused us to seek for still greater honors. The ray of light that has fallen across our pathway, giving hope and promise of better and brighter things further on, has but fired the zeal within us, and there is no way of satisfying this burning zeal save the feasting on the coveted goal—the riches and beauties of wisdom. One writer says: "As long as one's mind is shrouded in ignorance he is but the tool of others, and the victim of foolishness and gross absurdities. He will never experience those pleasures which come from a well-directed train of thought and which is akin to the dignity of a high nature. On the other hand, the person whose mind is illumined with the light of knowledge, and whose soul is lit up, is introduced as it were into a new world. He can trace back the stream of time to its commencement, and gliding along its downward course, can survey the most memorable events and see the dawnings of Divine Mercy and the manifestations of the Son of God in our nature." 'Tis not enough to know that we have faculties. 'Tis not sufficient to say that there lives in us the power to see, to hear, to feel, to reason, to think and to act; we must develop these powers until we can feel the benefit of the blessings that come from their use. We will never be able to reason for ourselves unless we learn to think for ourselves. The thinking mind is the active mind, and the active mind is the growing mind; the growing mind moves the man, and the man that moves helps to move the world. He moves step by step from the common level of events to things of greater height. He rises from pinnacle to pinnacle, never ceasing, never tiring, never stopping, ever growing, ever moving, ever rising till he finds the fountain head of all truth and all virtue. We are now face to face with a new order of things. Under this new regime we witness the foreshadowing of a higher sense of civilization, a higher standard of morals, a broader field of culture and a purer realm of thought.

Indeed, we are only in the shadow of this great light. 'Tis not the promise alone that brightens our sky. The dawn has appeared. The music of the morn has already been heard, and nations are awaking and rushing to crowd around the altar as worshippers at the shrine of learning. What lover of letters would doubt for a moment that if Thomas Carlyle could re-enter the world of letters and dignify the profession with the fertility of his brain, instead of captivating the world with his beautiful outline of heroes and hero worship, he would summon all his powers as an agency to do reverence, as a worshipper at the shrine, not of things material, not of men, but of *ideas.* This is the school to which we are crowding. In the development of our educational system we are enabled to find the highest ideals and center our thoughts on the highest and purest standard of life.

Only those who think, or those who seek to know the virtues of intelligence, and to enjoy the beauties of a pure and ideal life, can enter into the spirit of rejoicing over the approach of the time when each person will be measured by what is represented in his ability to exert a potent influence in shaping the destiny of things and helping to mold public sentiment. The mind can no more be allowed to remain dormant or inactive than the turf of the field, or the muscles of the body. It must be stirred up; it must be awakened from its stupor and quickened into a newness of life.

The opportunity for this general awakening was denied our parents, who were the victims of slavery, and they suffered the loss of the prestige and influence that naturally follows; but what was lost to our ancestry must be redeemed to posterity. We must center our work in the youth of our land and give them the broadest, deepest and highest training. The most liberal education should be provided for all. An education free from bias, free from proscription, free from any label that will mark them as Negro laborers, as Negro mechanics, as Negro scholars, but an education that will mark them as artisans, as skilled mechanics, as scholars, thinkers, as men and women with master minds and noble souls. In this will we find the reward for our labors and the hope of the race. I agree with the writer who says: "There is nothing to be compared with the beauty of an excellent character and the usefulness of a noble life. To the unlimited, unfettered spirit of man's mind that can rise above the mountain peaks and sweep across the ocean bounds. To that unequaled beauty of a pure and spotless soul. The whole earth, with all its beauties of art and skill, are counted as naught in the sight of God, as compared with a living creature, that represents in his body the image of his Creator, and in his mind and soul the divine principles of the mystery, the power, and glory of His Son."

'Tis not enough to know that schools and colleges exist, and to boast of the advantages and opportunities afforded us. We must lay hold upon them and become a part of them. We must, by our own efforts, out of our own means, build, own and control our own institutions for the training of our youths, and then establish enterprises of business for the practical display and use of the training received.

The great trouble about our system of education is that the masses have not yet felt the real good of it. To some it is no good, because they have simply gotten enough to misuse. You cannot satisfy a man's appetite by stopping him at the door of your dining room, where he can get only a smell of the dinner while he sees others eating. Of course he would turn away in disgust and call it all a farce. You cannot teach a man to swim by stopping him at the water's edge. You cannot convince a man that he is at the top of a mountain when you stop him at the base, where he can look up and see others above him; and you cannot show a man the virtue of education when you stop him at the school house door and deny him entrance while others crowd by and pass through. Let him in. Open the doors wide and let all come in and sit down to the intellectual feast. We want to bring the people out into the middle of the stream, into the deep water where they can be borne up by the strong tide of intellect and follow the current of popular ideas.

We must take them up and away from the foot of the mountain, place them on top, where they can bask in the sunlight of intelligence, where the atmosphere is pure and the virtue of education beams in every eye. God made man in his own image, prepared him a body, arranged for his food and raiment, stretched nature before him, and then commissioned him to go forth and subdue, replenish and have dominion over all. Yea more than this. He endowed man with reasoning faculties and for these faculties fixed no bounds; but left them to work out their own destiny and achieve their own triumphs.

I do not believe God intended for man's mind to remain undeveloped. He did not intend that His creatures should forever remain ignorant and shrouded in ignorance. Wherever He places talents there he expects to find evidence of growth and increase. Hence it is our duty to educate and prepare all for the intelligent use of what God has given them. If we expect to have a part in shaping events in this life; if we expect to be numbered among the learned, the strong, the molders of public sentiment, the masters of things material, free from abject menial servitude, we must educate the people.

Let this idea run all through our schools until it permeates the life of every boy, every girl, every man, every woman; making its influence felt in every home, every clime and among all nations.

THIRD PAPER.

WILL THE EDUCATION OF THE NEGRO SOLVE THE RACE PROBLEM?

BY PROF. KELLEY MILLER.

It is a hopeful sign when those who are vitally concerned in the outcome of the Negro problem are guided in their discussion by the light of evidence and argument, and are not impelled to foregone conclusions by transmitted prejudice and traditional bias. The article of Professor John Roach Straton in the North American Review for June, 1900, is notable for its calm, dispassionate, argumentative treatment, and for its freedom from rancor and venom. His conclusions, therefore, if erroneous, are all the more damaging because of the evident sincerity and helpful intention of the author.

With much erudition and argumentative skill Professor Straton sets forth the proposition that education has failed to check the Negro's degenerating tendencies or to fit him for his "strange and abnormal environment."

There are two leading divisions of the race problem:

1. The development of a backward race.
2. The adjustment of two races with widely divergent ethnic characteristics.

These two factors are, in the mind of many, antagonistic to each other. The more backward and undeveloped the Negro, the easier is the process of his adjustment to the white race; but when you give him "Greek and Latin and eyeglasses" frictional problems inevitably arise. Under slavery this adjustment was complete, but the bond of adjustment was quickly burst asunder when the Negro was made a free man and clothed with full political and civil privilege. The one great question which so far remains unanswerable is, can the two be readjusted on terms of equality? The solution of social problems belongs to the realm of statesmanship, philanthropy and religion. The function of education is to develop latent faculties. It was a shallow philosophy which prophesied that a few years of schooling on the part of the Negro would solve the race question. If the education of the colored man has not worked out the fulfillment which its propounders prophesied, it simply proves them to be poor prophets. The Negro, too, believed that if he could only learn to read and write, and especially if he could go to college, that he would be relieved of every incumbrance that beset him. Education was looked upon as an end and not as an agency. As his friends were destined to disappointment, the Negro himself was doomed to humiliation and chagrin. Education creates as many problems as it solves. It is both static and dynamical. When Professor Straton says, therefore, that education has not solved the race problem, he utters a truism. But if he means to imply that it has not had a wholesome effect upon the life of the Negro, his conclusion verges upon the absurd.

We are apt to be misled by the statistics showing the decline of illiteracy among Negroes. All those who can read and write are set apart as educated persons, as if this mere mechanical information had worked some great transformation in their nature. The fact is a very small per cent of the race is educated in any practical or efficient sense. The simple ability to read and write is of the least possible benefit to a backward race. What advantage would it be to the red Indians to be able to trace the letters of the English alphabet with a pen, or to vocalize the printed characters into syllables and sentences? Unless the moral nature is touched and the vital energies aroused there would be no improvement in conduct or increase in practical efficiency. Education has a larger function for a backward than for a forward race. To the latter it merely furnishes a key to an existing lock, while to the former it must supply both lock and key. The pupil who is already acquainted with the nature and conditions of a problem may need only a suggestion as to a skillful or lucky combination of parts in order to lead to its solution; whereas to one ignorant of the underlying facts and factors such suggestion would be worse than useless.

Even much of the so-called higher education of the Negro has been only a process of artificially forcing a mass of refined information into a system which had no digestive or assimilative apparatus. Such education produces no more nourishment or growth than would result from forcing sweetmeats down the throat of an alligator. Of education in its true sense the Negro has had very little. The great defect of the Negro's nature is his lack of individual initiative, growing out of his feeble energy of will. To overcome this difficulty, his training should be judiciously adapted and sensibly applied to his needs. Industrial training will supply the method and the higher culture the motive.

Professor Straton tells us that $100,000,000 have already been expended upon the education of this race. Princely as this sum seems to be, it is nevertheless utterly insignificant when compared with the magnitude of the task to which it has been applied. The city of New York alone spends $15,000,000 annually for educational purposes. And yet if we are to believe the rumors of corruption and the low state of municipal morality it will be seen that education has not yet done its perfect work in our great metropolis. Then why should we rave at the heart and froth at the mouth because a sum of money, scarcely equal to a third of the educational expenditure of a single American city, though distributed over a period of thirty years and scattered over a territory of a million square miles, has not completely civilized a race of 8,000,000 degraded souls?

The whites maintain that they impose taxes upon themselves for the education of the blacks. This is only one of the many false notions of political economy which have done so much to blight the prosperity of the South. Labor pays every tax in the world; and although the laborer may not enjoy the privilege of passing the tribute to the tax taker, he is nevertheless entitled to share in all of the privileges which his toil makes possible. And besides children are not educated because their parents are taxpayers, but in order that they may become more helpful and efficient members of the community. It would be wisdom on the part of the South to place the future generations under bonded debt, if necessary, for the education of its ignorant population, white and black. This would be far more statesmanlike than to transmit to them a legacy of ignorance, degradation and crime. Pride in a political theory should no longer prevent the appeal to national aid to remove the threatening curse.

Professor Straton underestimates the effect of culture upon a backward race when he minimizes the value of individual emergence. The individual is the proof of the race. The conception of progress has always found lodgment in the mind of some select individuals, whence it has trickled down to the masses below. May it not be that the races which have withered before the breath of civilization, have faded because they failed to produce individuals with sufficient intelligence, courage and good sense to wisely guide and direct their path? What names can the red Indian present to match Benjamin Banneker or Booker T. Washington, Frederick Douglass or Paul Laurence Dunbar? The Negro has contributed four hundred patented inventions to the mechanical genius of his country; how many has the aborigne contributed? The congressional library has collected fourteen hundred books and pamphlets by Negro authors. These works are, of course, in the main, commonplace or indifferent. But a people who have the ambition to write poor books will soon gain the ability to make good ones. Have any of the vanished races shown such aptitude for civilization? But these are exceptions. So are the eminent men of any race. When the exceptions become too numerous it is rather poor logic to urge them in proof of the rule. It is also a mistake to suppose that these picked individuals are without wholesome influence upon the communal life. They are diffusive centers of light scattered throughout the whole race. These grains of leaven will actually leaven the whole lump.

"We take these savages from their simple life and their low plane of evolution and attempt to give them an enlightenment for which the stronger races have prepared themselves by ages of growth." There is in this utterance a tinge of the feeling which actuated the laborers who had borne the heat and burden of the day when they objected to the eleventh hour intruders being received on equal terms with themselves. One answer suffices for both: "Other men have labored, and ye are entered into their labors." It is true that the Negro misses evolution and his adjustment to his environment is made the more difficult on that account. Education, therefore, is all the more essential and vital. The chasm between civilization and savagery must be bridged by education. The boy learns in a few years what it took the race ages to acquire. A repetition of the slow steps and stages by which progress has been secured is impossible. Attachment to civilization must take place at its highest point, just as we set a graft upon the most vigorous and healthy limb of a tree, and not upon a decadent stem. Must the Negro dwell for generations upon Anglo-Saxon stems and Cancerian diction before he is introduced to modern forms of English speech? The child of the African slave is under the same linguistic necessity as the offspring of Depew and Gladstone. He must leap, *instanter,* from primitive mode of locomotion to the steamboat, the electric car and the automobile. Of course many will be lost in the endeavor to sustain the stress and strain. Civilization is a saver of life into life and death into death. Japan is the best living illustration of the rapid acquisition of civilization. England can utilize no process of art or invention that is not equally invaluable to the oriental islanders. This has been accomplished by this young and vigorous people mainly through the education of picked youth. Herein lies the only salvation of the Negro race.

In the meantime the dual nature of the solution and its relative importance to both races is clearly indicated by Voltaire, the great French savant: "It is more meritorious and more difficult to wean men from their prejudices than to civilize the barbarian."

FOURTH PAPER.

WILL THE EDUCATION OF THE NEGRO SOLVE THE RACE PROBLEM?

BY C. H. TURNER.

The War of the rebellion is over, Negro slavery in America is no more, and the days of reconstruction have passed into history.

Dr. DuBois in speaking of that period wrote: "Amid it all two figures ever stand to typify that day to coming men: the one a gray-haired gentlemen, whose fathers had quit themselves like men, whose sons lay in nameless graves; who bowed to the evil of slavery because its abolition boded untold ill to all; who stood at last, in the evening of life, a blighted, ruined form, with hate in his eyes. And the other a form black with the mist of centuries, and aforetime bent in love over the white master's cradle, rocked his sons and daughters to sleep, and closed in death the sunken eyes of his wife to the world; aye, too, had laid herself low to his lusts and borne a tawny man child to the world, only to see her dark boy's limbs scattered to the winds by midnight marauders riding after niggers. These were the saddest sights of that woeful day; and no man clasped the hands of these two passing figures of the present-past, but hating they went to their long home, and hating their children's children live to-day."

Would some power had clasped the hands of these "two fleeting figures of the present-past!" Then those "marauders chasing niggers" would have been subdued and there would not be so many bloody threads in the weft of the history the New South has been weaving.

The "gray-haired gentleman" has left a grandson who has all the culture and education money and thrift can buy. He is thrifty and

Prof. C. H. Turner

PROF. CHARLES HENRY TURNER, M. S.

Charles Henry Turner was born at Cincinnati, Ohio, February 3, 1867. Both parents were of Negro descent. His mother was a Kentucky girl and his father a Canadian. Both parents were temperate and Christian in habits. Neither parent was college-bred, yet Charles' father was a well-read man, a keen thinker, and a master of debate. He had surrounded himself with several hundred choice books and one of the earliest ambitions of Charles was to learn to read these books.

The only education of our subject was obtained in the excellent public schools of Cincinnati, Ohio. From the Walnut Hills District School Charles passed to the Gaines High School, from which he graduated valedictorian of his class. From High School he passed to the University of Cincinnati, from which he graduated in 1891 wth the B. S. degree, and in 1892 with the M. S. degree.

When a youth in college, Charles hoped some day to be the head of a technological or agricultural school for Negroes, and much time and money was expended mastering those essentials that the head of a school should know. That youthful day dream has never been realized, but Charles has been an active teacher for years. Even before graduation he taught one year in the Governor Street School at Evansville, Indiana, and occasionally taught, as a substitute, in the public schools of Cincinnati, Ohio. From 1891 to 1893 he was assistant in Biology at the University of Cincinnati, Ohio. Since then he has been Professor of Biology at Clark University, South Atlanta, Ga. In 1901 he was dean of the Georgia Summer School.

By training Prof. Turner is a biologist who has contributed his mite towards the advancement of his favorite science. In the following list of some of the principal publications of Prof. Turner, those marked with an asterisk are contributions to biology.

*Morphology of the Avian Brain; "Jour. of Comp. Neur." (1891), 100 pp. 8 pls.

*A Few Characteristics of the Avian Brain. "Science" (1891).

*Psychological Notes on the Gallery Spider. "Jour. of Comp. Neur." (1892).

*Notes on the Clodocera, Ostracoda and Rotifera of Cincinnati. "Bull. Sci. Lab. of Den. Univ." (1892), 17 pp., 2 pls.

*Additional Notes on the Clodocera and Ostracoda of Cincinnati, 18 pp., (1893), 2 pls. *Ibid*.

*Notes on the American Ostracoda. *Ibid*, 11 pp., 2 pls.

*Preliminary Note on the Nervous System of the Genus Cypris. "Jour. Comp. Neur." (1893), 5 pp., 3 pls.

*Morphology of the Nervous System of Cypris. *Ibid*, (1896), 24 pp., 6 pls.

*Synopsis of the Entomostraca of Minnesota, etc., C. L. Herrick and C. H. Turner (1895), 525 pp., 81 pls. [C. H. Turner is only part author of this.]

Numerous abstracts and translations from German and French published in the Jour. of Comp. Neur.

Reason for Teaching Biology in Negro Schools. "Southwestern Christian Advocate" (1897).

Object of Negro Memorial Day (1899).

New Year Thoughts About the Negro. "Southwestern Christian Advocate" (1899).

*Notes on the Mushroom Bodies of the Invertebrates. "Zoological Bulletin" (1899), 6 pp., 6 figs.

*A Male Erpetocypris Barbatus, Forbes. "Zool. Bulletin" (1899).

*Synopsis of North American Invertebrates. V. Fresh-Water Ostracoda. "Amer. Naturalist" (1899), 11 pp.

Living Dust. "Southwestern Christian Advocate" (1901), xiii chapter.

*The Mushroom Bodies of the Crayfish and their Histological Environment. "Jour. of Comp. Neur." (1901), 50 pp., 4 pls.

enterprising, law-abiding and conscientious. He has inherited prejudices, yet he is sincere. He loves the South no less than did his grandfather; but he loves the Union more. He would die to save the Union;
he lives to glorify the South. He is known as the new Southerner and
he is evolving a New South.

The "marauder chasing niggers" has left a grandson who is illiterate, uncultured and thriftless. He despises manual labor, but is too
poor and too ignorant to live without doing it. Unfit to be the associate of the new Southerner, and feeling himself too superior to mingle
with Negroes, he broods over his hardships and bemoans his fate. He
is a Negro hater and thirsts for the excitement of a lynching bee. This
condoned clog to the progress of Southern civilization is known as
white trash.

The "form black with the mist of centuries" has left two grandsons.

One is a thrifty, law-abiding gentleman; too thrifty to be a beggar
and too busy acquiring an education or accumulating wealth or educating his race to be a loafer or criminal. In his home are all the comforts of modern life that his purse can afford. He loves his country
and his Southland, and is educating his children to do likewise. He
even contributes his mite to the literature, science and art of to-day.
He is modest and retiring and is known as the new Negro.

The other grandchild is a thriftless loafer. He is not willing to pay
the price of an education; but he likes to appear intellectually bright
and entertaining. He often works, but merely to obtain the means for
gratifying his abnormally developed appetites. He laughs, he dances,
he frolics. He knows naught of the value of time nor of the deeper
meanings of life. In the main he is peaceable and law-abiding; but,
under the excitement of the moment, is capable of even the worst of
crimes. This thriftless slave of passion, this child-man, this much condemned clog to the progress of Southern civilization is called the
vagrant Negro.

Prejudice is older than this age. A comparative study of animal
psychology teaches that all animals are prejudiced against animals
unlike themselves, and the more unlike they are the greater the prejudice. A comparative study of history teaches that races are prejudiced
against races unlike themselves, and the greater the difference the
more the prejudice. Among men, however, dissimilarity of minds is
a more potent factor in causing prejudice than unlikeness of physiog-

nomy. Races whose religious beliefs are unlike the accepted beliefs of our race we call heathens; those whose habits of living fall below the ideals of our own race we call uncivilized. In both cases we are prejudiced. When a highly civilized race is brought in contact with another people unlike it in physiognomy but in the same stage of intellectual advancement, at first each is prejudiced against the other; but when they become thoroughly acquainted prejudice gives way to mutual respect. For an example of this recall the relations of the nations of Europe to the Japanese.

The new Southerner is prejudiced against the new Negro because he feels that the Negro is very unlike him. He does not know that a similar education and a like environment have made the new Negro and himself alike in everything except color and features. Did he but know this he and the new Negro would join hands and work for the best interest of the South and there would be no Negro problem. At present he does not and cannot know this, for the white trash and vagrant Negro form a wedge separating the new Southerner from the new Negro so completely that they cannot know each other. Every unmentionable crime committed by the vagrant Negro, every lynching bee conducted by white trash, every Negro disfranchisement law passed by misguided legislators, every unjust discrimination against the Negro by the people drives this wedge deeper and deeper.

Render this wedge so thin that it will no longer be a barrier and the Negro problem is solved. This cannot be done by banishing white trash and the vagrant Negro; for that is neither possible nor practicable. The only way to accomplish the thinning of this wedge is to transform a large number into the new Southerners and the new Negroes. Will education do this?

In order to transform the majority of white trash and vagrant Negroes into new Southerners and new Negroes it will be necessary to instill into them the following regenerating virtues:

1. The manners of a gentleman. Not the swagger of the dude nor the cringing of a scapegoat, but the manners of a being permeated with the Golden Rule.

2. Cultured homes. Not necessarily extravagant mansions, but comfortable dwellings, wherein impoliteness, intemperance, slander and indecent tales have given place to politeness, temperance, intelligent conversation and refined pleasantries.

3. Business honesty. Not only punctual in the payment of debts, but also truthful in making sales.

4. Thrift. Not the ability to hoard as a miser does, but the ability to spend one's earnings economically, to purchase property and to lay by a little for a rainy day.

5. Christian morality. Not the ability to shout well, and pray well and testify well, but the ability to live the Christ life.

6. The ability to do something well that the world desires bad enough to be willing to pay a good price for it. This includes not only mechanical but also commercial and scholastic achievements.

7. Ability to lead in the light of modern civilization.

8. Love for justice and contempt for lawlessness.

Experience and thought convince me that the "highest education" is the only agency that will instill all of these virtues into a people without detriment to the multitudes that are forced to stop school before graduation. Highest education is a new phrase; but can we not truthfully say that there are three system of education in the world to-day: the lower or industrial education, the higher education and the highest education?

In each of these three systems the student begins his education by an attempt to master the English branches, and in each attention is given to developing the moral side of the pupil.

In the lower or industrial education, parallel with the elementary English training, or after its completion, the student learns how to work at one or more trades, but he gets no training in the higher English branches nor in languages nor science. This system may instill into students the majority of the regenerating virtues mentioned above, but it is impossible for this system to impart the ability to lead in the light of modern civilization. Without this virtue one is not fit to lead in this strenuous age. A race without competent leaders is doomed, and any system of education which does not furnish such leaders is defective and doomed. It has been well said that the advocates of the lower or industrial education are welding a chain that will bind the race in industrial servitude for ages.

In the higher education, after completing an elementary English training, the individual takes a collegiate course in science, literature, history and language; but no attention is given to industrial training. Such a course does instill into those who complete it all of the regenerating virtues mentioned above; but how about the multitudes that necessity forces to drop out before the course is completed? It is a sad, sad fact that the taste they have had of something different renders them not content to be servants, yet their training is not sufficient to enable them to be anything else.

In the highest education a thorough training is given in the common English branches, but parallel with it instruction is imparted in the care and practical use of tools. The elementary course is followed by a secondary course, in which, along with instruction in the elements of languages, literature and sciences, is given a thorough training in some trade. Above this come the colleges and technological schools, wherein the pupil specializes according to his natural tastes. In its ability to instill into those who complete it the regenerating virtues mentioned above this highest education ranks with the higher education. In this respect neither is superior to the other. But when it comes to fitting those who stop before the complete course has been mastered to successfully fight the battle of life, then highest education is infinitely superior to the higher education. Indeed it is the only education that helps abundantly not only the graduates, but also those unfortunate legions that drop out while yet undergraduates.

In attempting to solve the Negro problem, the industrial or lower education has been tried on the Negro and found wanting; the higher education has been tried upon both races and has succeeded but little better than the lower education; if we will cast aside our prejudices and try the highest education upon both white and black, in a few decades there will be no Negro problem.

Clark University, December 1, 1901.

Mrs. Rosetta D. Sprague

ROSETTA DOUGLASS SPRAGUE.

The subject of this sketch was born in New Bedford, Mass., June 24, 1839. She is the oldest child and the only living daughter of the late Frederick Douglass. At the age of five years she moved with her parents to Lynn, Mass., where the first narrative of Frederick Douglass, written by himself, was published. Its publication attracted widespread notice and stirred the ire of slaveholders in the vicinity from which he escaped. His many friends fearing for his safety arranged to send him abroad.

His wife has often told of the demonstrative and enthusiastic young father catching up his infant daughter and fervently thanking God that his child was born free and no man could separate them. Among the many friends who were solicitous for the family were two maiden ladies, Abigail and Lydia Mott, of Albany, New York, who were cousins of Lucretia Mott, the well-known philanthropist and friend of the Negro. These women, who conducted a lucrative business on Broadway, opposite Bleeker Hall, were also staunch Abolitionists. Being anxious for the welfare of the little six-year-old daughter of Douglass, they sought the privilege of caring for her while the father was abroad. The wife and three sons remained at their home in Lynn during the father's absence. Mrs. Sprague has frequently spoken of her stay with the Motts, who were in good circumstances, and with their one servant lived in comfort. Their little charge was amply provided for, and was made contented and happy. She had a time for play and a time for study. Miss Abigail gave her instruction in reading and writing and Miss Lydia taught her to sew.

At the age of seven Rosetta wrote her first letter to her father, and when her eighth birthday had passed she made a shirt to give him on his return from England. At this early age the child was painfully conscious of the trials and misery resulting from slavery. Many slaves had sought and obtained shelter with the Motts, and the anxious moments of their stay made a deep impression on her childish mind.

After the establishment of the "North Star," by her father in Rochester, N. Y., in 1847, the family were reunited in that place, a governess secured and for several months the children pursued their studies at home. Later the father was convinced that as he was a taxpayer he ought to avail himself of the privilege of the public schools; and, accordingly, sent his sons there. But the little daughter was sent to a private school but recently opened for girls. Tuition was paid in advance, the little girl was sent, but never saw the inside of the school-room nor met any of the pupils. Finally she with her brothers attended the public schools until the year 1850, when the Board of Education decided that Colored children should no longer be permitted to remain in the public schools. At the next meeting of the Board Mr. Douglass and some Anti-Slavery friends were present to debate the question why such distinction should be made. As the result of that conference the doors were opened to Colored children in that city.

Rosetta being the only girl of color in her room was subjected for a time to such indignities as only the vulgar are capable of inflicting. Her complaints pained her fond father, but his counsel was, "Daughter, I am sending you to school for your benefit; see to it that you are punctual in attendance, that you do not offend in your demeanor and cope with the best of them in your lessons—and await the results." The daughter strove to obey, and soon found herself appreciated by her teachers, who classed her as one of their best pupils. Her companions also changed and sought her aid in the preparation of their lessons. At the age of eleven years Rosetta became her father's assistant in the library. She copied for him, wrapped, addressed and mailed eight hundred copies of the "North Star" each week.

Rosetta Douglass married December 24, 1863, Nathan Sprague, who, like her father, had been a victim of the slave-holding power.

TOPIC X.

WHAT ROLE IS THE EDUCATED NEGRO WOMAN TO PLAY IN THE UPLIFTING OF HER RACE?

BY MRS. R. D. SPRAGUE.

The problems of life are manifold. Wherever we turn questions of moment are presented to us for solution and settlement. At no period in the history of the American Negro has his status as a man and an American citizen been so closely scrutinized and criticised as at the present time.

The galling chain and merciless lash were the instruments used to accomplish the humiliation and degradation of the African. Avarice was the factor in the composition of the character of a large number of the white men of America that wrought such ravishes in the well-being of the African.

To-day, after the short space of thirty-six years has passed over him, from the deep degradation of centuries the descendants of these Africans are wrestling with the situation as it exists to-day. Through the avarice of the white man in the past the black man's physical, moral and mental development was sacrificed. To-day egotism stalks abroad to crush, if possible, his hopes and his aims, while he is struggling from the effects of his thraldom.

This latter process is more subtle in its operation—placing, as it does, a weapon that can with confidence be used by the most inferior and degraded ones of the white race—so that *color* and not *character* is made the determining factor of respectability and worth, and as the target is to the archer, so is the Negro to the white man.

Notwithstanding that the presentation of such facts are not flattering to the white man or pleasurable to the black man, they are facts which are to be considered.

Rapid changes have already been wrought in the condition of the American Negro. His capabilities and possibilities as a factor in the nation have been marked and encouraging, and yet there are labors to be performed to further obtain and maintain his position in the land of his birth. The Negro is but a man, with the frailties that bound humanity, and cannot be expected to rid himself of them in any way different from methods adopted for the betterment of mankind generally. In view of much that has inspired the friends of the Negro in the years now past with faith in him and the interest and belief in him of his numerous friends at the present time, he is still an object of hatred to a considerable number of his fellow citizens.

Ages of deception, vice, cruelty and crime, as practiced by the Caucasian upon the African in this land, would in itself produce fruit in kind. We would submit a suggestion to those who are disposed to criticise very closely and to condemn in strong terms the delinquencies of the Negro. Allow the Negro two hundred and fifty years of *unselfish* contact to offset the two hundred and fifty years of Caucasian selfishness, and be as assiduous in his regeneration as you were in his degradation—then judge him.

The twentieth century in its infancy is striving to grasp what it pleases to call the Negro problem, when it is in reality only a question as to whether justice and right shall rule over injustice and wrong to any and every man regardless of race in this boasted land of freedom. The Negro is made the test in everything pertaining to American civilization. Its high principles of religion, politics and morals all receive a shock when a Negro's head appears, upsetting all theories and in a conspicuous manner proving that the structure of American civilization is built higher than the average white man can climb. At this stage of Afro-American existence the question is asked, "What role is the educated Negro woman to play in the uplifting of her race?"

As this is unquestionably the woman's era, the question is timely and proper. Every race and nation that is at all progressive has its quota of earnest women engaged in creating for themselves a higher sphere of usefulness to the world—insisting upon the necessity of a higher plane of integrity and worth—and thus the women of the Negro race should be no exception in this land of our birth. Feeling thus, this particular woman, previous to the question above presented, has already in considerable numbers formed various associations tending to the amelioration of existing conditions surrounding her race. The most notable of them is "The National Association of Colored Women," for several years presided over by Mrs. Mary Church Terrell of Washington, D. C., but now under the guidance of Mrs. J. Salome Yates, a woman of refinement, culture and education and an earnest worker in the cause of the advancement of the race. It is with pride I point to this body of women, as its scope is far-reaching, being composed of organizations from every part of the country.

There is no woman, certainly no woman in the United States, who has more reason to desire and more need to aspire for better opportunities for her brothers and herself than the Negro woman in general and the educated Negro woman in particular.

Avarice and egotism have done and is doing its work in retarding, but not entirely subjugating, the advances that a respectable number of the race are making.

The task that confronts the thoughtful woman as she surveys the field in which she must labor is not a reassuring one. It will be through a slow process that any good will be accomplished.

Much patient and earnest endeavor on the part of our women—a strong missionary spirit needs to be exhibited before any appreciable results may be reached. It will require the life-work for many years to rescue even a fractional part from the condition of to-day. Not only has the Negro race to be uplifted but the white race need to stand on a stronger platform than that of egotistical display of virtues which are not wholly theirs.

As long as they deny to the Negro the fact of his brotherhood and his consequent rights as a man, they are false to their God, and to the nation. Happily for us there have been a considerable number of the white race who are mindful of what is due to those of a race whose tendencies are upward and onward.

It is with feelings of deep gratitude, love and respect when we reflect upon the great work that was accomplished in the nineteenth century for the Negro by the truly great and good men and women of the white race. Now the twentieth century is confronted with the fact that there is more work yet to do, and the Negro has his part to bear in it. The progress of the race means much to the Negro woman, and as she goes forth adding her best energies to the uplifting of her people the work in itself will react upon her, and from a passive individual she will be a more alert and useful factor in the regeneration of her race and to the social system at large.

How to begin the work in a systematic manner for the further advancement of a people struggling amidst so much that is discouraging is puzzling to the would-be reformers within our own ranks. We would have the Negro, now that the mantle of freedom is thrown over him, and also as an acknowledged citizen, to fully understand and appreciate the fact that now that his destiny is in his own hands that he must make of himself a potential value.

In order to emphasize himself as a factor of value he must place himself in touch with the highest and best thought of past and present times.

Barring the barriers that avarice has placed in our way in the past or the growing egotism of our brothers in white at this stage of our progress, the women of the Negro race should put themselves in contact with all the women of this land and espouse all worthy efforts for the advancement of the human race.

The educated Negro woman will find that her greatest field for effective work is in the home. The attributes that are necessary in forming an upright character are each of them facts, the acceptance of them making or marring the character as they are accepted or ignored.

In view of this thought I cannot see that any different role should be adopted by us than by women in general in this land.

Industry, honesty and morality are the cardinal attributes to become acquainted with in forming an irreproachable character, and each and all of them must be dwelt upon in the home. Already the mothers all over the country are uniting themselves in the one thought—*the home.* No less should our women esteem it essential to place themselves in line with the progressive mothers in our common country. In advancing such a thought we are confronted with the fact that the development of the homes of this land has not been a day's work, and the improvement of the character of the homes will test the energies of the women who preside over them. The home life of the Negro has taken on a new significance during the past thirty or more years, and the zeal required to show the parents to-day their duties in the rearing of their children should be untiring. We have a few among us that are interested workers for the maintenance of good government in the home.

We would that in every city, town and village, where any number of the race reside, they would form aid societies for the maintenance of kindergartens and industrial schools, as well as to aid those already established, and before the twentieth century has reached its quarter century mark "The Colored Woman's Aid Societies" would have an astonishing effect on the manners and morals of those who come under its benefits.

It is a source of regret and deep concern to a number of our women that there is so little attention paid to the labors of "The Woman's Christian Temperance Union," when we reflect that through the medium of rum, and, I may add, red beads, African homes were devastated. We wonder at the apathy of our women in the matter of temperance. The homes of the race can but be humble and poverty-stricken so long as the men and women in them are intemperate. The educated women among us need to set the pace in discountenancing the social glass in their homes. In this transition stage toward a higher plane of civilization we need every faculty pure and undefiled to do the work that will lift us to a merited place in our land. Surely our women must see the necessity of urgent endeavor against a traffic fraught with so much that is inimical to the promotion of good citizenship and purer and better homes.

From the word of God we receive decided instructions against strong drink, as in the instance of the instructions concerning the character of John—his work was to be such that all his energies were to be called in action, and there was to be no weakening of them. "He was to be great in the sight of the Lord, and shall drink neither wine nor strong drink." We have a great work to perform in meeting the demands of the hour, requiring all the energy possible of a brain unclouded—pure and unsullied. The motto of the National Association of Colored Women, "Lifting as we climb," is in itself an inspiration to great activity in all moral reforms; and with a spirit of devotion for the welfare of humanity we embrace the work of the Woman's Christian Temperance Union in their motto, "For God and Home and Native Land."

If the educated Negro woman will rally to the support of the principles involved in the organizations already presented in this paper, I think they will be amply repaid in the results accruing from their labors.

SECOND PAPER.

WHAT ROLE IS THE EDUCATED NEGRO WOMAN TO PLAY IN THE UPLIFTING OF HER RACE?

BY MRS. MARY CHURCH TERRELL,
PRESIDENT OF THE NATIONAL ASSOCIATION OF COLORED WOMEN.

Should any one ask what special phase of the Negro's development makes me most hopeful of his ultimate triumph over present obstacles, I should answer unhesitatingly, it is the magnificent work the women are doing to regenerate and uplift the race. Judge the future of colored women by the past since their emancipation, and neither they nor their friends have any cause for anxiety.

For years, either banding themselves into small companies or struggling alone, colored women have worked with might and main to improve the condition of their people. The necessity of systematizing their efforts and working on a larger scale became apparent not many years ago and they decided to unite their forces. Thus it happened that in the summer of 1896 the National Association of Colored Women was formed by the union of two large organizations, each of which has done much to show our women the advantage of concerted action. So tenderly has this daughter of the organized womanhood of the race been nurtured and so wisely ministered unto, that it has grown to be a child hale, hearty and strong, of which its fond mothers have every reason to be proud. Handicapped though its members have been, because they lacked both money and experience, their efforts have, for the most part, been crowned with success in the twenty-six States where it has been represented.

Kindergartens have been established by some of our organizations, from which encouraging reports have come. A sanitarium with a training school for nurses has been set on such a firm foundation by the Phyllis Wheatley Club of New Orleans, Louisiana, and has proved itself to be such a blessing to the entire community that the municipal government has voted it an annual appropriation of several hundred dollars. By the Tuskegee, Alabama, branch of the association the work of bringing the light of knowledge and the gospel of cleanliness to their poor benighted sisters on the plantations has been conducted with signal success. Their efforts have thus far been confined to four estates, comprising thousands of acres of land, on which live hundreds of colored people, yet

Mrs. Mary Church Terrell

MRS. MARY CHURCH TERRELL.

In all matters affecting the interests of the women of her race, Mrs. Mary Church Terrell, of Washington, D. C., is a leading spirit. Three times in succession she was elected President of the National Association of Colored Women by most flattering majorities. When, according to the provision of the constitution, which limits the term of officers, Mrs. Terrell could not be re-elected president, she was made Honorary President.

She has twice been invited to address the National Woman Suffrage Association at its annual convention in Washington. Her public utterances have always made a profound impression on her hearers and no speakers associated with her have received more applause from audiences or higher praise from the public press than herself. Not many years ago when Congress, by resolution granted power to the Commissioners of the District of Columbia to appoint two women on the Board of Education for the public schools, Mrs. Terrell was one of the women appointed. She served in the board for five years with great success and signal ability.

Mrs. Terrell is the only woman who has ever held the office of President of the Bethel Literary and Historical Association at Washington, the foremost and oldest Lyceum established and controlled by colored people in America. Her splendid work as presiding officer of this organization had much to do with her other subsequent success in attaining similar positions in other bodies of deliberation.

Mrs. Terrell's life has been an interesting one. She was born in Memphis, Tenn., of well-to-do parents.

She graduated at Oberlin College in 1884 with the degree of A. B. In 1888 she received the degree of A. M. from Oberlin. She was for a while a teacher at Wilberforce University at Xenia, Ohio. In 1887 she was appointed teacher of languages in the Colored High School at Washington. She went abroad for further study and travel in 1888 and remained in Europe two years, spending the time in France, Switzerland, Germany and Italy. She resumed her work in Washington in 1890. In 1891 she was offered the registrarship of Oberlin College, being the first woman of her race to whom such a position was ever tendered by an institution so widely known and of such high standard. This place was declined because of her approaching marriage. In 1891 she was married to Mr. Robert H. Terrell, who is a graduate of Howard College and who was recently appointed by President Roosevelt to a Federal Judgeship in the District of Columbia, being one of the two colored men first to receive this high distinction. Mrs. Terrell has a daughter whom she has named Phyllis, in honor of Phyllis Wheatley, the black woman whose verses received the commendation of George Washington and many other distinguished men of her time.

Mrs. Terrell is now engaged by a lecture bureau. She has traveled extensively in the West, speaking before large audiences and everywhere her talks have received the highest praise. The Danville, Ill., "Daily News," speaking of her address before the Chautauqua of that town, says:

"Mrs. Terrell's addresses are the pure gold with less dross of nonsense than any lecturer that has come upon the stage at this Chautauqua. From the first word to the last she has something to say, and says it as a cultured lady in the best of English, which has no tinge of the high falootin or the sensational. Such speakers are rare. She should be paid to travel as a model of good English and good manners."

Mrs. Terrell's eloquent utterances and chaste diction make a deep impression, which must have influence in the final shaping of the vexed problems that confront the Negro race in this country. Her exceptional attainments and general demeanor are a wonderful force in eradicating the prejudice against colored women. She is making an opening for her sisters as no one else is doing or has ever done.

in the darkness of ignorance and the grip of sin, miles away from churches and schools.

Plans for aiding the indigent, orphaned and aged have been projected and in some instances have been carried into successful execution. One club in Memphis, Tennessee, has purchased a large tract of land, on which it intends to erect an old folk's home, part of the money for which has already been raised. Splendid service has been rendered by the Illinois Federation of Colored Women's Clubs, through whose instrumentality schools have been visited, truant children looked after, parents and teachers urged to co-operate with each other, rescue and reform work engaged in, so as to reclaim unfortunate women and tempted girls, public institutions investigated, garments cut, made and distributed to the needy poor.

Questions affecting our legal status as a race are sometimes agitated by our women. In Tennessee and Louisiana colored women have several times petitioned the legislature of their respective States to repeal the obnoxious Jim Crow car laws. In every way possible we are calling attention to the barbarity of the convict lease system, of which Negroes and especially the female prisoners are the principal victims, with the hope that the conscience of the country may be touched and this stain on its escutcheon be forever wiped away. Against the one room cabin we have inaugurated a vigorous crusade. When families of eight or ten men, women and children are all huddled promiscuously together in a single apartment, a condition common among our poor all over the land, there is little hope of inculcating morality and modesty. And yet in spite of the fateful heritage of slavery, in spite of the manifold pitfalls and peculiar temptations to which our girls are subjected, and though the safeguards usually thrown around maidenly youth and innocence are in some sections entirely withheld from colored girls, statistics compiled by men not inclined to falsify in favor of my race show that immorality among colored women is not so great as among women in some foreign countries who are equally ignorant, poor and oppressed.

Believing that it is only through the home that a people can become really good and truly great the National Association has entered that sacred domain. Homes, more homes, better homes, purer homes is the text upon which sermons have been and will be preached. There has been a determined effort to have heart to heart talks with our women that we may strike at the root of evils, many of which lie at the fireside.

If the women of the dominant race, with all the centuries of education, culture and refinement back of them, with all the wealth of opportunity ever present with them, feel the need of a mother's congress, that they may be enlightened upon the best methods of rearing their children and conducting their homes, how much more do our women, from whom shackles have but yesterday been stricken, need information on the same vital subjects. And so the association is working vigorously to establish mothers' congresses on a small scale, wherever our women can be reached.

From this brief and meager account of the work which has been and is still being accomplished by colored women through the medium of their clubs, it is easy to observe how earnest and effective have been their efforts to elevate their race. No people need ever despair whose women are fully aroused to the duties which rest upon them and are willing to shoulder responsibilities which they alone can successfully assume. The scope of our endeavors is constantly widening. Into the various channels of generosity and beneficence we are entering more and more every day.

Some of our women are now urging their clubs to establish day nurseries, a charity of which there is an imperative need. Thousands of our wage-earning mothers with large families dependent almost entirely upon them for support are obliged to leave their children all day, entrusted to the care of small brothers and sisters, or some good-natured neighbor who promises much, but who does little. Some of these infants are locked alone in the room from the time the mother leaves in the morning, until she returns at night. Not long ago I read in a Southern newspaper that an infant thus locked alone in a room all day, while its mother went out to wash, had cried itself to death. When one reflects upon the slaughter of the innocents which is occurring with pitiless persistency every day and thinks of the multitudes who are maimed for life or are rendered imbecile because of the treatment received during their helpless infancy, it is evident that by establishing day nurseries colored women will render one of the greatest services possible to humanity and to the race.

Nothing lies nearer the heart of colored women than the children. We feel keenly the need of kindergartens and are putting forth earnest efforts to honey-comb this country with them from one extremity to the other. The more unfavorable the environments of children the more necessary is it that steps be taken to counteract baleful influences upon innocent victims. How imperative is it then that as colored women we inculcate correct principles and set good examples for our own youth whose little feet will have so many thorny paths of temptation, injustice and prejudice to tread. So keenly alive is the National Association to the necessity of rescuing our little ones whose evil nature alone is encouraged to develop and whose noble qualities are deadened and dwarfed by the very atmosphere which they breathe, that its officers are trying to raise money with which to send out a kindergarten organizer, whose duty it shall be to arouse the conscience of our women and to establish kindergartens wherever means therefor can be secured.

Through the children of to-day we believe we can build the foundation of the next generation upon such a rock of morality, intelligence and strength, that the floods of proscription, prejudice and persecution may descend upon it in torrents and yet it will not be moved. We hear a great deal about the race problem and how to solve it. The real solution of the race problem lies in the children, both so far as we who are oppressed and those who oppress us are concerned. Some of our women who have consecrated their lives to the elevation of their race feel that neither individuals nor organizations working toward this end should be entirely satisfied with their efforts unless some of their energy, money or brain is used in the name and for the sake of the children.

The National Association has chosen as its motto: Lifting as We Climb. In order to live strictly up to this sentiment, its members have determined to come into the closest possible touch with the masses of our women, through whom the womanhood of our people is always judged. It is unfortunate, but it is true, that the dominant race in this country insists upon gauging the Negro's worth by his most illiterate and vicious representatives rather than by the more intelligent and worthy classes. Colored women of education and culture know that they cannot escape altogether the consequences of the acts of their most depraved sisters. They see that even if they were wicked enough to turn a deaf ear to the call of duty, both policy and self-preservation demand that they go down among the lowly, the illiterate and even the vicious, to whom they are bound by the ties of race and sex, and put forth every possible effort to reclaim them. By coming into close touch with the masses of our women it is possible to correct many of the evils which militate so seriously against us and inaugurate the reforms, without which, as a race, we cannot hope to succeed.

Through the clubs we are studying the labor question and are calling the attention of our women to the alarming rapidity with which the Negro is losing ground in the world of labor. If this movement to withhold employment from him continues to grow, the race will soon be confronted by a condition of things disastrous and serious, indeed. We are preaching in season and out that it is the duty of every wage-earning colored woman to become thoroughly proficient in whatever work she engages, so that she may render the best service of which she is capable, and thus do her part toward establishing a reputation for excellent workmanship among colored women.

Our clubs all over the country are being urged to establish schools of domestic science. It is believed that by founding schools in which colored girls could be trained to be skilled domestics, we should do more toward solving the labor question as it affects our women, than by using any other means it is in our power to employ. We intend to lay the Negro's side of the labor question clearly before our large-hearted, broadminded sisters of the dominant race and appeal to them to throw their influence on the right side. We shall ask that they train their children to be broad and just enough to judge men and women by their intrinsic merit rather than by the adventitious circumstances of race or color or creed. Colored women are asking the white mothers of the land to teach their children that when they grow to be men and women, if they deliberately prevent their fellow creatures from earning an honest living by closing their doors of trade against them, the Father of all men will hold them responsible for the crimes which are the result of their injustice and for the human wrecks which the ruthless crushing of hope and ambition always makes.

Through our clubs colored women hope to improve the social atmosphere by showing the enormity of the double standard of morals, which teaches that we should turn the cold shoulder upon a fallen sister, but greet her destroyer with open arms and a gracious smile. The duty of setting a high moral standard and living up to it devolves upon colored women in a peculiar way. False accusations and malicious slanders are circulated against them constantly, both by the press and by the direct descendants of those who in years past were responsible for the moral degradation of their female slaves.

Carefully and conscientiously we shall study the questions which affect the race most deeply and directly. Against the convict lease sys-

Mrs. Rosa D. Bowser.

MRS. ROSA D. BOWSER.

The writer of the subjoined article is a native of Virginia, and belongs in the front rank of educators of her race in this grand old commonwealth, which may justly boast of the eminence to which its black as well as white citizens attained before and since the war. The first president of the black republic on the West Coast of Africa, Joseph Jenkins Roberts, as well as the foremost Baptist leader, Lott Carey, were Virginians.

Mrs. Rosa D. Bowser was born in Amelia County, and was reared in the city of Richmond. She passed through the grades of the public schools, and completed her school work at the Normal School of that city under the instruction of its founder, Mr. Ralza Morse Manly, of Vermont, a distinguished educator in the North as well as the pioneer educator in Virginia among the Negro race. Mrs. Bowser received special training from Mr. Manly, having been instructed by him in the higher mathematics and Latin. She early developed a taste for drawing, painting and music, and made commendable progress in the fine arts. Mrs. Bowser's work as an educator has not been limited to the school room, in which she has been so efficient for the last twenty-five years, but she has been conspicuous in other and wider fields of usefulness among her people within and without the State.

This is evidenced by the following facts: She founded the Woman's League, which rendered signal service in the Lunenburg trials; she is President of the Richmond Mothers' Club; she is a member of the Executive Board of the Southern Federation of Colored Women; she is Chairman of the Executive Board of the Women's Educational and Missionary Association of Virginia; she is Chairman of the standing Committee of Domestic Economy, for the Hampton Conference; she is President of the Woman's Department of the Negro Reformatory Association of Virginia; and is one of the most conspicuous members of many benevolent organizations in Richmond. She is an eloquent and fascinating orator, bringing to that accomplishment, earnestness of manner, grace of gesture, and a charming personality.

tem, the Jim Crow car laws, lynchings and all other barbarities which degrade us, we shall protest with such force of logic and intensity of soul that those who oppress us will either cease to disavow the inalienability and equality of human rights, or be ashamed to openly violate the very principles upon which this government was founded. By discharging our obligation to the children, by coming into the closest possible touch with the masses of our people, by studying the labor question as it affects the race, by establishing schools of domestic science, by setting a high moral standard and living up to it, by purifying the home, colored women will render their race a service whose value it is not in my power to estimate or express. The National Association is being cherished with such loyalty and zeal by our women that there is every reason to hope it will soon become the power for good, the tower of strength and the source of inspiration to which it is destined.

And so lifting as we climb, onward and upward we go, struggling and striving and hoping that the buds and blossoms of our desires will burst into glorious fruition ere long. With courage born of success achieved in the past, with a keen sense of the responsibility which we must continue to assume we look forward to the future, large with promise and hope. Seeking no favors because of our color or patronage because of our needs, we knock at the bar of justice and ask for an equal chance.

THIRD PAPER.

WHAT ROLE IS THE EDUCATED NEGRO WOMAN TO PLAY IN THE UPLIFTING OF HER RACE?

BY MRS. ROSA D. BOWSER, OF RICHMOND, VIRGINIA.

In all ages of the world woman has been the central figure around which all joys and sorrows, all inspirations, all aspirations, and all accomplishments have circled. In all conditions of life, in all climes, in all Christian epochs, in all countries, she holds this position indisputable among the nations of the earth. For without her there would be no home circles, without the home circles there would be no races nor nations. Her office, of divine institution for the perpetuation of the human family, should not be lightly regarded by any class of people. Woman's primary duty is the systematic and wise ordering of the household. The infant looks into its mother's face and there receives its first impressions. These impressions are stamped upon the mind and heart of the child. The mother notices all the little disorders and griefs of the child from its birth throughout its life. The conscientious mother is ever ready to console, advise and sympathize in all grievances and perplexities which may confront her offspring. Hence there is great need for proper instruction to wives, mothers, and, in fact, to all women in anticipation of the responsibilities of a home, and the obligations of motherhood. It has been well said that the training of children should begin with their grandparents. The character of the homes of the land, the moral and immoral bearing of every settlement, town, and city, in a large measure depend upon the class of women—upon the idiosyncrasies of wives, mothers, and women in general, who by nature mould the sentiment of every department of human control. That society is ruled by women cannot be questioned. The age of complete dependence of women upon the stronger sex, has so far passed as to be foreign to the minds of the present generation. Not that the gentler sex is averse to the protection and tender solicitudes of the father, husband and brother, but it is of such common occurrence that women are thrown upon their own resources in the maintenance of the home, that they of necessity rather than from choice assume a degree of independence in various avenues of life.

Christianity is the medium by which woman has been exalted to her legitimate sphere in the world. The best colleges that a few years past closed their doors against her, have gradually put the latch strings on the outside. The coeducation of the sexes and the attendant results have displaced the old idea of the moral and intellectual inferiority of women. The learned professions are subject to her choice. She stands beside her brother as a partner, sharing equally with him in the world's work for humanity. Of one flesh God made all men. Hence they have the same general tendencies or inclinations, the same likes and dislikes, the same sympathies and the same indifferences, the same joys and the same sorrows manifested in a greater or less degree as their sensibilities have been cultured and developed. The Negro is no exception to this general rule. The centuries of servitude when he dared not of his own volition pursue courses for intellectual growth now place the Negro as an adolescent race, yet one that has made wonderful strides in improving its condition morally, intellectually and financially. The Negro is grateful for much in past experiences, which experiences have been rigid disciplinarians, urging him to *think* and *act* for himself. Therefore his hopes and aspirations grow stronger for more glorious results for the future. Compare the first thirty-six years *of* the independence of any civilized race with the progress made by the Negroes since their emancipation; who can, in a spirit of justice, say that the Negro has not made a very creditable record wherever the opportunity to show himself a man has presented itself. The Negro is grateful that there are many Southern as well as Northern friends in the dominant race who publicly commend him, and give him due credit for his energy and perseverance in making the best use of his time and talents. The fact is generally known that whatever success has been made was achieved through many difficulties. The best class of Negroes is not discouraged by the ravings and unjust criticisms of certain classes of people who do not know the Negro, having had little chance of intercourse with him even in the years prior to and during the Civil War. Yet he is far, very far from being contented with his present condition. The harvest is great, and many sheaves are yet to be gathered. He knows that the number whose eyes are opened to the beauties and utilities of life, and whose souls can discern the grand possibilities of the future, is a great contrast to the masses of the race that must yet be induced to appreciate the light of day. More teachers are needed to point out and supply this light. Who can better perform this duty than the unselfish, humane, intelligent Negro woman? Who can better feel the touch of sympathy and get out of self to help by lifting as she climbs? Who can better see the need than one who is interested in the lowly of her own household? Who but the educated Negro woman will feel more keenly the stigma of the depravity of her weak sister who has wearied of the struggle for a higher plane of living? To whom is the call to this duty more urgent? Will she answer? She must do so. Her advantages, intellectually and socially, demand that she should take a front rank in the crusade against ignorance, vice and crime. She is the lighthouse, giving warning of the hidden shoals and guiding away from the rocks which are wrecking the lives of many capable young men and women. These young people are anxious in many cases to be led into paths of purer man and womanhood. They incline toward leaders. But they will follow only good leaders in whichever course they take, whether the straight and narrow path of integrity and upright Christian character, or the broad road which leads to shame, degradation and death. They must and will follow leaders. But they require of leadership a reflection of their ideals. In other words, they require them to be as leaders all that they would admonish others to become—models of true, intelligent, morally pure women and men. Not only must these upright Negro women take their role as counselors and teachers, but it is highly essential that they be WITH the element to be uplifted, yet, certainly NOT OF it. It is impossible to help a fallen or weak sister to rise if the helper, like the Levite, pass by on the other side, and merely call out, Arise and stand in the beauty of pure womanhood—rather than like the Samaritan, she goes to her and lifts her to her feet. The touch of the hand, in proof of a heart full of sympathy, goes a long way in winning and holding a living, lasting evidence of the regenerating influence of charity to the recipient. The alarming death rate among the Negro population is largely due to ignorance of the laws of health, and the proper care of children. Such people need instruction in their homes, for you will reach them nowhere else. They will not attend public meetings nor church services; they feel out of place in them. Hence there is no way to reach such people other than by going among them. This act will not mar the reputation of a true leader, one whom they can emulate, and in whom they have confidence. It rather increases her influence; for they know she is NOT OF them, but WITH them in their efforts to improve. The magnitude of the work may sometimes cause one to shrink, when the progress seems slow. But all reforms require deliberation, endurance, and perseverance. Occasionally we get an encouraging comment which comes like a calm after storms of criticisms and abuse. Two of the daily papers of Richmond, Virginia, made very favorable statements in regard to the conduct of the colored people during the week of the carnival— October 7th-12th, 1901. For violations of the law there were about two hundred arrests, and not one colored person of the number. The colored schools came in for a liberal share of praise for their attendance during said week. All colored groups of schools were way up in the nineties. Baker School (colored), of six hundred and twenty-seven pupils, led the city schools, with 98.9 per cent of attendance. We hailed the announcements with delight, for they strengthened our belief that "Negro education" may not always be considered "a failure." We are stimulated to more earnest endeavor when we find persons of great minds and large hearts voicing such helpful sentiments as expressed by Mr. Joel Chandler Harris, in his article to the New York Journal, November 3, 1901, on "Negro Education," from which I quote:

"What is called the Negro problem is simply the invention of men with theories.

"The spectacle spread out before us is not in the nature of a problem.

"It is made up of the actual efforts and movements of a race slowly and painfully feeling its way toward a higher destiny.

"The conditions and circumstances being without parallel or precedent in the history of the world, it was inevitable that serious mistakes should be made; that misunderstandings should arise, that philanthropy should stretch out full hands in the wrong direction, that partisan politicians should pour out the vials of wrath.

"But what of it?

"The real progress of the race has not been retarded a moment. Nothing has been lost. And now, at last, the whole conservative and intelligent element of the race is placing itself under the leadership of men well qualified to lead it, and is making a new start.

"If the philanthropists and rich men of the country will hold up the hands of such Negroes as Booker T. Washington they will be able to forget in a few years that any serious mistakes have been made.

"More than that, they will be able to view leniently the mistakes that are still to be made."

And, I add, if the hands of such women as Mrs. Booker T. Washington of Tuskegee, and Miss Georgie Washington of Mt. Meigs, Alabama, be upheld by friends of the North, South, East and West, many skeptics would, in a comparatively short time, forget that they had at any time doubted the ability of the Negro to make for himself a creditable place in history. Such are the women needed to-day. Women who teach by doing. Women who can take a basket of soap on the arm, and in a gentle, winning way present it to homes that need it, while at the same time extol its merits in a pleasant manner. Women are needed who can teach the lesson of morality, cleanliness of soul and body, and the hygienic and economic management of the humble home, by showing them how to perform these acts, and furnish examples. Women who can arouse their sense of propriety to such a degree that by frugal habits they may abandon the one-room cabin in which a family of eight or ten eat, cook, sleep, wash and iron, for the neat two, three, or four-room well ventilated cottage. The laundry tub may be an excellent substitute when no better can be provided, but they will be taught to see the need of a genuine bath tub in every home. They will be taught that honest labor is no disgrace; that, however much education one may acquire, the deftness of the hands to execute the mandates of the mind tends rather to elevate the possessor, and hastens the day of a full developed man or woman with mind, heart, and hand trained to the best service—thereby dignifying labor. Above all, the thought must be impressed indelibly upon the hearts and consciences of the youth that the men can be no better than the women. Men are what the women make them. If a woman is refined, and exhibits a modest, dignified bearing, men can not fail to appreciate her demeanor and conduct themselves accordingly. While, on the other hand, boisterous, uncouth conduct upon the part of women will encourage boldness toward them, disrespect for them, and win the contempt of the men of a community for such women. Hence, wherever uplifting influence is needed, the result of the labor depends upon the compliant nature of the element, upon which they are working, whose persuasive power is more efficacious in directing the *upward* and *downward* trend of the masses. The women who can best appreciate this fact have the very grave responsibility of keeping the lesson constantly before the people—"Lest we forget, lest we forget." The so-called Negro problem must be solved by the Negro. The plane to which he must attain is limited by the energy and persistency of the most competent and sympathetic leaders, in piloting the followers in such a manner that they may realize that

> "Life is real, Life is earnest,
> And the grave is not its goal;
> Dust thou art, to dust returnest,
> Was not spoken of the soul."

FOURTH PAPER.

WHAT ROLE IS THE EDUCATED NEGRO WOMAN TO PLAY IN THE UPLIFTING OF HER RACE?

BY MRS. C. C. PETTEY.

Woman's part in the consummation of any project which has to do with the elevation of mankind is of paramount importance. With her influence eliminated or her work minimized failure is inevitable. This is true regardless of race or nationality. In the civilization and enlightenment of the Negro race its educated women must be the potent factors.

Mrs. Bishop C. C. Pettey

MRS. SARAH DUDLEY PETTEY.

Mrs. Sarah Dudley Pettey, the brilliant and accomplished wife of the late Bishop Charles Calvin Pettey, A. M., D. D., was born in the historic city of New Berne, North Carolina.

She is the daughter of Hon. E. R. and Caroline E. Dudley. Her father is a gentleman of great prominence. He was a member of the General Assembly of North Carolina during the reconstruction period, and has held important local, state and national positions, and his services are now in great demand as a political orator and editor. Her mother, the lamented Mrs. Caroline E. Dudley, was a lady of refinement and of natural gifts.

From environments, contact and association at home, Mrs. Bishop Pettey always had the instruction and advice of intelligent parents. At the age of six she could read and write. She entered the graded school of her native city, and after finishing her course she entered the State Normal School and remained three years; then she entered the famous Scotia Seminary at Concord, N. C., from which institution she graduated with distinction June, 1883.

In addition to her inherited gifts, Mrs. Pettey is a woman of great acquired ability. She reads the classics well, has a taste for the higher mathematics. She is a student of current events and a close observer of human nature. Upon graduating at Scotia Seminary she was, in October of the same year, tendered the position as second assistant in the New Berne graded school. Next year she was promoted to vice-principal, which position she held with credit and honor until she was married. For two successive summers she taught in the Craven County Teachers' Institute.

As a teacher, she was able, brilliant and magnetic. Popular with her associates, she was loved and honored by her pupils. She ruled with kindness and love, and punished with a flash of her eye. Well versed in the theory and practice of teaching, she soon won the sobriquet "Model Teacher."

She is a gifted musician; and for several years was the organist for one of the most prominent churches in her native city. On the morning of September 19, 1889, she was married to Bishop Charles Calvin Pettey, A. M., D. D. Immediately after her marriage she became the private secretary of her husband; and with him traveled extensively in the United States, Canada, Mexico, Great Britain and Continental Europe. She is an able writer and eloquent speaker.

For several years she has been General Secretary of the Woman's Home and Foreign Missionary Society of the A. M. E. Zion Church. As wife, mother and Christian worker, Sarah Dudley Pettey is a model woman, endeavoring to lead men and women upward and Heaven-ward.

The difficulties that the Negro must labor under, in his effort to rise, are manifold and peculiar. The critics of the Negro have assaulted him at the most vital point, viz., character. In their onslaught they have assailed the morals of the entire race. To meet this criticism the Negro must establish a character of high morals, which will stand out so conspicuously that even his bitterest foe will acknowledge its reality. In establishing this our women must lead. It must be understood that their virtue is as sacred and as inviolate as the laws of the eternal verities. They must not compromise even with an apparent virtuous sentiment; it must be real. Nothing great is accomplished without the shedding of blood. To convince the world of the virtue of the Negro race, Negro blood must be shed freely. Our young women must be taught that gorgeous dress and fine paraphernalia don't make a woman. They should dress modestly, becomingly and economically.

She is a true woman whose honor must not be insulted; who, though poorly paid, pursues her honest labor for bread and would scorn the obtaining of a livelihood any other way, regardless of the magnitude of the inducement. The foundation for this high sentiment finds its initiative in the home. Home life is the citadel and bulwark of every race's moral life. The ruler of home is mother. A faithful, virtuous and intelligent motherhood will elevate any people. The impress of mother follows her children to the grave; when .her form is changed and her physical existence extinct the footprints of her noble and pious life live long after her. Womanhood and manhood begin in the cradle and around the fireside; mother's knee is truly the family altar. True patriotism, obedience and respect for law, both divine and civil, the love and yearning for the pure, the sublime and the good, all emanate from mother's personality. If mother be good all the vices and shortcomings of father will fail to lead the children astray; but if mother is not what she should be all of the holy influences of angels cannot save the children. I would urge then, as the first prerequisite for our work, a pure, pious and devoted motherhood.

Secondly, a firm stand for right and truth in all things. Woman's power is her love. This pure flame lights up all around her. Her wishes and desires men love to satisfy. There are many things in society, politics and religion that ambitious men would seek to obtain by all hazards, but when woman takes her stand against these things she invariably wins. Our first stand must be for intelligence. No woman of to-day, who is thirty years of age, has the right to be queen of a home, unless she is intelligent. In this advanced day, to rear up a family by an illiterate woman might well be considered a crime. As a race, if we would possess the intelligence desired, our children must be kept in school, and not allowed to roam idly through the streets when the school-house is open. Since, in most of the Southern states, countless numbers of our people have been disfranchised, our educated women should institute a movement which will bring about compulsory education and a general reform in the educational system of the South. We need better schools and a higher standard of education for the masses. In our homes wholesome literature, periodicals, papers and books must be had. Mother must be acquainted with these herself. She introduces the little ones to them by the story form. This catchy method soon engrosses their attention, and they become wrapped up in them. Great care must be exercised in the selection of reading matter for our girls. Nothing is more hurtful than obscene literature.

When our homes become intelligent, we shall have intelligent states-men, ministers and doctors; in fact, the whole regime that leads will be intelligent. In public affairs woman has her share. She must speak through husband, son, father, brother and lover. Men go from home into the world to execute what woman has decreed. An educated wife formulates the political opinion of husband and son and though she may remain at home on election day, her views and opinions will find expression in the ballots of the male members of her household. The same thing is true in the church. I shall not dictate what woman should do here or limit her sphere of activity, but this I know she can with propriety—in her auxiliary work to the church she can become a mighty power. Woman's Missionary Societies, Christian Endeavor Societies, Sabbath School work, etc., afford a broad field of labor for our educated women. Her activity in all things pertaining to racial advancement will be the motive power in establishing firmly and intelligently an enlightened racial existence. Thirdly: The educated Negro woman must take her stand among the best and most enlightened women of all races; and in so doing she must seek to be herself. Imitate no one when the imitation destroys the personal identity. Not only in dress are we imitative to the extreme, but in manners and customs. When our boys and girls become redeemed from these evils a great deal will have been accomplished in the elevation of our race.

There are some noble women among other races whom we may imitate in virtue, morality and deportment. Those women come not from the giddy and gay streets of London, Paris or New York; but such women as Queen Victoria, Helen Gould, Frances Willard and others. These women have elevated society, given tone and character to governments and other institutions. They ornamented the church and blessed humanity. I can say with pride just here that we have many noble women in our own race whose lives and labors are worthy of emulation. Among them we find Frances Watkins Harper, Sojourner Truth, Phillis Wheatley, Ida Wells Barnett and others. Our educated women should organize councils, federations, literary organizations, societies of social purity and the like. These would serve as great mediums in reaching the masses.

I cannot refrain from mentioning public or street decorum here. Woman, as she glides through the busy and crowded thoroughfares of our great cities is eyed and watched by everyone. It is here that she impresses the world of her real worth. She can by her own acts surround herself with a wall of protection that the most vicious character would not dare attempt to scale or she can make it appear otherwise.

Beware then, mothers; accompany your daughters as often as possible in public.

In this advanced age, if the Negro would scale the delectable heights already attained by more highly favored races, our women must unite in their endeavors to uplift the masses. With concentration of thought and unity of action, all things are possible; these can effect victories when formidable armies and navies fail. The role that the educated Negro woman must play in the elevation of her race is of vital importance. There is no sphere into which your activities do not go. Gather, then, your forces; elevate yourself to some lofty height where you can behold the needs of your race; adorn yourself with the habiliments of a successful warrior; raise your voice for God and justice; leave no stone unturned in your endeavor to route the forces of all opposition. There is no height so elevated but what your influence can climb, no depth so low but what your virtuous touch can purify. However dark and foreboding the cloud may be, the effulgent rays from your faithful and consecrated personality will dispel; and ere long Ethiopia's sons and daughters, led by pious, educated women, will be elevated among the enlightened races of the world.

TOPIC XI.

HOW CAN THE NEGROES BE INDUCED TO RALLY MORE TO NEGRO ENTER-PRISES AND TO THEIR PROFESSIONAL MEN?

BY REV. H. T. JOHNSON, D. D., EDITOR CHRISTIAN RECORD.

Before an opinion uncomplimentary to the colored man's interest in the professional and business ventures of his race-variety can be of weight, there are several antecedent facts of primal value to be considered. If devotion to either class is lacking, it must be remembered, that shortcoming is traceable to causes which, however marked may be their effects in the Negro's case, are equally marked and striking in others of similar condition. Given centuries of environments and discipline hostile to the development of racial pride and co-operation, the result will not be unlike, whether the subject be the Red Man of America, the Yellow Man of Asia, the White Man of Europe or the Dark Descendants of Africa.

Time is an all-potential healer in the life of any progressive people and it is only when races are viewed in the light of extensive discipline and persistent struggles that achievements gratifying and reassuring are to be seen. The Rothschilds, Carnegies, Vanderbilts, and towering lights in the business and professional worlds at large are but well-favored children of a long-drawn ancestry, men in whose ancestral veins, the blood and iron of hope, pluck, anticipation and realization found outlet through the ravines and across the hill-tops of centuries bygone. However the claims of heredity may be made to appear in other directions, they carry weight when applied to an infant race and the traits which distinguish the more advanced varieties of the human family.

As it is futile to attempt the solution of any problem by eliminating any of its salient factors, so it would be well for us to admit the factor of unfavorable environment while that of an unfriendly heredity cuts so large a figure in the shortcomings and strivings of a race. The curse of slavery has so marred the visage of this otherwise comely and coming race that it will be the work of centuries to completely eradicate the

H. T. Johnson, D.D.

H. T. JOHNSON, PH. D., D. D.

H. T. Johnson, Ph. D., D. D., educator, minister, author, journalist, scholar, was born in Georgetown, S. C., October 10, 1857. Early life was spent in the public schools of his native town. Apprenticed to learn the printer's trade in his fifteenth year; worked for three years on the "Georgetown Planet" and "Charleston Independent." Gave up newspaper service for school teaching, in which occupation he earned sufficient means to enable him to enter the State Normal School in the Capital of his native State and subsequently the State University, at the same place continuing his studies with credit until the Fall of 1876, when Colored students were no longer allowed to enjoy such advantages by the Democrats who gained control of the State. For a time checkmated, young Johnson returned to the labors of the school-room until the autumn of 1878, when, having been licensed to preach a year earlier, he entered Howard University as a divinity student, graduating in the Spring of 1880.

While at Howard, Johnson took special studies in mathematics and the classics in the college department of the university. After preaching and teaching in his native State for two years, he resumed his student life, this time at Lincoln University, Chester County, Pa., graduating with honors in the class of '83. While at Lincoln he engaged in pastoral labors at Oxford, Kennett Square, Hosanah, Little Wesley and Morris Brown, Philadelphia; was ordained elder by Bishop Brown in Bethel Church, Philadelphia, June, 1883, having won the highest encomium for creditable examination passed in biblical, classical and metaphysical studies. The same year, the subject of our sketch was transferred to the New England Conference; was stationed at Chelsea, matriculated in the Boston University, where he studied for three years in the schools of Theology, Expression, Elocution, Voice Culture and Metaphysics, until from failing health he was compelled to change climate and sacrifice for a season at least his ambition for learning.

Between ministerial and educational services our subject applied his time in Tennessee until the winter of 1889, when he transferred to Arkansas and was stationed at Visitor's Chapel, Hot Springs, where he remained for two years. From here he was assigned the presiding eldership of the then leading district in the State, which position he held until the General Conference of 1892, which elected him to the editorship of the "Christian Recorder," the leading official organ of the A. M. E. Church, and the oldest and most widely known Colored newspaper in the world.

That the literary and moral worth of Dr. Johnson is recognized locally and in general is indicated by the place he holds in the confidence of the church. His two books, "The Preacher" and "Divine Logos," have been adopted in the ministerial course of studies of his church. He was the first course lecturer at Payne Theological Seminary at Wilberforce and is annual lecturer at Phelps Bible School at Tuskegee Institute at this writing. Is President of the National Association of Educators of Colored Youth, Treasurer of Douglas Hospital, Philadelphia, and Trustee of the New Jersey Industrial School at Bordentown, prior to its incorporation by the State Board of Education.

At the General Conference of 1900, Dr. Johnson was a popular candidate for the Episcopal honors of his church, and would have been numbered among the chosen ones had it not been for the triumph of foul methods rather than fair, as his votes on the first and only ballot (other ballots being thwarted) being in evidence.

As a man of liberal and progressive ideas and striking force of character, Dr. Johnson has already exerted an abiding influence in his race and generation.

awful results of its deeply imbedded hoof-marks. The lack of mutual confidence and inter-race alienation were among the most cherished tendrils to which the hot-bed of slavery gave birth for ages. That the sour grapes on which their ancestors fed should set on edge the incisors of their descendants is no less a deduction of common sense and history than the unavoidable finding of iron-clad logic.

The far-reaching effect of the unwholesome environment and heredity mentioned, is seen in the business and professional struggles of the more resolute and enterprising members of the race on every hand. While these endeavors are in many instances healthy and promising in character, the greater multitude are skeleton-like in shape and dwarfish in proportion, indicating to a pitiful degree the lack of blood to supply and brain to conduct the enterprise, it matters little whether it be of the professional or business type. The medical practitioner and undertaker are striking exceptions to the non-prosperous and unsuccessful class, although the good fortune of both is due chiefly to giant causes which account for the business and professional dearth of the race in other directions. While the physicians and funeral directors of the dominant race will not refuse service to colored applicants who seek them, the fee they charge, together with the cruel usages of certain social institutions, almost invariably drift or drive the trade in question in the direction of the professionals mentioned.

To trace the non-support of these classes to the conditions outlined exclusively will be to ignore other prime factors in the problem under consideration and render hopeless the remedies which may be applied toward an improvement of the case. However much in others or in conditions beyond his control lies the secret of the Negro's misfortune as a business or a professional venturer, the fact remains that he is himself responsible for much of the shortcomings which hamper his success and that in his hands resides the power to improve upon the disadvantages cited. The success achieved by business enterprises and professions conducted by men of the race in various communities of the different sections, clearly demonstrates the capacity of those who operate and establish their merit of the support of their peoples beyond the question of a doubt. In Wilmington, Del., Boston and New Bedford, Mass., Albany and Brooklyn, N. Y., and other places too numerous to mention, these enterprises and professions derive support mainly from white patrons, which fact is sufficient to dissipate every suspicion as to the demerit or inferiority of the articles handled or the agents patronized. Why Negro dentists, lawyers and doctors in the professions, merchants, farmers, butchers, smiths, produce and real estate dealers in the business world can prosper and succeed without the aid or patronage of their people, as is demonstrated in numerous instances, is a potential query the answer to which suggests a reply to the topical question under discussion.

On the list of sundry answers helpful to a successful investigation of our inquiry the good offices of the race acknowledged leaders and opinion moulders occupy a leading place. By constant precept and continuous example these leaders have it in their power to overcome the apathy of their followers or those within the range of their ministrations or influence as is true of no other agents. Chief among this class are the teachers and preachers of the race. In the contact of the former with children in the schoolroom and with their parents elsewhere the spirit of race-pride and race-patronage, if instilled and stimulated, cannot fail to produce the most gratifying outcome in the business endeavors of the race. Too much credit cannot be given the religious guides of the race for the interest and support inspired by them in this, as in all uplifting services toward their people, yet to the continuation of this devotion and the removal of their zeal must the eyes of the masses be directed until the royal harvest of a more prolific race-loyalty be seen and gathered on every hand.

But on its face value, may not the inquiry be construed as an impeachment of the loyalty or confidence of the race toward its leaders? That the indictment is rather well-founded, " 'tis true, 'tis pity, and pity 'tis, 'tis true." However specious may be the reasons assigned for this lack of support, the real and underlying cause is the absence of integrity, intelligence and race-pride on the part of the people themselves. The practice of constantly aiming to destroy the credit of those professional and business creditors who refuse to remain at the mercy of those who would serve only their own selfish aims, is a notorious failing which, the sooner outgrown or uprooted, the better.

In the attempt to solve the problem before us, the duty of business and professional men of the race toward their customers, clients, patients and the subjects with whom they severally deal, cannot be overlooked in the hope of success in our investigations. The duty which the former owe the latter can best be discharged by the application of ethical rather than ethnological standards, and this should be duly borne in mind, since it is the peculiar weakness of both sides to expect lenience and indulgence where probity and common sense require allowance for neither the one nor the other. If it be exacted that promptness and integrity characterize the actions of one let it be demanded that the same virtues be exercised by the other. If the race in other words would be induced to more liberally patronize its business and professional leaders, let the latter make it a point to furnish the articles and render the service and exercise the methods and manners which constitute the stock-in-trade of people who furnish standards in the commercial and professional worlds.

It may be, however, that after exercising the prerogatives and applying the principles defined, the results desired are not forthcoming. In that case it is possible that tact and faith combined with an enterprising genius may score the victory which surrenders itself only to the most patient and determined search. If the people are of mountainous proportions and are unyielding in their attitude of stolidity or unconcernment in the affairs of their business leaders, for the latter naught is left but to assume the role of Mohamet and go to the people.

In various ways the suggestion can be followed, but in no more feasible and effective way than by an appeal to their selfish and individual interests. On the principle that a people's pocket can be reached before their pride, it is suggested that those who would more largely secure their trade and patronage, do so by holding out to them the inducements common to co-operative business enterprises. The business represented by huge department stores operated by such merchant princes as John Wanamaker and Siegel & Cooper in their returns to their employees, and the offering of bargain inducements to their patrons in general, illustrate to a large degree what can be done on a smaller scale by business men of the race, provided the experiment be deemed worth the trial. The True Reformer's Organization is a purely Negro enterprise, representing interests running up into the millions, having as its mainspring of success the co-operative and profit yielding principle indicated.

The foregoing illustrations, references and suggestions cannot fail, at least in part, to answer the grave and momentous question on whose right solution so much of the race's future welfare depends.

SECOND PAPER.

HOW CAN THE NEGROES BE INDUCED TO RALLY MORE TO NEGRO ENTERPRISES AND TO THEIR PROFESSIONAL MEN?

BY PROF. J. W. GILBERT.

By proper education of the patrons, and merit on the part of Negro business enterprises and professional men, is a summary answer to the above question. It will be well for our present purposes to investigate this answer in detail. The natural inference therefrom—an inference whose justness is easily demonstrable—is that the education of the Negro race, so far and in such manner as it has already proceeded, is defective, when it comes to the question of training Negroes to support their own business enterprises and professional men. The very text books, not to mention the living teachers, in every department of education, whether professional or otherwise, are written by authors and for students other than Negroes. For every public, and well nigh every private educational institution of the land, the trustees of education have prescribed books which, besides suppressing whatever praiseworthy associations the race has had with the history and literature of our common country, never call the words of a Negro wise; nor his deeds noble. It is neither a sufficient nor true answer to the question, to say that Negroes have contributed nothing of educational or civic value to the literature or history of this country. Manifestly, then, our young people come out of school without confidence in the ability of their race to do what members of other races can do. This, I take it, is the reason why we find educated Negroes, as a rule, bestowing their patronage upon business enterprises and professional men of other races rather than upon their own representatives in the same vocation. This lack of confidence and race pride, characteristic of the educated as well as of the uneducated Negro, is the most destructive heritage bequeathed by slavery days to any once enslaved race in the history of the world. Hence, as a race, we need a thorough revision of our system of education which shall encourage the production of Negro authorship, on the one hand, and the confidence-and-pride-inspiring study of the worthfulness of the Negro's enviable record, on the other.

The schools are, however, only one of the agencies of education in the broadest acceptation of that term. Equally potent with scholastic

J. W. Gilbert, A. M.

PROF. JOHN W. GILBERT, M. A.

Prof. John Wesley Gilbert, A. B., A. M., was born at Hephzibah, Ga., July 6, 1864. Young Gilbert was left to the care of his widowed mother and his uncle John, for whom he had been named. He usually spent half the year on the farm and the other half in the public schools of the city of Augusta. After finishing the public grammar school course, he spent twelve months, all told, in the Atlanta Baptist College (then Seminary).

In January, 1884, Paine College opened in Augusta. He attended this institution eighteen months and graduated from it in June, 1886. In September of the same year he entered the Junior Class of Brown University, Providence, R. I. He graduated from this historic institution with honor in June, 1888. For excellence in Greek a scholarship in the American College, Athens, Greece, was conferred upon him at the end of his Senior year. In the spring of 1889, he married Miss Osceola Pleasant of Augusta, Ga. He attended the American College, Athens, Greece, during 1890-91. Under his supervision the site of Ancient Eretria, now Nea Psara, on the island of Eubola, was excavated and in collaboration with Prof. John Pickard, the only extant map of this ancient city was made by him. All the places of classic note in Greece were visited and studied by him. His M. A. degree was conferred upon him by Brown University upon the presentation of his thesis, "The Demes of Attica." He also took one semester of lectures in the University of Berlin, in 1891. He is author of several archaeological productions and has contributed articles on this subject to the *New York Independent* and other journals of like standing. He is at present a member of the Philological Association of America, and membership, which he accepts, in the Archaeological Institute, has also been tendered him. Ever since the fall of 1891, he has held the chair of Greek and German in Paine College, Augusta, Ga. Besides, he is a preacher of the order of Elder in the C. M. E. Church in America. As representative of that church, he was a delegate to the Ecumenical Conference, held in London, England, September, 1901. During the session he preached and lectured for a number of the largest and most intelligent audiences in England.

training, if not more so, is the cultivation of social sentiment in the community. Sentiment is higher than law, and the endeavor of all honest legislation should be to make laws expressive of the mandates of the highest and best sentiment. Any given community can almost always be trusted to act upon the impulse of sentiment, whether this comports with the law or not. Whether expressed or unexpressed, the social sentiment among Negroes—and it is seemingly often innate—is not favorable to the support of their own enterprises and professional men. Were it otherwise, we should now have prosperous wholesale and retail merchants, successful factories, large real estate agencies, considerable banks, solid insurance companies, better institutions of learning, well-paid lawyers, physicians, dentists, etc., and the reaction on the whole race would have been to change our status in the nation from that of mendicant denizens, as at present, to that of influential well-to-do citizens. This mutual helping of each other is expected of us, if we are to judge from the evidences given us from time to time by our white fellow citizens. For example, the white undertakers in Augusta, Georgia, have given up to the colored undertakers all their Negro patronage. The best white physicians do not seek Negro patients. Although greed for "the almighty dollar" keeps most white business men seeking Negro patronage, they do not, as a rule, try to prevent Negroes from patronizing Negroes except by striving to make it to their pecuniary advantage to patronize white men. In a word, it is natural, they allow, for birds of a feather to flock together. And this is true of the Jew, the German, the Irishman, of all except the Negro. As it is, the average Negro chooses rather to be discourteously and carelessly treated by a white professional or business man, often of inferior ability, than to be properly treated by a man of superior ability of his own race. Hence, to induce Negro patronage of Negro enterprises and professional men, there must be cultivation of the social sentiment of the Negro community by all possible means.

From every view-point the pulpit is the strongest factor in the cultivation of social sentiment. Some few preachers occasionally *"talk* on this line," but unfortunately for the influence of their admonitions, they themselves purchase their groceries and drugs, employ their physician and undertaker from members of another race. "A house divided against itself cannot stand," like many another passage and teaching form the "Book of God and the god of books," might as applicably be preached to a large number of Negro preachers as to their congregations. It is no "unholy compromise" of the gospel of saving grace to teach that the "Man of Galilee" came first unto his "own," and that to "follow after him" and his apostles in their doctrine of "first to the Jew," our religion should exemplify Christ by our acting on the principle, "first to the Negro." I would have this doctrine promulgated persistently, earnestly, constantly, from every Negro pulpit as the only hope of the Negro race, as such, and, therefore, of the perpetuity and progress of their churches. Nor should the publishing of the doctrine find place only in the congregations of the laity, but it should be proclaimed in the clerical conferences, conventions, associations, synods, assemblies, etc., for I recognize it as a case of "Physician, heal thyself."

This cultivation of sentiment in the purely religious bodies should be supplemented by similar efforts in the "thousand-and-one" societies of one sort and another among us. Let them incorporate it in their constitutions as a requirement for membership. It would not be amiss for our national race congresses and conventions to scatter broadcast and thickly over the whole land literature to this effect. Let that Negro individual or body be ostracized that does not subscribe to this doctrine, or fails to live in accord therewith.

To summarize, this training in the school room, preaching in the pulpit, proclaiming in social and civic organizations, promulgation from the rostrum, and broadcast distribution of literature, all tending toward the same end, it seems to me, would properly educate the popular mind and be productive of that social sentiment without which Negro enterprises and professional men are doomed either to utter failure, or, at most, to the eking out of a miserable death-in-life existence.

Now, as to those engaged in these enterprises and professions a few words may be befittingly said. In order to inspire the confidence and reasonably expect the patronage sought, there must be merit in the claims of the seeker. The business enterprise must present no appearance of hazard or mere adventure; for the mere matter of sameness of race does not warrant one in taking risks as a partner or patron in "wild-cat schemes." No man should expect or receive patronage solely because he is black; for your patron, besides generally being poor, is also black, and might as justly look for favors of you upon that score as you of him. The business, let us say of buying and selling, must show reason for its existence and firmness in its project. Besides capital, a common sense application of the economic laws of supply and demand, the principle of "low prices, quick sales," the proper estimates of the actual and prospective fluctuations of the market, these all must give evidences of your *raison d'etre,* your firmness of business, and your claim upon public patronage. It goes without saying that the quality of your goods or services must be second to none at the same price. In the professions Negro practitioners, if there is to be any difference in point of ability between them and other professional men, must be *exceedingly* well prepared for their chosen fields. This is imperative, because the presumption of the masses of Negroes, to say nothing of others, is that, on the average, the Negro professional man is not amply qualified for the pursuit of his profession. I would have Negro professional men spend much time in the study of their professions both before and after entrance thereupon. I should like to know that the average Negro preacher, physician, lawyer, etc., is better equipped for his work than the average professional man, whether white or black, who is now receiving the patronage of Negroes.

Finally, the business or professional man must be of the people and for the people, interested in their welfare of whatever sort, and promotive of the same as far as he is able. He must not be "seeking only what he may devour," but must give himself unreservedly to the people for their uplift in every good cause. I do not mean that there should be any "let-down" along moral lines, but I do mean to imply that a great many failures are due to the exclusive separation of not a few Negro professional men from the people unless when pecuniary gain is the sole purpose.

These principles have made others successful. They are but natural laws deducible from the philosophy of history. Therefore, if two and two make four, why should not an application of these laws induce, nay, compel Negroes to rally to the support of Negro enterprises and their own professional men?

THIRD PAPER.

HOW CAN THE NEGROES BE INDUCED TO RALLY MORE TO NEGRO ENTERPRISES AND TO THEIR PROFESSIONAL MEN?

BY J. R. PORTER, D. D. S.

In discussing questions of race building it is but just that we recognize the causes that have led up to the condition that may exist. If we are to suggest methods by which we may correct our weak points, we should first attempt to make plain what these are and then offer our remedy.

We have enterprises innumerable, enterprises of all classes and kinds, dignified and undignified, humble and pretentious, scattered all over this broad land. But these do not take on the sturdy growth of permanency and prosperity that usually attaches to the affairs of others. On the contrary we are surprised if they exhibit undue vitality and outgrow their long clothes.

Some of our businesses are lasting monuments to our commercial and professional ability, and stand out proudly against a background of restricted opportunities, while the unnumbered many fade into the shadow of the horizon and are lost to sight.

The questions that come to us are: Why is it so, and how may it be remedied? Are the causes for these economic conditions of commercial origin or social? Are they extrinsic or intrinsic? Are they the results of the unbusinesslike methods of our merchants, or the lack of appreciation of our buyers?

We glory that we are a full-fledged race. It is a splendid thing to glory over. But do we realize what we have missed in our sudden growth? Imagine a man, who has had no babyhood, no childhood, no youthhood; a man born into manhood, without the pleasures and experiences of boyhood; who has never fallen into a pond, battled with wasps, played truant, or done any of those innocent mischiefs that develop the boy both in body and in mind, and fit him for the strenuous duties of life. Imagine such a man and you have our race.

A nation in a day, is our record. We were born into cities, governments, laws, comforts, pleasures and schools. Aladdin's lamp has never accomplished anything so wonderful, and we rubbed our eyes and were amazed because everything had been prepared for us. This

Dr. J. R. Porter

J. R. PORTER, D. D. S.

Dr. J. R. Porter was born and reared in Savannah, Ga., among very pleasant home influences. He is the son of the late Rev. James Porter, of that city, well remembered as educator and musician, as one who loved his fellow man, and was eager to serve his race in any capacity. The son has partaken of these better qualities, and is earnestly following the father's footsteps.

J. R. Porter received his primary education in the West Broad Street Public School of his native city, and through assiduous application while a pupil of the public school, was enabled to enter Atlanta University on a two-year scholarship won in competitive examination. He graduated in 1886 with the degree of A. B., and after a year entered the Dental Department of Walden University, at that time Central Tennessee College. He received the degree of D. D. S. in 1889, and the following year was Professor of Operative Dentistry in his Alma Mater.

But this field was too narrow for his ambition. An active practice was more to his liking, and he wanted to get in touch with the people. With this in view he selected Birmingham as his field of labor.

The Doctor soon built up an excellent practice, and became indispensable both in public and religious affairs. He was the founder of the Alabama Penny Savings Bank of Birmingham, Ala., and the first Secretary of its Board of Directors. Whatever is of public interest has always appealed to him, and has had his hearty alliance.

But at that time Birmingham was a place of a few industries, and their interdependence was so marked, that to tie up one was to tie up all. In the strike of '92 and '93, the Magic City slipped from under the influence of the magician's wand, and was like any other broken and beaten town. The strike had ruined it, and Dr. Porter, like others, sought a better country. He chose Atlanta, Ga. He came here in the spring of '93. By faithfully attending to business, he has built up an excellent dental practice, and has become one of our most popular leaders. He is genial, thoughtful and reliable, and all classes feel very kindly toward him, because of his deep interest in them and their affairs. He is very much concerned in the young men and their future, and is a prominent officer in the Y. M. C. A., established by the colored men of Atlanta. He is conservative and just on all public questions, and earnestly desires to give his best to his people, because he has great faith in the ultimate adjustment of the abnormal conditions that so fetter them.

very munificence has hampered us. We have not had that development as individuals and as a people that would best fit us to grapple with each succeeding obstacle. Therefore we must patiently though painfully start from the beginning and travel over the same road, that each race has traveled, because individuals and races develop alike, and the same conditions that attach to the growth of one race, attach to that of all others.

A nation in a day is a splendid record. But a nation that came out of the wilderness, constructed its own cities, builded its own roads, made its own laws, established its own schools, devised its own comforts and pleasures, and in the contest with nature and poverty, wrestled until it won a new name, that nation with its scars, its experiences, and its development has far more to be desired, and has far more resources upon which to draw in its after contests than the former.

We entered the lists with these natural handicaps, and other conditions imposed upon us. We have made mistakes, and the wonder is that we have not made more, and that we have shown such splendid powers of adaptability. Shunted to the right and left, with our path continually obstructed, and our ambition jeered at, we have kept quietly and persistently on, until we can now show a very extensive catalogue of enterprises, that have grown and grown, until they are sufficiently important to call forth discussions of this character.

We have no definite figures of the exact amount invested in our business ventures. Though it is small when compared with the vast amounts invested by others, yet it is enormous when compared with our actual resources. The Negro merchant and professional man, have ceased to be novelties, and in many sections are making serious impressions on the business of both city and country.

We may still regard our enterprises as pioneer. We can even see the visible signs of our endeavors to learn a business while conducting it. Yet it is quite gratifying to notice an improvement. Our ventures are taking on more and more the general character of business, and losing the less desirable ones of race peculiarities.

What are the causes of so many failures among our enterprises, especially those that gave promise of great success? This question like the historic ghost will not down, but walks at unseemly hours, both by day and by night, calling for an adjustment of our commercial and economic sins, that it may go to its rest.

Our men do not have that thorough grasp of business principles, that comes with years of experience. One cause for our mistakes is that we do not have the opportunity of apprenticeship. The white youth enters an establishment, and step by step learns a business before he starts in it for himself. He thereby places a large factor of success to his credit.

The Negro goes into business without that intimate knowledge that is so essential, and stumbles into success or into failure. But this condition is gradually changing. We have been in active life long enough to have somewhat of an apprentice class of our own. Here and there we find men, who have, through this system gained a knowledge that gives them a decided advantage. It is through these means that we hope to improve the personnel of our merchant class, the character of our enterprises, and increase our patronage because of the excellency of the service.

One great need of our enterprises is the freedom of location. Experience and capital are both seriously hampered by want of proper place to house business. I have seen a prosperous merchant move across a street and fail. I have seen a splendid business carried around a corner and utterly destroyed.

If this is so with those who have choice of places, how much more must it be so with us who must take what we can get, and what wonder is it that we utterly fail, or that we imbibe the squalor and shiftlessness of the miserable places we must occupy. All life is subject to the same general physiological influences. Man and plant alike flourish in the sunshine, and fade and weaken in the damp and dark. Our business languishes as much from environment as from any other cause. Trade is a sensitive thing and increases or decreases according to fixed laws, and there must be more than goods to attract active patronage. Grant us this freedom of location and our road to success through business ventures would be much shortened.

I do not lay our failures to external causes alone. There are other and as grave ones within. Certain economic exactions must be complied with before success is ever assured. Some do not choose the pursuits for which they are best fitted, but strike out boldly and confidently, forgetful that adaptability is always an essential factor in success. Some are unable to carry out their plans from lack of capital. This has also kept many from getting the business training that is so necessary, and we therefore have less merchants and more store-keepers. We must know that business is progressive and demands an ideal. The whole system of Southern commercial life has been revolutionized, but the revolution is the product of a great evolution.

Under these conditions, have our business and professional men done their best to attract and hold the patronage of our people, or have they been content to drift along and catch whatever may come their way? Have they realized that they have obligations as well as those to whom they would sell? They have not done all of their duty, nor have they been as progressive as they might have been. Yet when we think of the severe handicaps they have had, we feel that they have done remarkably well. Life is a continual comparison, to-day with yesterday, this year with last. In the comparison we see better merchants, better stores, and higher business ideals among us. These appeal to us very sensibly, and we give more and more liberally of our patronage.

We are apt to forget the terrible handicaps that faced us as a people not so long ago, and the commercial ones that face our business men of to-day. We grow impatient with their mistakes and twit them because they are unable to display as large and as valuable a stock as some one else, or because of their shabby establishments. We are too exacting. We are not as generously inclined towards our enterprises as we should be, and it is only when we put ourselves in places that require patronage, that we can understand why so many fail. The power to discriminate between the useful and useless is born of experience and is of slow growth. The struggle between the right and wrong, the necessary and unnecessary is the heritage that came to us with our sudden birth of racehood. All fields of endeavor are new to us, and even when there are no restrictions, our adjustment must be slow.

For us to rally to our enterprises simply because they are ours, would bring temporary but not permanent success. The latter can only come by normal means. Abnormal conditions are not lasting. They may hold for a time and even prosper, yet they must ultimately fail, and then affairs will follow their natural tendency, and seek the normal. The restrictions that press us so, must in time yield to this law, and all efforts to rally to our enterprises from pride, and not from reason, must follow the same fate. There are a hundred cents in a dollar but no sentiment.   Lessen its purchasing value and you lessen the desire to purchase.

We may rally to enterprises simply because Negroes are the projectors, but we soon begin to cast about for reasons for our patronage, and if we find none to outweigh self-interest we soon drop off.   But if we find good reason for our support, we soon lose the idea of race pride, in the greater idea that our merchant is, a splendid business man.

The best agents for securing active support for our enterprises are the attractions that these enterprises hold within themselves.   Our intelligent and thrifty merchants, with their well appointed stores, and enlarged stock are to settle this problem of patronage, because they have within their keeping, the means to develop the normal conditions of trade and to build up a demand for their wares.

Mrs. Warren Logan

MRS. WARREN LOGAN.

Mrs. Warren Logan, whose maiden name was Adella Hunt, was born in a Georgia village after the close of the Civil War. When asked for this sketch, she said: "There is little to tell, as my busy life has been without romantic event. I was not born a slave, nor in a log cabin. To tell the truth, I got my education by no greater hardship than hard work, which I regard as exceedingly healthful."

It is known that she has an inheritance of blood, tradition and history of which any American woman might be proud.

Her early education was of a private nature. In 1881 she was graduated from Atlanta University as a bright member of one of its brightest classes.

Two years of teaching in an American Missionary School in a South Georgia town, where she was also a city missionary, prepared her for more advanced work, which opened to her at Tuskegee, Ala.

In 1883 Miss Hunt joined Mr. Washington, Olivia Davidson, Warren Logan and the handful of teachers who were the originators of the now famous Industrial School.

From the first she fitted into the activities and spirit of the school and became Miss Davidson's right hand helper. She succeeded to the position of Lady Principal when Miss Davidson became Mrs. Booker T. Washington. In this position Miss Hunt emphasized the academic side of the school and also urged the physical development of the girls. Her own line of teaching was the normal training of student teachers. Her services were constantly in demand for Peabody and other teachers' institutes in Georgia and Alabama.

In 1888 Miss Hunt was married to Warren Logan, treasurer of the Tuskegee Normal and Industrial Institute. Since that time she has ordered her household, written a little, read much, completed the Chautauqua Course, and kept abreast with the times. While she has given her best thought to her husband and children, she has kept in touch with the school and has lent a hand to the Woman's Club.

TOPIC XII.

WHAT ARE THE CAUSES OF THE GREAT MORTALITY AMONG THE NEGROES IN THE CITIES OF THE SOUTH, AND HOW IS THAT MORTALITY TO BE LESSENED?

BY MRS. WARREN LOGAN.

In these days of specialists among physicians and of specialists among students of social science it seems rather presumptuous for a teacher to attempt any formal discussion of causes and remedies for the high death rate among Negroes in the cities of the South. A few suggestions, however, may serve to draw more attention to this vital subject.

The sections of the cities inhabited by Negroes are generally the most unsanitary. The house in which the average Negro family lives is poorly built and too small. Frequently old houses are set aside as too far gone for any except Negro tenants. In many instances these dilapidated houses contain germs of disease which it is practically impossible for the young and the feeble to withstand. The food, fuel, clothing and general comforts of a family thus housed are insufficient. Food plays too large a part in the havoc made by death among Negroes. In many instances, there is great intemperance in both eating and drinking. With another large class there is actual scarcity of food and that, too, often of poor quality. Add to this, irregularity of meals and poor cooking and one can not wonder at the low state of health nor even at the excessive mortality.

One of the most serious phases of ignorance is criminal carelessness in regard to nutrition. Cooking is that part of household work which almost every woman undertakes and very few understand, and herein lies the foundation of disease.

The long death-roll among Negroes contains an excessive number of infants. Careful investigation shows that this slaughter of innocents is due in large measure to improper feeding. Some mothers must be away from their babies earning bread and shelter. Others leave their little ones for less worthy and less honorable purposes. Others neglect their offspring because they have a fancied or cultivated dislike of chil-

199

dren. It is a sad day for a people when happy motherhood declines. Man has devised successful substitutes for natural food for babies, but these should be used only when the best good of all concerned can be subserved thereby. Nature's ways are wisest and best, and parents must try to walk in those ways if they would have their children have life and have it abundantly.

Far be it from us here to attempt a technical discussion of tuberculosis, but in plain simple language, let us cite a few facts in regard to lung diseases among Negroes.

The oft repeated statement that the Negro slave did not have consumption, cannot be verified, for lack of authentic records on the subject. The Negro free, however, is dying of consumption and kindred diseases in appallingly large numbers.

Many theories in regard to consumption have been exploded, but it is acknowledged by all, to be an infectious disease. As such, ignorant people do not understand how to escape it; indeed, until anti-spitting laws are more universal and more rigidly enforced, every one may be exposed to these deadly germs. They respect neither race lines nor intellectual grades. The Negro, however, seems to be peculiarly susceptible to this class of ailments. I. Because of comparatively small lung capacity. 2. Because of general low nutrition. 3. Because of lack of bath rooms and their proper use. 4. Immorality. 5. General indifference to the incipient stages of the disease. Colds and coughs are passed by as matters of course with little or nothing done to prevent or cure them.

The physical life and death of man has a much more intimate connection with his moral life than is at first thought apparent. Too many children are robbed by Sin of a child's first right, viz.: the right to be well born. If parents have lived lives of shame and thereby weakened their bodies, the effects of this will be a sad legacy of weakness in the persons of their children. Men and women given to social impurity will hardly escape the notice of those about them. Their characters are imitated and shame and weakness, physical as well as moral, multiplied. "Sin conceived and brought forth Death."

Among people of low intellectual development and low moral standards, family love is below normal. With this defective class, there is much indifference to the life and death of their dependent relatives. The young and the aged are shamefully neglected. It is sufficient to be bereaved—better, the relieved, to say: "The Lord's Will be done." Remedies for these sad and unfortunate conditions are much more easily suggested than applied.

Better environment, greater comfort in the homes, come only as a return for money. Money will come as a return for labor. Money will come to those who earnestly desire it, because they will work for it. They will do whatsoever their hands find to do, accepting the pay such labor brings, but fitting and aspiring for something better. There is usually plenty of work for all honest, industrious Negroes in Southern cities.

Even money may not cause the old shanty to give place to a good house nor raise the standard of general comfort very materially, except as the demands of the family are enlarged as a result of education. No one factor will have such weight in the decrease of suffering and the reduction of the high death rate as enlightenment of mind.

The system of education in vogue in Southern cities will work slowly because up to the beginning of the twentieth century, school attendance has not been made compulsory. There are no truant schools, no reform schools. Idleness tends to vice. Idleness and vice are in no way conducive to health and longevity.

Many Negroes do not want education for themselves nor for their children. These people swell the death lists in Southern cities' health offices to such distressingly large numbers. They are often cared for and buried by funds from the city treasury. Would it not pay to try compulsory education? To try teaching them to help themselves, to save themselves?

To say that the home life of the masses must be improved is but another way of saying they must be educated.

Among the most potent forces in the uplift of a people are the school, the press, the courts and the church.

Under a system of compulsory education, the Negro would much sooner learn to observe the laws of health and thus to extend his life.

When newspapers in Southern cities are fairer in their attitude toward the black citizen, he will become a better citizen. It will increase his respect for others and greatly increase his self respect. He will then make more effort to live and to live well, because his life will seem more worth living.

Every state included under the "Land of the free and the home of the brave" should strive to make its criminal laws reformative rather than revengeful. A very considerable number of Southern Negroes come to their life's end in the prisons, which in no Southern state are all that prisons should be. From a health standpoint, most of them are all that prisons should not be.

It pays the municipality better to educate and reform its citizens than to convict and execute them.

A cultivated, spiritual ministry will emphasize the best teaching of the schools.

An active church will sustain a fair press; will uphold law and order; will supplement the work of the good doctor and in various ways try to reduce the number of funerals among the Negro population in Southern cities.

SECOND PAPER.

WHAT ARE THE CAUSES OF THE GREAT MORTALITY AMONG THE NEGROES IN THE CITIES OF THE SOUTH, AND HOW IS THAT MORTALITY TO BE LESSENED?

BY HON. H. A. RUCKER.

One who has never been taught to appreciate what health is and to understand hygienic laws can not become a safe guardian of his or her physical being. For when this being is attacked, as is constantly the case, by its millions of enemies, if all of its portholes have not been properly guarded it easily falls prey to disease and death.

As a race the Negro has had neither the time nor the opportunity to inform himself on the principles of health saving or in those of health getting—if there be such. Both prior to and since his emancipation his time, except nominally, has been the property of others from whom he has barely eked out an existence, and, from a humanitarian standpoint, has had but little interest in caring for his health.

During the years of his enslavement, his mortality, in proportion to his numbers and his environments, was no less than it has been since he became a free man—and the bald statement that his death-rate during the past thirty-eight years has greatly increased, may not be founded on facts. Fair play in discussing this phase of the subject demands careful and patient inquiry into the past history of a people

Hon. H. A. Rucker.

MR. H. A. RUCKER.

Out of the Southland—that awful crucible of prejudice and proscription,—like steel tempered by fire, and hardened for the practical uses of mankind, has come numerous valiant spirits, whose advent was so timely as to have seemed divinely inspired. Price and Cain, Elliott and Bruce, Cailloux, and others, who have joined the silent majority, did noble work and lived to see the race's redemption, but it has been left for newer and younger men to complete the structure on the foundation that was furnished by the "Old Guard." The modern age of politics and business in the sunny South—the home of nine-tenths of the Negroes—offers no brighter luminary than the Hon. Henry A. Rucker of Georgia. Young as years go, but mature in all the attributes that command success and popular esteem, the life of Henry A. Rucker is a priceless text-book for the aspiring Afro-American youth. Guided upward by nothing save the lofty counsel of a good mother and the inherent qualities of a true gentleman, he has scaled the heights, and for himself, has solved the problem of "how the fittest" may survive, and is giving to the whole race the key by which he wrought out so clear a solution. No *legerdemain* has worked his upward flight. The ingredients that he has utilized are simple, even if rare, and are within the reach of the least favored of human beings— honesty of purpose, fidelity to every trust and adherence to the golden rule. He has always been able to secure what was justly his without encroaching upon the sacred rights or legitimate possessions of another. Harboring no malice in his own bosom he has softened the wrath of his neighbor and demonstrated how clever diplomacy and a manly appeal to the finer instincts of a possible enemy yields richer returns than all the force and invective that a century could bring to bear. If the battle is to be fought out on lines of mental competition and personal worth rather than by balls and bayonets, Mr. Rucker has grasped the situation and the best evidence of the wisdom of his policy of inter-racial coöperation is the results he has individually achieved, and the commendation freely offered by the white and colored people who greet him day by day in the routine of duty. Atlanta owes much to the indefatigable energy and inexhaustible public spirit of Henry A. Rucker. He has been active in promoting all of her interests and that his services have been valuable is cheerfully admitted in the Board of Trade and industrial circles. He was conspicuous in advancing the prospects of the famous exposition of 1895, and is now striving to round out the work of securing a commodious federal building for the enterprising Georgian capital. He bore the brunt of the fight against the "Hardwick bill" and was potent in defeating both that infamous measure and the "Payne resolution." He has been repeatedly elected a delegate to the national conventions of the Republican party.

Since July 26, 1897, Mr. Rucker has been collector of internal revenue for the District of Georgia with headquarters in his own city, Atlanta. The receipts for the last fiscal year were more than double those of preceding years and exceeded in the same proportion the revenues gathered in any single year since the organization of the state. This marvelous showing is due partially to Mr. Rucker's prompt, thorough and painstaking plan of operation and of course in large measure to the national prosperity, growing out of President McKinley's shrewd financial policies. Brilliant as has been the past of this progressive Afro-American, the future holds out the promise of grander achievements. The race honors Mr. Rucker and holds him close to its heart, because he has proven himself a leader that can be trusted. When he commands "close ranks, steady, march," the Georgia populace goes forward in one conquering phalanx, determined, aggressive and undaunted, remembering that enduring power comes not by "fits and starts," but by clinching with mailed hand the rewards that have been won.

concerning whom little or no minute data of a national character was kept. However, this question may not properly enter into the subject, the contention being that the mortality among the race is excessive, which, if true, may be accounted for in part in the existence of certain acknowledged conditions.

Wherever the Negro has been cared for either by himself or by others he has enjoyed the same immunity from disease and death that those of other races have. And whenever neglected or abused, whether the failure or fault rests with himself or others, impaired health, decay of mind and body and death have ensued.

Compared with the masses but few Negroes at any time within the history of the life of the race in this country, have been properly guarded against exposure—the few who in ante bellum days were selected as house servants and to fill other kindred places, were measurably protected. And now the same classes and that of the more fortunate or business classes have limited protection from more than ordinary exposure.

The masses have always done the drudgery. And that too without knowledge or reference to health keeping. A common practice of employed Negroes is to go or be sent on short quick errands, leaving warm and, in this respect, comfortable places of employment without hat or wrap to breast chilling winds or atmospheric conditions many degrees removed from their places of services. In this practice is the exposure from sudden changes of temperature without preparation. The drayman, the cartman, the man in the ditch and others whose employment is in the open air are exposed not alone by the character of the work in which they are engaged but also by reason of the fact that six days of the week, those in which they labor, of necessity, their clothing is poor and shabby and their persons are ill kept. While the seventh day finds them as a rule well clad and well shod. Then their homes—no, their houses, partly because of circumstances beyond their control and partly on account of their improvident natures, are little more than shelters or huts.

These houses are built in what is known or accepted as Negro tenant districts, and those acquainted with the localities need no evidence to convince them that they are not sought as either health or pleasure resorts. They are the city alley ways and the low malarial districts where the noxious gases and foul vapors rise from emptying sewers.

More than two hundred years' application has made the Negroes agriculturists; they have been accustomed to labor and to plenty of nature's fresh, invigorating air; they have, because of conditions not proper to treat here, drifted from the farms and fields into the crowded cities, thence into the slums, to be infected with disease.

They have been thrust into prisons where they were provided with the poorest of covering and meanest food for their bodies; where scurvy and other loathsome diseases have made their impress upon them and where incentive to cleanliness is as distant as the North and South poles. Freed from prison life they have gone forth mingling with a class of people infecting them with their scales and spreading disease and death.

Then again the race is without proper places to care for its unfortunate, aged and infirm; without orphanages, reformatories and homes for its friendless. Institutions which are potent factors in the efforts of a people to prevent neglect and cure criminal tendencies.

All of these conditions are breeders of ills and conductors of death which must be and happily are being abated.

The remedy suggested is a knowledge coupled with an appreciation of health. Both to embrace the science of health preserving and of health getting; better homes and better habits, even to being "temperate in all things."

Acquired, accepted and practiced the mortality of the race will be materially lessened.

THIRD PAPER.

WHAT ARE THE CAUSES OF THE GREAT MORTALITY AMONG THE NEGROES IN THE CITIES OF THE SOUTH, AND HOW IS THAT MORTALITY TO BE LESSENED?

BY DR. JOHN R. FRANCIS.

In the study of the causes and remedy for the great mortality among the colored people of Southern cities I shall not waste time and words in an attempt to prove, by much statistical evidence, that which is already too well known to us as an admitted fact, viz.: a mortality of colored people in cities of the South, very largely in excess of that of the white people of the same communities.

Dr. John R. Francis

DR. JOHN R. FRANCIS.

Dr. John R. Francis, physician and surgeon, was born in Georgetown, D. C., in 1856. He attended the private and public schools of Washington, D. C., until his sixteenth year. His academic education was received at Wesleyan Academy, Wilbraham, Mass. He began the study of medicine under the tutorage of Dr. C. C. Cox, at that time dean of the Board of Health, and one of the foremost men in the profession of medicine in the District of Columbia.

His professional course was taken at the University of Michigan, from which he graduated with high honor in the class of 1878. Settling in the home of his boyhood, where he was well and favorably known, and where his parents before him were honored and respected, it is no wonder that he succeeded and stands as the leading Colored physician of Washington, D. C.

Dr. Francis was appointed in 1894 by the Secretary of the Interior to the position of first assistant surgeon of the Freedman's Hospital, with a salary of $1,800. He instituted several needed reforms in the treatment of patients. He installed the present training school for nurses, and, indeed, was so active in his reformation of affairs in the institution that those who know the facts admit that Dr. Francis, more than any other man, is responsible for the opening of the new era of the Freedman's Hospital, which led to its present flourishing condition. He is now, and has been for several years past, the obstetrician to the hospital.

He is the sole owner and manager of a private sanitarium on Pennsylvania Avenue, Washington, D. C. This institution has proven to be a panacea to the best element of Colored citizens.

It is a noteworthy fact that Dr. and Mrs. Francis have both served as members of the Board of Education of the District of Columbia.

I am fully justified, in the face of our present enlightenment, in entering, at once, into the discussion as to its causes.

If it be true that the animal organism is intended by nature to pass through a cycle, and that natural death is not a disease, but a completion of the process of life, it follows that the organism, with exceptions, as to any particular class of people born in health, is constructed to pass through this cycle and is not of itself,—that is to say, by its own organism,—capable of giving origin to any of the phenomena to which we apply the term disease. We must, therefore, seek for origins of the phenomena in causes lying outside the body, and affecting it in such manner as to either render the natural actions and processes irregular, or to excite actions and processes that are altogether new.

Writing out in correct lists all the groups of phenomena that make up the term disease, we will find that they invariably come from without. From my point of view all the groups of diseases are in truth accidents; exposure to some influence or influences that pervert function or create new motion. I must first refer to the cause to which at various times has been ascribed the responsibility for this excessive mortality, viz.: that innate vital weakness exists in the colored population of this country as a result of amalgamation. On this theory the black race when mixed with the Caucasian is the only one which produces with the latter a progeny of weakened innate vitality. I have never seen this statement supported by any trustworthy knowledge or information. On the other hand it has always been accompanied by the most absurd arguments which invariably tend to expose the mind of the writer as being prejudiced to the intermingling and the intermarriage between the two races. It is among the possibilities that physiological peculiarities account for dispositions to disease belonging to typical classes of the human family. No one has as yet been able to determine what these peculiarities are. Whether they are primitively impressed on a race, or are acquired is a question that can be answered only when the exact relationships of diseases to race are discovered. My own view is, that acquired and transmitted qualities and specific existing social peculiarities are sufficient agencies for the production of all the known variations of vitality belonging to peculiar races.

I am now thoroughly convinced that the causes of this great mortality of the colored people of the cities of the South are *poverty, pre-*

judice, and *ignorance.* For obvious reasons I will submit them in the following arrangement:

1. *POVERTY:*
    a. Contagious Diseases (close contact).—Diphtheria, scarlet fever, small-pox, tuberculosis, syphilis, etc.
    b. Unsanitary Nuisances (11,705 abated in the District of Columbia for year ending June 30, 1900).—Filthy alleys, cellars, bad drainage, garbage, filthy gutters, hog pens, filthy houses, filthy lots, stagnant water, filthy privies, leaky roofs, sewers, filthy yards, filthy streets, wells, etc.
    c. Unsanitary Homes.—Only those houses that are refused or abandoned by the white people are offered to the colored people for dwellings.
    d. Impure Food.—The large quantity annually condemned in the District of Columbia is an indication of that to which the poor is subjected.
    e. Impure Air.—Bad design and construction (small rooms) and unhealthy location.
    f. Impure Water.—Unhealthy sources, cheap, shallow and unhealthy wells, etc.
    g. Infantile Mortality.—Unusually large from *poverty* alone.

2. *PREJUDICE:*
    a. Idleness and Crime.—Late hours, broken rest, depraved association, tobacco, alcohol, syphilis, other diseases, etc.
    b. A Destitute Laboring Class.—Prejudiced employers, poor pay, excess of work, deficient rest, worry combined with physical exhaustion, unsanitary rooms, etc.
    c. Defective Homes.—Small rooms, poor ventilation, either no water supply, or a very bad one, neglect of sanitary measures by both landlord and agent, all the nuisances enumerated above, etc.

3. *IGNORANCE:*
    a. Diseases from bad hygiene (public, home, and personal).
    b. Induced diseases from physical strain.
    c. Diseases from combination of physical and mental strain.
    d. Disease from the influence of the passions.

e.　Disease from sloth and idleness.

f.　Disease from late hours and broken rest.

g.　Disease from food.

h.　Disease from water.

i.　Disease from alcohol.

j.　Disease from tobacco.

k.　Disease from errors of dress.

l.　Children of parents diseased or weakened from various causes.

The space allowed for this article will not permit the discussion of all the causes mentioned above. There are, however, a few that are worthy of our special consideration. For the purpose of condensation, I will attempt the elucidation of the importance of such causes as demand our most serious attention by incorporating them in the following discussion of the most important part of this article: *"How is this great mortality to be lessened?"*

In my opinion the remedy for this alarming condition exists in *education* and *money.* In other words our remedy is the same as that of other races. The only difference is that the barriers we must surmount are so very peculiar and so very much greater than that of other peoples we must do our best to, at once, recognize the fact and begin the work. I believe the goal is ours and if we will only struggle manfully and hopefully onward we will soon reach it. With

EDUCATION AND MONEY

as the remedy, the colored people must be taught that the first step towards the reduction of disease is to begin at the beginning, to provide for the health of the unborn. The error, commonly entertained, that marriageable men and women have nothing to consider except money, station, or social relationships demands correction.

The offspring of marriage, the most precious of all fortunes, deserves surely as much forethought as is bestowed upon the offspring of the lower animals.

It is well that we teach, in the school room and from the pulpit, about the condition that exists in the parental line, maternal and paternal. The necessity for such instruction is somewhat indicated, in the effect upon the prenatal state, of such conditions as scrofula or struma, of various forms of tuberculosis and syphilis, of epilepsy, of rheumatism, and of insanity. These are only a few. We have to contend even with hereditary proclivity to some forms of the acute communicable diseases, such as diphtheria and scarlet fever and also to immunity from the same.

We must furnish, by all available means and through every possible channel of information, persistent and systematic instruction in public, home and personal hygiene. We should utilize especially the power of the pulpit and influence the public school authorities to institute, in the colored schools throughout the South, special instruction on these subjects. The importance of such instruction is evident in the agitation which is now occurring among the educators in the schools of the Eastern states. If it is needed there then the need of it in the colored schools of the South must be urgent indeed.

We must give such education as will tend to a better general knowledge, especially of the two diseases which, I believe, more than any, should be the most dreaded as being the most prolific of injury to mankind and especially to the colored people on account of their ignorance of the communicability of disease combined with their poverty. I refer to the contagious maladies tuberculosis and the one called "specific" or syphilis, the moral as well as the physical blot on all civilized life. The former is well known nowadays to be one, if not the worst contagion to which the human family is subjected. In its various forms it is responsible, probably, for more deaths among the colored people than any one disease with a definite phenomenon. As less is known about the latter disease, syphilis, I must mention it a little more forcibly, however unpleasant and brief the utterance. The poison of the malady once engrafted into the living body, and producing its effect there, leaves, according to my professional experience, and observation, organic evils which are never completely removed. Various forms of disease of the skin; some forms of consumption; some phases of struma or scrofula; many forms of cachectic feebleness and impaired physical build—what are denominated delicate states of constitution—these and other types of disease are so directly or indirectly connected with the "specific" taint, it becomes impossible to be too careful in tracing it out, or in measuring the degree to which it extends in the field of morbid phenomenon, in our efforts to improve the vitality of the colored people and to enlighten them upon this class of diseases.

The widespread encouragement of thrift, industry and efforts among the colored people to gain a livelihood or, to put it more boldly, to get money and keep it, thereby obtaining the means with which to supply themselves with the necessaries of life, and possibly, with some of its comforts, will materially wipe out a large percentage of that class of diseases and death that proceed from such causes as worry, excess of work, physical and mental strain, late hours, broken rest, etc.

Washington, D. C., is considered a very clean city. It is, therefore, significant that the 11,705 nuisances, referred to in the foregoing, are an indication as to the great risk, from this source throughout the South. It is obvious at once that the colored people, who form the bulk of the poor class, are the principal victims to that which escapes official inspection.

Notwithstanding the fact that the colored population of the District of Columbia is less than one-third of that of the whites, in the year 1899-1900, there died in the homes located in the back alleys of the city 411 colored persons and eleven white persons, indicating to what extent these unsanitary homes are occupied by the colored people.

Space will not permit the further elucidation of the foregoing causes and remedies, which I have done nothing more than to touch upon. However, I cannot close without giving further emphasis to my views by offering in evidence the conditions, as to vitality, of the Jews. The facts are that this race, from some cause or causes, presents an endurance against disease that does not belong to any other portion of the civilized communities amongst which its members dwell. We do not have far to go to find many causes for this high vitality. The causes are simply summed up in the term "soberness of life." The Jew drinks less than the Christian; he takes, as a rule, better food; he marries earlier; he rears the children he has brought into the world with greater personal care; he tends the aged more thoughtfully; he takes better care of the poor; he takes better care of himself; he does not boast of to-morrow, but he provides for it; and he holds tenaciously to all he gets. It may be true that he carries these virtues too far, but I do most earnestly plead that if the colored people will only emulate the Jew, they, like the Jew, will win, like him they will become strong, and like him in scorning boisterous mirth and passion, will become comparatively happy and healthy.

FOURTH PAPER.

WHAT ARE THE CAUSES OF THE GREAT MORTALITY AMONG THE NEGROES IN THE CITIES OF THE SOUTH, AND HOW IS THAT MORTALITY TO BE LESSENED?

BY JAMES RANDALL WILDER, M. D., PHAR. D.

The American Negro finds himself, at the beginning of the twentieth century, seriously embarrassed by the many false and damaging accusations that have been made against him, not least of which is the charge of physical inferiority. The charge has been wholesale that the Negro differs from the white man physically, and that he is ethnically and strongly predisposed to certain fatal and contagious diseases. This stigma of disease has been placed upon him and repeatedly emphasized, but despite the fact that the effort has been made for years, by men learned in anthropology to find and prove the inherent inferiority of the Negro, based upon anatomical, physiological and biostatic peculiarity, to-day the bare statistical fact of his high mortality alone supports the calumnious fabrication. It is true that according to official statistics the Negro's death rate in this country is relatively high, but the causes of disparity are *extrinsic* and *remedial* and he was not stamped thus *ab initio,* but by the fiat of the Creative-will.

The Negro, identified as he is with the great human family, is subject to the same deteriorating influences that affect his fellow-man. Hence impure air and water, polluted soil from defective sewerage, adulterated food-stuffs, and the unhealthful conditions imposed during the school-going period of life—which are questions of public hygiene and general concern—contribute, in no small degree, to his mortality. But aside from these influences, common to all people, he is subject to others peculiar to himself, on account of the environments that govern him. The proverbial unreliability of statistics justifies the assumption that the Negro's death-rate is not as great as it is said to be. The occupations of the Negro tend to keep him in the back-ground and to encourage a neglect on the part of the census enumerator to record accurately all of the Negroes in a certain locality. But the Negro dies faster than the white man, and it is not my purpose to deny it, but to recite a few of the real causes of the disparity in the cities of the South, and to show how that mortality is to be lessened.

Dr. J. R. Wilder

JAMES RANDALL WILDER, M. D., PHAR. D.

James Randall Wilder was born at Columbia, S. C., and is the son of Charles M. Wilder, who was postmaster at Columbia, for many years. His mother was Maria Coleman, also a native of the Palmetto State.

Dr. Wilder is a man of spotless character, and enjoys a striking appearance, a magnetic personality, and a brilliant and versatile mind. His early training was received in the public schools of his native city. He spent a season in the classical department of Howard University, and from there he went to Howard Medical College, from which he graduated in the year 1888. Availing himself of the unrivalled opportunities afforded by the Freedmen's Hospital, he rapidly acquired both theoretical and practical knowledge, so that when he stepped into the world he possessed a preparation seldom equaled by the young practitioner. He has also the degree of Phar. D. from Howard.

He located in Washington, the capital of the nation, where today he enjoys a large and lucrative practice. His modest, sympathetic nature makes him an ideal man for the sick room. His ability has won prefessional recognition not only for himself but for others. He was for many years physician to the National Home for Destitute Colored Women and Children, and is today the examining surgeon for a number of benevolent and charitable organizations. He has been prominently connected with many of the business ventures of the colored people in the District of Columbia for the past ten years, and is ranked as a broad-minded, solid, public-spirited citizen—a grand object lesson for what is best and most progressive in the community. He has invested his earnings judiciously, so that today he has a competency seldom attained by a man of his years. The success gained, the making the most of himself, renders him the best advocate of truth, and a potent factor in the growth and development of the race. This plain, honest, earnest young man is a type of the generation since citizenship came—a splendid example of worth since the selfhood of the race has been partially recognized, and the members have been permitted to add their quota to the sum of human advancement and achievement. The hour calls for fact, not fancy— for flesh-and-blood examples of what has been done by the young manhood of the country. The interest here and now is due to the fact that he has had somewhat to say on a subject of vital moment, and has said it vigorously and eloquently. Here he is the champion of truth, performing a service in a dignified, scholarly manner, and so winning the praise and gratitude of all lovers of truth. His article must call a halt to those inconsiderate ones who persistently repeat what through haste and insufficient data has been given to the world as fact—as logical inference from scientific investigation.

Dr. Wilder has collected a large library of professional and literary works, and has never ceased to be a hard student. His home shows the taste of the scholar and wide-awake practitioner. He married Miss Sallie C. Pearson of Columbia, S. C., and to them have been born two children—Charles McDuffie and Susan Maceo.

Dr. Wilder belongs to that class of quiet, earnest souls who pursue the "even tenor of their way" and are doing most to establish truth, to refute error, content to let the "deeds, though mute, speak loud the doer."

(1) American slavery, with its unparalleled cruelty and bestiality has injured the Negro, intellectually, physically and morally. It has been claimed that the admixture of the Negro with the Caucasian has given us a resulting mulatto, weaker physically than either of the parent stock, but this statement is based upon hypothesis, and is not borne out by the facts in the case. It is true, however, that a resulting lowering of vitality has followed the admixture of *"kindred blood,"* which was almost unavoidable during the days of slavery as the result of certain well-known procreative practices that obtained on the part of the master, and on account of the itineracy of the Negro incident to his chattelism. In "those dark days" it was hard enough for the Negro to recognize his near kin on his maternal side, and it was infinitely impossible for him to trace the "family tree" from the paternal side. The evil effects of this consequent admixture of "similar" blood cannot be denied, and must bear a modicum of responsibility for the excessive mortality of the Negro of to-day.

(2) The fact that the great majority of the Negro women in the cities of the South are compelled to work steadily even while they are *enceinte,* doubtless often interferes with the normal development of the internal organs of their offspring, causing a lack of vitality which is not apparent to the casual observer, but which must make them an easy victim to disease.

(3) The same social and economic conditions that keep the expectant mother busy with her daily labors, also abbreviate her "lying-in-period," which not only weakens her physically, but deprives her newly-born offspring of its natural food—thus consigning it to an infant's grave, or so debilitating it that it succumbs to the first disease with which it becomes affected. It is bad enough to be bottle-fed, physiologists tell us, but it is infinitely worse to be hand-fed. The majority of the Negroes in the Southland are hand-fed from birth with food decidedly improper both as to quality and quantity, thus making defective the very substructure of their being. Is it any wonder that such a people die faster than another people, who nurse their young or have it done, or who give them pure cow's milk modified scientifically, or other artificial infant food prepared skilfully amid the best sanitary environments?

(4) The early motherhood of the Negro has its evil effects. The proper age for a woman to become a mother is at twenty-five years and usually before that time development is not complete, and the whole

organism is in a transition state. It is equally true that the use of any organ before it has attained its complete growth or development is damaging to that organ and interferes with its normal function, and "we cannot but believe that children developed in immature sexual organs must be deficient in true vital force and energy. It is often noticeable that a child apparently strong and vigorous, may have but little power to resist disease, or may even be strongly predisposed to some infirmity." The colored women in the section under discussion who become mothers, are usually multiporæ long before the twenty-fifth year.

(5)   The element of overwork must come in for its increment of responsibility in the excessive mortality of the Negro. While deficiency in exercise favors a lack of nutrition conducive to wasting in size, on the other hand too much work favors hypertrophy of vital organs and tissue degeneration. The average healthy man should work about eight hours per day and "should do work to the equivalent of 150 foot-tons daily." The American Negro's working hours, as a rule, are regulated, if at all, by the exigencies of the work to be performed, as it appears to an exacting employer.

(6)   The kind of work performed by the Negroes in the Southern cities includes all menial occupations, which conduce to accident and exposure. The death-rate among the laboring class of any community, irrespective and independent of its nationality, is necessarily greater than that of the well-to-do leisure class.

(7)   The manner of living of the majority of the colored people in the cities of the South—which is sometimes the progeny of ignorance, but oftener the result of necessity—is responsible, in a large measure, for their high mortality. They are crowded together on back streets, in lanes and ill-smelling bottoms, near ponds of stagnant water, on the banks of rivers—wherever their scanty means consign them. The ignorant among them, like the ignorant among any other people, ignore the teachings of hygiene, because they are ignorant, and not because they are black. They do not know the value of fresh air and sunlight and cleanliness, and hence are ignorant of the fatality attached to the unholy trinity —darkness, dampness and dirt, which is responsible for the tuberculosis that is charged to their "inherent tendencies." The pittance that is paid to the Negro in the name of wages forces him to crowd together in narrow and ill-ventilated sleeping apartments, which is decidedly unhealthful and favors the spread of contagious diseases. Thus smallpox spreads

rapidly in a Negro settlement, not because they are Negroes, but because their manner of living brings them into the most intimate contact with one another, so that whatever disease attacks one, rapidly spreads to all of the others who are not immune.

The lack of suitable clothing and proper food, as a result of poverty, weakens the Negro physically. The neglect of the bath through lack of time, is responsible for much of the heart, kidney and skin diseases so prevalent among the laboring classes of the colored people. It takes time to keep clean, and the laborer has no leisure. Ignorance of the seriousness of certain diseases like syphilis, scrofula and rheumatism, has played an important role in the drama of his mortality.

(8) Another fruitful cause of his excessive mortality arises out of his *struggle for existence.*. The exigencies of life are such with him that he does not heed the admonitions of nature made manifest in the early symptoms of disease, so that unwittingly he becomes habituated to discomfort and pain. When the common Negro laborer lays aside his implements of labor on account of sickness, the disease with which he is affected is well founded and passed beyond the abortive and often the curative stage, and very frequently when medical advice is obtained, it is of the dispensary or "physician to the poor" type, which too often savors of unconcern, inexperience and incompetency.

(9) The prevalent habit among the colored people of taking patented cure-all nostrums, which contain narcotics that insidiously benumb the sensibilities and mask the symptoms of disease, would naturally contribute to the mortality of any people.

(10) Not the least fruitful of all of the causes of the Negro's excessive mortality, is a lack of *resistance* to disease, engendered by the social conditions that obtain in the Southland. There he is so oppressed and persecuted that he finds himself not only an easy prey to disease, but an early victim to death. He has little to live for, and his religion promises him much after death, which, in a sense, he welcomes as a relief from his trials and troubles. This statement will not appear exaggerated when one considers the powerful influence that the mind has over the body. A cheerful, hopeful, contented mind, predisposes to a healthy body, and conversely, a discontented and despairful mind, interferes with the vital functions and invites disease and death.

(11) Lastly, in a consideration of the relatively high mortality of the Negro in the cities of the South, considerable weight must be given

to the *contracted* death-rate of the whites due to their superior social and financial condition. Their environments are, as a rule, as healthful as education can suggest and as money can obtain, and when disease overtakes them, they combat it not only with the skill of science, but with the power of will. The incentives of life, so lacking for the colored people, are theirs in all of their plenitude. The earth is theirs and the fullness thereof, and there is no power therein that they may not covet. This feeling, this knowledge, becomes a *vis-a-mente* that proves a potential factor in their struggle with disease. Despite this powerful influence however, and because of it, the *morbidity* of the white man in this country is great. I venture the assertion that his morbidity far exceeds that of the Negro—not because he is more prone to disease, but because he is enabled to live longer with disease on account of the influences to which allusion has already been made. The plain fact is, the Negro dies sooner and the white man lives longer with disease, which presents the unique question: Is it not more advantageous to the public good to die of a disease and be buried safely and deeply beneath the soil than to live with it and thus increase the opportunities of disseminating it?

(12)   The remedies for the excessive mortality of the Negro in the cities of the South are self-evident. He is a man and identical with other men structurally, so that whatever is health-giving and life-lengthening for other civilized peoples, is health-giving and life-lengthening for him. To be specific, his greatest need is an increase of knowledge along the line of hygiene, and a studious application of that knowledge. He must not only be taught to run the race of life intelligently, but he must not be hindered in the process of his running. He must know the life to lead, and then lead it. In this he must have the liberal co-operation of his employer, and his brother-in-white generally. He must be paid in accordance with the labor that he performs and must be allowed an equitable participation in the every-day affairs of life. Actuated by the hopes and aspirations that actuate other men, and given a man's chance in the struggle of life, his industry and genius will soon improve his condition and bring him material prosperity, upon which depends, in a measure, the development of moral, intellectual and physical growth. Leisure and opportunity, comfort and freedom from sordid cares and anxieties regarding the immediate necessities of life, must be secured, if a race is to find time for study and thought, and to develop its best moral and physical life. May not the Negro justly find some consolation in his

R. F. Boyd, A. M. M. D.

R. F. BOYD, M. D., D. D. S.

Dr. R. F. Boyd has clearly demonstrated by energy, pluck, ability and upright dealing with his fellowman, the possibility of rising from poverty's hard estate to honor's golden prize. Dr. R. F. Boyd was born and partly reared on a farm in Giles County, Tennessee, where he learned to hoe, to plow, to reap and to mow. When quite a boy he worked for the famous surgeon, Dr. Paul F. Eve, in Nashville, and attended as best he could night school in the old Fisk buildings on Knowles street. He taught his first school at College Grove, Tennessee. The Doctor would teach a school and at its close re-enter Fisk University or Central Tennessee College. In 1882 he graduated from Meharry Medical College, with the degree of M. D. He went to Mississippi and taught a high school at New Albany and practiced his profession till the fall of 1882, when he re-entered the Central Tennessee College to complete his college course, receiving at the same time an adjunct Professorship in Chemistry at Meharry and made teacher of Physiology and Hygiene in Central Tennessee by which he was able to pay his college expenses. In 1883 he was made Professor of Physiology in Meharry, which position, together with a position in the Literary Department, he held till he graduated from the College Department of Central Tennessee College, in 1886. In 1887 he graduated from the Dental Department of Meharry, receiving the degree of D. D. S., teaching in the school at the same time. In June, 1887, he opened his office in Nashville, where so many had tried and failed. In 1888 Dr. Boyd was made Professor of Anatomy and Physiology in Meharry; in 1890 he attended the Post-graduate School of Medicine at Chicago, from which he received a diploma. In 1890 he was made Professor of Hygiene, Physiology and Clinical Medicine, which position he held until 1893, when he was made Professor of the Diseases of Women and Clinical Medicine, which chair he still holds. In 1892 he took a specal course in the Post-graduate Medical School and Hospital of Chicago, on the diseases of women and children, among whom the greater portion of his practice is. One of the greatest needs of the colored people in the South is well regulated hospitals, where trained nurses can handle and care for the sick under skilled physicians. Until Mercy Hospital was instituted, there was no place of this kind in the South. It was Dr. R. F. Boyd who established and instituted this the largest and most complete hospital owned and controlled by colored people. There surgeons of our race do all kinds of operations and trained and graduate nurses of the race care for the sick under their management.

It is in this institution where the graduates of Meharry in the Medical and Nurse-Training Departments get their practical work. It is the great center to which colored physicians of the South may send cases to be operated upon by skilled physicians and handled by trained nurses. The death rate of this institution has been less than three per cent from all causes.

Besides this work, Dr. Boyd has taken a great interest in secret societies. As an Immaculate, he has gained a National reputation and has filled nearly all of the offices in the Supreme Lodge. As a Pythian he has served the Grand Lodge as Grand Medical Register, and has been honored by the Supreme Lodge as Supreme Medical Register, and is Surgeon General of the Military or Uniform Rank of that Order. The Ancient United Sons and Daughters of Africa is a creation of his own brain and he is at present Supreme Secretary of that Order. As a business man he ranks among the foremost of the race. He owns some of the best realty of the city, among which is the Boyd Building, 417-419-421-423 Cedar Street. This building has four business fronts, a hotel and restaurant, offices of various kinds and four large society halls, in which about forty societies meet. The Mercy Hospital was purchased by him solely, at a cash value of $6,000. Besides this he is the owner of other valuable property of Nashville and suburbs.

excessive mortality of to-day? May he not believe that "death is the philosophy of life?" May he not feel that his race is being strengthened by the dying of the weak, just as a tree is strengthened by losing its unsound branches? If so, then the future Negro in this country will be the fittest of "the survival of the fittest," and will represent the grandest type of physical manhood that the world has ever known.

FIFTH PAPER.

WHAT ARE THE CAUSES OF THE GREAT MORTALITY AMONG THE NEGROES IN THE CITIES OF THE SOUTH, AND HOW IS THAT MORTALITY TO BE LESSENED?

BY DR. R. F. BOYD.

This is a question of vital importance to us as a race and to the nation as well. Much thought has been given to it by the best thinkers of both races and many articles have been written by friend and foes. All kinds of solutions have been proposed and yet the great death-rate goes on. In the larger cities of the South our people die from two to three times as fast as the whites.

The number of premature deaths is on the increase; the infant death-rate is appalling; and consumption, a hitherto unknown disease among our people, is credited with one-fourth the victims of all ages.

All the powers of science and art are being taxed to the utmost to afford a complete solution to this problem. Every large city in the South is being awakened to the sense of the importance of this subject. And well they may; for the ignorance, the vice, the poverty, the habitation and the food that cause this alarming death-rate effect the whole community.

A proper knowledge and observance of the laws of health will give happiness to all.

Man is as subject to the organic laws as the inanimate bodies about him are to mechanical and chemical laws, and we as little escape the consequences of the neglect or violation of these natural laws, which affect the organic life, through the air we breathe, the food we eat, the water we drink, the clothes we wear, and the circumstances surrounding our habitation, as the stone projected from the hand, or the shot from the mouth of the cannon can escape the bounds of gravitation.

What we need is the gospel of the physical health to be preached from every pulpit, and in every school room and in every home. All strong motives of religion and the eternal world are taught from the pulpit and the Sunday school to enforce certain duties that are no more important to the well-being of man than the laws of health, which are so widely disregarded. These laws are God's laws as truly as any inscribed by Him on the Table of Stones.

The boards of health of our cities prescribe rules and regulations to insure the peace and happiness of the individual and the longevity of life which must apply to all in order that they might live out the expected term of life. What is the natural term of life? Physiologists have fixed it at a hundred years. Florens at five times the time required to per- fectly develop the skeleton. David says: "The days of man's life are three score years and ten; and if by reason of strength they be four score years, yet indeed is his strength labor and sorrow."

Under modern hygienic rules and regulations the days of man have been increased in civilized countries. Carefully prepared statistics show that while the maximum age has not increased in many centuries, the number of persons who survive infancy and reap a ripe old age is greatly increased.

According to the Secretary of the Chamber of Commerce of New York City, civilization largely interferes with the laws of evolution, by survivorship and by encouraging the waste which arises from it. We know that a human being soundly constituted continues in good health until he reaps a ripe old age, provided certain conditions are observed and no injurious accident befall him.

We might learn a lesson from the early Jews, or the ancient Greeks or Romans, if we had at our command statistics of their mortality. Doubtless they had a small death-rate! For they were strong and vigor- ous and observed the laws of hygiene. When these laws are properly observed, they decrease mortality and bring about greater health, com- fort and happiness to the individual and to the country at large. Those who would preserve health in themselves and in the community in which they live, who would reap the greatest benefits of earth, and live out the appointed time, must strictly conform to these essentials:

1. A constant supply of pure air.
2. Cleanliness of person and surroundings.
3. Sufficient nourishing food properly prepared and properly taken.

4. Sufficient exercise of the various organs of the body.
5. The proper amount of rest and sleep.
6. Right temperature.
7. Proper clothing.
8. Sufficient, cheerful, innocent enjoyment.
9. Exemption from harassing cares.

Conform strictly to these rules and all avoidable disease will be annihilated. On the other hand, where hygienic and sanitary science is not enforced, filth, decay and putrifying matter is sure to accumulate. In this we have suitable material for the propagation of disease germs, which cause all communicable and contagious diseases. These minute organisms exist in the atmosphere everywhere, and multiply by their own peculiar method of procreation; such as filth, heat and moisture.

A population under the influence of vice, poverty, filth, debauchery, foul air, poorly prepared food and crowded dwellings, or in low, damp localities, with no rule regulating their eating or sleeping, clothing or exercise, is sure to have a great degree of mortality.

With our thorough knowledge of how to prevent epidemics, most of the diseases that enter the body through the respiratory, digestive, cutaneous, circulatory, nervous, and genito-urinary systems should be less frequent. Taking the facts which I have here given into account one may see that not only do health and longevity depend upon laws which we can understand and successfully operate, but man has it in his power to modify to a great extent the circumstances in which he lives, with a view to the promotion of his well-being and preservation.

We know that the draining of a marsh pond banishes malaria; a change from the city to the country reinvigorates, and that those who live in the high, well drained portions of our cities have the smallest degree of mortality and that the greater comforts possessed by the affluent secure for them longer life than the poor who are not so favored. To diminish the mortality in the Southern cities will depend upon both the individual and social efforts as well as upon the public measures of the legally constituted authorities.

The dirty neglected portions of our city where refuse and rubbish, animal and vegetable matters are deposited and allowed to rest and send up their poisonous odors from house to house, must be looked after. The dwellings of our people must be improved. The old, dilapidated stables, in the narrow, filthy alleys; the low, damp basements and dark cellars, often below the ground, with an insufficiency of both light and air; the clusters of homes built in the bottom and low places, closely pent up, back to back so as to prevent ventilation with only one entrance to each, and a privy between; the over-crowded conditions of these uninhabitable quarters and the quality of the food taken by those who live in these disgraceful dwellings must be looked after.

Habits of living must be corrected and a crusade against ignorance and vice begun by society. I don't think I would miss it very far when I say that one-third of the colored people in our cities live in just such dwellings as I have described here; while most of the white population live in well-built houses in the healthy portions of the cities. Is there any surprise that there should be so great a disproportion in the mortality of the races? Compare the statistics of all the large cities and you will find that under similar conditions, this same proportion in mortality exists in the Northern and foreign cities, where the food and dwelling of the poor have the same difference. But this same difference exists nowhere in the world as it does in the South. It is almost impossible for a colored man to rent a respectable house anywhere in the cities; but the dark, low, damp, confined, ill-ventilated cellars and alley houses are rented for as much as comfortable quarters ought to bring. I don't wonder that the mortality of the Negro is so great; but I do wonder that it is not greater. Any other race of people would have been exterminated in twenty years.

The remedy for the high death-rate is the enactment and enforcement of laws against allowing the people to sleep in basements, cellars, old stables, alley houses, in low malarial sections of the cities, and making the penalty against the landlords so great, that they will not rent such places for dwellings. Regulate the kind of tenement houses and the number of persons who shall sleep in one room, the kind of food and rules for its preparation; break up these late church meetings in poorly ventilated houses, and the problem will be solved.

The infant mortality will be reduced one-half when our people learn that the care of a good conscientious physician is necessary, from generation to development, and through the entire stage of adolescence; not so much to cure, as to prevent disease. Our whole system of medicine is now turning upon prevention rather than cure. When the public is educated up to the point of paying physicians to prevent as well as cure diseases, then, there will be less sickness and fewer epidemics.

Then sanitary science, under the strict observance of hygiene, will reach perfection; the rude, gross habits of living will be corrected; a system of perfect drainage and ventilation will be inaugurated; pure air and fresh water supply will be furnished to every public and private house; only pure, unadulterated foods will be on the markets; every hotel, private and boarding-house will furnish properly prepared diets, and universal cleanliness will be the law.

Last, but by no means least, I call your attention to another most potent remedy for the diminishing of the great mortality of the race in the South. Besides the city hospitals, the whites have many other hospitals and infirmaries, supported by church and benevolent organizations where those that pay are at the hospitals because they can receive the constant attention of a physician and nurse. We need and should have such hospitals. The benevolently disposed people, the churches and societies of the cities could establish and well support them. In them, there would be pay wards and charitable wards. Each church and society supporting the hospitals could send their indigent sick to the charity wards and those who can pay, to the private apartments.

These hospitals would afford a much needed opportunity for young women of the race to prepare for trained nurses and afford better facilities for the physicians to practice surgery and study remedies.

We have established in the city of Nashville, the Mercy Hospital under the care and management of the Board of Trustees, composed of some of the best citizens and heads of our great universities. Among the directors are, Hon. J. C. Napier, President; W. T. Hightower, Treasurer; Dr. G. W. Hubbard, Dean of Meherry Medical College; Dr. P. B. Guernsey, President of Roger Williams University; Prof. H. H. Wright, Fisk University, and Dr. R. H. Boyd, President of the National Baptist Publishing Board.

The hospital is located at 811 S. Sherry street, Nashville, Tenn., in one of the most quiet, beautiful and healthful localities of the city. The site is high and well drained; the building large and commodious and up-to-date in all its apartments. There are two large wards; one for male and one for female, and private rooms, to which good pay patients are assigned where they will come in contact with no one but their physician and the nurse.

In this hospital great care is given to surgical work of all kinds and especially to abdominal surgery and gynecology. Colored physicians all over the South may send or bring their surgical cases here and get every advantage that can be provided by the best first-class hospitals and infirmaries all over the country. We have the best graduate-trained nurses in constant attendance and the resident physicians are men of the race who have made marvelous progress for two decades in all branches of their work.

Since the establishment of the hospital we have had a record of which few similar institutions can boast. During the first year we have had more than 140 surgical cases, including abdominal section and other major operations and yet the death-rate was less than 3 per cent from all causes.

Our operating room is well appointed, with an abundance of sunlight by day and gas light at night. Many of the physicians of the South have sent us cases for which we are very grateful. We have had cases from Alabama, Arkansas, Mississippi, Texas, Kentucky, Missouri, Florida and Georgia. Until the other cities of the South are able to afford the facilities and accommodations and the skill and experience of the Mercy Hospital we feel that it is the duty and should be the great pleasure of every colored physician to send his surgical cases to this hospital. I consider this one of the great factors to solve this vexed problem.

The causes of the great mortality among the Negroes of the large cities of the South are due to ignorance; vice; debauchery; poor food, illy prepared; unsanitary environments; their habitation in the overcrowded tenement houses; in old stables; damp cellars; and low, damp sections and in narrow, filthy alleys, where the foul air, improper nourishment, poor ventilation and the want of personal cleanliness, furnish the proper condition for the development of disease and death. Correct these conditions and educate the people up to a thorough knowledge of and a strict compliance of the laws of health and the problem is solved. The death-rate among our people will not only be lessened, but I believe the Negro will outlive any other people on earth.

Dr. W. F. Penn

DR. WILLIAM F. PENN.

Dr. Penn was born in Amherst County, Va., in 1870, and is accordingly thirty years of age. His parents took him to Lynchburg early in life and there entered him in the schools. From the Lynchburg schools he went to the Hampton Normal and Agricultural Institute and from there to the Virginia Normal and Collegiate College Institute, from which he graduated in 1891. After graduating he taught in the city schools of Lynchburg, Va., resigning to pursue a medical course in the Leonard Medical School, at Raleigh, N. C., from which he went, in 1893, to Yale University, New Haven, Conn., and graduated from the Medical Department of that world famed institution in 1897, taking high rank in all of his classes until the day of graduation.

His standing in his class may be seen in that he was the first Negro ever chosen in the Medical School as one of the editors of the Class Book, which goes down in history as a record of graduates, etc.

For a while he was one of the Internes at Freedman's Hospital in this city, under Dr. Williams, then Surgeon-in-Chief, and was regarded as one of the best informed and most skillful men on the staff.

Dr. Penn went to Atlanta in 1897 to practice medicine, and from the start took front rank.

By official preferment he is the physician to the following institutions of learning in Atlanta: Atlanta University, Clark University, Gammon Theological Seminary.

As a Christian gentleman he is well known to everyone in Atlanta, being a member and trustee of Loyd Street Methodist Episcopal Church. In 1899 he married Mrs. Lulu T. Wright, well-known in Georgia as one of the most polished and beautiful of Georgia women. Dr. Penn comes from one of the best of Virginia families and like his brother, Prof. I. Garland Penn, of Atlanta, Ga., is well-known to everybody, who holds high official position in the Methodist Episcopal Church.

SIXTH PAPER.

WHAT ARE THE CAUSES OF THE GREAT MORTALITY AMONG THE NE-GROES IN THE CITIES OF THE SOUTH, AND HOW IS THAT MORTALITY TO BE LESSENED?

BY WM. F. PENN, M. D.

The alarming mortality among the Negroes of this country is attracting a great deal of attention at this time. The causes that are responsible for this mortality are the following:

First—The Negro's bad sanitary surroundings. That these surroundings play an important part in the development of diseases among the Negroes, no one who has made any investigation into this matter will deny.

Second—The Negro's disregard for ventilation. I have seen hundreds of Negroes crowded in churches shouting and singing without a particle of fresh air being admitted.

Third—Loss of sleep. That many of the Negroes lose sufficient sleep to predispose them to disease cannot be denied. Many of them instead of going to their beds at night at reasonable hours, and taking their rest, can be seen at all hours of the night, after working hard all day, coming from churches, lodges, dances, barrooms and gambling dens.

Fourth—Drinking whiskey. It is a lamentable fact that many of the Negroes are whiskey drinkers. Now, it is an established fact that the man who drinks whiskey to excess does not only have changes produced in the various organs of his body, which render him an easy victim to disease, but, being an acquired disease, his chance for recovery is reduced in proportion to the extent of his drinking. Besides, he transmits to his posterity a hereditary tendency to disease.

Fifth—Syphilis. Of all the diseases known to the medical science, there is none that is so far-reaching in its effects as syphilis. One prominent writer says that a man who contracts this disease can never be cured, and that his ghost after him has the disease. That many Negroes have this disease there can be no doubt. Now, this disease not only destroys the lives of those who contract it, but it is transmitted from them to their descendants.

Sixth—The lack of money to furnish the proper medical treatment in sickness. That many Negroes die because of their lack of money to employ good physicians and to get the proper medicines is a sad fact. In many cases when the physicians are humane enough to give this class of Negroes their services free, they have not the money to buy the medicines prescribed. It is time that most of the cities of the South have physicians whose duty it is to give their services and medicines free to the poor Negroes, but in many cases these free services and medicines are too meager to do any good. We know that certain diseases, particularly those of the lungs, may be arrested or cured by change of climate. Now, there are very few of the Negroes with lung diseases who are able to go to a climate that might prolong their lives.

Seventh—Exposure. Many of the deaths among the Negroes are indirectly due to the kind of work they do. From necessity many of them have to work under conditions that are detrimental to their health. Having discussed briefly some of the causes that are responsible for the great mortality among the Negroes, I shall now proceed to give my ideas as to how the mortality can be lessened.

In order to lessen this mortality, the city authorities must do their duty in the matter of removing from the Negroes those bad sanitary surroundings to which many of their diseases are attributable.

I here quote from Dr. Culp's book on consumption. What Dr. Le Hardy says on the duty of the city authorities as to the matter of improving the Negro's sanitary surroundings:

"It seems to me that the authorities could easily reduce the death rate and protect these people, without increasing the expenses of the cities. They could prevent, under heavy penalty, the building of more than four houses upon a lot 60 or 62 feet front; require for each house an open space (yard) fully twice the area of the house; make it obligatory to leave an empty space between every second house; require that lots be thoroughly drained or filled before issuing building permits; that every wooden dwelling house shall be put upon brick pillars, at least 18 inches from the surface of the soil; this space to remain open for the free access of air; that no lying or sleeping rooms shall be made smaller than 12 by 10 feet, with fire-place or ventilation flue opening; forbid under heavy penalty privy vaults; require landlords where sewer connection is impracticable to build closets in such a manner that the pails can be easily removed and replaced by the scavenger, and forbid also that wooden fences be placed around or between yards. Such an ordinance, if vigorously enforced, will stop the building of ten or more houses, with as many vaults, upon a single lot."

The Negro must refuse to live in bad houses, they must keep things around them clean. They must not engage in those occupations in which they cannot keep good health. They must stop drinking whiskey, they must stop spending late hours at churches, lodges and barrooms and gambling dens; they must take at least eight hours' sleep every night. They must stop sleeping and living in rooms with persons who have contagious diseases. They must save some of their money, so that they may be able to get the proper medical treatment in sickness.

TOPIC XIII.

WHAT SHOULD BE THE NEGRO'S ATTITUDE IN POLITICS?

BY HON. GEORGE H. WHITE.

In presenting this subject to the public, I shall endeavor to treat it from a broad and liberal standpoint, eliminating all selfishness or individual political bias, and viewing the situation from the standpoint of an American citizen.

The first prerequisite to good government in a republic, is purity in the ballot. No stream can be pure unless its source is pure; neither can a republic hope for just and fair laws and the administration and execution of them, unless there is purity and fairness in the sources from whence these cardinal principles of government spring. Laws should be enacted for the whole people and not for individuals, races or sections —thereby securing the support and retaining the confidence of all the parts of our heterogeneous compact, to the end that a homogeneous whole may move in the same direction for the good of all concerned.

The Negroes ask for—and as a part of this republic—have a right to demand the perpetuation of these basic principles of our government. While we are young in citizenship, and admit having made many political mistakes, yet we are willing that the search-light of reason be thrown upon our acts, and a fair and impartial verdict rendered as to our conduct, when all the circumstances surrounding our variegated political history are taken into consideration. Liberated, enfranchised and turned loose among our former masters, who could not take kindly to our new citizenship, we naturally sought friendship and political alliance with those claiming to be our best friends—those who had been instrumental in obtaining our freedom. These new friends came largely from the Federal army, interspersed with many adventurers who followed in the wake of that army, seeking strange fields in which to ply their vocations. Many of these new-comers proved to be true friends to the Negro of the South and led us on and taught us as a faithful guardian would teach and care for his wards. But the great majority of them were wholly unscrupulous and worked upon the ignorance, inexperience and gullibility of the Negro, overtime, to place themselves into positions where

Hon. George H. White

HON. GEORGE H. WHITE, LL. D.

Mr. White was born in a log cabin, located at the confluence of "Richland Branch" and "Slop Swamp" in Bladen County, North Carolina, near the line of Columbus County, remote from cities and towns. His maternal grandmother was half-Indian and his paternal grandmother was Irish, full-blood. His other admixture is facetiously described as "mostly Negro." His early boyhood was a struggle for bread and a very little butter, his schooling being necessarily neglected. He usually attended two or three months in the year. Later, by dint of toil, and saving a few dollars, he was able to secure training under Prof. D. P. Allen, President of the Whitten Normal School at Lumberton, N. C., and afterwards entered Howard University at Washington, graduating from the eclectic department in 1877. Believing that he could best serve his race and himself as an advocate of justice, he read law while taking the academic course, completing his reading under Judge William J. Clarke, of North Carolina, and was licensed to practice in all courts of that State by the Supreme Court in 1879.

Although Mr. White has won marked success in several walks of life, as lawyer, teacher and business man, it is his political achievements that have won for him not only a national reputation, but have evoked no small degree of comment from the press and diplomats of many of the countries of the old world. It is worthy of remark that up to this time, at the age of forty-nine, he has never held an appointive office, his commissions coming invariably from the hands of the sovereign people direct. He was elected to the North Carolina House of Representatives in 1880, and to the State Senate in 1884; was elected solicitor and prosecuting attorney for the second judicial district of North Carolina for four years in 1886, and for a like term in 1890; was nominated for Congress in 1894, but withdrew in the interest of harmony in his party. He made the race for Congress in 1896 and was triumphantly elected by a majority of 4,000, reversing a normal democratic majority of over 5,000—a change of fully 9,000 votes, indicating in no uncertain tone the confidence and esteem in which he was held by his friends and neighbors. He was re-elected in 1898. His services as a legislator were conscientious and valuable. At the close of his second term, he delivered a valedictory to the country, which was universally praised as the best, truest and most timely expression of the Negro's plea for equality of citizenship that ever rang through the halls of Congress. The speech was widely circulated, and was favorably commented upon by the leading newspapers of the nation.

Mr. White has accumulated quite a handsome fortune, his wealth being estimated at from $20,000 to $30,000. His personal popularity and the respect for his ability are attested by the fact that several honorary degrees have been conferred upon him by a number of the noted educational institutions of the land.

Mr. White is a thirty-third degree Mason. For six years he was Grand Master of Masons for the State of North Carolina, having filled most of the subordinate offices in that body before his elevation to the Grand Mastership.

Since his retirement from Congress, Mr. White has been engaged in the practice of law in Washington, D. C., and so favorably has he impressed his qualifications upon the bench and bar of the national capital that one of the judges publicly, and without precedent, complimented him in open court and set his methods up as an example for other lawyers who practice there. Eminent as are his abilities, Mr. White is proverbially modest. Of strong character, well-balanced mind and an unswerving sense of justice, liberal in views upon all subjects, political, social or religious, companionable in private life, unostentatious in manner of living or in the bestowal of charity, ready to sacrifice personal convenience to serve the worthy, Mr. White is indeed a typical American. The Negro people, in slavery or freedom, as serfs or citizens, offer no model more inspiring, no picture more inviting.

.they had unlimited sway. The result that followed was most natural—the use of public trust for private gain, the looting of many of the Southern states, the political degradation of the Negro, and the complete estrangement between him and his former neighbors. When all these things were accomplished, these human cormorants betook themselves to their Northern homes to live in ease and splendor on the results of their pillage, while the black man was left in the South to endure disfranchisement, torture and murder on account of the malice and hatred begotten from his first political experience.

Surrounded by such environments, the suppression of his right of franchise, the open and notorious examples of fraud, ballot-box stuffing and intimidation practiced in every Southern election for the last thirty years, on the one hand, and the unfaithfulness, "Jungoism," the free offering of bribes and the continued practice of duplicity, on the part of those claiming to be his friends, on the other hand, no fair-minded man would expect to find complete political perfection among a people thus treated. Thus has the Negro been obstructed, not only in politics, but his civil rights have been denied him, and the doors of many industries are closed against him.

But let us turn our faces away from all the horrors of slavery, reconstruction and all kindred wrongs which have been heaped upon us, and stand up, measuring the full statue of an American citizen, upon the threshold of the new century as a New Man. The slave who has grown out of the ashes of thirty-five years ago, is inducted into the political and social system, cast into'the arena of manhood, where he constitutes a new element and becomes a competitor for all its emoluments. He is put upon trial, to test his ability to be accounted worthy of freedom, worthy of the elective franchise. After all these years of struggle against almost insurmountable odds, under conditions but little removed from slavery itself, he asks a fair and just judgment, not of those whose prejudice has endeavored to forestall—to frustrate—his every forward movement; rather those who have lent a helping hand that he might demonstrate the truth of "The fatherhood of God and the brotherhood of man."

In a nation like ours, blessed with peace, plenty and full of prosperity; filled with the spirit of "Expansion," sound money and a protective tariff; when there is a disposition to forget all sectional lines, and to know no North, no South, no East, no West, but having all to stand out in bold relief as one reunited whole, when one political party slaps the other upon the shoulder with a knowing look and a smile indicating the fraternal feeling everywhere present, the question naturally comes home to every colored American, "What should be the Negro's attitude in politics?" Constituting as we do, one-eighth of the entire population of this Nation, the Negro's political attitude should be a firm stand for the right, the support of honest men for office, the advocacy of strong, pure American policies, an unceasing contention for fair elections, a pure ballot, a complete repudiation of any party or man who seeks to bribe, or in any way to hamper or degrade him politically. Should he become self-effaced, politically? No, never! He should, at all times, contend wisely, firmly for every right accorded to other American citizens under the organic laws of the nation. He should identify himself with that political party which proves to be the most friendly towards him. There is very little in a name. Results should be sought, and the Negro should never waver until they are obtained. This will necessitate a division of the Negro vote. No fixed rule can be established as a political guide for him, any more than it can be done for any other people. The location, environment, men and measures sought to be obtained, should guide him. The political pathway for the future may seem dark and discouraging, but nothing daunted, we should continue to press forward, contending for every inch of our rights—no right which man enjoys aside from his own household should be guarded more sacredly than his right of franchise—a right which makes each one a sovereign in himself; a right which determines what laws shall govern us, who shall construe them and execute them.

I am not unmindful of the fact that the views here expressed, may sound rather Utopian. But in this age of rush and bustle for place, preferment and national gain, by individuals and the nation; and in an age when anarchists, lynchers and murderers set at defiance all law and government; in an age when, in certain sections of the country, the ballot-box ceases to stand as an exponent of the registered will of the people, but stands rather as a political cesspool of reeking rottenness, impregnating the national atmosphere with germs of discord that may yet stagnate and throttle the Union; in such an age, it is quite necessary that a halt should be called; a reckoning-had, and that these small, though dangerous political sores should be lanced from the body politic before they develop into putrifying cancers that will destroy the life of the republic.

T. Thomas Fortune

TIMOTHY THOMAS FORTUNE.

Timothy Thomas Fortune, the subject of this sketch, is an author, a journalist, an agitator, and a lecturer.

Mr. Fortune's grandmother was a mulatto, and his grandfather a Seminole Indian. Thomas was born of slave parents in Florida in 1856. His father took an important and active part in the reconstruction of Florida, being a delegate in the Constitutional Convention that framed the present constitution of Florida, and a member of the first five sessions of the reconstructed Florida Legislature.

During the Ku Klux Klan period, which followed, the father of Thomas had to stand for his life, which he manfully did by preparing his house to receive the night marauders. The father finally moved with his family to Jacksonville, Florida. Here young Thomas soon found a position as printer's "devil," which was the first step to that high position which he now occupies. He left his printer's "case" for two years in order to attend school and to work in the Jacksonville city postoffice.

In 1874 he was appointed mail route agent between Jacksonville and Chattahoochee; but he was soon promoted to the position of special inspector of customs for the first district of Delaware. A year later, 1876, young Fortune entered that school which has been an inspiration to so many negro youths, Howard University. After two years' study in this school he returned to the printer's trade. While in Washington he married Miss Smiley, of Florida.

In 1878 Mr. Fortune returned to Florida to try his hand at school teaching. After a year's experience at this work, he again returned to his first love, the printer's trade, but this time he went to New York City. Of course the other compositors objected to working with a "Nigger," but by the manly stand of the publisher, Mr. John Dougall, the "Nigger" remained, and after a short strike the white compositors were glad to return.

Mr. Fortune's real career as journalist began in 1880, when, with two friends, he began the publication of the *Rumor*, which, after two years, was changed to the *New York Globe*. After four years the paper was forced to suspend. Mr. Fortune immediately began the publication of the *New York Freeman*. A year later, 1885, the name of the paper was changed to the *New York Age*, of which Mr. Fortune is still editor.

His writings are, however, not confined to the editing of his paper. He is the author of several books, but "Black and White," and "The Negro in Politics," are perhaps the most noted.

Mr. Fortune was the first to suggest the Afro-American League, an organization in the interest of the Negro race. He was the president of the first convention of this league, which met in Chicago in 1890. His address as president of the convention was a scathing arraignment of the South.

Mr. Fortune was also elected chairman of the executive committee of the National Afro-American Press Association which met in Indianapolis, Indiana, in 1890.

The National Negro Business League was the outcome of a conversation between Booker T. Washington and Mr. Fortune. Mr. Fortune was elected chairman of the executive committee of the National Negro Business League which met in Boston in 1900, and also at its meeting in Chicago in 1901.

Mr. Fortune is, as might be suspected, a Republican in politics. In the presidential election of 1900 he took an active part in the political canvass of that year. He spoke in Indiana and in Missouri, advocating the re-election of President McKinley.

The whole energy of his life is devoted to the interests of the Negro race in America. He wields a sharp rapier. He is the complement of Booker T. Washington. Each is doing his own work in his own way; the one supplements the other's work.

From any view that may be taken of the present political situation, it is apparent that the time is ripe for the colored American to think and act for himself. If he reasons correctly, he will certainly reach the conclusion that right must some day prevail; and in order that he may enjoy the resultant blessings flowing from a pure ballot, the colored man must set the pace, and thereby place himself in a position to command respect and proper recognition. "He who would have equity must first do equity."

The Negro's loyalty to friends, his impressionable soul, his devotion to church, his yearning for education and enlightenment, his thrift, industry, devotion to country, fidelity to the flag shown upon hundreds of battle-fields, must be admitted and command the admiration of all fair-minded men. Let him add to all these attributes, purity in all things; let him cultivate a love for justice and fair play, live as an example for his neighbors, ally himself with the best men in the community or state where he lives, and the day must certainly come when his rights—political and civil—will be conceded to him.

Let us learn what is *right* and then dare to do the *right;* ever pressing forward to higher and nobler things; never lagging, but remember, "That constant effort will remove the mountain, and that continued dripping will wear away the stone."

SECOND PAPER.

WHAT SHOULD BE THE NEGRO'S ATTITUDE IN POLITICS?

BY T. T. FORTUNE.

There are some questions which, it seems to me, need no discussion, because the truths in them are self-evident; and yet, so perverse is the human understanding, that unanimity upon any subject of common interest is rare in social ethics; and by social ethics I mean the philosophy of organized government in all of its multifarious life.

How intricate and perplexing these questions are; even the uninitiated intuitively understand, although they cannot explain them; while ignorant and learned alike wrangle and often fight over the means to reach ends upon which there is no disagreement. There is, therefore, no phase of the Afro-American problem upon the proper solution of which there is not a substantial agreement among members of the race. The processes by which the solution shall be reached are the bases of the disagreements and discussions, which often defeat the common wish and aim.

"What should be the Afro-American's attitude in politics?" is a sophomoric, rather than a practical, question. What he should do at a given crisis is answered by what he has done ever since the right to vote was conferred upon him by the adoption of the war amendments to the Federal Constitution. Neither threats, fire, rope, nor bullet has been powerful enough to swerve him from pursuing the course made mandatory by his self interests. He may have pursued this course by the intricate processes of reasoning employed by educated men, or of intuition employed by the unlettered. The fact remains that his attitude has been one of sympathy and helpfulness towards those who were unmistakably sympathetic and friendly towards him and as unmistakably antagonistic and troublesome to those who were antagonistic to him. With him, as with the rest of mankind, "self-preservation is the first law of nature." What his attitude in politics should be now will be what it has been—governed absolutely by his self interests.

There will be nothing gained in the proper elucidation and comprehension of the subject under discussion by holding up holy hands of horror at the statement that selfishness, pure and simple, has governed and will govern the attitude of the Afro-American in politics. The purists, who prate of the common interest and loyalty to the flag as the first and highest duty of the citizen, are entitled to their view of the matter, but the fact remains and is true of the people of every ancient and modern government that self-interest will govern the actions of the voter. One of the components which is discriminated against and oppressed by legal enactment through popular clamor will invariably produce substantial unanimity of thought and action on the part of the pariah against the common interest, and, in the last analysis, against the flag itself, as the emblem of governmental discrimination and oppression. The Helots of Sparta and the Jews under the Pharaohs were of this sort. The Jews in Russia and Germany and the Irish in Great Britain are modern examples. The first concern of every man and of his own race is his own concern. He will oppose those who oppose him, whether as individual or state; he will look to his interests first and to those of his neighbor afterwards. The Afro-American is just like other people in this, as well as in all respects, despite the puerile contention of some, even of his own household, that he is not as other men. He will not love those who hate him nor pray for those who despitefully use him, although enjoined to do so in thunderous tones from every pulpit in Christendom. And, therefore, the Afro-American's attitude in politics will be governed, as it has been, by his selfish interests. And, why not? The banker's attitude in politics is governed by the policy that serves his selfish interests best; the manufacturer's attitude is the same. The same rule of conduct governs all men in their social and civil relations to the state.

In a republic, government by party is the fundamental basis of it. There must be parties or there can be no government; this is equally true of democracies and limited monarchies. The primary is the basis of party government. His selfish interests, of whatever sort, make it necessary for every citizen, who wishes to conserve those interests, to belong to some one party. Unless he is permitted to enjoy the rights and benefits of the primary, or party referendum, he cannot hope to enjoy the rights and benefits of the party of his choice—enjoy them to their fullest extent—for the right to vote, which does not carry with it the right to be voted for, leaves the citizen in a voiceless condition as to those specific interests in which he is concerned, and which can only be secured from the state through the action of his party. No man can speak for another as he can speak for himself, hence, in every party, men and special interests, such as railroad, bank, manufacturing and the like interests, habitually seek to put in control persons who will represent them, speak for them and vote for them upon any question of legislation which arises. It is because of this that there is great rejoicing among Afro-Americans when any man of theirs is put forward for his party in any official capacity whatever, and it is because of this that so few of them have been, and are put forward.

Wherever an Afro-American is found supporting, by his lung-power and ballot, a party which denies him participation in its primary (basis of party) government, then you have found a man who does not know what his attitude in politics should be; and, whether he should be pitied or despised, must remain a question for each individual to decide. The democratic party is the only party in the United States which denies to the Afro-American this basic right in party government. Logically enough, it is the only party in the United States which has always sought to prevent him from enjoying the rights of the elective franchise, the right to vote and to be voted for, and which has necessarily, to justify this policy, always sought in every conceivable way to degrade his manhood to the brute standard. A voteless citizen is always a social and political outcast; a voteless race in a composite citizenship will always constitute a problem more or less dangerous to the state—enemies, fostered in the bosom, as Cleopatra's asp, only to wound to the death. It has been the way of the world since the dawn of history.

It is creditable to the good sense and the manhood of the Afro-American people that they have constantly recognized and acted upon the theory I have here laid down, as the consistent one in politics. Their attitude has been manly and consistent; they have stood by their friends and defied their enemies, even when their friends have been lukewarm, or brutally indifferent, and this has been the attitude of their friends since 1876.

Through good and evil report they have refused to be seduced from their allegiance to the party of freedom, and their enemies have wreaked their vengeance, without hindrance, so that the attitude books of every Southern state bristle with a code of laws as infamous and oppressive as the slave code. But that does not affect the principle in the least, and the principle is the thing; it is the essence of all life. He who clings to it, though he may die, as the poor Indian has done, deserves and receives the respect of mankind. When it has been said of him that he was corrupt, purchasable, unreliable in politics and that the franchise should be denied to him by fair or foul means, because of this, by the kuklux klan terrorists, or red shirt brutalists—sufficient answer to it all, in my mind, has been that if he could have been seduced from his best interests, from his friends in party politics, without violence towards him, none would have molested him or made him afraid. That is a self-evident proposition in partisan ethics.

We do not terrorize and shoot and defraud people who vote with us. No, the Afro-American has instinctively distrusted his political enemies, even when they came to him bearing grapes in their hands and honey on their tongues. His attitude has been one of manly protest, wherever he was allowed to vote, or made to sulk in silence and indignation. And here has been and here is the rub. When you cannot coax a man against his will, as Jonathan did David, or purchase his birthright as Jacob did Esau, if you have the power you terrorize and shoot him into compliance. That is what the political enemies of the Afro-American have done and are doing, but patient as the ass and with the faith of Job, which passes

George Washington Murray.

GEORGE WASHINGTON MURRAY.

George Washington Murray was born September 22, 1853, of slave parents, near Rembert, Sumter County, S. C. Emancipation found him a lad of eleven summers, bereft of both parents. Without a friend upon whom to rely for either aid or advice in an impoverishing section, he entered upon the fierce combat then in progress for the indispensable bread of life. Among the waifs of his neighborhood in 1866, he learned the alphabet and acquired an imperfect pronunciation of monosyllables. In efforts to improve his meager stock of knowledge during the succeeding five years, he so industriously applied himself that in January, 1871, he entered a day school, while in session, for the first time, but as teacher, not scholar.

He taught until the Fall of 1874, when he successfully passed a competitive examination and secured a scholarship as sub-freshman in the reconstructed University of South Carolina. He was successfully employed as a teacher until February, 1890, when he secured an appointment as inspector of customs at the port of Charleston, S. C.

Entering the political arena in the contest for the Republican nomination for Congress in 1892, he successfully won the stake and was pitted in the general election against Gen. E. W. Moise, one of the most brilliant, wealthy and popular Democrats in the State, whom he finally defeated and was declared elected to the Fifty-third Congress.

He was again elected to the Fifty-fourth Congress, and counted out, but contested and was finally seated. He was again elected to the Fifty-fifth and Fifty-sixth Congresses, and counted out, and failed to be seated after strong contests.

Since his retirement from congressional contests, seeing the primary and crying need of his race is a larger per cent of the ownership of homes, and the impossibility of securing them in the desired space of time, under the prevailing circumstances, where the necessaries of life and rents consume the entire resources year after year, he has applied himself to the development of a scheme of buying large estates and cutting them into small holdings, and giving long periods of time in which to pay for homes, receiving about the usual rents as payments.

He now has about 200 families located on about 9,000 acres of land, and is adding from 2,000 to 3,000 acres to his territory each year.

He has already secured twelve letters patent on a multiple farming machine, that is destined to revolutionize farming methods.

Without his request upon the demand of the President himself, he was recently appointed Division Internal Revenue Deputy Collector for the district of South Carolina.

all understanding, he sticks to his principle of self-interest and waits; and the good proverb says, "All things come to him who waits." I believe it. And if every man of the race had the alternative of being shot in his tracks for clinging to his principles or life eternal for deserting them, the part of manhood and honor would be to stand up and be shot. As a matter of fact, thousands upon thousands of Afro-Americans have been shot to death by their political enemies since 1868, and perhaps thousands more will be shot in the future in the same way, and for the same reason and by the same heartless enemies, before the nation reaches the conclusion that an Afro-American citizen should have as much protection under the Federal Constitution as any other citizen with a white skin, despite the fact that the whole matter is largely one of state control and regulation. When cancers get on the body politic like this of disfranchisement and debasement of an entire element of the citizenship, they are usually cut out, as that of slavery, and its exceeding horrors, were.

Steadfastness, therefore, in the faith that moves mountains and patience which overcomes a world of wrong and injustice, will bring the reward as it has so often done with the race in the past. The reward is perfect equality under the laws of the Federal Government and of the several states. But our attitude must be one of absolute fidelity to the priceless sacred trust of citizenship, which comes to us out of the agonies of the greatest war of modern times. If we be true to ourselves, the great republic will be true to us "in God's way and time."

THIRD PAPER.

WHAT SHOULD BE THE NEGRO'S ATTITUDE IN POLITICS?

BY HON. GEORGE W. MURRAY.

To the casual observer the above query is easy of solution, but it is at the same time engaging the profoundest attention and thought of the wisest statesmen, and the greatest philanthropists and humanitarians.

It is especially difficult to the black victims of present political environments.

With a proportionate share of all the elements of strength, intelligence, wealth, business and character—the Negro's attitude politically should, and would, be the same as that of the other members of society.

The writer presumes that in dealing with the question at issue, he is territorially restricted to the ex-slaveholding portions of the United States, as the Negro's political status in the rest of the territorial limits of the country differs so little from that of other members of society.

As we see it, the mistake of the nineteenth century was the attempt to make the ex-slave a governor, before he had learned to be governed.

It seems that members of the race have not even yet learned that governments have their origin and growth in the necessities originating in the business and wealth of mankind, and have attained their greatest perfection where there is most business and wealth.

The naked, wandering savage has the lowest order of governments, because, in that state, he has need for no other, and could not support any higher.

If twenty intelligent and progressive men settle down in the midst of a hundred thousand such savages, they will immediately set about establishing business, accumulating wealth, and will very naturally organize in self-defense, and in time rule the ninety-nine thousand nine hundred and eighty others.

When just emerging from the shambles of two and a half centuries of slavery and inforced ignorance, penniless and without experience, it was a serious blunder to have placed the Negroes in such a position as to make them responsible for the government.

They were not only without the necessary intelligence and experience for its successful operation, but all the resources essential to its maintenance were in the hands of the minority class, and they were without the ability to compel any contribution for its support.

Placed upon the wrong track in the primary stages of emancipation, the race spent its energy in trying to control the kind of government that other people's business and resources made necessary, instead of trying to acquire the elements which would have made it welcome as part owners and rulers of that government.

Such conditions as resulted from the plans and policies pursued in the rehabilitation of civil government, after the War of the Rebellion, very naturally created great friction between the former master-class, possessing practically all the business, wealth and experience, though in the minority in many localities, and the former slave-class, without business, wealth and experience, on the other hand.

The master-class determined that in self defense it had to organize to repossess itself of governmental control, which was then in the hands of the slave-class, and withheld its support from the government, which the latter class was helpless to compel without the strong compelling arm of the Federal government, which the peaceful and considerate judgment of mankind would no longer sustain in maintaining such conditions.

Whereupon all over the South where the ex-slave class controlled merely, by reason of numbers, its power and influence failed, until to-day it finds itself absolutely shorn of power, even so much as is necessary to protect its property, family and life.

While it may be both unjust and unwise for a class in the condition of the former slave class to absolutely control a government made necessary by the resources of others, yet it is a cruel wrong to deprive it even of that influence that is absolutely necessary for the protection of family, property and life.

The paramount issue of Southern Negroes should not be political office, but the possession of such political influence as is necessary for the protection of their property and lives.

While it is desirable that as many Negroes as possible be provided for at the official pie-counter, the all important issue, in my humble judgment, is the equality of civil and political rights, without which we are in some measure worse off than slaves.

Deprived of that influence, which selfish interests always impel the master-class to give in defense of his property rights, the emancipated-class must possess a counter voting power somewhere within its own personality, which an untrammelled ballot alone affords.

Wisdom dictates that the Negro should speedily assume the task of producing such conditions as will give the needed influence.

This brings us to the question at issue, What should be the Negro's attitude politically?

In short, whatever attitude would prove most beneficial to him the Negro should adapt himself to it, until he shall have acquired sufficient strength along all lines to occupy and maintain an independent position, and shape the course of action to suit his fancy and convenience.

The difference in the treatment of colored men North and South is not half so much on account of a difference in the education and customs of the white people in the respective sections, as from the difference between the business, intellectual and political status of the members of the colored race itself in the two sections, coupled with the fact that the white man possessing practically all the business, wealth, culture and experience in the North, is divided into two political camps, each controlling influence sufficient to protect each constituent member, however weak, while in the South he is united in one political party, which wholly destroys the colored man's influence and partially his own.

In fact, in the North, the combined wealth, culture and influence of the entire party with which he is allied overshadows and protects his rights, both public and private, and this brings us to the question at issue, What should be the Negro's attitude politically?

Upon this question there are as many opinions as there were colors in Joseph's coat.

Some advise that we solidly vote the Republican ticket.

Others that we should all vote the Democratic ticket; still another class advise us to divide our vote, and another class advise us not to vote at all.

There may be a grain of truth in each one of the above theories, but for all times and occasions each one is essentially false.

Under present environments it appears that we accomplish nothing by voting the Republican ticket, and gain no more by voting the Democratic ticket than we would by not voting at all.

To us the all important task is to find a way to make our ballot effective.

Though, throughout the South, a cruel and savage spirit seems triumphant, let the Negro take courage, for God is still ruling, and the very machinery that has been set in motion for his political destruction is hastening the day of his political regeneration.

The reduction of the Negro's vote to an insignificant fraction which does away with the possibility of absolute Negro control, is not an unmixed evil, as it entirely destroys the foundation of the scarecrow of Negro supremacy, which has been used as a great welding hammer to forge the white race, with so many divergent views and opinions, into one political mass, while the standards of wealth and intelligence raised as a bar to his progress are causing the Negro, as never before, to bestir himself in efforts to reach them.

Thus it is seen that his would-be enemy destroys the welding hammer at one fell blow; sets in motion irresistible currents that will inevitably find outlets in the broad ocean of the political freedom of both races, and arouse in the Negro, by the standards set up, the very desirable incentive to make preparation for the enjoyment of the destined freedom which the fates seem bent on bringing him.

Once more the wonderful hand of Providence is using man's malice and prejudice as His own marvelous highway of hope to bring good results from evil intentions.

Let the poor, desponding Negro, way down in the valley of degradation and oppression, continue to be industrious, honest and frugal, and pray, and God will again hitch His own all powerful steeds of hope to his chariot of despondency and oppression, and, riding over the mountains of man's folly, manifested in unjust rules and practices, in defiance of His will, will draw him upon the broad eminence of joy, gladness and hope.

TOPIC XIV.

IS THE NEGRO AS MORALLY DEPRAVED AS HE IS REPUTED TO BE?

BY PROF. B. H. PETERSON.

The conclusion reached in this discussion will depend in part upon the viewpoint of the observation, upon the character of the judges and upon the logic employed. In considering any subject it is always best, fair and proper, to admit freely and fully the well known facts in the case. The book of books, which is an infallible code of morals, says that "there is none good, no not one." But there is none as depraved as he could be. In either direction, progression is possible.

Unfortunately, immorality is not a stranger to any people; and that it is to be found among the Negroes, should not excite wonder and amazement; for it grows out of their previous condition of servitude.

The horrible system of slavery, with its direful effects, is still felt to a greater or less degree by the American Negro. And the ex-slaveholders, from the very nature of the case, could not make their escape from its awful consequences. The market still has fruit from this system.

There can be little doubt that the arrangement which places one man or any number of men at the entire disposal and control of another, subject to his absolute and irresponsible will and power, is a system of things not the most favorable to moral excellence, whether of the master or the slave. The exercise of such authority must, from the very nature of the case, tend to foster the spirit of pride and arrogance, to make a man overbearing and haughty in temper, quick and irascible, impatient of restraint and contradiction. The passions of our nature, the animal propensities, ever ready to assume the mastery, and requiring to be kept in check with a firm hand, finding now no barriers to their indulgence but those which are self imposed, will be likely to break over those feeble barriers, and acquire unrestrained course and dominion. The tendency of the system to these results in morals, so far as the master is concerned, is inevitable. There may be some honorable exceptions, but the tendency is ever the same. It must and will be so while human nature is what it is. The temptation to the abuse of power over those who cannot or dare not resist to undue severity of punishment, where the passions

Prof. B. H. Peterson

PROF. B. H. PETERSON.

Butler Harrison Peterson, the subject of this sketch, is a native of the State of Florida. He was born of slave parents, just in time to be spared the horrible experiences of that slave system which swept over this country with such direful results.

When the war clouds of the Civil War passed over, he was sent to an ex-slave for private instruction. Shortly after the public school system was introduced into the state of Florida he entered as a regular attendant. Three very profitable and successful sessions were spent in these schools. Soon after entering upon the fourth term his mother moved to another part of the state, leaving him in the care of an aunt, who, loving money rather than education, took him out of school and hired him to a law firm as office boy, for $1.50 per month. This lasted for nearly two years. He then took a position as porter in a dry goods store, and then a clerkship in a small grocery store, owned and controlled by a colored man, the Rev. William Bell.

During this time Mr. Peterson showed signs of a thirst for knowledge. He had now become a member of the Baptist Church and was actively engaged in Sunday-school work. Having attracted the attention of a few friends, among them Mr. John J. Montth, an opportunity soon presented itself, which Mr. Peterson eagerly seized. This opportunity opened the doors of Cookman Institute, Jacksonville, Fla., at which place he remained two years. Mr. Peterson next found himself for three years a student of the St. Augustine Normal and Collegiate Institute, Raleigh, N. C. In 1883 Mr. Peterson entered Lincoln University, Chester County, Pa., passing successfully through the freshman, sophomore, junior and senior years. He tarried yet three years longer at Lincoln, taking the full theological course; and in 1889 returned home to begin work. His first position was as principal of the Oakland Graded School, Jacksonville, Fla. During the two years spent here, he was offered the chair of "ancient languages," Selma University, Selma, Ala., which he accepted and held for two years to the satisfaction of the President, Dr. C. L. Purse, D. D., and the Board of Trustees.

At this time matters over which he had no control so shaped themselves that this very pleasant and profitable work had to be given up. In 1893 Mr. Peterson became the first assistant teacher in the Phelps Hall Bible Training School, Tuskegee Normal and Industrial Institute, Tuskegee, Ala., and in connection with this work he is instructor in the Normal Department of Mental and Moral Science and Primary Mathematics. He is still here at work.

He is also pastor of one of the churches of the town of Tuskegee and spends a part of his vacations at the Summer Schools of the Hampton Normal and Industrial Institute and the University of Chicago.

In this brief sketch no reference is made to ways or means, but only the results are announced, the rosebush, however, has thorns as well as roses.

of the master are aroused, and there is no one to say, What doest thou? to the gratification of the baser appetites in their various forms, must be too great for ordinary and unaided human virtue. The tendency of such a system must ever be, not to progressive self refinement and moral culture, but to barbarism. We should expect to find in connection with such a civil polity, a state of society, of religion and morals somewhat peculiar—acts of violence and barbarity not infrequent, the street affray, the duel, the murderous assault, the unrestrained indulgence of the animal appetites. It would be quite natural and reasonable under such a state of affairs to expect this; and such, unless all history and experience be false, we find the world over, to be the general state and tendency of things wherever the system of slavery prevails.

Nor is the effect on the morals of the slave more favorable; on the contrary, it is even more disastrous. In proportion as the feeling of self respect and self dependence is taken away, and a man is taught to look upon himself as merely the tool in the hands of another, the instrument of another's will and pleasure, without responsibility of his own, just in that proportion the foundation of moral character is undermined. Nothing can be more demoralizing in its effect upon the character. Strip a man of all that constitutes manhood; of all self reliance and self respect; of all the rights which nature has conferred upon him, and all the faculties with which God has endowed him; take away from him all control and disposal of himself, all ownership of himself and all that can stimulate to activity, and incite to noble attainment and excellence, is gone at once. He sinks down to the level of the brute. What inducement is there for him to hope or strive for anything further or better than his present lot, and enjoyment which the moment may bring with it? He becomes as a matter of course improvident and reckless, content with the gratification, so far as may be, of his merely animal appetites; indolent, for why should he be otherwise?

Deceptive and dishonest, for what motive has he to be honest? He is governed only by fear of the lash, with little thought of anything future, with little knowledge of that hereafter whence are derived the most powerful motives to present virtue. His mind is shrouded in ignorance, his moral nature almost wholly uncultivated, his condition is little above that of the beast with whom he toils, and with whom he perishes. As in the case of the master, so in the case of the slave; some will rise above the influence that surround and drag them down, and, in spite of all these depressing and demoralizing influences, will maintain their integrity. But such is not the rule, such is not the tendency of the system. No one who has either reflected on the matter or observed the actual working of the system can honestly suppose that it is. It is a notorious fact that, as a general rule, wherever this system exists, the slave is indolent, deceptive, dishonest, improvident, not to be trusted away from the eyes of honest people.

Such a system having a growth of two hundred and fifty years, would it be reasonable to expect that thirty-five years could eradicate entirely the work done during the two hundred and fifty years? While this is all true, can any one with so many facts and figures all about him, entertain a doubt as to the Negro's progress along all lines of human activity and toil? The Negro has either advanced, morally and religiously, or the proud Anglo-Saxon's standard of morals and religion is a hopeless failure. Considering the depths from which he came, the fact that he has come at all, or any part of the way, shows at least some progress.

A journey through this country, especially the South, the home of the Negroes, and an inspection of the homes and surroundings, and coming into near contact with them, will serve to change a great many baseless and unfair criticisms found afloat among a certain class of people, of whom Mr. Wm. Hannibal Thomas' book, entitled "The American Negro," is the mouthpiece. One room log huts, dirty floor, the home of the Negro, for large families during the period when slavery existed, are giving away to neat little cottages, sometimes two-story buildings, with rooms, furniture and surroundings sufficient to make each member of the family comfortable, and secluded enough to avoid the temptation to immoral conduct. And these homes, together with lands attached, in a great many cases are owned by the colored people whose morals are called in question. Some of the most fashionable weddings of the day are celebrated among the Negroes. Births out of wedlock, the plurality of wives and divorced cases, have decreased among the Negroes 65 per cent. Womanhood, virtue and honor are defended at any cost, at the proper time and place.

The Negro got the idea imbedded in him during his servitude that religion and morality, like the Jews and Samaritans, had no dealings with each other. To-day this idea has lost its power and influence. The professors of religion and leaders of the people stand first and foremost with the people, and are expected to take the lead in all matters of reform.

The church property owned and controlled by the Negro tells its own story. The Sermon on the Mount is taking a hold of the Negro as never before. If I should offer an adverse criticism on the Negro's religion, it would be that, as he understands it, he has a surplus of religion. But he is surely grasping the idea that God is a Spirit, and "they that worship Him must worship Him in spirit and in truth." There are to be found among the Negroes those whose words are as good as gold. The true significance of morality is being better understood and practiced by the Negro. The newspaper gossip and sophistical reasoning to the effect that some Negroes have been apprehended for immoral conduct, and therefore all Negroes are immoral, would astonish all creation if applied to the white race. Let us be fair and try the Negro by the same logic that the white man.is tried by.

A very sure and hopeful sign is the fact that the Negro is ashamed of any immoral conduct which he hears has been committed by any member of his race. The mere desire of better things is indicative of a better state of affairs. A straw often shows which way the wind is blowing. It is a historical fact that any race which has been subdued and ruled over by another race will imbibe, imitate and copy after the dominant race, and especially is this true if the conquered race live in and among the conquering race. It follows, then, that if the Negro is wholly immoral, his white neighbor needs to move a pace in the moral world.

Other causes might have been assigned accounting for the Negro's previous immorality, but slavery comprehends them all. But for the sake of emphasis and showing the contrast, let us note the following: Granting that the Negro as a mass is ignorant. Is he as ignorant as he was? If he is, then in what light shall we regard the philanthropists of this country North and South who have done and are doing so much for the Negro's elevation? The public school system, so well organized and maintained throughout this country, and patronized so largely by the Negro youth, *either* means the Negro's advancement morally or a lack of wisdom on the part of those who administer the nation's affairs. I realize that a people could advance intellectually without advancing morally at the same time. But such is not possible in this country where the Bible is made the basis of our education. A mere reference to this topic is all that is needed.

The Negro is poverty stricken, this needs no demonstration. But is he as poor as he has been? The banks, county records and business enterprises of the country are living witnesses to the Negro's advancement along this line. How could a man wholly depraved come into such relationship with a moral man and get along so well? "How can two walk together except they be abreed," asks the faithful prophet.

The time was when the Negro could not take out a policy in a life insurance company, because he was regarded immoral, and would soon die out and bring the company under obligations to his estate. To-day the Negro can hold a policy in almost any insurance company of whatever nature it may be. This is a case where the Negro's advancement in morals is admitted and he himself not a judge in the case. Negro lawyers consult with white lawyers, Negro doctors consult with white doctors, Negro teachers consult with white teachers, Negro preachers consult with white preachers, Negro workmen of whatever kind confer with the whites of like occupation, and, sometimes, the process is reversed, the white mechanics go to the Negro mechanics for counsel. In all of this, the Negro's upward march is admitted. And there is no advancement worthy of the name of advancement that does not include moral strength, worth and improvement.

We hail with joy the rapidly approaching time, under the sunlight of civilization and Christianity, when the color of the skin and the texture of the hair will not be badges of reproach, humiliation, degradation and contempt. True merit will yet be the worth of the man, under the wise and just government of a beneficent God and Father, who "of one blood made all nations for to dwell upon the face of all the earth." The poet Burns labored under no misapprehension when he wrote the following lines:

> " Is there for honest poverty
>   Wha hangs his head, and a' that?
> The coward slave! we pass him by;
>   We dare be poor for a' that—
>   For a' that, and a' that,
>   Our toils obscure, and a' that!
> The rank is but the guinea's stamp—
>   The man's the gowd for a' that.

> " What, though on hamely fare we dine,
>   Wear hodden gray, and a' that?
> Gie fools their silks, and knaves their wine;
>   A man's a man for a' that—

Prof. A. U. Frierson

AUGUSTUS ULYSSES FRIERSON, D.D.

Mr. A. U. Frierson was born in the State of South Carolina a few years before the Civil War. His parents were slaves, and, of course, were uneducated. After some preparation in the public schools, he entered Biddle University, from which he graduated with honor in 1885. The same year he entered the theological department of the same university, graduating therefrom in 1888.

The Summer of 1885 was spent as teacher and preacher to the ex-slaves of the Choctaw Indians, Indian Territory. He worked under the Freedman's Board of the Presbyterian Church. For several years he acted as pastor of different Presbyterian churches in North and South Carolina.

In 1891 he was called to the chair of Greek language and literature of Biddle University, which position he holds at this writing.

In 1893, his alma mater conferred upon him the degree of D. D.

For a' that, and a' that,
   Their tinsel show, and a' that;
The honest man, though e'er sae poor,
   Is king o' men for a' that.

" A prince can mak a belted knight,
   A marquis, duke, and a' that;
But an honest man's aboon his might—
   Guid faith, he maunna fa' that!
For a' that, and a' that,
   Their dignities, and a' that;
The pith o' sense and pride o' worth
   Are higher ranks than a' that.

" Then let us pray that come it may—
   As come it will, for a' that—
That sense and worth, o'er a' the earth,
   May bear the gree, and a' that.
For a' that, and a' that,
   Its coming yet, for a' that—
When man to man, the warld o'er,
   Shall brothers be for a' that!"

SECOND PAPER.

IS THE NEGRO AS MORALLY DEPRAVED AS HE IS REPUTED TO BE?

BY PROF. A. U. FRIERSON.

A question so pertinent, so comprehensive, so thoroughly charged with what must give rank and standing to a people in the eyes of the world, ought not to be superficially considered, nor lightly and rashly answered. On the surface it would seem to involve a simple yes or no. But slight reflection reveals the fact that the yes or no fails to satisfy the conditions. That the answer to this question has long since been removed from the realm of the simple negative and affirmative, becomes very evident from what has been, and is still being, said *pro* and *con*.

The moral status of the Negro of the United States has long since given rise to a debated question. This debate waxes hotter and hotter, and the lines are more closely drawn as the years go by. For it is impossible to think of the future of the Negro apart from his moral status. His future will be bright, gloomy, or blighted, in proportion as he is able or not able to set to his account true moral worth. I speak of the Negro by limitations, as I feel that only the American Negro, and that, too, of the United States, can be contemplated by the query under consideration; hence, by the discussion.

That my answer will be in line of an *emphatic* negative will appear from what follows. I know full well the tremendous task I have set myself by this position. In doing this, I must take up the defensive as well as offensive alike against a large per cent of people, outside of the Negro race, who set themselves up as an authority on all questions affecting the Negro, and, mark you, from their decision there is no appeal; as also against the *know-alls* within the ranks of the race. But I am not deterred by this, since I feel that I owe it to the friends of the race; to those of the race who honestly strive to do what is right, and to myself, to utter no uncertain sound in responding to this important question.

For the encouragement of a weak and struggling people and their friends, for the better enlightenment of mankind in general, touching the moral status of the Negro, I place in evidence and offer in support of my negative the following considerations:

First: As far as my knowledge goes, the sum total of the considerations and discussions tending to show and set forth the moral turpitude of the Negro, leave out, if they do not ignore wholly, a most vital element. Any conclusion, therefore, reached, must eliminate the same, and in the degree that this element is important, the conclusion will be inconclusive and defective.

I contend, in the outset, that any just and charitable answer to this question must take into account the fact that the Negro is not unlike the other children of Adam, in that he is possessed of an inherent immoral tendency. Yet how many, speaking to this subject, reckon from this point? I think all sane people, at least, are agreed that since the fall, conformity to the moral standard, as set up by our Creator, is *relative* and not *absolute*. I think it would be a very light task to prove this assertion true, on the best authority known to man—the Bible. A single instance will suffice to put to silence all dissenters. David, "the man after God's own heart," gives us a life whose complexity at once presents the elements of *passion,* tenderness, generosity, and *fierceness.* From this life flowed a character blackened by adultery and murder. Rather checkered, measured by a perfect moral standard.

Grant that the Negro is a child of Adam, and I score one of the most important points on the side of my negative. Weighed in the balance of a perfect moral scale, "There is none good, but one, and that is God."

Second: When talking or writing on this subject, men seem to forget also that this inherent or natural immoral tendency in the Negro has had the impetus of the most debasing influences of a baser system of slavery, covering a period of two and a half centuries. This is not a defense, nor by any means an apology, for the shortcomings of the Negro, which are too many by far, but it is a plea for fairness in making up a verdict which is very far-reaching in its consequences.

In my humble opinion this thought is sufficient to temper, at least, the criticisms of the most rabid and reckless assailants of Negro morals. Let friends and foes alike think, if they can, what two hundred and fifty years of training means in a system whose principal tenet was that a Negro had no wish or will of his own—either morally or otherwise—a mere thing, acting only as it is acted upon. Under this system the next most natural thing would be and was the breaking down and beating back of every bar to the baser passions, except when its observance, perchance, contributed to the physical vigor and resistance of the Negro, thus rendering him more valuable and indispensable to his master. Add to this, if you please, the fact that there were few, if any, formal marriages; the "shanty" system instead of the home; no responsibility in the training of boys and girls that naturally came to the so-called homes; no safeguard thrown around the morals of the tender years of boyhood and girlhood, but, on the other hand, everything most favorable and conducive to the development of bad morals. Out of this condition, unless the superior—the master—had a very high moral sense, which was highly improbable, if not impossible, under the existing circumstances, little could justly be expected of the inferior—the Negro. Yet, in spite of all this, the Negro gave the world a very few rapists of whom we hear so much nowadays, and on whose account we are so often called upon to defend him from the viewpoint of our question.

As regards this particular crime, I digress here to say that my faith is small. For this reason, there was a time when the commission of it was more opportune and easy than now. For example, during the Civil War, when it was scarcely, if ever, heard of. I have introduced this subject here simply to say this, that human nature is one and the same in mankind, and the argument that natural tendencies do not assert themselves alike in a slave and a freeman under like favorable conditions, is open to serious objections, if not in a degree fallacious. The pertinence of this reference will also appear when attention is drawn to the fact that the tendency of the race to criminality, hence, to moral worthlessness, is more largely hypothecated upon this than upon any other single crime. By a similar process of reasoning it would not be difficult to show that all the races of the world are moral reprobates. For what escape would there be for any measured by its criminal class? I, therefore, contend, finally, that the standard by which the Negro is measured is seriously at fault, if not wholly wrong. Coming out of the most untoward circumstances, with less than a half century in which to outlive and unlearn the deadly doings of two hundred and fifty years, who can lay claim to more or to so much as the Negro? Measure him by the depths from which he came as well as by the heights which you would have him attain, when taking his moral pulse.

Third: I note the work of the press, which is largely in the hands of, and controlled by, those least friendly to the Negro's progress. Hence, a magnificent contribution is daily made from this quarter, to his moral impeachment. I think it is never, perhaps, properly considered, that the class generally held up by the press is one and the same with that already noticed under the preceding head—the criminal. Further, news gatherers are at great pains to ferret out and dole out to the public daily whatever serves to excite, and especially whatever shows the moral crookedness of the Negro, and that the years of freedom already enjoyed by him have simply brought forth a generation of vipers. Too often, from the lowest to the highest court, the records are so manipulated as to show the moral obliquity of the Negro. It is a potent fact that public opinion of the Negro is largely, if not wholly, based upon press reports, whether it pertains to religion, politics, morality, or otherwise. I hold, therefore, that it is largely misinformation that brings the Negro into bad odor in this regard, and earns for him the opinion that he is on the decline or "moral lapse," if you please. Then, too, the dying testimony of what is commonly called the worthless Negro, is given wider publicity and greater credence than the precept and example of ten thousand living, straightforward, upright Negroes. I say this because the opinion obtains so widely that the Negro is growing worse.

Fourth: That the Negro is not as morally depraved as he is generally reputed to be, and that those who are foremost to note and proclaim it do not believe it themselves, I place in evidence the following: 1st. A considerable number of Southern states has passed laws restrictive, if not prohibitive, of the removal of the Negro from his holy (?) confines, and this, too, where most is seen and known of him. What! Make it a misdemeanor to influence to emigrate or to deport a people whose presence is a standing menace to the good morals of those who enact measures and those who uphold them? Do not they make themselves liable to mild criticism? Other countries and sections of countries seek to rid themselves of all incubus of whatever kind. Of this we have numerous examples in the scum from Europe and other parts of the world unloaded upon our shores annually. 2d. Let the Negro with all his moral depravity initiate any movement looking toward his withdrawal even from one part of our country to another. The scene of such activities attracts special attention, and unsought advice is poured upon his "worthless" head; words of warning flow apace, and direct steps are taken to defeat the end in view. In view of this fact, the Negro is seldom allowed to organize, secretly, for mutual protection and helpfulness, in some sections; and, when organized, he is always looked upon with grave suspicions. That people should go so far out of the way to circumvent the legitimate endeavors of the undeserving, to my mind, is the most unnatural thing to be sure. "Consistency, thou art a jewel!"

Fifth: What people regard as a most discouraging sign touching the Negro of this country, I consider a most portentous and hopeful one. I refer to it here, because it bears decidedly upon my answer, and is strictly in line therewith. As shown by the census of 1890 and 1900, the increase of the Negro has suffered a positive check, if not back-set. In explanation of this, one theory and another has been advanced. Some have seen that he, like the American Indian, is on the road to a kindred fate—final and utter extinction. Others have consigned him to this or that destiny, according as they have felt kindly or unkindly towards him. True, he has increased less rapidly, but more surely, because of his stricter observance and growing regard for the proper and God-appointed channels to this end. His propagation by marriage, in which case one man is the husband of one woman, and one woman the wife of one man, would naturally tend to this.

I might record and add to what has already been said, a rich and varied experience, growing out of actual contact with, and work for, my people covering twenty-four years—a period in which no year has passed without leaving something done or suffered. But time and space will not permit.

Finally, out of the unfavorable moral conditions to which the Negro as a child of Adam is heir; out of the most untoward circumstances, surrounding him in the dark days of his enslavement; out of the traductions to which he is exposed at the hands of a most cruel and relentless foe—the printing press; out of the mock trials and false convictions visited upon him by the courts, too often manned by his oppressors; out of the barriers put in the way of his withdrawal from the midst of those who pronounce him without moral worth; out of the glaring inconsistency of all dissenters; out of the pure and spotless lives of ten thousand women—the wives, mothers, sisters and lovers—of as high souled and moral men as the world ever saw or produced, I here and now once again and forever record my most unconditioned and emphatic *no* to the query I have in some measure tried to answer.

I have attempted no fine analysis of the case, but simply tried to point out a few facts more or less familiar to all.

THIRD PAPER.

IS THE NEGRO AS MORALLY DEPRAVED AS HE IS REPUTED TO BE?

BY MRS. M. E. C. SMITH.

This question is as grave as it is suggestive. There being a marked difference between *character* and *reputation,* its discussion naturally leads to a consideration of the Negro as he really is, and not as he is represented. The delineation of the Negro's true character is one of the most effectual means of refuting the calumnious epithets so constantly hurled at him—a veritable blasphemy against his higher and better nature.

Has the Negro a higher and better nature? We shall see.

To separate him from the rest of the human family would be to dispute the great truth, that has been so long accepted, by all thoroughly Christianized nations—the Fatherhood of God, and the brotherhood of man. "Of one blood God formed all nations, for to dwell upon the face of the earth." Man, in his first estate, was supremely moral, being created in the righteous image of his Maker; had man continued in this

Mrs. M. E. C. Smith.

MRS. MARY E. C. SMITH.

Mrs. Mary E. C. Smith, daughter of Peter H. Day, was a native of New York city. Her education was provided for, by her energetic widowed mother, to whom she ascribes the secret of her success. From early childhood she showed strong power of mind, and inherited from her mother that force and determination of purpose which prefigure success in whatever is undertaken. As a pupil she was prompt and energetic, and never failed to win one of the Ridgeway prizes for good scholarship, which were given annually to successful contestants. She was an excellent Bible student, and when ten years old was elected a teacher in the Sunday-school. At this age she was impressed with the idea that it was her duty to go to the South to instruct her people, who were just emerging from bondage.

By a strange coincidence she was led to Florida, when she had finished her school course, the very place she had named when in an outburst of childish enthusiasm, while preparing a geography lesson, she had said: "O, mother, how I long to go there and teach my people!" The "land of flowers" has been the principal field of her labors as a teacher. Her ability as a teacher was soon discovered, and in 1890 she became principal of the Normal Department of the Edward Waters College, under the presidency of Prof. B. W. Arnett, Jr. Hundreds of students are better citizens because of her faithful teaching and Christian influence. As a church and Sunday-school worker she has few equals. The earnestness of purpose with which she performs the slightest duty is an example worthy of imitation.

condition, he would have been perfectly innocent and happy, favored with the exalted privilege of direct communion with God, inspired only by Him who is the Great Source, all light and perfection, from whom emanates nothing dark, unholy or unclean.

But man fell, and was driven from Eden. Hence, he began to wander away from God, in spirit and purpose; the tempter had been admitted and man's heart grew very deceitful and desperately wicked. The command of God, however, as written in Genesis, 1st chap., 28th verse, was inviolable. The earth *must* be peopled; thus man continued to wander, and his heart became proud and defiant, even to the resistance of the will and purpose of God. So far did the distance become between man and his Maker and so greatly abounded his wickedness, that at last God gave him over to his own evil imaginations.

The inhabitants of the antediluvian world, as a consequence of man's first transgression, fell lower and lower in the scale of good morals. They became so confirmed in wickedness, so totally depraved, that God destroyed them all, save one man and his family, whom He accounted as righteous, for the sake of his faithful obedience, and whose seed He preserved for the repeopling of the earth. The races, whether Semitic, Hamitic or Japhetic, as springing from the three sons of Noah, all partook of some of the natural proclivities of their revered and ancient grand-sire. What Canaan lacked in the line of perfection in the moral ethics of his day, may be directly attributed to heredity. The lineage of the Negro has been directly traced through Cush to Ham; hence, to argue the total moral depravity of the sons of Ham is but to concede the total moral depravity of the entire human race, as emanated from Noah in the postdiluvian age.

To assert that the Negro has no defects, and is morally good, would be to deny him as one of the legitimate heirs of the family of Noah, and deprive him of his natural inheritance. On the contrary, the Negro is joint-heir to *all* the virtues and *all* the infirmities of the other members of the human family. He is just as good and equally as bad as his fairer-complexioned brothers.

"Multiply and replenish the earth," was the eternal fiat. The subsequent confusion of tongues, and the dispersion of the people even to the remotest parts of the globe, were but links in the chain of God's design. The entire globe must be peopled, not a portion of it; hence the sons of men continued their migration until they were lost to each other.

The history of civilization discloses to us the land of the Hamites, as the cradle from whence sprang all learning, literature and arts, but man's heart still being deceitful, proud and wicked, continued to wander away from the true God; and, notwithstanding his acquired knowledge, and the very high state of civilization to which he had attained, he forgot God, and was allowed to drift into pagan darkness and superstition. These people were scattered, and their land despoiled, and they fled for refuge far into the wilderness where they were left in thick darkness:

"Grouping in ignorance, dark as the night," with
"No blessed Bible to give them the light."

Had any other division of the human family been subjected to the influences of the same depressing climate, for an equal length of time, as were the Hamites, and surrounded by the same degrading circumstances, having no light without the assistance of divine counsel, their degeneration would have been equally as great as these descendants of Ham, when first began their involuntary migration into this country. The subsequent training which the Negro received in the school of bondage, while, in some respects, may have been a very potent lever in raising them from the pit of darkness and superstition, was not that which would best serve in the development of his higher moral nature.

Prior to the beginning of colonial slave traffic, the Negro, as found in his original home, the dark continent, was innocent and simple in his habits, possessed of a very high regard for truth and virtue. And, though very ignorant and superstitious, the result of his paganistic worship, vice and immorality was to him almost unknown. He was a lover of the beautiful, and in disposition easily entreated; and, because of these *very* tractile elements in his character, he fell an easy prey to the machinations of his more wily and crafty brother Japhet.

A study of the American Negro since his most remarkable advent into this country, after being decoyed from his fatherland, portrays him as a mild, impressionable and submissive being—extremely imitative and very easily led or controlled. Those who speculated upon him, as human chattel, very often took advantage of his traits of character in order to further their own interests, and perpetuate the abominable institution of slavery.

The Negro was so tractile in disposition and so easily trained for good or bad that he was frequently developed in the practice of deceit, hypocrisy, tattling and numerous other weaknesses, as the result of the course of training which he received from those who were directly responsible for his physical and moral well being. That peculiar nature of his education in the school of bondage, which taught him that his owner's will was supreme, divested him of his very high regard for virtue; and, wherever resistance was presumed, coercion soon forced him to yield, and he instinctively bowed to the inevitable. Thus, the females drifted into the belief that their bodies were the absolute property of their owners, and that they had no sacred personal rights which he, their self-imposed master, was bound to respect. But, like begets like. What wonder, then, that the seed of unrighteousness, which was implanted in the modern American Negro, before his birth, should spring up and bring forth abundantly of the same kind? Whatever is immoral about the American Negro of to-day was bequeathed to him by his unrighteous ancestors of fairer hue.

A closer inspection of the Negro's home life reveals him as an upright, religious character, and, even under the most adverse circumstances of his unholy environments, he was in many instances so tenacious of his preconceived standard of good morals that he defended his principles even to the extent of yielding his life.

The Negro's native integrity and fidelity were so thoroughly relied upon that during the Civil War, which arrayed in fratricidal strife the two sections of our beloved country, the heroes of the South left their homes and went forth to battle, feeling perfectly secure in entrusting their wives, their daughters, and, in many instances, their fortunes, in the hands of their faithful Negro servants, who remained true to their trusts, caring for, and defending, their precious charges, even at the risk of their own lives. To their credit, it may be inscribed that, although they were aware that victory for the South and the return of their masters meant the prolongation, if not the perpetuation, of their unjust bondage, they swerved not from their posts of duty, and took no advantage of the situation, thus proving the high standard of their moral character.

In the darkest days of thralldom the dominant powers relied upon the Negro's higher moral sense; to the nurse was entrusted almost the entire care of their offspring, and numerous other duties of great responsibility were frequently imposed upon their male and female Negro servants, who invariably proved their high sense of honor, based upon their highest conception of good morals.

Notwithstanding the efforts made to keep the Negro ignorant and degraded, ever and anon, the scintillations from his superior nature would flash out like a burning meteor and exhibit him as he was designed by God his Father, who is no respector of persons. In this connection, we cannot help referring to the beautiful character of Phyllis Wheatley, whose life was absolutely pure, and who was so remarkably inspired by the poetic muse that, even in the darkest days of Negro bondage, she forced the recognition of mankind. Her genius flashed forth as a beacon light to her benighted brethren as a token of assurance to them of the fulfillment of the promise, "Ethiopia shall again stretch forth her hand unto God." Benjamin Banneker, the great mathematician and astronomer, was another instance, in those remote days of darkness, that the Great Dispenser of all light, and truth, imparted His gifts alike to all; and there were others, but for our purpose, these names must forever stand as exponents of that higher and better life that was pent up within the Negro's breast, as a dimly-lighted torch, enshrouded under the mantle of slavery, which needed only the removal of the garment to be clearly seen; and thus, surrounded by the igniting influences of the atmosphere of liberty, would burst forth into all the effulgency of a brilliant light.

As a rule, the modern Negro of America, since his liberation from the shackles of his unjust bondage, has put forth strenuous efforts to uplift himself. And he has succeeded beyond his own most sanguine expectations; having had so many obstacles to overcome, he should not be measured by the heights he has attained, but by the depths from which he came. Out of the depths cried the Negro unto God; and He heard him! A few have arisen far above the masses, and are by their noble examples beckoning the others to come on. The general response is, "We are coming," up out of the cesspool of darkness, ignorance and immorality to the higher plane of virtue, knowledge, purity, and true righteousness which exalteth nations.

That there are dark sides to the picture of the Negro's career since his emergency from that dreary school of bondage, must be admitted, but many of his defects are directly traceable to his imitative propensity. To his own sorrow, he imitates the BAD, as well as the good.

Like the Indian, the fire-water which he has learned to imbibe has divested him of his manhood, and robbed him of his virtue, and it is a sad truth that he is encouraged in this personal debasement of himself by his brother in white, who is still, in many instances, taking advantages of his weak traits, offering him every inducement to continue in his course of self-degradation.

Thirty-six years of light and privilege have wrought wonders for the Negro, but these are scarcely a day, when compared with the long night of over two hundred years of bondage; it is impossible for him in this short period to have totally eradicated the evils for which he was not wholly responsible, but which were entailed upon him at his birth.

Those deflections in the Negro's practice of his code of good morals, which are so often exhibited as an argument against the entire race, are but the results of the development of his weaknesses, by the methods of former years, which he now, finds it so hard to overcome. But those who transgress the general rule of uplifting are the exceptions. To God be the glory for the present Negro, measured, not by the few, who have overlooked their most sacred rights and privileges, but by the many who are daily demonstrating, by honest toil and labor, that they have the highest regard for all that is pure, ennobling, and virtuous.

The Negro's inspiration for poetry, music and the fine arts, proves conclusively that there dwells within him a higher and better nature, which needs only to be developed to its fullest capacity to convince the world beyond the possibility of a successful contradiction that his standard of good morals is as elevated as that of mankind in general. As it is impossible for any fountain to pour forth pure and impure water at the same time, so is it impossible for total depravity to exist in the same mind where dwells that finer sense or appreciation of the beautiful, which originates music, poetry and the fine arts. Again, we refer the world to such beautiful examples as our own dear Edmonia Lewis, B. T. Tanner, now abroad; Paul Lawrence Dunbar, Frances W. Harper, Madam Salika, Flora Batsen Bergen, Nellie Brown Mitchell, Virginia Adele Montgomery, Hallie Quinn Brown, and scores of others; some, perhaps not quite so famous as those mentioned, but who along the line of the higher inspiration of the Negro, refute any argument that may be opposed. As an ensign of the very high standard of Christian ethics attainable by the race, we mention with heart-felt gratitude our dear Amanda Smith, the leader among hundreds of other noble Christian women, who have given not only their lives to God and their race, but feel themselves responsible for the general uplifting of mankind wherever found, knowing that there is no difference with Him, for whom they labor, "whether Greek or Jew." There is no difference, whether high or low, rich or poor, bond or free, white or black; all have a part in the common salvation of Him who came to lift the world up to its original standard of morality by sacrificing His own pure life, and who said, "And I, if I be lifted up, will draw *all* men unto me." The essential need of the human family is charity. Our Saviour said of the Christian graces, "And now abideth these three, Faith, Hope and Charity, but the greatest of these is CHARITY." The time was when there was very little, if any, faith in the Negro's ability to rise and equip himself as a man; afterwards there came a faint glimmer of hope, which commingled with the slowly but gradually increasing faith, proved a blessed and powerful agent in the line of effectual assistance. The Negro began to rise, and he has, with the omnipotent aid of God, his Father, continued his rising until the present, with wonderfully good results, as must be conceded by all minds unbiased by prejudice.

Still there is much land to be possessed, and one thing is yet lacking in the attitude of those who scrutinize him daily for the purpose of rendering an unfavorable judgment. "Charity suffereth long and is kind." Suffer in this connection means to bear; those who claim to have attained a higher standard of morality should bear patiently the infirmities of the Negro, while he is rising, knowing full well that his inherent weaknesses are not of his own begetting, and that it will require some time to overcome the inertia of wrong instruction and practice. But "thanks be unto God, who giveth the victory," to all who obey Him, the Negro as well, God requires simply the earnest effort on his part, and then accomplishes the work Himself.

The highest type of morality is that which generates a disposition on the part of its possessor to have compassion for the lowly and extend a helping hand toward the elevation, comfort and restoration of their inferiors. It has been wisely asserted that "an idle brain is the devil's work-shop." In view of this truism it is wisdom to keep the hand and brain well employed. Booker T. Washington comprehended this fully when he commenced the great work which he is now so successfully prosecuting at Tuskegee. Like the sainted bishop, Daniel A. Payne's, Booker T. Washington's standard of true morality was far above the average of his race. The range of his vision being so extensive, he saw clearly the situation of his people, and without hesitation undertook, in his own way, the work of ameliorating the condition of the masses with the hope of uplifting them to a higher plane of truth and virtue. His motives being pure, his success has been thus far commensurate with the scope of his prodigious undertaking. Notwithstanding his being misunderstood and misinterpreted by many, he has, with unswerving purpose, pursued the trend of his own honest convictions, proved his fidelity to the race, and convinced the world of his unshaken faith in the ultimate success of his enterprise. He is still practically demonstrating his obedience to the Moral Law, as summed up in the Divine command, "Thou shalt love thy neighbor as thyself." Many noble women, also of the race, having outrun their less-favored sisters and reached the highest standard, are now extending their hands to assist others in making their ascent into the more etherial atmosphere of that highest sense of good morals. Thousands, with organization as their watchword, have banded themselves into associations and federations under the significant motto, "Lifting as we climb." The Negro race, under the combined influence of its army of noble workers, both male and female, is fast journeying the upward way of truth and virtue; new heights it is gaining every day.

The little leaven of purity will be unceasingly applied until the whole lump of Negro humanity is raised upon the lofty plane which will force the recognition of his antagonistic brother and convince him that the same high sense of morality governs the Negro as does the Caucasian, or any other highly civilized race upon the globe.

God grant that the refining fires of truth may burn until all the dross of prejudice shall be melted and consumed, when,

> " Man to man united,
>   The whole world shall be lighted,
>   As Eden was of old."

TOPIC XV.

IS THE YOUNG NEGRO AN IMPROVEMENT, MORALLY, ON HIS FATHER?

BY EDWARD MACKNIGHT BRAWLEY, A. M., D. D.

A generation has come since the passing away of the period to which the old Negro belonged, and this generation has lived in the period of the new Negro. Is this new Negro an improvement morally on his father? Zealous friends of the race stoutly maintain that he is; while enemies assert that he is not as good. It is the purpose of this article to present some facts which will prove that the young Negro, in spite of his dreadful inheritance, has, by the aid of generous friends and the grace of God, lifted himself to a higher moral plane than that upon which his unfortunate father stood.

It is well, however, to note carefully at the very beginning, that we are not dealing with exceptions in this discussion, but with the race as a whole. At a river bank the water sometimes appears to run up stream, while if one will but look in the middle, he will see the river in full force gliding smoothly on to the ocean. So in all matters belonging to the realm of morals we must discard the narrow vision, and, taking the broad view of the Christian philosopher, sweep the entire horizon.

Let us first, as an antecedent matter, consider some reasons why the young Negro should be expected to be better than his father.

1. His father had no moral training. His very person was the victim of a prodigious theft, and his labor was daily stolen. Could such a man be effectively taught honesty? To have taught the slave the elements of morals meant the quickening not only of his moral, but also of his intellectual nature; and such a thing would ultimately have developed resistance on the part of the slave. No true instruction in morals was possible in a condition of slavery. Look over the entire moral code as set forth in the Ten Commandments, and the impossibility of teaching effectively those great truths to slaves—American slaves—becomes apparent. The old enslaved Negro was destitute of true moral training; and very much of what was offered to him as such was nothing more than "sounding brass," and he knew it and could not profit by it.

2. And while the old Negro did not have true moral training, he

E. M. Brawley, D.D.

REV. EDWARD MacKNIGHT BRAWLEY, A. M., D. D.

Edward MacKnight Brawley was born at Charleston, S. C., March 18, 1851. His parents, James M. and Ann L. Brawley, were both free. Before the Civil War, in order that he might secure good educational advantages, he was sent to Philadelphia, Pa., where he passed through the grammar school; then he entered the Colored High School, of which Prof. E. D. Bassett was principal, and there prepared for college. In the fall of 1871 he entered Bucknell University, where he was graduated Bachelor of Arts in the class of 1875. During his college course he also pursued theological studies and was ordained for the ministry on the day after his graduation, by a council composed largely of professors of the university. He was the first colored student to attend Bucknell, and in 1878 he secured from his college the degree of Master of Arts. In 1885 the State University of Louisville, Ky., conferred upon him the degree of Doctor of Divinity, and Rev. E. M. Brawley has this distinction, that he has held this degree for a longer time than any other living colored Baptist minister. For eight years he was State Missionary in South Carolina for the American Baptist Publication Society.

In 1883 he was called to the presidency of Selma University, Selma, Ala., and devoted several years to educational work. He then became District Secretary for the South for the American Baptist Publication Society, which work he resigned in 1890 to accept the call to the pastorate of the First Baptist Church of Petersburg, Va., the oldest colored Baptist Church in the country, which he subsequently left to go back to the work of the Society, at its earnest solicitation. He has also served in the pastorate at Greenville, S. C., Darien, Ga., and Palatka, Fla. He has done considerable newspaper work, and has devoted much time to religious writing, many pamphlets and books along race and denominational lines having been written by him. He is now Editorial Secretary of the National Baptist Publishing Board, of Nashville, Tenn., under the auspices of the National Baptist Convention. Dr. Brawley's qualifications and experience well fit him for his present position, for he has made a specialty of Sunday-school and denominational literature.

did have positive training in the opposite direction. For the very system under which he lived was a training in evil. His ancestors had been stolen; he himself was stolen; his civil liberty was stolen. Could he form any adequate conception of property rights? And is it now a matter of surprise to us that the old man sometimes did a little stealing himself in order to relieve a hungry stomach? He was not taught the sacredness of the married life. Indeed, he was not taught to marry at all. He was, as a rule, simply told to live with a woman whom he might *call* his wife, and when the good pleasure or the necessities of his master demanded that she should be sold away, to take another woman and live with her and call her wife, also. He was not allowed to develop the idea of fatherhood toward his children, for they were not his, but rather mere chattel, to be sold at the pleasure of his master. The two great vices charged against the Negro race are theft and adultery. Whatever truth there is in this charge is due to the long training slavery gave. Indeed, slavery was largely a training in moral evil. Antecedently, therefore, we expect the old Negro to be worse than his son.

But, now, what are the positive arguments to prove that the young Negro is an improvement morally on his father?

1. Slavery has been abolished, and the young Negro has not felt it. He has, therefore, missed its direct evil training. It is not denied that he is damaged because he was trained by a father who was brought up in slavery; but it is claimed that he has not received from his father, and cannot receive, as much injury as his father received from the system of slavery.

2. The young Negro now has the gospel. The many thousands who came to Christ in the days of slavery, and are now at rest from their earthly toils and sufferings, are not forgotten. That they were saved is due to the fact that, owing to God's infinite goodness and mercy, a little knowledge and a little faith can save a sinner; and God pitied our fathers. But the young Negro now has the gospel in its fullness. He gets it from the pulpit, from the Sunday-school, and daily in scores of our highest literary institutions. The gospel is the power of God unto salvation, and our youth, constantly learning it, have in large numbers been made to feel its power. Their lives having thus been purified and ennobled, beautiful and strong Christian characters have resulted.

3. Many young Negroes have been thoroughly trained for the ministry, who have led strictly upright lives and have taught others to do

the same; and many others, not ministers, have enjoyed systematic training in ethics. Is it conceivable that the combined work of this class of our young people has accomplished nothing in the moral uplifting of the race? Such work must and does count powerfully on the right side, or else the gospel is a failure. Just as heathen nations have been redeemed and regenerated, having put away their savage life and accepted civilization and Christ because the gospel was preached to them, even so has our race been saved; and just as no other people ever received the gospel without being immeasurably blessed and lifted up, so also is that true of the Negro. And it is further true of all men that the more gospel privileges they enjoy, the better will be their condition. For the kingdom of evil is sure to be overthrown, and the kingdom of Christ established on the earth. And thus the young Negro cannot help being a better man morally than his father.

4. The young Negro is living in an age of higher morals and necessarily partakes of its superior advantages. The age of brute force is fast passing away. When after our great civil war the adjustment of our troubles with England was arranged by arbitration rather than settled by war, an immense stride in civilization, men say, was made. Very true, but why not say that the men in control of the two great nations involved were moved to act as they did because of their strong ethical principles? And from that time until now the moral advance of the world has been rapid and steady. The new Negro is living in this higher and better age, and his moral constitution has been built up and made strong because of it. The principles of international comity are fast spreading among the nations. And just as the economic principles of the trust are being applied to religious organizations, even so the stronger ethical principles that are moving the nations are inducing Christian white men to come nearer to their brethren in black, and to treat them more as *men, brethren,* than has ever been done before. And thus both external and internal forces have combined to make the young Negro morally better than his father.

5. And, last of all, the young Negro is turning his social and political disadvantages to his best interest by relying calmly upon the justice and wisdom of God's moral government. Life is, indeed, but a conflict of forces, but the intelligent young Christian Negro knows that the universe does not operate by chance. He feels the full force of what Charles Sumner said in his eulogy on Abraham Lincoln: "In the provi-

J. Simeon Flipper, D.D.

REV. J. SIMEON FLIPPER, D. D.

The subject of this sketch was among the first to enter Atlanta University the first day it opened, 1869, and there remained until 1876. He taught school in Georgia for several years. He was converted in 1877 and joined the A. M. E. Church at Thomasville, Ga. He was licensed both to exhort and to preach. In January, 1880, he joined the Georgia Annual Conference. In 1882 was elected secretary of the Georgia Conference, which position he held for five consecutive years. In this same year he was ordained a Deacon by Bishop W. F. Dickerson and sent to Darien, Ga., where he prepared for and took care of the session of the Georgia Conference.

In 1884 he met the Georgia Conference at Valdosta, Ga., and was ordained an Elder by Bishop W. F. Dickerson, and was stationed at Quitman, Ga., remaining there two years. In January, 1886, he was transferred by Bishop James A. Shorter to the North Georgia Conference and stationed at Big Bethel A. M. E. Church, Atlanta, Ga., the city in which he was born. His mother had been a member of this church and its old members knew him when a boy. There he remained four years with great success, raising the largest amount of dollar money that had up to that time been raised in the State; by this he became one of the dollar money kings of the connection for 1886 and was awarded a gold badge by the Financial Department of the A. M. E. Church. Thus, in six years after entering the ministry, he became pastor of the largest church in the State at the age of twenty-seven years. In 1889 he was assigned to Pierce's Chapel, Athens, Ga., and served it three years. In 1892 he was made Presiding Elder of the Athens District, which place he filled for three years. In 1893 he preached the annual sermon to the students of Allen University, Columbia, S. C., when the faculty and Trustee Board conferred on him the title of Doctor of Divinity. In 1892 he was a delegate to the General Conference of the A. M. E. Church, which met in Philadelphia, and served as a member on the committee on statistics.

In 1895 he was stationed a second time in Atlanta, at Allen Temple, A. M. E. Church, remaining here four years with great success and entertaining the session of the North Georgia Conference in his last year. He was elected again to the General Conference, which met at Wilmington, N. C., in May, 1896, and served on the committee on revision of discipline.

In 1899 he was elected not only a delegate but the leader of his delegation to the General Conference, which met at Columbus, Ohio, in May, 1900. Here he was elected without opposition chairman of the Episcopal Committee, the most important committee of the church; it is composed of all the leaders of the delegations from all parts of the church, and before this committee the Bishops appear for an examination in their moral, religious and official character; it fixes the boundaries of the districts and assigns the Bishops to their fields of labor.

He is now a trustee of Morris Brown College, Secretary of the Trustee and Executive Boards, Treasurer of the Theological Fund, Chairman and treasurer of the dollar money committee of the Atlanta, Ga., Conference, Book Steward, Chairman of Committee on Fourth Year's Studies. He is a prominent craftsman and for one year was Deputy Grand Master of the Most Worshipful Union Grand Lodge, A. F. and A. M. of Georgia, Grand Representative of the Stringer Grand Lodge of Mississippi to the Grand East of Georgia, with the rank of Grand Senior Warden. He is now a Trustee of the W. E. Terry Masonic Orphan and Widows' Home and Industrial School, located at Americus, Ga., Associate Editor of the "Voice of Missions," the missionary organ of the A. M. E. Church, published in New York.

One of the greatest events of his life was the receiving of Rev. Jas. M. D'wane of the Ethiopian Church from Pretoria, Transvaal Republic, South Africa, into the A. M. E. Church, and through him eighty preachers and two thousand eight hundred members.

dence of God there is no accident—from the fall of a sparrow, to the fall of an empire or the sweep of a planet, all is controlled by divine law." And thus he lives undisturbed by the wrathful elements that are at play around him. His full confidence in God at this trying hour, and his firm belief that the wrath of man will yet be turned to his advantage, are but the evidence that he trusts intelligently; and the fact that he does so, and does not become an anarchist, is the proof of his higher moral life. If it be said that his father did not become an anarchist, the answer may be that slavery had dispirited him. But the young Negro is not dispirited. He knows enough and has spirit enough to make this country tremble; but whatever knowledge and spirit he has which could be used for evil, he has restrained and will yet further restrain, because he has abiding confidence in God, and knows that "giant right is more than might;" and this confidence has aided in making him a better man than his father.

SECOND PAPER.

IS THE YOUNG NEGRO AN IMPROVEMENT, MORALLY, ON HIS FATHER?

BY REV. J. S. FLIPPER.

The difficulty of considering this question deepens as we consider the young Negro from every phase of life. Universally it cannot be answered in the affirmative, for the Negro is divided into classes as well as are other races, and as no people are universally, morally good, so such cannot be expected of the Negro.

The Negro possesses an upper class, a middle class, and a lower class, and in a consideration of these classes we shall look for an answer to the question. The upper class consists of those who have made extraordinary progress, morally, religiously, mentally and materially; who have outstripped their fellows in the race of life and attained a standard of civilization commensurate with their opportunities and proved to the civilized world that under favorable circumstances the Negro is as capable of a high development in civilization as any other race. This class is an improvement, morally, upon their fathers. For their opportunities have been such as to render them more capable of a higher conception of morality and of their duties to their fellowmen, and in proportion as a man is enlightened on morality does he improve in morality, other things being equal, and reaches a higher type of manhood. Morality is always affected by one's religious views. The moral binds us to our fellowmen, and the religious to our God; and a man may in many respects be better than his fellowman but he can never be better than his God. If a man has low and meagre ideas of God his ideas of man will be low and meagre whatever may be his conceptions of the law, government, and the character of his Creator will be his ideas of duty to wife, children, neighbors and country.

The educational qualifications on moral and religious lines must furnish some of the rules by which the standard can be gauged for the man who has by liberal and extensive educational facilities gotten the capacity to know his God and His moral government over His creatures must rise in moral improvement and stand out as the towering mountain above the plain that surrounds it. And on this line the upper class of Negroes, by reason of religious and educational advantages, are an improvement morally on their fathers, whose opportunities for moral improvement were very meagre, indeed.

The middle class of Negroes are not equal to the upper class in attainments. Their educational advantages have not been so great as those of the upper class, and yet their moral development has been correspondingly as great. The moral law of God has been heard as distinctly by them as by the upper, but they have not that discriminating judgment that enables them in every instance to distinguish between the morally wrong and the morally right, and yet there has been awakened in them a consciousness of certain things due to their fellowman and to their God that has kept them in a way that they could not be charged with wilful moral wrong, and their conservatism has placed them in a manner nearer to the morally right than to the morally wrong. And the young Negroes of this class are an improvement morally on their fathers. Solomon hath said, "As a man thinketh, so is he." Good character cannot arise out of low thoughts, but it must emanate from pure, noble, God-fearing and elevating thoughts and ideas. Correct ideas of life practically embodied in conduct can lift man above the low, sensual, evil walks of life. Now that there are many young Negroes with correct ideas of life cannot be denied. Now the lower class of Negroes are those whose ideas are distorted; who are conscience-seared, and who have no regard for God nor man; and as the upper and middle classes have ascended

E. C. Morris, D. D.

REV. E. C. MORRIS, D. D.

On May 7, 1855, near Springplace on the Connesauga, in the chestnut hills of North Georgia, of slave parentage, was born E. C. Morris, now the President of the National Baptist Convention, which is the largest deliberative body of Negroes in the world, the editor-in-chief of the Sunday School series issued by the National Baptist Publishing Board, the President of the Arkansas Baptist State Convention, and pastor of the Centennial Baptist Church of Helena, Arkansas. His early education was through the common school, but practically from nature and necessity. From earliest childhood he was peculiarly interested in men and things; hence, now possesses a large stock of knowledge concerning human nature, is an advocate of prudence, conservatism and manliness in all affairs bearing upon the relation of the races in this country. He stands for self-help and racial integrity and believes that when man has acknowledged his inability and failure to ameliorate the ill conditions in this country, God will settle the same and cause the deserved recognition of all men, black and white.

He saw with his father the first train that passed through North Georgia, though the spectacle was quite an amusing draft on his youthful nerve, for, says he, "Had I been older than five years, it is questionable that my father, by whose hand I was led, could have detained me from the urgent business I felt I had back home when that mysteriously terrible locomotive came rushing down the track seemingly intent upon spending its fury upon no one else but me."

When Elias was ten years old, his parents, James and Cora Morris, moved into Alabama, settling at the little town of Stevenson. But Elias had a short while before begun living with the late Rev. Robert Caver, his brother-in-law, at Stevenson, and so lived until he arrived at the age of twenty-one. Mr. Caver taught the young man the shoemaker's trade and the latter earned his bread upon the shoemaker's bench until thirty and three years old. He felt a call to the gospel ministry immediately upon his conversion at the age of nineteen, which took place just at the time when he had grown so inimical and impatient toward a revival that had been going on for several days in the church at Stevenson that he had plotted mischievous disturbance of the meeting.

He grew in grace and general ability, and in 1879 accepted a call to the pastorate of the Centennial Baptist Church of Helena, Arkansas, which position he has held continuously to the present time. His ability as an organizer is fully recognized among his people. He established and for the first two years edited the first religious paper published by the Negroes in the State of Arkansas. In 1884, he organized the Arkansas Baptist College and for sixteen years has been Chairman of its Board of Trustees. For nineteen consecutive years he has been annually elected President of the Arkansas Baptist State Convention. In 1894 he was elected President of the National Baptist Convention, whose constituency numbers about a million and a half, and has been elected every year since to the same position. Under his leadership, this society has been firmly unified and has enjoyed the greatest prosperity in its history. It was his address before this Convention at Washington, in 1893, that inspired an indomitable and uncompromising determination in the minds of the colored Baptists to begin publishing interests of their own. It was his active brain that conceived the idea of the National Baptist Young People's Union Board, which Board is located at Nashville. And so his progressive acts have multiplied as he has advanced in age and responsibility. Dr. Morris is an acknowledged adviser of the colored people of his community, in all matters relating to their general uplift. He is a friend to humanity and a lover of his race. He is a possessor and advocate of wholeheartedness and sincerity, being charitable to a difference or a fault. His influence begins at home and spreads abroad, and all distinctions that he bears are borne with gentlemanly modesty, believing leadership to him a duty rather than an honor.

in the scale of moral civilization, so the bad class of Negroes have descended in the scale, their finer sensibilities having become blunted by vice and crime, so that education on moral and religious lines has no charms for them. Sinai's majestic summit and moral law are as chaff to them, and as freedom has given a greater and better opportunity for the morally good to improve and rise, so it has given the same for this class to descend and become more and more corrupt. Indeed, they have gone lower than their fathers on this line. But the character of a race is not to be judged by its degraded element, but by the upper and middle classes, which form the major portion of any race and give it a standing along the line of moral and religious civilization. We conclude by saying that the young Negro is an improvement morally upon his father.

First, because freedom has given to the young Negro aspirations for a purer life, which his father did not have.

Second. The moral atmosphere of the young Negro's home life is better than that of the old Negro.

Third. The young Negro's educational advantages give him higher conceptions of life and duty than those had by his father.

Fourth. The young Negro has a more enlightened pulpit than his father had to preach a broader and more comprehensive gospel to him, and to thus give him more correct ideas of life.

Now these superior advantages, which the young Negro has, make it possible for him to outstrip his father in moral accomplishments, and the arguments of his enemies to the contrary notwithstanding, the educated young Negro presents a striking contrast in point of morality to the old Negro.

THIRD PAPER.

IS THE YOUNG NEGRO AN IMPROVEMENT, MORALLY, ON HIS FATHER?

BY REV. E. C. MORRIS, D. D.

The subject of this article is a very important and delicate one; important because it forms the base from which all the advancement made by the race for the last past thirty-six years must be measured, and delicate because it makes comparison between father and son. If there has been no improvement in the race, morally, since its emancipation from slavery, then no real advancement has been made; and to say that the Negro has made no advancement would be sufficient to call forth universal derision.

It must be admitted in the beginning that to do full justice to the subject, much study and space is required. In the absence of comprehensive statistics on the subject and the time in which to compile the same, several standpoints of reasoning must be assumed, and these will be taken up in no regular order, one being important as the others. I do not attempt to go upon or set up a system of scientific theories either, but simply to state and connect obvious facts. The past and present moral status of the race is involved, but I shall not go beyond that period in which the race was emancipated, and will include, as the fathers, such as were the heads of families at that time and those who were born about that time, constituting largely the heads of families now, as the respective parties to the comparison.

What is here said in comparison of father and son is not intended as unfavorable criticism even where the language may appear uncomplimentary, but rather to make a truthful statement of the virtues found in both. I wish also to be understood as placing myself with those who have faith in the race, to the extent that I believe a large majority of the freedmen and their descendants are moral, and should be counted with the good and upright in heart. Such a decision cannot be reached, however, from a surface examination or outward appearances. For it is a notorious fact that in all the years of the Negro's life in this country, he has been subjected to the most menial occupations such as would, in a large measure, prejudice the disinterested observer against any high opinion of his morals. The subject is by no means a new one, but has been investigated and discussed for a long time by great writers and thinkers. Opinions have been expressed which are by no means favorable to the race—by no means favorable because of the ignorance of the party expressing the opinion. Many of these opinions have been formed and influenced by what is seen of the Negro in the crowded streets of great cities, at railroad depots, or at steamboat landings; or upon the great cotton, rice and sugar plantations, where thousands of Negroes who are employed only as day laborers, meet. But these do not represent the majority of the Negroes. Nor should opinions be formed, of the moral status of this people, out of what may be seen of them at such places as above referred to, any more than the morals of a great city like New York or Chicago should be judged by what is seen of the motley crowds that gather about the wharfs and in the congested streets and other places where the lowest element of society is to be seen in the majority. The Negro fathers of forty years ago were as good as the circumstances and conditions of that day required, and many of them showed themselves to be superior to the requirement. It is to be admitted that environment and teaching have much to do with moral development, and that neither of these were, as a rule, favorable to the fathers. The contraband life of the Negroes during the war was perhaps the best that could be provided at that time. But it was far from being conducive to good morals, and was not, in a moral sense, an improvement upon the plantation life prior to the war, when almost all the slaves were huddled by families in one room cabins of what was known as "the quarters." It was fortunate for the race and the fathers that the contraband life was of short duration, and the heads of families among the Negroes, as fast as they could get their loved ones together, began to settle in families all over the Southland. The privilege of being a free man, to come and go at will, had its evil effect upon the fathers for a few years, but they soon became enveloped with the desire that their children become educated and otherwise cultured, as were the children of their white neighbors.

The desire to educate and accumulate for the good of the children became the restraining point in the lives of the fathers, and a very appreciable change for better morals was noticeable in the latter sixties and early seventies.

Immediately following the close of the war, a great many missionary agencies set to work among the Negroes for the purpose of improving them morally and intellectually. These agencies operated among the old and young alike, but not with the same results; for it soon became known that very little change could be wrought among the aged ones whose superstitious notions of religious worship and peculiar ideas about "white folks' religion" made it a difficult task to teach them. Notwithstanding their superstition, the aged Negroes were singularly kind and respectful to their white neighbors and permitted the white teachers— for nearly all teachers were white at that time—to have absolute control of their children both as to home and school life.

One of the attributes of morality is a happy conscience, or happiness, for there can be no true happiness where there is no morality. Hence, there existed an appreciable element of morality among the fathers, for, as a rule, no happier or more contented people could be found anywhere. I speak of the whole race. One may be a good servant or a good neighbor, and yet not a good man. Opportunities have much to do with developing the attributes of the soul. Many of those noble qualities which go to make a good man were latent in the fathers, for there had been no opportunity for the development of these qualities.

The home is the foundation place of all that is good and grand in a race or nation. Wisdom and virtue are inseparable from a good home. Hence, to make the comparison which my subject calls for, we must inquire into the home and religious life of the present generation. The young men from eighteen to twenty-one years of age who are, so to speak, in embryo with respect to questions affecting the progress of the race, are not included in the summary we make and should not be considered directly, in measuring the moral status of the race. As to the homes of the fathers forty years ago, very little can be said. But late statistics show that there are over three hundred thousand homes and farms owned by the Negroes in the United States, which indicates that nearly two millions of the nine million of our people live in their own homes. The figures are very significant when it is remembered that the race started forty years ago, four million and a half in number of individuals, with practically no homes. The property value of the homes now owned is conservatively put at one billion dollars—not a bad showing for a people who commenced forty years ago at zero in wealth. But the accumulation of wealth does not always mean that the owner is moral, yet the accumulation and maintenance of good homes present a better argument in favor of the good moral inclination of the people accumulating and maintaining these homes than can be produced in words. These mean more than the mere ownership of a house and lot, or a sixty acre farm; a respect for the first institution set up by the Creator is thereby shown and that in that institution (the family) is one to love and honor; and that there an altar is to be erected around which all are to kneel and worship God; they mean that morality, the foundation of all true greatness, is to be enthroned there. The establishment and maintenance of so many Christian homes among our people has brought forward a demand which is a barometer of the moral changes, and shows conclusively that the race is improving morally. This demand is for the right kind of men as preachers and teachers. The time was when a man who could read and write, no matter what his character, could find a place to preach and teach among our people. This does not obtain now so much as before, and the people are demanding that their teachers and spiritual advisers be men and women whose lives and characters are living epistles of virtue. If proof of this point were necessary, one would need only to refer to the continued upheavals in various communities, in the schools and churches, where war has been made upon those persons whose lives have been such as to arouse suspicion that they were unworthy the offices held. The fact that these demands are being made for a pure ministry and a competent and worthy corps of teachers is encouraging.

In passing judgment upon the moral status of the young Negro, or in comparing this status with that of the father who has gone from the stage, we will necessarily have to apply the multiplication process, for it will require a life fully lived in all its details to constitute the sum total of a well built character. Therefore, the *whole* truth about the morals of the present generation will be known only to the next. The processes used in the moral development of the race have been gradual and almost imperceptible in progress, but they have been in progress, nevertheless, and promise great results. The man who sowed his seeds yesterday does not expect to reap a harvest to-morrow. Cultivation is to follow planting. The warm spring rains, the hot rays of a summer sun are to come and moisten and warm the soil around the roots, cause the blade to shoot forth and then harden the stalk and the grain. These are to be followed by the cool winds and frosts of autumn before harvest comes. The planting of moral principles in the present generation of Negroes has been done; the cultivating process is now going on by means of the buying of homes, entering into business and agricultural pursuits, building churches and schools and in educating the youth. These facts point to the moral trend of the mind of the present generation, but per-haps none of them in the same degree as the religious desire of the colored man.

A larger per cent of the Negroes in this country are members of the Christian churches than of any other race of people. Notwithstanding the criticism to the contrary, they are as practical in their Christianity as any set of people. The matter of divorce has been a great problem to many of the most thoughtful men of the race, and the frequent resort to the courts to obtain divorces has been used as an argument against the growth of the moral sentiment in the race. But the very fact that such meets with opposition and is disapproved by the good people is evidence in favor of the Negro's morals. Then again, the class of Negroes who have but little respect for the marriage vow are, as a rule, those who are indolent, worthless and without a home and making no effort to obtain one. But, happily, this class form but a small minority.

Another virtue in the Negro's character which comes only from a moral sentiment is gratitude. He loves his benefactors and would gladly repay them for all they have done for him, if he were able to do so. If the mind was filled with sensuality, deception, hatred and like vices, there would be no room for that noble characteristic, gratitude, which is so prominent in the present generation. His gratitude extends beyond the individual benefactor to the flag of his country; overlooking present conditions and remembering past favors, he is always ready to dare and die for his country's honor. We conclude by saying that the fathers who came up out of slavery, unlettered and untrained, did well. The present generation of fathers, or heads of families, by reason of superior advantages, are doing far better. The race as a whole for the last past thirty-six years has made a history for itself which will form the apex of its glory when it has passed through a century of training under its changed condition from slavery to freedom.

FOURTH PAPER.

IS THE YOUNG NEGRO AN IMPROVEMENT, MORALLY, ON HIS FATHER?

BY MRS. ARIEL S. BOWEN.

The most important and vital factors in the development of a race are physical strength, intelligence and morality, these three, but the greatest of these is morality.

The individual or the race possessed of either or both of the first two, and that utterly ignores the third, can never attain to the full status of man, nor reach the zenith of full racial development or the pinnacle of civilization. To-day we hear much about the survival of the fittest and the "superior race and the inferior races." The earnest, thoughtful student of life and its affairs immediately raises the question, To whom do such titles "fittest," "superior" and "inferior" refer, and why? The history of a people shows the advance and growth of that people. Their development can be traced from the crude barbarous or semi-barbarous

Mrs. Ariel S. H. Bowen

MRS. ARIEL SERENA HEDGES BOWEN.

Mrs. Ariel Serena Hedges Bowen, wife of Dr. J. W. E. Bowen of Gammon Theological Seminary, Atlanta, Ga., was born in Newark, N. J. Her father was a Presbyterian clergyman in that city. He had graduated from Lincoln University, Pa., and had organized churches in New York State. Her mother represents one of the oldest Presbyterian families of that State. Her grandfather was a bugler in the Mexican war, and was a Guard of Honor when Lafayette revisited the United States. Her parents removed early to Pittsburg, Pa., where she attended the Avery Institute. She completed the Academic course of this school. Her parents then moved to Baltimore, Md., where her father became pastor of Madison Avenue Presbyterian Church, and finally of Grace Presbyterian Church. She was sent to the High School of Springfield, Mass., where she remained and graduated with honor in a large class in 1885. She also took the Teachers' Course and Examination and passed a creditable examination and was favorably considered as teacher for one of the schools of that city. She was then called to teach History and English Language in the Tuskegee Institute, Tuskegee, Ala., under Prof. B. T. Washington.

In the year 1886 she was married to Dr. J. W. E. Bowen. She became a Life Member of the Woman's Home Missionary Society of the Methodist Episcopal Church. She removed to Atlanta with her husband in 1893. She became Professor of Music in Clark University in 1895. She is the State President of the Georgia W. C. T. U., No. 2. She has written very largely, among which may be mentioned, "Music in the Home." "The Ethics of Reform," etc. She is an accomplished vocalist and musician with the piano and pipe organ. She is busily engaged in temperance and reform work, together with training and fitting her family of one boy and three girls for life. She is regarded as one of the foremost and best cultured women of her race. She reads Greek, Latin and German with facility, and is a superb housekeeper.

state in which physical prowess predominated through the period of intellectual development where the mind begins to grasp new ideas and where new ideals of higher and nobler purposes are sought after. Then came the greater perfection, the nobler aspiration, the purer, higher civilization, growing out of the purer thought and purer life of a purified people. This is true of all races, therefore the Negro race is no exception, and is entitled to the same justice that is accorded to every race that has had its rise and fall.

The writer takes it that the young "Negro" and his father are to represent only the ante-bellum and the post-bellum Negro. To go beyond that, to take him in his earlier state in the native wilds of his fatherland, before the Anglo-Saxon missionary reached him and gave to the world a true picture of his morality, would be to present to the world some startling facts that would not only put to shame the "young Negro," but also the hosts of men of all nations who glory in the progress they have made in morals.

It can be proven by the best authorities that many of the heathen Africans, though crude in ethics, were pure morally.

But the discussion resolves itself into two very important questions. What was the moral condition of the Negro before the war, and what is his moral condition to-day? Before the war, what a picture comes before us at these words, what a panorama of deeds passes before our mind's eye. Years of gross darkness, darkness that deepens into the blackness of the pit, those days that seem like a hideous nightmare to the hoary headed, and the story of which sounds to the youth like a heart-rending and nauseating recital. Yet, it was not all dark, some would say; perhaps not, but the bright spots only tended to intensify the darkness.

What morals were chattels expected to have, and who gave to these chattels their moral code? It was certainly not of their own making. What could be the moral condition of a race to whom family rights were forbidden and whose business, next to labor, was to propagate solely for the master's gain? The words mother, father, were used only in the language of the "big house."

Womanhood, the foundation stone of moral eminence, passed through a crucial ordeal, and it is to be greatly wondered at that the Negro woman emerged with even the crudest type of moral capacity.

Every line on every page of the history of those dark days teem and reek with the abandon of licentiousness, nor could this be otherwise. It was the natural sequence of a debasing system. It is no disparagement upon the noble few whose garments were kept unspotted, nor upon those who would have reached towards higher ideals, if they had been masters of themselves, to say that the ante-bellum Negro did not possess a great degree of morality. There can be no other conclusion drawn from such demoralizing conditions.

The moral status of the Negro is to-day an all-absorbing theme, and is discussed pro and con by friend and enemy in other races, and by the optimist and pessimist of his own. Comparisons concerning his morals and moral growth are made as all other comparisons are made concerning him, not between his present and former condition, nor between his condition and that of any other people at the same stage of development, under the same conditions and environments. On the contrary, inconsistency is ever present in the attempts to show the world existing facts. Whenever an attack was made upon the system of slavery, the defenders of the system immediately pointed to the poor slaveholder and the dearth of Negro criminals as points in favor of a time when the Negro enjoyed the blessings of a "mild and humane system."

When the progress of the black race in America is placed in the balance, the lowest and most degraded and careless of the masses who have not come out of a state of inertia are brought into comparison with the noblest types that have ascended the scale of life. What wonder then that there is so much adverse criticism; what is needed is a search for facts and an unprejudiced putting of all that appertains to the Negro, and a just acknowledgment of the results attained.

That the American Negro has made an advance along all lines that make for the higher development of a people cannot be denied. He has improved morally in a corresponding way. The limit of this paper will not permit a statistical comparison, but a few points may be noticed in passing. His moral instinct is quickened and his moral nature asserts itself in higher forms of life under the new conditions. He has started at the fountainhead and the purity of his home and hearthstone is a magnificent memorial to the purity of the black woman.

Were it possible to give in numbers the correct estimate of these beautiful homes and their characters, even the most bitter of his enemies and the pessimists of his own race would look with doubt upon the pernicious libels disseminated in the periodical literature of the day.

The dark picture of the Negro's shortcomings is thrown on the canvas and so familiar has it become that not a few seldom think that there is another picture which the Negro himself knows to be truer to life and more prophetic of his real nature, taken from real life, and one that ought to give inspiration and hope to all seekers after facts.

The Negro ministry has made rapid and marked progress in moral achievements for itself and also for the race in their wide influence upon the same. There is a constant and ever-increasing demand coming from the people for a higher and nobler service in the pulpit, and the demand is being met in a comparative measure. Moreover there are professional men whose lives prove the possessors' estimate of virtue and are being spent in bringing others up to these lofty ideals.

The noble army of teachers, most of whom are women, are not to be overlooked or underestimated. Next to the faithful mother, these noble women have lived and worked for the race. They have proved themselves ever against untoward conditions. Their work and worth should not be reflected against because of the few whose lives are not up to the standards of true womanhood. It is undeniably true that the virtues of Solomon's virtuous women may be duplicated in multitudes of our women teachers.

A word concerning the criminal record of the Negro might be worth considering. It is here that the moral weakness of the race is said to be most manifest. We are told that figures do not lie, and an appeal from the records is not to be considered for a moment. Yet, he who wants facts and is in search of the truth must appeal and must make personal investigation.

As yet statistics, the press and history, have not given a truthful, unbiased record of the Negro of to-day as he really is. One side has been faithfully followed, and elaborately and painfully portrayed, but of the other side only here and there an item, a reference and a charitable surmise rewards the seeker after knowledge. A careful study of the environments of the so-called criminal class, also the courts of justice before which the criminals are arraigned, would develop some interesting, not to say startling, facts; for example, "it has been shown by Prof. Branson, of the Georgia State Normal School, that while the illiterate Negro population of the state furnish three convicts per thousand, the Negroes who have profited by the public schools furnish only one convict per thousand." Many of the criminals start from the court-room and are the victims of injustice.

Such untoward conditions serve rather to stamp out every vestige of nobility rather than inspire to a reaching out after higher ideals.

The young or post-bellum Negro is steadily improving morally. In the face of strong opposition, in his moral development, just as he does in mental, financial and civil growth, against all the opposing forces that would hinder his growth and relegate him to the lowest stratum of mankind, he is forcing his way up the stream. His spiritual and moral nature is beating under the animal nature which for so long a time held him as a slave. He now does right for right's sake, and loves the pure and good. He honors the women of his race and is raising her to nobler plains in his thoughts and life.

The Negro woman is asserting herself also and is building for herself a character that rests upon a foundation of personal purity. This she is doing not only for herself, but for others. The building up of pure homes is her chief concern and in them she reigns with womanly queenliness.

Social reform receives her attention, and in these walks she may be found teaching the young the single standard of purity for both sexes. Her way is the roughest, her path most closely beset with snares, but her works show for themselves.

If there had been no advancement along moral lines, the Negro's material and intellectual attainments would count for very little in the world of affairs, for he would degenerate to a mere mechanical factor in human society and become a tool in every case in the hands of a stronger race. But he has added to his material and intellectual strength a greater and higher force, viz., that of moral worth, which at once raises him to higher planes in the social and civil world, and brings him into contact with his enemies and oppressors.

The Negro has met and overcome the great barriers to his progress one by one. Despite the snares that are all about his path, and their hidden evils that seek to hold him in thralldom, yet he bursts his chains and marches forward with renewed purpose and greater zeal.

Yes, the young Negro is embodying nobler ideas in his nature and reaching forward after higher ideals because of his superior advantages. He is to face a future pregnant with struggles of a higher order and of a more diverse character, than the struggles of an earlier day. He enters into competition, not with one race only, but with all the races of mankind. As the knowledge of the fierceness of the battle comes to him, he raises himself from his lethargy and in the strength of his manhood he goes forward.

He who doubts not the Negro's growth and development along intellectual and financial lines cannot gainsay his steady and sturdy growth in moral and social power.

TOPIC XVI.

THE NEGRO AS A WRITER.

BY REV. J. Q. JOHNSON, D. D.

It would be extravagant to set up any claims of greatness in behalf of Negro writers. The Negro has yet his contribution to make to the literature of mankind. We fully believe that he has a message to deliver. The making of a writer is a matter of centuries. England was a long time producing a Shakespeare or a Milton, Italy a Dante, Russia a Tolstoi, France a Hugo or a Dumas, Germany a Goethe and a Schiller. America, active in invention and commerce, has not yet produced a name worthy to stand by the side of those just mentioned. All really great writers have not only a national or racial, but also a universal quality in their productions. So far the greater part of our literary effort has been of historical compilations. We have accumulated a large mass of material for the future historians. Williams' "History of the Negro Race" is an example of this kind. In this way we have recorded the deeds of distinguished Negroes in every avenue of life. Such works have kept alive the hope and kindled the aspirations of the race. A most interesting work of this kind is that of Prof. E. H. Crogman, "The White Side of a Black Subject." In this book we have the serious and earnest efforts of the race recorded. Here we learn of educators like Booker T. Washington and J. W. E. Bowen, lawyers like T. McCants Stewart and S. A. McElwee, women physicians like Halle T. Johnson and Georgia Washington. Books of this kind are in almost every Negro home in the land.

The Negro as a writer of prose is nowhere seen to a better advantage than in Dr. Blyden's "Christianity, Islam and the Negro Race." Here we find the Negro in command of the best English style. Whatever may be said of his opinions, his mastery of a forcible, spirited, nervous expression reminds one of Macauly and Addison. Probably the best book from the standpoint of scientific, historical investigation is the work of Dr. DuBois on "The Suppression of the African Slave Trade."

Bishop B. T. Tanner, in his "Dispensations in the Church," has made a real contribution to our race literature. In this he establishes the

J. Q. Johnson, D. D.

REV. J. Q. JOHNSON, D. D.

Rev. J. Q. Johnson, D. D., was graduated from the Collegiate Department of Fisk University in 1890; from the Hartford Theological Seminary in 1893. He taught mathematics at Tuskegee for one year; the John F. Slater fund published his report of the fifth Tuskegee Negro Conference in its series of "Occasional Papers." He has been President of Allen University, Columbia, S. C. His pastoral work has embraced some of the strongest and most influential churches in the A. M. E. connection. Associated with him was his brilliant and cultured wife—Mrs. Halle Tanner Johnson—the first woman who ever passed the State Medical Board of Examiners of Alabama. Her recent death was a loss to the race.

Dr. Johnson is among the foremost men of his church. He is among the best read men of the race. He is an able preacher and a strong, forceful writer. One of his characteristic points is his ability to say much in little. He goes right to the point without wasting time with needless *words*. He received Doctor's degree from Morris Brown College, Atlanta, Ga. He studied two years as a post-graduate student at Princeton University.

Hamitic origin of the ancient Egyptians and shows that Ham is not one whit behind Japheth and Shem in achievement. Dr. R. L. Perry's work, "The Cushite," is a very excellent work along the same line. In this department there is yet much work for the Negro scholar.

In Paul Lawrence Dunbar, the race has struck its highest note in song. A high and worthy tribute has been paid this writer by William Dean Howells. His lyrics have not only a genuine race flavor, but at the same time they appeal to the universal heart. Dunbar's work is of the first class. He has made a real contribution to the literature of the country. His name must now appear in any Manual of American Literature. The success of this writer is a matter of note. His poems and stories are in most of the popular magazines and his books on all news stands. It is clear from this that, whenever a Negro writes anything worth reading, his productions will be in constant demand.

Mention must here be made of the commendable work of Chas. W. Chestnutt, another popular writer of the race. The lamented Dr. A. A. Whitman and Mrs. Frances W. Harper are two poets well-known to the public. Some think that Whitman is a greater poet than Dunbar.

In a short sketch like this, it is impossible to do justice to the literary achievements of the race. A whole volume might be written on the great work done by the Negro press. Here we have many strong writers —men of such mould as Fortune, Stewart, Mitchell and H. T. Johnson. Then, too, there are noted names as magazine writers—Scarborough, Kelly Miller, D. W. Culp and B. T. Washington and H. T. Kealing.

The Negro has been a failure nowhere. In war, there stands Toussaint L' Overture and Maceo; in education, B. T. Washington; in oratory, Frederick Douglas; in art, H. O. Tanner; in letters, Phyllis Wheatley and Paul Lawrence Dunbar. These and others like them are our prophets of the future. Being thus judged by our best men, it doth not yet appear what we shall be. The Greeks are great in a large measure because they wrote of themselves. So the Anglo Saxon, and any race for that matter. The Negro must do the same. His story will not be adequately told till it is done by himself. The Negro poet, novelist and historian have a vast wealth of material before them. Every southern city and plantation are vocal with the past history of our race. From the past and the present, from our achievements and our suffering, the Negro writer, whether poet, novelist or historian, will deliver our message to the world.

SECOND PAPER.

THE NEGRO AS A WRITER.

BY WALTER I. LEWIS.

On the stage, on the platform, in the pulpit and in conversation, the Negro has demonstrated a power in the use of speech that has well won him a merited distinction. This fluency and force of language, so often found in striking disparity to his other attainments, has armed critics and students of his racial peculiarities with the opinion that talking is his peculiar forte.

Such an opinion does not obtain, however, in the face of noble examples of this race who have the art of forcibly and correctly writing great thoughts.

The great cause of the Christian religion has furnished the field for more writers of this race than any other. This is noted not as a fault, but rather to confirm the fact that since the emancipation, the training of the Negro, both at school and in his home, has been largely religious, owing to his inborn susceptibility to religious impressions, and his well known proneness to abide by the teachings of his fathers; it is no marvel that the major portion of his written thoughts should be deeply tinged with religious ideas.

Even in his occasional contributions to current literature, and when he is making an attack or a defense, right often does the religious effusion predominate.

Until about twenty years ago, rare were the instances where Negro writers had produced books and other productions on other than religious subjects. And even at the present the number of secular writers is not large, considering the opportunities for writers of this class and the profits available. There are certain advantages, strange to relate, that the Negro has, that might be called natural. The great realm of thought, through which fiction and mental analysis holds undisputed sway, is not circumscribed by caste and other invidious discriminations as are most other avenues, through which the bravest souls essay to traverse, but are either crushed down or are ejected. Perhaps this is why, in cases that have doubtless come under the observation of all readers of the productions of Negro writers, there is a tendency toward recklessness.

But it will be equitable and fair to take under consideration only

Prof. W. J. Lewis

WALTER I. LEWIS.

Walter I. Lewis was born near Chester, S. C. No record having been kept, it is not possible to determine the date of his birth. Walter is the third of seven children that were born to William Charles and Mollie Lewis who were slaves to a man by the name of W. T. Gilmore.

He successfully passed from the common schools to the preparatory department of Biddle University.

Walter I. Lewis graduated with the second honor of his class of five from Biddle University, in Charlotte, N. C., and at once began his life-work, public school teaching, at Spartanburg, S. C.

After teaching in that city for three years, two of which he succeeded in securing a sufficient donation from the Peabody Fund to have the school term increased from five to nine months, he accepted an appointment under the Freedmen's Board of the Presbyterian Church, to take charge of their parochial school in Columbia, Tenn.

Special inducements were offered him to take a position in the newly organized graded schools of that city, and he resigned the parochial school after serving one year, and accepted work with the graded school. This he found congenial and won special distinction in using the phonetic method of teaching primary pupils, that system being newly introduced there then.

Having a turn for political contests he vigorously entered local political campaigns, generally on the winning side, and won some distinction as a campaign orator.

Mr. Lewis came to Florida in 1890, as corresponding secretary of the Afro-American Chautauqua Association, whose president was the lamented Dr. J. C. Price.

The failure of that enterprise was a withering blow to Mr. Lewis.

After remaining in Florida for nearly a year, at Tallahassee, Mr. Lewis became field correspondent and agent for the Florida Sentinel, then published in Gainesville.

In 1892, Mr. Lewis got a position as city editor on the Labor Union Recorder of Savannah. For a time his activity seemed to be equal to the task of redeeming that paper, but the entailments of indebtedness were too great. It went under.

He was urged to go to Jacksonville to enter the office of the Jacksonville "Advocate"; the inducements being flattering he went. He served the "Advocate" until the "Daily American" was established. He was on the "Daily American" as its city editor, and was on deck when that sheet went down.

In the winter of 1895-96, necessity demanded a better daily news for the colored people of Jacksonville. This was secured at the office of the "Metropolis," one of the most successful afternoon papers that is published in the whole South.

Mr. Lewis was put on as reporter for his race, on the staff of the "Metropolis," and has held this place continuously ever since.

He is a firm believer in the survival of the fittest in all things, and declares this is the key to the solution of the race problem.

those Negro writers, who have won more or less distinction as such, while discussing the Negro as a writer.

From Alexander Dumas to the latest celebrity among Negro writers, the close observer of racial traits is furnished with vivid evidences of methods of thought that are peculiar to this people. In imagery, there is that floridity that goes dazzling to the sublime with a brilliancy that is captivating. If sorrow is depicted, his course through its horrible depths brings a shudder over the most listless reader. If happiness is to be portrayed, the coziest nook in Elysium is laid bare. If anger pleads for expression, no bolt from Vulcan's anvil has ever fallen with so crushing a clang.

The Negro writer is prolific in detail. Situation follows situation in rapid success, demanding close attention to keep clear of the meshes of involvement. The writings of the Negro are full of soul. If, at times, there is a lacking of aptness in conventional adjustments, the hiatus is beautifully abridged with a freshness and wealth of expression that fully atones.

The Negro writer has it largely in his power to demonstrate the higher possibilities and capabilities of his race. As long as there is a Charles W. Chestnut, or a Paul Lawrence Dunbar, a T. Thomas Fortune, and others, whose writings are read by the thousands of literary people of this country and England, so long will there be an irrefutable argument for the intellectual worth of the Negro race.

It is within the power of the Negro writer to practically and profitably demonstrate the oft repeated aphorism, "Genius is not the plant of any particular soil."

It should be a matter of some congratulation to the Negro that the great publishing houses of this country are not, and never will be, located at the great centers of race prejudice. A manuscript of merit can easily find publication. Within recent years it has been noticed that the vein of seriousness that has run through the writings of Negro authors is fading away, and a jollity that is his own is taking its place. Most of the men and women of the race, who have written enough to win public notice, are known to be persons of a cheerful and jovial disposition. For such a person to live in the role of the miserable is at least a misrepresentation.

The Negro's aptness in detecting the facetious, even in things that are serious; his laughing soul that places a bouquet of joy and sunshine where the somber draping of woe would so often be found, is his God-given stock in trade upon which he can do business for generations to come. This secret is being discovered by him. This discovery will yet furnish the great world of letters with men and women of this race, who will place millions under tribute to graciously acknowledge the beneficence.

The way to favor and preferment for the Negro writer is to be made by himself. The epic of his race awaits a writer. The drama of an unwritten history covering about four centuries will welcome the facile pen of some gifted son or daughter. The well nigh inexhaustible field of folk-lore of his own people is ready to be told to the world, whether in the crude dialect of the race, or in Americanized English, it matters little. It will make no difference. The English speaking people of both continents will read it if it is written by a master. It is not at all taken for granted, admitted, or intimated, that the Negro writer of the present century is oblivious to any of these facts. Just as the "coon" melodies have captured the musical realms of this country, and will remain in the saddle for some time yet; just as Negro singers and actors are honorably invading the progressive end of the American stage, so will Negro writers swarm in the great field of writers, bringing with them a supply of freshness of genius, that will rejuvenate and give fresh life to the literature of this country.

This is a domain that mocks at legislative restrictions, caste, exclusionism and what not. Those who will enter and maintain their ground will be few. All of the stars in the heavens are not fast flying meteors. There never was such a thing as an army of sages.

Mindful of the fact that his antecedence is small in the world of letters, the Negro writer is the more ardently inspired when he looks beyond and catches sight of golden fields into which no swathy hand has thrust a sickle.

The world wants more joy; the world cries for more sunshine; the world begs for a laugh. Mankind gloats over the depiction of deeds both noble and ignoble. The world delights in that which is novel. The Negro is a son of caloric. His presence is sunshine. He tells a story leaving nothing out. He is himself a novelty, and it will not be too far in the twentieth century before he will take pity on the world and mankind and write them what they like.

Prof. G. M. McClellan

GEORGE MARION McCLELLAN.

The objection is often raised against schools of higher education for the Negro race that these people need instruction, not in Latin, history, geometry and moral science, but in scientific farming and geometric bed making. The leaven of truth in this assertion makes a plump denial hard to return; while its leaven of error is a reminder of the old antislavery assumption that till the end of time the Negro must be a hewer of wood and drawer of water, with no mental life to speak of. This error is best confuted by proof of the race's actually wide range of intellectual demands, imaginative sympathies, moral questionings; and for this reason, if for no other, one thanks Mr. George Marion McClellan for venturing on the publication of his verses. This gentleman is a graduate of Fisk University, as he tells us in the interesting and modest preface to his volume. Thus he belongs to the first generation since the War. His parents, he indicates, were slaves, and his early home was upon the "Highland Rim" of Tennessee, amid the poverty of a freedman father's little farm. These things well weighed, the refined love of nature, the purity of sentiment, the large philosophy, the delicacy of expression which his poems display, are sufficiently marvelous. One must, perhaps, deny him the title of "poet" in these days when verse writers are many. His ear for rhythm is fatally defective, while, so far as one may judge from the few dates appended to the poems, the later productions seem not to be the best. Nevertheless, his little volume stimulates to large reviews and fair anticipations. It is a far cry from "Swing low, sweet chariot"—an articulate stirring of poetic fancy, but hardly more than that—to Mr. McClellan's "September Night in Mississippi":

"Begirt with cotton fields, Anguilla sits,
Half birdlike, dreaming on her summer nest
Amid her spreading figs and roses still
In bloom with all their spring and summer hues.
Pomegranates hang with dapple cheeks full ripe,
And over all the town a dreamy haze
Drops down. The great plantations stretching far
Away are plains of cotton, downy white.
Oh, glorious is this night of joyous sounds,
Too full for sleep Aromas wild and sweet
From muscadine, late-booming jessamine
And roses all the heavy air suffuse.
Faint bellows from the alligators come
From swamps afar where sluggish lagoons give
To them a peaceful home. The katydids
Make ceaseless cries. Ten thousand insects' wings
Stir in the moonlight haze, and joyous shouts
Of Negro song and mirth awake hard by
The cabin dance. Oh, glorious is the night!
The summer sweetness fills my heart with songs.
I cannot sing; with loves I cannot speak."

If many thoughts and feelings such as these lie folded in Southern cabins, let us not deny, for their unfolding, the genial influences of literature and history and the sciences. The race that possesses such powers, even though undeveloped in the great majority of its members, needs Fisk and Atlanta educated pastors and teachers.

THIRD PAPER.

THE NEGRO AS A WRITER.

BY G. M. McCLELLAN.

"The pen is mightier than the sword." It would have seemed idle to have said this at the mouth of the mountain pass at Thermopylæ with Leonidas and his immortal Spartan heroes all lying dead amid the wreck made by the mighty host of Xerxes. A century afterward, at Cannæ, one sixth of the whole population of Rome lay dead on the battlefield by the sword thrust. Where was the might of the pen to compare with this? The might of the sword at Thermopylæ, together with the concluding events at Salamis, turned back the Persian hordes and thereby saved the Greek civilization for Europe. Again, after the blood of Cannæ, at Zama, Hannibal was utterly broken and Carthage, with her attending civilization, was doomed to everlasting death, while Rome, her mighty adversary, with her eagles and short sword, carried her dominion and her splendid civilization from England to India. One more great movement in the world illustrating the power of the sword is too tempting to pass by in this connection. From the deserts of Arabia a fanatical dreamer came forth claiming a new revelation from God and as a chosen prophet to give the world a new religion. His pretentions at first caused his expulsion from Mecca, together with a small and insignificant band of followers. Yet because of these it was not long until there came from out the desert the sound of the marching of a mighty host, heralding the approach of the Arab, the despising and despised. Before these barbarous hordes the principalities of the East were doomed to crumble and yield up their accumulated treasures of the ages, and so triumphant were these invaders from the desert they decided to appropriate for themselves the whole world, and from this they were not *dissuaded* until Charles Martel sent them back from Tours and out of Europe, together with their hateful civilization. So it would seem from these and all other mighty movements of races and tribes, men and nations, the sword has ever been the arbiter. Yet over all the mighty sweep of events and the *stupendous* results of the sword-thrust throughout the ages, comes this insinuating claim, "The pen is mightier than the sword." And when we consider the whole of accumulated philosophy, the onward march of science and human thought, and the consequent development of the human race, the comparative might of the sword becomes insignificant before the less demonstrative power of the conquering pen. And here comes the question, which in some phase or other comes up in all great questions of America, "What part has the Negro in the might of the pen?" Nobody doubts that the great movements of the world at present, let their primary manifestations be military or political, scientific or industrial, have any other great lever than knowledge and sentiment brought into notice and activity by writers.

The chief agencies for the dissemination of thought and discoveries are the newspapers, magazines, literary journals and books of fiction. The newspapers have the most immediate and controlling influence over the action of men in the business and political world. To undertake to estimate with anything like exactness the part the Negro has in molding sentiment through the press and giving the consequent direction to the action of men would be a task impossible in the very nature of the case.

It shall be, then, the purpose of this article to discuss in a general way the Negro as a writer in all lines in which he has essayed to express thought. It would be easy to dispose of the question in two ways. One would be to separate all that he has done as far as that would be possible, and put it over against the production of the white race and thus so minimize it by comparison that its power would likely to be *underrated*. Another way would be to magnify all that has been done as especially praiseworthy, because the production comes from the Negro, thus overrating its significance, forgetting that whatever power any writing can have can only be in proportion to its real merit in the thought-world, regardless of all source from which it came. Overrating the Negro as a writer is more likely to be done in passing on his attempts in *literary* art than in any other field. But in literary lines the number who can command attention and be worthy of notice is very small. One does not have to go far to see that the most effective work, so far as creating sentiment is concerned, and thereby *wielding* power in the great moving forces of this age, the Negro as a writer is best evinced by the Negro press. We have many newspapers, and after thirty years we have not been able to produce one single great newspaper, nor for many good reasons one single great editor who is a power in the land. Indeed, the most of the many papers of ours that come from the press have but little in them that can attract the intelligent minds of the race. There is, however, among us too great a tendency to ridicule the Negro press unreservedly, and though much of the ridicule many be deserved it remains true that the accumulative power of the Negro press is hardly appreciated as it deserves to be. They who write for us and fight our battles are essentially our only spokesmen, and as ignored as our articles and editorials would seem to be by the white press, it is true nevertheless that the white newspapers take close notice of what the Negro writers have to say. They may not ordinarily deign to appear to take notice, but let any publication be made in our most humble sheets that seems to them to be dangerous or too presumptuous to let pass, and it will be seen then that the white press takes notice and the power of the colored press will become apparent. I have said that we have not yet produced one single great paper, nor one great editor, as white papers and editors are great, and to this I think there can be justly no exceptions taken, for we are lacking in nearly all the accessories to make such greatness possible, but we do have a few papers and editors of marked power. The two most exceptional papers of power that have come under my notice are the New York Age, edited by Mr. T. Thomas Fortune, and the Richmond Planet, edited by Mr. Mitchell. These two papers and their editors have been, and are yet, valiant warriors for the race and of incalculable benefit to the race. As a terse, caustic and biting editorial writer Mr. Fortune is hardly surpassed by any one, and his paper for years has been uncompromising in fighting all adverse issues in the race question. Almost the same thing can be said of the Richmond Planet, and more than any other, perhaps, has this paper been valiant in waging war against lynching. These two papers, together with a host of others, have set forth the power of the pen and have accomplished far more to offset the adverse sentiment created by the white press than can ever be fully determined. There is another class of Negro writers than those I have mentioned that gets an occasional hearing in the white papers of the South and is of great value to the race. Any one familiar with the strictures of the South, knows that the Negroes themselves have essentially no chance to discuss through the white newspapers the great questions which are ever to the front concerning them, and their position in the South, and also but very little more in the newspapers of the North, unless in the South the Negroes write some articles to say amen, and highly sanction the white man's dictums and positions on the Negro questions that happen to be up. But there are a few who are able to write on some questions in our defense without compromise, and yet so skillfully as not to offend. In speaking of the attitude of the white press, and its representations, it is not assumed that there is no disposition of fairness on the part of the writers of the white press. Many of the great editors mean to be fair from their standpoint. The Southern white people are prejudiced and supersensitive on some points beyond all reason, and in all questions between the Negro and the white man, as man to man, the assumptions, without an exception, are arrogant beyond all naming, so that it comes about at any point of issue, where men differing, usually would permit the opponent his views as fitting from his side of the question, what the Negro has to say, if he is emphatic and decided, is called impudence. The writer must be skillful, then, to write uncompromisingly and yet not be of the "impudent." There are a few men among us who are able to write for the Southern white papers with reserve, yet without compromise, greatly to our advantage. Among those few, prominent are Prof. G. W. Henderson, of Straight University, New Orleans, and President W. H. Councill, of the College, Normal and Industrial School at Normal, Alabama. Prof. Henderson is a graduate of Middlebury College, Vermont, and Yale Theological Seminary, having taken the fellowship from that institution and studied in Germany two years. His writings show his scholarship and refinement. He has been persistent and valiant in all race matters, especially in educational lines in Louisiana, and his articles, though uncompromising, have from time to time found a hearing and forced respect from the great dailies of New Orleans. President Councill is the most widely accepted in the Southern white press of all Negroes. On some points of disagreement between the Negroes and the white people he concedes more to some of the white man's claims than any other Negro who writes. Secondly, he is truly a great man, and has gained his right to a hearing in intelligent sources. As a writer, pure and simple, he is forcible; and while the whole of his attitude many not be accepted generally by his own race, there is no doubt about his uncompromising attitude and loyalty to his own race first and last, and any one who has followed his articles in newspapers and leading magazines have surely seen that the apparently sometimes too generous bouquet throwing to the white brother is fully offset by the terrible blows given that same white brother for his sins against the Negro race. This is especially seen in his symposium article in the April number of the Arena, 1899. It would be impossible in the limitation of this article to mention the many Negro writers who are acceptable in leading magazines, and to a greater extent in the great weekly journals of this country. Only one or two can be mentioned: Rev. H. H. Proctor, pastor of the First Congregational Church at Atlanta, Ga., is a graduate of Fisk University and Yale Theological Seminary, and he is a young man of exceptional ability as a writer on timely questions, but as an article writer is often seen in the Outlook, the New York Independent, and such papers. Above them all is Bishop Tanner, of Philadelphia. For diction, fine style, conciseness and logical conclusions, one must go far to find his superior. In the way of history, text books on various subjects, and scientific presentation, not much has yet been done among us. Mr. Geo. W. Williams, the Negro historian, has done more in that field than any other. Dr. D. W. Culp has written a treatise on consumption and other medical subjects that have attracted attention and favorable criticism.

It now remains to speak of the writers in literary art. In this field there are many who have certainly made praiseworthy attempts, and of the ladies who cannot be classed with those who have truly made a place among successful literary artists, but whose writing has attracted attention and in character is literary, most complimentary things can be said of Mrs. Frances E. W. Harper, of Philadelphia; of Mrs. Fanny Barrier Williams, of Chicago; of Miss Edna Matthews, of New York, and of Mrs. Cooper, Washington, D. C. Mrs. Cooper's book, "A Voice from the South," is a work in purpose and execution of decided merit. In real literary art, perhaps there are only two in the whole race who have reached a place of genuine high rank among the critics, namely, Dunbar and Chestnut. There are four poets, however, who have attracted much attention and favorable criticism, and of these I will speak in turn. It is in order to speak of Mr. A. A. Whitman first, because he appeared first of all and in one particular of excellency he is first of all four. His "Rape of Florida" is truly poetry and as a *sustained effort,* as an attempt *in great lines,* it surpasses in true merit anything yet done by a Negro, and this assertion without one qualifying word. He failed as a poet? Certainly. Mr. Whitman made attempts in lines in which Shelley, Keats and Spenser triumphed, and with such mediocrity only possible to him in such a highway, what else could follow beyond a passing notice, though his "Rape of Florida" is a production of much more than passing merit. Aside from the mediocrity of the work attempted in Spenserian lines the man himself in his lack of learning, in his expressible egotism, was derogatory to his ultimate success, and his styling himself as the William Cullen Bryant of the Negro race was sickening in the extreme. Mr. Whitman died recently, but not before he had done all in literary excellence that could be hoped from him. It remains true, however, that he was worthy of a much better place than is accorded him as a Negro poet, and it is to be regretted that his work is so little known among us.

Ten years after Mr. Whitman, Paul Dunbar came forth as a new singer, and got the first real recognition as a poet. As a poet, pure and simple, as a refined verse maker in all directions, Mr. Dunbar surpasses Mr. Whitman by far in the truest significance in the term poet, and he is justly assigned the first place among Negro poets. For many reasons Mr. Dunbar is famous, and to enter into any extended discussion of his work in this connection is needless. Mr. Dunbar is the first Negro to attempt poetic art in Negro dialect. To speak the truth, however, it must be said that there is no such thing as a Negro dialect, but in the bad English called Negro dialect Mr. Dunbar has in verse chosen to interpret the Negro in his general character, in his philosophy of life, in his rich humor and good nature, and the world knows how well he has succeeded. Robert Burns has shown how the immortal life of all beautiful things can be handed down for all time in dialect, but it can scarcely be believed by any one that great poetry can ever be clothed in the garb known as Negro dialect. But for some pathos and to put the Negro forward at his best in his humorous and good natured characteristics the so-called dialect is the best vehicle, and in these lines, and these lines only, is Mr. Dunbar by far greater than all others. Out of those lines he is still the first poet, Whitman not excepted, but he is first with nothing like the difference in real merit and the fame he has above all others. But in passing from him, here is Dunbar at his best, dialectic and otherwise:

> " When de co'n pone's hot—
>   Dey is a time in life when nature
>   Seems to slip a cog an' go,
>   Jes' a-rattling down creation,
>   Lak an ocean's overflow;
>   When de worl' jes' stahts a-spinnin'
>   Lak a pickaninny's top,

An' you feel jes' lak a racah,
  Dat is trainin' fu' to trot—
When yo' mammy says de blessin'
  An' de co'n pone's hot.

" When you set down at de table,
  Kin' o' weary lak an' sad,
An' you's jes' a little tiwhed
  An' purhaps a little mad;
How yo' gloom tu'ns into gladness,
  How yo' joy drives out de doubt,
When de oven do' is opened,
  An' de smell comes po'in out;
Why, de 'lectric light o' Heaven
  Seems to settle on de spot,
When yo' mammy says de blessin'
  An' de co'n pone's hot.

" When de cabbage pot is steamin'
  An' de bacon good an' fat,
When de chittlins is a-spuller'n'
  So's to show you whah dey's at;
Tek away yo' sody biscut,
  Tek away yo' cake an' pie,
Fu' de glory time is comin',
  An' it's 'proachin' mighty nigh,
An' yo' want to jump an' hollah,
  Dough you know you'd bettah not
When yo' mammy says de blessin',
  An' de co'n pone's hot.

" I have hyeahd o' lots o' sermons,
  An' I've hyeahd o' lots o' prayers,
An' I've listened to some singin'
  Dat has tuck me up de stairs
Of de Glory-lan' an' set me
  Jes' below de mahstah's th'one,
An' lef' my hea't a-singin'
  In a happy aftah tone;
But dem wu'ds so sweetly murmured
  Seemed to tech de softes' spot,
When my mammy says de blessin',
  An' de co'n pone's hot."

This is not so great a poem as the "Cotter's Saturday Night" by
Burns, because the spiritual element and the whole scope of the tenderest

concerns of the family and of life in that poem are left out of this. But in Dunbar's poem, where only the festival is pictured, the scene is so intensified that one feels the warmth and sees the glow of the evening fire and inhales the appetizing odors of the coming homely cheer, and can see back of these the tender care and ineffable love of the "Mammy," who puts the crowning touch upon her love with the blessing. As far as it goes, "When the co'n pone's hot" is great precisely in the same lines that the "Cotter's Saturday Night" is great.

Mr. Dunbar has also written a number of novels and short stories. It has not been my good fortune to see "The Stories from Dixie;" but the novels I have bought and read. If there were no Charles Chestnut, Mr. Dunbar's novels would have to be discussed in this connection, and he would have to be put down as the very first Negro novel writer, mainly, however, because there would be no other; but with Mr. Chestnut in the field, no true admirer of Mr. Dunbar will ever discuss the prolific diffusions of his, bearing the name novels, in any connection with Dunbar, the poet. There is only enough space left in this article for the poets, to barely mention the names of Mr. Daniel Webster Davis, of Manchester, Virginia, and Mr. James D. Corrothers of Red Bank, New Jersey, and to give a selection from each and let their poems speak for them as writers. Both of them have received notice in the best magazines and favorable criticism elsewhere. Both owe their distinction mainly to their work in dialectic verse which, I fear, is too much like the "ragtime" music, considered quite the proper dressing for Negro distinction in the poetic art.

Here is to "De Biggis' Piece ub Pie," by Mr. Davis:

"When I was a little boy
    I set me down to cry,
Bekase my little brudder
    Had de biggis' piece ub pie.
But when I had become a man
    I made my min' to try
An' hustle roun' to git myself
    De biggis' piece ub pie.

"An' like in bygone chil'ish days,
    De worl' is hustlin' roun'
To git darselbes de biggis' slice
    Ub honor an' renown;
An' ef I fails to do my bes',
    But stan' aroun' an' cry,

Dis ol' worl' will git away
Wid bof de plate an' pie.

"An' eben should I git a slice
I mus' not cease to try,
But keep a-movin' fas' es life
To hol' my piece ub pie.
Dis ruff ol' worl' has little use
Fur dem dat chance to fall,
An' while youze gittin' up ag'in
'Twill take de plate an' all."

The one more selection from Mr. Davis will show him as a poet outside of dialect:

A ROSE.

"The rose of the garden is given to me,
And, to double its value, 'twas given by thee;
Its lovely bright tints to my eyesight is borne,
Like the kiss of a fairy or blush of morn.

"Too soon must this scent-laden flower decay,
Its bright leaves will wither, its bloom die away;
But in memory 'twill linger; the joy that it bore
Will live with me still, tho' the flower's no more."

Mr. James D. Corrothers writes:

"A THANKSGIVIN' TURKEY.

"Cindy, reach dah 'hine yo' back
'N han' me dat ah Almanac;
W'y, land! t'morrer's Thanksgivin'!
Got to git out an' make hay—
Don't keer whut de preachah say—
We mus' eat Thanksgivin' day,
Uz sho' uz you's a-libbin.

"You know whah Mahs Hudson libs?
Dey's a turkey dah dat gibs
Me a heap o' trouble.
Some day Hudson g'ine to miss
Dat owdashus fowl o' his;
I's g'ine ober dah an' twis'
'At gobbler's nake plumb double.

"Goin' pas' dah t' othah day,
Turkey strutted up an' say,
    'A-gobble, gobble, gobble,'
Much uz ef he mout remahk,
'Don' you wish 'at it wuz dahk?
Ain't I temptin'?' S' I, 'you hah'k,
    Er else dey'll be a squabble.

" 'Take an' wring yo' nake righ' quick,
Light on yo' lak a thousan' brick,
    'N you won't know whut befell you.'
'N I went on. Yet evah day
When I goes by that a-way,
'At fowl has too much to say;
    'N I'm tiahd uv it, I tell you.

"G'ine to go dis bressed night
An' put out dat turkey's light,
    'N I'll nail him lak a cobblah.
Take keer, 'Cindy, lemme pass,
Ain't a-g'ine to take no sass
    Off no man's turkey gobblah."

And now for the last and the greatest Roman of them all in literary art—Mr. Charles W. Chestnut, of Cleveland, Ohio. I have never seen him, and at present the only personal acquaintance I have with him, is a brief letter of a dozen or more lines; but Mr. Chestnut, revealed by his novels, I know well. The chief distinction one finds in reading Mr. Chestnut from all other Negro story-writers, so far as there are such, is that he is truly an artist and that his art is fine art. Secondly, and this is of the greatest concern to Negroes in any thought of the Negro as a writer, he is the best delineator of Negro life and character, thought and feeling, of any who has attracted notice by writing. It is not possible to give in this connection any quotations from Mr. Chestnut's work that may speak for him, but it is fitting in this article to speak of the character of some of Mr. Chestnut's stories, and, as far as possible, suggest the ground and purpose of his fiction. Perhaps, to mention the stories, "The Wife of His Youth," "The Wheel of Progress," and "The House Behind the Cedars," would serve best for this occasion. There are some situations of the Negroes too full of ineffable pity for utterance. Who has not sat at some time in a Negro church and heard read the pitiful inquiry for a mother, or a child, or a father, husband or wife, all lost in the sales and separations of slavery times—loved ones as completely swallowed up in the past (yet in this life they still live) as if the grave had received them. At such a reading, though it was given with unconcern, one heard the faithful cry of faithful love coming out of the dark on its sorrowful mission.

And in this realm Mr. Chestnut tells us of a mulatto boy who marries a woman of Negro type, and who was old enough for the boy's mother, but had, at that time, youth enough left to make the disparity of age at the time of little objection, especially in the times and situation where there was little objection to marriages of any sort. But the youth escapes from slavery and in the far North receives education, development and culture, and in time earns a competence that makes life desirable and opens up vistas to new happiness, for the old life is now only a memory of what the new man once was, and the new man is on the borderland of new love and marriage befitting all his advancements, while the mulatto slave boy, the slave girl, the black slave-wife and the slave connections are left forever behind. But in all these twenty-five years the black slave wife is still living, still ignorant and yielding all the while to age until she is an old woman. But there was one thing that did not yield to age and time, and that was her love for her boy husband, and, what was more, her sublime and unwavering faith in the constancy of her "Yaller Sam," after whom she sends inquiry after inquiry, and year after year tramps from place to place in her search, with faith and love divine ever leading her on, until one day in a Northern city, to which place she had finally traced him, she stopped at his very door to humbly inquire of the strange gentleman she saw for her "Yaller Sam," never dreaming that it was he to whom she spoke, though he knew her and had to face the bitter tragedy of it all. But Mr. Chestnut's art enables him to take care of so sorrowful a case satisfactorily.

"The Wheel of Progress" touches another phase of pathetic situations arising out of the mixture of people and sentiments in the South. The story tells of an ostracized Northern white teacher who, from young womanhood, labors away her life for the Negroes, until her age and health reach that degree of disadvantage that her position as teacher, once her medium of charity, becomes her only means for a living. In the meantime the Negroes whom she and others helped to uplift and develop, and to whom, because of race distinction, most all avenues outside of menial labor are closed, except preaching and teaching, had become her competitors. In the conflict that arose over the reappointment of the white missionary teacher and a young Negro to the place the pitiful situation is again taken care of by Mr. Chestnut's fine art. "The House Behind the Cedars," until his latest, "The Marrow of Tradition," was his most ambitious attempt. In this book the story of an Octoroon family is put forth in all the pathos and tragedy that is the lot of so many Negroes who belong wholly to neither race.

Mr. Chestnut's latest book, "The Marrow of Tradition," is a strong and vigorous presentation of the colored man's case against the South in the form of a dramatic novel. This book especially deserves a wide reading among the Negroes, who have none too many friends to plead their cause. Mr. Chestnut, as one truly high-rank novelist among us, ought to have such a hearing among the eight millions that would give him all the advantages of a successful novelist from a financial standpoint as a return for his labor, which is by no means for himself alone.

In closing, it is but fair to say, while the artists of high rank among us are few in number, in an article discussing the Negro as a writer, in mentioning names at all, it must necessarily follow that there are very many names not here mentioned that would deserve to be if in such an article as this there were any intention or necessity to mention the whole list of Negro writers who write well and with power in every department of letters.

M. W. Gilbert, D. D.

REV. M. W. GILBERT, D. D.

The subject of this sketch was born July 25, 1862, at Mechanicsville, Sumter County, South Carolina. His parents were slaves and his father, a Baptist minister, is still alive. Mr. Gilbert began his early school life during the reconstruction period, at Mechanicsville, and continued it at Mannville, in an adjoining township, until 1879, when he entered Benedict College (then Benedict Institute) at Columbia, South Carolina. He remained in Benedict till the spring of 1883, when he graduated from a classical course specially designed to fit him for a Northern college. In the fall of 1883, after a searching examination, he entered the freshman class of Colgate University and remained in that institution four years, until his graduation in 1887 with the degree of A. B. During his college course Mr. Gilbert particularly distinguished himself in the languages and oratory. During his sophomore year he won in an oratorical contest the First Kingsford Prize. Although the only colored man in his class, yet he was so highly esteemed by his classmates that he enjoyed the unique distinction of being elected every three months for four years as Class Secretary and Treasurer. In addition to this he was elected Class Historian in his senior year. His alma mater conferred on him the degree of A. M. in 1890. Immediately after his graduation Mr. Gilbert was called to the pastorate of the First Colored Baptist Church at Nashville, Tenn. He remained in this position three years and a half and then he accepted the call of the Bethel Baptist Church of Jacksonville, Fla. He was not permitted by his denomination to remain long in this pastorate; for after one year in it, on the nomination of the American Baptist Home Mission Society of New York, he was elected to lead in the educational work among the colored Baptists of Florida. He presided one year over the Florida Institute at Live Oak, and he led in 1892 in the founding of the Florida Baptist Academy (now college) at Jacksonville, Fla. The cares and anxiety involved in this work threatened his health and in 1894 he resigned this position to accept the pastorate of a young church organization in Savannah, Ga., having in the meantime declined an election to the presidency of State University at Louisville, Ky. In 1894 he was elected Vice-President and Professor of History, Political Science, and Modern Languages, in the Colored State College at Orangeburg, S. C. He served in this capacity two years and after re-election for a third year he resigned to re-enter upon his life-work in the gospel ministry. He served a few months after this in the office of General Missionary and Corresponding Secretary of the Baptist State Convention of South Carolina, but this work militating against his health he gave up to enter upon the pastorate of the Central Baptist Church at Charleston, S. C., where he now is. Mr. Gilbert received three years ago the degree of D. D. from Guadalupe College of Seguin, Tex. In 1883 Dr. Gilbert was married in Columbia, S. C., to Miss Agnes Boozer. Seven children have been born to them, five of whom are still living. Dr. Gilbert is much in demand as a public speaker on great occasions and his services are frequently sought by some of the best churches of his denomination.

TOPIC XVII.

DID THE AMERICAN NEGRO PROVE, IN THE NINETEENTH CENTURY, THAT HE IS INTELLECTUALLY EQUAL TO THE WHITE MAN?

BY M. W. GILBERT, D. D.

The necessity for asserting and maintaining the affirmative of the above question is due to the deep-seated prejudice against the Negro, which prejudice is the unfortunate fruit of the Negro's past enslavement. It is not surprising that those who for centuries held the Negro as a chattel should regard him as a being essentially inferior to themselves, and time is required, in the changed condition of affairs, to completely eradicate this idea. Even now, despite the remarkable development of the Negro since his emancipation, occasionally some Rip Van Winkle, awaking from a long sleep, essays to deny the complete humanity of the Negro race. A true believer in the Scriptures must be equally a believer in the fatherhood of God and the brotherhood of all men. For the divine record declares that God "hath made of one blood all nations of men for to dwell on all the face of the earth." Language, physiology and psychology confirm the truthfulness of Scripture on this issue. The mission of Christianity to preach the gospel over the inhabited world is based upon this great idea. Science and Holy Writ assert the intellectual equality of all men of whatever race or color, so far as real capacity and possibilities are concerned.

The position and relative importance of a race or nation in the world's history are determined more by its antecedents and environments than by the original endowments of each individual that constitutes it. Two different races, having the same antecedents and subject to the same environments, will produce the same results. In answering the question as to whether the Negro has demonstrated his intellectual equality with the white man during the century just closed, our inquiry must necessarily be confined to the closing third of that century; for prior to the emancipation of the race the colored people were generally in an enslaved condition. Opportunities for education, citizenship, and the development of manhood, were few, and at best could apply to but few of the race. Although our inquiry is limited to only one-third of the century just closed, nevertheless we can safely assert that in that short period the Negro has demonstrated by actual results his intellectual equality with the white man.

1. The Negro has demonstrated in thirty-five years a capacity for education equal to that of the white man. This remark does not apply alone to his primary education, but also to the highest. He has entered already every intellectual field that is open to him, and he is achieving success in every one that he has entered. Within a third of a century one hundred and fifty-six institutions for the higher education of the Negroes have been founded, and from these and Northern colleges there have been more than seventeen thousand graduates. These colleges are located chiefly in the South, and their courses of studies are as high as their neighboring white colleges; in some instances they are higher. Some of these graduates have evinced great ability and brilliancy in mastering the most difficult studies included in the curriculum. The existence of Negro colleges and the successful graduation of Negroes therefrom is a strong argument for his intellectual equality. Nor has the Negro simply demonstrated his ability to master the literary courses of the college, but also his capacity to acquire the knowledge and training to fit him for life in the various professions. Within a third of a century the race has produced thirty thousand teachers, five hundred physicians, two hundred and fifty lawyers, and a large number of others who have entered the ministry, politics, and editorial life. If there is doubt on the demonstration of the Negro's ability to acquire education in his own colleges, we need only to mention the fact that his ambition has led him to some of the leading Northern universities where he studied at the side of white men, and even there he has demonstrated his essential intellectual equality with the white man by winning, in several well-known instances, some of their highest honors for scholarship, proficiency and oratory.

2. The Negro has demonstrated his capacity for imparting an education to others after he has himself received it. He is an essential and established factor in the public school system of the South. It is he that is intrusted with the primary education of his people, and it is due largely to him that his people in thirty-five years have reduced their illiteracy 45 per cent. During those thirty-five years he has become professor of law, medicine, theology, mathematics, the sciences, and languages. In the colleges devoted to the education of the colored men,

there are colored professors who have become eminent in their departments and who would fill with credit similar chairs in white institutions
of learning. All of the colored state colleges of the South are under the
management of Negroes as presidents and professors.

3. The Negro has also demonstrated his productivity in the field of
authorship. In this particular he has shown a white man's capacity. In
calling attention to the Negro's achievement in this particular, it may be
well to note the fact that the Negro's white neighbor, although he lives
in a clime similar to that which produced in Greece, philosophers like
Plato and Aristotle and poets like Homer, Euripides, and Sophocles, and
in Italy poets like Virgil and Horace, has not produced a philosopher
or a first-class poet, with all the leisure he enjoyed while the Negro has
been engaged in enforced labor for him. In the highest field of thought
as in philosophy and the works of imagination the South presents a
barren field. In the sphere of authorship usually entered by white men
the Negro has already worked his way. He has already produced meritorious books on mathematics, sociology, theology, history, poetry, travels,
sermons, languages, and biographies. There have been three hundred
books written by Negroes.

4. Nor has the Negro's mind followed slavishly in the beaten path
of imitation. He has demonstrated that he possesses also a high order
of intellect by his inventive genius. The "lubricator" now being used
on nearly all the railroad engines in the United States was invented by
a colored man, Mr. E. McCoy, of Detroit, Michigan. Eugene Burkins, a
Negro, was inventor of the Burkins' Automatic Machine Gun, concerning which Admiral Dewey said it was "by far the best machine gun ever
made." Many other useful inventions in the country are credited by the
Patent Office to the Negro.

5. The Negro has also demonstrated in thirty-five years his capacity
for organizing, controlling, and directing great and diversified interests.
Capacity to organize, maintain, and direct presupposes a high order of
mind. Executive ability requires accompanying intellectual ability and
not mere brilliancy. Unaided and alone the Negro has set on foot great
ecclesiastical organizations which he is maintaining and developing with
much credit to himself. In all these organizations, leadership to the few
has been cheerfully conceded by the masses. As a church builder, with
little means at his command, the Negro stands without a peer. Within
the last thirty-five years of the nineteenth century the Negro has founded

high schools, academies and colleges, and he is successfully supporting and managing them. If it is fair to estimate the ability and worth of men by real achievements, then it must be conceded that the foremost man for real ability throughout the entire South is a Negro, and we refer to the eminent founder and developer of the Tuskegee Institute in Alabama. It is unquestionable in our mind that the greatest enterprise conceived and executed by any one mind, in the entire South, during the past forty years, was that conceived in the brains of a single Negro, the child of a slave mother, that resulted in the world-renowned Tuskegee Institute. The results at Tuskegee will demonstrate that the highest order of mind in the South, as well as the most famous, is in the keeping of the Negro. The leading Presbyterian institution of learning in the South for the education of colored men is now managed successfully by Negro scholars. We refer here to Biddle University.

6. In business and politics the Negro, despite the odds arrayed against him, is succeeding reasonably well. He is constantly undertaking new business enterprises, and wherever the government or state has intrusted him with official position the intelligent Negro has discharged his public functions with credit to the government and glory for himself. Whenever failure is recorded against the Negro it is not due to his lacking the mental endowments equal to that of the white man, but because he was denied the white man's favorable past, and because a white man's opportunity is denied him. Equality of opportunities and equality before the laws should be cheerfully granted him. Criticism against him is savage and un-Christian, if these doors are closed against him.

J. W. Cromwell

JOHN WESLEY CROMWELL.

John Wesley Cromwell, the twelfth child and seventh son of Willis H. and Elizabeth Carney Cromwell, was born at Portsmouth, Va., September 5, 1846. In 1851 the family moved to Philadelphia, where he entered the public schools and subsequently the Institute for Colored Youth, graduating in 1864.

He taught at Columbia, Pa., after which he established a private school in his native town. Under the auspices of Northern charitable associations he taught at Spanish Neck and Little Gunpowder in Maryland, Providence Church, Scott Farm, Charlotte County and Wytheville, Va. On the inauguration of the public school system he became principal of the Dill's Bakery School in Richmond, Va., and in the following summer taught near the scene of the Nat Turner Insurrection in Southampton County in the same State.

Mr. Cromwell took an active part in the reconstruction of Virginia, was delegate to the first State Republican Convention, did jury service in the United States Court for the term at which the case of Jefferson Davis was calendared, and was a clerk in the reconstruction Constitutional Convention. A shot, fired with deadly intent, grazed his clothing while at Spanish Neck, where the church in which the school was taught was burned to the ground, and he was twice forced to face the muzzles of revolvers in Virginia, because of his work as an educator.

In 1871 he entered the law department of Howard University, graduating therefrom in 1874. In 1872, after a competitive examination, having distanced two hundred and forty applicants, he received a $1,200 appointment in the Treasury Department, in which he was twice promoted, by the same method, within twenty months. In 1885, in the early days of the Cleveland administration, he was removed as an offensive partisan, having established and conducted since 1876 "The People's Advocate," a weekly journal of more than local influence. He then began the practice of law in connection with his journalistic work. In 1889 he was tendered and he accepted a principalship of one of the grammar schools of Washington, D. C., the position he still holds.

In 1875 he was chosen at Richmond the president of the Virginia Educational and Historical Association and was four times re-elected. He has served two terms as the president of the "Bethel Literary," with which he has been officially connected for twenty years. He was one of the original members of the American Negro Academy founded by Rev. Alexander Crummell, and is its corresponding secretary.

In 1873 he was married to Miss Lucy A. McGuinn, of Richmond, Va. Six children survive of that marriage, the eldest being Miss Otelia Cromwell, the first Colored graduate (1900) of Smith College, Mass. In 1892 he married Miss Annie E. Conn, of Mechanicsburg, Pa.

In 1887 he became a member of the Metropolitan A. M. E. Church under the pastorate of Rev., now Chaplain, T. G. Steward.

Among his addresses and papers are "The Negro in Business," "The Colored Church in America," "Nat Turner, a Historical Sketch," "Benjamin Banneker," "The Negro as a Journalist," and other historical and statistical studies. The first named, published for a syndicate of metropolitan newspapers in 1886, found its way in one form or other in nearly all the representative papers of the land.

TOPIC XVIII.

WHAT PROGRESS DID THE AMERICAN WHITE MAN MAKE, IN THE NINE-TEENTH CENTURY, ALONG THE LINE OF CONCEDING TO THE NEGRO HIS RELIGIOUS, POLITICAL, AND CIVIL RIGHTS?

BY JOHN W. CROMWELL.

The status of the Negro at the close of the eighteenth and the opening of the nineteenth centuries was substantially the same, North and South. These well-defined geographical sections on both sides of Mason and Dixon's line were not as extensive then as now. Ohio, Kentucky and Tennessee were the only states west of the Alleghanies; Florida was a foreign possession, Alabama and the region beyond were to be numbered with the United States at a subsequent period.

The colored population in 1800 was 1,001,436, free and slave, or 18.88 per cent of the entire population; 893,041 were slaves, of whom there were in round numbers 30,000 in the states of New Hampshire, Rhode Island, Connecticut, Pennsylvania, New York and Delaware; 20,000 were in New York alone. In 1900 the total population is 76,303,387, with 8,840,789 persons of Negro descent, or 11.5 of the aggregate population.

The year 1800 marks the beginning of an epoch of increasing hard-ship for the Negro, both in church and state. It was also characterized by fierce aggressiveness by the slave power, stimulated by the invention of the cotton gin by Eli Whitney and the impetus which it gave to the growth and importation of cotton. The acquisition of the Louisiana Purchase from France added to the possible domain of slave territory and affected the current of political action for more than half a century.

During this period the Negro was a most important figure, both in church and state, the occasion if not the cause of perplexing problems. In the field of religion and politics, especially, has his status attracted world-wide attention.

At a very early day the Methodist and Baptist churches had the largest number of colored followers in both town and city; but these as yet were not assembled in distinctive organizations. The right of the Negro, not only to govern but to direct his religious instruction, was bitterly contested, sometimes by force, at other times by law. The high-handed manner in which the ordinary rights of worship were denied the Negro led to the withdrawal of the majority of colored Methodists in Pennsylvania, New York, Maryland and South Carolina, and ultimately to the formation of the two denominations, the African Methodist Episcopal and the African Methodist Episcopal Zion Churches, that became independent before the end of the first quarter of the last century.

As to the recognition of the right of colored Baptists to church fellowship, the white Baptists were more liberal, for we find an association of white churches recognizing the existence of a colored Baptist church at Williamsburg, in 1790.

The first colored Episcopal society was received into membership on the express condition that no delegate was to be admitted in any of the diocesan conventions.* As early as 1801 Rev. John Chavis, a Negro of North Carolina, was licensed by the Hanover Presbytery of Virginia as a missionary to his own people.† The incompatibility of an ordained minister of the same denomination being a slave was recognized in the manumission of Rev. John Gloucester, the slave of Rev. Gideon Blackburn, of Tennessee, on the organization of the first colored Presbyterian church of the country, at Philadelphia, in 1807, and the subsequent settlement of Rev. Gloucester as its pastor.‡

That the white Baptists really manifested greater liberality in this period is obvious, because we also find Jacob Bishop, a Negro, the pastor of the first Baptist church of Portsmouth, Virginia, for a few years.** The church was a large and influential one, and the predecessor of Bishop, Rev. Thomas Armistead, had served with distinction as a commissioned officer in the Revolutionary War.

To-day at all the general conferences of the M. E. and M. E. South— both white—and of the A. M. E., A. M. E. Zion, and C. M. E. denominations—all colored—fraternal delegations are exchanged with all the courtesies bestowed by the two former on the two latter that should prevail among brethren. A further concession is seen in the fact of

---

*History of the Protestant Episcopal Church in America. Samuel Wilberforce.

†History of Education in North Carolina.—United States Bureau of Education.

‡Semi-Centenary Discourses.—Rev. William Catto.

**Rise of the Baptists.—R. B. Semple.

the elections of colored ministers of recognized scholarship and fitness to important secretaryships and an editorship by the powerful M. E. Church. Another illustration is the organization about thirty years ago by the M. E. Church South of its colored membership into the C. M. E. denomination and the liberal provision made by the former connection for secondary education in the Payne Institute, at Augusta, Georgia.

The Protestant Episcopal Church that forbade St. Thomas, Philadelphia, and St. Phillips, New York, to aspire to membership in diocesan conventions repealed this resolution after the breaking out of the Civil War and delegates from these and other colored parishes throughout the North and West, at least, find free admission.

Sixty years ago the application of so promising and talented a you_g man as Alexander Crummell to be matriculated as a student in any of the Episcopal divinity schools created a great shock in church circles, and his rejection is set forth at length in Bishop Wilberforce's History of American Episcopalianism; yet both at the New York and Philadelphia theological seminaries numerous colored clergymen, Episcopalian and others, now graduate with honor and distinction.

To-day in the House of Bishops there are two colored prelates of African descent, Rt. Rev. S. D. Ferguson, the Bishop of Africa, and the Rt. Rev. James Theodore Holly, the Bishop of Hayti; the former a native of South Carolina, the latter of the District of Columbia. Their welcome to the pulpits of many of the most exclusive Episcopal Churches and to the homes of their parishioners is in marked contrast to the greeting of the Negro by the same communion only two generations previously.

In the general assemblies of the Presbyterian Church to-day the presence of colored commissioners is no novelty, and the faculty of Biddle University, composed of colored professors, by the will of the Presbyterian Board of Education, shows what this conservative body has done in the recognition of Negro scholarship.

The conventions and associations of the Baptist Church in the South, where the bulk of the black race dwell, are still on the color line, yet there is progress towards true fraternal feeling here. Some years since "The Religious Herald," of Richmond, Virginia, the leading journal of that denomination in the South, announced among its paid contributors the name of a prominent colored divine.

It must be said, nevertheless, that during the first half of the nineteenth century the record of the white church on the Negro shows not only a temporizing, but a cowardly spirit. This was true in some respects of the Congregational Church;* instead of leading, the church followed the state. The anti-slavery sentiment which was unmistaken in the later years of the eighteenth century became with the growth of commercialism and national expansion, quiescent and subservient to the slave power. The right to vote, which in colonial days was generally exercised by colored freeholders, was subsequently either restricted or wholly denied. North Carolina, Maryland and Tennessee in the South, and Pennsylvania in the North, disfranchised their colored suffragists. The wave of disfranchisement then, as on the threshold of the twentieth century, dashed from one state to another. In the North repeated efforts were made to concede to the Negro his complete political and civil rights. Though the sentiment in his behalf became stronger at every trial of strength, yet with a single exception—Wisconsin—each result was decisive against the concession of the franchise to the Negro. It was only after a bloody civil war, in which thousands of lives were sacrificed and billions of treasure were expended, that the nation conceded to the Negro, first, his freedom, next his civil rights, finally his political franchise.

One hundred years ago there were but few colored schools, even in the free states, and these only in the larger towns and cities. Philadelphia was in the lead, with New York a second and Boston a third.

Connecticut, in the third decade of the nineteenth century, would not permit Prudence Crandall to maintain a school of colored girls. The means employed to break it up stands a blot on the name of the commonwealth. A resolution of the National Convention of Colored Men, held at Philadelphia, to establish a college for the education of colored youths, at New Haven occasioned both fierce excitement and bitter hostility.

Negroes could ride only on the top of the stagecoach when traveling, and Jim Crow cars prevailed on the introduction of railroads. Angry mobs were frequent. Churches and schools were the common target of attack. In the opening of the West to settlement public sentiment there against the Negroes found emphatic expression in Black Laws forbidding with heavy penalties their permanent abode in that section. These laws have only been removed in the memory of men still living. In many communities, however, these laws were a dead letter, just as to-day there

---

*Slavery and Anti-Slavery.—Wm. Goodell.

J. M. Cox, D. D.

JAMES MONROE COX.

James Monroe Cox was born in Chambers County, Alabama, February 26, 1860. While he was yet a boy his parents moved to Atlanta, Ga., and in the public schools of that city he received his first educational training. Having a desire to go to college and receive the best training possible for life's work, he entered Clark University. He took high rank in his studies, completing the classical course in 1884, and graduated from Gammon Theological Seminary in 1886, being the first student to receive the degree of B. D. from that institution. The year following his graduation from Gammon he was appointed teacher of ancient languages in Philander Smith College, Little Rock, Ark. In the fall of 1887 he was married to Miss Hattie W. Robinson, a young woman of culture and refinement, who after graduating from Clark University in 1885, taught two years in the public schools of Macon, Ga. They have five interesting children, and their married life has been singularly happy and helpful. After a professorship of eleven years in Philander Smith College he was appointed president of the institution. As president he has served for five years, and under his administration the school has had a strong, healthy growth, until now it numbers almost five hundred students. A much-needed addition to the main building has been completed at a cost of fourteen thousand dollars, the faculty has been increased, and through the efforts of the students he has raised some money, which forms the nucleus of a fund for a trades school. He is a member of the Little Rock conference of the M. E. Church, and has twice represented his brethren as delegate to the General Conference,—at Omaha, Neb., in 1892 and at Cleveland, Ohio, in 1896. His influence over the young people committed to his care is great, and he is striving to send out strong, well-rounded, Christian characters, and thus erect monuments more enduring than granite or marble. Last year Gammon honored him with the degree of D. D.

are isolated localities in Indiana and Illinois, as in Georgia and Texas, where no Negro is permitted to permanently abide.

Through the Anti-Slavery and Abolition agitation, carried on by such reformers as William Lloyd Garrison, Wendell Phillips, Frederick Douglass, John G. Whittier and Horace Greeley, the organizations of the colored people themselves, and their appreciation of the meager educational advantages afforded them prior to Appomattox, the sentiment of the country yielded one by one the rights and privileges of citizens, until colored members of state legislatures in more than half a dozen Northern states, delegates to city councils, a judgeship each in Massachusetts and Michigan, and state elective officers in Kansas—in none of which communities was the colored voting population of itself sufficiently numerous to elect—evidences the remarkable revolution in public opinion towards the Negro throughout the North.

In the South, since 1867, there have been more than a score of congressmen, including two senators, state legislators by the hundreds, councilmen, police officers, city and county officials without number; but nearly all of these were obtained by the numerical preponderance of the Negro rather than any liberalizing of dominant white sentiment.

SECOND PAPER.

WHAT PROGRESS DID THE AMERICAN WHITE MAN MAKE, IN THE NINE-TEENTH CENTURY, ALONG THE LINE OF CONCEDING TO THE NEGRO HIS RELIGIOUS, POLITICAL, AND CIVIL RIGHTS?

BY REV. J. M. COX, D. D.

The very language of our subject assumes that the Negro is entitled to religious, political and civil rights, and limits our task to showing the extent these rights have been conceded to him by the American white man. In considering this, as well as other subjects that concern the race, it is well to bear in mind the fact that men make conditions and conditions also make men. The truth of this statement is strikingly demonstrated in the reactionary influence which slavery had upon the American white man. The chains that bound the Negro and made him a chattel, also fettered the mind and soul of the white man and caused him to become narrow and selfish. Lincoln's proclamation gave freedom alike to slave and master, and now the progress made by each along all lines of human development will depend upon the extent he leaves behind slavery conditions and thinks on purer and higher things. Living in the past, meditating upon the time when he was owner of men and women, the white man must still be a slaveholder. If he can not hold in subjugation human beings, he will arrogate unto himself the rights of others and use them to further his own selfish ends. The Negro also must get away from slavery conditions, if he hopes ever to be a man in the truest sense of the word and have accorded him the rights of a man. Time and growth are determining factors in what is known as the Negro problem. The white man must grow out of, and above, his prejudice, learn to measure men by their manly and Christian virtues rather than by the color of their skin and the texture of their hair. The Negro must devote himself to character-making, wealth-getting, and to the faithful performance of all duties that belong to him as a man and a citizen, for, he may only hope to receive his rights to the extent that he impresses the white man that he is worthy and deserving of them. We repeat, it will take time to accomplish these things, but when they are accomplished, rights which now the white man withholds, and which it seems he will never concede, will, like Virgil's golden branch, follow of their own accord. Viewing the subject in the light of the above stated facts, we believe that much progress was made by the American white man in the nineteenth century along the line of conceding to the Negro his religious, political, and civil rights.

In fact, the progress made in this direction stands without a parallel in the annals of history. It surpasses the most sanguine expectation of the Negro's friends, and even of the Negro himself. Although the white man is not entirely rid of his prejudice in religion and the color line is written over the entrance to many of his temples of worship, yet he recognizes the Negro as a man and a brother and accords to him religious rights and privileges. The Negro worships God according to the dictates of his own conscience, and the laws of the land protect him in this worship. He is a potent factor in all religious and reformatory movements and works side by side with his brother in white for the overthrow of vice and sin and for the hastening of the time when man and nations shall live and act in harmony with the principles of the Christian religion. He sits in the councils of the leading denominations of the country and assists in making their laws and determining their polity. He is accorded a place on the programs of the different young people's gatherings and is listened to with the same attention which other speakers receive. He bears fraternal greetings from his to white denominations, and is courteously received and royally entertained. In international assemblies and ecumenical conferences he enjoys every right and receives the same attention that others enjoy and receive.

But this progress is further evidenced by the profound interest manifested by the white man in the Negro's religious and moral development and by the strong pleas on the part of the nation's best and ablest men for the complete obliteration of the color line in religion and for dealing with the Negro as with any other man. Millions of dollars have been given for the building of churches and schools and hundreds of noble men and women have toiled and suffered that the Negro might be elevated. The bishops of the Methodist Episcopal Church, representing two and a half million members, said in their address to the General Conference, at Omaha, in 1892: "We have always affirmed them (the Negroes) to be our brothers of the same blood and stock of all the races which compose one common humanity. As such, we have claimed for them the same rights and privileges which belong to all other branches of the common family.

His political rights. He, who but yesterday was a slave, is now a citizen, clothed with the elective franchise. This is marvelous, and all the more so, because the ballot is a wonderful force. It is the ground element of our American civilization. In its exercise the poor man counts as much as the rich, the ignorant as much as the learned, and the black as much as the white. Indeed, the free and untrammeled use of the ballot makes its possessor a veritable sovereign and gives him power over men and their possessions. Opinion is divided as to the wisdom of giving the Negro citizenship at the time it was given him. We think no mistake was made. It came at the time the Negro needed it most. It was the weapon with which he defended himself when he had but few friends. The Negro has not been a failure in politics. The very leaders who urge our young men to let alone politics, will, on the other hand, point out Bruce, Douglass, Pinchback and others as the most worthy and conspicuous characters of the race. That a reaction has set in, and the Negro is being deprived of the ballot, should occasion no alarm and little surprise.

The grandfather clause in the different state constitutions will serve as a check to the white man's progress along educational lines, but a spur to urge us on. These seeming setbacks in the concession of political rights I count as progress, and place it to the white man's credit.

The decision of the Supreme Court at Washington against the constitutionality of the Civil Rights Act of 1875 has had its effect, and to-day we find the Negro more discriminated against in his civil than in any other class of rights. Then, too, the social bugbear has had much to do with this discrimination. However, progress has been made. It has been slow, of course, because of the channel (public opinion) through which it has been compelled to come. In many sections of the country the Negro enjoys the most of his civil rights. He is admitted to the hotels, theaters, and other public places, and on public conveyances he is furnished fair accommodations. We believe in the ultimate triumph of right. Let us be patient. There is a disposition on the part of the better class of white people to do the fair and just thing by the Negro. This class will continue to increase, and some day the Negro will enjoy all of his rights, and our fair country will indeed be the land of the free, as well as the home of the brave.

Prof. N. W. Harllee

N. W. HARLLEE, A. M., A. B.

The subject of this sketch was born a slave in Robeson county, near Lumberton, North Carolina, July 15th, 1852. His father was a Methodist preacher who exhorted the plantation slaves, and was noted as "a natural mathematician." His mother was deeply religious.

Mr. Harllee is a self-made man, for he taught himself to read and write after being taught to spell about a third through Webster's blue-back spelling book, and with this small beginning he laid the foundation for a collegiate education and for the active work of life.

In 1881 he was elected register of deeds in Richmond county, N. C., where he had taught school for a number of years, and in 1882 was appointed United States postal clerk on the Carolina Central Railway and transferred to Charlotte, Columbia and Augusta Railway, which position he held till 1885. In 1879 he was graduated at the Biddle University, Charlotte, N. C., with honors. In 1885 he went to Texas and engaged in the profession of teaching, and served for a number of years as principal of the Grammar School No. 2 of Dallas, Texas. Afterward he was promoted to the principalship of the Colored High School of the Dallas City Public Schools, which position he now holds.

Professor Harllee has taken an active part in the educational work of his state, and has served as president and secretary of the Teachers' State Association of the state of Texas; he has also held the position of Superintendent of the Colored Department of the Texas State Fair for eight years, and still holds that position. He is a practical staff reporter on the Dallas Morning News, Dallas, Tex.

Mr. Harllee was married to Miss Florence Belle Coleman of Dallas, Tex., 1891, and has three children, Lucretia, Chauncey Depew and Norman W., Jr.

He is author of "Harllee's Tree of History," a new and graphic method of teaching history; also Harllee's "Simplified Long Division," a new graphic method of teaching long division; also Harllee's "Diagram System of Geography."

He has for a number of years advocated the establishment of a State University for the youth of Texas, and is also working with the Rev. W. Lomas and D. Rowens to establish an industrial school for his people at Dallas.

He is also chairman of the Y. M. C. A. board of education of Dallas, and along with Messrs. Rice, Darrell, Polk, Weems and Anderson is conducting a successful Y. M. C. A. night school for all ages and sexes.

TOPIC XIX.

THE NEGRO AS A LABORER.

BY N. W. HARLLEE.

For two hundred and fifty years the American Negro has been a drawer of water and a hewer of wood. He felled the trees and turned the forest into fields of cotton and corn; he drained the swamps and turned them into fields of rice; he graded the highways and made them possible for railroad transit and traffic. In summer he was to the white man, his owner, an umbrella; in winter, to the same owner, he was his winter wood, and always a ready servant with hand and brawn, as bread and meat and shelter.

The question of labor is one of bread and meat. To the bread-winner it means much; to the unemployed it often lends a charm for crime; for after all, the unemployed needs food, clothing, medicine, a shelter and employment alike for body and mind.

But the subject of labor is not a new one, and, indeed, it has been made a question of many complex phases introduced by prejudice from white trade unions. Also, climate makes an important factor, hence the different sections of our country employ to a large extent different kinds of labor, suited to the prevailing industries, thrift and enterprises.

We may consider at once the two general classes of labor, the crude and the skilled. For generations the black man, as a crude laborer, raised "King Cotton" in the cottonfields of the South. He has had no competition as a crude laborer; he still holds a trust on the fleecy staple; his right there is none to dispute.

But to-day a new and brighter era opens before us. We are to manufacture cotton as well as raise it. We are to advance and keep pace with the mental training of our children and provide employment for them in every avenue. As the Turk weaves his carpet and darns his shawl and as the Chinese prepares his silk, so the black youth must be trained to change cotton into cloth.

Trained hands and trained minds are inseparable companions. If we educate our boys and girls, we create in them a desire, we thrust upon them a stimulus which pushes them out into the active world, and, if only with polished brain and soft hands, they wander from place to place seeking the shady side of active, stern reality.

Since we, by educating our boys and girls, create new appetites, new desires, new activities, we set in motion new forces; then we ought the more to create new enterprises, open new avenues, establish new business or improve the old so as to meet the new relations, the awakened appetites, the growing activities and the employment of the new forces in the culture of cotton and the establishment of cotton mills.

We commit a crime by creating appetites and then failing to appease them.

The education of our children should no longer be a mere theory, but a matter of real practical nature, such as will benefit the bread-winner, the home-seeker, the higher citizenship, the welfare of the greatest number.

While I favor the higher education of the youth of the nation, I also think the youth ought to learn trades, to wear the overalls at the forge, at the work-bench, to adjust the machinery in the work-shop and the factory. I would have the youth able to design and build a house as well as to live in one, to raise potatoes as well as to eat them, to produce as well as consume. For many years the great majority of the youth must be common laborers, whatever their education, whatever their social condition or station; then it follows as the day follows the night that they should be educated with the trend of the mind and in connection with environment.

In the days of slavery many of our young men and women were trained along certain lines; the young men such as skilled carpenters, blacksmiths, stone masons, bricklayers, and the like, and the young women were trained in dressmaking and the like, and these boys and girls grew up having a kind of monopoly in their respective lines, although controlled by their owners. But for a quarter of a century very little attention has been paid to trade learning in many sections of the South.

This condition confronts us to-day; however, it is claimed that it is no fault of the children that they do not learn trades, and it is further urged by many parents that the blame does not lie at their hands; but that it is the fault of the times, of conditions and circumstances; and still others claim that the trade unions are the main cause. Many claim that, if their children are trained along certain lines, they will be debarred by the opposition of the trade unions. But these excuses seem too trivial. The opposition of the labor organizations should urge greater activity in superior trade learning in every pursuit, so that when the white striker walks out of the shops the black man, skilled, trusted and tried, should walk in and demonstrate his ability to do better and more work than the outgoing striker.

We are to take no steps backward in industrial and intellectual progress in the opening days in the dawn of the new century. A thinking people is a prosperous people. We are to be measured by what we can accomplish, not by the color of the skin, the texture of the hair, the color of the eye or the contour of the head. But we are to be measured as skilled farmers, mechanics, printers, artists and scholars.

This age demands substantial progress in every department of industry, in the home, at the fireside, in the shop and on the farm. To labor with skill, to facilitate and hasten its benign results with trained hands and cultivated brain, must ever be the fiery incentive of our people, in order that they may keep abreast of the times in all practical operations as skilled laborers, and, as such, vindicate their usefulness as citizens.

As laborers and citizens, the black face must stand for integrity in the community, the emblem of sterling worth, the black diamond intrinsic in value.

The time has come when one person ceases to employ another because he is of color, but he employs the one who can give more than value received. The race needs to bring the hand and the head nearer together.

The boy who has completed a college education should, in the course of time, raise more corn to the acre, if he be a farmer, than his uneducated father; for his knowledge of geology should better fit him to know the condition and nature of the soil; if a mechanic, his knowledge of geometry and of physics should enable him to be an adept.

The question of labor during the last few years has become, in many respects, intensely sectional. North of Mason and Dixon's line, the color of the skin has to do with the employment of the colored man along certain lines of skilled labor. While this is true in the South, the prejudice is not so rank as in the North, except where the colored laborer comes in contact with the Yankee or the foreigner.

SECOND PAPER.

THE NEGRO AS A LABORER.

BY PROF. R. G. ROBINSON, B. L.

So artful is nature that she does not permit man to break one of her laws for his pleasure without a sacrifice on his part; that for every action there is a corresponding reaction; and so the laws of compensation hold good in the dealings of man with man, races with races, and nations with nations. Slavery, as ignominious as it was, had a dual effect. The master race, forming what might be termed a landed aristocracy, looked upon manual labor as degrading; while it of necessity became the natural sphere of the weaker. Thus the spirit of work became engrafted into the very being of the Negro. This is the path all races have trod.

The basis of the South's industrial system was Negro labor; and although the Emancipation Proclamation changed the whole structure from a base of slave labor to that of free labor, nevertheless the Negro remained virtually in the same position, but with enlarged opportunities. This was a legacy greater than the ballot, for it is vastly more important to a man to be able to earn an honest living than to be privileged to cast a ballot, and doubly so if the element of doubt as to its being counted enters into the privilege. It was a cruel change from that of an irresponsible creature to that of a man clothed with the responsibility of self-support and of American citizenship—a change that would have staggered any race, but the Negro has acted nobly his part.

To say that the Negro is a valuable citizen, and a necessity in the development of the South, is to put it mildly. It can best be appreciated when we remember that since the war the Negro has earned seventy-five billions of dollars, and out of this vast amount he has saved the pitiful sum of five hundred millions; thus contributing to the wealth of the South seventy-four billions and a half of dollars. It is estimated that four-fifths of the labor done in the South is done by the Negro. The theory advanced by those who claim themselves to be immunes from that dreaded disease of Negrophobia is, that the industrial education of the Negro will inevitably inspire a similar movement for the industrial training of the poor whites, and the resultant competition means a further complication of the race problem, which will only be solved by the ultimate separation of the races. This theory is as unique as it is

Prof. R. G. Robinson, B. L.

PROF. R. G. ROBINSON.

Prof. R. G. Robinson, B. L., the subject of our sketch, was born in Hamilton, Bermuda Islands, B. W. I., February 16, 1873. In pursuit of education he came to the United States at the early age of eleven, going directly to New Hampshire. In the fall of '85 he entered Dow Academy in Franconia, N. H. By economy and thrift he maintained himself in this institution for eight years, graduating in 1893, second in his class. During this course he was several times elected president of the Autonomation Literary Society. His conduct and standing was very tersely stated by one of his professors, when he said that "he was courteous and obliging under all circumstances, clear and logical in his deductions and conscientious as a Christian."

He immediately entered Dartmouth College in the class of '97. During his college course he was prominent in athletics, at the same time holding a good position in his class. Despite the fact he was one of the two colored men in a class of a hundred and twenty-eight, yet at the close of Freshman year he was unanimously elected class auditor for the ensuing year. He was a charter member of the Ruskin Society, a society for the cultivation of the histrionic art in Dartmouth College. In 1897 Dartmouth gave him the degree of Bachelor of Letters. Says President Tucker of Dartmouth: "He is a man of clear and earnest purpose, possessing tact and good executive ability."

After graduation he was elected to the chair of English language and literature in the Tuskegee Institute, but resigned at the close of the year and was elected principal of one of the city schools of Montgomery, Ala., which position he held until elected by the Freedmen's Aid and Southern Educational Society as principal of the La Grange Academy, La Grange, Ga.

In 1899 he was married to Lily Belle, the daughter of Wm. Hill, the wealthy truck gardener of Montgomery. Mrs. Robinson is a graduate of the A. & M. College at Normal, Alabama. They have a son, Mason Francis.

Prof. Robinson has a brother who is a member of the Boston Bar. He graduated from Dow Academy in Franconia, N. H., in 1893; attended Oberlin College and received the degree of LL. B. from Boston University. In 1898 he was a member of the Boston Common Council.

original, and bids fair to revolutionize the laws of economics. But to the contrary the laws of trade and labor are as imperious as all the enactments of necessity. The South is fast regaining her lost treasures and bids fair to become not only an agricultural section, but with her wonderful oil and mineral resources to be the rival of the North. Coupled with her wonderful resources is the free Negro labor, which is the cheapest in the world outside of Asia, and will not only be in demand but will ultimately enter into all industries, driving all before it. It is a certainty that capital will inevitably seek and secure the cheapest labor. Besides cheapness, other qualifications have made, and will continue to make, him indispensable to the South's development and make him far superior to the foreign element for which a few seem to clamor.

Coming out of slavery ignorant, irresponsible, no name, no home, no "mule," there is no better way to measure the influence of Christian education than by the increased ability to earn, to save and to wisely invest money. The spirit of home-getting and the eagerness for education are very hopeful signs. We proudly quote from a lengthy editorial in a recent issue of the Atlanta Constitution: "The building up of wealth follows a sharpening of intellect. If the untutored colored man of the past quarter of a century could amass nearly a half a billion of dollars, why may not the educated Negro, during the next quarter of a century, quadruple the amount?"

As a skilled laborer it will take time for the race to make a mark, because here he will meet with sharper competition. This is the opportunity of the industrial school. The lack of sufficient numbers of skilled colored mechanics and because of the existence of prejudice, the employer shows timidity in attempting to supplant white labor with Negro labor. This fear will decrease as the supply increases. We indorse industrial training for the masses, but as efficient as it is, it is not sufficient. The tendency of these schools is to make the training of the hand of primary importance and that of the brain secondary. This might suffice for a while, but in this age of progress, of invention, when the genius of the age seems to have directed all its power to the invention of labor-saving machines, the demand for brainy mechanics is increasing so rapidly that the industrial school of to-day will wake up to-morrow only to find itself behind the times.

The Northern section of our country, with its large manufacturing interests and the constant demand for skilled labor, has encouraged the combining of labor into trades unions as a means of protection against the encroachments of capital. Because of the social side of these organizations the Negro has been debarred, with some exceptions. The unions will operate against him just as long as the interests of the unions are not in jeopardy and the supply of skilled colored mechanics is insufficient. But in the South, where Negro labor is plenty and agriculture is the chief occupation, the Negro will always have a practical monopoly, and his opportunities in all the trades in the North, as well as in the South, will increase in proportion as he becomes an educated, thrifty, law-abiding land-owner. The time has come when the Negro can no longer afford to play upon the sympathies of his friends, but as a man among men he must be pre-eminently fitted for his place; fitted in intellect, in the knowledge of his craft and in sobriety.

As a common laborer the Negro in his ignorance has had to battle against great odds. Too often his employer, who built the courts, run them and owns them, but who made the Negro shoulder the expense, feeling that he has the right of way and in his eagerness to get something for nothing, has forced the Negro through necessity to do the very thing for which he condemns him. Despite these great odds, industry and uprightness in any man, be he white or black, makes him a valuable member of any community.

THIRD PAPER.

THE NEGRO AS A LABORER.

BY MISS LENA T. JACKSON.

The wide scope of this subject, and the limited time given for research, together with the absence of statistics, make it impossible at this time to present more than a brief sketch. I propose to continue my research and investigation and at some later date to present the subject in a very much enlarged form, giving the condition of the Negro as a laborer in all the leading cities of the United States. In the present sketch mention will be made of only a few cities.

The Southern cities, with their stately residences and business houses that were constructed in ante-bellum days, bear emphatic testimony to the skill of the Negro in the mechanic arts. All of the labor of the South

Lena T. Jackson

LENA TERRELL JACKSON, M. A.

Lena Terrell Jackson was born December 25, 1865, in Gallatin, Sumner County, Tenn. Her father died in her early childhood; hence the responsibility of her support and education fell upon her mother.

This mother determined to give her daughter the advantage of a good education. Accordingly at the age of seven years the daughter was placed in a private school and remained there until the autumn of 1876, when, having finished the course of study in the private school, she was entered as a pupil in the Belle View City School and remained there three consecutive years.

She completed the course of study in the Nashville City Schools in June, 1879. In September, 1879, she entered the Middle Preparatory Class of Fisk University and remained at Fisk six years, graduating from the Collegiate Department in 1885.

During the six years spent at Fisk she taught school during the summer months in the rural districts and with the money thus earned helped to support her mother and maintain herself in school. She also assisted her mother in her family work after school hours.

After graduation, in 1885, she was elected as a teacher in the Nashville Public Schools, having resigned two similar positions, the one at Birmingham, Ala., and the other at Chattanooga, Tenn., to accept the Nashville appointment.

In 1894 she was assigned to the Junior Grade in the colored High School and two years later to the Chair of Latin in the High School, which position she is still filling.

Following out the principles of economy that are so thoroughly inculcated in the minds of Fisk students, her first thought after completing her course of study was turned towards the acquisition of real estate and the purchase of a home for her mother, who through so many struggles and sacrifices had made it possible for her to obtain a college education.

Her hopes in this direction have been realized to some extent; and she has secured not only a home, but considerable other real estate.

at that time was done almost exclusively by the Negro. Plantation owners trained their own blacksmiths, wheelwrights, painters and carpenters. The Negro was seen as a foreman on many Southern plantations during ante-bellum days. Education has greatly improved his ability to labor, and to-day in every vocation he is found as a laborer, competing successfully with other laborers. Notwithstanding the fact that prejudice and labor organizations are arrayed against him, the character of his work is such, and his disposition as a laborer such, that his services will always be in great demand.

Negro laborers are given employment on large buildings alongside of white laborers, and generally give entire satisfaction. In the city of Nashville, Tenn., during the present year, in the construction of the Polk Flats, two Negro laborers were employed with a number of white laborers; a strong pressure was brought to bear upon the foreman to displace the two Negro laborers and fill their places with white men. The request was promptly denied. This is conclusive proof that had the character of the Negroes' work not been eminently satisfactory the reverse would have been the result.

The Negro is found in all the occupations that are characteristic of a progressive people, namely, barbers, blacksmiths, brick and stone masons, carpenters, coachmen, domestic servants, firemen, farm laborers, mail carriers, merchants (grocers), millers, shoemakers and repairers, waiters, nurses, seamstresses, housewives, washerwomen and milliners.

Trades and Industries.—As stone and brick masons the wages range from $2 to $3 per day. Huntsville, Ala., has a brickyard that is owned and controlled by Negroes. This firm secures the contract for a large number of houses in Huntsville and the adjoining towns.

There is a town in the northern part of Virginia in which the entire brickmaking business is in the hands of a colored man, a freedman, who bought his own and his family's freedom, purchased his master's estate, and eventually hired his master to work for him. He owns a thousand acres or more of land and considerable town property. In his brickyard he hires about fifteen hands, mostly boys from sixteen to twenty years of age, and runs five or six months a year, making from 200,000 to 300,000 brick. Probably over one-half the brick houses of the place are built of brick made in his establishment, and he has repeatedly driven white competitors out of business.

As firemen the Negro has shown himself courageous and faithful to his trust. During a great fire in Nashville, Tenn., a few years ago, it was conceded by all that the progress of a disastrous fire was checked and much valuable property saved by the heroic efforts of the colored fire company. Unfortunately, however, the captain of the company and two of his comrades were sacrificed. In all the large cities colored fire companies are to be found, and in every case they are making a good record.

In some sections of Texas and Mississippi Negro plantation owners are often found.

Just after the close of the war the highest ambition of the Negro was the ministry. But there has been a remarkable change in that direction and Negroes are now found in all the professions. The Negro physician has made an enviable record. One of the leading surgeons in the West is a colored physician. He is the founder of a large hospital in a western town, and is also surgeon-in-chief of one of the largest hospitals in the country. The Negro has also gained some distinction at the bar. A large number of Negroes are teachers, and an increasing number of these are young women.

Clerical Work.—Negroes are given employment as clerks in the government service at Washington, D. C. There is a large number of railway-mail clerks, with salaries ranging from one thousand to fifteen hundred dollars a year. Nashville, Tenn., has three mail clerks who have held their respective routes for more than ten years.

Common Laborers.—This class includes porters, janitors, teamsters, laborers in foundries and factories. The usual wages paid for this class of work is $1 a day.

The barbering and restaurant businesses, toward which the Negro naturally turned just after emancipation, for which their training as home servants seemed especially to fit them, are not so largely followed now owing to the fact that the best talent of the race have entered the professions. Yet, however, in some places the Negro restaurant keeper does a thriving business. In Chicago, Illinois, there were two fine up to date restaurants which did a good business. One of these employed white help exclusively.

The Negro blacksmiths and wheelwrights do a good business, sometimes taking in from $5 to $8 a day.

As shoemakers and repairers, and furniture repairers and silversmiths, the Negro is successful, and is kept busy. In painting there is a colored contractor in Nashville who does business on a large scale. He is proprietor of his own shop, employs a large number of men, and secures the contract for a large number of fine dwellings. His patronage is confined mostly to white people.

Nashville has a steam laundry owned and operated entirely by colored men, and it has a large white patronage. In the rural districts most of the Negroes devote themselves to farming, either working on the farms of others or are themselves proprietors of farms.

Domestic Service.—In this field of labor both men and women are found. The average wages paid the men is $15 a month and board. The women receive from $5 to $12 a month, according to age and work. In addition to their wages they also receive lodging, cast-off clothes, and are trained in matters of household economy and taste. At present there is considerable dissatisfaction and discussion over the state of domestic service. Many Negroes often look upon menial labor as degrading and only enter it from utter necessity, and then as a temporary makeshift. This state of affairs is annoying to employers who find an increasing number of careless and impudent young people who neglect their work, and in some cases show vicious tendencies.

The low schedule for such work is due to two causes: One is, that from custom many Southern families hire help for which they cannot afford to pay much; another reason is that they do not consider the service rendered worth any more. This may not be the open conscious thought of the better elements of such laborers, but it is the unconscious tendency of the present situation, which makes one species of honorable and necessary labor difficult to buy or sell without loss of self-respect on one side or the other.

Day Service.—A large number of single women and housewives work out regularly in families, or take washing into their homes; and, like house servants, are paid by the week, or if they work by the day from 30 to 50 cents a day. This absence of mothers from home not only occasions a neglect of their household duties but also of their children, especially of girls. Aside from house servants and washerwomen, many of the women are seamstresses and readily find employment in white families. Some do a remunerative business in their own homes. The Negro woman is especially successful as a trained nurse, and a considerable number of the brightest and most intelligent among the young women are entering upon that calling.

Conclusion.—The closing years of the nineteenth century indicate remarkable advancement on the part of the Negro in all industrial lines; but the twentieth century will doubtless furnish opportunities which will enable him to carry these beginnings to their legitimate fruition.

W. E. Partee, D. D.

WILLIAM E. PARTEE, D. D.

Rev. William E. Partee, D. D., was born at Concord, N. C., of Christian parents in the year 1860 and at an early age placed in the common schools of his native town. He was left an orphan at the age of ten, but by determination and the help of friends he gained an education. When but sixteen years of age he taught a country school. He was graduated from the collegiate and theological departments of Biddle University and was licensed to preach in 1883 and ordained in 1884 by the Presbytery of Catawba and entered upon his life work by serving as pastor of Westminster Presbyterian Church at Concord, N. C., for more than three years, among his early playmates and companions.

In the year 1887 he took charge of a mission church and school at Gainesville, Fla., serving acceptably in that work for more than four years and standing faithfully by his people during that memorable epidemic of yellow fever in 1888. In 1892 he was called to the pastorate of Laura Street Presbyterian Church in Jacksonville, Fla., which position he occupied for nearly seven years. During two years of that time he was also principal of one of the city graded schools. In 1896 he was sent as commissioner from the Presbytery of East Florida to the General Assembly of the Presbyterian Church at Saratoga.

In 1898 he resigned from his work in Jacksonville to take charge of the First Presbyterian Church of Richmond, Va. Thus he has been engaged for many years in the active work of the ministry, always doing earnest and faithful work and held in high esteem by the people of every community in which he has labored.

He was married in 1886 to Miss Edith I. Smith, of Lynchburg, Va., who proved a worthy and efficient helper in his work, and uncomplainingly shared with him the trials and vicissitudes which fall to the preacher's lot in life for fourteen years. Then the Master called her to rest from her labors.

TOPIC XX.

THE NEGRO AS A CHRISTIAN.

BY REV. WILLIAM E. PARTEE, D. D.

To form a correct estimate of the Negro as a Christian we must take into account the "depths from which he came."

Back of his forty years of freedom lie more than two hundred years of bondage, in which he was forced to obey the will of another absolutely and kept in ignorance. All real manhood was repressed and every ambition curbed. Though under the control of the Christian Church and people of the South, and living on the farms and in the homes and families of their masters, mingling in their lives and their society, and subject to their moulding influence, yet, as a rule, the moral principles and qualities necessary to a religious life were not taught him, neither was he encouraged to cultivate them.

There was no lawful marriage, no true home, but husband and wife were the property of a master who used or abused either as he chose; their children grew up under the same conditions and were encouraged or forced into unchastity, lying, stealing and betraying of one another under the teaching that there was no moral wrong to them since they were the property of another who was responsible for their acts. There could be no growth in morals, and there can be no true religion without morals. To say the least they came out of bondage with a dwarfed moral nature, and to this day suffer more or less from the effects of it. The carnality of slavery has not yet ceased to bear fruit, as we all know. Ever and anon it shows itself in those horrible acts which the newspapers report in full.

It takes long and weary years to root out of a race or nation evils that have become fixed in its nature. But while there is much to be deplored as to laxity in morals among the masses there has been constant and steady improvement in this regard. It is no doubt true that any race, kept in bondage under similar conditions, and for the same length of time as the Negro was, would come out of it in no better condition, and would, perhaps, show no better record in forty years than this race has shown, and especially so if that bondage were preceded by heathenism.

Dr. Haygood has said, "The hope of the African race in this country is largely in its pulpit. No people can rise above their religion; no people's religion can rise above the doctrines preached and lived by their ministry."

The Negro began almost unaided and alone in this particular. As to their religion they were very largely left to themselves during slavery. Their ministers were ignorant and unlettered. Many of them were pious, but many were ungodly and unscrupulous. So theirs was a religion largely without the Bible. It consisted of bits of Scripture here and there, of glowing imaginations, of dreams and of superstitions; yet it was the best they knew.

Then many years of freedom had passed by before fully equipped ministers could be provided them. During those years faithful servants of God, unlettered, did their best to be the true religious leaders of the people (all honor to them), but they necessarily came short in many respects and could not carry the people up to the higher plane of religious life.

With these things before our minds we say that the race has shown a remarkable growth in the essentials of true Christian manhood. Their notions may, in some things, be crude; their conceptions of truth may be realistic; they may be more emotional than ethical; they may show many imperfections in their religious development; nevertheless is it true that their religion is their most striking formative characteristic. So susceptible are they that no other influence has had so much to do in shaping their better character, and what they are to become in their future development will be largely determined by their religion.

While in their church and social life there are some elements of evil and superstition, some of which are the inheritance of past ages in the fatherland, while others have been developed in this country by the conditions of life during the years of slavery, still any fairminded person who takes the pains to correctly inform himself will acknowledge that these are being gradually but surely eradicated.

As a Christian he commends himself in his faith and devotion. Though his religion may sometimes be defective in its practical application to the principles of right conduct and living, God, heaven, hell and the judgment day are realities to him. He believes the truths of the Bible to be real, and thus he is sound in the faith so far as he understands it, and that is more than can be said of many who are better informed than he. What a rare thing to find one an infidel! Where can you find a people more susceptible to religious teaching?

The emotional nature is highly developed, and they are quick to respond to whatever appeals to their sympathies and affections. Emotion has its place in religion and is not to be ignored, but to be properly used and controlled and directed. To move any one we must first reach the feelings; if these can be aroused they may develop into a conviction that the subject of them should adopt a given course of action, and he accordingly does so. I am not sure after all that we should seek to repress such to any great extent. It may be a point in his favor, for since he is easily and powerfully impressed by strong appeals, he is the more readily brought under the influence of the wise teacher or leader. It is true in some cases that mere physical excitement is mistaken for being "filled with the spirit," and thus some swing to the extreme in this direction. It is noticeable, however, that this is being rapidly outgrown and more self-control is being practiced. After all it does seem that being easily moved and swayed may furnish the lever by which the wise and prudent may begin to lift them to the higher ground of religious life. No doubt in most cases there is deep down beneath the easily overwrought feelings a true religious disposition, with much spirituality and divine energy.

Benevolence is rightly regarded as an important matter in Christian living. In proportion to his means the Negro excels in this. Hundreds of churches, and many schools and colleges have been built out of their poverty. To sum up and place on record their gifts for the extension of Christ's kingdom would perhaps show to the world an unequalled record of self-sacrifice and devotion to a cause. Show that a cause is a worthy one and they are ready to give according to their ability to help that cause. To give help to ministers of the gospel and other Christian workers is not only regarded as a duty but as an honor and a pleasure. On the whole they are kind at heart, generous to the distressed, obliging and considerate. Love to friends and forgiveness of enemies are marked characteristics.

The statement has been often made that loose notions as to morals are held. To some extent this may be true. Let us bear in mind that the large majority are poor and are common laborers, and more than half the race are illiterate. Compare them with this class of any race in this or any other country and I dare say they will suffer but little by the comparison. Some have made much of the fact that in many places whole families by necessity live in one or two-room cabins. While this is unfortunate and to be regretted, it is nevertheless true that you can find even in such conditions in the majority of instances that purity and virtue are as much respected as among those who live in roomy homes where every privacy is afforded. They are not any worse, certainly, and, perhaps, are better in this respect than the multitudes of other races who live in the cellars and attics of crowded tenements in our great cities.

Let us not make the mistake of including all in one general class, and *that* the worst, but while acknowledging that there is great room for improvement, let us recognize in the vast mass of multitude who, in education, morals and religion, are the equals of any people.

The correspondence between the profession of the heart and the outward life is often not what it should be, but is not that true also of many Christians of any race? There are Christians of highest education who enjoy abundant and varied opportunities of enlightenment and culture who fail to show in all their outward life what they profess in their heart to be. Some do fall into the error of trying to separate between the religion of the heart and that of the life, but generally they are learning the better way. Where so large a percentage of the people cannot read and write, how can you expect of them the highest degree of moral and religious life? Taking into account the disadvantages and limitations under which they labor, you rather wonder that they have reached so high as they have in Christian living. We must consider the past history of the race, its present disadvantages, environment and opportunity, if we would justly estimate its Christianity. We must base our judgment upon the developed Negro if we would be fair. Education helps us to be better Christians just as it helps others and, and as we get more knowledge of Bible truths such as education can give us we will be better Christians. Educated ministers are fast displacing the uneducated, and those whose moral and Christian character fall below the standard are being crowded out, and schools and colleges are sending out every year hundreds of educated Christian men and women who raise the standard of right living in any community where their lot is cast.

The material prosperity of the Negro may be placed in evidence as to his Christianity. With all the odds against them and starting up from absolute poverty, the race now owns farms, homes, schools, churches, bank accounts and personal property amounting to five hundred and fifty mil-

Rev. L. B. Ellerson

REV. L. B. ELLERSON.

Rev. L. B. Ellerson, A. M., was born at Cheraw, S. C., in 1869. Mr. Ellerson's father having died when the son was but an infant, Mr. Ellerson was left to be reared under the fostering care of his mother alone. He spent his youthful days in the public schools of his native town until he was sixteen years old. At that time he was happily converted to Christ and received the impressions that he was called to the gospel ministry. At the same time he united with the Presbyterian Church. In 1886, Mr. Ellerson entered Biddle University at Charlotte, N. C., to pursue such a course as would prepare him for the ministry. He remained at Biddle University until 1893, when he graduated from the classical course with honor, taking the Philosophical Oration. In '92 Mr. Ellerson was the successful contestant for the medal given by the Alumni to the Junior Class. During his course at Biddle, Mr. Ellerson spent his summer vacations, teaching in the district schools of North and South Carolina. In June, 1893, Mr. Ellerson was employed to do missionary work near Asheville, N. C. He continued in this work until September, 1893, at which time he entered the Theological Seminary of the Presbyterian Church at Princeton, N. J., for the purpose of completing his course for the ministry. During the first two years of his course of Theology at Princeton he continued to come South in summer and engage in teaching during vacations. He graduated from Princeton Theological Seminary in 1896. He and two others being the only colored students in a class of sixty-nine young men. Besides keeping up the studies of the last year, Mr. Ellerson supplied the pulpit of Dwight's Chapel at Englewood, New Jersey. Here he remained until September, 1896, when he came to South Carolina and was ordained to the full work of the gospel ministry by the Fairfield Presbytery, the same Presbytery having licensed him the preceding year.

During Rev. Ellerson's course at Princeton he was at one time engaged to supply the pulpit of Siloam Presbyterian Church at Elizabeth, N. J. At another time he was employed to assist the Rev. H. G. Miller, pastor of Mt. Taber Presbyterian Church, in New York City, during the illness of the pastor. Upon his ordination by Fairfield Presbytery in 1896, Rev. Ellerson was placed in charge of the church and school work at Manning, S. C. Here he worked very successfully preaching and teaching until November, 1898, when he was called to the pastorate of Berean Presbyterian Church at Beaufort, S. C. At the same time he was made principal of Harbison Institute. Rev. Ellerson labored with a marked degree of success on the Beaufort field from November, 1898, to April, 1901, when he was urged to accept a call from the Laura Street Presbyterian Church at Jacksonville, Fla., where he is at present prosecuting the work of his church with success. For a young man of his age, Rev. Ellerson evidently stands high in the estimation of his fellow Presbyters. This is evinced by the fact that he has already filled some of the highest offices in the gift of his brethren. In 1898 he was unanimously chosen moderator of Fairfield Presbytery at Camden, S. C. In 1899 he was made the choice of Atlantic Synod for moderator at Columbia, S. C., and in 1900 he was unanimously elected to represent the Presbytery of Atlantic in the General Assembly which met in St. Louis, Mo.

He has filled each of these offices with credit and ability. The degree of A. M. was conferred upon him by Biddle University, his Alma Mater in 1900.

lion dollars. It is remarkable that this has been acquired in forty years. God's word teaches that nations prosper in material things as they get close to God.

Thus looking upon the brighter side we are led to commend in many things the Christianity of the Negro race and to believe that as a people higher ground is aimed at. Though yet a long way off from perfection, yet ever onward and upward are they tending.

SECOND PAPER.

THE NEGRO AS A CHRISTIAN.

BY REV. L. B. ELLERSON, A. B., A. M.

If it is true that man is naturally a religious being, then it is preeminently true in the case of the Negro. If the Negro is anything at all he is religious. It matters not in what walk of life you find him or what may be his personal or individual character, it is a very rare case indeed when you find a Negro who indulges in doubt as to the existence of a supreme being or the existence of a future state of rewards and punishments. With him these are fixed points of belief. But as much as may be justly said regarding the Negro's natural piety, it must be observed and admitted by all who know the Negro best that his religion is very much defective in its practical application to the principles of right conduct and living. And this, we perceive, is the main point at issue, for when we discuss the Negro as a Christian we must of necessity feel called upon to distinguish between his native piety and his applied Christianity. We wish it understood, too, that the general observations made here refer to the masses of Negroes rather than to the individual.

We unhesitatingly affirm that individuals of our race have risen to as true and as high a Christian status as has mankind anywhere. And although we know and confess that the masses of our race have not yet come up to the genuine standard of the New Testament Christianity— even in apprehension—yet it must be observed that their religion contains many features that are highly commendable. Chief among these features are, first, his simple, child-like, unwavering faith in God. Nor can this condition be wholly attributed to ignorance or thoughtlessness, as some might hold; for, indeed, we have produced some men of as rare ability as move among the human throng; yet it is almost as difficult to find an atheist, an agnostic, or an infidel of any sort among us as it is to find a "needle in a haystack." The Negro believes in the God of the Bible.

Second. Because the Negro is naturally emotional he is usually earnest and fervent in the exercise of his religious worship, as far as that goes. He likes the strong, passionate appeal which for the time being, at least, tickles him into laughter or moves him to tears and sweeps him off his feet in its flight. The earnestness and fervency are all right but too often these run to the extreme and so constitute by far too large a portion of his Christianity.

Third. Again, the Negro's religion is characterized by benevolence. I believe that history has no record of a people who, out of their want and poverty, have given so much to benevolent causes as have the Negroes in this country. Is it not wonderful to reckon the millions of dollars that have been given by us for erecting and maintaining church edifices, schools and other benevolent institutions since emancipation? It is perfectly safe to affirm that no people have exceeded us along this line. But with all of these good things that can be justly said to the credit of our religion, the fair-minded must still admit that when we come to the daily application of the principles and practices of Bible Christianity we are lacking. If this be true, there is a cause. What is it? We believe that the cause was stated in part when we referred to the natural emotional element in our makeup. That element too often causes us to run off with the sentiment, having left the substance behind. Another cause, and, perhaps the main one, is to be found doubtless in the same way in which we find the causes of defects in our race along other lines, i. e., from defective leadership and instruction along this particular line. We would be understood. The crying need of our race to-day *is* and has been a *competent* ministry to lead and instruct the masses in the application of the principles of right life and conduct from the standpoint of Bible Christianity. To-day the church, especially in our race, is the center of both our social and Christian life. Like priests, like people. All honor to the pioneers who did their best in their circumstances and who served well their day and generation. But this is another age; this, a brighter day—one that demands improvement along all lines, and especially in the pulpit of my race. The pew is advancing, hence the pulpit had better push on. The key to the situation, then, is nothing more nor less than

Rev. W. H. Brooks, D.D.

REV. WALTER H. BROOKS, D. D.

Rev. Walter H. Brooks, D. D., has a very unusual and interesting history. He was born a slave in Richmond, Va., August 30, 1851, his parents belonging to different masters. In 1859 his mother's master died, and arrangements were made to sell her and her six children, she being allowed to select a purchaser if she could find one. Through a white friend his father bought Dr. Brooks' mother, together with two of the youngest children. Walter H. Brooks and an elder brother were bought by a large tobacco manufacturing firm in Richmond. In 1861 the breaking out of the war affected the tobacco trade, and many of the tobacconists were obliged to sell or hire out their slaves. Walter and his brother David were hired by their mother, who, each quarter of the year, managed to pay the amount agreed upon. For the next three years both of the boys worked, thereby aiding their mother in paying their hire. After the war Walter H. Brooks, for a short time, attended a primary school in Richmond, taught by a young lady from the North.

In October, 1866, he had received one year's instruction when he went to Lincoln University, Chester County, Pa. He remained there seven years, graduating in 1872, and then entered a theological class for one year. During the second year of his seminary life he was converted and became an elder in the Presbyterian Church. He expected to become a Presbyterian preacher, but in 1873 his ideas having made him a subject to baptism, he joined the First African Baptist Church of Richmond, Va.

For a short time he was a clerk in the postoffice at Richmond, Va., but in 1874, having resigned his position, he entered the service of the American Baptist Publication Society in the State of Virginia. Having been ordained in December, 1876, in April, 1877, he accepted the pastorship of the Second Baptist Church of Richmond, Va., where he succeeded in paying off the entire debt of the church. In June, 1880, he was sent as a delegate for the Virginia Baptist State Convention to the Baptist General Association in session at Petersburg, and he was the first Colored delegate received by that body. In September, 1880, he resigned the charge of the church and went to New Orleans, La., to commence work in the American Baptist Publication Society's employ, but his wife's failing health caused him to return to Virginia in 1882.

In November, 1882, he was called to the pastorship of the Nineteenth Street Baptist Church of Washington, D. C., where he has been ever since.

Roger Williams University, Nashville, Tenn., and State University, Louisville, Ky., both honored him with the title of Doctor of Divinity; while his alma mater, in June, 1883, conferred upon him the degree of M. A.

Recently he was elected a trustee of the United Society of Christian Endeavor, to represent the Colored Baptists of the world.

Dr. Brooks has distinguished himself as a temperance advocate, and for a number of years has been the Chaplain of the Anti-Saloon League of the District of Columbia.

His article, printed some years since in the "National Baptist" of Philadelphia, Pa., on "George Liele, the Black Apostle," and his more recent paper on the "Beginnings of Negro Churches in America," have won for him many praises.

For twenty-eight years Dr. Brooks has been in public life, and his power as a speaker still gives him a commanding influence in the pulpit and on the platform.

Dr. Brooks married Miss Eva Holmes, of the family of Rev. James H. Holmes, of Richmond, Va., and this union resulted in the birth of ten children—eight of whom are living, four boys and four girls—the oldest born being 27 years of age, the youngest four years.

a more consecrated and intelligent Christian ministry for our race throughout the length and breadth of this land. And we are hopeful; for the "signs of the times" portend the coming of better things. Already bright streaks of gray high up upon the eastern horizon herald the dawn of a new and brighter day. Every branch of the Christian church in our race is putting forth strenuous efforts to supply the pulpits of the race with competent ministers. Let this glorious day be hastened and soon Ethiopia will stretch out her hands to God.

THIRD PAPER.

THE NEGRO AS A CHRISTIAN.

BY REV. WALTER H. BROOKS, D. D.

The Christian religion is eminently adapted to the wants of humanity. It has always had a charm for lowly and oppressed peoples. It was, therefore, the one thing, above all others, which gave comfort and hope to the American Negro during the night of his long bondage.

The story of the enslavement and marvelous deliverance of God's ancient people; of Daniel, the prophet, and the Hebrew youths, whom God protected and honored in the house of their bondage; the psalms of David, the sweet singer of Israel; the inspired narratives of Jesus of Nazareth, the Christ of God; the Biblical account of the faith, sufferings and triumphs of the apostles; and the manifold promises of God, made to all who served Him in truth, and patiently wait for their fulfillment, could not fail in influencing the conduct and life of America's Negro slaves. It was in circumstances like these the Christian Negro, many years ago, sang out his hopes, his sorrows, and his soul-yearnings in melodies peculiarly his own, whose plaintive strains have been echoing around the globe for a generation and more.

The balm of Gilead was never so soothing to the wounds of an Israelite as the Gospel of Jesus Christ was, in the dark days of slavery, to the oppressed and sorrowing soul of the unfortunate Negro. It is not surprising, therefore, that at least one-fourth of the entire Negro population of the country was devout Christians forty years ago, while the entire Negro population was nominally believers in the living and true God, and in Jesus Christ, the Savior of the world.

Whether the Negro Christian has lost some of his old-time love for Christ, and his zeal for the sanctuary, is, in the minds of some, an open question. We, however, believe that the Savior and the sanctuary are dearer to the Negro than ever. Indeed, so far as the census, which was taken by the United States in 1890, proves anything as to the matter of religion, the Negro is the most religious citizen of the country. Here is an extract from that report: "The Negro population of the country, exclusive of Indian territory and Alaska, according to the census of 1890, is 7,470,040. As the churches report 2,673,197 Negro communicants, exclusive of Indian territory and Alaska, it follows that *one* person in every 2.79 of the Negro population is a communicant. Excluding Indian Territory and Alaska, the total population is 62,622,250, and the total of communicants 20,568,679. The proportion here is 1 communicant in every 3.04 of the population. In other words, while all denominations have 328.46 communicants in every 1,000 of the total population, the colored organizations reported have 357.86 communicants in every 1,000 of the Negro population." According to this showing, *more than a third* of the entire Negro population of the country was enrolled as active members of the churches, ten years ago. At the same time, *less than a third* of the white population was connected with the churches of the land.

It remains to be seen whether the census of the United States, which is now in process of completion, will show any change in the relative strength of the Negro and white churches of the country.

It is certain that the Negro Christian is displaying commendable zeal in erecting spacious houses of worship; in acquiring school property; in giving the Gospel to the heathen in Africa, and in other parts of the world; in raising funds for the cause of education, and in providing himself with a religious literature of his own making.

In the quality of his religion, we dare say, there is room for improvement. But the changes mostly needed for his highest good are intellectual, material, social, commercial and political in nature, rather than religious.

The Negro Christian is as a rule as good as he knows how to be. He often errs, *not knowing the Scriptures.* He sometimes plunges headlong into the ditch of shame, because his spiritual adviser and instructor is a "blind leader of the blind."

Christian schools, however, are giving us better leaders every year,

Rev. Henry H. Proctor

REV. HENRY H. PROCTOR, B. A.

Henry Hugh Proctor was born near Fayetteville, Tennessee, December 8, 1868. After completing the public school course of his native town he studied in Fisk University, Nashville, Tenn., from which school he was graduated with the degree of Bachelor of Arts, June, 1891. That fall he entered the Divinity School of Yale University, graduating three years later. He was assigned by the faculty to the post of honor among the chosen orators of the class. He at once entered upon the pastorate of the First Congregational Church of Atlanta, Ga.

Mr. Proctor has lectured extensively in many parts of the country, his best-known lecture being "The Black Man's Burden." He has been active in preventing legislation in Georgia adverse to the colored race, especially measures designed to restrict the franchise and cut down public school facilities of the Negro. He is correspondent for a number of Northern periodicals, and extracts from his sermons are published weekly in the "Atlanta Constitution," the leading daily of the South. At his recent seventh anniversary as pastor many letters of congratulation came from all parts of the country, one being from Principal Booker T. Washington, whose esteem and friendship he enjoys.

and the time is hastening when the Negro Christian of America shall be respected and loved because of his intelligence, his Christian piety, his zeal for God's cause, his manly bearing, his general worth as a moral and material contributor to the well being, both of the state and of the country which claim him as a citizen, and because of his excellent spirit and gentlemanly deportment.

FOURTH PAPER.

THE NEGRO AS A CHRISTIAN.

BY REV. H. H. PROCTOR.

In the historic development of Christianity race and religion have had a reciprocal relation. Conversion has involved a mutual conquest. The religion has modified the race, and the race has modified the religion. Every race that has embraced Christianity has, by developing that element of truth for which it has affinity, brought to the system its own peculiar contribution.

In the Semitic race, the high priest of humanity, Christianity, was born. "Salvation is of the Jews." Israel's code of ethics was the highest known to antiquity. It was but natural that the Hebrew should leave upon the new-born system the impress of his genius for ethics.

Hellenism may be regarded as the complement and contrast of Hebraism. Hebraism revealed the transcendence of Jehovah. Hellenism declared the divinity of man. The Greek, pre-eminent in philosophy as a pagan, became, as a Christian, pre-eminent in theology. He blended the complemental conceptions of divinity and humanity. If the contribution of the Hebrew was ethical, that of the Greek was theological.

The Latin mind, practical rather than speculative, political rather than theological, established the *Civitas Dei* where once stood the *Civitas Roma.* This ecclesiastical masterpiece of human wisdom "may still exist in undiminished vigor," says Macaulay, "when some traveler from New Zealand shall, in the midst of a vast solitude, take his stand on a broken arch of London Bridge to sketch the ruins of St. Paul's." Truly the Church of Rome has left upon Christianity an ineffaceable political impress.

The Teutonic mind—fresh, vigorous, even childlike in its simplicity and love of reality, accustomed to enjoy the freedom peculiar to lands where the national will is the highest law—would not brook the inflexible dogmatism of the Greek nor the iron ecclesiasticism of the Roman. The Teuton loved liberty in religion as well as in other things, and asserted his right to stand before his God for himself. The free spirit revealed in Christianity through Luther can never die. "Christianity as an authoritative letter is Roman; as a free spirit it is Teutonic."

The Saxon, pre-eminent in capacity for developing ideas, has so assimilated Christianity as to become its noblest representative. Enterprise and energy, vigor and thrift, striking characteristics of this great race, are becoming part and parcel of our Christianity. This is the missionary age, and it is the enterprising Saxon, unchecked and undaunted by sword, flame or flood, that is encircling the globe with a girdle of divine light.

And yet our Christianity is not complete. Notwithstanding its moral stamina, its philosophic basis and its organic solidarity, its free spirit and its robust energy, do we not feel there is something lacking still? Does not our Christianity lack in its gentler virtues? To what nation shall we look for the *desideratum?* Shall it not be to the vast unknown continent? If the Jew has modified our religion by his ethics, the Greek by his philosophy, the Roman by his polity, the Teuton by his love of liberty, and the Saxon by his enterprise, shall not the African, by his characteristic qualities of heart, bring a new and peculiar contribution to Christianity?

The Negro is nothing if not religious. His religion touches his heart and moves him to action. The result of his peculiarly partial contact with Christianity in America is but an earnest of what his full contribution may be confidently expected to be. The African's mission in the past has been that of service. "Servant of all" is his title. He has hewn the wood and drawn the water of others with a fidelity that is wonderful and a patience that is marvelous. As an example of patient fidelity to humble duty he stands without a peer.

His conduct in the late war, which resulted in his freedom, was as rare a bit of magnanimity as the world ever saw. The helpless ones of his oppressor in his power, he nobly stayed his hand from vengeance. And at last, when he held up his hands that his bonds might be removed, his emancipator found them scarred with toil unrequited, but free from the blood of man save that shed in open, honorable battle.

His religious songs are indicative of his real character. These songs embodied and expressed the only public utterance of a people who had suffered two and a half centuries of unatoned insult, yet in them all there has not been found a trace of ill will. History presents no parallel to this. David, oppressed by his foes, called down fire, smoke and burning wind to consume his enemies from the face of the earth. But no such malediction as that ever fell from the lips of the typical American slave; oppressed, like the Man of Sorrows, he opened not his mouth.

Truth is stranger than fiction. Harriet Beecher Stowe's "Uncle Tom" was more than a character of fiction. He was a real representative of the Christian slave. Recall that scene between Cassy and Uncle Tom. Unsuccessful in her attempts to urge him to kill their inhuman master, Cassy determines to do it herself. With flashing eyes, her blood boiling with indignation long suppressed, the much-abused Creole woman exclaims: "His time's come. I'll have his heart's blood!" "No, no, no," says Uncle Tom; "No, ye poor lost soul, that ye must not do! Our Lord never shed no blood but his own, and that he poured out for us when we was his enemies. The good Lord help us to follow his steps and love our enemies." Uncle Tom's words are not unworthy of immortality.

> "Howe'er it be, it seems to me,
>   'Tis only noble to be good;
> Kind hearts are more than coronets,
>   And simple faith than Norman blood."

Humility, fidelity, patience, large-heartedness, love—this is Africa's contribution to Christianity. If the contribution of the Saxon is Pauline, that of the African is Johanine. Paul, with his consuming energy, carrying the Gospel to the uttermost parts, stands for the white man; John, the man of love, leaning on his Master's bosom, is typical of the black. The white man and the black are contrasts, not contraries; complementary opposites, not irreconcilable opponents.

The Jew has given us ethics; the Greek, philosophy; the Roman, law; the Teuton, liberty. These the Saxon combines. But the African —"latest called of nations, called to the crown of thorns, the scourge, the bloody sweat, the cross of agony"—the African, I say, has the deep, gushing wealth of love which is yet to move the great heart of humanity.

FIFTH PAPER.

THE NEGRO AS A CHRISTIAN.

BY REV. S. KERR.

My purpose in writing upon this subject is to investigate God's disciplinary and retributive economy in races and nations, with a hope of arriving at some clear conclusion concerning the.Negro as a Christian.

First, it may be just and proper to view the races of mankind in respect to growth and mastery. The principles of growth and mastery in a race, a nation, or a people, are the same all over the globe. The same great agencies needed for one quarter of the globe, and in one period of time, are needed for all quarters of the globe, for all people and for all time, and consequently needed for this American nation.

The children of Africa in America are in no way different from any other people in respect to Christianity. Many of the differences of races are accidental and oftentimes become obliterated by circumstances, position and religion.

Go back to a period in the history of England, when its rude inhabitants lived in caves and huts, when they fed on bark and roots, when their dress was the skins of animals. Then look at the eminent Englishman of the present day—cultivated, graceful, refined, Christianized. When we remember that his distant ancestors were wild and bloody savages, and that it took centuries to change his forefathers from rudeness and brutality into enlightened, civilized Christians, there is no room to doubt the susceptibility of the Negro to Christianity.

The same great general laws of growth continue unchangeable. The Almighty neither alters nor diminishes these laws for the convenience of a people, of whatever race they may be. The Negro race is equally susceptible of growth in Christianity as in civilization.

At once the question arises—Is the Negro race doomed to destruction? Or, does it possess those qualities which will enable it to reach a high degree of moral and Christian civilization? To the first of these questions I reply that the Negro race is by no means doomed to destruction. It is now over five hundred years since the breath of the civilized world touched powerfully, for the first time, the mighty masses of the pagan world in America, in Africa and the isles of the sea, and we see everywhere that the weak heathen tribes of the earth have gone down before

Rev. S. Kerr

REV. S. KERR.

To give anything like a true sketch of Mr. Kerr's life and labors both in and out of the ministry would fill a good-sized volume rather than a page of this book, as his life has been replete with thrilling, romantic incidents. The Rev. Mr. Kerr graduated with honors, having received the degree of A. B. from Rawden College, Leeds, England. He returned at once to the West Indies, where he labored three years.

In 1859 he did extensive missionary work in the Turks and Caicos Islands, where, in 1860, he accepted the appointment of Registrar of Births and Deaths. In 1863 he accepted the appointment of Assistant Master of the Government Schools at Grand Turk, and was afterwards appointed Head Master. In 1864 he filled the dual role of Inspector of Schools and missionary, and he passed unscathed through the great hurricane of 1866 which devastated the whole colony, destroyed all the schools and public buildings, as well as 2,500 dwelling houses, including Mr. Kerr's personal property. In 1867 he was sent as missionary to Hayti, where, as everywhere, he did good work. In 1873 he was appointed professor in the National Lyceum College for boys and young ladies, where he did effective and extensive missionary work in Cape Hatien, Grande Riviere and Dondon, and maintained considerable influence with the Haytien officials and authorities.

In 1880 he was advanced to the Priesthood of the Episcopal Church of America, by the Rt. Rev. J. Th. Holly, D. D., LL. D., Bishop of Hayti. In 1882 he was delegated to represent the Episcopal Church in the United States, and to collect funds for the building of the same in Hayti. On landing in New York, his reception by Bishop Horatio Potter was cordial in the extreme—the same by Bishops Littlejohn, of Long Island; T. A. Starkey, of Northern New Jersey; T. M. Clark, of Warwick, R. I.; M. A. De Wolf Howe, Central Pennsylvania; William C. Doane, Albany; Alfred Lee, Primate, Delaware; W. B. Stevens, Pennsylvania; H. A. Neely, of Maine; A. C. Coxe, Western New York. He occupied the pulpits of the leading Episcopal Churches in New York—Old Trinity, Grace Church, St. Chrysostom's, St. Paul's, St. Philip's and others. The leading churches in Brooklyn, Yonkers, Newport, R. I., Newark, N. J., Orange, N. J., Syracuse, Saratoga Springs, Utica, Buffalo, Rochester, Albany, Newburg, Poughkeepsie, Sing Sing, Barrytown, Tarrytown, Philadelphia, Germantown, Ashebourne, Reading, Cheltenham and many others.

In 1883 he was sent to Jamaica, W. I., and the following year he was appointed by the Provincial Synod (under the auspices of the Society for the Propagation of the Gospel—London, Eng.) Rector of the Panama Railroad Church and Arch-deacon of the Church of England Mission, and Chaplain to the Panama Canal Company. In 1889 he made an extensive missionary tour through Central America, where he performed religious services at the opening of the Nicaragua Canal, coming in touch with several Indian tribes, and gaining considerable knowledge of their manners and customs in their crude condition.

In 1890 he returned to the West Indies and was transferred to the Diocese of Florida and made Rector of St. Peter's Episcopal Church in Key West, where he has a large parish and congregation and where he is highly esteemed by all classes, white and colored.

the civilized world; tribe and nation have dispersed before its presence. The Iroquois, the Pequods, the brave Mohawks, the once refined Aztecs and others have gone, nevermore to be ranked among the tribes of men. In the scattered islands of the Pacific seas, like the stars of the heavens, the sad fact remains that from many of them their populations have departed like the morning cloud. They did not retain God in their knowledge. Just the reverse with the Negro. Destructive elements, wave after wave, have swept over his head, yet he has stood unimpaired.

Even this falls short of the full reality of the Negro as a Christian, for civilization at numerous places has displaced ancestral heathenism, and the standard of the cross, uplifted on the banks of its great river, showing that the heralds of the cross have begun the glorious conquests of their glorious King. Vital Christian power has become the property of the Negro. Does God despise the weak? No, the Providence of God intervenes for the training and preservation of such people.

But has the Negro race any of those qualities which emanate from Christianity? Let us see. The flexibility of the Negro character is universally admitted. The race is possessed of a nature more easily moulded than that of any other class of men. Unlike the Indian, the Negro yields to circumstances and flows with the current of events, hence afflictions, however terrible, have failed to crush him; his facile nature wards them off, or else through the inspiration of hope their influence is neutralized. These peculiarities of the Negro character render him susceptible to imitation. Burke tells us that "imitation is the second passion belonging to society, and this passion arises from much the same cause as sympathy." This is one of the strongest links of society. It forms our manners, our opinions, our lives. Indeed, civilization is carried down from generation to generation, or handed over from a superior to an inferior, by means of imitation. A people devoid of imitation is incapable of progress or advancement, and must retrograde. If it remains stagnant, it must of necessity bring its own decay. The quality of imitation has been the grand preservative of the Negro in all lands. Indeed, the Negro is a superior man to-day to what he was three centuries ago.

I feel fortified in the principles I have advanced by the opinions of great, scrutinizing thinkers. In his treatise on Emancipation, written in 1880, Dr. Channing says: "The Negro is one of the best races of the human family; he is among the mildest and gentlest of men; he is singularly susceptible to improvement." Kinmont declares in his "Lecture on

Man" that "The sweet graces of the Christian religion appears almost too tropical and tender plants to grow in the soil of the Caucasian mind; they require a character of the human nature of which you can see the rude lineaments in the Ethiopian, to be implanted in and grow naturally and beautifully withal." Adamson, the traveler who visited Senegal in 1754, said: "The Negroes are sociable, humane, obliging and hospitable, and they have generally preserved an estimable simplicity of domestic manners. They are distinguished by their tenderness for their parents, and great respect for the aged—a patriarchal virtue which, in our day, is too little known." Dr. Raleigh, also, at a great meeting in London, said: "There is in these people a hitherto undiscovered mine of love, the development of which will be for the amazing welfare of the world. * * * Greece gave us beauty; Rome gave us power; the Anglo-Saxon unites and mingles these, but in the African people there is the great gushing wealth of love, which will develop wonders for the world."

I feel that the Almighty, who is interested in all the great problems of civilization, is interested in the Negro problem. He has carried the Negro through the wilderness of disasters, and at last put him in a large open place of liberty. There is not the shadow of a doubt that this work which God has begun, and is carrying on, is for the mental and spiritual elevation of the Negro.

Rev. J. H. Anderson.

REV. J. H. ANDERSON, D. D.

Rev. J. H. Anderson was born June 30, 1848, in Frederick, Md. Dr. Anderson is what is called a self-made man, he having attended school only six months in his life and studied a short time under a private tutor. By hard, persistent efforts and close application to books, Dr. Anderson has risen to a point in scholarship and prominence that only a few college Negroes have reached. He is noted as a pulpit orator and platform speaker. He has attained to some prominence as a writer and takes front rank as a preacher in his denomination. For his scholarly attainments and usefulness as a minister of the gospel, Livingstone College conferred upon him, in 1896, the degree of doctor of divinity. Dr. Anderson was one of those heroic liberty-loving souls who went to the battlefield in the Civil War to fight for their and their race's freedom.

TOPIC XXI.

DOES THE NORTH AFFORD TO THE NEGRO BETTER OPPORTUNITIES OF MAKING A LIVING THAN THE SOUTH?

BY REV. J. H. ANDERSON.

Colonization is a condition of cosmopolitan society as it is of races. As "birds of a feather flock together," so the different races in the American civilization form settlements or colonies, as far as possible. The truthfulness of this statement is seen in the thickly-settled German, Irish, Jewish and Italian communities in the North. Their race affinities produce natural and social relations promotive of their varied interests. The Negro's civil and social privileges are more restricted in the South than in the North, owing to which fact the Negroes of the South are more united than the Negroes of the North. In the North a few individuals may rise to intellectual, professional, business and mechanical distinctions, but from general employment in the skilled industries, business enterprises and political preferment he is debarred, and, being cheaply and conveniently accommodated in almost every respect by the whites, he is not under the same necessity as the Southern Negro to establish and operate business enterprises. It is rather inconvenient to establish and maintain Negro business enterprises and schools in the North, for the reason that there are no thickly settled communities. A Negro lawyer, doctor, dressmaker, music teacher, hair dresser and mechanic do well in some instances, because they receive patronage from the whites. It is not so much the prejudice of the whites nor the indifference of the Negro as it is the peculiar conditions of the North that prevent the Negro from enjoying the business enterprises and founding race institutions. The few new institutions and even churches in the North are largely sustained by donations from the whites. Renting houses and purchasing property and living in the North are commensurate with the large scale and competition along all lines of industry, and social life is so active that the most rigid economy and business tact are essential to success in any kind of business in the North.

The Negro who embarks in business in the North has not only to compete with his own people, but with the shrewd Yankee, who seeks to monopolize all interests that have money in them. The Negro of the North for the most part appears to be content with his superior civil and social privileges. He breathes the air with more perfect liberty, enjoys life free from violence, is vindicated and redressed at law and recognized in his citizen rights, and, like the Pharisee, thanks God that he is not like the ex-slave of the South, and this is the height of his ambition. Three-fourths of the freeholding and tax-paying Negroes in the North are from the South, and Southern Negro labor is preferred in the North as in the South. Waiters, domestic servants, janitors, teamsters, laundrymen and coachmen from the South can find employment in the North. Any industrious Southern Negro can find common labor to do in the North.

Before the formation of labor unions and federations in the North, the Negro skilled laborer found employment, but after deciding to exclude the Negro from membership these unions became an effective dictating power to employ when Negroes applied to them for work.

The tax-payers in many Northern sections favor mixed schools because it is less expensive to have them. They would not be justified in maintaining separate schools for the few Negro pupils. Of course, race favoritism, competition and prejudice, combine to exclude Negro teachers, and yet a few Negro teachers are employed to teach in the mixed schools. That Negro children, procuring their education by Negro teachers in the Negro schools, can better appreciate race efficiency and dignity there can be no question. The Northern Negro is ill fitted for living in the South, it being difficult for him to adapt himself to the conditions of the South, yet it is quite easy for the Southern Negro to adapt himself to the North where full and free expression is equally accorded to all, and where no legal discriminations are made and where the social question is left for adjustment by the parties nearest concerned. In the North the Negro has the opportunity of advocating the interests of his Southern brother in a way that would not be tolerated in the South, and thus the Northern Negro can assist in the formation of a proper sentiment in his favor. The Northern Negro is, therefore, a necessity to the Southern Negroes, and vice versa. The Negro's destiny is to be worked out in the South because he has greater numerical strength and superior advantages in the South, notwithstanding the civil, social and legal restrictions upon him. The lesson of self-dependence and self-effort is forced upon the Southern Negro as not upon the Northern Negro.

When the Southern Negro was emancipated, his first thought was

Prof. W. H. Councill

PROF. W. H. COUNCILL, PH. D.

W. H. Councill was born in Fayetteville, N. C., in 1848, and was carried to Alabama by the traders in 1857, through the famous Richmond Slave Pen. In Alabama he worked in the fields with the other slaves. He is a self-made man, having had only few school advantages. He attended one of the first schools opened by kind Northern friends at Stevenson, Ala., in 1865. Here he remained about three years, and this is the basis of his education. He has been a close and earnest student ever since, often spending much of the night in study. He has accumulated quite an excellent library, and the best books of the best masters are his constant companions, as well as a large supply of the best current literature. By private instruction and almost incessant study, he gained a fair knowledge of some of the languages, higher mathematics, and the sciences. He was Enrolling Clerk of the Alabama House of Representatives in 1872-4. He was appointed by President Grant Receiver of the Land Office for the Northern District of Alabama in 1875. He was founder and editor of the "Huntsville Herald" from 1877 to 1884. He founded the great educational institution, Normal, of which he is president, and has been for a quarter of a century. He read law and was admitted to the Supreme Court of Alabama in 1883. But he has never left the profession of teaching, although flattering political positions have been held out to him. He has occupied high positions in church and other religious, temperance, and charitable organizations, and has no mean standing as a public speaker.

Prof. Councill has traveled quite extensively in Europe, and was warmly received and entertained by the Hon. W. E. Gladstone and His Majesty, King Leopold, of Belgium.

And thus by earnest toil, self-denial, hard study, he has made himself, built up one of the largest institutions in the South, and educated scores of young people *at his own expense.*

Prof. Councill is proud to be known as a friend to Africa. He is co-operating with Bishop Turner in the redemption and civilization of that continent. Normal, under Prof. Councill, is educating native Africans for this purpose. He has received the degree of Ph. D. from Morris Brown College.

Prof. Councill is author of "The Lamp of Wisdom." He writes extensively for the leading magazines and newspapers of the country.

education, and, adhering steadfastly to this idea, he has made a progressive education since his emancipation that has astounded the civilized world. No school-loving race can be kept down or back. Brought here a heathen, the Negro soon exchanged fetichism for Christianity, and, having been trained in the school of servile labor for centuries, he learned how to labor so that when his emancipation came he was prepared to strike out on lines of self development, and he has made in thirty-six years a progress in the acquisition of wealth that is without a parallel in history.

The prejudices of the whites against the Negro have rather helped him, in that they have stimulated him to make greater efforts to reach the independence of the white man.

Having lived in both sections of our country, I am prepared to say that the Negro can do better towards working out his destiny in the South than in the North.

SECOND PAPER.

DOES THE NORTH AFFORD TO THE NEGRO BETTER OPPORTUNITIES OF MAKING A LIVING THAN THE SOUTH?

BY PROF. W. H. COUNCILL.

A comparison of the opportunities which different sections hold out to any class of our fellow citizens should not be regarded as hostile criticism. No man, no country suffers by the truth.

We cannot answer this question by yes or no. The North affords the better opportunities in some things, while in others the South gives the Negro the better opportunity for making a living. If we are correct in putting a broad and educated mind as the foundation for every useful superstructure, we are forced to admit that the opportunity for laying this foundation is better in the North, where a century of thought on popular education has developed the finest public school system in the world. While this brings the Northern Negro in contact with the great Anglo-Saxon mind, and fits him for making a living and for business in that atmosphere, he has to undergo a kind of mental acclimatization before he can effectively and usefully enter into work in the South, where the atmosphere at every turn is different from that in the North. For twenty-five years I have been brought in direct contact with Negroes reared or educated in the North, and I do not recall one who did not have to un-Northernize himself in many respects before he could harmonize to usefulness in the South. It is to the credit of our Northern brethren that they are thus willing to sacrifice a part of their individualism in order to serve their race in the South. In my long experience I have not met a quarter dozen who have not cheerfully put aside their selfishness for the common good of their associates and their work. Indeed, I have found my Northern brethren more willing and helpful in this regard, perhaps, than Southern Negroes, who are more self-assertive and persistent in their make-up, a spirit imbibed from the general character of independence and domineering found in the South. But the Southern Negro, reared in harmony with Southern institutions, having assimilated prejudices and counter-prejudices, can use to greater advantage his small amount of education and training.

In a country where competition is sharp, as in this country, and where any kind of excitement is resorted to in order to give advantage to the competitors, the minority race, especially in inferior circumstances, must suffer along lines of battle for bread in which the masses engage. Thus it is, while the Northern Negro enjoys high privileges of an intellectual character among the classes, he is bumped, shunned, and pushed to the rear among the quarreling, scrambling masses.

There are scattered far and wide a few Negroes in the North who are doing well in business. They get the patronage of their white neighbors. There are few communities in the North where the Negro population is strong enough to support a Negro in business, if the race lines were drawn in business. I think the voluntary collections of like tribes and races of men, as Italians, Jews, Chinese, Poles, Norwegians, Swedes, and the like, in settlements in our large cities and some country districts, show clearly the gregarious disposition of like peoples; and from time out of mind each tribe, clan or race, has depended upon itself for patronage and support. In order for the Negro to succeed in any considerable degree in business in the North, it would be necessary to increase the Negro population in that section. As I have intimated above, there are few fields for operation in the North for Negroes, regardless of their ability to succeed, for there are few cases where Negro patronage is not limited to the Negro population. While occasionally a few Negroes may get patronage from the other clans and tribes it is nevertheless true that as a general rule the aim is to keep the trade in the family, as it were. Every whip of tribal differentiation and prejudice is applied to enforce a rigid observance of this general rule. I think that we may logically conclude that the opportunity for that training and education which could make the Northern Negro immediately useful to the mass of the race, and the opportunity to gather material wealth, are not ideal in the North.

Ninety-two per cent of the Negro population reside in the South, where slavery left them. Under normal conditions there should be ninety-two per cent of Negro wealth, thrift and energy in the South. The opportunity to accumulate wealth and the accumulation are different. The Southern Negro is a wealth producer. He does four-fifths of the agricultural labor of the South and thereby adds four-fifths to the wealth of the South derived from agriculture, the leading Southern industry. If the whole of the billion dollars to the credit of the Negro race were placed to the credit of the Southern Negro alone, it would be less than half of what he should have saved since the war. The Negroes of the South handle more money than New England did one hundred years ago, and yet New England would be glad to place her barrels of gold and silver at nominal interest—so rich has she grown, although in the chilly winds of the Northeast.

The opportunities for the Southern Negro are as good for material gain as are enjoyed by any other people in this country. The census of 1890 shows two hundred and twenty-four occupations followed by the wage-earners of the United States. The Negroes are represented in every one of these occupations—grouped under five heads: Professional, Agriculture, trade and transportation, manufactures and personal service. The Southern Negro, while not in all of them, occupies in the South the vantage ground in those that bring the most independence in living. We must not forget that agriculture is what we might call the staple industry of the South.

I am indebted to Hon. Judson W. Lyons, register of the United States Treasury, for the following statistics, showing the wonderful influence of Negro labor in the commercial industries of the world: More cotton is exported from the United States than any other article. In the last ten years, 30,000,000,000 pounds of cotton, valued at $225,000,000 have been exported. The United States produces more cotton than all the balance of the world. The cotton manufactories of Great Britain, Germany,

France, Belgium, and Italy depend upon our cotton exports. Ten years ago, $354,000,000 were invested in cotton manufactories, employing 221,585 operatives, who received for wages $67,489,000 per annum. The South produced from 1880 to 1890, 620,000,000 bushels of corn, 78,000,-000 bushels of wheat, and 97,000,000 bushels of oats. The Negro performed four-fifths of the labor of the South, as we have seen. Therefore, his share in the average annual production in the last ten years would be 6,988,000 bales of cotton, valued at $209,640,000. In the last ten years the Negro's part of the production of corn, wheat, oats and cotton was $431,320,000 per annum. The entire cotton acreage of the South would form an area of 40,000 square miles. Negro labor cultivates 32,000 square miles of this space.

Fifty-seven per cent of the Negro race are engaged in agricultural pursuits, and 31 per cent are engaged in personal service. Therefore, 88 per cent of the wage-earners of the race in the South are engaged in these two pursuits, or, in other words, 88 per cent of the wage-earners of the race have opportunity for profitable employment.

Where the masses of the Negroes are found and can get paying work, as they can in the South, there we must expect the greatest prosperity among Negroes. Our expectation is highly gratified in this case in the South. No doubt if the ninety-two per cent Negro population were to exchange places with the eight per cent, the opportunities now held out in the South would be transferred to the North. Our opportunities over those enjoyed by our Northern brethren are the creatures of accidents rather than of our meritorious invention.

The opportunities to win character and wealth afforded the Negroes of the South by agriculture and domestic service are probably better than are enjoyed by any other class of people in the world. The field is broad and ripe and the Negro must now see and seize these opportunities or they will pass from the race forever. No peasant population ever had more favorable environments. The Negro does not only do four-fifths of the agricultural labor of the South, but he has the opportunity to own four-fifths of the land he cultivates.. This opportunity is not enjoyed by any other peasant class in the world. As I see it, the greatest success for the Negro race in America lies in the farm. There he meets the least resistance and obtains the greatest sustenance. There color prejudice is almost unknown, while everywhere in the mechanic arts, prejudice is bitter, competition is sharp, and the chances for success are small. This is a matter which the Negro must seriously consider now, or weep over his procrastination. The drift to the cities to exchange the free, honest, healthful, plenteous conditions of farm life for the miserable slums, sin, and squalor of city life must be checked. Our boys and girls must be educated for the farm.

It would be hard to find a people better suited for domestic and personal service than the Negro. In all the elements which are necessary for personal and domestic service, the Negro cannot be excelled. He is not treacherous. He forms no plots and schemes to entrap his master. He resorts to no violent incendiary measures of avenging himself against his master, but he humbly and tamely submits to the conditions, ever looking for betterment through superhuman agencies. If the South would only look this matter squarely in the face, it would admit that it has the best service on earth, and would vote liberal appropriations for the development of Negro education of every character.

It may seem to persons not informed incredible, but it is no less a fact that where racial prejudice runs highest in the South and the demarcation between the races is most distinct along social lines, there the Negro is most prosperous, and, strange to say, advances most rapidly in material wealth. Self-help, self-dependence, faith in self, seem to spur to success as nothing else does. The drug store is the creature of Anglo-Saxon prejudice in denying Negroes accommodations at the soda-water fountains run by white men. In a score of channels the Negro is pushed on to success by Anglo-Saxon discrimination. What seems a curse is in reality a blessing to the race. Anglo-Saxon prejudice forces the Negro to take advantage of his great opportunity to get rich.

TOPIC XXII.

WHAT IS THE NEGRO TEACHER DOING IN THE MATTER OF UPLIFTING HIS RACE?

BY PROF. A. ST. GEORGE RICHARDSON.

An examination into the earliest records of history will reveal a fact that is not observant to the casual reader—that man, as an individual, has ever been groping in darkness, seeking hither and thither to find a ray of light that would safely guide him and lead him through the mystic vale of doubt and uncertainty—be a "light to his pathway, a lantern to his feet."

To this end he has lent all his energies and directed all his forces. Long and tedious have been the ways and the journeys, yet onward and upward has he continued to travel, through storm and tempest, amid trials and vexations, until finally, after many centuries of progressive endeavor and honorable achievements, he has reached the loftiest pinnacle of fame, and there, on its rugged summit, has inscribed in letters of gold the result of his many conquests in literature, science and art, in religion, philosophy and commerce.

We use the generic term man as embracing all the various descendants of the sons of Noah. For each race-variety has in its turn played its part in producing the high degree of civilization that it is now our heritage and privilege to enjoy. Each has been an important factor in the development of some element that is essentially its own.

In thus reviewing the early history of the world we also find that the peoples who sat in darkness were brought to the light only through the agency of the teachers of the times in which they lived. Who made Egypt renowned? Were they not her great teachers, whose pupils came from far and near to learn, as it were, the foundation steps of our great civilization? Who in China is better known to the world than the great teacher Confucius? Who gave to Greece her renown for philosophy and art? Was it not Aristotle and Plato? Mention Rome, and the names of Quintilian and Cicero are recalled to our minds as the foremost educators. The Israelites had their prophets to instruct them, until the Great Teacher came to earth to enlighten all mankind. What was best

Prof. Arthur Richardson.

PROF. ARTHUR ST. GEORGE RICHARDSON.

Far out in mid-Atlantic ocean about 700 miles east of New York lies the group of sunny isles known as the Bermudas. On one of these beautiful coral formations called St. Georges was born, July 5, 1863, the subject of this writing. Arthur was sent to Canada in 1878 to attend the public schools of St. Johns, N. B. Being an apt pupil he soon finished the curriculum of studies of the grammar schools and in 1880 entered the high school from which in three years' time he was graduated.

Not considering his education complete at this point, Arthur matriculated at the University of New Brunswick at Fredericton, in the fall of the same year, being the first and only colored young man to enter this institution of higher learning. As in the high school so now in college young Arthur distinguished himself among his classmates by winning a scholarship and at times leading his class in Greek. He was graduated from the university with honors in classics, June, 1886.

He was then elected principal of the Wilberforce Collegiate Institute at Chatham, Ont., where he served one year, increasing the attendance, and greatly improving the work of the school. The following year, 1887, he returned to his native home and visited his parents from whom he had been separated nine years. The next year after his return to Canada he was invited by Bishop W. J. Gaines to come to Georgia and assume the principalship of Morris Brown College in Atlanta. After much hesitancy, Mr. Richardson accepted the invitation and took charge of Morris Brown College when it was a school of small proportions and modest pretensions. Here Professor Richardson served ten successive years, each year adding something to the fame and increasing popularity of the school.

In 1898 he was offered the Presidency of Edward Waters College in Jacksonville, Fla., by Bishop W. J. Gaines, who felt that the educational work in Florida then needed just such a person as Professor Richardson had proven himself to be in Georgia. Resigning his position in Atlanta he came to Florida and at once set to work to restore Edward Waters College to the confidence of the people. In a year's time the school was again assuming the flourishing condition that it once had.

The great fire of Jacksonville, May 3, 1901, caused him to lose all his possessions in the destruction of the college buildings, nevertheless he has held on unflinchingly to the work and at great sacrifice and loss has kept the school together, and is now serving his fourth year at the head of this institution.

and noblest in the systems of the famous teachers before the advent of Christ was crystallized into the method adopted by the Son of Man. He came to elevate the whole man, to shed light into his whole being—his mind, his body, and his soul.

Many and various have been the devices of mortal man to imitate the plan of the Master; and yet, after centuries of earnest endeavor, we have but recently begun to recognize the fact that complete success in the education of man lies in the secret of training the whole man—mind, body and soul.

Passing over the long period of scholastic apathy in European history, we come to a more recent epoch of intellectual awakening in the founding of great universities and stately colleges. These several institutions, through the instructions given by their most eminent teachers, have of themselves made the respective places of their establishment famous in both hemispheres.

Between the periods of the Revolutionary and Civil Wars in America, educational interests seemed to be centered mainly in the cultivation of the intellect as the only part of man that required special training.

The abolition of slavery and the consequent endeavor to enlighten the freedmen gave rise to a new phase of educational activity. This new ideal was the training of the body and the soul along with that of the mind. This system naturally reduced the length of time usually devoted to mind culture in proportion as time was required for the training of the hand and the cultivation of the moral side of man.

Foremost among the early teachers to inaugurate this system were Mrs. Frances Ellen Watkins Harper, Mrs. Sarah J. Early, and Bishop John M. Brown. As a result of their efforts in this direction we have Wilberforce University, the first school by Negro teachers to follow the plan of the Great Teacher. Since the establishment of Wilberforce in the North, many similar institutions have been founded in order to give the "brother in black" an opportunity to show to the world what the Negro teacher is doing and can do towards uplifting his race.

It is a difficult matter to estimate the good that a true teacher can do, be he of whatever race-variety. But to calculate on the noble work of the majority of the self-sacrificing and virtuous Negro teachers is a task beyond the ability of man. Bishop Daniel A. Payne, the apostle of an educated ministry, is known throughout the country for the noble work he did in teaching the people at large as well as his immediate pupils both how to live and how to die. Almost every educated Negro preacher has at some period of his scholastic career served in the capacity of a teacher, and therefore, after his advent to the gospel, ministry has continued to instruct the people under the same principles of teaching.

To be a teacher in the strict sense of the word requires the possession of certain qualities of mind and soul, and the power to exercise these qualities in such a manner as to awaken in the mind of another thoughts similar to those of the person assuming to teach, and thereby causing the mental activity on the part of the learner to become knowledge and power. We, therefore, hold that the Negro teacher has acted along the method here described, and has thus been the means of enlightening the masses of the colored people that lay claim to any degree of education whatever. What the Negro teacher has accomplished has been done not from a selfish motive or a mercenary point of view, but primarily because he has endeavored to do his part toward elevating the race with which he is identified. If it is true that the salvation of the Negro lies in his being educated, then to the Negro teacher must be attributed the greater portion of his salvation.

Again, the majority of the Negro teachers are Christian men and women of high moral character, and as such are shining lights in the community in which they may be engaged in teaching. The good they thus do is not confined to the school or class-room, but permeates every sphere of society, ennobling and enriching the thoughts and minds of all with whom they may have dealings, both by their chaste conversation and by their upright and godly lives. The Negro teacher, therefore, wields an influence for good, not only by precept, but what is considered far better, also by example. Furthermore, the Negro teacher in the day school invariably becomes a teacher in the Sunday-school of the town where he happens to be living. And here again he exerts a power for good, confirming and strengthening the teachings of the past week.

Aside from his professional duties, the Negro teacher is often called upon to decide on matters of grave importance. In many cases he is the attorney for individuals who are unable to secure the services of a competent lawyer. In this capacity he often acts as justice of the peace, as well as a peacemaker, thereby allaying strife and contention. From early morn till late at night the Negro teacher is besieged by questions of every sort and kind, which he must satisfactorily answer to the benefit of the inquirer, be he farmer or blacksmith, preacher or vagrant. In fact, the Negro teacher in the rural districts answers the purposes of a bureau of information.

Such is the lot of the average Negro teacher. That there are exceptions need not here be stated. From what he has done on a small scale may be inferred what is being done on a larger basis of operation by the best and most renowned of the Negro teachers.

In nearly every Southern state of the Union may be found some one or two famous educators and teachers of Negro descent. Prof. Jno. R. Hawkins of North Carolina, Commissioner of Education of the A. M. E. Church, has established Kittrell College. Prof. J. C. Price gave us Livingston College in North Carolina. Prof. E. A. Johnson of Virginia has written a worthy history of the Negro race, now in use as a text-book in many public schools. In South Carolina we find results of the great work in science by Prof. J. W. Hoffman. Georgia is proud of Prof. R. R. Wright, President of the State Industrial College at Savannah, orator and historian; also Prof. W. H. Crogman, scholar and author. In Florida the names of Prof. T. de S. Tucker, Prof. T. V. Gibbs, and Prof. T. W. Talley stand high as eminent scholars and professional teachers. Alabama is rich in having the foremost men of the race as her great teachers— Prof. B. T. Washington, founder and principal of Tuskegee Institute, and Prof. W. H. Councill, President of the State Normal and Industrial College at Normal. And thus we might mention each state and her eminent Negro teachers; but it is not necessary; the above suffices our purpose. And yet we would not conclude without referring to the noble work of Prof. W. S. Scarborough, of Wilberforce, Ohio. He has gone a step beyond the ordinary and given us a Greek text-book that has been adopted in many schools. Moreover, his contributions to the leading magazines and periodicals are eagerly sought and read by the best scholars of the day, without reference to race.

With this accumulated force of intelligence, radiating its numerous beams of light in every section of the land, one need not seek far to find an answer to the query: "What is the Negro teacher doing in the matter of uplifting his race?"

As we endeavored to show in the beginning that it was through the instrumentality of their teachers that many countries acquired fame and gave to posterity a name honorable and glorious, so now the Negro teacher in his weak strength is laying the foundation for successive generations to build upon—a foundation more durable than stone or granite, more valuable than rubies or diamonds—the cultivation of the morals, the training of the hand, and the enlightenment of the mind. With an informed mind, a skillful hand, and an upright conduct, there is no reason why the Negro should not take his place upon the stage of action, play well his part in the drama of life, and meritoriously receive the plaudits of the gazing nations of the world.

SECOND PAPER.

WHAT IS THE NEGRO TEACHER DOING IN THE MATTER OF UPLIFTING HIS RACE?

BY PROF. E. L. BLACKSHEAR.

When the Negroes were set free the first aim of thousands was to learn to read and write. Gray-haired veterans of the plantations sat side by side in the day schools as well as in the night schools with the smallest pickaninnies. And all seemed eager to learn the mysterious arts of the schoolroom. The school-book, in the eyes of the unlettered slave, was a sort of fetich to which he attributed the power of the white man. The young slave could follow his master to the door of the schoolhouse, but thus far and no farther. The mysterious rites and ceremonies which went on within were forbidden him. Human nature has ever been curious to know that the knowledge of which is prohibited, and so the slave had a great curiosity to master the printed page and to be admitted to the privileges of the schoolroom. It was not surprising that the whole race tried to go to school, and it need not surprise us if, in the enthusiasm for book-learning, from which the race had been so strictly debarred, too much stress may have been placed on mere book learning and too much confidence placed in the formal processes of the schoolroom. But, better even this exaggerated enthusiasm than indifference to all education of the schoolroom. The race would soon learn that the blue-back Webster's Speller was not the magic wand that would turn all troubles and difficulties into success and prosperity; that the ability to spell B-a-Ba, k-e-r-ker, baker, would buy no bread of the baker; while the power to read, "Do we go up by it!" with painful praiseworthy effort, would help the ex-slave but little as he strove to "go up by" the dangers ahead of him.

But they went to school, all of them at first, or all that could possibly

Prof. E. L. Blackshear.

PROF. E. L. BLACKSHEAR.

Prof. E. L. Blackshear was born in Montgomery, Ala., in 1862. He was educated in the negro public schools of Montgomery. So rapid had been his progress that he graduated from Tabor College at the age of eighteen.

Prof. Blackshear is now principal of Prairie View State Normal School and Industrial College of Texas.

The following is the testimony of Prof. Blackshear concerning his grandmother. These words give us a glimpse of the bright side of slave life, and of the ideal "mammy" of the ante-bellum Southern plantation home:

"My grandmother was a remarkable woman. She idolized my mother, the only child that slavery had allowed her to keep. When grandma was sold from Georgia to Alabama, the humanity of her Georgia owners caused them to sell mother and child to the same people.

"My grandmother, although ignorant, had a profound belief in education. But if she knew absolutely nothing of the world of letters, she had something as good, perhaps better—a warm, honest, loving heart and Christian principles. She had genuine hatred for dirt and disorder, a regard, amounting to a fearful reverence, for white people of 'quality,' and a great and ill-disguised contempt for common, shiftless, 'darkies,' and low-bred whites. She was the best type of the faithful and efficient slave. But it was as a cook that 'Grandma's' reputation was known in two States. To my youthful imagination she was a magician; things she cooked for the white folks seemed so good to me. I think now of the batter-cakes, the light rolls, the syllabub, the sally-lunn, the ship-ships and the wafers grandma made. The light-bread she made is made no more. It is a lost art, an art that died with grandma."

do so, either by day or by night. It is not recorded that the chickens of that time had rest, but it must be that they did, for verily, in the first mad rush of letters, even chickens must have been forgotten by a race whose predilection for them has furnished the point for many a joke, as well as the occasion for painful if not indignant regret on the part of those whose fowls may have been abstracted. And it is a hopeful sign for the future of the Negro that while his first wild enthusiasm for the school-house has been moderated, his real desire for educational improvement continues strong and steady. He will go to school—the public school—when he can, and the higher institutions for his race are all filled to their capacity and are expanding. Will not this thirst for knowledge on the part of a so lately savage race bear good fruit both for the Negro and for humanity?

But who were to teach these black fanatics, seeking initiation for the first time, in the long and gloomy history of their race, into the mysteries, elusinian, of a modern, and, to them, totally foreign cult? A faithful band of Christian missionary white women gave answer by coming in the face of an inevitable social ostracism to light the torch of thought in a region hitherto unblessed by a single ray of education's light. The first Negro schools were taught by these white ladies at Charleston, at Atlanta, at Montgomery, at New Orleans, at Austin, and at the other great centers of the South's Negro population. The success of the first labors of this devoted band led to the foundation of permanent institutions for the elementary and later for the normal and collegiate instruction of the Negro youth. At Nashville, at Atlanta, at Raleigh, at Memphis, and at New Orleans institutions were founded which have become great schools and have contributed beyond measure to the process of civilizing the Negro as a mass—a process confessedly still far from completion. Complicated and annoying as the race problem assuredly is and will be for years to come at the South, it would be far worse—much farther away from even a hopeful degree of solution—but for the work done by the missionary colleges.

The missionary schools, of which Fisk, Atlanta, Straight, Roger Williams and Central Tennessee may be taken as types, furnished the first Negro school teachers and the Negro owes to these schools, founded and maintained in the spirit of the purest Christian philanthropy, a debt he can never repay in either kind or equivalence. The nearest like payment he can make is to imitate the beautiful, pure, devoted, lives of the missionary teachers. Too much cannot be said in praise of their labors. Perhaps if only the missionary Christian teachers had come and the political missionaries had remained at home, all might have been better.

But the missionary schools could reach but few. How was the great mass of the colored population to be educated? This was the question, and it was a most serious one. But the answer came not from the federal government, as some expected—that source from which so many had looked to get the mythical "mule" and the legendary "forty acres"—it came from the South, from the wasted resources of the former master. History furnishes no precedent as it affords no parallel to the action of the ex-slaveholders—a dominant race—in entering at once—before any opportunity had been afforded for recuperation from the losses of the Civil War—on the expensive work of giving a public school system to their former slaves—now technically, at least, their political equals. And nothing can be gained by the Negro in refusing gratitude to the South for this most magnanimous act and policy. An instance of this unselfish policy of the South in its attitude toward Negro education is seen in the history of Texas, the most liberal as well as the most progressive of the Southern commonwealths. The Constitutional Convention of 1876, which of course was Democratic, framed the present state constitution of Texas, and in it absolutely equal provision is made for both the elementary and the higher education of the Negro youth of Texas. And it is to the credit of Texas as an enlightened state as well as fortunate for her Negro population, that in the distribution of the magnificent school fund of the state, no discrimination is made between the races.

The Negro public schools are doing a great work for the elevation of the colored people. In a silent, unobtrusive way, these schools are leavening the thought and life of the race. The status and progress of the Negro are too commonly gauged by the deeds of the loafing and criminal element. The honest, law-abiding Negro who has a home, is getting a little property, has a small bank account, and is educating his children to useful citizenship, attracts little or no attention. But a race that has in a generation since chattel slavery gotten property worth by reliable estimate upward of $400,000,000 has been doing something. All of such a race are not either lazy, vicious, or immoral. The public school is doing effective work for the Negroes of the South in awakening in them a desire for better ways of living and higher ideals of conduct. Much remains to be done but that already accomplished is an earnest of better work yet to be done.

The Negro public school teacher has been more than a mere school-keeper. No class of educators in any race has done more, all things considered. The colored teacher has been a herald of civilization to the youth of his people. His superior culture and character have acted as a powerful stimulus to the easily roused imagination of the colored youth, and the black boy feels, in the presence of the black "professah," to him the embodiment of learning, that he too can become "something." At first he does not know what that something is, but he determines to be "somebody" and to make a place and a standing for himself in the world. In this way the colored school teacher is leading his race "up from slavery;" that is from the slavery of ignorance and superstition, of intellectual and moral inertia, of aimlessness and shiftlessness, into the freedom of intelligence, of energy, ambition and industry. Lincoln removed the formal yoke of a legal bondage, but the colored teacher is helping his race to get free a second time from a bondage just as galling— the bondage of intellectual and moral blindness and of industrial independence. Booker T. Washington is such a teacher—a teacher, indeed, and the leader of a race. And what Mr. Washington, himself a product of the missionary schools, is doing in a large way as the teacher and leader of the entire Negro race in America, hundreds, yea, thousands, of colored teachers in city and village, in the malarial river bottoms and among the pine-clad hills, are doing in a local but no less effective, though less comprehensive way. These colored men and women, many of whom are people of genuine culture and character, are giving their lives to the upbuilding of a race. And it is for them a labor of love.

These teachers teach by example as well as by precept. Their homes are models in neatness and refinement that are readily imitated by the other colored people of the community. It is to the credit of the colored teacher that he is, with rare exceptions, a model in his moral conduct and home life, and sets a high standard for his race, which they invariably— some of them—seek to follow. The colored teacher, too, has always been conservative and has been the wise adviser of his people. Himself dependent on the sentiment of the best white people of the community, he has usually won the confidence and respect of the white people, and they in turn have given him their moral support in the work of improving the minds, morals, and habits of the Negro youth of the community. In this way it is throughout the entire South—the best white people of the community by maintaining public schools for the Negro youth and by co-operation with the colored teacher, and often by personal interest in the work of both teacher and pupil, are actually aiding most effectively if not really directing the educational development of the colored race.

It is also greatly to the credit of the colored teacher in the South that he has not gotten above his race or tried to leave them, but has remained at his post and in his place doing the duty Providence has assigned and content to leave results to God and the future.

THIRD PAPER.

WHAT IS THE NEGRO TEACHER DOING IN THE MATTER OF UPLIFTING HIS RACE?

BY T. W. TALLEY.

As soon as the clouds of the Civil War had cleared from our country and the Negro had become a free man, the question immediately presented itself as to how he could be made worthy of citizenship and capable of exercising the rights and privileges of free government.

Free government exists through intelligence and integrity in citizens. The whole system of slavery in which the Negro had been schooled was such as to leave him without either intelligence or integrity. It rather taught him that deception was a better way to recognition than decency; and that whatever supplied his wants, regardless of its nature, was the means to be used. As the Negro stepped forth from the darkness of bondage into the light of freedom, the eye of his mind accustomed to the blackest and lowest was not ready to exercise the function thus suddenly thrust upon it. It was blinded and needed treatment that it might be so reconstructed as to guide and lead aright in this new atmosphere to which it had suddenly gained admission. The Negro came from slavery in want of training, and training is requisite to citizenship.

A man, to be trained symmetrically, must be trained mentally, morally and physically. Although this symmetrical training is much a result of personal effort, the effort must be directed by an intelligent, interested teaching. It is to such teaching that the Negro school teacher has directed and is directing his efforts.

Prof. T. W. Talley

PROF. THOMAS WASHINGTON TALLEY.

Thomas Washington Talley is a native of Bedford County, Tenn. His boyhood was spent upon his father's farm where he imbibed a love for nature. Some of the experiments made by him, as a child, with some of the lower animals, have proven most valuable aids in answering scientific problems encountered in later years.

In 1883 he entered the preparatory department of Fisk University, and after three years of study was admitted to college.

He began teaching in the public schools of his native state at the age of twelve. By teaching during his summer vacations, and by obtaining state scholarships through competitive examinations, he secured the larger portion of the means necessary for his support in college. He graduated from the classical course of Fisk University in 1890, receiving the degree of A. B. From 1890 to 1891 he was a member of the Fisk University Jubilee Singers, who raised funds for the building of the Fisk Theological Seminary. In this company it was his duty aside from singing, to present the needs of the school. This he did with much eloquence and his appeals were always answered by liberal contributions.

In 1892 he received the degree A. M. from his alma mater for special work done in Natural Philosophy, Latin and German.

On October 1, 1896, he matriculated in the Graduate Department of Central Tennessee College (now Walden University), having spent the two preceding summers in resident work along the lines indicated by his courses of study in the institution. He selected courses leading to the degree of Doctor of Science.

He has been chiefly engaged in educational work and has held the following positions: Instructor in Mathematics and Music, Alcorn A. & M. College, Westside, Miss., two years; Professor of Natural Sciences, five years, and Vice-President two years in the State N. & I. College, Tallahassee, Fla. He at present occupies the chair of Natural Philosophy and General, Analytical and Industrial Chemistry in the Tuskegee Institute, Tuskegee, Ala.

He is a member of the American Ornithologists Union, the Michigan Ornithological Club, a Vice-President of the Florida Audubon Society, and a Fellow of the American Negro Academy. He is considered an authority in Biology and Chemistry.

The first schools established distinctively for Negroes in our country were supported and taught by philanthropic white people of the North. At the date of the founding of these schools there were practically no Negro teachers, but in these institutions, fostered by consecrated white men and women, Negro boys and girls began to receive training through which they developed into the first teachers of the race.

These schools, begun by philanthropy (although at first they did primary work) have developed into the Negro colleges, normal schools and industrial schools of the South. These schools of higher learning are still manned largely by white men and women. Thus the work of the Negro teacher is almost entirely limited to a few state colleges and to the public schools of the Southern cities and of the country districts. The especial point of excellence which characterizes the work of the Negro teacher is its interestedness. Whatever may be the sentiment in other sections, in the South—the real home of the Negro—every Negro's standing is gauged by the standing of the whole race in case of those who are most kindly disposed to him, while those who are illy disposed judge all by the lowest of the race. There is little or no recognition of individual merit except in so far as it meets the approval of his Southern white neighbor. Such being the case, the Negro teacher, realizing that their own elevation comes only through and in so far as the whole race is elevated, have a double stimulus for zealously doing their best work; first their love for the race which naturally springs up between those of the same blood and of the same descent, and second a selfish reason—their personal elevation, which only comes through the elevation of the whole race. Such interested teaching is not without its effect. Illiteracy is disappearing from day to day. A consultation of the latest census reports, and a contrasting of them with those previously taken, will show that the Negro has wiped out some of his illiteracy and is increasing in wealth, intelligence, etc.—yes, in all that which will finally force his recognition as a full-fledged American citizen without any "ifs," except that he be as any other man in possessions, in mind, and in character.

The Negro teachers are more and more studying the needs of their race and are shaping their work to meet the demands of the times. The Negro race formerly sang, and still sings, with much fervor of spirit: "You may have all this world; Give me Jesus." In the days of its ignorance, the Negro race observed this beautiful song in letter, but not in spirit. The Negro teachers have caught the spirit and are beginning to spread it among the ignorant masses. These teachers go into the Sunday schools and there teach the race to keep the spirit, "You may have all this world; Give me Jesus." They teach them that Christ is far above and is to be preferred to the whole world, but they also teach them that which is equally good, and that is, getting a hold on a portion of the goods of this world is a splendid preparation for getting a hold upon the things which lead up to heaven. In other words, the Negro teachers have become the great preachers of wealth getting, not because they would have the race carnally-minded, but because they know that no race of paupers can ever amount to anything or enjoy the full rights of citizens.

To the end of replenishing the empty treasury of the race the Negro teachers are encouraging their fellows to gain a skillful use of the hand. Many of them are enthusiastic to the extent that they would see every Negro school in the land teaching skill in the trades and in the tilling of soil. In this movement for the education of the hand the Negro teacher is meeting with encouragement on all sides. Such an education cannot fail to work great benefit for the race, and help to give it standing. Given an intelligent Negro mass, masters of the trades and of science of agriculture, there need be no fear for the Negro's future. The only mistake which it seems that the Negro teachers may possibly make at this time is, that having pictured in their minds the benefit of having a mass skilled in industry, and noting the present popularity of industrial training, they may lose sight of the fact that the skilled hand must be backed by and rest upon a mind trained to logical thinking. Industrial training does much indeed toward mental training, but by no means does it, nor can it, do all. There is quite a tendency at present aside from industrial training to limit the mental training of the race to the "3 r's," viz., reading, writing and arithmetic. The highest industrial attainment is not possible with such a limitation. The making, the repairing and the manipulation of machinery calls for a knowledge of natural philosophy and higher mathematics. The masterly tilling of the soil demands one learned in chemistry and botany—botany, which we know is not even a stranger to Latin. So we might go through every industry and point out that its perfection is conditioned on the highest mental training. Let the Negro teacher, while loving industrial training for his race, not learn to despise that which appears on the surface to be merely a mental gymnastic, but which, when examined more carefully, proves to be that only which furnishes a condition for the best and the highest even in that which he may most love.

Since social conditions in the South are such as to necessitate a system of separate schools for whites and Negroes, and since this necessitates the establishment of a large number of extra schools, it inevitably results in the shortening of school terms and the cutting down of the salaries of teachers. I have found some Negro country schools in Alabama paying the teachers from twelve to fifteen dollars per month, and the length of the school term was only four months. In these cases I did not find the teachers worrying over the small salary, but they were working to have the Negro patrons, from their own scanty purses, lengthen the school term. In not a few cases the Negro teachers observed were thus lengthening out the school term from one to two months every year.

The Negro teacher is also here and there founding institutions of higher learning. He is getting a hold on the churches, the state, benevolent societies, and individuals, and is causing them to contribute money and goods to educational centers which are to prove most potent levers in lifting the race to a higher level.

The fact that at present a large number of the states of the Union are basing suffrage upon an educational qualification enhances the value of the literary work to be done by the Negro teacher. In some states in the South the educational qualification is avowedly adopted by the whites to eliminate the Negro from the body politic. The Negro teachers are not sleeping over the interests of their race in this matter. They are working quietly, but earnestly. Most of them have the resolution which I heard expressed during the past summer by a Negro country school teacher, viz.: "I intend that all my pupils shall learn to read, write, and have the qualifications for voting if nothing more."

This, then, is what the Negro teacher is doing in the matter of uplifting his race: he is giving to it literary training, teaching it to skillfully use the hand, and encouraging it to accumulate property. He is lengthening school terms and founding institutions of learning. He is entering into the inner life of his people; and is implanting ideas and ideals there which will make them strong and respected by all the races of mankind.

FOURTH PAPER.

WHAT IS THE NEGRO TEACHER DOING IN THE MATTER OF UPLIFTING HIS RACE?

BY PROF. H. L. WALKER.

After a lapse of some thirty-eight years, or a little better than a generation, we are asking the question, "What is the Negro Teacher doing in the matter of uplifting his race?" In so brief a period of years it would seem to savor of arrogance to ask a question so seemingly fraught with significance, so inopportune and, too, about a people so recently freed from bondage that they have not yet had the time to grow a generation of teachers. It took England more than a generation to grow an Arnold at Rugby. It took France more than several generations to produce a Guizot, and Pestalozzi, whose reputation as a teacher widens with the universe, is the product of years of experimental accumulations of Swiss ingenuity. And yet it may be pardonable arrogance on our part to say that at this first milestone in our educational career we pause here long enough to take an inventory of what the Negro teacher has done and is still doing in the matter of uplifting his people. In the pioneering or experimental period of Negro education there were no Negro teachers, but it is safe to say that as early as 1875 a few Negroes, daring to rush in where angels would fear to tread, began the profession of school teaching. It is from this date that we may safely begin to reckon the services of the Negro teachers as a class. I make bold to lay down the proposition that wherever God has ordained intellect that intellect is capable of the highest development; for mental ability is a divine endowment. The intellect may be the possession of an Indian, a Mongolian, an Arab, a Negro, a Hindoo or a Caucasian. Textures may differ, but all mental organisms are the same in color, fiber, and mode of operation and development. It must then follow that the proper training of the intellect must produce the same results upon all races when properly applied. That training which has made the Mongolian, or the German, or the Caucasian race great and powerful will of necessity, under similar conditions, produce like results in the Negro race. Let us now see what the facts show. It is largely through the instrumentality of our schools that Negroes have been taught to place a higher and a proper valuation upon their citizenship, and the importance of the ballot when it is wielded for the maintenance and perpetuation of good government. As a class

Prof. H. L. Walker

PROF. H. L. WALKER, A. B.

Prof. H. L. Walker was born near the city of Augusta, Ga., in the year of 1859. His parents, Wesley and Adline Walker, were the property of slave owners to whom they rendered allegiance until 1864 and 1865, when Sherman took his triumphal march through Georgia and the Carolinas. At the fall of the Confederacy young Henry went with his parents to Wilmington, N. C., where they spent about a year, during which time young Henry for the first time saw the inside of a school, taught by those pioneering teachers from the North. At the close of this year the family left Wilmington and went to Augusta, Ga., which city has been the scene of our subject's boyhood and the basis of his literary career. The public schools of Augusta were completed by 1874 and upon the recommendation of all of his teachers young "Henry," as he was familiarly called, was matriculated at the Atlanta University, one of the most noted of Negro colleges in the South. In this institution he studied for eight years, coming out in 1882 with the class honor and the degree of A. B. His parents died during his early boyhood, even before he had entered the Atlanta University, so that in his efforts to complete his collegiate career he had to rely largely upon his own resources, and the very kind assistance of his foster parents, and other friends whose protege he was.

Prepared for his life work, he left school in June, 1882, and was immediately elected principal of the Mitchell Street Graded School, Atlanta, Ga., his examination papers being the best offered for this position. In the following month—July—he was also elected President of the Georgia State Teachers' Association for Colored Teachers, of which body more will be said later. As a student at College our subject was studious, popular with professors and students, and acquired that assiduity and strict adherence to business that has since characterized all his subsequent life. In the profession of teaching he continued to rise higher and higher each year, holding positions of trust and honor under each of the State's superintendents of education down to the present incumbent. For eighteen years he has held sway in the public school of the city of Augusta, during which time Mr. Walker has officered the Second Ward Grammar School, the famous Ware High School and at present the First Ward High School, which position he still fills with dignity and credit to himself and race. As Peabody expert, Mr. Walker, by appointment of the successive State superintendents of education, has occupied the lecture platform in all parts of the State, with the best lecturers, white and Colored, that money could command, and they have all cheerfully conceded his ripe ability to master and handle successfully such subjects as have been assigned him from year to year. As a practical school man and well-informed scholar, Mr. Walker is always at home. As a Peabody lecturer he has often been pronounced one of the best in the State. Every Summer his services are in demand in various parts of the State. For ten years Mr. Walker was the honored President of the Georgia State Teachers' Association, Colored, and no man has since filled that honored chair whose administration has in any way rivaled the success of Mr. Walker. During his ten years the association was built up as it has never been since. The intelligence of the State—white and Colored—came together in these annual meetings and made this gathering of educators and leaders the most representative body in the State.

Mr. Walker is easy of address and modest in all things, never contending for honors. Several years ago, at its annual exercises, his alma mater conferred upon him the degree of A. M. as a deserved tribute and recognition of the literary work he has accomplished. As a polished orator Mr. Walker has been heard with profit and delight in all parts of the State. Some of his addresses before the State Teachers' Association are considered real gems of literature.

of citizens Negroes are peaceable and law-abiding, and must not be reck-
oned with the migratory hordes of anarchists, nihilists, and the wreckers
of law and order that infest our Eastern·and Western shores. In our
schools, too, Negroes have learned that it is theirs to petition respectfully for the enjoyment of their rights, and the redress of grievances so
often unjustly imposed upon them. In the last two decades the influence
of the schools, colleges and industrial institutions and seminaries of all
kinds has wrought wonderful changes in the home life of the Negro race.
Purer homes now abound; intemperance is giving way to sobriety and
economy; love and order have driven out hate and confusion; the golden
rule and the Bible are taken as the measurement of conduct; and, where-
ever Negro communities are found, cozy little cottages, and often palatial
homes with thoughtful and convenient appointments, have taken the
place of the very many little one-room huts in which all the whole range
of domestic life was wont to be performed. In these new homes a better
and more intelligent class of children is being reared to fit in the scheme
of our advancing civilization. These are very hopeful signs of a better
generation and a brighter day for the American Negro.

Our Negro teachers and leaders have instilled into the race a desire
for the accumulation of property and wealth, and the keeping of bank
accounts. "Put money in thy purse," "Put money in thy purse." This
advice from Shakespeare is ripening in the minds of all thoughtful Negroes, and the results are being universally manifested. In the United
States the valuation of Negro property runs far into the millions. In the
state of Georgia alone Negroes are paying taxes on $15,629,811 worth of
property; of this amount $1,000,000 represents the increase of a single
year—1900 to 1901.

In the domain of literature and the varied professions the education
of the Negro has furnished us as lawyers, Hon. D. Augustus Straker,
Detroit, Michigan; Hon. R. B. Elliott, late of Columbia, South Carolina;
Hon. Jno. R. Lynch, Washington, D. C., paymaster United States Army;
Hon. J. W. Lyons, Augusta, Georgia, register Treasury, Washington, D.
C.; Hon. H. M. Porter, Augusta, Georgia, lawyer at the bar.

As statesmen Negro education has produced Hon. Frederick Douglass,
"The old man eloquent," late of Washington, D. C.; Hon. B. C. Bruce,
ex-registrar Treasury, late of Washington, D. C.; Hon. Geo. W. Murray,
ex-member Congress, Columbia, D. C.; Hon. Geo. H. White, ex-member
Congress, North Carolina.

As poets, Mrs. Frances E. N. Harper and Paul Lawrence Dunbar are samples of a splendid class.

As musicians it might suffice to say that Blind Tom, Black Patti and Madam Selika are only samples of a large class.

Negro education has furnished us pulpits better filled with intelligent men, devout and pious; and with modern churches that are in harmony with the Christian demands of the age. In the Ecumenical Conference recently held in London, the Negro clergy represented there were from all parts of the civilized world, and the high tribute paid to their ability and ecclesiastical character was the comment of all the English papers. Our bishops and eminent pulpit divines are largely young men, the product of our Negro schools. Dr. C. T. Walker, now of the Mt. Olivet Baptist Church, New York, and the foremost pulpit orator in all the Baptist ranks, perhaps, is a native of Georgia soil, and a product of our Georgia schools. But I must not prolong this account with a long list of bishops, D. D's., LL. D's., M. D's., diplomats, artists, painters, mechanics, inventors, and successful business men, who are the product of Negro education, but before closing this humble effort it is but proper that we should make mention of some of the men who are universally regarded as masters in the profession of teaching, and who in themselves are great benefactors of the Negro race. The following educators have wrought much in the matter of elevating their race in all the essentials of right-living. The most conspicuous figure just now in the firmament of Negro educators is President Booker T. Washington, who has at his command both the hand and the heart of the American people. The far-reaching influences of his work at Tuskegee, Alabama, where, perhaps, more than 1,300 Negro youths are taught all the useful and honorable methods of labor, are too well understood to merit further comment here. President J. H. Lewis, president of Wilberforce University, Ohio, has and is still doing a work that will tell on ages and tell for God in the matter of developing Negro ability along the lines of higher intellectual manhood. Prof. R. R. Wright, president of the State Industrial College, Savannah, Georgia, is a pioneer in the work of uplifting the Negro youth, and his excellent work recently begun at the state college is already teeming with fruit. Miss Lucy C. Laney is a woman of rare and well-developed intellectual attainments. The Haines Normal and Industrial School, with all of its influence for good, will ever be an imperishable monument to her memory. Her reputation as a woman of ability and culture is universal. Prof. W. H. Council, of Alabama, is hardly second to President B. T. Washington in his noble work in Alabama of uplifting Negro youth.

In professors, W. S. Scarborough, who holds the chair of Latin and Greek in Wilberforce University, Ohio; Prof. W. H. Crogman, chair of Latin and Greek, Clark University, Atlanta, Georgia; Prof. Kelly Miller, chair of mathematics, Howard University, Washington, D. C.; Prof. J. W. Gilbert, chair of Latin and Greek, Paine College, Augusta, Georgia; and Prof. W. E. B. DuBois, chair of science and economics, Atlanta University, Atlanta, Georgia, we have the ripest examples of high-class scholarship. These men, steeped in the love and sciences of all ages and people, have won respect and recognition in all the institutions, and among all educators of world-wide reputation, both European and American. They are only samples of a large class of educated Negroes who have given a very high literary tone to Negro intelligence. In an account like this, which necessarily must be brief, it must not be expected that we could elaborate into details about any one of the features above mentioned. In mentioning them thus briefly it is only our purpose to call attention to the great work now being accomplished by the Negro teachers.

In closing these brief lines it might be well to consider several charges made against the educated Negro. It is charged that education teaches Negroes how to commit crime, etc. Because some educated Negroes commit crime and do wrong that is no more of an argument against the education of the Negro race than it would be an argument against the education of the Caucasian race, because some educated white men commit crime and do wrong. If a man has indigestion from eating the wrong kind of food that ought not to be taken as an argument against eating. Educated Negroes as a class are among our best American citizens.

Again, there are still some "back numbers" belonging to the old school of thought who still charge a lack of ability on the part of Negro scholars to absorb and assimilate the same amount of intelligence that the Caucasian race does.

In our humble school career in the state of Georgia we have sat on the same seat with the boys and girls of the Caucasian race, and, often, in the recitation room, under the same professor in the higher classics and sciences, we have shared the same book with them, and yet at the time of reckoning term standing we have seen those white professors give the members of these mixed classes their class rating in their various subjects, and the average percentage of Caucasian and Negro pupils in all these subjects would be a matter of significant comment.

In many instances like these, both in the North and South, the ability of our Negro scholars is so forcibly demonstrated; and what the Negro teachers may yet do for their race and for civilization will be left as a rich inheritance for the enjoyment of an advancing civilization. Of all teachers it may be said that he who shapes a soul and fits it for an eternal habitation in the blissful Beyond has erected for himself a monument that eclipses in grandeur and architectural beauty all the conceptions of a Solomon, though Solomon was the wisest of men.

Dr. D. W. Onley

DR. D. WATSON ONLEY.

Dr. D. Watson Onley, the eldest child of John E. and Mary J. R. Onley (nee Wheele), was born in Newark, N. J. When but two years old his parents moved to Brooklyn, N. Y. He was early taught to read and write by his mother, afterward he was sent to the Raymond Street public school, Prof. Chas. A. Dorsey, principal. Here he showed a capable mind, by his easy mastery of all the subjects assigned him, and by his standing among his fellows.

At the age of thirteen, by force of circumstances, his progress in school was checked, his parents having changed residence, going to Florida, transferred him to entirely new scenes, environments and conditions. After attending school in Jacksonville, Fla., for three years, he entered the college preparatory course of Atlanta University.

In 1876, returning North, he entered and took a collegiate course in Lincoln University, after which he took two years' technical course in Boston, Mass.

In 1880 he married an accomplished young lady of one of the first families of Charleston, S. C., Miss Ella L. Drayton. Two charming and accomplished daughters of this happy union are Charlotte E. and Mary M., the elder one a graduate of the Normal school at Washington, D. C., and a teacher in its public school. The younger daughter is at present a pupil in Normal School.

In 1885 he returned to Jacksonville, Fla., began business as architect and builder. After three years of prosperous business, he launched upon the world the first steam saw and planing mill, owned and operated entirely by colored men to manufacture lumber in all its forms for house building. The plant grew rapidly, increasing in facilities and continued prosperous until by the hand of an incendiary it was swept by fire. The State Normal and Industrial College of the State needing a practical and efficient man to take charge of their technical department, solicited his services, where he taught all branches of architectural and mechanical drawing, manual training, uses and care of wood-working machinery and steam engine.

Not being thoroughly satisfied with his surrounding conditions, he struck out for a new line of work, that of dentistry, which, after three years of hard study, struggle and sacrifice, with the cares and responsibilities of a family upon him all the while, he finished at Howard University, dental department, and immediately opened an office in Washington, D. C., where he enjoys a lucrative practice. His life has been a busy one, and his success only represents what many have accomplished who have on hand a good stock of push.

TOPIC XXIII.

IS THE NEGRO NEWSPAPER AN IMPORTANT FACTOR IN THE ELEVATION OF THE NEGRO?

BY DR. D. W. ONLEY.

In answer to this question I would say that the press next to the school has done more for the intellectual advancement, hence, elevation, of the Negro, than anything else. When I say press, I mean specifically the Negro press, which is an integral part of the American press of the country. It is his positive mouthpiece, effective when other audiences are denied him. Before Negro newspapers, the Negro had nothing to set forth his claims and true status. The race consequently speaks through the press to plead its cause.

Reviewing the history and growth of the Negro press of this country since it was launched by John B. Russwurm in New York City, March 30, 1827, to the present, comparing style of form, character of matter, increase of circulation, widespread and universal interest, the great host of contemporaries that have joined in making a vast throng of channels through which we can advocate our cause without fear of having it misrepresented or smoothed over, but bringing forth our opinions to truly enlighten the world. The general support given speaks volumes for the good it has done in elevating the Negro.

In conducting the Negro newspaper of to-day as compared with fifteen years ago there is a marked change. The success then in maintaining and increasing the circulation depended largely in appealing to the vanities of the subscribers in parading their name in print, calling attention to many things of no consequence to the public, less to themselves; but to-day in a very large degree that is changed; it has become distasteful, which is a very healthful sign along the lines of improvement of taste.

While it is true the majority of Negroes care little but for local news, doings of their own race, care but little for the news of the great wide world, it must be conceded a step far in the right direction if they can be interested at all. The Negro press, like all others, had to begin at the bottom and grow, not patterned particularly after any other paper, but fashioned to suit the tastes, conditions and interests of its customers. It is the privilege of the editor, not only to shape public opinion, pointing out the policy that alone will conserve to our best and lasting interest, but to develop the tastes, and so elevate the race which he serves. Through the press the editor sees that the interests, as far as our freedom and rights are concerned, are in no wise abridged, circumscribed or destroyed. In a large measure this has been one of the great benefits to the race; through the medium of the press we have been awakened to our condition, and our rights, and we jealously guard and clamor for their enjoyment and recognition. Although dark clouds of prejudice and lawlessness obscure our pathway, yet we are surely though slowly moving on in the pathway already blazed before us.

In the hands of the Negro, the press has been an educator to the whites as well as to the Negro, reflecting his manhood and capacity; this, too, has elevated the Negro's appreciation of manhood and appreciable standing among men.

Before Negro newspapers we were unknown in history, art and science. Like the Negro exhibits at all the great fairs, they have served to open the eyes of the blind, and to remove an ignorant prejudice which was against us.

To-day we find the leading journals of this country clipping and editorially commenting upon topics discussed and articles appearing originally in Negro newspapers, and more than this, find the Negro newspapers for sale on the principal stands where newspapers are to be had, indicating the demand. In this city it would be hard not to find the "Colored American" and "Washington Bee" at the newsdealer's. "Yes, we keep them," I have heard to the query about the above papers; "they are good sellers." Now what is true in this city is no doubt true in other places where the local papers have secured recognition from their standing and worth.

The Negro newspaper has taken such a stand that its columns are read by white patrons, many of whom take pride and interest in noting the advancement of their brother in black.

Many newspapers published by whites have taken advantage of this condition, and the Negro's interest in the press, and have set aside columns devoted to his individual interest; have procured competent Negro reporters to gather all facts and doings of the race of special interest to it, and are published daily.

Walter W. Wallace

WALTER N. WALLACE.

Walter N. Wallace, the organizer of the Colored Co-operative Publishing Company, of Boston, Mass., publishers of the "Colored American Magazine" and many other race publications, was born at Boydton, Mecklenburg County, Va., in 1874.

His mother was Nannie J. Ellerson, who has the distinction of being one of the first graduates of the Hampton Normal School. Mr. Wallace is the oldest grandchild of that institution. His father Merritt Wallace was also a student of Hampton, and after leaving that school he settled in Boydton, in educational work, where he became one of the most prominent and energetic citizens of his community. He was at one time Deputy Treasurer and Commissioner of Revenue for the county.

At nine years of age Mr. W. Wallace was sent to school in Richmond, where he completed the grammar course, then spending two years preliminary training at the High, before entering the State College (Virginia Normal and Collegiate Institution, at Petersburg), where he spent another two years. While at this college he was prominent in athletics and a member of the institute band.

Later, determining upon the study of medicine, he entered the Leonard Medical College, where he spent two years in theory, then turning his face northwards he came to Boston in 1896, where he secured a position as prescription clerk in a prominent drug store, there becoming more practically acquainted with medicines.

In May, 1901, he launched his pet scheme, the "Colored American Magazine," and under his editorial care there is now no question of its future, as it has passed far beyond the experimental stage, and is now an assurity.

The confidence which has been displayed by him and his associates in the belief "that a man is what he makes himself," is wonderful, for they have, through strenuous effort, brought the magazine up to an actual circulation of over twenty thousand copies per month, with a steady increase each month, besides publishing many Race books, which are the equal of any in merit and mechanical makeup.

Personally, Mr. Wallace is of a kind and modest disposition and hardly realizes that he has accomplished within such a short while a thorough new departure in Negro journalism. If ever persuaded to forget for a moment, and be drawn from his business cares, you will find him a pleasant entertainer, both in music and conversation, for beneath his seeming austere countenance there lies an urbane streak of humor, piquant with wit and pleasant cynicisms, much to be enjoyed.

This has increased the circulation by thousands of new subscribers who eagerly seek to know just what is going on among them. The causes of non-support of the Negro press is no argument that the press has not been elevating, nor any argument against its possibilities. This is largely a condition due to poverty, illiteracy and inferiority of paper, but time will bring about a change. In the hands of the Negro the press has been a success. Failure in management and poor financial profit have been to one and all engaged in the pursuit, yet the net result shows success, not failure; and its success demonstrates the possibilities of the race, notwithstanding the lack of encouragement.

·

SECOND PAPER.

IS THE NEGRO NEWSPAPER AN IMPORTANT FACTOR IN THE ELEVATION OF THE NEGRO?

BY WALTER N. WALLACE.

In its entirety, yes. The power of the press is indisputable. To the Negro youth of the land it should be put, as a beneficent educator, next to our schools. In its pages they should be able to read the good being accomplished by our prominent race-men in this glorious fight now on; this will cultivate a desire to emulate them. They will read of the bad being daily done and will learn to abhor such dastardly actions. With such a mission to perform our newspapers should contain the essence of truth and good and sensible instructions; for its power of assimilating bad influences is equal to the good which would accrue.

The Negro journal is an important factor, because it is a source through which the younger generation should and must become acquainted with the good accomplished by members of the race, with the possible exception of a favored few whom the ordinary press seems to think is all that is worth speaking of. Important because the rank and file is utterly ignored and positively unnoticed by the American white press (except as an example of the demonstrative inability to be an intelligent and thrifty citizen), and from which they pick from day to day the lowest as a type of Negro capabilities.

In order to fully explain the position taken in this matter we will be compelled to deviate from the main question.

To rightly diagnose the cause, for the seemingly apathetic manner in which the race appreciates its journals we must place the blame upon the right parties.

A few hundred dollars, a set of type and a press do not make a newspaper. A man with an education does not always make an editor. Many of our editors grow discouraged over their failure to arouse a support to their journals, blaming the race for non-appreciation, when the fault lies with themselves. Do they give their readers news? If a local sheet, they deal in stale generalities. If a general sheet, they confine themselves to locals of no general interest.

Let our journals arise, procure competent help, give the news, regardless of class, as the newspaper is for the masses. Make a business of the paper, run it on strict business plan, have good printing, be careful with proofs, avoid all mistakes as nearly as possible; study their patrons' tastes and cater to them, for it is not dealing fairly to require the masses to purchase for race pride when they should receive the worth of their money.

Petty animosities should not fill their pages with vituperation, which is shocking to refined sensibilities; neither should the reading public be forced to search for original matter with a microscope. He should ever be on the alert to champion the Negro's cause and never wholly sink his originality within the narrow confines of party bounds. Stand up for truth, and censure wherein, in his wide judgment, he feels it necessary so to do. Never let his paper travel in a rut, plenty of room for expenditure of gray matter.

We have many Negro journals which should be a source of pride to the race at large, others, we are sorry to say, do not deserve support and should make room for those which do.

A press association should be formed and the happenings sent from one to the other and used in brief by out-of-town journals and be fully detailed by local journals. More unity is needed and is a thing to be encouraged and maintained. Our journals depend too much upon chance MSS. than upon active reporters for their news.

Much could be said of the many sacrifices and labors of many of our editors, but we believe that the most good can be accomplished by fewer and better newspapers, than with "quantity without quality."

In our article we place great stress upon truth; we believe the goal for which all the Negro journals are laboring is to find "the means for the best good of the race," and why waste energy in useless toil?

Richard W. Thompson

RICHARD W. THOMPSON.

Richard W. Thompson stands in the front rank of those who are making history for the Negro race in this century. A native of Kentucky, he has spent most of his life in Indiana and was educated in the common and high schools of Indianapolis. His career of thirty-five years is quite an interesting one, abounding in well-directed efforts that have done much to give character and dignity to the Afro-American youth of the land. At an early age he evinced a remarkable aptitude for public affairs, and at school showed proficiency of the highest order in such studies as political economy, civil government, history, literature. He was especially happy in the art of English composition, his papers on current problems attracting wide attention in his home community. Losing his father when very young, he was largely dependent upon his own exertions for a livelihood and throughout his school days worked at a variety of pursuits.

In 1879 he became associated with Messrs Bagby & Co., in the publication of *The Indianapolis Leader*, the first journalistic venture launched in the Hoosier State, and later on mastered the trade of printing. Taking as naturally to newspaper work as "a duck to water," he made himself an indispensable quantity on the *Leader* staff and at seventeen, was city editor. At the same time in connection with his school duties, he kept books for Dr. F. M. Ferree, secretary of the Marion County Board of Health. When *The Indianapolis World* was launched in 1883, Mr. Thompson took charge of the city department and at different times during the palmy days of that sheet, held nearly every position on it from work at the case to foreman of the mechanical department and managing editor. He was the first managing editor of *The Indianapolis Freeman*, in which position he was a marked success. Later, as editor of the *Washington Colored American*, he won national fame as an accomplished journalist, a graceful, versatile and forcible writer and a clear and courageous thinker upon all questions that affect the Negro's social, political and industrial development. He leads rather than follows popular sentiment, and at no time while the editorial tripod was in his hands did he take a stand upon any issue that failed to meet the hearty endorsement of the race and which was not accepted as the expression of the best thought and principle of our people. In argument his style is logical and conservative. As a spicy paragrapher, originator of attractive news features, and as a keen observer of popular tastes, he has few equals and no superiors in the army of Afro-American journalists. He has done special work for prominent papers of both races, and furnished much "copy" for private individuals, always giving complete satisfaction.

Mr. Thompson has been fortunate in the matter of official recognition. At the age of fifteen he served as page in the Indiana Legislature, being the first colored boy so appointed. After attaining his majority he became a clerk in the Marion County Auditor's office, and in 1888 he led a class of seventy-five in a civil service examination, earning an appointment as letter carrier. He came to Washington in 1894 and was appointed clerk in the counting division of the Government Printing Office, enjoying the distinction of being the first colored man to be assigned to a clerical position in that department. Mr. Thompson is now connected with the United States Census Bureau and is regarded as a faithful and efficient assistant.

Busy as Mr. Thompson must necessarily be, he has time to aid in promoting race movements and organizations, being an active spirit in the National Afro-American Council, the Pen and Pencil Club, and St. Luke's P. E. Church. He is now serving his third term as President of the Second Baptist Lyceum, a cosmopolitan debating forum that has won a national reputation.

THIRD PAPER.

IS THE NEGRO NEWSPAPER AN IMPORTANT FACTOR IN THE ELEVATION OF THE NEGRO?

BY RICHARD W. THOMPSON.

The question is both pertinent and timely. In the past two decades the necessity for the preacher, the teacher, the lawyer, and the doctor has not been open to dispute. Every father and mother, no matter what their social standing or their worldly means, have striven honestly, faithfully and persistently to enroll their favorite boy in the ranks of one or the other of these callings, as if they were the only open highways toward distinction, or the goal denominated "success."

In contemplating the professions which make for racial grandeur, racial opportunities, and protection from assault, many of us forget the importance of the Negro *press* as a factor in the elevation of the masses. It is not too much to say, in this connection, that of the primary levers to which the race must look for support, none contribute more toward endurance, permanency, and virility than the press. We have the pulpit, the schoolhouse, the field of politics, and the arena of business. Each has its bearing in the development of a larger life and a more perfect manhood for the Afro-American; but, conceding all due respect to the noble men and women who stand in the vanguard of each of these missions, no one of them is more potent or far reaching in its effect than the press. From the pulpit comes the precepts that direct moral and religious thought; the schoolhouse stands for a broader intellectual culture; the field of politics gives us our practical experience in the science of government, affording us an opportunity for actual participation in the shaping of legislation and in giving vitality to public policies. The press, however, occupies a most unique position with reference to all of them. It is the fulcrum upon which all these activities must depend for useful service. The press is the concentrated voice of the masses; the mouthpiece of the age; the universal censor—directed by popular opinion—from whose verdict there is no appeal. The press is the medium through which the great work of the church is disseminated over land and sea, and gives to the world the sweetening influence that the spoken word offers only to a single parish. It magnifies the labors of educational leaders and is itself an indispensable adjunct to the growth of intelligence. In the political field the press has long been recognized as an institution more powerful than any individual, and from the post of messenger or handmaiden of the people—a mere pur-veyor of current happenings—it has come to be the master mind in the economy of nations. To the business world it is a "guide, counselor and friend," and correctly analyzes the ingredients that bring material prosperity to the civic organization, of which all of us are a part. That distinguished autocrat of autocrats, Napoleon, once exclaimed, with a bitterness born of impending destruction: "Hostile newspapers are more to be feared than bayonets." And why not? It holds in its grasp the power of life and death, success and failure, happiness and misery.

These facts amply justify the assertion that the Negro newspaper is an all-important factor in the elevation of the race. Caucasian journals, while general in their news features, too often lack breadth in their opinion department, when the race question is a burning issue, just as religious denominations, the trades and political parties require "class" papers for the exploitation of their particular lines of thought, the Negro has found that only through his own "class organ" can he obtain a sturdy defense of his character, the record of his laudable achievements, and the advocacy of his rights as a man and a citizen. So the Negro journal came, and it is here to stay. The Negro journal had its origin in the direst necessity, and that necessity was never more apparent than at the opening of the twentieth century when the Declaration of Independence seems not broad enough to include the colored American, when the Con-stitution of the United States is perverted from the sacred intent of its framers and the spirit of disfranchisement is rampant throughout the land.

This demand for a Negro journal was first met between 1827 and 1834 by unpretentious sheets in and about New York City. But it was not until 1847 that race journalism became a positive factor, when that intrepid spirit, Frederick Douglass, launched "The North Star." This great man built up a circulation upon two continents and wielded an influence not exceeded by any subsequent race venture. That paper blazed a wide path, and in its path followed enterprise after enterprise, developing the sentiment for liberty and keeping in touch with the newer requirements of the hour. No reliable census of the many race journals has been kept. They have sprung from every state and section, but their span of life in most cases has been so brief and sporadic that only rough estimates have been attempted. To-day, perhaps, three hundred are in existence, a few taking high rank in literary quality—others struggling desperately for maintenance. The majority are printed at a positive loss, as regards dollars and cents. It is doubtful if any of the survivors are supported exclusively from revenues derived from subscriptions and advertising. It is a stinging indictment of our much-lauded "race pride" that the greater proportion of our Negro journalists are compelled to depend for a living upon teaching, preaching, law, medicine, office-holding, or upon some outside business investment. In character and make-up, these papers are as widely varied as the localities and environments from which they spring. Many are crude specimens of the "art preservative," dealing heavily in "boiler plate"—to use a professional term— and very lightly in original matter. A few have taken steps out of the beaten path and are giving striking evidence of what the resourceful and energetic Negro journalist could do under circumstances more encouraging. Our editors are, for the most part, men of strong personality, with standing and influence in their respective "bailiwicks." Without notable exception they speak for manhood, for race elevation, and for material development in every avenue of industry.

How many of us have paused and candidly considered just what Negro journalism is doing for the uplift of the masses? Notwithstanding the hard fact that the editorial work of many writers is done late at night, after protracted hours of labor in other fields; and notwithstanding that where a journalist is able to give his entire time to the business, he is often sole solicitor, clerk, compositor, pressman, collector, office boy, and editorial staff combined—despite all these disadvantages, the beneficent effect of the Negro press is felt all over the land. The dozens of able men and women who are engaged in this noble work, most of them doing so at a tremendous sacrifice, are true patriots, bearing burdens from which the timid shrink, leading cheerily where none but the brave dare follow, contending with malicious opposers, every inch of ground, this sturdy band struggles on year after year, hoping patiently for the "joy that cometh in the morning." Through their efforts Negro writers have been given a fair hearing, and, while the Caucasian journal is giving space to the police court episodes of our lower orders, the alert Negro sentinel finds in the church, the schoolroom, the inventor's studio, the author's desk, and in honorable political or social station, a most fertile field for his operations. Negro newspapers have aroused in us the commercial and industrial spirit, and are giving employment to hundreds of young colored men and women as bookkeepers, stenographers and canvassers. They are lending practical aid in solving the race's labor problem by yearly instructing and providing employment to printers, book-binders, pressmen and other artisans. They are building up a market for Negro labor, and neutralizing to a great extent the baleful influence of the trades unions' hostility. The Negro editor has increased the self-respect of the race by collating and publishing the creditable achievements of our people, furnishing a periodical compendium of history and placing the Negro in his most favorable light before the critics of the world. The truly representative Negro journal reflects the sober judgment of the race upon topics of general interest. It largely fixes our status as thinkers and philosophers of the times. The rights of no people can be ruthlessly invaded whose press is fearless, pure, upright, and patriotic. No people can forever be denounced as ignorant, vicious, and shiftless who support a press that is intelligent, moral, and thrifty.

Let it be remembered here, however, that the picture has its somber tints. Negro journalism, speaking generally, is not a paying investment. The fault does not lie wholly with either the public or the publisher. As a mass we are not a reading people and the bulk of us neither know nor appreciate the value of the work that the race paper is doing. Some of us take and pay for Caucasian journals for their news features—which is eminently fitting and proper—but the Negro journal should not be made to suffer in the unequal competition, for the latter fills a want which the former cannot or does not reach. One dollar to the race paper is often worth as much as ten to the wealthy corporation behind our great metropolitan dailies. It is not alone our illiterates who fail to support our journals. The educated classes are not as loyal to the cause as their means, learning, political interest and race pride suggest that they should be. True, it frequently happens that our papers fall into the hands of characterless adventurers who are "anything for a dollar," and it is felt that the best method of rebuking their self-constituted and erratic leadership is to treat them with silent contempt. To this no thinker can offer a reasonable objection. A journal that does not represent the highest impulses of a community does not deserve support. The personal organ, the scandalmonging sheet, the political and social blackmailer, the confidence-destroying campaign dodger, and the subsidized traitor to racial manhood are all under a ban, and should have no place in the homes of self-respecting Negroes. In this category should also be classed the colorless journal, that smirks in the recesses of cowardice. We should be faithful, however, to those that are honest and straight-forward. We should strengthen their arms by our moral and financial resources. Booker T. Washington aptly points out how difficult it is for a needy man to resist the temptation of the bribe-giver, and tells pathetic-ally of the uphill work of making a Christian out of a hungry mortal. Support the right kind of editors and the result will be a press that is progressive, healthful, and fearless—an institution of which all may justly be proud.

Is the ideal race journal attainable? I say, YES—when the two ele-ments necessary to the transaction—the public and the publisher—are able to meet on a common ground, in the spirit of co-operation and fair dealing. The chasm between the journalist and his rightful constituency must be bridged by mutual confidence and mutual sympathy, or neither can reap the great benefits that lie in concentration of forces.

The ideal journal is that one which places racial weal above private gain—which exalts patriotism above pelf. It is controlled by men big enough and broad enough to eschew petty personalities and to avoid cheap sensationalism. It is piloted by men who breathe the atmosphere of freedom, whose inspiration is not drawn from the committee rooms of political parties, and whose course is not dictated by scheming poli-ticians. It is the antithesis of sycophancy. The ideal journal is backed up by men who are far-sighted enough to perceive that success through trickery is short lived, and that character is the only foundation upon which an enduring structure can be built. It is conducted by men who know by experience that genuine worth will ultimately be appreciated, and that refined taste, sound judgment, and a saving sense of proportion will produce a newspaper that may stand as a model to posterity.

Journals of this type, sincere, earnest, and consistent—and in the future their names will be legion—are without question the key-stone in the arch of those forces which make for the permanent elevation of the Negro people. Such journals are prime factors in the race problem.

TOPIC XXIV.

ARE OTHER THAN BAPTIST AND METHODIST CHURCHES ADAPTED TO THE PRESENT NEGRO?

BY REV. GEORGE F. BRAGG, JR.,

At first the asking of this question is a most natural one, seeing that the great body of Negroes are attached to either one of the above churches, and it would seem at a first glance that these religious organizations are pre-eminently suited to the Negro race: But, we hope to show that not only are other churches adapted to the "present Negro," but one of these other churches meets the Negro's need better than either one of those above mentioned. Of course it is hardly necessary for me to state that our showing is conceived in the very best spirit, and with the fullness of Christian love towards our Baptist and Methodist brethren. Did I not believe that the church of which I am a member is best suited for the Negro, I would at once renounce attachment thereto and embrace most lovingly the one which I thought more efficiently equipped to minister to the complexed and diversified needs of my race. On account of a multitude of reasons, not necessary to state here, Negroes naturally drifted into that form of Christianity presented by the Baptist and Methodist churches. With the innate feeling and strong tendency to warmth, fervor, animation and excitement, it is not at all surprising that people so strongly emotional should gravitate in that direction. Whatever may be my own criticisms with respect to the defects in these two systems, which render them inferior to the church of which I am a member, and therefore less suitable to the needs of the race, I much prefer stating my side of the question and leaving my readers free to draw their own conclusions. That portion of the Universal Church, known in this country as the Episcopal Church, to my mind, is better suited and equipped for the amelioration of the condition of the Negro than any other.

The Negro is specially fond of "regularity" in religious as well as political affairs. In this respect the Episcopal Church comes to him not as something new but as the living exponent of the old-time religion and the old church which has actually descended to him, through all the ages

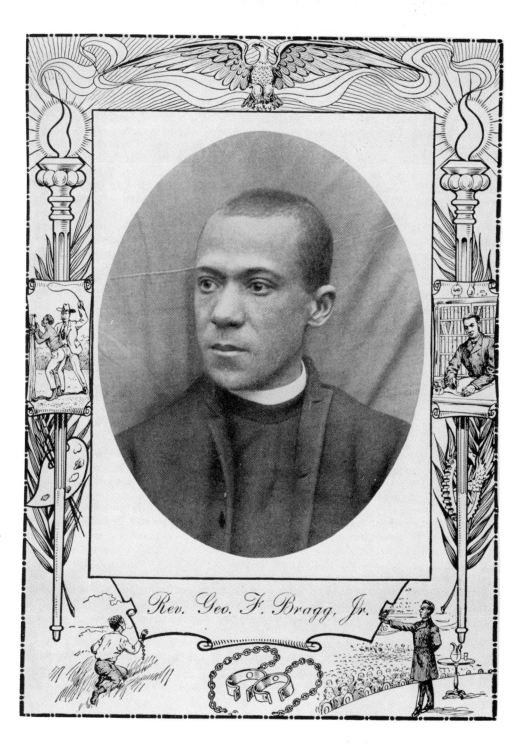

Rev. Geo. F. Bragg, Jr.

REV. GEORGE F. BRAGG, JR.

George Freeman Bragg, Junior, Priest and Rector, was born in Warrenton, N. C., January 25, 1863. Shortly after his birth his parents, George F. and Mary Bragg, removed to Petersburg, Va. It was in this latter place that their son was reared and educated; remaining there until ordained to the Episcopal Ministry, he left to take charge of his first work in Norfolk, Va. Mr. Bragg was educated, first, in the Episcopal Parochial School, then in the St. Stephen's Normal School, and in the Bishop Payne Divinity School, all of Petersburg, Va. His education, however, was supplemented by private tuition by a master in languages, under whom he studied Latin, Greek. Hebrew and philosophy. In 1881 he was appointed a page in the Virginia Legislature, and a little later, by the Speaker, promoted as the postmaster of that body. In 1882, though not of age, he founded and edited the "Virginia Lancet," the first Colored weekly published in the "Black Belt" of Virginia. This newspaper he conducted for some four or five years, and on January 12, 1887, in St. Stephen's Church, Petersburg, Va., he was ordained Deacon by Bishop Whittle of Virginia. He immediately left for Norfolk, Va., where he began his ministry at the head of the little Episcopal Mission of that city. He remained in Norfolk for nearly five years, and during that time formally organized Grace Church, secured the lot, built a new church and rectory and improved the old school building. A very large day Industrial School was carried on by Mr. Bragg in connection with his work. While here, in June, 1887, Governor Fitzhugh Lee, of Virginia, appointed him one of the State's Trustees of the Hampton Normal and Agricultural Institute, where he served for four years, resigning only because of leaving the State.

In December, 1888, he was advanced to the priesthood by Bishop Whittle in St. Luke's Church, Norfolk, Va. In the Fall of 1891 he accepted an invitation to become the Rector of St. James' Church, Baltimore, Md. The church, although one of the oldest of the connection, had been very much run down. During a ministry there of ten years, he has wrought remarkable improvement. He has increased the communicant list from sixty-three to nearly two hundred, and advanced the church well-nigh to complete self-support. The old church, which was in a Jewish neighborhood, has been sold during the present year, and a handsome brick structure erected in another section of the city. Mr. Bragg, during his residence in Baltimore, has founded a splendid charitable institution, the Maryland Home for Friendless Colored Children, and two young men have been sent into the ministry of the church directly through his efforts. For many years the Rev. Mr. Bragg was Secretary of the Annual Conference of Episcopal Church Workers among the Colored people. And in addition to his many other arduous labors he has found time to edit the "Afro-American Ledger," a weekly of this city, the "Church Advocate," and the "Maryland Home," monthly publications.

Mr. Bragg is a well known figure in all public movements for race amelioration, and is a veteran newspaper man, having been Secretary of the National Press Convention for four years, beginning with the presidency of the late Rev. Dr. W. J. Simmons.

past from the very hands of Christ down to this present time. It has historic continuity and claims none less than the Blessed Master as its founder. She is not founded upon the Bible, for she gave to the world this blessed book. Her sons inspired of God wrote it. And the claim of historic continuity can be established and proven in the ordinary way that we attest other historical facts. The church, then, that Jesus Christ founded and concerning which He said the "Gates of hell should not prevail against it," must of necessity be "adapted to the present Negro."

The Negro needs the faith once delivered to the saints, not in shreds or left to pick it out for himself, but the whole faith. This the Episcopal Church offers him. A complete faith, naturally, is to be found in a comprehensive church. The Episcopal Church is most comprehensive. She believes more in turning in than in turning out. Men are not brought into the fold to be "turned out" for every little thing, but they are brought in to be built up, established and rooted and grounded in Him. The church, then, is adapted to the present Negro because she gives him not opinions and theories, but the living faith of the ages and a living Christ as potential to-day as when He trod this earth clothed in flesh. And this church is most comprehensive, taking in all sorts and conditions of men, and by grace dispensed through sacraments, ordained by Christ Himself, seeks to bring to the fullness of stature as realized in Jesus Christ.

The Episcopal Church is pre-eminently adapted to the present Negro, for the present Negro is most eager to learn, and, above all other religious bodies, she is a *teaching church.* More Scripture is read at one Episcopal service than is ofttimes read in a month in the services of other churches. She has a liturgy which is the sum total of all that is good and grand in the ages past, and the constant and almost imperceptible influence of her most excellent system of public worship, as indicated in the Book of Common Prayer, silently but effectively issues, in moulding and mellowing good Christian character. She teaches not only through the prayer book, but by the yearly round of feast, festival and fast, of which, like a great panorama the acts and incidents in the life of her Lord are constantly set forth before those who have ears to hear and eyes to see. More than that, she teaches through symbolism. Many persons, and a considerable number of Negroes are here included, are endowed with but little brain. But they have eyes, and what they take in with their eyes help to rivet and fasten in their memories what they seize upon with what brain they possess. Our children begin to take in the surrounding objects with their eyes long before their minds are sufficiently developed to act, and the same is true in the present matter. The Episcopal Church, therefore, is especially adapted to the present Negro because she is adequately and sufficiently equipped to touch him at that portion of his being which will respond in unison with what she has to offer for his improvement. Her service addresses itself to his natural senses, as well as to his mental powers, however strong or weak they may be.

The Episcopal Church is adapted to the Negro because her worship is hearty, beautiful, uplifting and inspiring, though simple and easy, furnishing the greatest opportunity for active participation therein by the ignorant as well as the learned. The worship of the Episcopal Church harmonizes most beautifully with the strong religious fervor of the Negro, and as a vehicle for offering up those intense longings and aspirations of his heart, is without an equal.

The Episcopal Church is adapted to the Negro because she believes so persistently and thoroughly in "a change of heart." Of all religious bodies not one lays such emphasis on the absolute necessity of "a change of heart" as does the Episcopal Church. Stamped upon every page of her divine liturgy, and permeating the beautiful prayers of her offices, and inwrought in her hymnology, is this deep and firm recognition and teaching with respect to a change of heart. All her sacraments, disciplinary offices, instructions and the like, are with the design of helping her children, through the aid of the Divine Spirit, in proving the genuineness of their change of heart by a conspicuous, powerful and beautiful change of life.

The Episcopal Church is adapted to the Negro because she offers a government that is congenial and pleasant to his sunshiny nature, and which, while it amply protects him in the enjoyment of all the blessed privileges of religious culture, saves him the disaster and confusion of a democracy, which, when realized, is but another name for anarchy and confusion.

The government of the Episcopal Church is jointly shared by her clergymen and laymen, and the stability and security of its government is firmly attested by the past ages of experience and notable achieve-
ents.

In conclusion the Episcopal Church is the church for the Negro, because she is both willing and able to supply his every need, and under

Rev. John W. Whittaker

REV. JOHN W. WHITTAKER.

Rev. John W. Whittaker, A. M., a prominent Congregational pastor, was a poor boy who made his way up through many hardships. He was born at Atlanta, Ga., December 23, 1860. Of his father he knows very little. His mother was a devoted Christian whose life greatly influenced his character. When old enough, he was put to work to help support the family. While an office boy at Atlanta he met a young man, Lewis G. Watts, a thorough Christian and fond of reading, who cultivated Mr. Whittaker's friendship and took a great interest in him. Whenever with Mr. Whittaker he questioned him in arithmetic, grammar and the news of the day.

In this way a desire for an education was awakened in Mr. Whittaker. He decided to go to school. He began his education in the summer of 1876 in a country school in a suburb of Atlanta. From here he went to the Starr's Grammar School. His examination revealed the fact that he had considerable general information, but it was so unsystematic that it was very difficult to tell to what grade he belonged. He was, however, classified as a senior with conditions and was graduated with honor at the close of the school year. Then he matriculated in Atlanta University, where he studied seven years, completing the college course in 1884. He studied theology at the Hartford Seminary, graduating in 1887.

During these years of study Mr. Whittaker partly supported himself by teaching in the summer and working out of school hours, which was an immense drain upon his strength, and once he broke down under it. Through the kindness of friends he was enabled to spend two summers in the North farming. This change, he feels, was the saving of his life. June 1, 1887, at Springfield, Mass., where he held his first charge, he was ordained. In 1888 he was married to Miss Anna J. Connover, of Hartford, Conn.

Mr. Whittaker educated himself to labor for his people in the South. He was not content to remain in the North. After a very successful year at Springfield, he resigned to accept a call to the Knowles Street Congregational Church of Nashville, Tenn. For three years he was chaplain of the Tuskegee Normal and Industrial Institute. For seven years and four months he was pastor of the First Congregational Church of New Orleans, La., and three years he had charge of the First Congregational Church of Savannah, Ga. Recently he has been recalled to Tuskegee to be the Financial Secretary of the Tuskegee Institute.

Mr. Whittaker is a preacher of force and power. In every place he pastored he was remarkably successful. He has often been honored by his church with positions of trust and responsibility. He was one of the Louisiana Commissioners of the Negro Department for the Atlanta and Cotton States Exposition.

her loving nurture and constant training in the end will graduate him into a well-rounded Christian man of symmetrical character and beauty.

SECOND PAPER.

ARE OTHER THAN BAPTIST AND METHODIST CHURCHES ADAPTED TO THE PRESENT NEGRO?

BY REV. JOHN W. WHITTAKER.

It would seem from the immense following of these churches that this question would require a negative answer, but it is only in appearance and can be accounted for.

In the days of slavery the Methodist and Baptist churches predominated in the South.. The great mass of the slaves attended these churches with their masters and there they were converted and became members. They were thoroughly indoctrinated in the teachings of these churches. At the same time, there were other denominations existing among the slaves: Catholic, Episcopalian, and Presbyterian. In some portions of the United States, where these denominations were in the lead, they have a very large Negro following, whose attachment to these religious sects is so strong that they could be satisfied in no other. They belong to these denominations by birth and training. All that is sacred and dear to them is wrapped up in the history of these bodies. At the present time, it is a fact that the Negro is found in every religious denomination known among men. So it can not be said with truth that no other than Baptist and Methodist churches are adapted to the Negro. The needs of the Negro, from a religious point of view, demand all sects.

How does it come about then that the Baptist and Methodist so largely predominate to-day? These denominations, just after the War of the Rebellion, required no educational qualification for the ministry; and missions were opened by them everywhere an opening was to be found, and every man, learned or ignorant, who felt himself called to preach, was licensed and sent forth to preach in his way and to build up churches. These men were for the most part ignorant and superstitious, with very vague ideas of religion. Their chief object was to draw the people and every other consideration was sacrificed to that end. They pandered to the ignorant and superstitious notions of the Negro, ridiculed intelligence, and prejudiced their followers against it. They had no thought of progress, but taught the people to be satisfied with what their fathers before them did and had; not to believe in this Bible religion which has sprung up since the war; to prefer the old-time preacher who, without any learning, gets up and opens his mouth and lets God fill it with words to utter.

Back of all this there was one ever present motive—the pastor's support, the running expenses of the church, and the keeping up of a house of worship. All this had to be collected from the congregation. Hence the preacher's position hung upon his getting and holding a congregation. In the Methodist Church, a clergyman's advancement depends chiefly upon his ability to increase his membership and to raise money. Therefore, every Baptist and Methodist pastor felt the very great necessity there was upon him of getting as great a crowd as possible and gathering all the finance he could from it. This many did, regardless of the method employed.

Thus it was that these two denominations got hold of the masses and preoccupied the field.

The other denominations went to work in an entirely different way. They did not seek in the first place the spread of their sects, but the *elevation* of the Negro. They realized that the Negro needed to be developed into strong, self-reliant, and independent characters; that the masses were not moved by duty and did not appreciate the obligation of duty. They are a prey to their feelings, which sway them to the right hand and to the left. They live on their feelings. So engrossed are they in their feelings that they neglect duties and ignore obligations. That is why the religion of so many is such sad rubbish. God gave man reason to rule over his actions. But it was plain that, in the great mass of the Negro, reason is yet a child, ruled over by its playmates—the feelings, passions, and appetites. This is not the kind of foundation upon which to build a true religious life.

Therefore, these denominations went to work to educate the Negro. They put the emphasis on education. Schools instead of churches were established. Their theory was that men should not only be converted, but they also should be educated and made intelligent Christians. They did not discount brains, did not consider ignorance in itself a mark of virtue, nor that learning disqualified a disciple of God for the best service of his Lord and Master. In their polity, the school and the church stood side by side. In their view, an example of higher and better things must be set. Men of intelligence, power, thought, and strong characters, filled with the spirit of the Lord Jesus Christ, must be raised up from among the people to lead them and to teach them.

They were slow in establishing churches. Whatever churches they set up were pastored by men of learning and character. They were unwilling to stoop to the people, but sought to bring the people up to them. Everything was done according to the custom of the most intelligent and cultured. The preaching was of a high order, yet adapted to the needs of the people. The music was the very best. Thus a model church was set up, suited to the needs of its communicants. As fast as men were trained and prepared for the work of the gospel ministry, they were sent forth to take charge of newly-organized fields. This work went on with considerable opposition, but the influence that went out from these churches and schools was felt in the whole community. They were centers of light and wholesome Christian instruction. They were Mt. Sinais from which the laws of liberty, education, and progress were sent out to the people far and near.

These churches were, in intelligence, far removed from the masses. There was very little effort put forth to reach them. That was not the object now. That work was to come on later. The members of, and the attendance upon, these churches were mainly those who had been sufficiently taught to appreciate them.

The ignorant and prejudiced dubbed these churches high-tone. They said: "Only the educated and well-dressed can go there. The people in that church have no religion. They have only book religion. You must know how to read to go there. Why, you can't shout or say amen. I don't want anything to do with that church. It's too cold for me." Thus there grew up in the minds of the masses generally a prejudice against these denominations. And the fact that these churches were for a long time in the hands of white pastors was used to stir up opposition to them. The clergymen of the Methodists and Baptists made much of it to tear them down and to build up themselves.

Then, again, the members of these educated churches did a great deal to widen the breach by such remarks as this: "We do not want any head handkerchief people in our churches." They often spoke in a way which gave the impression that they felt themselves better than the commonality of their brethren; and whenever visitors came to these churches, the members did not extend them that cordial welcome which makes one feel at home and want to come again. This was often done unconsciously. These members had been apt students, who faithfully copied their instructors. The very atmosphere of these churches was New England, which was cold and formal as compared with our Southern ways. Thus our untrained brethren did not feel at home in their midst.

As time goes on and education becomes more general, these hindrances and difficulties to the progress of the other denominations begin to pass away. The prejudice against them wanes. The Baptist and Methodist are forced to change their tactics; their people begin to clamor for a more intelligent ministry. The churches of the other denominations fell into the hands of young colored men who had been educaied and trained to take these places.

The passing of these churches into the hands of the native pastors was the beginning of a new era in our Southern church history. The North had set the standard and carried out its purpose to raise up educated men and women to take up the work. The labor of these churches heretofore was one of education and preparation. Now it becomes one of development and expansion. Up to this time, they cared for the few. Now they are to reach out for the masses. Previously these churches had been in great measure supported by Northern aid, but now they have to deal with all the problems connected with running a church, such as gathering and holding a congregation, securing pastor's support, and all the expense of keeping up and maintaining a house of worship. Hence the necessity is upon them to reach the masses if they expect to exist, not only to save souls, but also that their forces may be strengthened and made more efficient; and they stand to-day as good a chance in this race as do the Methodists or Baptists. Their past work in an educational line in behalf of the Negro in general has given them a lasting hold upon the hearts of the people, who feel that they owe these denominations a debt of gratitude which can never be paid. Most of the Methodist and Baptist leaders of to-day were trained in the schools of these denominations. So they enjoy the best wishes of the communities in which they exist, with very few exceptions. The way is open to them to grow if they will only seize it and use it for all it is worth.

[*Note by the Editor.*—We assume that the membership of neither the Baptist nor the Methodist churches would claim for a moment that theirs

Rev. O. M. Waller

REV. OWEN M. WALLER.

Rev. Owen Meredith Waller, rector of St. Luke's P. E. Church, Washington, D. C.; Associate of Arts of Oxford University, England; Graduate of the General Theological Seminary, New York, was born in Eastville, Va., in 1868. When but five years old his parents settled in Baltimore, where he was sent at an early age to the St. Mary's Academy. In 1881 he went to Oxford, England, where he entered St. John's Classical School, pursuing studies there until 1889, when he returned to New York city. He graduated from the General Episcopal Theological Seminary in 1892, and was ordained to the Deaconate by Bishop Potter, after which he accepted a call as assistant rector to St. Phillip's Church, New York.

He declined the principalship of Hoffman Hall of Fisk University, Nashville, Tenn., to accept a call to St. Thomas' Church, Philadelphia. Having passed all examinations before reaching the required age to enter the priesthood, it was only after his election to St. Thomas' that he became eligible for advancement.

Bishop Potter arranged for the ordination to take place in the Colonial Church of St. John, Washington, D. C. Here in the presence of the Chief Justice, Cabinet Officers, Senators and other men of national note, Mr. Waller was formally elevated to the priesthood. After a rectorship of three years' successful work in this historic parish, during which its centennial was celebrated, Mr. Waller was elected rector of St. Luke's Church, Washington, D. C., in succession to the Rev. Dr. Crumwell.

In size he is above the medium and of athletic build. He is a perfect type of the physical manhood of his race, graceful in manner and address and is clear and eloquent in his style of oratory.

Success has crowned his work from the beginning. Mr. Waller combines all the essentials necessary of a leader of men along religious lines. He understands humanity. His methods inspire the confidence of men, and they reverence his gospel. He appeals to the intelligence and reason, never to passion and prejudice. He has the faculty of saying much in little, and saying it with directness and force.

Mr. Waller was married in 1893 to Miss Lillian M. Ray, of Brooklyn, N. Y. Three bright boys have blessed this union by their advent into the home.

is the only church suitable to the Negro race. But we think it would be unfair to leave the discussion of this topic without correcting an erroneous impression given by the Rev. J. W. Whitaker in the paper above. Perhaps not more than one other church has done more for the education of its Negro ministers and membership than has the Methodist Episcopal Church through its Freedmen's Aid Society and by other methods. This education commenced immediately after the war. We have reason to believe that the Baptist is a close second to the Methodist Church in this matter of educating the Negro. It is possible that some of the Negro Baptist and Methodist Churches that are entirely separated from the white churches of the same denomination may come under the category of especially ignorant ministry and membership; but even these exclusively Negro churches began the work of education soon after emancipation. We suspect that the two churches under criticism as given above preferred not to wait until the freedmen became cultured before attempting to save them.]

THIRD PAPER.

ARE OTHER THAN BAPTIST AND METHODIST CHURCHES ADAPTED TO THE PRESENT NEGRO?

BY REV. O. M. WALLER.

I have no hesitancy in saying that not only are there other churches adapted to the training of the Negro than the Methodist and Baptist churches, but, in my opinion, some are better suited to the present needs of the Negro, and chief, if not indeed the first, among these is that branch of the Apostolic Catholic Church known as the Protestant Episcopal Church. I advance the following arguments to sustain this statement:

First, the Negro is under a spell of religiosity; a conception of religion that freely recognizes and imbibes its sentiment, but just as frankly rejects its stern practical duties and obligations. The Negro's religion is a poem—a sentiment—indeed, a velvet-lined yoke. He, therefore, stands sadly in need of an influence that will regulate his super-emotional nature, and not one that adds fuel to an existing conflagration that threatens to forever consume the only power in the human being that can ultimately work out his salvation, viz., the human will.

His religiosity needs to be directed to the deep channels of true religion, and there harnessed as a mighty Niagara to produce practical right-eousness in daily living.   No church is better adapted to this end than the Protestant Episcopal.   (a)   She seeks after the example of her Mas-ter's method to develop the permanent power of the will, rather than the unstable prop of emotionalism.   This is evidenced in her majestic litur-gies and dignified but helpful services.   (b)   In doctrine, discipline and worship the Protestant Episcopal Church is the school of mental, moral and spiritual training, that a people but now coming to the light from the darkness and degradation of bondage so terribly need.   (c)   Again, her ministry, bishops, priests and deacons are her people's leaders; secure in the tenure of their office from factional machinations, they are fearless in the advocacy of righteousness; not with their ears to the ground, but with eyes looking upward, their pulpits speak plainly "Things pertaining to the Kingdom of God."   Nothing at this stage does the Negro stand in greater need of than fearless and positive guidance in the "ways of righteousness."

Second: The present Negro needs opportunity and latitude for self-development in a church where he must measure himself with the high-est standard of Anglo-evolution.   As long as the Negro is content to compare himself, in Negro associations, with himself, he must be satis-fied to know only that things equal to the same thing are equal to one another.   But, both in the lay membership and in the ministry of the Protestant Episcopal Church, the Negro coming into contact with the best results of modern forces, not only rises up to higher standards, but is saved from the insidious evils of conceitedness by ever seeing the vistas beyond him.   Withal, the doors are open to the Negro, here more truly so than in any church of like prestige and heritage. Two Negroes are on the bench of the Protestant Episcopal Church.   Nearly a hundred have been elevated to the diaconate and priesthood, meeting all require-ments and thereby teaching the same level as other men.   Such a showing cannot be made by any church of like history.

Third: We have been told of late to teach the Negro history, and I add that no lesson will be so potent as identification with a historic church that has come down the centuries to us, in unbroken integrity, from the hands of Christ through the spiritual loins of the Apostles.   I advance the following argument to show that the Protestant Episcopal Church will meet this need of the Negro: At Acts 11:42, we read as follows: "And they continued steadfastly in the apostles' doctrine and fellowship and in the breaking of bread and in prayers."

It may be readily seen from these words, drawn as they are directly from the scholarly Greek of St. Luke, that the Apostolic Church was distinctly marked by four observances or characteristics:

(a) Their steadfastness in the Apostles' doctrine.

(b) Their steadfastness in the Apostles' fellowship, dealings, doings, ministry or form of government.

(c) Their steadfastness in the breaking of the bread, or the Holy Communion; Holy Baptism being included in the Apostolic doctrine.

(d) Their steadfastness in the Apostles' manner of praying or in the set forms of prayer, at first, for twenty-five years in the Temple and the synagogues of the Jews.

These being the four marks of the church at that time, is there now in existence any church having these selfsame marks? Without any doubt, Christ was the founder of that visible body of Christians, the church in Acts II. Does that church exist to-day? It must, because Christ said: "The gates of hell shall not prevail against it."—Matt. 16:18.

THEN WHICH IS IT, AND WHERE IS IT?

The church is certainly a visible body of Christians, not founded by a man or men, but by Jesus Christ. Having a divine founder it is then a divine society, seeking men to save them from the degrading power of sin and everlasting punishment in hell. It is not then, as is so commonly and popularly thought, a human society founded by Luther, 1530; Calvin, 1541; Knox, 1560; Robert Brown, 1582; Roger Williams, 1639; John Wesley, 1739; or Swedenborg, 1783. In brief, the church founded by Jesus Christ is the Kingdom of Heaven on Earth, as Christ so often described it (Matthew 13:47, 5:19, 13:44); endowed with power from on high transmitted through her unbroken line of the Apostolic ministry, but obedient to her Divine Founder, who is at the right hand of God in heaven.

This church of four distinct marks in the Acts existed before the completion of the New Testament at least some sixty years, and it was the church that by the inspiration of the Holy Spirit pronounced the New Testament inspired, and rejected other books claiming to set forth the life of Christ, three hundred years after it was founded. The Old Testament is the document of the Jewish Church, that church having been in existence for a thousand years before its document was completed. Therefore, this church of the Acts cannot be set aside for one claimed to be founded upon the Bible.

For three hundred years then, this Apostolic Church existed with Apostolic doctrine, ministry, sacraments, and prayers before she gave the New Testament to the world with her certificate that it was the Inspired Word of God.

The Protestant Episcopal Church of America as the daughter of the Church of England, has ever possessed, and does now possess and hold more sacred, these four marks that identify her unmistakably with the primitive and Apostolic Church, as a true branch of the same.

First, as to doctrine this church holds and defends the pure teaching of the early church, without taking from or adding to the same. There are few, indeed, who would question this.

The Holy Trinity (John 14:16, 26; Acts 2:33; Gal. 4:6).

The Incarnation of God's Son (Luke 1:35; John 1:14; Matt. 1:23).

The Redemption of Man by Christ Jesus (Matt. 1:21, 20:28; Gal. 1:4).

Regeneration and Holy Baptism (Titus 3:5; Rom. 6:4; Gal. 3:27).

The Holy Communion (Matt. 26:26-28; Mark 14:22-24; Luke 22:19-20).

Confirmation (Acts 8; Heb. 6:2).

The Resurrection of the Dead (Luke 14:14; John 11:23).

The Judgment (Acts 17:31; Heb. 9:27).

Belief in these statements and other fundamental teaching of Holy Scripture is in accord with the mind of the Apostolic Church.

Secondly, as to the unbroken line of bishops, priests and deacons, who have succeeded for more than eighteen centuries other ministers Apostolically ordained, that has been most jealously guarded and maintained by the Episcopal Church.

There may be some who have never given any study to the Apostolic succession of ministers in the church founded by Christ. No one could well doubt the fact or deny the doctrine who had patiently investigated the matter. The New Testament is itself witness to the fact that the Apostles appointed others to do Apostolic work and to be their successors; at least thirty Apostles are mentioned in the New Testament. Among them were Paul, Matthew, Barnabas, Andronicus, Silas, Luke,

Titus, whom St. Paul appointed Bishop of Crete, and Timothy, whom he appointed Bishop of Ephesus. There were also at least ten others whose names are recorded, space does not permit us to mention.

Now, if the original twelve could have eighteen successors, certainly they could, and have had a continual line of successors down the centuries. The titles of the three orders of the ministry may, at first, mislead the unlearned.

(1) In the New Testament the highest order was Apostles. The second, "ordained in every city," were Presbyters (Presters or Priests), also called Bishops and the lowest order Deacons.

As the Apostles began to die off, the title "Apostle" was limited to them and to their successors who had probably seen Christ, at the same time the title "Bishop" was set apart to denote the highest order which succeeded the original Apostles. This is stated by Clement of Alexandria in the second, and Jerome in the fourth century. While Theodoret, writing in 440, says: "The same persons were in ancient times called either presbyters or bishops, at which time, those who are now called bishops were called Apostles. In process of time, the name of Apostles was left to those who were sent directly by Christ, and the name of Bishop was confined to those who were anciently called 'Apostles.'" From Palestine the church spread to Asia Minor, Greece, Rome, Gaul, Spain and England, carrying with her the Apostles' doctrine, ministry, sacraments and prayer.

In 597, when Gregory the Great, Bishop of Rome, sent Augustine to England, he found there the church with the four marks. After awhile the Bishop of Rome, by political methods, gained great influence over the English Church in so much that he was receiving from England greater revenues than the king. When the tremendous revolt against the papacy came about in Europe in the sixteenth century the English people simply ejected the pope's emissaries and with them, Italian influence and corruption from England and the English Church, the church remained essentially the same she had been for centuries.

The word "Reformation" signifies the footing of something into a new shape. It is therefore not the destruction of the old and the substituting of the new, but rather the reshaping, cleansing and revivifying of the old. The melting down of the family silver and the reshaping it on new models is not to acquire new silver. Perhaps it was so distorted by abuse that it required new shaping.   This was very much the case with the Church of England.

The reformation in England was effected on very different lines from that on the continent of Europe.   Luther, Calvin, Melancthon, and others were individuals attracting to themselves multitudes of other individuals and together they establish societies of Christians.   The Apostolical churches on the continent did not, as such, participate in the reformation movement.   In England the reformation, i. e., the reshaping, restoring and cleansing, was more wisely conducted.   The church there had existed since the days of the Apostles.   For six hundred years it remained independent of the Roman world power, and it was only after the Norman Conquest that the papal authority became well established in England.   When a reformation seemed necessary, it was conducted, not by individuals leaving the national church, but by the whole Church of England.   In A. D. 1532 the quarrel of Henry the Eighth with the pope led to the overthrow of the Roman power in England.   Henry is not to be credited as a reformer, much less as the founder of any church. He never made any attempt to found a church.   When he was born, in 1491, he found the church existing in England, and when he died, in 1547, he left the same church, but cleansed and independent.   The ancient church was not changed, and the old religion did not give place to the new.   The papacy was opposed to the independence of the national churches for which the Church of England had always contended.

Accordingly, when the power of the pope was broken and thrust out of England, the church was at liberty to restore Apostolic purity and freedom to the nation and the individual.

Parliament prohibited the payment of money to the pope and appealing from English to papal courts.   In 1539 the Bible was given to the people to read in their native tongue.   The services were read in English instead of Latin.   The chalice was given to the laity.   The worship of the Blessed Virgin Mary was abolished and praying to departed saints forbidden.   These reforms were conducted by the archbishops, bishops, priests, and deacons and laity, i. e., by the whole church.   The pope was not without his adherents during this period, who opposed these changes most vehemently.   But these traitors to the Church of England found they could not stem the tide for an open Bible and pure religion.   In 1569 Pope Pius Fifth created the great sin of schism by commanding all in favor of papal power in England to withdraw from the English Church and form an Italian party. In 1685 the Italian Church supplied this party with a bishop. To-day the Italian mission in England is doing all in its power to make headway against the Church of England, but in vain.

We can now come briefly to the Episcopal Church in America. She was established in the American Colonies under the oversight of the Bishop of London. In 1609 the Church of England planted her first church on American shores at Jamestown, Virginia. After the Revolution, the church in this country became the American Episcopal Church, receiving the Apostolic ministry from the ancient Apostolic Church of England. Samuel Seabury of Connecticut, was consecrated at Aberdeen in 1784 and William White of Philadelphia, and Samuel Provoost of New York were consecrated at Lambeth Palace in 1787. These were the first three bishops with jurisdiction, and thus was the Apostolic Succession maintained in the Episcopal Church in unbroken line from the days of the Apostles.

In conclusion, the Protestant Episcopal Church has ever continued steadfast in the sacraments of prayers, and by these four undeniable and unmistakable marks shows that she is a true branch of the same church described in Acts 2.

The question for the Negro now becomes, not which church do I like or prefer, not to which church did my parents belong, but which church did Christ found for me to be trained in.

TOPIC XXV.

THE NEGRO AS A BUSINESS MAN.

An Address Before the National Negro Business League.

BY T. W. JONES.

There has been so much controversy concerning the Negro, so much said and written about his alleged inferiority, such an attempt made to establish relationship between him and the monkey, that even in this new century there exists, in some quarters, grave doubts as to his origin, and a general misapprehension as to his nature, capabilities and purposes. But research into the primeval history of man evinces the fact, beyond the possibility of skepticism, that mankind had only one common origin. We are taught that in the beginning God created man in His own image, and breathed into his nostrils the breath of life, and that man became a living soul. The closest and most thorough analysis of the blood of different races fails to detect the slightest difference in the color, size, shape or quality of its corpuscles. The fact that one people are white, another yellow, another red, another brown, and yet another black has its cause in the working of a law of nature which we do not fully understand. Sacred history plainly teaches that the Negro is a man like other men and that of one blood God created all nations; hence there can be no racial barrier to a successful business career, in the general constitution of a black man.

What was the business of the Negro in the land of his nativity, or at the time of his emancipation in this country, does not so much interest us now, except as it may help us to appreciate his capacity for business at present.

Life for our forefathers in Africa was very plain and very simple. The multitude was engaged with problems little more difficult than the acquirement of food and drink and rest, raiment not being a necessity; hence their only business, aside from frequent wars with kindred tribes, was to explore a way to the fruit tree, the water brook and the shade, and so their years were principally filled up with the business of merely satisfying those three physical wants—hunger, thirst, and rest.

J. W. Jones.

HON. THEODORE W. JONES.

The Hon. Theodore W. Jones was born during the temporary residence of his parents in the beautiful city of Hamilton, Ontario, September 19, 1853. His parents soon returned to New York, their native State, and there remained until he was twelve years old. In 1865 this family decided to make Illinois their home and settled in Chicago.

Mr. Jones was one of a very large family; his parents were poor and unable to give him even a common school education. Compelled to support himself, at the age of fifteen years he was driving an express wagon. He was an industrious boy, full of pluck and energy. Without money and by his own unaided efforts, step by step, he pressed on and soon built up a most successful express and moving business.

Discouraged by no difficulty, the ambitious young expressman turned his attention toward acquiring an education. He was a diligent student. Through the aid of private tutors and the "midnight oil," he was able, when twenty-five years of age, to enter Wheaton College, Wheaton, Ill., where he remained three years. Leaving college, he returned to his business in Chicago and has been exceedingly prosperous.

Mr. Jones is the owner of a large brick storage warehouse, Twenty-ninth Street and Shields Avenue, and other valuable property in this city. In his employ are three lady clerks and about fifty men, all colored.

In 1894, Theodore W. Jones was elected on the Republican ticket to the responsible position of County Commissioner of Cook County, Ill. He ably and well performed the duties of this office.

That he labored earnestly and unselfishly to advance the interests of the colored people we need relate only the following fact: During Mr. Jones' term of office the colored people of Cook County drew $50,000 yearly salary. This was about seven times the amount paid into the county treasury by our race.

He is a valued member of the National Negro Business League. He was present in Boston at the organization and has organized a branch league in Chicago, known as the Business Men's League of Cook County. This league entertained the National League in Chicago, August 21, 22, 23, 1901.

When human slavery was established in the colonies, those of our race, either fortunate or unfortunate enough to be brought to these shores were instructed mainly in the care of cotton, tobacco and rice crops; and from these few Southern industries we could not turn aside. Slavery deprived the Negro of the little responsibility devolving upon him in his savage state—that of providing food and drink and finding rest. No responsibility was allowed to devolve upon him, other than to perform allotted work, not even the selection of his wife; and when children were born to him, he was not confronted with the problem of how he should provide food and shelter for them, nor wherewith they should be clothed. He and his issue being the property of his master, like swine or cattle, their issue were alike stalled and fed by the owner. With but few exceptions, this was the condition of the Negro when the Proclamation of Emancipation was issued, thirty-eight years ago.

From that eventful day onward, the mighty aspiration of the ex-slave for education and material development has written a new page in the history of the world's progress. Let us now examine the record made, and call to our assistance the statistics of the Government that we may truthfully answer the question, can the Negro succeed as a business man? We are indebted to ex-Congressman George H. White for the information that since the dawn of our freedom the race has reduced its illiteracy at least 45 per cent; that we have written and published nearly 500 books; have edited fully 300 newspapers; have 2,000 lawyers at the bar, a corresponding number of practicing physicians, and 32,000 school teachers. We own 140,000 homes and have real and personal property valued at $920,000,000. The census of 1890 shows that 20,020 persons of African descent were engaged in business, and there were more than 17,000 barbers not included in those figures; and be it remembered that this showing was made more than ten years ago.

It is true that we have produced no skilled master mechanics or great speculators; no commercial princes or merchant kings. These are beyond our immediate reach and reserved for later growth. But we have today, on the floor of this convention, colored men who represent nearly every business enumerated in the census reports—wagon-makers, watchmakers, grocers, druggists, bankers, brokers, bakers, barbers, hotel keepers, caterers, undertakers, builders, contractors, printers, publishers, decorators, manufacturers, tailors, insurance agents, coal dealers, real estate agents, collectors, the proprietor of a brick yard, the owners of a cotton factory, and the president of a coal mine. The number engaged, and the capital invested, may not reach very pretentious figures, but the beginning has been made. Aside from the above, we have produced soldiers whose valor has reached world-wide reputation, poets, artists, teachers and professional men and women of recognized ability. There are hordes of others pursuing the humbler walks of life eager to acquire by education a higher ideal of manliness and womanliness, and to learn the ways of advanced civilization and approved citizenship. These achievements have been wrought by us under the most adverse conditions. We have wearily toiled by day and by night; have made bricks without straw; helped ourselves and taken advantage of small opportunities; though these are days of increasing combinations of capital, growing corporations and gigantic trusts, which greatly lessen the possibilities of individual success. Surely there is in the black man the same capacity for business, the self-same spirit, purpose and aspiration that there is to be found in the white man, and he is as much entitled to the blessings of life, and to share its honors and rewards, as the descendants of other races, notwithstanding Senator Tillman's recent plea for lynching Negroes, and the plaudits and acclaim of a Wisconsin audience.

Despite the fact that the door of nearly every large factory, shop and department store is closed against us, despite the fact that prejudice stalks our business streets with unblushing tread and dominates in all the commercial centers of our common country—yet we are not here today pleading for special legislation in our behalf; we are not here whining to be given a chance; we are not here, even to complain of our hard lot, or to find fault with conditions which we cannot change. This, we conceive, would be a very poor programme to attract the attention of the business world, but we are here, representing hundreds of thousands of dollars, thus demonstrating that we have achieved, at least in a small measure, one of the things which, by common consent, is taken as evidence of progress, ability and worth. We have made money, have saved money, and are succeeding in many profitable business enterprises which require the possession of skill and executive ability to direct and control.

The Jew traces the industrial strides of his people from the first footsore peddler to their present position of affluence in the financial world, and so without reciting further the early struggles and hindrances experienced by our pioneers in business, sufficient is it to say that we have men who should be placed in the class with Nelson Morris, A. M. Roths-child and Mandel Bros. Not that they can compare with these men in the sum total of their wealth; no one expects this. But that they began life without a dollar, have accumulated property and acquired influence, and are today men of public affairs, able to stand, persevere and prevail in the fierce struggles and competitions of business life. These mer-cantile strides the members of our race are taking in the face of proscrip-tion and oppression, in the face of the administration of unjust laws and in the face of disfranchisement and barbarous lynchings, such as no other men ever had to face. In fact we are prospering under conditions which would not only fill other business men with hopelessness and despair, but would surely drive them into bankruptcy.

It is not true that the business patronage of the Negro is confined to his own race, nor is it true that he is a cringer, and solicits patronage among the whites because of the fact that he is a colored man. We have long since learned that we are entitled to no more consideration because we are black than other men are who chance to have red hair, big mouths, or mis-shapen feet. If you will pardon personal mention, I would say that in my business as a furniture mover, few customers, indeed, have I among my own people; nor do I ask to remove any man's goods because of the color of my complexion or the texture of my hair; but because I have put brains into my humble calling and made the business of moving furniture a science. What is true in this instance is true in all others, where progress is made. We are grasping opportunities and compelling adverse circumstances and forces to work together for our profit. Under the wise leadership of Booker T. Washington, we are finding our bear-ings and casting anchor in the dark and muddy waters of industrial con-ditions in which we were sent adrift without rudder, compass or means of existence less than thirty-eight years ago.

It is not strange that, as business men, we have made some failures. It is a long way from the depth of the valley to the summit of the moun-tain; from a barbarian to a master mechanic; from the jungles of Africa to a successful business career, and from the slave cabin to the professor's chair. We have not all outgrown the feeling of dependence instilled in us by more than 250 years of chattel bondage; many of us yet shrink from responsibility, and lack the requisite amount of ambition. We rec-ognize our shortcomings, our peculiar environments and the limitations of our experience and powers. We are beginning to learn that if the

Negro is to become more and more a factor in the business world he must take a more active part in all of the trades, competitions, industries and occupations of life. Again, he is learning, slowly perhaps, but surely, that he must outgrow the weakness and confusion resulting from distracted purposes; that he must have one aim, and be one thing all the time. He must stop doing things in a slipshod and half-way manner and become more thorough. He must put the force of a strong character and a determined will power into whatever he undertakes, and he must stop stumbling and falling over impediments, especially of his own placing.

The Negro is, however, affected by nothing now which education and personal endeavor will not in time remove. For example, we take the liberty to refer to our honored President, Booker T. Washington, who about forty-two years ago was born a slave in Virginia. At an early age he began the battle for himself untutored and untrained in all the ways of life. What he has since accomplished is a sufficient answer to those who claim that the Negro is void of any capacity for doing business, and that his offspring has no chance to rise in the world. For twenty years Booker T. Washington has not only been president of a great industrial institution, but has had very largely the acquisition, management, investment and expenditure of its finances. In recent years there has scarcely been a month in which he has not been offered positions in important and influential business enterprises, as well as in the affairs of government. His career is evidence that there is plenty of room at the top for Negro boys who have sense enough to rise to the level of their opportunities. The lack is not so much of opportunities as of men. It is a fact which cannot be gainsaid that success still is, and most likely always will be, a question determined very largely by the individual. For the man or woman who has made thorough preparation and is willing to do hard work a place will always be waiting, irrespective of race or color.

The tone of this convention clearly indicates that the Negro will succeed as a business man in proportion as he learns that manhood and womanhood are qualities of his own making, and that no external force can either give or take them away. It demonstrates that intelligence, punctuality, industry and integrity are the conquering forces in the business and commercial world, as well as in all the affairs of human life. Permit me, in closing, to quote the language of President McKinley addressed to the students at the Tuskegee Institute. "Integrity and

Andrew F. Hilyer

ANDREW FRANKLIN HILYER.

The subject of this sketch was born in slavery near Monroe, Walton county, Georgia, August 14, 1858. In the early fifties his maternal grandfather, Overton Johnson, was set free, given some money and sent North. He went to Cincinnati and began a free man's life as a cook and steward in a hotel. In a short time, by strict economy, he had saved some money from his earnings. This, with the money brought from the South, enabled him to open "The Dumas House," well known to the older residents of Cincinnati. In 1862 he sold this business, moved to St. Louis and opened a hotel in that city, where he was at the close of the war. In 1866 he sent for the remainder of his family in the South, consisting of his youngest son and a daughter and her four children, the eldest of whom was Andrew Franklin Hilyer.

About the time of their arrival in St. Louis business reverses threw the now enlarged family upon their own resources, and young Andrew, though but eight years old, was "hired out." He early developed a burning desire for an education, and took advantage of every opportunity that he could find to study and to learn. He soon learned to read. With this key he opened up to his enquiring mind a wide vista of knowledge and saw through many things which before had seemed dark. The family remained in St. Louis two years, but in very poor circumstances. During this period Andrew was able to attend school but little, yet he was so anxious to learn several persons gladly gave him instruction. It was during these struggles that he formed his purposes in life. He solemnly resolved to make a man of himself and to graduate from college.

In 1868 the entire family moved to Omaha, Neb., where their circumstances gradually improved and Andrew was enabled to attend school a part of each year. His mother died in 1871, and the next year he went to Minneapolis, Minn. Here was located the State University, and his opportunity to go to college had now come. To make this possible he learned the trade of a barber and pursued his studies, graduating from the Minneapolis High School in 1878 and from the University of Minnesota in 1882.

He soon came to Washington, entered the service of the Government and took up the study of law, and in 1885 graduated from the Howard Law School.

Mr. Hilyer takes an active interest in the progress of his race along all lines, but he has especially urged upon their attention skilled labor and business as very important factors in the progress of the race.

In 1886 he married Miss Mamie E. Nichols, a descendant of one of the older Washington families, who graces a happy home. They have been blessed with two boys, whom they are trying to rear and educate to become good men.

industry," he said, "are the best possessions which any man can have, and every man can have them. No man who has them ever gets into the police court or before the grand jury or in the work-house or the chain gang. They are indispensable to success. The merchant requires the clerk whom he employs to have them; the railroad corporation inquires whether the man seeking employment possesses them. Every avenue of human endeavor welcomes them. They are the only keys to open with certainty the door of opportunity to struggling manhood. If you do not already have them, get them."

For our encouragement, reference has been made to a portion of the history of the distinguished President of this convention, and also, for the same purpose, quotation has been made from a speech of the honored President of his country. We thus have before us the example of the former and the precept of the latter—each a leader in his own sphere, the one black and the other white. By following the example of the one and the advice of the other, the Negro will not only succeed as a business man, but the early dawn of the present century will yet witness the best achievements and the loftiest conceptions of a once enslaved race.

SECOND PAPER.

THE NEGRO AS A BUSINESS MAN.

BY ANDREW F. HILYER.

The resistance of the white people to the progress of the colored people is least along the line of business. The colored people themselves have only to develop a larger spirit of race help in business and a magnificent future is just ahead for them.

In addition to little capital and much inexperience the colored merchant has to contend against a hostile public opinion, which seems to resent his efforts to improve his own condition and that of his own race, when he assumes to tear himself away from the mass of his fellow laborers and attempts to keep store like a white man.

Strange enough this hostile feeling is shared in, more by the colored than by the white people, especially along certain lines of business not of a semi-social nature. It is a matter of common complaint by colored business men in those classes of business in which they must compete with white merchants that they do not get their share of the trade of their own race and that their patronage comes very largely from the white race. At present the pathway of the colored man to success in business is very much handicapped by this unfriendly public opinion. His problem is to win the confidence of the public in his ability and purpose to serve them as well as or better than his competitors.

Individuals, here and there, have won this public confidence to a surprising degree and are demonstrating day by day the ability of men and women to do business according to approved business methods. The hostility of the whites is but another manifestation of the general feeling of race prejudice; but the hostility of the masses of their own race can only be attributed to envy and ignorance. For every colored man, woman and child should rejoice in the success or upward step of any colored person, because it is an inspiration and a hope to thousands of others to follow his example. Only the strongest and most progressive few of any race can be successful pioneers. The masses of all races are LED to attempt only what they see persons of their own kind doing. Every community of colored people needs, as a powerful uplifting force, a few captains of industry who will lead his people along the pathway of home-getting and the undertaking of business enterprises. For business will develop their sense of independence and personal responsibility and give strength and symmetry to character. No better service can be performed for the race at this time than to turn the light upon those successful business men and women of the colored race in every community, so that our youth may see them, know them, and take inspiration and courage from their example.

The real leaders of the race are those who lead in doing. It has been said that ninety per cent of all business enterprises among the highly favored white race finally fail in the lifetime of their promoters. The conditions of success in business for the white race are so exacting, uncertain, changeable and inscrutable that only ten per cent retire from the contest victorious. When we recall the fact that the colored people have come so recently from savagery, through the barbarism and debasing effects of American slavery, into the light of the present-day civilization, we should expect them to be slow in getting a footing in the shifting and ever-changing sands of the business world, while in slavery they were deprived of every opportunity to learn anything about the art of business or even to drink in its spirit. It was one of the essential conditions of the slave system that they should be taught to distrust each other; and they learned this lesson well. We must expect that it will take some time to unlearn it. Along with this blighting feeling of distrust the seeds of envy and jealousy were carefully sown. These seeds must have fallen in good soil, for they sprang up and increased wonderfully, and now constitute the thorns and weeds in the pathway of the colored man's success in business.

In view of their economic, educational and political history, we should naturally expect the colored race to make in the first generation of their freedom more progress in education and general culture, more progress in the building of churches and in the acquisition of homes and lands than in the exacting arena of business. At any rate such has been the fact. The entire race is passing through a hard and severe economic struggle. The whole nation is in the throes of a great social distress, on account of the presence of this colored race with physical aspects so different from the main body of the people. The colored people are being put to a severe test. They are being tried as it were by fire. They are face to face and in competition with the most efficient, the most exacting people the world has ever seen. The dross is being driven off. The race is being purified and strengthened for the contests which are to follow. The colored man or woman who would succeed in business must meet not only the competition of his white neighbor with his superior capital and training, but also the blight of distrust and the jealousy and envy of many of his own race. His course is by no means plain sailing. He has foes within his race as well as foes without; enemies in front and enemies in the rear. And yet, in spite of all these adverse conditions a very creditable beginning has already been made in the business world— a beginning that promises well for the future. The business movement among the colored people has not as yet attained great volume, but its foundations have been laid broad and deep. The number of persons engaged in business is quite large, and the classes already invaded by individuals of the colored race cover almost every class of business in which persons of the white race are engaged.

THE CAPITAL OWNED BY NEGROES.

The colored people are rapidly acquiring property. This is a matter of common, every-day observation. The value of property owned by them is no less than five hundred millions of dollars. In Georgia alone, where separate records are kept, their assessed valuation exceeds fifteen millions, one million of which was added in the past year. The assessed valuation is only about forty per cent of the actual value. From all over the country equally encouraging reports are sent out of the steady progress of this people in the acquisition of landed property. Although tens of thousands are shiftless, thousands are saving money. It is being stored up slowly but surely for future use. Much of it is already invested in business. A larger part of this property and money will be turned into business channels as fast as the race, by its patronage and support, evidences its desire to advance this business movement.

THE EXTENT OF THE BUSINESS MOVEMENT AMONG THE NEGROES.

In order to obtain reliable data for a study of the progress of the colored people in the skilled trades, in business, in getting homes and in building churches and other institutions, the United States Commission to the Paris Exposition of 1900 sent out the writer in February of that year as an expert agent to visit the chief industrial centers of the South and secure the data for the purpose of making the facts collected, a feature of the Negro exhibit. In every city or town visited the colored people took great pride in showing their successful business establishments; and they all had some to show. In every place a beginning had been made. The writer personally visited, inspected and collected data from one hundred and forty-three business establishments of considerable importance owned and conducted by colored men and women. They range from a grocery store, with stock and fixtures of the value of five hundred dollars, to a bank, which, on the day of my visit, had a cash balance in its vault of $82,000. Only the best business places were visited. There were hundreds of small shops in the cities and towns visited, all of which evidenced the breadth of the business movement of the people.

THE ATLANTA UNIVERSITY CONFERENCE.

The results of this hurried trip corroborates in a remarkable degree the report of the Atlanta University Conference. "The Report of the Negro in Business" was made in 1899. In that year the conference made an investigation of this subject under the direction of Prof. W. E. B. DuBois, professor of sociology in that university. This report is a most valuable contribution to the study of the race problem. Prof. DuBois has shown commendable zeal in studying the race problem, while so many others are content to discuss it. The data for his study were collected principally by the alumni of Atlanta University and are thus entitled to a high degree of credibility.

Reports were received from one thousand nine hundred and six colored men and women in business, showing the kind of business, time in business, and the amount of capital invested. Almost every kind of business carried on by white people was represented, thus evidencing a desire and a reaching out on the part of the Negro that will produce great results in years to come. Only establishments of considerable importance were solicited and reported.

Time in business: Four-fifths had been established five years or more; one-fifth more than twenty years. Sixty-seven more than thirty years. This shows a remarkable longevity in business that is highly gratifying.

Capital invested: Complete returns were not received from all; only 1,736 establishments reported capital. Their aggregate capital was $5,631,137. Prof. DuBois estimated that the total amount invested by American Negroes in business managed by themselves in 1899 was $8,784,000. Compared with the immense sum of money invested in business in the United States, this seems meager enough; but when we consider the poverty of the colored people at the beginning of their freedom, the saving and investment of nearly $9,000,000 in business enterprises conducted by themselves in one generation is a most creditable showing.

By far the larger part of the capital of the colored people is as yet invested in enterprises conducted by white persons. In the city of Washington, where the idea of the advantage to the race in having a number of successful business enterprises has been very much agitated, only about one-fifth of its wealthy colored people have any investments in enterprises conducted by colored men, as shown in the report of the Hampton Conference for 1898. A like proportion will doubtless be found in other cities.

THE CENSUS OF 1890 ON NEGRO BUSINESS.

According to the census of 1890 (the returns from the census of 1900 on this subject not being available at this writing), taken twenty-five years after the war, the colored people had representatives engaged in every business listed in the census schedules. It is true that the number of persons engaged and the capital engaged in some branches of business were not imposing, yet an effort had been made—a start, a beginning had been made in every branch of business carried on in this country. The census of 1890 does not in all cases make a distinction between "proprietor" and occupation. Hence, it is not always easy to pick out the "proprietors." The tables have been gone over very carefully. Only those occupations have been selected about which there can be no doubt that the persons listed are "proprietors." The total number of persons of Negro descent engaged in business in 1890 was 20,020.

It is obvious to any one who has paid even a little attention to it that there has been a considerable increase since 1890, in the number of such business ventures and in the capital employed.

THE NATIONAL NEGRO BUSINESS LEAGUE.

As an evidence that the race is rapidly advancing along business lines, a conference or convention of colored business men was called by Mr. Booker T. Washington to meet in Boston August 23-24, 1900, for the purpose of making a showing of the progress of the race in business and to give encouragement and impetus to the business movement. The success of this convention was a pleasant surprise to many persons. Over two hundred delegates reported in person, and nearly two hundred additional reported by letter. The tone of the reports they brought from their several localities was uniformly hopeful. Most of the delegates present lived outside of New England, some coming from as far south as Florida and Texas, and as far west as Nebraska. A permanent organization was formed, called The National Negro Business League, the purpose of which is to keep its members in touch with one another. Their "Proceedings" were published by Mr. J. R. Hamm of No. 46 Howard street, Boston, in a handsome volume of two hundred and eighty pages, and constitutes one of the most valuable contributions to the study of the progress of the colored people.

This business league held its second annual convention in Chicago in August, 1901. This meeting also was a great success in every way, and received, if possible, more attention and space from the public press than the previous meeting in Boston.

A recent study of the colored business enterprises of Washington, published by the writer, shows that there are in the National capital 1,302 colored "proprietors" in all kinds of business and professions. Their capital exceeds seven hundred thousand dollars, and they transact more than two million dollars worth of business annually, affording employment to 3,030 persons.

Among the more conspicuous examples of successful enterprises conducted by colored men in the United States may be mentioned the following: Thirteen building and loan associations, seven banks, about one hundred life insurance and benefit companies, several mining companies, one street railway company, one iron foundry, one cotton mill, one silk mill, three book and tract publication houses, one of them having a plant valued at $45,000; over two hundred newspapers and three magazines. One of these newspapers has 5,000 subscribers and a plant costing $10,000. One firm of truck gardeners, near Charleston, South Carolina, over 500 acres under cultivation, has been in the business over 30 years and ships several carloads of garden truck to Northern markets every week. The railroad company considers its trade of such importance that it has built a siding to their farm and the cars are loaded directly from their warehouses. This is probably the most extensive individual or partnership business carried on by colored men anywhere in the United States. Noisette Bros. is the name of the firm. Near Kansas City, Kansas, there is a colored man, Mr. J. K. Graves, who owns and cultivates over 400 acres of land. He has been engaged principally in raising potatoes. His crop last year was over 75,000 bushels, which, with the other things raised and sold, was worth about $25,000. Within a radius of thirty-five miles of his farm, he says that there are 312 Negro farmers, horticulturists, gardeners, truckers, potato growers and dealers, most of whom are up to date and have all modern appliances necessary to carry on their business.

Mr. C. C. Leslie, a dealer in fish in Charleston, South Carolina, has $30,000 invested in the business, in nets, boats, ice-houses, real estate, etc., and ships to Northern markets from three to five carloads of fish per week during the busy season.

In Charleston the most prosperous butchers are colored men. In Columbus, Mississippi, there is a colored butcher who owns his abattoir and supplies the best trade of his town with meat. Some of the most prosperous fish, produce and poultry dealers in the markets of Washington are colored men. One firm has been in business continuously over thirty years, the sons succeeding the father in the business. Several have maintained their stands over twenty years.

A pawnbroker in Augusta, Georgia, has $5,000 capital. The largest and best equipped drug store in Anniston, Alabama, is owned by a colored physician. He has a considerable wholesale trade in patent medicines and druggists' sundries.

One of the best equipped ready-made clothing stores in Columbia, South Carolina, is owned by a colored man. He carries a stock of ten thousand dollars.

A stock breeder in Knoxville, Tennessee, is worth $100,000, and has $50,000 invested in blooded horses.

A photographer in St. Paul, Minnesota, does a business of $20,000 a year. Another in New Bedford, Massachusetts, began as an errand boy, learned the photographic art thoroughly, saved his money, bought out the white proprietor, and now conducts the leading studio in that old and aristocratic city.

The caterers of Philadelphia and Baltimore have long been noted for their success in business, although they have lost some ground from white competition during the last few years. There are yet several with capital above $5,000.

The caterer at the great naval banquet at Newport in honor of Admiral Sampson and our navy upon its return from the victories in the war with Spain, where the very unusual task was accomplished of serving one thousand men in a very satisfactory manner, was a colored man.

The foregoing are only a few of the many examples of success that individuals of the colored people have achieved in business. They are cited by way of "a bill of specifications." They show conclusively that, in spite of many adverse conditions, it is possible for a colored person, by perseverance and honesty, to succeed in business.

Rev. J. H. Morgan.

REV. J. H. MORGAN.

Rev. J. H. Morgan was born in Philadelphia, Pa., November 15, 1843. His father was Rev. John R. V. Morgan. His mother's maiden name was Mary Ann Harmon. At his mother's death, which occurred when he was fourteen years old, he was adopted into the family of James T. Robinson of Philadelphia. Becoming dissatisfied at some fancied slight, he left without authority, determined to provide for himself, and be his own man. He soon found that the job was not so easily done, as thought about, nevertheless he was determined to win out, so he kept at it, and being of a jovial disposition he soon made friends, and had the happy faculty of keeping them. He started in the business of selling home-made pies and cakes along the wharves. After a short time he gave up this business for that of cabin boy on a passenger boat plying between Philadelphia and Bristol, Pa., making Bristol his home. At the breaking out of the Civil War he was very anxious to enlist as a soldier, but they informed him at Trenton, that it was a white man's war and they were not taking colored men, as their ankles set so near the middle of their feet, that when they said forward march, they would be as likely to go backward as forward, so he hired as a cook in an officers' mess and went to the front with Company C First Regiment N. J. V. six months' men. He was not down there long before he lost all his desire to become a soldier, when the opportunity came for him to enlist. While in Alexandria, Va., he started in to learn the barber trade, and on his return home worked as a journeyman at his trade until he set up in business for himself.

In 1876 he organized a mission at Poughkeepsie, N. Y., and being young and enthusiastic, he requested at the next conference to be sent to the mission to build it up. Bishop Payne demurred, but after his persistence in the matter, he consented, saying, "Well I will let you make your own appointment this time, but will be expecting to hear from you before the year is out, asking for a change." So after ordaining him an Elder in Sullivan Street Church, May 12, 1878, he was stationed at Poughkeepsie. There he had some misunderstanding with the people, which caused them to promise to "cut his bread and butter short," which promise he says was the only one that they made, that they faithfully carried out. One day they fed his family on wind pudding, air sauce and balloon trimmings, and right here Bishop D. A. Payne became a prophet, because he heard from him, and his time was short, as in a few days after he received an appointment to Albany, N. Y., and was returned the following year on account of effective service done. At the following conference he was elected as delegate to the General Conference at St. Louis with Rev. W. F. Dickerson, John F. Thomas and C. T. Shaffer. On his return from the conference he was transferred to N. J. Conference and stationed at Princeton, N. J., and with the exception of four years spent in the N. E. Conference, one in the N. Y. Conference, he has remained in the N. J. Conference. Rev. Morgan is the recognized historian of the conference, and was its secretary for a number of years, and was the Vice-President of the first Board of Church Extension. The Reverend is known in his conference under the cognomen of 'The Only Morgan"—his description of things and events gaining for him this title. He was made Presiding Elder by Bishop H. M. Turner, and he thus describes his return from the Presiding Eldership to one of the weakest appointments in another conference: "Milton, or some one, says that the devil was nine days falling from heaven to hell; I made the trip in less than twenty minutes." Bishop H. M. Turner's second wife and the subject of this sketch were converted in and became members of the same church at Bristol, Pa. He was considered an exceptionally good superintendent of the Sabbath school before he was a member of the church. It was during the time that he was a local preacher at this church that he learned the lesson of his life, "I had a fair smattering of an education and, being in business, I was always consulted in the affairs of the church."

THIRD PAPER.

THE NEGRO AS A BUSINESS MAN.

BY REV. J. H. MORGAN.

It becomes more and more evident every day of our existence, as individuals, and as a race, that a grave mistake has been made by those who have heretofore, or may be now, making claim to leadership of making higher education the main and only route to the full development of the race. The higher education is in the order of specials. It is true that we need the artistic structure, but we need first a foundation upon which to rest it. We seem to have started with the idea that the structure has already been laid, which is true as concerns the other man. But we have not laid one foot ourselves, but are endeavoring to build upon another's, and as often as we build and finish the structure, the other man, by virtue of owning the foundation and that upon which it rests, claims and takes all (under the fixed rule that the people who own the land will rule it), and the last state is worse than the first, unless this happens at a time of life when the experience will become a lesson, well learned, and time allotted for a new start along the proper lines. It is, therefore, very evident that the essential thing in the line of individual and race development, is business. Business, we discover, when properly defined, leads in its various ramifications to all roads to success

Business defined.—"The state of being anxious; anxiety; care. The act of engaging industriously in certain occupations. The act of forming mercantile or financial bargains, more generally an abundance of such acts done by separate individuals."

Crabb thus distinguishes between business, occupation, employment, engagement, and avocation: "Business occupies all of a person's thoughts, as well as his time and powers; occupation and employment occupy only his time and strength; the first is most regular—it is the object of his choice; the second is causal—it depends on the will of another. Engagement is a partial employment; avocation a particular engagement; an engagement prevents us from doing anything else; an avocation calls off or prevents us from doing what we wish. A person who is busy has much to attend to, and attends to it closely; a person who is occupied has a full share of business without any pressure; he is opposed to one who is idle; a person who is employed has the present moment filled up; he is not in a state of inaction; the person who is engaged is not at liberty to be otherwise employed—his time is not his own—he is opposed to one at leisure."

Business, trade, profession, and art are thus discriminated: "The words are synonymous in the sense of a calling, for the purpose of a livelihood; business is general; business, trade and profession are particular; all trade is business, but all business is not trade. Buying and selling of merchandise is inseparable from trade; but the exercise of one's knowledge and experience, for the purpose of gain, constitutes a business; when particular skill is required, it is a profession; and when there is a particular exercise of art, it is an art; every shop-keeper and retail dealer carries on a trade; brokers, manufacturers, bankers, and others, carry on a business; clergymen, medical or military men follow a profession; musicians and painters follow an art."

The distinction between business, office, and duty: "Business is what one prescribes to one's self; office is prescribed by another; duty is prescribed or enjoined by a fixed rule of propriety; mercantile concerns are the business which a man takes upon himself; the management of parish concerns is an office imposed upon him, often much against his inclination; the maintenance of his family is a duty which his conscience enjoins upon him to perform. Business and duty are public or private; office is mostly of a public nature; a minister of state, by virtue of office, has always public business to perform; but men in general have only private business to transact; a minister of religion has always public duties to perform in his ministerial capacity; every other man has personal or relative duties which he is called upon to discharge according to his station."—Crabb: Eng. Synon.

There has been a vast number of theories advanced as regards the solving of the Negro problem. But the idea of business seems to have only a minor place, which, to our mind, should be one of the leading factors. It seems that the race has been educated away from itself. It is not an uncommon thing to see young men who have splendid educational abilities, versed in the languages, with check aprons on, scrubbing marble steps, and doing other menial labor. Their plea is, when questioned along this line, "I cannot get anything else to do." To what advantage then, has the hard earned money of their parents and friends been expended to educate them? Their fathers did as well as, if not better, than they without it, and cannot this man, with the advantage of education, "turn up something"? There is something radically wrong with the plan of education. The old man could plod over the farm in his antiquated way, and earn money enough to keep things going, and educate his son, but when that son's education has been completed, he has not the ability, or business tact, with modern improvements, to build upon the foundation laid by his less cultured father. Let this cultured boy get down to business. For him, here is the route laid down.

Secretary of Agriculture, Hon. Mr. Wilson, in discussing the productive possibilities of the South and the problem of Negro labor, makes the following observations: "The pressing question is, what is the laborer down South who has been growing cotton, and is not getting enough for his product, to do in the future to enable him to live comfortably, not to speak of the improvement of his condition, education, and all that?"

The cotton crop leaves very little that is valuable for domestic animals after the picking is done, thus differing from the corn crop of the Northwestern states. There is a by-product, the cotton seed, that is exceedingly valuable, and much good work is being done by scientists at experiment stations to show how valuable cotton seed is for feeding purposes.

The nitrogen element in cotton-seed is greater than that of any of the grains; it is richer in nitrogenous matter than peas or beans; richer than gluten, meat or oil cake. The Northern feeder and the European feeder have been using this by-product of the cottonfields with great advantage, while the loss of its fertilizing qualities to the South has been very great.

The South has more marked advantages over the North with regard to production. It has heat and moisture, the two great factors of production, and if the cotton grower is to diversify his crops, he must use those natural advantages. The dairy cow and mutton sheep would succeed admirably in the South, but something for them to eat must be provided first. The winters in the South are mild, grasses, grains, legumen can be sown in the fall and grow abundantly in the winter, upon which the dairy cow and mutton sheep may thrive and prosper. From one-fifth to one-fourth of all the fat of the milk on the farms of the United States is lost because people do not thoroughly understand when to churn cream. The churning process is an art, having much science underlying it. But the cotton grower of the South only needs to learn the way, while the man who teaches him can understand the science. Much yet remains to be discovered in the art of breeding animals, but enough is known to indicate to the instructor of the colored cotton grower of the South, who is to be diverted into work of this kind, to enable him to breed his. herd intelligently. The South can prepare the spring lamb much earlier than the North can. The Southern land owner understands horse raising. There is always a greater demand for saddle horses than is supplied. The world wants carriage and draft horses, and good roadsters. Early spring chickens—the broilers—can be produced down there because of the milder winters, and milder springs than we have, and the Northern market can be supplied. Should the market be over supplied we can send this product abroad in the refrigerating compartments of steamships.

The colored man is learning the trades at Tuskegee; he is mining coal, and working the manufacture of iron at Birmingham. We quote this gentleman, who is without doubt authority on this special line, and therefore worthy of serious and careful consideration, to support the point we make, that this problem must be worked out along lines, especially along business lines.

BUSINESS OPPORTUNITIES.

Hawaii, Porto Rico, and the Philippines are absolutely ours. The Philippines are said to be as large as the New England States, including New York and New Jersey; Hawaii about the size of New England; Porto Rico the size of Connecticut. Hawaii, with a population of 109,-000; Porto Rico, 900,000; Philippines, 8,000,000, and very few whites; a climate in which the Anglo Saxon, it is said, cannot stay for any great length of time. And it is rich in all those things which are desirable by the white man. These acquisitions must be developed by American genius and capital, and as the white American cannot stay there the year round to develop the same, what better agent to do this work than the Afro-American who has been schooled in American ideas and customs and usages. Is not this an opportunity given by Providence to commence business building? The race should cease pleading to be "The Wards of the Nation;" cease waiting for something to turn up, or have somebody to do something for them, but should unite their forces and turn up something for themselves. The people who own the country, if intelligent and thrifty, will rule and run it. What Coleman has done in North Carolina in a business way, could be done in a majority of the states to a greater or less extent. Small factories could be arranged for, where our people could be employed in producing the commodities of life. Some time ago it was said that a large tract of land had been arranged for, backed by a number of Tammany Hall capitalists; factories were to be built to give employment to the settlers, deeds for lots were to be given at a nominal cost. The project was opposed by some of our so-called leaders, because it was backed by Tammany; but it is the very thing needed, no matter who backs it up; it is the business men who run the country; it is they who put the millions to work and keep the mighty dollar in circulation; we must enter the business world and by pluck, tact and thrift, live while we are living, and die when we cannot do otherwise. The man who thanks Almighty God when the news of disaster comes from land or sea that no loss comes to him is not so wise in the sight of God, or man, as he who can thank God that the interest on accrued stock had advanced an hundred fold before the crash came.

TOPIC XXVI.

THE NEGRO AS A FARMER

BY PROF. GEORGE W. CARVER.

The above subject is by no means an easy one to discuss, as reliable data are fragmentary and widely scattered; yet I am sure that I have been able to collect some interesting and valuable facts and figures bearing upon this important question. There is no doubt that the Negro as a tenant farmer is a failure; this we are forced to admit, but we do so with a justly proud feeling that it is not an inherent race characteristic, but the result of conditions over which we had little or no control. Failure is inevitably and indelibly stamped in the foreheads of any class of average tenant farmers, regardless of race or color.

In American agriculture the Negro has always held, and is yet holding, an important place; in fact, far more, as a rule, than has been accredited to him. Lest our judgment be too harsh in this particular, I have thought it wise to briefly scan the beginning and development of agriculture in the United States. In 1492 the first settlers found the Indians carrying on agriculture in a crude and limited way, by the women; their farm machinery consisting of their fingers, a pointed stick for planting, and the bones of animals and the shell of the clam for a hoe; with nothing more than a squatter's right as a voucher for the ownership of their farms. Prof. McMaster's History of the People of the United States, George K. Holmes, assistant statistician of the United States Department of Agriculture, in his "Progress of Agriculture in the United States," and other high authorities, tell us that the white man came, poor in the materials of wealth, a stranger in a strange land with a strange climate. His tools were but little, if any, improvement on those of the Indians, and agriculture as we know it to-day was an idealistic dream. The plow was an exceedingly crude thing and but little used, the hoe forming the principal implement of industry. After a piece of land had been continuously "cropped" until worn out, it was abandoned, or the cows turned upon it for a while. It is further said that the poor whites, who had formerly been indentured servants, were the most lazy, the most idle, the most shiftless and the most worthless of men. Their huts were

Prof. Geo. W. Carver, M. Ag.

PROF. GEORGE W. CARVER, M. AG.

A few years ago there was graduated at the Iowa Agricultural College a young colored man of unusual promise. His name was G. W. Carver, and his specialty the care and production of plants. Not long after graduation he was engaged by Booker T. Washington as a teacher and assistant in his famous industrial school, and to-day the young man is Mr. Washington's most trusted adviser, while his reputation has gone abroad as a scientist and an original investigator of no mean order.

Born during the period of the Civil War, he was separated from his parents when but six weeks old, they having been sold to some distant slave-holders. The infant was puny and ailing, and his master regarded him as worthless. A family named Carver took the babe and his brother, a little older. It was with them the child had a home for nine years. About that time the little black boy developed a remarkable love for plants, and so much knowledge of their structure and life, that he was given the name of "the plant doctor." Mr. and Mrs. Carver were proud of the boy's talents and made much of him, and it was their evident satisfaction in him that aroused the jealousy of their own children, who at last drove the two colored boys away from home. Northward they turned their faces, to the land where white and black have equal chances in life, as they fondly believed. The little "plant doctor," who had picked up the elements of an education, wanted, above all else, to enter some good school. The boys were driven from pillar to post, but, being devotedly attached to each other they held together, until in Kansas they thought best to separate.

During these years, young Carver had tried many kinds of work. At length he found himself at Winterset, Iowa. It was there the wife of a physician encouraged him to go to Indianola where she thought he could enter college and earn his way by doing laundry work. He went there, but didn't get the work, and it was while there that a young lady, a well known Iowa artist, became interested in him. Under the pretext of securing his help in correcting some drawings, she went to the mean quarters he occupied and found him starving to death. There was no work for him, no money. For weeks, he had subsisted upon corn bread and tallow. She then arranged for him to go to the Iowa Agricultural College, where she had influential friends and where she believed he would have a chance.

But, even at the Agricultural College of Iowa the color line was sharply drawn by the students. Persecution and ill-treatment were resorted to. But young Carver said, "I will bear it. I must get an education. Here I can get work and I will suffer anything rather than give up the one chance of my life to obtain a schooling." His old and intimate knowledge of plants stood him in hand, and he was given charge of the greenhouses. True, he was shunned by many, his place at table was with the servants, but he had warm friends and he was, by force of character, winning the good will of all. One day an Indianola lady, who had come to know him before he left that place, went to visit him at his college. Dressed in her best, she accompanied him, though against his protestation, to dinner, taking a seat at the servants' table.

The next time this lady visited the college the colored student sat at the table with the faculty. In the military drill he had taken the highest honors. When he was graduated it was with distinction. He wrote the class poem. He had succeeded in winning and holding friends.

Some time ago he spent several weeks in Washington, D. C., and there the most kindly attention was extended to him by Secretary Wilson, who never fails to recognize merit wherever he may find it.

The name of G. W. Carver is now enrolled on the fellowship list of more than one scientific institution.

scarcely better than Negro cabins, the chimneys were of logs, the chinks being filled with clay. The walls had no plaster, the windows had no glass, and the furniture was such as they themselves made.

The grain was threshed by driving horses over it in the open field. When they ground it they used a rude pestle and mortar, or placed it in the hollow of one stone and beat it with another. Beef or pork, generally salted, salt fish, dried apples, bread made of rye or Indian meal, milk, and a very limited variety of vegetables, constituted the food throughout the year. When night came on his light was derived from a few candles of home manufacture. The farmer and his family wore homespun. If linen was wanted, the flax was sown and weeded, pulled and retted, then broken and swingled, for all of which processes nearly a year was required before the flax was ready for the spinners, bleaching on the grass, and making and wearing. If woolens were wanted, sheep were sheared and the wool was dyed and spun and woven at home.

It was almost invariably true of all the settlers that the use and value of manures was little regarded. The barn was sometimes removed to get it out of the way of heaps of manure, because the owner would not go to the expense of removing the accumulations and putting them upon his fields. Such were the dreary conditions of the farmer's life in colonial days, living all the time very closely upon the margin of subsistence. Those conditions continued for some time after the Republic had been established, and were not measurably ameliorated until the present century had well advanced, until an improved intelligence—the dissemination of information, and the work of the inventor, had begun to take effect.

From the above we see how strikingly similar were the life, methods of agriculture, and the results obtained from the sturdy New Englander, who represented the best blood, bone and sinew of the old world, with its almost prehistoric civilization, to that of the American Negro, whose intellectual star is just beginning to rise above the horizon. Over two centuries and a half ago the Negro found his way as a slave to America, in a little Dutch trading vessel, cheap labor being the chief motive which prompted such a gigantic scheme. The experiment flourished and grew, and at about the close of the eighteenth century six million slaves had been brought to this country. The major part of all the cotton, corn, cane, potatoes, tobacco, and other agricultural products, were planted, cultivated, harvested and prepared for, and, not infrequently, marketed by, the slaves. In fact, they were the agricultural backbone of the South. Since cotton forms the largest, and has been the most important agricultural product in the South, I think a hundred and nine years of its production will prove interesting and valuable: In 1791, 8,889 bales were produced, and the second cotton mill built at Providence, Rhode Island! the first one being built at Beverly, Massachusetts, in 1787. From this time on the acreage planted, the output and the number of cotton mills and spindles increased. The estimated area planted in cotton alone in 1852, 6,300,000 acres, and the census report of 1860 showed 1,262 cotton mills and 5,235,727 spindles in the United States, with an output of 4,861,292 bales. Despite the depressing effect of the four years of civil strife, it took only five years to almost completely regain the highest point reached in previous years. In 1889 and 1890 we find in the United States 19,569,000 acres planted, giving an output of 7,311,322 bales, with 905 cotton mills operating 14,088,103 spindles. In 1898-99 the acreage increases to nearly 25,000,000, with an output of 11,189,205 bales, representing a money value of $305,467,041. Such is the history, production and growth of the cotton industry in the United States, and were we to trace the other staple products we would find them none the less interesting, since they were produced largely by Negroes as slaves before the war, and as freedmen after the war. This applies especially to Southern products.

Whatever of truth there is in Mr. Van de Graff's grave apprehensions for the Negro, he with us must admit that the ills of the black tenant farmer are simply the ills of the Southern farmer in a more or less aggravated form. It is also true that the curse of such a system falls the heaviest on the smallest and most ignorant tenant farmer, who is the least capable of self-defense. For years we have been content to let the preachers preach, the lawyers argue, the philosophers predict, the teachers and the doctors practice with scarcely a question as to our priority of right. We have, in the face of the many oppositions which come to every race similarly situated, labored with endurance, patience and forbearance, until the birth of the twentieth century dawns upon us, steadily marching on, with something over $263,000,000 worth of unencumbered property to our credit. Now as to the number owning farms and following agricultural pursuits as a livelihood, we are pleased to submit some figures from the last census report, from Crogman, in his "Progress of a Race," and from other authorities. Beginning with the little District of Columbia, with an aggregate area of 8,489 acres and 269 farms, there are seventeen Negro farmers, five of which own their land in whole or in part. Their farms contain 29 acres, of which 25 are improved. The total value of the land is $23,300, and the appurtenant buildings are worth $390; live stock to the value of $489; and farm incomes for 1899 amounting to $4,244. Ten farms, aggregating 258 acres, are operated by Negroes as cash tenants. The reported values are, land, $114,600; buildings, $9,200; implements and machinery, $1,200; and live stock, $1,383. The total incomes for these farms in 1899 were $10,300. Two farms, together consisting of 21 acres, valued at $149,630, are operated by Negroes as salaried managers. Of the 17 farms operated by Negroes, only 1 contains less than three acres; 7 contain from 3 to 9 acres; 5 from 10 to 19 acres; 2 from 20 to 49 acres; and 2 from 50 to 99 acres, giving an average size for all of 18.1 acres.

In the state of Delaware the farms constitute 85 per cent of the total land surface of the state, which is divided up into 9,687 farms, of which 8,869, or 91.6 per cent, are operated by whites, and 818, or 8.4 per cent, by Negroes. Of the latter class 297 are operated by owners, and 35 by part owners. The value of their farms, including implements, machinery and live stock, together with the value of implements, machinery and live stock on the farms which other Negroes operate as tenants, is $495,187.

In Arizona we find that three Negro farmers operate their farms as salaried managers. Twelve own farms containing 1,511 acres, with farm property valued at $60,422; one leases a 39-acre farm for cash, and has implements and live stock worth $130. The total investment by Negroes in agriculture, exclusive of farms owned by them and leased to others, is, therefore, $60,552, which is a rather encouraging showing for Arizona.

Messrs. Walker and Fitch, graduates of Hampton Institute, in 1896, made a careful canvass of one congressional district in Virginia, and found as follows: Out of a total acreage of 1,944,359 acres, one fifteenth, or 125,597 acres, is owned by the Colored people, roughly estimated at $1,000,000. These figures mean farm owning chiefly, as $79,611 represent the total city property. They also report that in Gloucester county, 25 years from the above date, the Colored people owned less than 100 acres of land. To-day they own 13,000 acres of land free from any encumbrance. Mr. Fitch further adds that he has traveled quite thoroughly through more than ten counties of Virginia, with horse and buggy, during the present year (1896), and that in no county through which he traveled did the Colored people own less than 5,000 acres of land. He found also that much of the improved farming was being done by Colored men, and that the strong public sentiment against moving to cities was having the desired effect.

Again, the statistician reports, in 1890, 12,690,152 homes and farms in the United States, and of this number the Negroes own 234,747 free from all encumbrance, and 29,541 mortgaged; giving the percentage of mortgaged property owned by Negroes as 10.71, while the whole percentage of mortgaged property for the whole country is 38.97. It is further stated that of all the property held by Negroes, 88.58 per cent. is owned without encumbrance. Since so much has been accomplished in the Negro's pioneer days of freedom, may we not predict with a considerable degree of assurance that the next decade and a half will far exceed our most sanguine hope? The virgin fertility of our soils, and the vast amount of cheap and unskilled labor, have been a curse rather than a blessing to agriculture. This exhaustive system of cultivation, the destruction of forests, the rapid and almost constant decomposition of organic matter, together with the great multiplicity of insect and fungus diseases that appear every year, make the Southern agricultural problem one requiring more brains than that of the North, East or West. The advance of civilization has brought, and is constantly bringing, about a more healthy form of competition. The markets are becoming more fastidious, and he who puts such a product upon the market as it demands, controls that market, regardless of color. It is simply a survival of the fittest.

We are also aware that the demands upon agriculture were never so exacting as they are now. All other trades and professions are holding out their inducements to the young men and women who are ready and willing to grapple with life's responsibilities. One says, "Come and I will make you a Gould." Another, a Rockefeller; still another, an Astor—with all the luxuries their names suggest. Too many of our own farmers illy prepare their land, cultivate, harvest and market the scanty and inferior crop, selling the same for less than it cost to produce it. I need not tell you that the above conditions imperatively suggest the proverbial mule, implements more or less primitive, with frequently a vast territory of barren and furrowed hillsides and wasted valleys. Instead of the veritable Klondyke, of which their dreams are made sweet, another mortgage has been added as an unpleasant reminder of the year's hard labor. With this inevitable doom staring them in the face, is it any wonder that so many of the youth of our land flock to the cities with the hope of seeking some occupation other than farming? The above conditions, together with the seemingly higher civilization of the city folk, I claim, are largely responsible for this. But be this as it may, in the light of what has been accomplished, I see for us a very bright star of hope in the education of two-thirds of the brightest and best of our youth in scientific agriculture.

The many excellent schools, colleges, nature study leaflets, farmers' bulletins and reading courses, conferences, convocations, congresses, fairs, and the like, are all powerful educational factors designed to lead the race into higher agricultural activities. The agricultural schools, and higher institutions of that character, are wisely laying much stress upon stock raising, dairying, horticulture, landscape gardening, poultry raising, and every manipulation incident to the successful operation of this great industry. These subjects have been taught almost wholly to young men, but recent experience has taught, not only in this, but in other countries, that many of these studies seem especially suited to women; and many are taking the advantages offered by schools in the matter of learning the technique of poultry raising, dairying, horticulture, landscape gardening, and the related sciences, along with their academy or college work, and as a reward are finding pleasant, profitable and healthful employment. Nature study, with the first principles of agriculture, is compulsory in many of the primary schools, and ere another decade is indelibly placed upon the historical records of the greatest events of the greatest century, it will find us wonderfully in advance in this particular.

Every year we see a perceptible increase in the funds for public education, and magnificent schools and colleges, with better paid professors, springing up here and there, stand out as beacon lights to this new and wonderful epoch. The wisdom of spending these ever-increasing millions upon the youth of our land becomes from year to year a matter of less concern as we seek to give our boys and girls a broader education than that of a pure scientist. It is very encouraging to note the course taken by our young men and women who have gone out from those institutions—the way they have acquired land, built homes, and are devoting their entire time and talent in that direction. I have no fears but what we, in the course of time, will do our part both nobly and well in the matter of feeding a hungry world.

SECOND PAPER.

THE NEGRO AS A FARMER.

BY H. A. HUNT.

In a chapter on this subject it may not be out of place to give some little attention to the early history of the Negro as a farmer in America.

Without stopping to discuss the motives of the sea captain who brought over the first load of Negroes to America, or why the Northern colonists discontinued, at a comparatively early date, the use of slave labor, let us note a few things about the Negro in the South.

The fact that they could easily endure the summer sun of the cotton belt; that they learned quickly the simple methods of farming used in the cultivation of cotton, rice, sugar-cane, and tobacco; that they required but little in the way of food, clothing, housing and medical attention, and the further fact that they possessed a peculiarly happy and light-hearted disposition, all tended to make them especially valuable to the Southern planters.

It seems that slave labor was looked upon, at a comparatively early date, as being not only desirable, but absolutely necessary to the growth and development of the Southern colonies.

For several years after the settlement of Georgia no slaves were allowed to be used in that colony, but, finding that the colony seemed to be doomed to failure, the "trustees" permitted the introduction of slaves and the colony began immediately to prosper.

The following lines attributed to George Whitefield—the famous minister—in referring to his plantations in Georgia and South Carolina, give a fair idea of the feelings of the Southern colonists on the subject of slave labor at that time. He speaks thus about his Georgia plantation: "Upward of five thousand pounds have been expended in the undertaking, and yet very little proficiency made in the cultivation of my tract of land, and that entirely owing to the necessity I lay under of

Prof. H. A. Hunt

PROF. HENRY A. HUNT.

Henry A. Hunt was born in Hancock County, Ga., in 1866. He attended the public schools of Sparta, the county seat, until 1882, when he entered Atlanta University and was graduated from the college course in 1890. He also completed the course of instruction given in the Industrial Department of that university. He kept up his expenses, in a measure, by working as a carpenter during his vacations and during his spare hours while in school. He was considered a most promising young man and a thorough scholar by his professors and schoolmates. He became a professing Christian while pursuing his college course. In all of the athletic sports of the university he took an active part and served as captain of the base ball team for several years. He graduated with the highest honors of his class. Through a most flattering recommendation from the Superintendent of the Public Schools of Atlanta, Ga., he was called, in 1891, to the principalship of the Charlotte Graded School, which position he filled acceptably, until he resigned, during the same year, to accept the superintendency of the Industrial Department of Biddle University, Charlotte, N. C. In 1896 he was given, in addition to his industrial work, the superintendency of the Boarding Department of Biddle University. These two positions he is now filling in a most acceptable manner. Mr. Hunt's work and close touch with the young men of the university have been most gratifying. He encourages and takes part with them in all of their sports, being the leading spirit in their athletic association. He is a noble example of the manly man and his influence over the students for straightforward and manly endeavor has been truly helpful. The respect and esteem in which he is held by the graduates and undergraduates are most noteworthy. In August, 1900, Mr. Hunt called together the farmers of Mecklenburg and surrounding counties for the purpose of holding a farmers' conference. A permanent organization was effected, of which he was made president. The influence of these annual conferences is far-reaching and will no doubt result in great good to the farming class of western North Carolina. He was for several years the president of the Queen City Real Estate Company of Charlotte, N. C., an organization designed to help those wishing to obtain homes. He was forced to relinquish this work because of other duties. Mr. Hunt is a strong and courageous young man, he is firm in his convictions and believes the royal road to success is attained through the faithful performance of each day's duties. His sympathies are near to the interests of the working classes. As a college-bred man he urges his people to become skilled artisans and to build up reliable business enterprises and thus become independent. His kindness of heart and plain honest dealing with his fellow-man, along with his intellectual attainment, have won for him a host of friends and made him a popular man with all the people.

While attending Atlanta University, Mr. Hunt met the girl—Miss Florence S. Johnson, of Raleigh, N. C.—who in the year 1893 became his wife and to whom much of whatever success he has attained is attributable. To them there have been three bright and beautiful children born—two girls and a boy.

making use of white hands. Had a Negro been allowed I should now
have had a sufficiency to support a great many orphans, without ex-
pending above half the sum which has been laid out." How different are
his expressions concerning his South Carolina plantation, where slavery
existed: "Blessed be God! This plantation has succeeded; and, though
at present I have only eight working hands, yet, in all probability, there
will be more raised in one year, and without a quarter of the expense,
than had been produced at Bethesda for several years past. This con-
firms me in the opinion I have entertained for a long time that Georgia
never can or will be a flourishing province without Negroes are allowed."

With the invention of the cotton gin slave labor became still more
valuable, the South more prosperous, and the planters verily believed
that cotton was king and South Carolina the hub of the universe.

But, while it is true that the Negro became an indispensable factor
in the material prosperity of the South by his work on the plantations,
yet he did not at that time occupy a position that could be dignified with
the name of farmer. During the days of slavery the Negro occupied a
position more closely akin to that of a farm animal than that of a farmer.
Of course there were exceptions but we are speaking now of the masses.

The Negro having been looked upon by his master and schooled to
look upon himself and his fellow bondmen as possessing none of the
intelligence and virtues essential to success in life, there is little wonder
that a comparatively small number of freedmen took advantage of the
opportunities offered immediately after the close of the Civil War to
become land owners. Indeed, when we take into account the fact that
there was a sort of caste feeling among the slaves, with the "field hands"
as the "mud sill," and all glad of any opportunity offered to rise above
the despised position, the great wonder is that so many were willing to
continue an occupation considered so degrading. The fact is, that it was
to a very great extent simply a matter of accepting cheerfully the inevitable that held so many of the freedmen to the farms and to farm life.

Among the positive forces that operated in taking the Negro from the
farm there was, perhaps, none stronger than the desire to have his
children educated—the opportunity for which being very poor in the
country districts—many of the very best and most thrifty among them
left the farms for the towns and cities.

But whether on the farm or in the city, only a few years of freedom
and its attendant responsibilities were necessary to enable the more

intelligent ones of the ex-slaves to see the importance of not only knowing something, but owning something as well, if they were to entertain any hopes or aspirations above those of the "field hand," and it was from this class of Negro farm hands that the real Negro farmer came into existence. While there were many who showed decided intelligence, sound judgment and shrewd business sense by the manner in which they managed their affairs, still the great masses had arisen, if at all, only from the position of the master's farm animal in slavery to that of his less cared for farm hand in freedom.

The condition just described represents the state of affairs during the first few years after the war, as indeed it does present conditions, except that the number of those who may be called farmers is constantly increasing and the number of mere farm hands is growing proportionately smaller. We should keep constantly in mind the distinction between the man who tills his own land and the one who works the land of another, the former is the farmer, the latter the farm hand.

The distinction just noted would seem to be entirely justifiable as ownership of the land is the first requisite for the proper interest in, and love for the work being done, to entitle a man to the name of farmer.

In order to properly appreciate the opportunities and advantages of farm life to himself and his children, there must be that love for the farm itself, its rocks, its woods, its hills, its shady rills and its meadows that can come in no other way than through the proud sense of ownership. There must be the feeling of kinship for the very soil itself; the birds, the bees, the flowers must all be held dear to the heart of him who would know nature's choicest secrets and reap rich harvests from her beautiful storehouse.

In no field are the prospects brighter for the nego than in that of agriculture. There are thousands of acres of land in the South and Southwest that may be purchased upon terms so favorable that the land being purchased, may, by proper management, be made to yield sufficient income to meet the payments.

In the combination of a mild climate, cheap land, with easy payments, ready markets and previous training of the Negro, God seems to be offering special inducements for him to come out from the condition of a landless tenant—that may grow into a serfdom worse than slavery—to that of worthy, independent and self-respecting land owners.

There is no field in which he meets so little of the unreasoning and unreasonable prejudice as in farming.

The products of the farm are the necessaries of life and people do not stop to question too closely as to whence they come or by whom produced.

Owing to the growth of manufacturing in the South, especially of cotton goods and the consequent removal of large numbers of the poor whites into the cities and towns, just now would seem to be the high tide of the Negroes' opportunity to become an independent class of citizens; and we should be careful to seize it at its flood, or all the rest of our life's voyage may be bound in shallows and miseries more distressing than those already passed.

The opportunity for buying land, becoming independent and even wealthy, are, indeed, grand, but the fact must ever be kept in mind that the present favorable conditions will not obtain indefinitely. Let the tide of European immigration once turn southward and competition immediately becomes sharper, and the further progress of the Negro decidedly more difficult.

If the Negro would put himself in position to successfully withstand this competition that will inevitably come, let him begin now by purchasing his stronghold—the farm—and fortify himself, or he may awake, when it is too late, to find himself without a home or the means with which to secure it.

Let us note just here one of the most solemn obligations resting upon those who stand as leaders of the Negroes, viz.: The duty of impressing upon the masses the absolute necessity for purchasing land and the great need, yes, the absolute necessity of doing so *now.*

It is not the purpose of the writer to create the impression that the leaders of our people are neglecting their duty, or that the masses are letting their opportunities for material betterment pass unimproved, but rather to arouse both leaders and followers to the necessity for greater activity in their work. Indeed when all things, favorable and unfavorable, are taken into account, there is much to be thankful for and hopeful over in the present condition of the Negro farmers.

In almost every community in the South there are to be found Negro farmers who are not only making a decent living, but buying land and improving it, building comfortable dwellings, improving the grades of their farm animals, giving liberal support to their schools and churches and bringing up their children in a manner that is altogether creditable and calculated to make of them good citizens.

It is encouraging to note the increased interest on the part of many young men on the subject of farming, as evidenced by the increasing popularity of the agricultural and mechanical colleges, and the lively interest taken by them in the farmers' conferences held in various parts of the South. The number of Negro farmers who read agricultural journals and make intelligent use of the bulletins issued by the agricultural departments of the various states and the United States, is constantly increasing.

Lest there be some doubt as to the truthfulness of the favorable conditions just mentioned, let the figures speak. Since last year the Negroes of the single state of Georgia have purchased 66,000 acres of land and added $380,000 to the value of farm lands. (Prof. W. E. B. DuBois in The Independent, Nov. 21, 1901.)

Indeed it seems that if in one particular line of work more than any other the Negro has won for himself a place in the history of this country's progress that work has been upon the farm. If one section of the country has profited more than another by his toil, that section is the South, whose forests he has felled, whose roads he has built, whose soil he has tilled, whose wealth he has created, and whose prosperity he has made possible. Then let us not be discouraged, but turn our faces to the sunlight of heaven and put forth our very best endeavors, confidently expecting to reap the full rewards for our labors and attain the full measure of manhood as a race in this "the land of the free and the home of the brave."

H. E. Baker

HENRY E. BAKER.

Henry E. Baker is one of the most useful men in Washington. His life stands out in strong contrast to that of so many of our educated colored men who have come to Washington, obtained positions in the government service, and shriveled up so far as public usefulness is concerned. He is an active member of the Berean Baptist Church, being its treasurer, an office he has held for several years. For ten years he has been secretary, the executive office, of the Industrial Building and Savings Company, and a director of the Capital Savings Bank. His most notable characteristic is his public spirit, having been connected with almost every well-directed movement in this city for the last fifteen years, looking to the betterment of the condition of his race, especially in the matter of opening up business opportunities for them. The estimation in which he is held by those who know him best is attested by the fact that he is almost invariably called to the position of treasurer in every organization of which he is a member. Born just before the War in Columbus, Miss., he attended the public school of his home and also the Columbus Union Academy. He passed the entrance examination at Annapolis, and was admitted into the Naval Academy as cadet midshipman in 1875, where he remained nearly two years. In 1877, he was appointed "copyist" in the United States Patent Office, where he is at present employed, and where he was promoted, through the several intervening grades, to the position of Second Assistant Examiner at $1,600 per annum. He attended the Ben-Hyde Benton School of Technology in this city from 1877 to 1879; entered the law department of Howard University in 1879, graduating in 1881, at the head of his class, and from the post-graduate course in 1883.

He was married in May, 1893, at Lexington, Ky., to Miss Violetta K. Clark, of Detroit, Mich., who graces a cozy home at 2348 Sixth Street, N. W.

TOPIC XXVII.

THE NEGRO AS AN INVENTOR.

BY H. E. BAKER.

It is quite within the mark to say that no class of men of modern times has made so distinct a contribution to what is popularly called "modern civilization" as have the inventors of the world, and it is equally within bounds to say that the American inventor has led all the rest in the practical utility as well as in the scientific perfection of his inventive skill. Within the century just past the inventors of America have done more than was done in all the preceding centuries to multiply the comforts and minimize the burdens of domestic life. What Washington and Grant, Sherman and Sheridan did for the glory of America was done, and more, by Whitney, Morse, Thompson, Howe, Ericsson, Colt, Bell, Corliss, Edison, McCormick, and a host of other Americans, native and naturalized, to promote the progress of American inventive skill, and thus firmly to establish this country in the front rank of the enlightened nations of the world.

The true measure of a nation's worth in the great family of nations is proportionate to that nation's contribution to the welfare and happiness of the whole; and similarly, an individual is measured by the contribution he makes to the well being of the community in which he lives. If inventions therefore have played the important part here assigned to them in the gradual development of our complex national life, it becomes important to know what contribution the American Negro has made to the inventive skill of this country.

Unfortunately for the seeker after this particular information the public records of the United States government offer practically no assistance, since the public records distinguish only as to nations and not as to races. The Englishman and the American may instantly find out how each stands in the list of patentees, but the Irishman and the Negro are kept in the dark—especially the latter.

The official records of the United States Patent Office, with a single exception, give no hint whatever that of the thousands of mechanical inventions for which patents are granted annually by the government, any patent has ever been granted to a Negro. The single exception was the name of Henry Blair of Maryland, to whom the public records refer as "a colored man," stating that he was granted a patent for a corn harvester in 1834 and another patent for a similar invention in 1836.

It is altogether safe to assume that this Henry Blair was a "free person of color," as the language of those days would have phrased it; for the government seemed committed to the theory that "a slave could not take out a patent for his invention." And this dictum gave rise to some rather embarrassing situations on more occasions than one. For instance, in 1857, a Negro slave, living with his master in the state of Mississippi, perfected a valuable invention which his master sought to have protected by a patent. Now, in law, a patent is a contract between the government and the inventor or his assignees. The slave, although the inventor, could not under the law be a party to a contract, and therefore could not secure the patent himself. His master applied for the patent, but was refused on the ground that inasmuch as he was not the inventor and could not be the assignee of a slave, he could not properly make the required oath. The master was not satisfied with this interpretation of the law by the Commissioner of Patents, and at once appealed from the latter's decision to the Secretary of the Interior, who, in 1858, referred the case to the Attorney-General of the United States. This latter official, who was Hon. Jeremiah S. Black, of Pennsylvania, confirmed the decision of the Commissioner of Patent, and neither master nor slave was ever able to get a patent for the slave's invention. This case is reported on page 171 of volume 9, of "Opinions of Attorneys-General, United States."

Another instance of a similar character occurred a few years later, in 1862, when a slave belonging to Jefferson Davis, President of the Confederacy, invented a propeller for vessels. He constructed an excellent model of his invention, displaying remarkable mechanical skill in wood and metal working. He was not able to get his invention patented, but the merits of his invention were commented upon approvingly by a number of influential Southern newspapers, and his propeller was finally put in use by the Confederate navy. With the barrier of slavery cast aside, a new opportunity was opened to the Negro inventor, and the purpose of this article is to show what use he has made of that opportunity.

It must still be borne in mind that the records of the United States Patent Office do not show whether a patentee is a Negro or a Caucasian, and that to ascertain what the Negro has accomplished in the field of invention other sources of information had to be utilized; and finally, that the very omission from the public records of all data calculated to identify a given invention with the Negro race completely destroys the possibility of arriving at any definite conclusion as to the exact number and character of negro inventions.

Judging from what has been duly authenticated as Negro inventions patented by the United States, it is entirely reasonable to assume that many hundreds of valuable inventions have been patented by Negro inventors for which the race will never receive due credit. This is the more unfortunate since the race now, perhaps, more than ever before, needs the help of every fact in its favor to offset as far as possible the many discreditable things that the daily papers are all too eager to publish against it.

It appears that no systematic effort was ever made by the government to collect information as to the number of inventions by Negroes until January, 1900, when the then Commissioner of Patents, Hon. Charles H. Duell, undertook the task. Previous to that time the United States Patent Office had received numerous requests from all parts of the country for information on that point, and the uniform reply was that the official records of the Patent Office did not show whether an inventor was colored or white, and that the office had no way of obtaining such information.

Notwithstanding this fact, however, an employee of the Patent Office had undertaken to collect a list of such patents, and this list was used in selecting a small exhibit of Negro inventions first, for the Cotton Centennial at New Orleans, in 1884; again for the World's Fair at Chicago, in 1893; and, lastly, for the Southern Exposition at Atlanta in 1895. But it was reserved for the United States Commission to the Paris Exposition of 1900 to make the first definite effort to obtain this information, and at its request the following letter by the Commissioner of Patents was addressed to hundreds of patent lawyers throughout the country, to large manufacturing establishments, to the various newspapers edited by colored men, and to prominent men of the race:

DEPARTMENT OF THE INTERIOR,

UNITED STATES PATENT OFFICE.

WASHINGTON, D. C., Jan. 26, 1900.

DEAR SIR:

This Office is endeavoring to obtain information concerning patents issued to colored inventors, in accordance with a request from the United States Commission to the Paris Exposition of 1900, to be used in preparing the "Negro Exhibit."

To aid in this work, you are requested to send to this Office, in the enclosed envelope, which will not require a postage stamp, the names of any colored inventors you can furnish, together with the date of grant, title of invention, and patent number, so that a list without errors can be prepared.

You will confer a special favor by aiding in the preparation of this list by filling in the blank form below, and sending in any replies as promptly as possible. Should you be unable to furnish any data, will you kindly inform us of that fact?

Very respectfully,

C. H. DUELL,
Commissioner of Patents.

NAME.	NUMBER.	DATE.	INVENTION.

The replies to this letter showed that the correspondents personally knew of and could identify by name, date and number more than four hundred patents granted by the United States to colored inventors. The letters also showed that nearly as many more colored inventors had completed their inventions, and had applied to patent lawyers throughout the country for assistance in obtaining patents for their inventions, but finally abandoned the effort through lack of means to prosecute their applications. The list of the patented inventions as furnished mainly by the letters above named is printed below, and shows that, beginning first with agricultural implements and culinary utensils, which circumscribed the character of his earlier employment, the Negro inventor gradually widened the field of his inventive effort until he had well nigh covered the whole range of patentable subjects.

A study of the list will disclose the fact that the Negro inventor has very often, like his white brother, caught the spirit of invention, and not being contented with a single success, has frequently been led to exert his energies along many different lines of inventions.

Elijah McCoy, of Detroit, Mich., heads the list with twenty-eight patents, relating particularly to lubricating appliances for engines both stationary and locomotive, but covering also a large variety of other subjects. The next is Granville T. Woods, of Cincinnati, whose inventions are confined almost exclusively to electricity, and cover a very wide range of devices for the utilitarian application of this wonderful force. Mr. W. B. Purvis, of Philadelphia, comes next with sixteen patents relating especially to paper bag machinery, but including a few other subjects as well. Mr. F. J. Ferrell, of New York, has ten patents on valves adapted for a variety of uses. Then comes ex-Congressman Geo. W. Murray of South Carolina, with eight patents on agricultural implements. Mr. Henry Creamer has seven patents on steam traps, and more than a dozen among the number have patented as many as five different inventions.

Time and space will not admit of any extended notice of many individual patentees, but mention should be made of a few of them.

Granville T. Woods is called the "Black Edison" because of his persistent and successful investigations into the mystery of electricity. Among his inventions may be found valuable improvements in telegraphy, important telephone instruments, a system for telegraphing from moving trains, an electric railway, a phonograph, and an automatic cut-off for an electric circuit. One of his telephone inventions was sold to the American Bell Telephone Company, who is said to have paid Mr. Woods handsomely for his patent. Mr. Ferrell's inventions in valves laid the foundation for a large and highly successful manufacturing and commercial enterprise which he now conducts in the city of New York.

Mr. Elijah McCoy succeeded in placing his lubricators on many of the steam car and steamboat engines in the northwest and also on some of the ocean steamers, and from these he receives a valuable annual royalty.

Mr. Matzeliger, of Massachusetts, is credited with being the pioneer in the art of attaching soles to shoes by machinery; and Mr. Joseph Lee, of Boston, is said to have placed his kneading machine in many of the first-class bakeries and hotels in Boston and New York, from which he receives a substantial royalty.

So far as is known to the writer Miss Miriam E. Benjamin, of Massachusetts, is the only colored woman who has received a patent for an invention, and the principle of her invention, that of a gong signal, has just been adopted in the United States House of Representatives in signalling for the pages to attend upon members who want them for errands. Formerly the pages were signalled by members clapping their hands, and the noise incident to this method was frequently a great disturbance of the House proceedings. The new system just adopted involves merely the pressing of a button on the member's chair, and this rings a small gong while displaying a signal on the back of the chair.

Another invention by a young colored man which has attracted considerable attention is the rapid-fire gun by Mr. Eugene Burkins, of Chicago. This gun has been examined by officers of the War and Navy Departments, and has been pronounced a valuable contribution to the scientific equipments for military and naval warfare.

The following description of Mr. Burkins' gun appeared in Howard's American Magazine some months ago:

"A brief description of the gun is not exactly out of place, although the Scientific American and other technical journals have long since given it to the world. It is an improvement upon all that has yet been done in the way of ordnance, and the principles involved in its construction can be applied to any size of gun, from a one-inch barker to a thirty-six-inch thunderer. The model as it now stands weighs 475 pounds, measures four inches at breech, and is constructed of the finest of gun brass at a cost of $3,500. There is a magazine at the breech in which a large number of heavy shells can be held in reserve, and in the action of the gun these slip down to their places and are fired at the rate of fourteen a minute, an improvement on the Maxim gun of four shots. The gun is elevated upon a revolving turret with electrical connections, enabling the gunner to direct the action of the machine with a touch of his finger. Firing, reloading and ejection of shells are all effected by electricity, and a child could conduct the work of manning the gun as easily as anyone."

These inventions show how completely in error are those who constantly assert that the Negro has made no lasting contribution to the civilization of the age, and they prove conclusively that under favorable environment he is capable of performing his whole duty in the work of mankind whether it be tilling the earth with his hoe or advancing the world by his thought.

LIST OF COLORED INVENTORS IN THE UNITED STATES AS FURNISHED FOR THE PARIS EXPOSITION, 1900.

Inventor.	Invention.	Date.	Number.
Abrams, W. B.	Hame Attachment	Apr. 14, 1891.	450,550
Allen, C. W.	Self-Leveling Table	Nov. 1, 1898.	613,436
Allen, J. B.	Clothes Line Support	Dec. 10, 1895.	551,105
Ashbourne, A. P.	Process for Preparing Cocoanut for Domestic Use	June 1, 1875.	163,962
Ashbourne, A. P.	Biscuit Cutter	Nov. 30, 1875.	170,460
Ashbourne, A. P.	Refining Cocoanut Oil	July 27, 1880.	230,518
Ashbourne, A. P.	Process of Treating Cocoanut	Aug. 21, 1877.	194,287
Blair, H.	Corn Planter	Oct. 14, 1834.	
Bailey, L. C.	Combined Truss and Bandage	Sept. 25, 1883.	285,545
Blair, Henry	Cotton Planter	Aug. 31, 1836.	
Bailey, L. C.	Folding Bed	July 18, 1899.	629,286
Bailes, Wm.	Ladder Scaffold Support	Aug. 5, 1879.	218,154
Bailiff, C. O.	Shampoo Headrest	Oct. 11, 1898.	612,008
Ballow, W. J.	Combined Hatrack and Table	Mar. 29, 1898.	601,422
Barnes, G. A. E.	Design for Sign	Aug. 19, 1898.	29,193
Beard, A. J.	Rotary Engine	July 5, 1892.	478,271
Beard, A. J.	Car-coupler	Nov. 23, 1897.	594,059
Becket, G. E.	Letter Box	Oct. 4, 1892.	483,525
Bell, L.	Locomotive Smoke Stack	May 23, 1871.	115,153
Bell, L.	Dough Kneader	Dec. 10, 1872.	133,823
Benjamin, L. W.	Broom Moisteners and Bridles	May 16, 1893.	497,747
Benjamin, Miss M. E.	Gong and Signal Chairs for Hotels	July 17, 1888.	386,286
Blackburn, A. B.	Railway Signal	Jan. 10, 1888.	376,362
Blackburn, A. B.	Spring Seat for Chairs	Apr. 3, 1888.	380,420
Blackburn, A. B.	Cash Carrier	Oct. 23, 1888.	391,577
Blue, L.	Hand Corn Shelling Device	May 20, 1884.	298,937
Binga, M. W.	Street Sprinkling Apparatus	July 22, 1879.	217,843
Booker, L. F.	Design Rubber Scraping Knife	Mar. 28, 1899.	30,404
Boone, Sarah	Ironing Board	Apr. 26, 1892.	473,653
Bowman, H. A.	Making Flags	Feb. 23, 1892.	469,395
Brooks, C. B.	Punch	Oct. 31, 1893.	507,672
Brooks, C. B.	Street-Sweepers	Mar. 17, 1896.	556,711
Brooks, C. B.	Street-Sweepers	May 12, 1896.	560,154
Brooks, Hallstead and Page	Street-Sweepers	Apr. 21, 1896.	558,719
Brown, Henry	Receptacle for Storing and Preserving Papers	Nov. 2, 1886.	352,036

Inventor.	Invention.	Date.	Number.
Brown, L. F.	Bridle Bit	Oct. 25, 1892.	484,994
Brown, O. E.	Horseshoe	Aug. 23, 1892.	481,271
Brown & Latimer	Water Closets for Railway Cars	Feb. 10, 1874.	147,363
Burr, J. A.	Lawn Mower	May 9, 1899.	624,749
Burr, W. F.	Switching Device for Railways	Oct. 31, 1899.	636,197
Burwell, W.	Boot or Shoe	Nov. 28, 1899.	638,143
Butler, R. A.	Train Alarm	June 15, 1897.	584,540
Butts, J. W.	Luggage Carrier	Oct. 10, 1899.	634,611
Byrd, T. J.	Improvement in Holders for Reins for Horses	Feb. 6, 1872.	123,328
Byrd, T. J.	Apparatus for Detaching Horses from Carriages	Mar. 19, 1872.	124,790
Byrd, T. J.	Improvement in Neck Yokes for Wagons	Apr. 30, 1872.	126,181
Byrd, T. J.	Improvement in Car-Couplings	Dec. 1, 1874.	157,370
Burkins, Eugene	Rapid-Fire Gun		649,433
Campbell, W. S.	Self-Setting Animal Trap	Aug. 30, 1881.	246,369
Cargill, B. F.	Invalid Cot	July 25, 1899.	629,658
Carrington, T. A.	Range	July 25, 1876.	180,323
Carter, W. C.	Umbrella Stand	Aug. 4, 1885.	323,397
Certain, J. M.	Parcel Carrier for Bicycles	Dec. 26, 1899.	639,708
Cherry, M. A.	Velocipede	May 8, 1888.	382,351
Church, T. S.	Carpet Beating Machine	July 29, 1884.	302,237
Cherry, M. A.	Street Car Fender	Jan. 1, 1895.	531,908
Clare, O. B.	Trestle	Oct. 9, 1888.	390,753
Coates, R.	Overboot for Horses	Apr. 19, 1892.	473,295
Cook, G.	Automatic Fishing Device	May 30, 1899.	625,829
Coolidge, J. S.	Harness Attachment	Nov. 13, 1888.	392,908
Cooper, A. R.	Shoemaker's Jack	Aug. 22, 1899.	631,519
Cooper, J.	Shutter and Fastening	May 1, 1883.	276,563
Cooper, J.	Elevator Device	Apr. 2, 1895.	536,605
Cooper, J.	Elevator Device	Sept. 21, 1897.	590,257
Cornwell, P. W.	Draft Regulator	Oct. 2, 1888.	390,284
Cornwell, P. W.	Draft Regulator	Feb. 7, 1893.	491,082
Cralle, A. L.	Ice-Cream Mold	Feb. 2, 1897.	576,395
Creamer, H.	Steam Feed Water Trap	Mar. 17, 1885.	313,854
Creamer, H.	Steam Traps	Mar. 8, 1887.	358,964
Creamer, H.	Steam Traps	Jan. 17, 1888.	376,586
Creamer, H.	Steam Trap Feeder	Dec. 11, 1888.	394,463
Creamer, H.	Steam Trap	May 28, 1889.	404,174
Creamer, H.	Steam Trap	Aug. 18, 1891.	457,983
Creamer, H.	Steam Trap	Nov. 21, 1893.	509,202
Cosgrove, W. F.	Automatic Stop Plug for Gas Oil Pipes	Mar. 17, 1885.	313,993
Darkins, J. T.	Ventilation	Feb. 19, 1895.	534,322
Davis, I. D.	Tonic	Nov. 2, 1886.	351,829
Davis, W. D.	Riding Saddles	Oct. 6, 1896.	568,939
Davis, W. R., Jr.	Library Table	Sept. 24, 1878.	208,378

Inventor.	Invention.	Date.	Number.
Deitz, W. A.	Shoe	Apr. 30, 1867.	64,205
Dorticus, C. J.	Device for Applying Coloring Liquids to Sides of Soles or Heels of Shoes	Mar. 19, 1895.	535,820
Dickinson, J. H.	Pianola	Detroit, Mich., 1899.	
Dorticus, C. J.	Machine for Embossing Photo	Apr. 16, 1895.	537,442
Dorticus, C. J.	Photographic Print Wash	Apr. 23, 1895.	537,968
Dorticus, C. J.	Hose Leak Stop	July 18, 1899.	629,315
Downing, P. B.	Electric Switch for Railroad	June 17, 1890.	430,118
Downing, P. B.	Letter Box	Oct. 27, 1891.	462,093
Downing, P. B.	Street Letter Box	Oct. 27, 1891.	462,096
Dunnington, J. H.	Horse Detachers	Mar. 16, 1897.	578,979
Dorsey, O.	Door-Holding Device	Dec. 10, 1878.	210,764
Edmonds, T. H.	Separating Screens	July 20, 1897.	586,724
Elkins, T.	Dining, Ironing Table and Quilting Frame Combined	Feb. 22, 1870.	100,020
Elkins, T.	Chamber Commode	Jan. 9, 1872.	122,518
Elkins, T.	Refrigerating Apparatus	Nov. 4, 1879.	221,222
Evans, J. H.	Convertible Settees	Oct. 5, 1897.	591,095
Faulkner, H.	Ventilated Shoe	Apr. 29, 1890.	426,495
Ferrell, F. J.	Steam Trap	Feb. 11, 1890.	420,993
Ferrell, F. J.	Apparatus for Melting Snow	May 27, 1890.	428,670
Ferrell, F. J.	Valve	May 27, 1890.	428,671
Ferrell, F. J.	Valve	Apr. 14, 1891.	450,451
Ferrell, F. J.	Valve	Nov. 10, 1891.	462,762
Ferrell, F. J.	Valve	Jan. 26, 1892.	467,796
Ferrell, F. J.	Valve	Feb. 2, 1892.	468,242
Ferrell, F. J.	Valve	Feb. 9, 1892.	468,334
Ferrell, F. J.	Valve	Jan. 17, 1893.	490,227
Ferrell, F. J.	Valve	July 18, 1893.	501,497
Fisher, D. A.	Joiners' Clamp	Apr. 20, 1875.	162,281
Fisher, D. A.	Furniture Castor	Mar. 14, 1876.	174,794
Flemming, R. F., Jr.	Guitar	Mar. 3, 1886.	338,727
Goode, Sarah E.	Folding Cabinet Bed	July 14, 1885.	322,177
Grant, G. F.	Golf-Tee	Dec. 12, 1899.	638,920
Grant, W. S.	Curtain Rod Support	Aug. 4, 1896.	565,075
Gray, R. H.	Baling Press	Aug. 28, 1894.	525,203
Gregory, J.	Motor	Apr. 26, 1887.	361,937
Gray, R. H.	Cistern Cleaners	Apr. 9, 1895.	537,151
Grenon, H.	Razor Stropping Device	Feb. 18, 1896.	554,867
Griffin, F. W.	Pool Table Attachment	June 13, 1899.	626,902
Gunn, S. W.	Boot or Shoe	Jan. 16, 1900.	641,642
Haines, J. H.	Portable Basin	Sept. 28, 1897.	590,833
Hammonds, J. F.	Apparatus for Holding Yarn Skeins	Dec. 15, 1896.	572,985
Harding, F. H.	Extension Banquet Table	Nov. 22, 1898.	614,468
Hawkins, J.	Gridiron	Mar. 26, 1845.	3,973
Hawkins, R.	Harness Attachment	Oct. 4, 1887.	370,943
Headen, M.	Foot Power Hammer	Oct. 5, 1886.	350,363

Inventor.	Invention.	Date.	Number.
Hearness, R.	Sealing Attachment for Bottles	Feb. 15, 1898.	598,929
Hearness, R.	Detachable Car Fender	July 4, 1899.	628,003
Hilyer, A. F.	Water Evaporator Attachment for Hot Air Registers	Aug. 26, 1890.	435,095
Hilyer, A. F.	Registers	Oct. 14, 1890.	438,159
Holmes, E. H.	Gage	Nov. 12, 1895.	549,513
Hunter, J. H.	Portable Weighing Scales	Nov. 3, 1896.	570,553
Hyde, R. N.	Composition for Cleaning and Preserving Carpets	Nov. 6, 1888.	392,205
Jackson, B. F.	Heating Apparatus	Mar. 1, 1898.	599,985
Jackson, B. F.	Matrix Drying Apparatus	May 10, 1898.	603,879
Jackson, B. F.	Gas Burner	Apr. 4, 1899.	622,482
Jackson, H. A.	Kitchen Table	Oct. 6, 1896.	569,135
Jackson, W. H.	Railway Switch	Mar. 9, 1897.	578,641
Jackson, W. H.	Railway Switch	Mar. 16, 1897.	593,665
Jackson, W. H.	Automatic Locking Switch	Aug. 23, 1898.	609,436
Johnson, D.	Rotary Dining Table	Jan. 15, 1888.	396,089
Johnson, D.	Lawn Mower Attachment	Sept. 10, 1889.	410,836
Johnson, D.	Grass Receivers for Lawn Mowers	June 10, 1890.	429,629
Johnson, I. R.	Bicycle Frame	Oct. 10, 1899.	634,823
Johnson, P.	Swinging Chairs	Nov. 15, 1881.	249,530
Johnson, P.	Eye Protector	Nov. 2, 1880.	234,039
Johnson, W.	Velocipede	June 20, 1899.	627,335
Johnson, W. A.	Paint Vehicle	Dec. 4, 1888.	393,763
Johnson, W. H.	Overcoming Dead Centers	Feb. 4, 1896.	554,223
Johnson, W. H.	Overcoming Dead Centers	Oct. 11, 1898.	612,345
Johnson, W.	Egg Beater	Feb. 5, 1884.	292,821
Jones & Long	Caps for Bottles	Sept. 13, 1898.	610,715
Joyce, J. A.	Ore Bucket	Apr. 26, 1898.	603,143
Latimer, L. H.	Manufacturing Carbons	June 17, 1882.	252,386
Latimer, L. H.	Apparatus for Cooling and Disinfecting	Jan. 12, 1886.	334,078
Latimer, L. H.	Locking Racks for Hats, Coats and Umbrellas	Mar. 24, 1896.	557,076
Lavalette, W. A.	Printing Press	Sept. 17, 1878.	208,208
Lee, H.	Animal Trap	Feb. 12, 1867.	61,941
Lee, J.	Kneading Machine	Aug. 7, 1894.	524,042
Lee, J.	Bread Crumbing Machine	June 4, 1895.	540,553
Leslie, F. W.	Envelope Seal	Sept. 21, 1897.	590,325
Lewis, A. L.	Window Cleaner	Sept. 27, 1892.	483,359
Lewis, E. R.	Spring Gun	May 3, 1887.	362,096
Linden, H.	Piano Truck	Sept. 8, 1891.	459,365
Little, E.	Bridle-Bit	Mar. 7, 1882.	254,666
Loudin, F. J.	Sash Fastener	Dec. 12, 1892.	510,432
Loudin, F. J.	Key Fastener	Jan. 9, 1894.	512,308
Love, J. L.	Plasterers' Hawk	July 9, 1895.	542,419
Love, J. L.	Pencil Sharpener	Nov. 23, 1897.	594,114
Marshall, W.	Grain Binder	May 11, 1886.	341,589

Inventor.	Invention.	Date.	Number.
Marshall, T. J.	Fire Extinguisher	May 26, 1872.	125,063
Martin, W. A.	Lock	July 23, 1889.	407,738
Martin, W. A.	Lock	Dec. 30, 1890.	443,945
Matzeliger, J. E.	Mechanism for Distributing Tacks	Nov. 26, 1899.	415,726
Matzeliger, J. E.	Nailing Machine	Feb. 25, 1896.	421,954
Matzeliger, J. E.	Tack Separating Mechanism	Mar. 25, 1890.	423,937
Matzeliger, J. E.	Lasting Machine	Sept. 22, 1891.	459,899
McCoy, E.	Lubricator for Steam Engines	July 2, 1872.	129,843
McCoy, E.	Lubricator for Steam Engines	Aug. 6, 1872.	130,305
McCoy, E.	Lubricator	May 27, 1873.	139,407
McCoy, E.	Steam Lubricator	Jan. 20, 1874.	146,697
McCoy, E.	Ironing Table	May 12, 1874.	150,876
McCoy, E.	Steam Cylinder Lubricator	Feb. 1, 1876.	173,032
McCoy, E.	Steam Cylinder Lubricator	July 4, 1876.	179,585
McCoy, E.	Lubricator	Mar. 28, 1882.	255,443
McCoy, E.	Lubricator	July 18, 1882.	261,166
McCoy, E.	Lubricator	Jan. 9, 1883.	270,238
McCoy, E.	Lawn Sprinkler Design	Sept. 26, 1899.	631,549
McCoy, E.	Steam Dome	June 16, 1885.	320,354
McCoy, E.	Lubricator	June 16, 1885.	320,379
McCoy, E.	Lubricator	Feb. 8, 1887.	357,491
McCoy, E.	Lubricator Attachment	Apr. 19, 1887.	361,435
McCoy, E.	Lubricator for Safety Valves	May 24, 1887.	363,529
McCoy, E.	Lubricator	May 29, 1888.	383,745
McCoy, E.	Lubricator	May 29, 1888.	383,746
McCoy & Hodges.	Lubricator	Dec. 24, 1889.	418,139
McCoy, E.	Dope Cup	Sept. 29, 1891.	460,215
McCoy, E.	Lubricator	Dec. 29, 1891.	465,875
McCoy, E.	Lubricator	Mar. 1, 1892.	470,163
McCoy, E.	Lubricator	Apr. 5, 1892.	472,066
McCoy, E.	Lubricator	June 6, 1893.	498,809
McCoy, E.	Lubricator	Sept. 13, 1898.	610,634
McCoy, E.	Lubricator	Oct. 4, 1898.	611,759
McCoy, E.	Lubricator	Nov. 15, 1898.	614,307
McCoy, E.	Lubricator	June 27, 1899.	627,623
McCree, D.	Portable Fire Escape	Nov. 11, 1890.	440,322
Mendenhall, A.	Holder for Driving Reins	Nov. 28, 1899.	637,811
Miles, A.	Elevator	Oct. 11, 1887.	371,207
Mitchell, C. L.	Phoneterisin	Jan. 1, 1884.	291,071
Mitchell, J. M.	Cheek Row Corn Planter	Jan. 16, 1900.	641,462
Moody, W. U.	Game Board Design	May 11, 1897.	27,046
Morehead, K.	Reel Carrier	Oct. 6, 1896.	568,916
Murray, G. W.	Combined Furrow Opener and Stalk-knocker	Apr. 10, 1894.	517,960
Murray, G. W.	Cultivator and Marker	Apr. 10, 1894.	517,961
Murray, G. W.	Planter	June 5, 1894.	520,887
Murray, G. W.	Cotton Chopper	June 5, 1894.	520,888
Murray, G. W.	Fertilizer Distributer	June 5, 1894.	520,889

Inventor.	Invention.	Date.	Number.
Murray, G. W.	Planter	June 5, 1894.	520,890
Murray, G. W.	Combined Cotton Seed	June 5, 1894.	520,891
Murray, G. W.	Planter and Fertilizer Distributer Reaper	June 5, 1894.	520,892
Murray, W.	Attachment for Bicycles	Jan. 27, 1891.	445,452
Nance, L.	Game Apparatus	Dec. 1, 1891.	464,035
Nash, H. H.	Life Preserving Stool	Oct. 5, 1875.	168,519
Newman, Miss L. D.	Brush	Nov. 15, 1898.	614,335
Newson, S.	Oil Heater or Cooker	May 22, 1894.	520,188
Nichols & Latimer.	Electric Lamp	Sept. 13, 1881.	247,097
Nickerson, W. J.	Mandolin and Guitar Attachment for Pianos	June 27, 1899.	627,739
O'Conner & Turner	Alarm for Boilers	Aug. 25, 1896.	566,612
O'Conner & Turner	Steam Gage	Aug. 25, 1896.	566,613
O'Conner & Turner	Alarm for Coasts Containing Vessels	Feb. 8, 1898.	598,572
Outlaw, J. W.	Horseshoes	Nov. 15, 1898.	614,273
Perryman, F. R.	Caterers' Tray Table	Feb. 2, 1892.	468,038
Peterson, H.	Attachment for Lawn Mowers	Apr. 30, 1889.	402,189
Phelps, W. H.	Apparatus for Washing Vehicles	Mar. 23, 1897.	579,242
Pickering, J. F.	Air Ship	Feb. 20, 1900.	643,975
Pickett, H.	Scaffold	June 30, 1874.	152,511
Pinn, T. B.	File Holder	Aug. 17, 1880.	231,355
Polk, A. J.	Bicycle Support	Apr. 14, 1896.	558,103
Pugsley, A.	Blind Stop	July 29, 1890.	433,306
Purdy & Sadgwar	Folding Chair	June 11, 1889.	405,117
Purdy, W.	Device for Sharpening Edged Tools	Oct. 27, 1896.	570,337
Purdy, W.	Device for Sharpening Edged Tools	Aug. 16, 1898.	609,367
Purdy, W.	Device for Sharpening Edged Tools	Aug. 1, 1899.	630,106
Purdy & Peters	Design for Spoons	Apr. 23, 1895.	24,228
Purvis, W. B.	Bag Fastener	Apr. 25, 1882.	256,856
Purvis, W. B.	Hand Stamp	Feb. 27, 1883.	273,149
Purvis, W. B.	Paper Bag Machine	Feb. 12, 1884.	293,353
Purvis, W. B.	Fountain Pen	Jan. 7, 1890.	419,065
Purvis, W. B.	Paper Bag Machine	Jan. 28, 1890.	420,099
Purvis, W. B.	Paper Bag Machine	June 24, 1890.	430,684
Purvis, W. B.	Paper Bag Machine	Aug. 19, 1890.	434,461
Purvis, W. B.	Paper Bag Machine	Sept. 2, 1890.	435,524
Purvis, W. B.	Paper Bag Machine	Sept. 22, 1891.	460,093
Purvis, W. B.	Electric Railway	May 1, 1894.	519,291
Purvis, W. B.	Paper Bag Machine	May 8, 1894.	519,348
Purvis, W. B.	Paper Bag Machine	May 8, 1894.	519,349
Purvis, W. B.	Paper Bag Machine	Dec. 11, 1894.	530,650
Purvis, W. B.	Magnetic Car Balancing Device	May 21, 1895.	539,542
Purvis, W. B.	Paper Bag Machine	Mar. 9, 1897.	578,361
Purvis, W. B.	Electric Railway Switch	Aug. 17, 1897.	588,176
Queen, W.	Guard for Companion Ways and Hatches	Aug. 18, 1891.	458,131
Ray, E. P.	Chair Supporting Device	Feb. 21, 1899.	620,078

Inventor.	Invention.	Date.	Number.
Ray, L. P.	Dust Pan	Aug. 3, 1897.	587,607
Reed, J. W.	Dough Kneader and Roller	Sept. 23, 1884.	305,474
Reynolds, R. R.	Non-Refillable Bottle	May 2, 1899.	624,092
Reynolds, H. H.	Window Ventilator for R. R. Cars	Apr. 3, 1883.	275,271
Reynolds, H. H.	Safety Gate for Bridges	Oct. 7, 1890.	437,937
Rhodes, J. B.	Water Closets	Dec. 19, 1899.	639,290
Richardson, A. C.	Hame Fastener	Mar. 14, 1882.	255,022
Richardson, A. C.	Churn	Feb. 17, 1891.	446,470
Richardson, A. C.	Casket Lowering Device	Nov. 13, 1894.	529,311
Richardson, A. C.	Insect Destroyer	Feb. 28, 1899.	620,362
Richardson, A. C.	Bottle	Dec. 12, 1899.	638,811
Richardson, W. H.	Cotton Chopper	June 1, 1886.	343,140
Richardson, W. H.	Child's Carriage	June 18, 1889.	405,599
Richardson, W. H.	Child's Carriage	June 18, 1889.	405,600
Richey, C. V.	Car Coupling	June 15, 1897.	584,650
Richey, C. V.	Railroad Switch	Aug. 3, 1897.	587,657
Richey, C. V.	Railroad Switch	Oct. 26, 1897.	592,448
Richey, C. V.	Fire Escape Bracket	Dec. 28, 1897.	596,427
Richey, C. V.	Combined Hammock and Stretcher	Dec. 13, 1898.	615,907
Rickman, A. L.	Overshoe	Feb. 8, 1898.	598,816
Ricks, J.	Horseshoe	Mar. 30, 1886.	338,781
Ricks, J.	Overshoe for Horses	June 6, 1899.	626,245
Robinson, E. R.	Electric Railway Trolley	Sept. 19, 1893.	505,370
Robinson, E. R.	Casting Composite	Nov. 23, 1897.	594,286
Robinson, J. H.	Life Saving Guards for Locomotives	Mar. 14, 1899.	621,143
Robinson, J. H.	Life Saving Guards for Street Cars	Apr. 25, 1899.	623,929
Robinson, J.	Dinner Pail	Feb. 1, 1887.	356,852
Romain, A.	Passenger Register	Apr. 23, 1889.	402,035
Roster, D. N.	Feather Curler	Mar. 10, 1896.	556,166
Ross, A. L.	Runner for Stops	Aug. 4, 1896.	565,301
Ross, A. L.	Bag Closure	June 7, 1898.	605,343
Ross, J.	Bailing Press	Sept. 5, 1899.	632,539
Ross, A. L.	Trousers Support	Nov. 28, 1899.	638,068
Ruffin, S.	Vessels for Liquids and Manner of Sealing	Nov. 20, 1899.	737,603
Russell, L. A.	Guard Attachment for Beds	Aug. 13, 1895.	544,381
Sampson, G. T.	Sled Propeller	Feb. 17, 1885.	312,388
Sampson, G. T.	Clothes Drier	June 7, 1892.	476,416
Scottron, S. R.	Adjustable Window Cornice	Feb. 17, 1880.	224,732
Scottron, S. R.	Cornice	Jan. 16, 1883.	270,851
Scottron, S. R.	Pole Tip	Sept. 21, 1886.	349,525
Scottron, S. R.	Curtain Rod	Aug. 30, 1892.	481,720
Scottron, S. R.	Supporting Bracket	Sept. 12, 1893.	505,008
Shorter, D. W.	Feed Rack	May 17, 1887.	363,089
Shanks, S. C.	Sleeping Car Berth Register	July 21, 1897.	587,165
Smith, J. W.	Improvement in Games	Apr. 17, 1900.	647,887
Smith, J. W.	Lawn Sprinkler	May 4, 1897.	581,785
Smith, J. W.	Lawn Sprinkler	Mar. 22, 1898.	601,065

Inventor.	Invention.	Date.	Number.
Smith, P. D.	Potato Digger	Jan. 21, 1891.	445,206
Smith, P. D.	Grain Binder	Feb. 23, 1892.	469,279
Snow & Johns	Liniment	Oct. 7, 1890.	437,728
Standard, J.	Oil Stove	Oct. 29, 1889.	413,689
Standard, J.	Refrigerator	July 14, 1891.	455,891
Stewart, T. W.	Mop	June 13, 1893.	499,402
Stewart, T. W.	Station Indicator	June 20, 1893.	499,895
Stewart & Johnson	Metal Bending Machine	Dec. 27, 1887.	375,512
Stewart, E. W.	Punching Machine	May 3, 1887.	362,190
Stewart, E. W.	Machine for Forming Vehicle Seat Bars	Mar. 22, 1887.	373,698
Spears, H.	Portable Shield for Infantry	Dec. 27, 1870.	110,599
Sutton, E. H.	Cotton Cultivator	Apr. 7, 1874.	149,543
Sweeting, J. A.	Device for Rolling Cigarettes	Nov. 30, 1897.	594,501
Sweeting, J. A.	Combined Knife and Scoop	June 7, 1898.	605,209
Shewcraft, Frank	Letter Box	Detroit, Mich.	
Taylor, B. H.	Rotary Engine	Apr. 23, 1878.	202,888
Taylor, B. H.	Slide Valve	July 6, 1897.	585,798
Thomas, S. E.	Waste Trap	Oct. 16, 1883.	286,746
Thomas, S. E.	Waste Trap for Basins, Closets, etc.	Oct. 4, 1887.	371,107
Thomas, S. E.	Casting	July 31, 1888.	386,941
Thomas, S. E.	Pipe Connection	Oct. 9, 1888.	390,821
Toliver, George	Propeller for Vessels	Apr. 28, 1891.	451,086
Tregoning & Latimer	Globe Supporter for Electric Lamps	Mar. 21, 1882.	255,212
Walker, Peter	Machine for Cleaning Seed Cotton	Feb. 16, 1897.	577,153
Walker, Peter	Bait Holder	Mar. 8, 1898.	600,241
Waller, J. N.	Shoemaker's Cabinet or Bench	Feb. 3, 1880.	224,253
Washington, Wade	Corn Husking Machine	Aug. 14, 1883.	283,173
Watkins, Isaac	Scrubbing Frame	Oct. 7, 1890.	437,849
Watts, J. R.	Bracket for Miners' Lamp	Mar. 7, 1893.	493,137
West, E. H.	Weather Shield	Sept. 5, 1899.	632,385
West, J. W.	Wagon	Oct. 18, 1870.	108,419
White, D. L.	Extension Steps for Cars	Jan. 12, 1897.	574,969
White, J. T.	Lemon Squeezer	Dec. 8, 1896.	572,849
Williams, Carter	Canopy Frame	Feb. 2, 1892.	468,280
Williams, J. P.	Pillow Sham Holder	Oct. 10, 1899.	634,784
Winn, Frank	Direct Acting Steam Engine	Dec. 4, 1888.	394,047
Winters, J. R.	Fire Escape Ladder	May 7, 1878.	203,517
Winters, J. R.	Fire Escape Ladder	Apr. 8, 1879.	214,224
Woods, G. T.	Steam Boiler Furnace	June 3, 1884.	299,894
Woods, G. T.	Telephone Transmitter	Dec. 2, 1884.	308,817
Woods, G. T.	Apparatus for Transmission of Messages by Electricity	Apr. 7, 1885.	315,368
Woods, G. T.	Relay Instrument	June 7, 1887.	364,619
Woods, G. T.	Polarized Relay	July 5, 1887.	366,192
Woods, G. T.	Electro Mechanical Brake	Aug. 16, 1887.	368,265
Woods, G. T.	Telephone System and Apparatus	Oct. 11, 1887.	371,241
Woods, G. T.	Electro-Magnetic Brake Apparatus	Oct. 18, 1887.	371,655

Inventor.	Invention.	Date.	Number.
Woods, G. T.	Railway Telegraphy	Nov. 15, 1887.	373,383
Woods, G. T.	Induction Telegraph System	Nov. 29, 1887.	373,915
Woods, G. T.	Overhead Conducting System for Electric Railway	May 29, 1888.	383,844
Woods, G. T.	Electro-Motive Railway System	June 26, 1888.	385,034
Woods, G. T.	Tunnel Construction for Electric Railway	July 17, 1888.	386,282
Woods, G. T.	Galvanic Battery	Aug. 14, 1888.	387,839
Woods, G. T.	Railway Telegraphy	Aug. 28, 1888.	388,803
Woods, G. T.	Automatic Safety Cut-out for Electric Circuits	Jan. 1, 1889.	395,533
Woods, G. T.	Automatic Safety Cut-out for Electric Circuit	Oct. 14, 1889.	438,590
Woods, G. T.	Electric Railway System	Nov. 10, 1891.	463,020
Woods, G. T.	Electric Railway Supply System	Oct. 31, 1893.	507,606
Woods, G. T.	Electric Railway Conduit	Nov. 21, 1893.	509,065
Woods, G. T.	System of Electrical Distribution	Oct. 13, 1896.	569,443
Woods, G. T.	Amusement Apparatus	Dec. 19, 1899.	639,692
Wormley, James	Life Saving Apparatus	May 24, 1881.	242,091
Williams, P. B.	Electro-Magnetic Electrical Railway Track Switch	Apr. 24, 1900.	648,092
Williams, P. B.	Electrically Controlled and Operated Railway Switch	Jan. 15, 1901.	666,080

TOPIC XXVIII.

WHAT THE OMEN?

BY PROF. W. S. SCARBOROUGH.

The all-absorbing question now before the American people seems to be the race question. Our magazines and papers generally—dailies and weeklies as well as monthlies—are deluged as it were with articles on the Negro people—the Negro as a citizen—his status, his future, the sort of education best adapted to his needs as a man and a citizen, and kindred subjects. In fact no phase of the Negro's life fails of discussion at the hands of the most flippant penny-a-liner as well as the gravest thinker. All have theories of some sort and they do not hesitate to express them—whether they are visionary or practical.

If theories alone could have solved this problem, long ere this would race friction have been removed; it would have been a question of the past, but unfortunately for the race, unfortunately for the people at large, many of those who knew least about the subject and who had no remedy for the troubles complained of—have had most to say and they have generally said it in the most reckless way, regardless of facts. Only now and then do we have a calm view of the situation with reasonable suggestions as to the best course to follow.

As we enter upon the twentieth century, it will be well for black and white to get together and understand one another and ascertain as far as possible what is best to do in the light of facts before us.

One thing is certain—the white man does not yet know the Negro. Strange as it may seem, the Northern white man does not know him after many years of close observation, neither does the Southern white man, for all the years gone by in which the Negro has lived in his midst. The observations of both in fact only leave the Negro largely an unknown quantity to either. I have claimed heretofore that there is a life that the white man knows nothing of. It is found in the hovel as well as in the cultured home, in the school and the church. It is a life in the bud-time of race pride and another race prejudice; and it is swelling to the blossoming. *What will be the fruit?*

To know the race one must do more than occasionally to visit it here

414

Prof. W. S. Scarborough.

PROF. WILLIAM S. SCARBOROUGH, A. M., LL. D.

William S. Scarborough, now Vice-President of Wilberforce University, Wilberforce, Ohio, and Professor of Greek and Latin in the same institution, was born in Macon, Ga., February 16, 1852. He received his early education in his native city before and during the Civil War. In 1869 he entered Atlanta University where he remained two years in preparation for Yale University, but, instead, entered Oberlin College, Oberlin, Ohio, in 1871, and was graduated from the Department of Philosophy and the Arts with the degree of A. B. in 1875. He spent a part of the following year in Oberlin Theological Seminary in special study of the Semitic languages and Hellenistic Greek.

In 1877 Professor Scarborough was elected as head of the Classical Department in Wilberforce University. In 1881 he published through A. S. Barnes & Co. (New York) a Greek text book—"First Lessons in Greek"—the first and only Greek book ever written by a Negro. This book was widely used by both the white and colored schools of the country, especially in the North. Professor Scarborough has also written a treatise entitled "The Birds of Aristophanes—a Theory of Interpretation"—aside from numerous tracts and pamphlets, covering a variety of subjects—classical, archaeological, sociological and racial. He has written many papers for various societies to which he belongs. In 1891 he was transferred to the chair of Hellenistic Greek, Payne Theological Seminary. In 1897 he was again re-elected as Professor of Latin and Greek in the University and Vice-President of the same.

He has contributed largely to the press of the country, including the leading magazines. He is one of the editors of the A. M. E. Sunday-school publications, having filled that position for a number of years. He is a member of a number of associations: American Philological, American Dialect, American Social Science, Archaeological Institute of America, American Spelling Reform, American Folk-Lore, American Modern Language, American Political and Social Science, the Egyptian Exploration Fund Association and the American Negro Academy, of which he is First Vice-President. He has several times been one of the orators at the Lincoln League banquet of the State of Ohio. At a conference held by the leaders of the race in the city of Columbus, Ohio, he was elected President of the Afro-American State League designed to further the interests of the Negro throughout the country. Professor Scarborough has traveled extensively in Europe. He was a delegate to the Ecumenical Methodist Conference held in London in 1901, representing the African Methodist Episcopal Church.

We take the following from the "New York Age" of July 18:

"While in Boston Prof. W. S. Scarborough of Wilberforce University was delightfully entertained by the colored graduates of Harvard University and Amherst College at a reception given in his honor at the home of Mr. G. W. Forbes, a graduate of Amherst. Speeches were made by Messrs. Forbes, Morgan, Trotter, Lewis, Williams and others eulogistic of the life and services of the professor in behalf of his race. The professor replied, thanking them for the honor conferred upon him. Next year it will be twenty-five years since Professor Scarborough first became connected with Wilberforce University as its classical professor and he intends to mark the event by publishing a volume of his philological papers. These papers have all been read before the American Philological Association at its various annual sessions. Twenty years ago Professor Scarborough was first elected to membership in this body at Harvard University. This year the association again met at this venerable seat of learning and by way of commemorating the event Professor Scarborough read a paper on Thucydides. It is some of these papers that the professor intends to put into more tangible form for future use."

and there, must see more than even a close examination of schools and churches, instructed, aided and supported by white philanthropy, will disclose. The toadying, the servile representatives of the race, the politicians, the dependent ones—all must be passed by and the people found. *To know the Negro one must be with him and become a part of his life —see what he is doing, and above all, to know what he is thinking.*

Go into the schools and churches where there is not a shadow of white influence to check freedom of speech or tinge thought and what do we see and hear? In every case we find those from the oldest to the youngest with some ideas upon the race question and ready to express them. Not so with white children. They are not thinking about the color of their skin or the texture of their hair or their rights and privileges or the deprivation of these rights, the contempt and ostracism following them everywhere; but the Negro child, on the other hand, of every shade of color has these almost constantly in mind, for they are thrust upon him. *He can think of little else.*

In such schools, in such communities, the field work, the social gathering, the literary society, the routine of school or church or community life, the platform—all are tinctured deeply with these ideas and these are expressed in some form on every possible occasion. All these questions are in a large degree to the race, as far as interest is concerned, at least, the momentous, the ever-present, ever-burning topic.

No youth of the white race feels the weight of any subject agitating the mind of the public as these colored youth feel this one. What is the omen, when boys and girls alike make it a common question, in some form or other for all their daily work? It has been said that the two races are growing apart, that there is as much race prejudice in the one as in the other. In many respects this is true, though the prejudice on the part of the Negro is a thing of natural growth from certain causes, not an inherent quality. The fact that the Negro is rising without anything like adequate recognition—at least other than a patronizing one— is one of these causes. As here and there the Negro comes to the white man's higher level, among the best he is confronted with that "Ah-you-are-here." Ah, which means more than words can express and he straightway feels his pulses stirred to the defensive counter spirit of "I-am-and-what-are-you-going-to-do-about-it?" The result is the two mutually draw back from each other.

Among the middle classes where the level of the whites intellectually and financially is more readily and more rapidly being reached by the greater number of Negroes there is still more prejudice to be found. It is here where the Negro has his fiercest battle ground; it is here where he finds his greatest opposition. It is only following out the idea of the French writer who said, "Mediocrity alone is jealous." The constant desire of this class of white people to rise to the highest level aggravates them upon seeing a Negro reaching out for or obtaining in any way that which they may have or may be seeking, and they "take it out" by greater assumption of superiority especially over those of the race who have reached their own plane of living, and here again is a creation of a counter prejudice.

Growing refinement brings with it to the Negro all that sensitiveness which is accorded to refined people wherever found, and naturally he recoils from rebuffs, insults, and contumely, and holds himself aloof more and more only as business demands contact. He has no growing reason to revere the whites as a mass, and if nations are proverbially ungrateful, what more can be expected of individuals, no matter how much fine theorizing there may be upon the subject of what the Negro owes to the white man.

With this increasing prejudice, for reasons named, there is a growing race pride. This is taking firm root among the young people of the Negro race who are being taught to respect those of their own number who have obtained honor and distinction through merit. The school-boy and school-girl are studying the history of their own race with eagerness. They are finding out that it is not an altogether degraded people from which they have sprung, and with the gathering evidences about them of education, refinement, even wealth, and high character, they see no good reason why they should be despised for mere color or the possession of some imperceptible drops of Negro blood, as in many cases. This is a laudable pride based upon both the past and present and, as we have said, they are more alive to all that pertains to race matters than any other set of young people whom we are able to mention.

What is the omen? Think you that the growing generation will tamely submit to the endless continuance of present and past grievances? Think you that this thoughtfulness of the Negro youth will be without some sort of fruit? Will these not have as much influence upon their ignorant brother masses as have the whites over the ignorant masses of their own color? I repeat, the white man does not thoroughly know the

Negro. He does not begin to see all that boils and seethes and ferments in the brains of this growing class. It is well for the nation to learn wisdom from the mouths of babes and sucklings. And when these prattle of race issues it is an omen not to be unheeded.

TOPIC XXIX.

WHY THE NEGRO RACE SURVIVES.

BY PROF. T. DE S. TUCKER.

It requires no stretch of thought to understand our constant and earnest interest in everything which concerns our environments. Every question and issue of national significance have for us a vital consideration for weal or woe. We scan with greedy eagerness the expressed policy of the statesman, we hang with bated breath on the eloquence of the sentiment moulder, we probe with tremulous care the feelings of the community to find out if we have been pushed to the rear or given a fair chance in the race to a higher life—our final place in American life.

While we are not, and should never be, unmindful of all interests which appertain to others in this vast country of which we form such a necessary part, it is natural and right that our first thought should be of our own welfare.

The position we are to definitely assume and maintain in the distinctive American civilization now in process of formation, is yet concealed in the womb of futurity; we can neither anticipate nor force it against the period of its advent. While we are passing through this slow process of development, it is well at times to take a reckoning of our race powers by way of encouragement to such as may become faint and weary in the combat. All are not strong, all are not determined, all are not forceful. The fiercest courage will now and then lose its force when battling against steady odds. Moreover, our shortcomings, like the shirt of Nessus, are not only with us ever, but they are on constant exhibition to shame, mortify and humiliate us. While it is not sensible to shut our eyes to these painful reminders of the obstacles to our progress, while it is even best to invite a searching scrutiny of them to the end that they may be torn off by heroic methods, if need be, after all an occasional study of our strong parts is a help in the struggle.

DISCARD SELF GRATULATION.

In the attempt to reflect on the staying powers of the race, I have not the remotest idea of pandering to conceit or vanity, to the contrary, I

418

Prof. J. de S. Jucker.

THOMAS de S. TUCKER.

Thomas de S. Tucker first saw the light of day at Victoria, in Sherbro, Sierra Leone, West Coast of Africa, on the 21st day of July, 1844. His mother was the youngest daughter of James Tucker, hereditary chief of Sherbro. The founder of the family, about two hundred years previous, was an Englishman, from whom the surname is derived.

On the paternal side, Tucker comes of an ancient noble family in the east of France, the de Salieres, of Marseilles. His father, Joseph, although descended from this noble lineage, was an ardent admirer of Napoleon Bonaparte, whose checkered fortunes he followed to the disastrous field of Waterloo.

In accordance with the custom of the country, the wife being deemed of higher social standing than the husband, the son took the maternal surname. Tucker was sent, at a tender age, to a school located in the family territory. Such was his rapid progress that in a few years he had acquired English sufficiently enough to read and write it about as well as the average child of his age in this country.

In the summer of 1856 he came to the United States to complete his education. Having just completed the English course in the public schools of Oberlin, Ohio, he entered college and completed the course in 1865. He then crossed over into Kentucky and opened day and night schools for the education of the newly freed race.

From Kentucky he removed to Louisiana, where the climate was more congenial to his tropical constitution. During his residence of many years in that State he was employed most of the time in the customs service with chances of preferment to higher and more lucrative posts, which he never sought nor cared for. His tastes have always inclined him to the more quiet and private walks of life, where he can promote the welfare of his fellow men, without show and the applause of the giddy crowd.

President Grant once advised him that he intended to offer him the Liberian Mission, but Tucker was so indifferent in the honor that he made no effort to be commissioned.

Anxious to pass away from official duties, he studied law and entered on practice in New Orleans. This profession was so fully in keeping with his tastes he hoped to pursue it the rest of his days. Finding that his legal training practically restricted him only to Louisiana, he removed to Florida and located at Pensacola. He was admitted to practice, and with it he rose rapidly both in knowledge of the common law and in securing a paying clientage. He stood high with the bar, from judge and attorneys to officials. He saw every prospect of realizing the fond dream of his ambition when once again a call of duty to serve God's humble children came in stentorious tones. The State in 1887 had founded a Normal and Industrial School for the training of Colored teachers. A telegram unexpectedly announced that Tucker had been elected by the State Board of Education to take the management of it. He demurred, he objected; but leading Colored men and the Chief Executive importuned and requested his acceptance of the place. By patient perseverance and tact he succeeded in enlisting the hearty good will of all classes to the maintenance of the institution. The history of his work is a part of the educational records. Many men and women of worth and saving influence in their respective communities in Florida owe their training to the devoted consecration to duty of this native of the "Dark Continent." The school itself will ever remain a lasting monument to his tireless, efficient devotion to the welfare of his race.

He retired from the field of his labors at the close of the fourteenth year, carrying with him universal regret for his departure, and the esteem and respect of the whole State and the acclamations of good will, especially of the people of the capital in which the Normal School is located.

decry any disposition to extol and magnify whatever we are subject-
ively, and whatever we have achieved. The fierce conflicts we have undergone and the terrible crucible through which the cruel hand of fate
promises to pass us, dispel the idea of self gratulation. Life for us in
the conflict ahead is all stern and serious. Wounds and scars will for
generations yet to come be the decorations for our leaders in thought
and action; there is no niche in the edifice consecrated to our present
and coming heroes for fulsome, windy flatteries airing their importance
to the galleries. Hearts true and stout charged with big emotions to
raise and elevate their suffering kind to a higher plane, should be the
only thinkers to claim our considerate attention and command our
homage.

THEME UNDER CONSIDERATION.

In the theme I have chosen for this paper, I shall endeavor to show
that the latent and active attributes of the negro eminently. adapt him
to be classed among the survivals of the fittest in the family of races.
Before proceeding, however, to a formal discussion of the subject, it might
not be amiss for a minute or two, to take a running retrospect of the race
since its advent into its present civil life.

The three decades which mark the close of our Civil War have perhaps not only written history more broadly in the behalf of humanity
in general as interpreted by Christian civilization, than any other similar period, but they have been the most momentous in shaping the
national life by moulding and settling policies of a lasting nature. The
admission of millions, of what is termed an alien race into the solution
of an untried problem of government by the people, rendered that problem still more difficult, hence, wild and extravagant speculations bearing
on the future of the Negro and the questionable influence of his changed
relations on American life, became the current literature of the country
for two decades. Friends spoke in fulsome praise or doubtful measure,
according to conviction, while enemies protested in exultant tone that
a generation or two hence would suffice to write the Negro's epitaph.
But even in that early period of his infancy, had the nation been disposed to study him with other than preconceived, erroneous views, it
might have perceived traits which justified the wisdom implied in his
changed condition. Thus far, if he has not risen to the dizzy heights to
which the hopes of ardent enthusiasts invited him, he has at least, not

only belied the gloomy fate of inglorious extinction, but he is going forward with steady strides to realize an honorable destiny in common with the many other people of the Republic.

ORIGIN OF A STRONG RACE.

A strong race, like marked personality, is the product of varied and opposing agencies. As in nature when conflicting elements struggle for the mastery and bear the impress of the strongest, so in the evolution of a forceful people, its character takes on the form of the means that has been most efficacious in moulding it. There is no instance in the authentic annals of the human family where a masterly people has emerged into greatness from the tame school of gentle methods. Trials keen and severe, have first slashed, cut and tortured the entire being in mind and soul to fit it for the new life it is to enjoy in accordance with its destined end. What has ever been thus will always be so.

QUALITIES INDICATING THE NEGRO'S SURVIVAL.

In this law of nature, in the formation of dominant powers, the Negro has no favor to expect. He must pass through the fiery furnace and be shorn of dross to leave the solid matter which is to constitute the framework of his strength. First among the many qualities of survival which distinguish him as an enduring race, is patient endurance and fortitude under affliction. The elastic temperament of the race in the ability to adapt itself to varying conditions, in swaying with the force of the tempest until the fury of it is spent, in seizing with instinct on circumstances that tend to save, is something not only amazing, but marvelous. No oppression however heavy, no ebullition of wrath however fiery, can swerve him from the road he has chosen to attain his purpose as a part of the pulsating life of this nation. From a dogged determination to butt aside forces which contained the elements of his salvation, the Indian has passed into a retreat closed to contact with the active life of the dominant power of the land. On the other hand, the future of the parent race of the American Negro in the dark continent is bright with hope from its ready assimilation of the civilizing agencies of European civilization. In obedience to this self-evident law of survival, Japan has entered on a new existence, while its neighbor, China, the home of a kindred race, bids fair to become the easy prey of Western greed.

STRENGTH, NOT WEAKNESS.

Now this easy swaying to conditions, when his welfare is in hazard, and for which the superficial thinker twits the negro with lack of manliness, is one of the strongest elements of his being. Were he less malleable than he is, less ready to concede where contention can only work him woe, were he wont to resent in wild and reckless fury, real or fancied wrongs, were he too obtuse to perceive and profit by the passing advantage, were he to remove his cause from the bar of reason, and the verdict of a calm judgment he would neither be imbibing the civilization of his native land, nor would he have achieved a tithe of the wonderful progress which is to-day the vindication of his freedom, and at the same time the shame and confusion of those who foretold his ignominious passing away. Patience pure and simple, coupled with, and gracing a quiet heroism, has enabled him to bridge over the earlier days of his trials, and confirm his status in the body politic to the general acceptance of the American people.

THE NEGRO'S WARFARE, MORAL AND MENTAL.

The honor which waits on material contest counts for little to the Negro's advantage. Indeed, if the strife with which he is confronted were to be waged on such an issue, the result could be foretold in advance. His warfare is moral and mental, and by the arts of peace he is to be left a cipher or rise in triumph to honorable destiny. Physical courage which the negro shows largely in common with other races has its trophies blazoned in marble and brass only to crumble beneath the corroding tooth of time. The warfare of mind and heart which ever calls in evidence only the highest courage of man's nature leaves its achievement to immortal fame to grow with the ages till time surrenders it to Eternity.

WHAT HAS BEEN ACCOMPLISHED.

By the exercise of this gentle but potent virtue of learning to labor and to wait, we have mined our way into the heart of educational authorities to grant such of our sons and daughters as are competent the privilege of becoming preceptors to the youth of the race. By the nurture of the same virtue, our slender means have tickled the greed of capital to call us away from obscure streets and narrow lanes that we may enjoy a wider range of selection of homes befitting higher tastes and growing ambition. Go, if you will, into the Southern section of our country where the bulk of our race resides, and there you will find by this same sturdy persistence to wait on time for a reward that schools, colleges, churches and business enterprises are being built and maintained. Prejudices which retard our progress are crumbling to pieces.

THE OPTIMISTIC TEMPERAMENT.

The cheerful sunny temperament of the Negro is another of the many sturdy qualities which declare his fitness to withstand the blows of adverse fortune. His long training in the school of mental and moral darkness wherein he had need to cultivate a sanguine temperament to buoy him up, stands proof against dark forebodings and pessimism. The grotesque and the ludicrous find in him a joyous patron. Where others count and bewail their woes, he sees only sunshine. Gloom and sorrow melt away at his approach, while his features are ever radiant with mirth and joy. His head is up and erect with every sense attuned to the bright, and dead to the doleful. He thanks God that the lot apportioned him is fashioned by infallible wisdom, while he munches with contentment the humble crust that honest toil has brought him. Malevolence towards his fellow men is at the most a passing emotion. Wealth and the happiness attendant on it, he neither envies nor mars. He asks a chance to live, no matter how sumptuously others may fare beyond his condition. Such a being is forever beyond the pale of anarchy, and other tendencies which work to the detriment of society. In this portraiture I have drawn no ideal, but the average Negro as he is known of all men.

In peace and in war such a being is an invaluable factor in a nation's well being. As he does not envy the class which fortune has blest with good things of this world, he therefore breeds no feeling of ill will by which he might seek to level conditions, while he is equally ready to assume his share of the dangers consequent on the maintenance of the existing order of affairs.

PATRIOTISM OF THE RACE.

Another marked characteristic of race strength is love of country. The only race in this country which has more than a shadow of excuse to be indifferent to the nation's welfare is the Negro. Not unlike the dog in the fable whose devotion to his master's interest was recognized only after the sacrifice of life in that master's service, the Negro's love for his country in the civil service, on the tented field, and wherever sincere devotion should command the highest commendation, is commonly rewarded with cold indifference, or at least with damnable praise, and yet when driven, as it were, with brutal kicks and cuffs from the service and defense of his country's honor, he hangs on to the outer folds of its flag with a grim determination to maintain its glory as though that duty had been specially entrusted him by heaven. And herein again he shows the instinct of self-preservation, as people who would seek to become an appreciable power in the public affairs of their country, must be alive to every vital interest pertaining to it. To become rooted it must maintain an unyielding grasp. That the Negro is to-day only a passive member in the affairs of government, does not argue that his unflagging patriotism will not finally gain its reward. That he is quietly working now at long range to prepare himself for citizenship, means that he will in due time enter into that rich inheritance. The foaming stream is not the water carrying most matter into the ocean; the deep current which gives no evidence on its surface is the hydraulic force which forms the Delta. And so it is with the latent influence of Negro patriotism. In every essential matter pertaining to national welfare, however keen his grievance, fancied or real, his regard for the honor of the government and the maintenance of its power, induces him to throw his head-gear in air, out-yell the lustiest lung in the crowd and attest his enthusiasm by demoniac courage on the field of battle.

The chief magistrate of the nation is stricken down in the vigor of manhood and in the fullness of power. In the exercise of his great office morally and otherwise, without going out of his way, he might have benefited the race. But although he had no special claim to the Negro's regard, yet his untimely taking off has been lamented by none more sincerely than by our race. In country, in town, in state, in every section, the Negro is broadly American. Nothing that concerns this country is foreign to him, but with all there is to discourage him, what is the outcome of such steady, magnificent devotion to duty? Geologists affirm that the wondrous chasm of Niagara is the creation of trickling drops of water during myriads of ages. In like manner, the fervent, unflagging patriotism of the Negro is slowly but surely crumbling away the granite of American prejudice to give him a permanent place in the national life of this country. A nation, the bulk of which comes of a race whose love of fair play is proverbial and goes with them into every land and clime, will be constrained in the end to recognize and confirm the merit the race is developing as a strong pillar in the edifice of state.

In the heat of that terrific contest at Waterloo where charge after charge of the imperial guard seemed likely to consign the fate of Europe to the absolute sway of the little Corsican, Wellington exclaimed, to such of his staff as still remained around him, "Hot pounding this, gentlemen." But the day was at last won, and the endangered constitutional liberty of Europe leaped forth from the sea of blood, to inspire man with new hope and aspiration. As a race, we are struggling for life. Our hopes and fears are trembling in the balance against might, power, and moss-covered prejudices. A continuous pounding, directed by the impulse of a will to do, dare and succeed, will bring us victory.

But, says the carping critic, if the Negro were less patient, forbearing and more combative, if he risked less for country, and gloried more in deeds of heroism for his personal defense, he would be truer to his self-preservation. Other races placed in condition quite similar to the Negroes have tried the experiment, and failed. They opposed simple brute force to intelligence, and they went down in the contest either to extinction or to servitude. The Britons gave way to Saxon numbers and tougher sinews, the latter bent the neck to Norman intelligence, bided their time and brought the victor down to an equality of rights and privileges. If the Negro should attempt another way, he would soon be undone.

ADAPTABILITY TO ENVIRONMENTS.

Again the adaptability of the race to environments constitutes one of the means of his endurance. In servitude as in freedom, no conditions have yet been so vigorous that the negro has not been able to adjust himself with ease. Indeed, it is not a figure of speech to assert that wherever he has suffered the most, there he has given the best proof of his vitality. His acquisition of wealth, his possession of material means in general, has been most rapid in parts where he has most obstacles to confront and encounter. He not only laughs at his misfortunes, but turns them to account. When he is ground down beyond the point of greatest resistance, he leaves for new and untried regions, with a radiant hope for a better fate. He goes to the semi-arctic lands of the West, readily becomes domesticated, and so insinuates himself into the hard, prosaic customs of the country that he at once becomes, in so far as he is not debarred from the rules of labor organizations, a sharp competitor with the wage-earner in the strife for bread. His blood has no lazy microbes to dam the current of its movement. Assure him of reasonable compensation, and his brawny arm is bared to the pick and the mattox. His ax and hoe and plow drag out wealth from mine and soil.

ACTIVE EVERYWHERE.

Wherever his lot is cast, there he enters with zest into the live sentiment of the community. No thought born of enterprise within the scope of his comprehension, no undertaking to enhance the common wealth fail to enlist his good will. He will at least talk for it and praise it, even if he has not a cent to invest. However limited by industrial conditions to few and humble ways of acquiring a livelihood, his scanty earnings are on the market to give healthy circulation to the arteries of trade. Merchants welcome him to open doors, and small dealers meet him with graceful smiles knowing he has come to apply the move-on ordinance to the jingling coin in his pocket. In church and school, in the pulpit and on the rostrum, his desire to fall in with the prevailing spirit to promote the betterment of the community, is equally pronounced.

Take as a sample the spirit of the race to absorb elevating influence from the dominant class. The African Methodist Episcopal Church is a race organization which justly challenges the admiration of every one of us no matter of what creed or sect. A race which in about one generation from a condition of base servitude can be so lively to a sense of its spiritual wants and the public weal as to advance enough to create such an organization is no mean factor in any age or country. In the show of this receptive capacity, it declares its eternal fitness to live and thrive under the blaze of the most searching civilization in the history of the world.

Take moreover, the many worthy bodies founded in the last quarter of a century for moral, mental and social elevation. All these have been inspired by the thought that if the race would hold its own, it must emulate the spirit of the country and age in which it lives.

Truly, if our coming to this land was involuntary, the genius of our being has built a home which can only be abandoned at our own will.

THE END.

I am admonished that this paper must come to a close. I am compelled to omit even by mere mention many of the exemplary virtues of the race. I have, however, touched on just enough to furnish the enquiring mind with deductions. Even the pessimist is constrained to admit that, under the circumstances, as a whole, the race has made a remarkable record, and that chiefly, because of the qualities with which he is endowed. Many historic races who have dominated mankind, made less rapid progress than we, at the point we have reached. This remarkable advancement may be ascribed in the main to the superior attributes which give us a flexible and well balanced temperament.

The hardships the race undergoes in this period of development constitute the necessary training school and the virtues which spring thence are intended as much for the betterment of the other race as for our own. We are to soften their stern qualities, while our life is to take on some of the iron of their soul.

That our nature will be largely modified by the necessities of our growth must be an accepted fact, but our merit, worth and fitness in American life will substantially be the product of our qualities as they are to-day. The past gives us assurance of glorious possibilities to come. Just how far and to what extent we are to realize the fruition of our cherished dreams of rising to the full heighth of honorable manhood rests chiefly with us. God has endowed us with the capacity to suffer and undergo the trials incident to race development. If we can recognize the need for this training, severe though it be, if we do not chafe and fume and fret and get angry because our deliverance has not come, we may well be comforted in the meanwhile that any device of man to deny us a share in the government of a common heritage in this land consecrated by heaven to suffering humanity, will prove a complete failure.

Rev. F. J. Grimke, D.D.

FRANCIS J. GRIMKE, D. D.

Francis J. Grimke, clergyman, was born near Charleston, S. C., November 4, 1850. Son of Henry and Nancy (Weston) Grimke; attended school in Charleston; entered Lincoln University, Chester County, Pennsylvania, in 1866, and graduated in 1870 (A. M., D. D.); graduated from Princeton Theological Seminary in 1878. Ordained pastor of the Fifteenth Street Presbyterian Church the same year. Remained until 1885. Took charge of Lama Street Presbyterian Church 1885-1889. Returned to Fifteenth Street Church, Washington, D. C., in 1889, where he is still. Has published articles in the New York Independent and New York Evangelist. Wrote monographs on "The Negro: His Rights and Wrongs; The Forces For and Against Him." In 1898, "The Lynching of Negroes in the South; Its Causes and Remedy;" "Some Lessons from the Assassination of President William McKinley," 1901; "The Roosevelt-Washington Episode; or, Race Prejudice," 1901. Address, 1526 L Street, Washington, D. C.

TOPIC XXX.

THE SIGNS OF A BRIGHTER FUTURE FOR THE AMERICAN NEGRO.

BY REV. F. J. GRIMKE, D. D.

Extracts from his sermon on the race problem.

"Some of these days all the skies will be brighter,
Some of these days all the burdens be lighter,
Hearts will be happier, souls will be whiter,
Some of these days.

"Some of these days, in the deserts uprising,
Fountains shall flash while the joybells are ringing,
And the world, with its sweetest of birds, shall go singing,
Some of these days.

"Some of these days: Let us bear with our sorrow,
Faith in the future—its light we may borrow,
There will be joy in the golden to-morrow—
Some of these days."

That is my faith; I am no pessimist on this Negro problem. Terrible as the facts are, cruel and bitter as is this race prejudice, and insurmountable, almost, as are the obstacles which it sets up in our pathway, I see a light ahead, I am hopeful, I look forward to better times. And I want to tell you this morning what the ground of this hope is.

(2.) I am hopeful, because of the progress which the Negro is making in intelligence and in wealth. Think of what our condition was at the close of the war, and of what it is to-day, in these respects. That we are progressing, there can be no doubt; indeed, in view of all the circumstances, our progress has been marvelous.

Take the matter of wealth. Since freedom, hundreds and thousands of our people have become property owners in the South. Many of them are prosperous and successful farmers; thousands and hundreds of thousands of acres of land have come into their possession, hundreds and thousands of them in the cities own their own homes, and are engaged in small but lucrative business enterprises of one kind or another. They are now paying taxes on some three hundred million dollars' worth of property. That is not a very large sum, I admit, considered as the aggregate wealth of a whole race, numbering some seven or eight millions; but whether much or little, it indicates progress, and very considerable progress, and that is the point to which I am directing attention. The acquisitive faculty in the Negro is being developed; his eyes are being opened more and more to the importance of getting wealth; and slowly, but surely, he is getting it.

Educationally, the same is true. Thirty years ago there were but few educational institutions among us, but few professional men—doctors, lawyers, ministers—ministers of intelligence—teachers; but few men and women of education. Now, there are thousands of well-equipped men and women in all the professions, and thousands upon thousands of men and women of education in every part of the country. Not only are there institutions founded especially for our benefit, crowded with students, but all the great institutions of the land are now open to us, and in all of them, with scarcely an exception, are to be found representatives of our race; and the number in such institutions is steadily increasing. The last report of the Commissioner of Education shows that in the common schools of the sixteen former slave States and the District of Columbia, there are enrolled 1,429,713 pupils, and that in these schools, some twenty-five thousand teachers are employed. It also shows that there are 178 schools for secondary and higher education, with an enrollment of over forty thousand pupils. There are, of course, thousands of our people who are still very ignorant, but that there is vastly more intelligence in the race now than at the close of the war, no one will pretend to deny. The colleges and universities, the high and normal schools, are turning out hundreds of graduates every year. The educational outlook for the race is certainly very encouraging.

In view of these two factors—the growing desire on the part of the Negro for material possessions, the fact that he is actually acquiring property, and his growing intelligence—I see signs of a brighter future for him. These are elements of power that will make themselves felt. You may deprive a poor and ignorant people of their rights, and succeed in keeping them deprived of them, but you can't hope to do that when these conditions are changed; and the point to which I am directing attention here, is that this change is taking place. All that has been done, and is being done to stimulate in the Negro this principle of acquisitiveness, and to increase his thirst for knowledge, is a harbinger of a better day. Every dollar saved, or properly invested; every atom of brain power that is developed, is a John the Baptist in the wilderness, crying, Make straight the pathway of the Negro. In proportion as the race rises in intelligence and wealth, the valleys will be filled and the mountains will be leveled, that now stand in the way of his progress, in the way of the complete recognition of all of his rights. Ignatius Donnelly, in that remarkable book of his, "Doctor Huguet," which some of you, doubtless, have read, would seem to teach the opposite of this. He attempts to show that never mind what the intellectual attainments of the Negro may be—he may be a Doctor Huguet, learned with all the learning of the schools, and cultured with all the culture of the ages— still there is no chance for him, there is no hope of his being recognized. The story as told by him is, at first, quite staggering and terribly depressing. But when we remember that, according to the story, there was but one Doctor Huguet with a black skin, and that he was poor, and that all the rest of his race were poor and ignorant, light breaks in upon the darkness, the awful pall which it casts upon us, is at once lifted. How will it be when instead of one Doctor Huguet there are hundreds and thousands of them, scholarly men and women, cultivated men and women, men and women of wealth, of large resources? It will be very different. If the Negro was indifferent to education; if he was actually getting poorer, then we might lose heart; but, thank God, the very opposite is true. His face is in the right direction. He may not be pressing on as rapidly as he might towards the goal, as rapidly as some of us might wish to see him, but it is a matter for congratulation, that he is not retrograding, nor even standing still, but is moving on. Poor? Yes, but he isn't always going to be poor. Ignorant? Yes, but he isn't always going to be ignorant. The progress that he has already made in these directions shows clearly what the future is to be. Knowledge is power; wealth is power, and that power the Negro is getting. He is not always going to be a mere hewer of wood and a drawer of water; he is not always going to be crude, ignorant. American prejudice is strong, I know; it is full of infernal hate, I know, but in the long run it will be found to be no match for the power which comes from wealth and intelligence.

(3.) I am hopeful because I have faith in the ultimate triumph of right. You remember what Lowell says in his "Elegy on the Death of Dr. Channing:"

" Truth needs no champions: in the infinite deep
   Of everlasting Soul her strength abides,
From Nature's heart her mighty pulses leap,
   Through Nature's veins her strength, undying tides.

     *   *   *   *   *   *   *   *

" I watch the circle of the eternal years,
   And read forever in the storied page
One lengthened roll of blood, and wrong, and tears—
   One onward step of Truth from age to age.

" The poor are crushed; the tyrants link their chain;
   The poet sings through narrow dungeon-grates;
Man's hope lies quenched;—and, lo! with steadfast gain
   Freedom doth forge her mail of adverse fates.

" Men slay the prophets; fagot, rack, and cross
   Make up the groaning records of the past;
But Evil's triumphs are her endless loss,
   And sovereign Beauty wins the soul at last."

     *   *   *   *   *   *   *   *

" From off the starry mountain-peak of song,
   The spirit shows me, in the coming time,
An earth unwithered by the foot of wrong,
   A race revering its own soul sublime."

And in the "Ode to France," from which I quoted on last Sabbath, the same glorious thought is expressed:—

     "And surely never did thine altars glance
     With purer fires than now in France;
     While, in their bright white flashes,
        Wrong's shadow, backward cast,
          Waves cowering o'er the ashes
        Of the dead, blaspheming past,
          O'er the shapes of fallen giants,
        His own unburied brood,
          Whose dead hands clench defiance
        At the overpowering good:
     And down the happy future runs a flood
        Of prophesying light;
     It shows an Earth no longer stained with blood,
     Blossom and fruit where now we see the bud
        Of Brotherhood and Right."

That is my faith. The wrong may triumph for the moment, but in its very triumph is its death-knell; it cannot always prevail. God has so constituted the moral universe, has so planted in the human heart the sense of right, that ultimately justice is sure to be done. "Ever the Right comes uppermost," is no mere poetic fancy, but one of God's great laws. In the light of that law, I am hopeful. I know that things cannot go on as they are going on now, that the outrageous manner in which we are at present treated cannot always continue. It is bound to end sooner or later.

(4.) I am hopeful, because I have faith in the power of the religion of the Lord Jesus Christ to conquer all prejudices, to break down all walls of separation, and to weld together men of all races in one great brotherhood. It is a religion that teaches the fatherhood of God and the brotherhood of man, a religion in which there is neither Greek nor Jew, barbarian, Scythian, bond or free. And this religion is in this land. There are, according to the statistics of the churches for 1898, excluding Christian Scientists, Jews and Latter Day Saints, 135,667 ministers in the United States, 187,075 churches, and 26,100,884 communicants in these churches. This would seem to be a guarantee that every right belonging to the Negro would be secured to him; that in the struggle which he is making in this country for simple justice and fair play, for manhood recognition, for such treatment as his humanity and citizenship entitle him, back of him would be found these 135,667 ministers, 187,075 churches and 26,100,884 church members. But, alas, such is not the case. These professed followers of the Lord Jesus Christ who came to seek and to save the lost, who was the friend of publicans and sinners, whose gospel was a gospel of love, and who was all the time reaching down and seeking to befriend the lowly, those who were despised and who were being trampled upon by others;—the Christ of whom it is written, "And he shall not judge after the sight of his eyes, neither reprove after the hearing of his ears; but with righteousness shall he judge the poor, and reprove with equity for the meek of the earth;" and who, in speaking of himself, said, "The spirit of the Lord God is upon me; because he hath sent me to bind up the broken hearted, to proclaim liberty to the captives, and the opening of the prison to them that are bound; to comfort all that mourn; to give them a garland for ashes, the oil of joy for mourning, the garment of praise for the spirit of heaviness;"—these professed followers of this wonderfully glorious Christ, instead of standing back of the poor Negro in the earnest, desperate struggle which he is making against this damnable race-prejudice, which curses him because he is down, branding him with vile epithets, calling him low, degraded, ignorant, besotted; and yet putting its heel upon his neck so as to prevent him from rising; despising him because he is down, and hating him when he manifests any disposition to throw off his ignorance and degradation and show himself a man;—in this struggle, I say, against this damnable race-prejudice, these professing Christians are often his worst enemies, his most malignant haters and traducers.

In saying that the religion of the Lord Jesus Christ is in this land, I do not therefore, base my assertion upon the fact, that there are 135,667 ministers in it, and 187,075 churches, and 26,100,884 professing Christians. No. The American Church as such is only an apology for a church. It is an apostate church, utterly unworthy of the name which it bears. Its spirit is a mean and cowardly and despicable spirit. "One shall chase a thousand," we are told in the good Book—and "two shall put ten thousand to flight." And yet with 135,667 preachers, and more than 2,000,-000 church members in this land, this awful, black record of murder and lawlessness against a weak and defenseless race, still goes on. In the presence of this appalling fact, I can well understand the spirit which moved Theodore Parker—that pulpit Jupiter of his day—when in his great sermon on "The True Idea of a Christian Church," he said, "In the midst of all these wrongs and sins—the crimes of men, society and the state—amid popular ignorance, pauperism, crime and war, and slavery, too—is the church to say nothing, do nothing; nothing for the good of such as feel the wrong, nothing to save them who do the wrong? Men tell us so, in word and deed; that way alone is safe! If I thought so, I would never enter the church but once again, and then to bow my shoulders to their manliest work, to heave down its strong pillars, arch and dome, and roof, and wall, steeple and tower, though like Samson I buried myself under the ruins of that temple which profaned the worship of the God most high, of God most loved. I would do this in the name of men; in the name of Christ I would do it; yes, in the dear and blessed name of God." And I would do it, too.

But, in spite of the shallowness and emptiness and glaring hypocrisy of this thing which calls itself the church; this thing which is so timid, so cowardly that it dares not touch any sin that is unpopular, I still believe that Christianity is in this land. To-day it is like a little grain of mustard seed, but it has entered the soil, has germinated, and is springing up. It is like the little lump of leaven which the woman hid in three measures of meal; but it has begun to work, and will go on working, diffusing itself, until the whole is leavened. God has promised to give to his Son the heathen for his inheritance, and the uttermost parts of the earth for his possession; and in that promise this land is included. Christianity shall one day have sway even in Negro-hating America; the spirit which it inculcates, and which it is capable of producing, is sure, sooner or later, to prevail. I have, myself, here and there, seen its mighty transforming power. I have seen white men and women under its regenerating influence lose entirely the caste feeling, to whom the brother in black was as truly a brother as the brother in white. If Christianity were a mere world influence, I should have no such hope; but it is something more than a mere world influence; it is from above; back of it is the mighty power of God. The record is, "To as many as received him to them gave he power to become children of God, even to them that believed on his name, which were born, not of blood, nor of the will of flesh, nor of the will of man, but of God." It can do what no mere human power can do. Jesus Christ is yet to reign in this land. I will not see it, you will not see it, but it is coming all the same. In the growth of Christianity, true, real, genuine Christianity in this land, I see the promise of better things for us as a race.

TOPIC XXXI.

NEGRO CRIMINALITY.

BY JOHN HENRY SMYTH.

We have need to felicitate ourselves as members of a great though oppressed race, that an Armstrong, the founder and promoter of this institution of practical learning, was given to us and to the nation, and that through his influence and example, Tuskegee and other similar institutions have grown into vigorous youth. Two of these seats of industrial education, through a system of race conferences, have given to us who are deprived of a popular press an opportunity to be heard in our own behalf upon subjects, the public discussion of which, through literary mediums, has been monopolized by members of the other race. Our moral delinquencies have been discussed recently at the North and in the South—at times in a sensible and at other times in a nonsensical way; arguments have been made to the world by orators and writers seemingly more interested and concerned in making the worse appear the better reason than in philosophically looking into facts or honestly seeking to discover truth. From much that has been said, it would appear to one unacquainted with the American branch of the Negro race that within thirty-five years it has become criminal, although for nearly three centuries it has been a stranger to wrongdoing, law abiding and not law breaking. Such radical change, if change there has been, in individuals or classes of people, is rare, abnormal, and must be accounted for in some other way than by the wholesale charge of inherited savagery and innate moral obliquity. Crime from an hereditary standpoint may not justly be chargeable to one race of men to the exclusion of another, to the black race more than to the white, to the yellow races more than to the white or black.

The first crime was in the first family. The sacred writings teach that God gave, mid the thunderings of the heavens, the smoking of the mountain, and the consternation of the people, the criminal code in the ten commandments, which may be found in the traditions of heathen peoples, somewhat modified, just as in the written laws of all Christian nations. Had crime not existed prior to this heavenly edict, there would

434

Prof. John H. Smyth

JOHN HENRY SMYTH, LL. D.

John Henry Smyth, LL. D., ex-U. S. Minister Resident and Consul-General to Liberia, was born in the city of Richmond. His parents were Sully Smyth of Lynchburg, Campbell County, Va., and Ann Eliza, formerly Goode of Chesterfield County, Va. He received his first instruction from a lady of his own race, at a time when the laws of Virginia made it a penal offense to teach Negroes any other thing than manual labor. At the age of seven years he was sent to Philadelphia to be educated. He attended the public schools of that city four years and two private schools under the control and direction of friends or Quakers. He graduated from the Institute for Colored Youth, May 4, 1862. He displayed a decided taste and aptitude for the fine arts early in life, and at the age of sixteen years he became a student of art, and was admitted a member of the Life School of the Academy of Fine Arts, Philadelphia, a year before graduation. In 1870 he graduated from the Law School of Howard University. The same year he married the daughter of Rev. John Shippen, of Washington, D. C., Miss Fannie Ellen, a lady whom he had the pleasure of instructing in the first elocution class of Howard University.

For eighteen years he was in the service of the United States, beginning as a first-class clerk and ending as United States Minister and Consul-General. For seven years he taught in the public schools of Pennsylvania, practiced law in the District of Columbia, North and South Carolina. On retiring from the diplomatic service in Liberia, two distinctions were conferred upon Mr. Smyth, by Liberia College, the honorary degree of LL. D., and by the President of Liberia, the Honorable Hilery Richard Wright Johnson, the order of Knight Commander of the Humane Order of African Redemption. There were only two Americans so honored by the Black Republic. At present Mr. Smyth is at the head of the Negro Reformatory Association of Virginia, a corporation resident in Virginia, with authority to establish reform schools for delinquent Negro minors of both sexes in Virginia.

The first school of the association is the Virginia Manual Labor School, Hanover, Va., with 1,800 acres of land, 800 of which is under cultivation. The good people of Mr. Smyth's native city, Richmond, and friends in Massachusetts, Connecticut, Rhode Island and New York have made possible the purchase of the plantation known as Broad Neck, Hanover.

The principal benefactor was Mr. Collis P. Huntington of New York, who was pleased to make a contribution of $12,000 toward this worthy and necessary charity.

have been little apparent reason for this ancient pronouncement through a Hebrew medium. The conclusion seems then to be irresistible—that mankind coveted, stole, lied, were disobedient to parents, were adulterers and murderers from the earliest times, and only ceased to be so, measurably, in proportion as the sanctions of law were strong or weak. The Christian religion and civilizations other than Christian, with their religions, growth, and development under the influence of good, wise, and godly men, have contributed more than all else, to the decrease of crime and among all classes and conditions of men. "Thou shalt not" stays the course of crime.

The history of the black or African race, since the decadence and destruction of the cities of North Africa and the Nile Delta and the loss of prestige of the peoples who held sway in them, has been shrouded and obscured, and hence gratuitous arguments are made in regard to the savagery and bestiality (which it is claimed we inherit) of the progenitors of Negro Americans that are wholly unsupported by reliable data. The acts of the Puritan fathers of New England and of the cavaliers and Huguenots of the South, toward Indian and Negro heathen in the New World—men of whom it has been facetiously said that, "they fell first upon their knees and then upon the aborigines,"—these acts, together with the horrors of the middle passage and the unrequited toil of centuries, of which the blacks were victims, must be taken into account in considering the matter of crime in connection with this race, and go far to explain a condition which otherwise would be abnormal. The baleful influences of a dead and buried past account for crime among the old and the young Negro Americans, the responsibility for which rests upon the United States rather than the Southern states, upon this nation rather than any part of it.

In Virginia and Maryland there were indentured white slaves. When the system was abolished the same conditions plagued the colonists that annoy us now. Mr. Doyle, in his work entitled *English Colonies in America,* says, "The liberated servant (white) became an idler, socially corrupt and often politically dangerous." The whites became an irresponsible, shiftless, and criminal class, just as the Negroes have become to an alarming extent since freedom. There are to-day in certain sections of the South whole neighborhoods of whites almost without moral sense and near to barbarism. It will not be pretended, however, that there has not been and is not now, criminality among the Negro race just as there was during the years of its oppression; but a condition upheld and approved by the constitution, laws, and public sentiment of the nation cannot do other than plead guilty to having contributed to this result which has so greatly affected the estimation in which good men, equally with bad men, the innocent as well as the guilty of our race, are held by the whites. I am not clanking my chains as a Negro in remembering the past, and only do so in accounting for what the unreasoning and unsympathetic are disposed to regard as abnormal criminality in the American Negro.

Negro parents under the old regime were parents physically only. The government of their children was in the hands of others. Obedience to parents enjoined by the decalogue was not rendered by children, was not encouraged by others, nor could it have been enforced by parental authority. Filial affection in the slave-child existed to an appreciable degree notwithstanding these disadvantages. Parents and children came into the possession of freedom not sufficiently understanding nor appreciating the relation of each to the other. While I am clearly of opinion that it may not be successfully shown that Negro children are more criminal in inclination than other children, their home-training, or, rather, their lack of home-training, is greatly responsible for what of criminality there is among them. Negro parents, as a rule, seem disposed not only to give larger liberty to their children than they ought, but they give absolute license in too many instances. In illustration of this fact, in cities particularly, children are allowed to go from their homes in the night-time and wander the streets amid their baleful associations until nine, ten, eleven o'clock and longer. And when they return home they do so unattended. The accounts given by them as to where they have been cannot be relied upon. Further, children are not required to be respectful to their elders of either sex. This condition does not obtain alone among children of ignorant and poor parentage, but absence of good manners is also often found among children and youths who have had fair common and high school advantages. This license has led directly and unerringly to the formation and cultivation of habits more likely to debase than elevate them. To venture criticism of parental laches or of the conduct of the young, to admonish or advise different manners and conduct from that which the inclination of the young seems to suggest, would be to run the risk of being regarded as officious or meddling, and thereby of inviting insult. Parents whose children are known to be of the class pictured are themselves timid and indisposed to insist upon obedience from them, for fear of offending them and causing them to go away from home. The inexperience and ignorance of childhood and youth, coupled with the grant of too great liberty, are responsible for the too general tendency to wrong doing.

Negro parents who were themselves victims of oppression as well as those who were born under the benign influences of freedom, have crude and unwise notions about the duty of requiring their children to do some kind of work. Too many Negro children are guarded from soiling their hands and developing their muscles with necessary and useful toil. The struggling, industrious widow as well as the well-conditioned housewife whose husband has a good home and makes a good living, seeks to relieve her children of work. This encouragement of laziness can have but one outcome—the living in the sweat of others' faces than their own. Under conditions such as these, parents possessed of radically ignorant and wrong notions about rearing their children, unconsciously cultivate tendencies which lead to criminality. To the extent that a child's mind becomes familiar with higher conditions and mind-work, to that degree does physical exertion in the way of mere muscle-work become distasteful, and as a result the child becomes less efficient as a mere bread-winner by the sweat of his brow. Education is chargeable with producing a condition for which parents and not school teachers are responsible. Complete and entire reform in our system of home-training of our boys and girls will go far to relieve youthful Negroes of just censure for ill-breeding. How far all these reflections are applicable to the rearing and training of white children is for white parents to consider.

Mr. Philip Alexander Bruce, in a recent publication in the *Contemporary Review,** accounts for moral delinquencies in the young of the race by the very natural and normal disposition of Negroes, where numerically strong, to segregate themselves from the whites. In London one finds a French settlement. In nearly every large city in the United States, Germans live together. Italians, Swedes, and Norwegians settle among their congeners. It is not contended that they are

---

The American Negro of To-day. Contemporary Review, February, 1900.

less law-abiding and loyal citizens as a consequence of their nearness of living and association. Mr. Bruce enlarges upon the thought thus: "The worst impression made by that society (a Negro community) is seen in the temper of the children. Whatever may be said in condemnation of the old system, it at least not only compelled the parents to restrain, and if needful to punish their offspring for bad conduct, but it also created an atmosphere of order and sobriety in the plantations which had a more or less beneficial influence on the character of the young. As the case now stands the only discipline to which the little Negro is subject is that exercised by parents too untrained themselves to understand how to govern him properly, and in most instances too ignorant to have any just idea as to the difference between right and wrong in the ordinary affairs of life. What is the result? The child grows up without any lessons in self-control and self-improvement, or any intelligent appreciation of the cardinal principles of morality. If the child is a boy, he leaves his parents almost as soon as he can earn his own support and only too often leads for years the life of a vagabond. All the worst impulses of his nature are further encouraged by this wandering and irresponsible existence. Is it strange that, under the operation of this influence alone, the number of black criminals in the Southern states is increased to an alarming degree?"

What good effect could result from restraint exercised or punishment inflicted by parents whose judgment and will were dormant? It is only when a parent governs and controls, ignorant though he may be, that the best results can be expected to follow. Judgment, affection, and concern for the child must enter into the method of his training if the rearing is to be beneficial and helpful.

To my mind but one merit can be claimed for the old system of enslavement—a discipline as to labor which produced the best results to the master class and made the slave orderly and systematic in the performance of his tasks. Though smarting, even now, under the resultant influences of a destroyed system, we can afford to do justice to the good men and women of the white race who constituted a part of the system. Slavery as it has been known in the outside world, is not slavery as it was in the genteel and pious homes and households of the South. Here the "people" were treated almost as members of the family, "uncles" and "aunts" and "mammies" and playmates. They were necessary supplements, sharers of all great occasions of joy or sorrow, of feasts and sufferings. And the tenderest and most watchful care was bestowed on them. Consideration for the servants was the test of the "quality." Mutual influences went to make as pure, high and beautiful a civilization as the system was capable of. And no philanthropist on earth has ever had a deeper horror for the evils that have been represented as slavery in the South than many of the "quality." Nor anywhere was the wise abolition of slavery more earnestly studied and desired than by the good people of the Southern states.

In the discussion of the criminality of the Negro, too much importance is attached to mere statistics. In any discussion of an ethical character mere statistics may not be relied upon. I shall present a few which are entirely authentic but which prove little, in my opinion, prejudicial to the Negroes of to-day as compared with the Negroes of the past, and could not unless figures could be adduced, alike authentic, showing the criminality of the Negroes as bondmen; neither can comparison between the criminality of the blacks and whites be cited to the Negroes' prejudice in the light of the disparity between the races in every essential element of race growth. The foregoing facts greatly detract from any comparative criminal exhibit in which Negroes of to-day are made to figure.

The last United States census furnishes some figures which seem to be more in the Negro's favor than against him. Persons of all races in the penitentiaries of the United States in 1890 were 45,233, of which number 14,687 were colored. Prisoners in county jails, 19,538, of which number 5,577 were colored. Inmates in juvenile reformatories, 14,846, of which 1,943 were colored. Of a total of 73,045 almshouse paupers, only 6,467 were Negroes. Of murderers there were 2,739 Negroes out of a total of 4,425. In 1850 there was one criminal to 3,500 of population; in 1890 one criminal to 645 of population; whites, one to every 1,000, and blacks, one to every 284. Take the ignorance of the Negro as to secular matters, the moral torpor in which he necessarily exists, his poverty, the presumption of guilt when charged with crime, his inability to defend himself, his being forced to plead to an information or indictment *in forma pauperis;* could crime charged and established against him be less than it is? Ought not the record to be worse rather than better? Of the 14,846 juvenile delinquents given an opportunity to re-enter society and walk in the straight path through reformatories, only 1,943 were Negroes. With the doors of almshouses swung wide to 73,046 paupers, racial pride prevented poor Negroes entering these homes of mercy, and only 6,467 allowed themselves to become objects of public charity. With a larger percentage of unskilled than skilled Negro laborers in 1890, only 2,253 of 6,546 convicts whose employments were known were in the penitentiaries of the land. Of 45,233 criminals but 253 were persons who had enjoyed higher educational advantages, and not a single educated Negro figures in the enumeration.

What are the remedies for existing criminality, and how may its increase be checked? Popular secular education for whites and blacks, compulsory, if possible, erected on a broad basis of Christianity, is the only safe, enduring, moral, and economic remedy. Mere secular education may not be relied upon to restrain crime, and we must honestly own that our only hope is in the diffusion of true religion. The church should take the initiative in this matter, the state, aye, the nation should come to the assistance of the church, and of those states in which the burden is too great for them to bear it successfully. If the Holy Scriptures be not the basis of all worthy knowledge our civilization is a fraud. Individual philanthropy has done much towards aiding in the matter of education, particularly so-called higher education. May not individual wealth help to minimize ignorance, dissipate poverty, help the feeble in mind and morals of the race to robust Christian manhood? "For many men of great possessions, the voice of conscience is effective, as the contemplated grasp of the tax-gatherer could never be. Around them they see ignorance to be banished, talent missing its career, misery appealing for relief. They know that the forces of the times have brought them their large fortunes, only through co-operation and the protection of the whole community; so with justice in their hearts, as well as generosity, they found the benefactions which are doing so much to foster the best impulses of American life; and in this response to public duty they find conferred upon riches a new power and fascination."

The reform schools for juveniles throughout the North and West, and those in Virginia, represent Christian agencies for the reduction and destruction of crime in its germinal state, and are a display of wise and humane statesmanship on the part of legislators. The white people of Virginia, ever responsive to appeals in behalf of human need, made possible the Virginia Manual Labor School at Broad Neck Farm, Hanover, Virginia. It was this sentiment in behalf of moral reform among Negro children and youths that brought to the aid of this institution the interested concern of a man of wealth and national influence, whose sympathy for the poor and ignorant of his countrymen, white and black, is as broad and far-reaching as ignorance and human suffering.* This reformatory, opened September 12, 1899, and aided by the state February 5, 1900, began with a nucleus of five Negro boys, and has now under its guardianship fifty-two children. It has thus early demonstrated conclusively that saving and redemptive elements of character exist in Negro children no less than in those of other races; also that for tractableness and responsiveness to kindly influences, delinquent Negro children show themselves of legitimate kinship to that race among whom, as the classic writer tells us, "the gods delighted to disport themselves—the gentle Ethiopians."

I know how disposed as a race we are to wilt, to lose heart, and complain, in the glare of new exhibitions of prejudice, such as harass us in our native Virginia, and our brethren in other parts of the country. To such, I put the question: "By courage can we not lessen misfortune? Yes! A thousand times yes! Courage turns ignoble agony into beautiful martyrdom. Its alchemy is universal. Is the stake a misfortune to the martyr? It is his dearest fortune. Is oppression, prejudice, or ignorance, a misfortune to the reformer? It is the very condition of his reform. Is misunderstanding, injustice, suspicion, or contempt a misfortune to the earnest man or woman anywhere who is trying to guide his life by a more celestial trigonometry than petty minds can conceive? In one sense these things are to be deplored but in another and deeper sense nothing is to be dreaded that can be faced and known by an unfrighted human spirit. A misfortune bravely met is a fortune, and the world is full of people happy because bravely unhappy."

---

*The late Mr. C. P. Huntington of New York.

TOPIC XXXII.

THE AMERICAN NEGRO'S OPPORTUNITIES IN AFRICA.

BY WILLIAM H. HEARD.

The Liberian government takes charge of all persons landing as emigrants and looks after their comfort preparatory to their settling; but if one prefers he may secure board in the best of families at a cheap rate until settled. As the government gives each settler from fifteen to twenty-five acres of land, and allows him to choose his own plot, it takes a little time to settle. He must locate and survey his land and build his hut. All new-comers build the hut, as it is cheap and quickly built. From fifteen to fifty dollars will put up a good thatch hut which will answer all purposes for at least three years. The land cleared, coffee, ginger, sugar-cane, edoes, cassada, oranges, limes, plums, bread-fruit, pawpaws, can be planted. It takes three years for coffee to yield; five to six for oranges, limes, bread-fruit, etc. Edoes, cassadas and such bread-stuffs yield in three or four months, and ginger and sugar-cane once a year. From these two commodities an income at once is had. All of the above fruits and products are obtainable from neighbors while yours are maturing. This is the condition of the farmer. But should you go out as a professional or business man you have a wide field and little competition. Any educated person will find ready employment by individuals or the government and a remuneration in keeping with the vocation. Citizenship is the result of a deed to your land and this is obtained at your option; and citizenship means an election to any office save that of President and Vice-President. It requires a residence of five years to be elected to one of these offices. Attorney Wright, Professor Stevens, Rev. Frazier and others filled national positions before they had been citizens five years. The government needs strong men to assist in running the Republic, and such, if loyal, are always welcomed. The merchant of Liberia receives the greatest profit of any merchant on the face of the globe—not less than one hundred per cent on the purchasing price—and a hundred and fifty per cent on the selling price. Rent is cheap, taxes low, and duties moderate, so that everything is in favor of the merchant.

442

W. H. Heard, D. D.

DR. WILLIAM H. HEARD.

Dr. William H. Heard, ex-Minister Resident and Consul General to Liberia, was born in Elbert County, Georgia, of slave parents and therefore was a slave himself until Lee surrendered to Grant in April, 1865. He was only fifteen years of age at this period. He began his education at this age, attended South Carolina University, Clark University and Atlanta University at Atlanta, Georgia; taught school twelve years, was elected to South Carolina Legislature from Abbeville County in 1876, appointed railway postal clerk in 1880, but resigned this position in 1883 and entered the ministry at Macon, Georgia. He pastored churches in Athens and Atlanta, Georgia; Aiken and Charleston, South Carolina; Philadelphia, Pennsylvania; Wilmington, Delaware; Harrisburg, Pennsylvania, and was appointed Minister Resident and Consul General to Liberia by President Grover Cleveland February, 1895. He served this position with honor to his race and to himself. He is one of the most successful ministers in his denomination, and has served the best appointments, both as pastor and as presiding elder. He is now the pastor of Allen Temple, Atlanta, Georgia; has written a book called the "Bright Side of African Life," which has a large circulation. He is now President of the Colored National Emigration Association

The scientist finds the widest field imaginable—silver, gold, precious stones, herbs, coal, iron and such articles are as plentiful as the leaves on the trees—they never fall. All that is needed is a scientific eye to see these things.

The zoologist could make a fortune in one year catching insects and shipping them to colleges in America, England, Germany and France.

Why so many of our young people, educated and refined, will don white aprons and stand behind chairs and watch other people eat is a problem, if there is one, that needs to be solved. Many of our educated girls, when they can work on people's heads and feet, and present a card with some big word on it, as "chiropodist," which means foot-cleaner, are perfectly satisfied. All of this must be done, but it does not require a knowledge of Latin, Greek, French, German, and all the sciences to do this successfully; yet it is the highest ambition of many of our young people, while Africa invites them to higher walks.

In America cotton is the staple in many of the Southern states. The farmer plants and grows this staple to obtain clothing and the necessaries of life, and, if possible, lay by a dollar for a rainy day. In Liberia coffee holds the same relation to the farmer as cotton in America; yet it is planted like the peach tree or apple tree. It takes about five years to yield, but when it begins to yield it increases yearly, costing about five cents a pound to clean, hull and ship to market, giving a clear profit of from two to five cents on the pound, while there is no real profit in cotton growing. Liberia would yield cotton as prolifically as Arkansas or Mississippi, if cultivated. The Englishmen are turning their attention to cotton growing in West Africa.

Cassadas takes the place of the American sweet potato, but is much easier produced, as the greatest cost is the labor of planting. It produces without cultivation, and, as there is no frost in West Africa, once planted it will produce for twenty years. It is a root as is the sweet potato.

The upland rice of West Africa grows anywhere and everywhere it chances to fall upon the ground. Very little attention is given to cultivation, yet it could be made an export which would yield the farmer a most valuable income. Corn grows as prolifically in Africa as in the bottoms of Georgia and Alabama. Planting is the hardest task.

The palm tree grows as the pine in Georgia or North Carolina, and the nut which it produces is as large as, or larger than, a horse chestnut.

These nuts contain an oil that answers all the purposes of bacon, lard and butter in America. The greatest task is to have a boy climb the tree and cut them down. This oil fries your fish, seasons your greens, shortens your bread and answers all the purposes of lard or butter.

There are hogs, cows, sheep and goats in West Africa, but no meat can be cured, therefore all bacon is shipped from abroad.

Rubber farms are much more profitable than turpentine farms, for the reason that it costs so much less to produce rubber and the profit is so much greater. Rubber is produced at from fifteen to twenty cents per pound and sold at from seventy-five cents to one dollar per pound. While all of these products are used on the ground, with a few exceptions, yet all of them are profitable commodities for export.

We have presented this array of facts to sustain our position that the Negro will be benefited by returning home to Africa as fast as he is self-reliant and independent. But he must be a man; boys cannot stand the hardships of pioneer life.

Mrs. Lena Mason.

MRS. LENA MASON.

Mrs. Lena Mason, the Evangelist, was born in Quincy, Ill., May 8th, 1864. Her parents, Relda and Vaughn Doolin, were devout Christians, and they brought up their daughter Lena, as far as they knew how, in the nurture and admonition of the Lord, so that Lena became a Christian at a very early age. She attended the Douglass High School of Hannibal, Mo. She also attended Professor Knott's School in Chicago. She married March 9th, 1883, to George Mason. Of this union six children were the result— four boys and two girls; of these only one, Bertha May, survives.

At the age of 23 Mrs. Mason entered the ministry, preaching for the first three years to white people exclusively, and later preaching to mixed congregations. She now belongs to the Colored Conference. Mrs. Mason has preached in nearly every state in the Union, and the preachers are few who can excel her in preaching. She has, since she has been preaching, been instrumental in the conversion of 1,617 souls. Her five months' work in colored and white churches in Minneapolis will never be forgotten by those who were greatly benefited by her services. Mrs. Mason possesses considerable ability as a poet, and has written several poems and songs that do not suffer by comparison with poems by the best poets. Mrs. Mason is powerful in argument and picture painting. Rev. C. L. Leonard, pastor of the Central German M. E. Church, in speaking of Mrs. Mason, says: "I desire to express my highest appreciation of Mrs. Mason's church and effective evangelical work in my church and in many others. Mrs. Mason is now making a tour of the South, and by her lectures and sermons is doing a work among the colored people that will bear good fruit in the future. One only needs to hear Mrs. Mason lecture and preach to understand how it is that one never tires listening to her."

TOPIC XXXIII.

THE NEGRO AND EDUCATION.

BY MRS. LENA MASON.

1. Said once a noble ruler,
    Thomas Jefferson by name,
    "All men are created equal,
    All men are born the same."
    God made the Negro equal
    To any race above the grave,
    Although once made a captive
    And sold to man a slave.

2. Of all the crimes recorded
    Our histories do not tell
    Of a single crime more brutal,
    Or e'en a parallel.
    It was said by men of wisdom (?)
    "No knowledge shall they have,
    For if you educate a Negro
    You unfit him for a slave."

3. Fred Douglass' young mistress,
    Moved by a power divine,
    Determined she would let the rays
    Of knowledge on him shine,
    But her husband said, " 'Twill never do,
    'Twill his way to freedom pave,
    For if you educate a Negro
    You unfit him for a slave."

4. But there is no mortal being
    Who can the wheels of progress stay;
    An all-wise God intended
    He should see the light of day.
    God drew back the sable curtains
    That shut out wisdom's rays,
    He did give unto him knowledge
    And unfit him for a slave.

445

5. But God's works were not completed,
   For he had made decree,
   Since all men àre born equal,
   Then all men shall be free.
   He removed the yoke of bondage,
   And unto him freedom gave;
   He did educate the Negro
   And unfit him for a slave.

6. When the Negro gained his freedom
   Of body and of soul,
   He caught the wheels of progress,
   Gave them another roll.
   He was held near three long centuries
   In slavery's dismal cave,
   But now he is educated
   And unfitted for a slave.

7. He's able to fill any place
   On this terrestrial ball,
   All the way from country teacher
   To the legislative hall.
   He has proved himself a hero,
   A soldier true and brave,
   And now he's educated
   And unfit to be a slave.

8. We have lawyers and we've doctors,
   Teachers and preachers brave,
   And a host of noble women,
   Who have safely crossed the wave.
   We are pressing on and upward,
   And for education crave,
   For it's written now in history,
   We shall never more be slaves.

TOPIC XXXIV.

A NEGRO IN IT.

BY MRS. LENA MASON.

1. In the last civil war,
   The white folks, they began it,
   But before it could close,
   The Negro had to be in it.

2. At the battle of San Juan hill,
   The rough-riders they began it;
   But before victory could be won
   The Negro had to be in it.

3. The Negro shot the Spaniard from the tree,
   And never did regret it;
   The rough-riders would have been dead to-day
   Had the Negro not been in it.

4. To Buffalo, McKinley went,
   To welcome people in it;
   The prayer was prayed, the speech made,
   The Negro, he was in it.

5. September sixth, in Music Hall,
   With thousands, thousands in it,
   McKinley fell, from the assassin's ball,
   And the Negro, he got in it.

6. He knocked the murderer to the floor,
   He struck his nose, the blood did flow;
   He held him fast, all nearby saw,
   When for the right, the Negro in it.

7. J. B. Parker is his name,
   He from the state of Georgia came;
   He worked in Buffalo, for his bread,
   And there he saw McKinley dead.

8. They bought his clothes for souvenirs,
    And may they ever tell it,
    That when the President was shot
    A brave Negro was in it.

9. He saved him from the third ball,
    That would have taken life with it;
    He held the foreigner fast and tight,
    The Negro sure was in it.

10. McKinley now in heaven rests,
    Where he will ne'er regret it;
    And well he knows, that in all his joys
    There was a Negro in it.

11. White man, stop lynching and burning
    This black race, trying to thin it,
    For if you go to heaven or hell
    You will find some Negroes in it.

12. Parker knocked the assassin down,
    And to beat him, he began it;
    In order to save the President's life,
    Yes, the Negro truly was in it.

13. You may try to shut the Negro out,
    The courts, they have begun it;
    But when we meet at the judgment bar
    God will tell you the Negro is in it.

14. Pay them to swear a lie in court,
    Both whites and blacks will do it;
    Truth will shine, to the end of time,
    And you will find the Negro in it.

Joseph D. Bibb, A. M.

PROF. JOSEPH D. BIBB, A. M.

Prof. Joseph D. Bibb comes from the city of Montgomery, Ala., of excellent parents. His early life was spent among pleasant surroundings and he received his primary education at the Swain Public School of that city. While quite young he entered Fisk University, where he was prominent because of his splendid scholarship and original ideas. Being impressed with the idea that Negroes were the natural and best teachers for the Negro youth, he left that institution and entered Livingstone College at Salisbury, N. C., at the head of which was the justly celebrated Dr. J. C. Price. Here he received the degree of A. B. in 1886.

He was not contented with his academic attainment, but completed the courses of law and theology, and has constantly applied himself to the fulfillment of his high ideal.

After graduating he spent his first year as instructor in the State Normal at Montgomery, ten years as principal of the public school, in which he received his training, and two years as professor of Hebrew and Bible history at Morris Brown College, Atlanta, Ga. Neither of these nor the minor fields of usefulness satisfied his ideal, and it was not until he entered the active ministry that he felt that satisfaction that comes with fitness. He is now laboring acceptably as a minister in the A. M. E. Church and is recognized as one of its most scholarly divines.

The world needs men who will use all of their cultivated powers to bless and to lift up their fellowmen, who will dedicate themselves to their fullest energies and their energies to their people. Such a man is the subject of our sketch.

TOPIC XXXV.

THE NEGRO'S ADVERSITIES HELP HIM.

BY PROF. JOSEPH D. BIBB, A. M.

In this hour when the sun is just beginning to climb the horizon of a new day in the life of the Negro race, there is an imperative need for close observation and serious, earnest thought. We cannot content ourselves with appearances. We cannot trust the decision reached mainly through our emotional nature. We must bring the whole personal conscious man into our meditation in order that we may see and comprehend that hand of God laid in love upon the Negro of this country.

All problems in a nation's life must be unraveled and solved by that nation. It may take advantage of foreign influences and examples, incorporate and utilize them, but the real work must be done by the nation itself. The same principle obtains in problems affecting individual life or the life of a race. To adjust the Negro in harmonious relationship to American civilization is a question that depends for solution not so much upon the nation as upon the thought and life of the race itself. The Negro seen through the refractory medium of fear and prejudice is regarded as an unhealthy member, yet it is evident that he is a vital member and cannot be removed by the surgeon's scalpel. It is necessary, therefore, that this unhealthy member should be toned up to harmony with the great organism of which he is a part.

"No cross, no crown," is a trite saying, yet it has lost nothing of the beauty of strength of originality, but, rather, it has grown to be the sustaining, inspiring motto of all men as they plod up the hill of life. Great souls do not whine and fret in adversity. The men and women who lay the foundation of great institutions that bless mankind, that fling rainbows on the black bosom of the tempest, do not tremble and falter because of the clouds and mountain peaks, but onward and upward they go until the victory is won. The church came up by the way of the cross. If you would know the path of civilization, look for the great battlefields in the world's history. The greatest battles of reform in church and state have been fought, and the right has conquered. The Negro to-day reaches his hand out and plucks the best fruitage of the highest and grandest age known to man. Even liberty, a plant that grows luxuriantly only when watered with human blood, and rooted in the hearts and affections of a free people, is within the very grasp of the American Negro.

The history of the free American Negro is one continuous and unbroken chain of success. I shall lay the proof of the statement before you as we advance. Did you ever consider the agencies at work for the amelioration of the condition of the Negro in this country? Here and there counter-forces may appear to hinder the too rapid advance of the Negro, but such is the inevitable law of growth. Life is conditioned upon its ability to absorb and assimilate the good and reject and expel the bad. What are these counter-forces, these hostile external relations? Do they tend to destroy the equilibrium of the race, or, rather, do they conduce to its stability and strength? The answer is obvious. The Negro is being sharpened and fashioned here under Providence into a better and nobler manhood. He is suffering no more than all infant races suffered. Slavery and oppression is the school in which races are trained for the enjoyment of the fullest life. God has a purpose in thus dealing with the Negro. The power of his individuality, his highly developed religious nature, his disposition to linger in peace in whatever condition he finds himself; his preserving a truly magnanimous spirit in the very face of an unwarranted and violent opposition, foretell his future history. He is contributing his part toward the industrial development of the South and the religious elevation of the nation. Many of his redeeming qualities are often regarded as evidences of puerility and barbarism.

Character cannot be built in a day, neither in an individual nor in a race, but the Negro is old enough now to be an American citizen. He has reached the years of maturity; his character is formed, and what is good for the most advanced citizen is good for him. He demands equal and exact justice; he will content himself with nothing less. There are divine purposes in each life, in each race and nation. How well these purposes are subserved is left with the individual, the race or the nation.

Afflictions are a wholesome discipline, and the people who would survive the wreck of nations must fight their way up under the inexorable law of God, through trials, through tribulations, through persecution and through blood. I do not wish in any way to condemn the agitation of the hour in the name of justice, and civil political liberty, but rather to urge it in a reasonable way. Agitation, says Wendell Phillips, is the method that puts the school by the side of the ballot box. Agitation prevents rebellion, keeps the peace and secures progress. Every step she gains is gained forever. Muskets are the weapons of animals. "Agitation is the atmosphere of brains." Sir Robert Peel defines it as the marshaling of the conscience of a nation to mold its law. Injustice cannot stand before exposure and argument and the force of public opinion. No sharper weapon of defense will be required against the wrongs which afflict the South." No race can rise higher than its ideal. To teach the Negro that the evils of his environments will crush him forever, that a servant is and must be servile in disposition and in general habit of mind; that hair and skin and the shape of the head stamp him an inferior, is a doctrine of creation without God in it.

No, let him know and feel that he is a man with the great ever-expanding capacity of a man, and that a step beyond him is Deity. Let him see himself mirrored in Hamlet's sublime outbursts of admiration: "What a piece of work is man, how noble in reason, how infinite in faculties, in reform, how express and admirable; in action how like an angel in apprehension how like a god." Let him know that he has and will yet realize in his racial life the loftiest ideal of civilization. The Negro has profited immeasurably by the lessons, stern and severe—taught him in this country.

Yet these adverse forces are but ministers of Heaven, awakening his sleeping energies and accelerating his motion towards racial unity and organization. They are stern, at times, inhuman teachers, but so long as the Negro considers himself inferior, so long as a barber discriminates against his father and brother, so long as a waiter feels himself disgraced if he waits upon one of his own race, and the washer-woman if she washes for her sisters, so long as we loathe to serve only our own kith and kin these rough and severe teachers are absolutely indispensable.

The power that permanently lifts a people is within that people, so also the forces that degrade them. You cannot change public opinion by drifting with its current. You cannot present yourself in a slavish attitude and then demand a free man's portion. In that attitude you are neither feared nor loved, but tolerated. You are regarded an excrescent growth on the body of civil society. But it cannot always be thus.

How can this race fail? In this day a million new homes, comfortable homes of cultured black men, are built above the ruins of the slave's log cabin of yesterday. Wilberforce and Morris Brown, Tuskegee, Biddle and Livingstone, each gallantly manned by black men, and thousands of schools dotting the South—all immortalizing Christian philanthropy—are sending forth annually torch-bearers of truth to light the paths the race must pursue in the great civilization of to-day. How well these advantages will subserve his progress, his interest—depend upon the confidence and faith which they will inspire in him toward himself. Responsibility alone educates. Skill comes by constant practice. Any reason alleged that the Negro is not yet prepared for the leadership of his people, whether in the church or institutions of learning or in politics, or whether in any of the various avenues of business or of life, weakens the character of the race, and augments and quickens the prejudice of the enemy both within and without the race.

Our rightful leaders may be comparatively inexperienced, but experience is not acquired by inactivity. It took the Civil War to make Grant. The Northern missionary at the time when it tried the souls of men following in the wake of battle came to break the long night of ignorance that had settled down upon the Negro; but they have done their duty and gone to their reward. God bless them. The Negro is now prepared to take care of himself. Let the child crawl, he will learn to walk. Lift up the men and women of your own race. Let some great, towering example of Negro manhood and thrift and virtue and wisdom point the youth to the pole star of redemption. Trust the Negro now, and the future will take care of itself.

I repeat, if this and coming generations are taught to believe the crushing and slanderous dictum of natural inferiority, what hope is there for the salvation of the race, for a man can rise no higher than his ideal? These great, honest, sincere souls in the race, who show their love as do fathers to their children, rebuke because they love. Moses, the great leader of and lawgiver to the Israelites—a people who gave to the world its noblest song, its widest proverbs, its sweetest music—throws down the Table of the Ten Commandments in righteous indignation when he found them worshiping idols, but the next day his heart, gushing forth love for his people, he found his way in prayer to God, seeking forgiveness for his idolatrous people. This was but an expression of his burning zeal for the safety and progress of his people. So do I regard the scathing criticism given within the race by its own men. All other criticisms are questionable. But grant that the negro likes the idea, worships the idea of white supremacy, with its institutions and customs, vitalized apparently with the energy of violent opposition to his moral and industrial development; I cannot believe that he will always be thus.

Necessity is not merely the mother of invention, but the soul of the law of progress—the genius of civilization. It is here in the closing period of the Nineteenth Century effulgent with the light of all the historic past and marvelous achievements that the Negro must stand or fall. Here in the wilderness where peaks of cultivated mountain-tops in the near distance invite him onward and upward; here under the full ordered sun of the brightest day the world has seen he must work out his salvation with fear and trembling.

TOPIC XXXVI.

THE AMERICAN NEGRO AND HIS POSSIBILITIES.

BY GEO. L. KNOX.

History has, since time begun, shown the rise, decline and fall of empires, nations, races and individuals. It is but fair to say that the fate of the Negro has been cast along these lines that were as fixed as the stars in their courses. There have been exceptions to the laws of civil and political change. We have read with joy the triumph of the black man of ancient times, his power in battle, his eminence in letters, his skill in science, his genius as an agriculturist, his patience as a herdsman. In the great cycles of changes, it stands to reason that the wheel of civil and political fortune will again revolve in the Negro's favor.

The history of the black man's past in no wise serves to usurp the functions of present duties. Notwithstanding the fact that there are lowering clouds and muttering thunders, yet there is every indication of a day, to express it boldly, that is coming that will outshine the glittering sun.

'Tis not much that the American Negro asks in this racial warfare; his aid has always been scant and rare; he has been thrown on his own resources, buffeted about until he has become hidebound, as it were, to those circumstances which have been so hurtful to the progress of other nations.

Slavery, while a curse, has been a redeeming institution to the American Negro.

It was that purgatorial step between African slavery and American wealth. It was a necessary evil to prepare us for this most advanced civilization of the world. Since that refining period, the Negro has proven that he has the elements that make him a fit part of this great country. There are those among us who have reached fame in nearly all of the avenues of life. I take this as an index to the total possibilities of the race. The masses, however, are to be reached. The abilities of the few will not answer for the sins of the many. Crispus Attucks, whose blood stained Boston Commons, the black soldiers of the wars of

454

George L. Knox

GEORGE L. KNOX.

The subject of this sketch, George L. Knox, was born in Wilson County, Tenn., September 16, 1841. He was a slave, spending his early life on the farm and in following the vocation of shoemaker, which he learned while serving a master.

In 1862 he joined the Union forces in the Civil War; after the termination of that terrible crisis he went to Indianapolis, where he learned the tonsorial art. He did not stay any great while in that city, but went to Greenfield, Ind., not many miles away, where he concluded to make his home. He established himself in business in a small way, and by dint of persistency, thrift and integrity, such as has marked his course ever since, he, in a few years, succeeded in gaining a competence. He took an active part in politics as a Republican, of which party he has been an unswerving member up to this time. He won great respect for himself and family among the whites, and the older Greenfieldians never visit Indianapolis without dropping in to see George, as they so familiarly call him.

In 1895 he moved to Indianapolis and finally became the sole proprietor of the Bates House barber shop, said to be the most elegant shop in the country. He is a member of the M. E. Church, which has greatly honored him by sending him as a delegate-at-large to the general conference in New York in 1888, and to Omaha, Neb., in 1892. He has filled numerous offices in the local church.

He has been very active and prominent in Republican councils in his new home. Has served as delegate-at-large to the National Convention that met in Minneapolis, Minn., 1892, where Benjamin Harrison was nominated for the Presidency. He was selected as an Alternate Delegate-at-large to St. Louis, Mo., in 1896, when President McKinley was nominated. His voice has been heard all over the state in advocacy of the principles of his party.

In 1892 he took charge of the Freeman and since that time he has given the publication considerable attention, the results of which are shown by its very large and very wide circulation. The active management of this well-known paper is in charge of his son, Elwood C., who is rapidly developing as a man of business and affairs.

our country down to that memorable engagement at El Caney, will stand for Negro patriotism. Professors Washington, Councill and thousands of others who are holding up the torch of learning will stand for Negro intellect and citizenship, but behind all of these stand the Negro masses that are not sufficiently quickened. These must be prodded up, that they reach the front ranks of the procession. It is but justice to the Negroes, however, to say that the doors of opportunity do not swing wide for them. It ought to be otherwise, and I believe it will be otherwise when a better understanding exists between the races as to their aims and objects. The white man is quick to judge the Negroes by those he meets in his every-day life. Unfortunately, these are too much in evidence, giving color to the charge that all Negroes look alike. The better Negro is not, as a rule, seen; his works, as a rule, are not known; his refinement, his morals and industry are not advertised—hence a wrong notion as to the bent and intent of the race is noised abroad. Prejudice is not confined to one side alone; both races show it to a hurtful extent.

Hon. Robert Allen, one of the most noted criminal lawyers of Texas, said to a jury: "While it is true that we all have some trace of race prejudice against the Negro, which makes it hard for us to do him justice, I can not see why it is so; I know it should not be so. If the Negro owes us something, we also owe the Negro something. It is a mutual debt of gratitude that we owe each other. We as a race are inclined to think that the white man is against us naturally. It is true to a great extent, but we have reasons for thinking that the white man thinks more of the law-abiding, intelligent, taxpaying Negroes than he does of that set that turn up on election day, looking for something. It may be that the white man is jealous of the Negro's success, but I rather think that it is a mistaken notion. It is not toward the better class that he hurls his hatred, but against that class that the Negro himself is learning to fear. Until the colored man changes his position and conditions it will be useless for him to look for that consideration and respect that is accorded his more fortunate brother and fellow-citizen. The Negro must not conceive the idea that he has no friends among those now in supremacy; neither must he entertain the belief that fortune will come to him without effort on his part, or that citizenship will receive the proper recognition without improvement in his morals and political attitude. These are the days of newer and greater things in every conceivable direction. The Negroes are taking but a small part in their creation, glory and profit. If there are men among us who can be the means of bringing better conditions to the great Negro masses, and who can weed out the slow, dull, plodding process of evolution, they should not be denied the opportunity. The masses seem to be hedged about by a wall of indifference. Negroes have such little respect for their own kind that the thing is becoming proverbial. Now they pretend otherwise in self-defense.

You think of some little device for testing race love; try it—it will do the rest. The white people have found that nothing is to be feared of colored people when it comes to helping racial cause. The individual who is loudest in defense of his race generally gets the most generous cursing from Negroes. Newspapers are often held in abomination by Negroes. A Negro editor would be mobbed if he told the truth about Negroes; they say, let the white people do it. Negroes who engage in business of any kind are usually criticised most severely by Negroes who are incapable of engaging in any kind of business for themselves. They are always full of suggestions as to how Mr. "A" and Mr. "B" should conduct or run their business; still they have nothing substantial to offer. Criticisms coming from such a source simply amount to nothing. It is about time for all of us to stop going out of our way, and making occasion, where none exists, to blackguard the Negro, and instead encourage him to industry and correct living and increase our efforts to make him a steadier laborer and better citizen. It is hardly fair to place the whole race under a common condemnation because of the slothfulness and lawlessness of some of its members; it would hardly be fair even if this percentage were larger than it is, and it is hardly worthy of a people to continue nagging at, and seeking to arouse further prejudice against its own race. No man can reach the elevated plane of good character and worth who drags behind him a great load of little and mean dislikes for his fellowman. The possibilities of higher professional standing of colored men and women depend upon the unity and determination of the colored people to push their professional and business men to the front. I appeal to you as a race to cultivate race pride, not race prejudice. Stand up like men and women and cultivate unity and protect and defend each other's interest. Let the elevation of one be the joy of the other, instead of pulling down those who are trying to elevate themselves and the race. The possibilities of colored professional men will be great to the extent that the colored people will allow their greatness. Their destiny is with the colored race.

This world is not a place of peace and unmixed happiness. There has always been a struggle of individuals and races for existence and mastery.

It is beginning to dawn on the Negroes generally, that if they would be saved, they must save themselves. The idea that they were to enter at once into all the walks of American life without violent protest has been dissipated through the actual occurrences of the last four decades. It would be too long a story to rehearse the reasons for the seeming undiminished prejudices.

In the interest of truth, the exact truth, we feel free to say, however, that the reasons are not to be charged altogether to one race. There is much that can yet be done on the Negro's side that would tend to put a better face on the matter. There has been undergoing a gradual change in the minds of the thoughtful of both races concerning education and politics as it concerns the Negroes, which has, indeed, upset the first calculations of many, but which, after all, has a tendency to broaden the foundation on which racial progress must rest. The Booker T. Washington theory of education has come to stay; not because he advocates it; not because rich men are sustaining his school, but because he has an institution that meets the requirements, the demands of the day. It is a pity, but true, that the race as a rule has entertained inflated notions about the matter of education. It rather looked forward to an education that vied with the whites, with their centuries of leisure and their myriad routes for employment. Education that unfits the individual to grapple with his surroundings, his environments, is a misfit. The masses of any race do not hope to be educated as its classes do. Those who oppose Mr. Washington's theory advance the argument, but those intimately acquainted with the race must admit that the Negro parent slaves himself to make a fine lady or gentleman out of the daughter or son, whereas the poor white parents hope and endeavor to turn out breadwinners, notwithstanding they have no color conditions to overcome. The lady and gentleman idea, doubtless, was born of the slavery period, when the so-called "great" received flattering attention from master and slave. The desire to be the recipient of such attention, or to have it bestowed on their kind, was the result of association and infantile minds, which have not as yet left the will free to have the children taught to feel that the conditions must determine the education. Happily, we may say that the notion of turning out ladies and gentlemen instead of women and men is on the wane. The trades, the fields, the shops are, as they should now be, given greater consideration. Mr. Washington eternally dwells on the theory of doing something, producing something, and especially do we recommend the field, with its thousand-avenued opportunities. Competition in the products of the field is fair. The school prepares the farmer as well as it does the classic. A company of Negroes, equipped to make a wagon throughout, will at least make living wages, even should the article be sold for a few dollars less in order to make it go. Material is always the smaller item of expense. The public will not question the nationality of the makers. Reputation for good work is always understood to be a condition.

Other enterprises, with a small output of capital, would insure wages if no more. Do Negroes receive fair wages generally? If the Negroes have dreamed that they were to move unscathed in the industrial procession as they found it existing when they obtained their freedom, they have long ere this been rudely awakened. It is not always prejudice with shop owners and proprietors that prevent them from employing Negroes; it is that general mass prejudice that puts an emphatic veto on any such intentions. It resolves itself into a business proposition with him. The store owner allows no philanthropy in his business. He is dictated to by that course which insures him the greatest prosperity. He may not be wholly free from prejudices, but it is not that which determines his actions, it is the prejudice of the masses. He will not sacrifice his existence by opposing it. It is a mistake to wail at the class who is at the mercy of the masses. It is more than probable that they would do different if free to do so.

The question is often asked, can the Negroes work out their own salvation? Will they do it? The answer is: they have it to do or reap the very bitter consequences. The wardship idea is not the part of the American institution as it concerns them. Competition, deadly competition, is the pass word. The white man gives no quarter nor takes any; nothing but sheer force, absorption, extinction, annihilation, or what not in the commercial, industrial competitive sense. Nothing is longer conceded; no special place for the white man, for the black man, but for the man with the greatest pull. White barbers, white waiters, white coachmen, are no longer "curios;" they are persistent in their efforts to establish themselves, having no regard for peculiar races with peculiar occupations. It means that the Negroes must hustle and rustle, create avenues, open new vistas, announce new projects, and thus avoid alms-seeking and poor houses in the end.

Politics has played an undue part in perpetuating prejudices. It has contributed much in the way of wealth to many of the race. It has honored thousands by places of trust, honor and profit; it has been the means of developing the latent abilities of the village Hampdens, Pitts, Gladstones, Websters, Clays and Calhouns. It has been the means of demonstrating fealty to party, and to country. For this a glorious apostrophe is due those who have proven no cravens at any stage of the race's career. If there were but that picture on which to look, the occasion of this very lecture would not be necessary. The triumphs in political, civil, church, scholastic, and army life have been attested by such men as Douglass, Bruce, Washington, Langston, Revels, Walters, Turner, Derrick, Grant, Pinchback, Councill, Lyons, Cheatham, White and Dancy, not to speak of a host of younger men of journalistic careers, that, according to opportunity, compare favorably with those of greater reputations. But beyond all of this stands that grim complement in the way of civil depression, political stagnation, if not utter palsy. The courts have rendered their functions to the mobs in some localities, and all but anarchy sits enthroned. The white man has been held to blame altogether for the reversed picture. It is not quite the case. Slavery left a legacy of hate when it gave away to freedom. The older Negro, better groomed in the art of preserving peace, did not forget the depth from which he sprang. He was ever pouring oil on the troubled water, trying to bring peace out of confusion; as a consequence that period immediately subsequent to the war period was eventful, as it concerned the prospective peace of the races and general prosperity. It is the new Negro, the latter day product, who knows nothing but freedom, freedom modified by native propensities, idleness and a groveling disposition, that is causing the trouble. He does not understand the philosophy of the situation, and cares less—like the Andalusian, his mule, his guitar, and it ends right there. This strenuous American life demands work of every individual in some form; it revolts at the idler.

Disfranchisements owe their rise as much to the indolence and vice of too large a class of Negroes as they do to prejudice on the part of the whites. No respectable class of men, white or black, is going to be governed by a hoodlum element whose bellies are the main objects of their existence. The Indianapolis *Journal,* one of the most influential northern dailies, is right when it says that Booker T. Washington will not be disfranchised; it means further that his class will not be disturbed.

It will concern us but little as to what this country may do to the whites to spur them up to their duties, providing that is their object. The whites are not on trial; it is the Negroes. If the disfranchisements are the means of creating better Negroes they will have builded better than they knew. If they reduce hoodlumism, creating Washingtons, we will not be concerned about the hoodlums of other races. The decline and fall of disfranchisement are the two last acts of the great political drama. The Negroes have it in their power to hasten or prolong the day. What will they do with it? Our lives are measured by that which we are and that which we do. The two elements most essential to a successful life, are character and achievement. Character is the excellence of spirit. It consists not in external deeds, but in the thought, feeling and purpose enshrined in our character. In the sight of God and in the eyes of our own spirit it depends not so much upon the words we speak or the things we do, but the thoughts we think and the feelings we cherish are the purity, power and integrity of our spiritual nature. The first and best object of life is character; what we do may command the admiration of mankind, but to be is better than to do. The measure of our spiritual excellency lies within us. It is in the heart rather than the deed. Beauty, purity and generosity may appear in the external act, while the motive prompting it may be mean, ignoble and selfish. Sweet truth, purity and noble traits of character may be enshrined within the soul and the life be so modest that they may not manifest themselves to the public gaze.

When asked why Antipater was not dressed in purple, Alexander, replying, said: "These men wear their purple on the outside, while Antipater is royal within." It is the soul throbbing with a generous feeling and a noble impulse. The soul is loyal to the claims of truth and virtue. So you can see it is better to be loyal from within than to make a display from the outside. If our race expects to meet the possibilities we must learn what it takes to make true characters. It is not the exhibit from the outside, it is what we are, as we are judged from our actions, by the fruits we bring forth.

Character is the cultivated power; shun the examples of the world. How many persons ever made a careful analysis of their own character or labored to develop the good and suppress the evil? The first object of life is character, but an object no less important is achievement. Character is power, but power is of no use only when it is applied. A cistern of water may contain a latent force enough to do the work of a thousand men or overturn mountains, but only when its latent powers are developed into the form of steam and applied to the arm of iron for the accomplishment of a purpose is it of any good to the world. A man of moral force must apply his power to become a blessing to mankind. Character must go forth into the deed if it accomplishes that whereunto it was sent. Public sentiment is beginning to measure a man, not so much by his culture as what he can do with his culture. It demands efficiency as well as scholastic acquirement. We must understand that the demands are different now from what they were in times gone by. A man must accomplish something if he expects to meet the possibilities that await him and his race. I do not object to education; I rather love education; but how must a man be educated? His feet, his eyes, his hands, his head, must all be educated; and when he is thus educated he is prepared to meet the emergencies that await his race. As a race, thus educated, we can not be hindered from taking position in life as American citizens. We often say that everything is against us, and it seems so; but while this seems the case we must be doing something individually and as a race. The conditions of successful achievements are a correct idea of intelligence, persistence and courageous labor. First we must have purpose in life or, in other words, an object in view. A life that is aimless is a sad spectacle, not so bad perhaps as a ruined life, but not much more admirable. The Hindoos believe that the destiny of mankind was lost in the personality by absorption in the Brahma, and most persons are so aimless in life and so devoid of any higher or nobler purpose that they lose their individuality in the great Brahma of society. A man is an individual, not a mere unit in a mass; a personality, not a mere member of a body politic. Did you ever think what a fearful lack of that which is noble in humanity is contained in the world? It ignores that which is highest and best in human nature—man's freedom and power of self-organization and self-determining influence in the masses of men. We are too apt to fall in the same line or take on the same personalities of those around us for the emancipation from bondage of social errors, evils, spiritual freedom and individual aims. To float with the current is easy; a chip can do that, but a man ought to be able to stem the tide when necessary. Put manhood, womanhood into the world as a spiritual force to mold, purify and elevate. Go forth into an active life with a noble purpose, and attaining it achievement will be of the highest success. The greatest issue of the day and the demands of the hour have not been made fundamental in our homes; the duties of the home have not been pressed on the youth until they stand out erect in the possession of a sterling womanhood and manhood, respecting and respected in whateve sphere they find their vocation. Character—character, resting upon the foundation of integrity, has not been as it ought the burning theme of every day's instruction, until it becomes the very soul of every boy and girl. Without character a man had better be as dumb as a fish and as ignorant as a snail. Intelligence, skill, industry, economy, endurance, courage and power will be so many elements of destruction unless character shall dominate the life and be expressed in the actions. My hands and yours have a work to do; my head and yours have a duty to perform. Here is the only solution for the Negro problem. It may not be out of place for me to here emphasize the need of our working in harmony with our environments. Our destiny is American in place and American in spirit. It is nonsense to talk of emigration of the masses. We endured slavery 243 years and stayed here, and we shall still be here when lynch law shall have spent its force, and with us shall be our white brother.

It is the dictate of wisdom to develop friendship, to teach unity, to rivet the ties of fraternal love. It is the policy of annihilation to deepen the chasm between the races. God forbid the day when the white educators of the land shall no longer be willing to spend and be spent for the moral and intellectual uplift of our masses. Let us be done with sowing the seed of bitterness; we can only reap the whirlwind of destruction. Because an inflamed sentiment drove black miners from Pana, Illinois, every community is not repellent. Because a man rose in the Christian Endeavor meetings in Detroit and tried to cast bad reflections on our race, every Christian Endeavorer is not our enemy. We shall be wise when we find our friends of whatever locality, of whatever faith, of whatever rank, or of whatever race, and pour into their open bosoms the full measure of our confidence. So shall we hasten the day of our final disenthrallment. There is one thing the Negro must be proud of before he can reach the height and possibilities that await him, he must learn to be proud of his race and color. No race can be successful until it does these things. I would not change my color, because I am proud of it. If there is any one thing that will clog the wheels of our material progress, it is the fact that some of us try to overreach ourselves. We should not become dazzled at the splendor and magnificence of those who have had hundreds of years to make this country what it is to-day. No man is a success who has not a fixed sign post, an aim in life to attain unto. A man should get that amount of education that will best fit him for the performance and attainment of his object in life. Too much Greek will do you no good with a white apron on. I do not say that you should not study Greek if you intend to fill a chair in some institution of learning. I do not say that you should not read medicine if you intend to become a physician, or law if you desire to follow the profession. If we watch our chances, and take timely advantage of the opportunities offered us, our race will greatly improve and we will be wage workers, skilled artisans, and eventually land owners and a wealthy class of citizens of this country. I advise you to learn trades; learn to become mechanics. We have the ability and capacity to reach the highest point, and even to go further in the march of progress than has been made by any people.

TOPIC XXXVII.

IMPORTANT LESSONS FROM THE AWFUL TRAGEDY.

BY E. E. COOPER.

We stand in the shadow of a national sorrow.

In an hour of national pride and jubilation, with the eyes of the world upon the greatest republic since the eagles of Rome overspread the earth, in the fullness of his powers and the prime of his usefulness, the Chief Magistrate of the Republic was stricken down by the hand of an assassin. It is meet here that I should refer in the opening of my address to this third assassination in the history of our country, for the purpose of illustrating the short story that I have to tell you and to point a moral and adorn a tale which may not be without value to us. For it is true that

> "Lives of great men all remind us
> We may make our lives sublime,
> And departing leave behind us
> Footprints on the sands of time."

William McKinley was the incarnation, not only of the possibilities of the humblest American boy who, by diligence, integrity and devotion to the best interests of the country, rose by steady strides to the highest dignities in the gift of the people, but he was also the embodiment of that grand sweep of American business genius which has spread over the world, and promises to predominate it. If this man who now rests from his labors with his honors full upon him represented anything, it was the logic of business development in its largest and best sense, for, as Governor of Ohio and member in Congress and President of the United States, his name is indissolubly associated with the commercial promotion, protection and expansion of American trade.

He was not only a great executive and a great legislator, but, when yet a youth, when the great Republic was in the agony of possible dissolution, he heroically shouldered a musket and went to the front as a private to preserve the union of the states bequeathed to us by the noble fathers and the heroism of the American revolutionary soldier in that memorable struggle, the first victim of which was Crispus Attucks, the

E. E. Cooper.

EDWARD E. COOPER.

For twenty-five years following Emancipation and the new opportunities which that great event brought, many of the brightest minds the colored race has produced, had been endeavoring to solve the perplexing and important problem of how to make a newspaper, published in the interest of the colored people, a profitable business enterprise. The number of such newspaper ventures whose managers failed to solve the problem mounts well up into the hundreds.

In the early spring of 1893, Mr. Edward E. Cooper, fresh from conquests in race journalism in Indianapolis, came to Washington and established "The Colored American," a weekly newspaper whose circulation last year was put down at 12,000 copies per week, and numbers among its readers residents in every clime where our flag floats. Mr. Cooper interpreted the "want" for such a newspaper.

His first venture in journalism was "The Colored World," published at Indianapolis. This was quite a success, but he gave it up to accept a position in the Railway Mail Service. On leaving the Mail Service he again embarked in journalism and established "The Indianapolis Freeman," an illustrated weekly. This was a new feature. "The Freeman" quickly jumped into great popularity and soon gained national fame. Having made "The Freeman" a success, he decided to go to Washington for a larger field of endeavor. Mr. Cooper is undoubtedly the best all-around newspaper man the colored race has yet produced.

Edward E. Cooper was born near the little town of Smyrna, Tenn., and attended the old barracks school for colored children on Knowles Street, Nashville, south of the Nashville and Chattanooga depot; which school afterwards became the nucleus of Fisk University. He began life selling papers, etc., on trains; then worked on a farm two years. He next went to Indianapolis, attended the public schools and graduated from the high school. In 1883, he married Miss Tenie Jones, one of the most cultivated young ladies of Paris, Ky.

Mr. Cooper freely acknowledges that his wife has been the balance-wheel in his life that has brought him what success he has gained.

lineaments of whose personality have been chiseled in marble and will stand a monument upon Boston Common, to show a "Man's a man for a' that and a' that," and that the rank is but the guinea's stamp.

Ah, well, we faithful hearts and true, who were never false to a friend, who have always loved the flag, even when the flag waved not over us, who fought with Washington at Valley Forge and with Perry at Lake Erie, with Jackson at New Orleans, with Shaw at Fort Wagner, and with Butler at New Market Heights, who went up San Juan Hill with Theodore Roosevelt and the immortal Rough Riders and followed little Joe Wheeler in Luzon, who, although a Southern brigadier, as a reconstructed unionist in a reunited country showed in Cuba and Manila that he had the same regard for a black soldier as for a white one when he was loyal to the flag and faithful to his country, are here to mourn our loss. This great heart that loved his country and gave his life to it and for it is stilled in death!

The assassin! What of him? It is a matter of notorious fact that he was so obscure in the life that he had led and had contributed so little to the public weal in the place where his hands found labor that he was utterly unknown and went down to the quicklime that consumed his miserable remains, to the chaos from which we all spring, stigmatized with at least two cognomens and with the reputation of having contributed nothing to the wealth of the Republic or the happiness of mankind. There are millions of him in Europe and America who keep in perpetual jeopardy the splendid civilization evolved out of the tumult of Egypt and Rome and the Dark Ages. And the very genius of logical business development sprung out of the bosom of Moroe on the Nile and of Tyre where ancient Afro-Phœnicians ruled the blue waters of the adjacent seas and of the lordly Egyptians, who were African in their fiber, historians to the contrary notwithstanding, were the founders of the commercial spirit that dominates the world to-day. More than that, they laid the basis of our literature and of our philosophy. As Lord Byron hath beautifully said:

> "Ye have the Pyrrick dances yet—
>   Where has the Pyrrick phalanx gone?
> Of two such lessons, why forget
>   The nobler and the manlier one?
> Ye have the letters Cadmus gave;
>   Think ye he meant them for a slave?"

Now, Cadmus was a black African slave captured in war; so was Aesop, the world's greatest fabulist; so was Terence, among the grandest of Rome's lyric poets; so was Pushkin, the national poet to-day of Russia; so was Alexander Dumas the first, the greatest, not only of French novelists, but of novelists of all times and the infinite storehouse from which all novelists draw, Honore De Balzac and Charles Dickens to the contrary notwithstanding.

But of this vile assassin, Leon Czolgosz, why do I make this exordium here upon the violent taking off of the President beloved by all the people, and my animadversion upon the character of the man who lifted his hand against the supreme representative of the greatest Republic upon earth and the most prosperous nation? It is an incident in the life of government that the supreme head of it shall be subject to the vicissitudes of its maniacal, fanatical and criminal classes, those who live by their wits or those who dream of a condition of society unattainable, as human nature is constructed, such as Edward Bellamy has pictured in "Looking Backward." I wish it distinctly understood that I refer to this matter simply to draw attention to the fact that Czolgosz, the obscure assassin of the highest representative of the logic of business development in this country, is inseparably linked as the Siamese twins to the mobocrat, and that any effort made to root out the anarchist in this country will fail, and should fail, unless the mobocrat is rooted out at the same time.

It is written in the stars. God has said, "Righteousness exalteth a nation, but sin is a reproach to any people."

And what business development can we have when the dark shadow of anarchism and mobism overshadows the land like the dark cloud that covered the children of Israel in their confusion, when in their perversion they had turned their faces from the God of their destiny? No, there can be no business development in this country while our laws are so lax as to allow irresponsible individuals or organizations to clog the wheels of industry or to waste unnecessarily the red blood that gives life to a virile human form. 'I say, with our grand President, throttle the anarchist that would shoot a President or a successor to a President. Yes, but if you leave the Southern mobocrat to shoot John Jones, an unknown entity, the element of anarchism remains pregnant in the body politic and is liable at any time to show its venomous head.

Who could have told when the whole nation was hopeful that a John

Wilkes Booth lurked reluctant in the body politic to cut down the wisest and the most humane and the most lovable of all the Presidents? Ah, my friends, you can't protect the President of the United States from the assassin and leave unprotected in any corner of the republic its meanest citizen, because, as Alexander Pope has wisely said, "We are all but links of one stupendous chain. Break a link of that chain and the power of that chain is destroyed."

TOPIC XXXVIII.

HOW TO HELP THE NEGRO TO HELP HIMSELF.

BY W. R. PETTIFORD.

Since the emancipation of the Negro in this country philanthropists have contributed largely to the establishment of schools and colleges for his education. Some of these institutions have been the means of affording the Negro literary instruction, and others have given him more practical benefits in industrial training. These methods of helping a race that was necessarily groping in the darkness of illiteracy are not only commendable from the viewpoint of humanitarianism and sound philanthropy, but it must be conceded that some such help was indispensable to any real advancement of the Negro in the matter of education. For all such assistance it can be said that the Negro is truly appreciative and, for the most part, has earnestly striven to demonstrate his profound gratitude by eagerly taking hold of the opportunities thus afforded for his enlightenment. The industrial schools, Hampton, Tuskegee, and others, have done much in a practical way for the Negro in giving him a knowledge of trades—a class of training that must prove of inestimable value to him in his endeavor to earn a living honestly and honorably. That person who has been taught how to do something well, who has been so equipped as to be able to do with skill what the world is willing to pay a desirable price for, has been done an incalculable service, and one for which society as well as the individual himself has occasion to feel grateful.

So generously have the Negro's friends contributed toward his education and so marked are their continued efforts in this direction that it would appear somewhat bold for anyone to offer a suggestion at this time looking to any additional contributions from this source for the purpose of materially advancing the masses of that race along other lines. On the other hand, when it is remembered with what avidity the beneficiaries of these funds have seized the opportunities offered, and the splendid results so far realized; and when the further facts are borne in mind that the improvement of one class of the population never fails to inure to the benefit of the entire community, it may not, after all, require

W. R. Pettiford, D. D.

REV. WILLIAM R. PETTIFORD, D. D.

It is difficult to present a life's record so as to furnish a correct estimate of the man in question. Particularly is this true if we attempt to give upon a page the account of a long life of active and useful service.

Among the leaders in Christian work in the state of Alabama, Dr. W. R. Pettiford ranks very high, having but few, if any, superiors. As a business man he is unexcelled. Twelve years of unremitting toil and unbroken success in the banking business demonstrate the truth of this assertion.

In presenting this sketch we could not do better than quote from the Cyclopedia of the Colored Baptist of Alabama, by Rev. C. O. Boothe, D. D.:

Rev. W. R. Pettiford, D. D., son of William and Matilda Pettiford, was born in Granville county, North Carolina, January 20th, 1849. He was, when a boy, of an industrious turn of mind, working faithfully at whatever his hands found to do. At one time he was with the tanner, and at another time he was running his father's farm.

At the age of 21 years he united with the Baptist Church of Rocksboro, Person county, North Carolina, and was immersed by the Rev. Ezekiel Horton of Salisbury. While he was serving this church as clerk he told his mother the secret, which he greatly desired that she would not reveal, that he felt called to the gospel ministry. Brother Horton often put up at their home, hence soon got possession of the secret.

Dr. Pettiford now says: "When I was called into an examining council and learned that my secret was out, I was very much frightened, but the advice given upon this day has ever been helpful to me."

At the commencement of Selma University, 1877-78, he joined Brother Woodsmall, becoming a member of the pioneer faculty of the school. It was here that he was seen as the patient, studious, industrious man—loved by tender youth and trusted by those of riper years.

He was called to ordination by the Berean Baptist Church, Marion, Ala., and dedicating hands were laid upon his head in Marion, Ala., in the midst of the Conventional Session held there in November, 1880. After this he severed his connection with Selma University to enter the pastorate in Union Springs.

As teacher and financial agent he made such a record that unprecedented prestige was given to his work at Union Springs, where for two years, by his labor of love and sacrifice, he laid the foundation for permanent Christian work that shall stand throughout all time.

For a brief period Dr. Pettiford worked under joint appointment of the American Baptist Home Mission Society and the Home Mission Board of the Alabama Baptist State Convention as lecturer for ministers. In this capacity he accomplished a great work. Many ministers to-day look back to those days when they sat in institutes conducted by him as the times of their greatest inspiration for mental and spiritual development.

As president of the Alabama Penny Savings Bank he has a reputation as extensive as the country of which he is a citizen. There is no city of importance where this bank has not done business. It has gained the reputation of being a safe business, having survived several panics to which many other similar institutions have succumbed.

Dr. Pettiford has managed to find some time to write. He is the author of the following treatises: "Divinity in Wedlock," "God's Revenue System" and "The Centenary," all of which do him honor and his fellow man service. But this sketch would be incomplete if it were closed without stating this truth: That much of the Doctor's success is rightly attributed to the sympathy and help of his life companion, formerly Miss Della Boyd, to whom he was joined in bonds of wedlock November 22, 1880. Three children have graced their home, being systematically trained for usefulness in life.

unusual temerity in one to venture upon the suggestions which are to follow in this article. When it is noted, too, with what care, discrimination and rare judgment such contributions have been directed in the effort to lift the Negro out of his unfortunate condition, and with what earnestness, consistency and sincerity of purpose such aid has been given, the conclusion is irresistible that any other needed help will come if the method suggested is shown to be practicable and gives promise of beneficial results.

While the school has wrought wonders for the Negro, as it has for all civilized races, it cannot be hoped or expected that all desirable improvements in the development of a people can be accomplished through this agency. All the virtues may be taught in the school-room, but the student gets only a theoretical idea of what is intended to be conveyed to his mind, and necessarily so. He has not yet learned to be practical and cannot, until he is brought in contact with the actual and serious responsibilities of life, see the real, practical phase of things as they actually exist. He needs to learn the practical value of economy and thrift, of constant industry and frugality. If he would build on a certain and safe foundation, he must do so by honestly earning every dollar he can and wisely saving as much of it as his actual necessities will permit. Nothing so strongly encourages this spirit in the Negro as a savings bank operated in his community by persons of his own race. The powerful influence exerted in this direction by such institutions may be shown by some impressive figures which have been secured from reliable sources: Atlanta, with no such institution to stimulate its colored population to save, has only 1,000 colored depositors in the associated banks of that city out of a total colored population of 30,000; or one out of every thirty. Richmond, with a thriving institution of this character, has 5,000 colored depositors out of a total colored population of 45,000; or one out of every nine. Birmingham boasts of 5,000 colored depositors (4,000 of whom deposit with the bank with which the writer is connected) out of a total colored population of 20,000; or one out of every four. These three thriving Southern cities, blessed with equal prosperity and promise, furnish convincing proofs of the great power for good exerted by such institutions. If Atlanta, which in other respects equals either of these two cities, were favored with the presence of a bank of the kind mentioned, a much larger percentage of its colored population would be filled with the spirit of economy and the desire to save.

If such institutions are materially helpful to the Negro, if they tend to inculcate right principles and encourage habits of industry and frugality; and if it be true that the uplifting of one class benefits the entire community, is it not within the bounds of legitimate reasoning and fairly good common sense to suggest that it would be well to have these beneficial agencies established, as far as possible, in cities containing a large Negro population; taking care, however, that none is established until it becomes apparent in each instance that such an institution can be wisely, safely and successfully conducted in the proposed community?

The writer has had a great many inquiries in the last few years for information and advice looking to the organization of savings banks by colored men; but it has been noted that in nearly every case the element of doubt, fear and backwardness developed when the promoters were brought face to face with the problem of how to begin such a business and conduct it successfully. They found the problem a difficult one, just as all problems are difficult until they are understood. Here then is where the wealthy friends of the Negro, the Northern and Southern philanthropist, can be of invaluable help. It would be well if a few such friends would become interested in the work of assisting in the establishment of such banks, to be conducted by competent colored men in such cities as offer favorable conditions for institutions of the character mentioned. They could form themselves into a board for the general supervision of the work, and then engage the services of an experienced and thoroughly competent man to give personal attention to it. This man should comprehend every detail of the banking business, and he should be willing to meet and advise with those who are to have in hand the conduct of the institution and instruct them in all the details of its proper management before the doors are thrown open to the public. He should then give daily attention to the operation of the bank for two or three months, or until the officers are able to proceed safely without him. By this time a similar work should await him in another locality. He should, however, keep in constant communication with the president of the newly established bank and so arrange his engagements as to be able to return to it from time to time, as the work elsewhere will permit, in order that he may oversee the management and give such helpful counsel as the situation may demand. With the right kind of men at the helm, educated, popular with their people and possessing unquestioned integrity, it would not be unsafe at this stage to trust the management to their hands for a few days at a time, after it has been ascertained that all departments of the business are being conducted intelligently and without friction.

So that instead of having only three or four communities in the country reaping the good results of such forceful agencies for the moral and material elevation of their citizens, we will have at least a few more to assist in spreading the gospel of economy and thrift. The expense attached to such an undertaking would be represented in the salary paid the organizer, and perhaps a stenographer, and the traveling and other necessary expenses of both. Their services would not be required for a longer period than five years, at most, and the real good accomplished would be incalculable.

The plan is not impracticable. The few savings banks now being operated by colored men had no such help. They overcame the difficulties under which they necessarily began, and they have succeeded admirably. Cannot others succeed as well, especially after such difficulties are effectually removed? New Orleans, Memphis, Nashville, Louisville, Montgomery, Atlanta, Charleston and other cities offer fruitful fields for this work. But let it be understood that such assistance as is here suggested should in no case be attempted until the citizens of a given community have first evinced a proper interest in the enterprise, such interest, indeed, as would leave no doubt of their earnestness in the matter. The only real danger, in any instance, or, perhaps, it may be better to say the chief danger, lies in an unwise selection of a locality for the establishment of this kind of business. But this question might be safely determined, after proper investigation, by those who furnish the funds.

Lest there be persons in the North, who, not being altogether familiar with conditions as they exist between the races in the South, should doubt the wisdom of the undertaking because of a fear that the idea might meet with disfavor on the part of the dominant race, it may be well to suggest that the writer's personal experience in connection with the conduct of a similar institution for nearly twelve years in an extreme Southern community, has justified the opinion that the very reverse is true. The bank referred to has enjoyed ever since its establishment the moral support and cordial good wishes of the white people of that section. And the reason for this is apparent. Perhaps the true reason is nowhere more aptly and succinctly given than by the editor of the

Charleston *News and Courier,* who, in commenting on an address delivered by Mr. Booker T. Washington, said: "The Negro with a bank account, with houses and lands, with education in the practical things of life, is a far better citizen and a safer and more desirable neighbor than the Negro who is steeped in ignorance and who has really no part in the life of his country." The wise, progressive, far-seeing citizens of the white race recognize and admit the influence for good exerted upon the colored population by banking institutions operated by members of that race, and they welcome and encourage the establishment of them in any community.

It is hoped that some little grain of merit may be found in these suggestions. There has been no desire in the preparation of this article to aspire to any literary effort. That would not be possible in one who makes no pretensions in that direction. It is submitted with the hope that the ideas here sought to be expressed may find favor with those who practice the doctrines of true philanthropy—that class of Americans who find genuine happiness in doing good wherever good can be done, and who believe that no harm can come of helping the Negro to help himself.